# CHRONIN

## VOLUME 2: THE SWORD IN YOUR HAND

Alison Wilgus

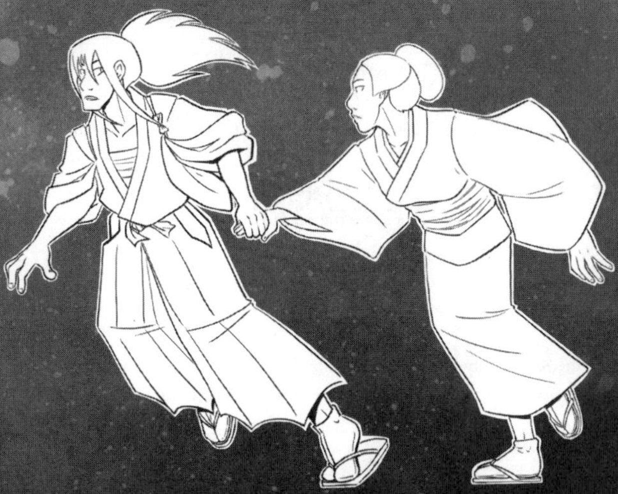

TOR

A TOM DOHERTY ASSOCIATES BOOK • NEW YORK

For everyone who needed to make a book
to figure out their own damn selves.

CHRONIN VOLUME 2: THE SWORD IN YOUR HAND

Copyright © 2019 by Alison Wilgus

Final interior artwork was created digitally in Adobe Photoshop on a Cintiq 12WX.

Digital inks by Niki Smith, with additional inks by Alison Wilgus and Robin Kaplan

A Tor Book
Published by Tom Doherty Associates
120 Broadway
New York, NY 10271

www.tor-forge.com

Tor® is a registered trademark of Macmillan Publishing Group, LLC.

The Library of Congress Cataloging-in-Publication Data is available upon request.

ISBN 978-0-7653-9164-3 (trade paperback)
ISBN 978-0-7653-9290-9 (ebook)

Our books may be purchased in bulk for promotional, educational, or business use. Please contact your local bookseller or the Macmillan Corporate and Premium Sales Department at 1-800-221-7945, extension 5442, or by email at MacmillanSpecialMarkets@macmillan.com

First Edition: September 2019

Printed in the United States of America

0  9  8  7  6  5  4  3  2  1

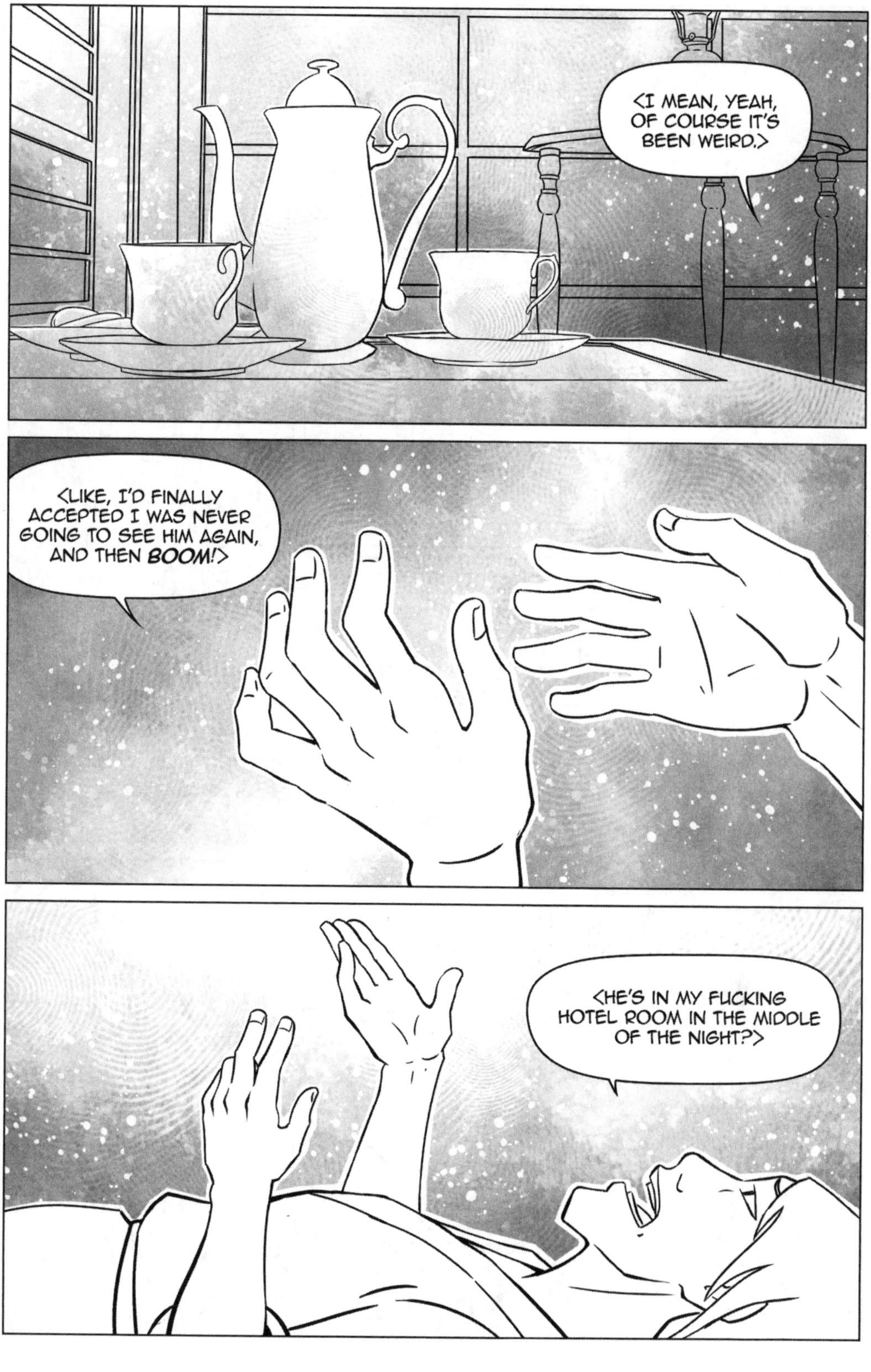
<I MEAN, YEAH, OF COURSE IT'S BEEN WEIRD.>
<LIKE, I'D FINALLY ACCEPTED I WAS NEVER GOING TO SEE HIM AGAIN, AND THEN *BOOM!*>
<HE'S IN MY FUCKING HOTEL ROOM IN THE MIDDLE OF THE NIGHT?>

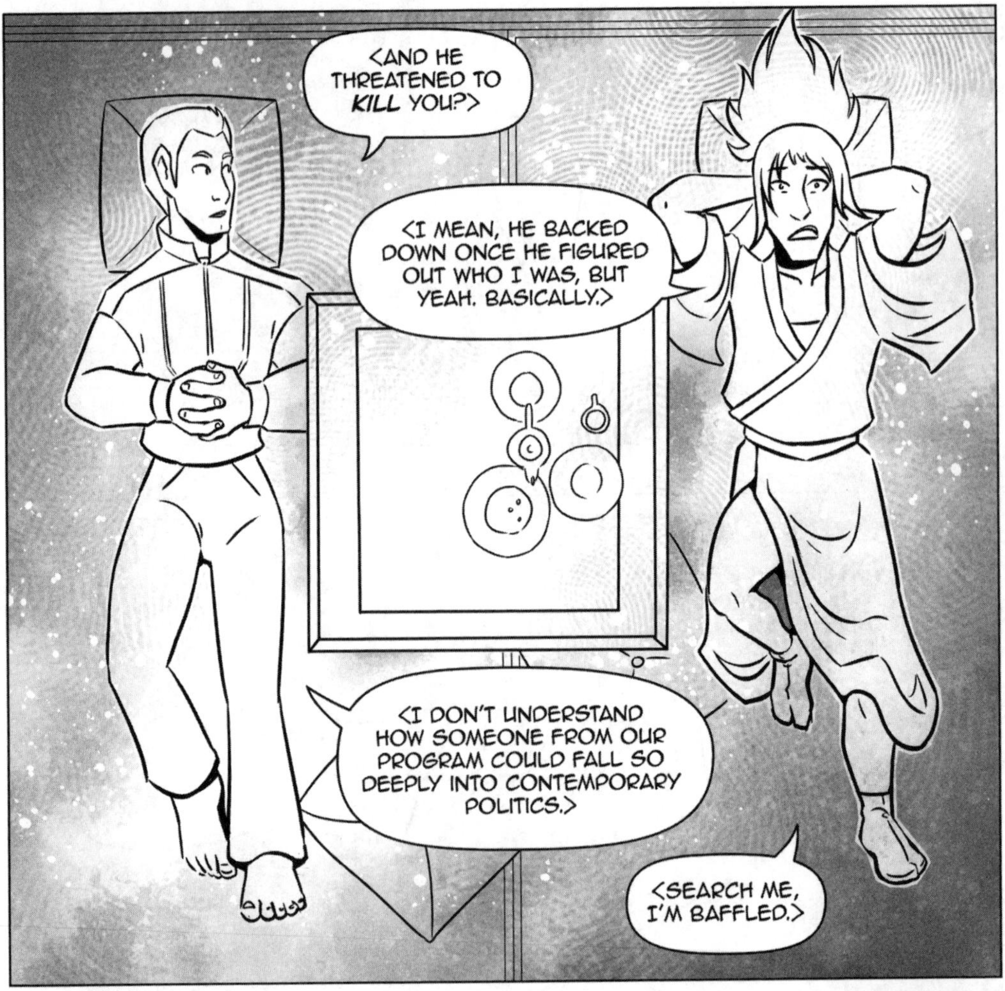
<AND HE THREATENED TO KILL YOU?>
<I MEAN, HE BACKED DOWN ONCE HE FIGURED OUT WHO I WAS, BUT YEAH. BASICALLY.>
<I DON'T UNDERSTAND HOW SOMEONE FROM OUR PROGRAM COULD FALL SO DEEPLY INTO CONTEMPORARY POLITICS.>
<SEARCH ME, I'M BAFFLED.>

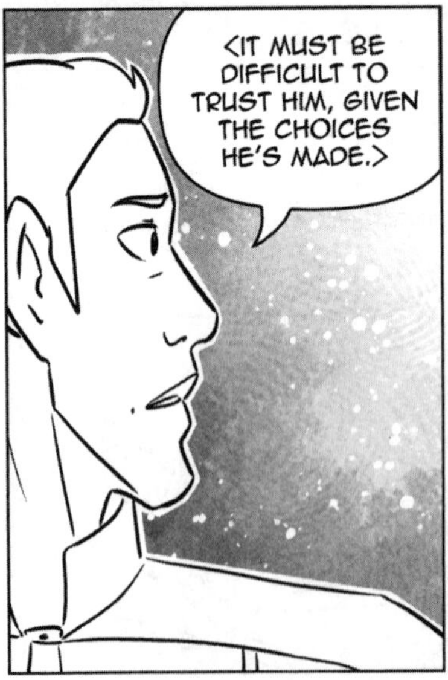
<IT MUST BE DIFFICULT TO TRUST HIM, GIVEN THE CHOICES HE'S MADE.>

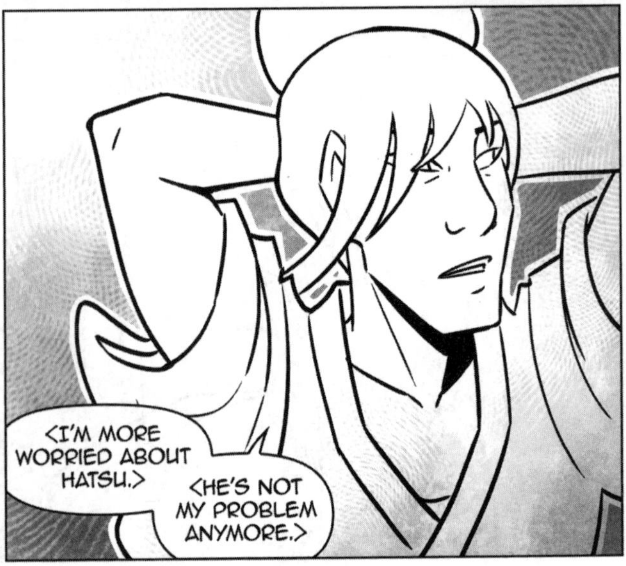
<I'M MORE WORRIED ABOUT HATSU.>
<HE'S NOT MY PROBLEM ANYMORE.>

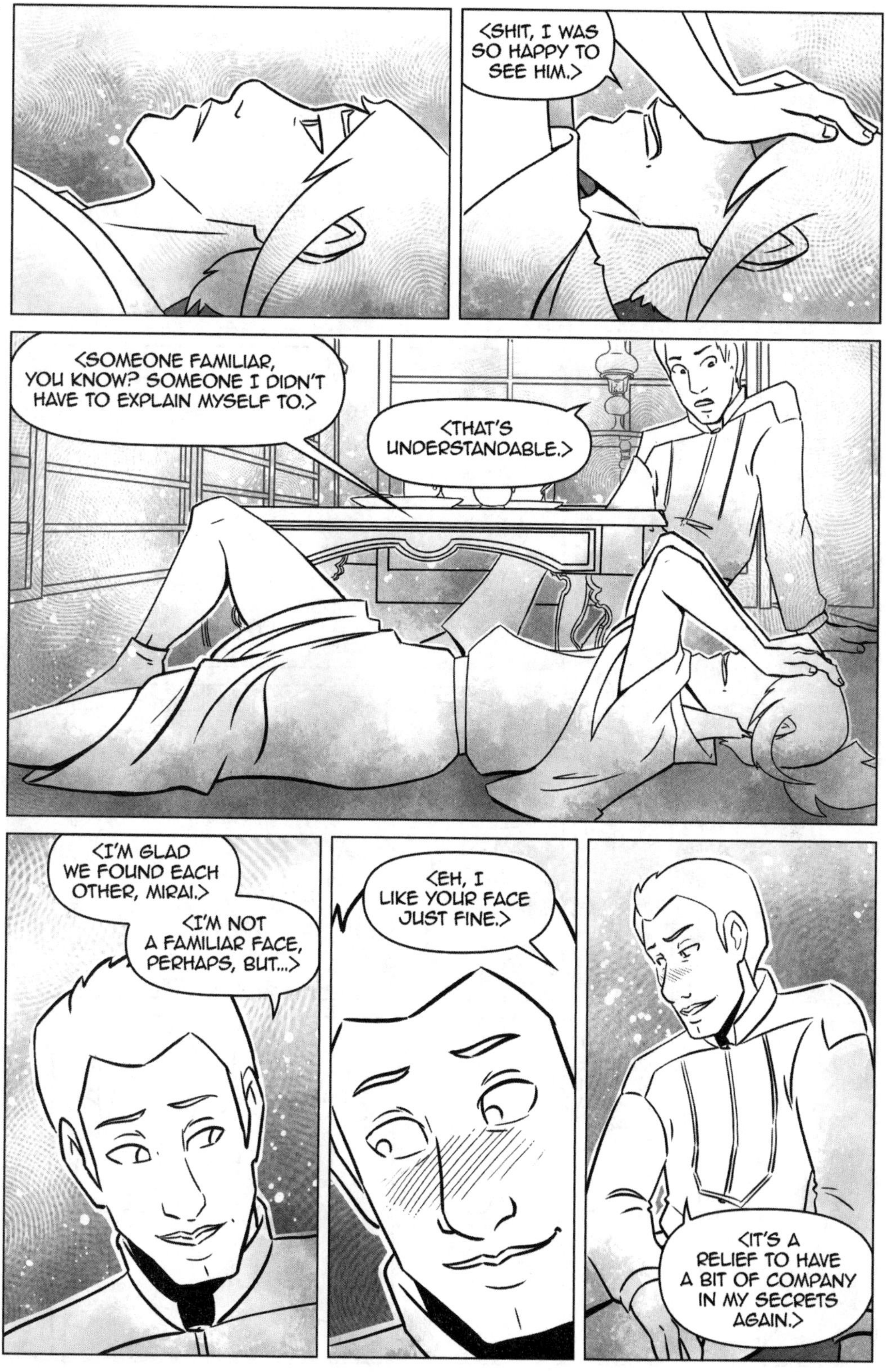

<SHIT, I WAS SO HAPPY TO SEE HIM.>
<SOMEONE FAMILIAR, YOU KNOW? SOMEONE I DIDN'T HAVE TO EXPLAIN MYSELF TO.>
<THAT'S UNDERSTANDABLE.>
<I'M GLAD WE FOUND EACH OTHER, MIRAI.>
<I'M NOT A FAMILIAR FACE, PERHAPS, BUT...>
<EH, I LIKE YOUR FACE JUST FINE.>
<IT'S A RELIEF TO HAVE A BIT OF COMPANY IN MY SECRETS AGAIN.>

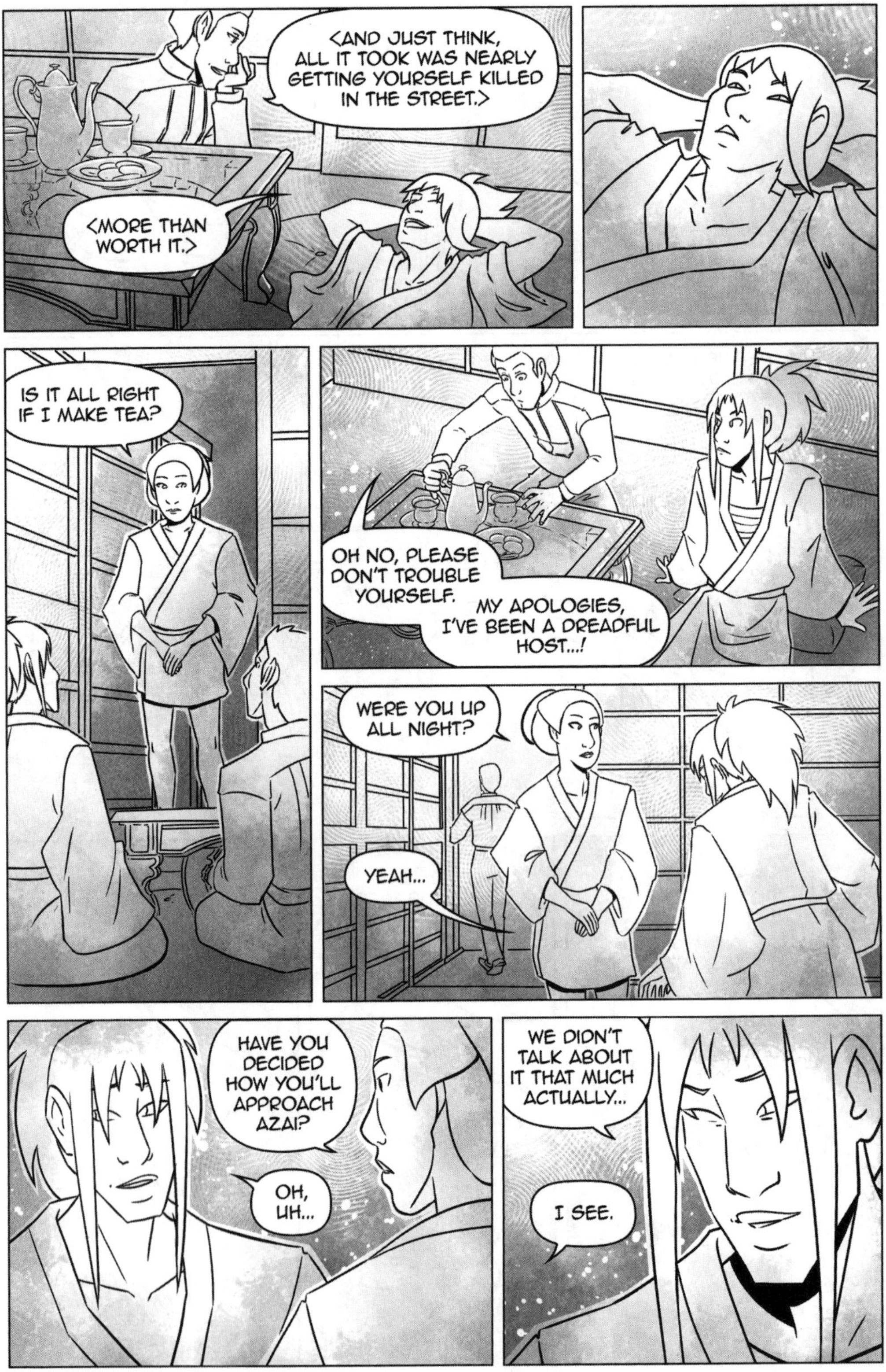
<AND JUST THINK, ALL IT TOOK WAS NEARLY GETTING YOURSELF KILLED IN THE STREET.>
<MORE THAN WORTH IT.>
IS IT ALL RIGHT IF I MAKE TEA?
OH NO, PLEASE DON'T TROUBLE YOURSELF.
MY APOLOGIES, I'VE BEEN A DREADFUL HOST...!
WERE YOU UP ALL NIGHT?
YEAH...
HAVE YOU DECIDED HOW YOU'LL APPROACH AZAI?
OH, UH...
WE DIDN'T TALK ABOUT IT THAT MUCH ACTUALLY...
I SEE.

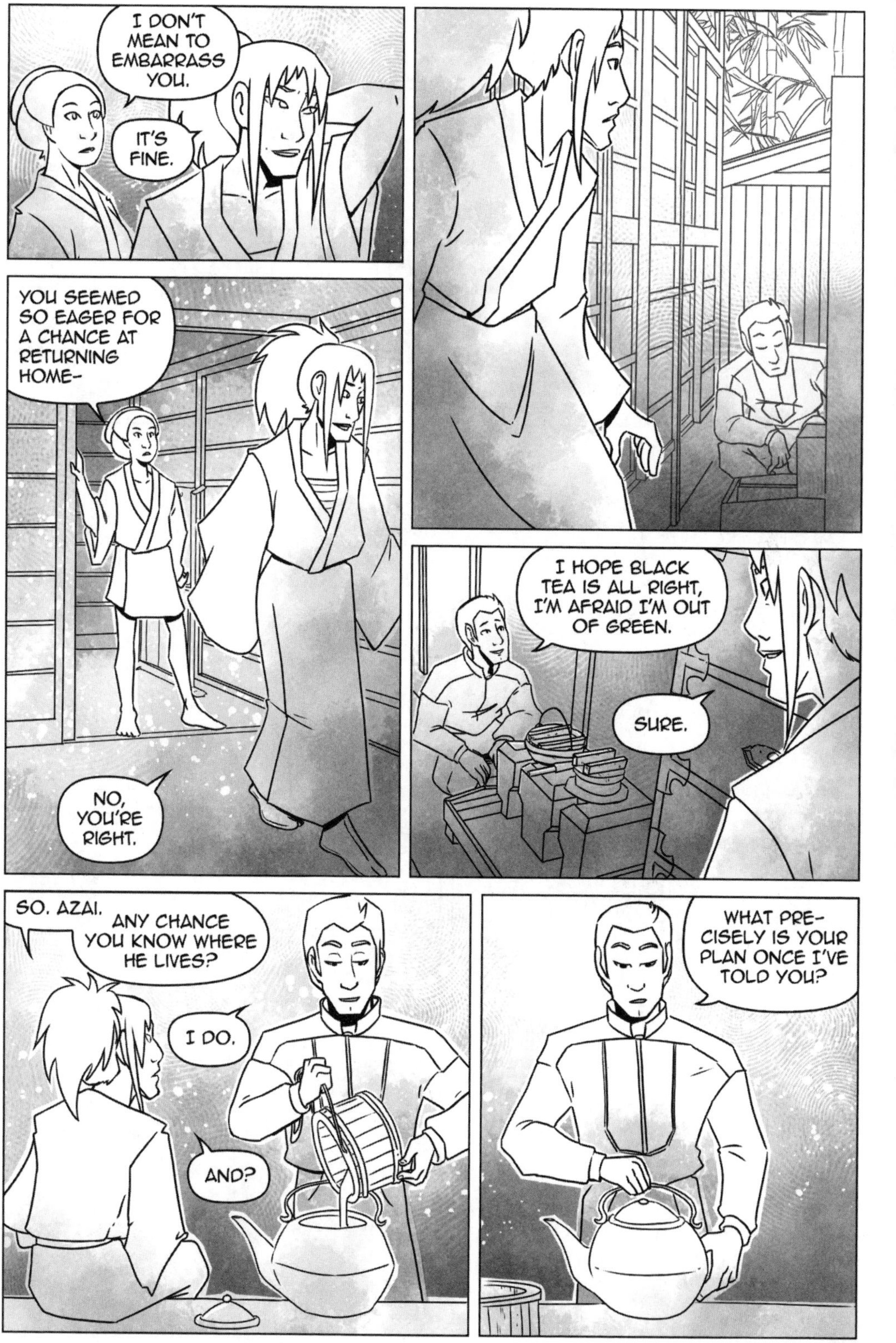
I DON'T MEAN TO EMBARRASS YOU.
IT'S FINE.
YOU SEEMED SO EAGER FOR A CHANCE AT RETURNING HOME-
NO, YOU'RE RIGHT.
I HOPE BLACK TEA IS ALL RIGHT, I'M AFRAID I'M OUT OF GREEN.
SURE.
SO. AZAI.
ANY CHANCE YOU KNOW WHERE HE LIVES?
I DO.
AND?
WHAT PRE-CISELY IS YOUR PLAN ONCE I'VE TOLD YOU?

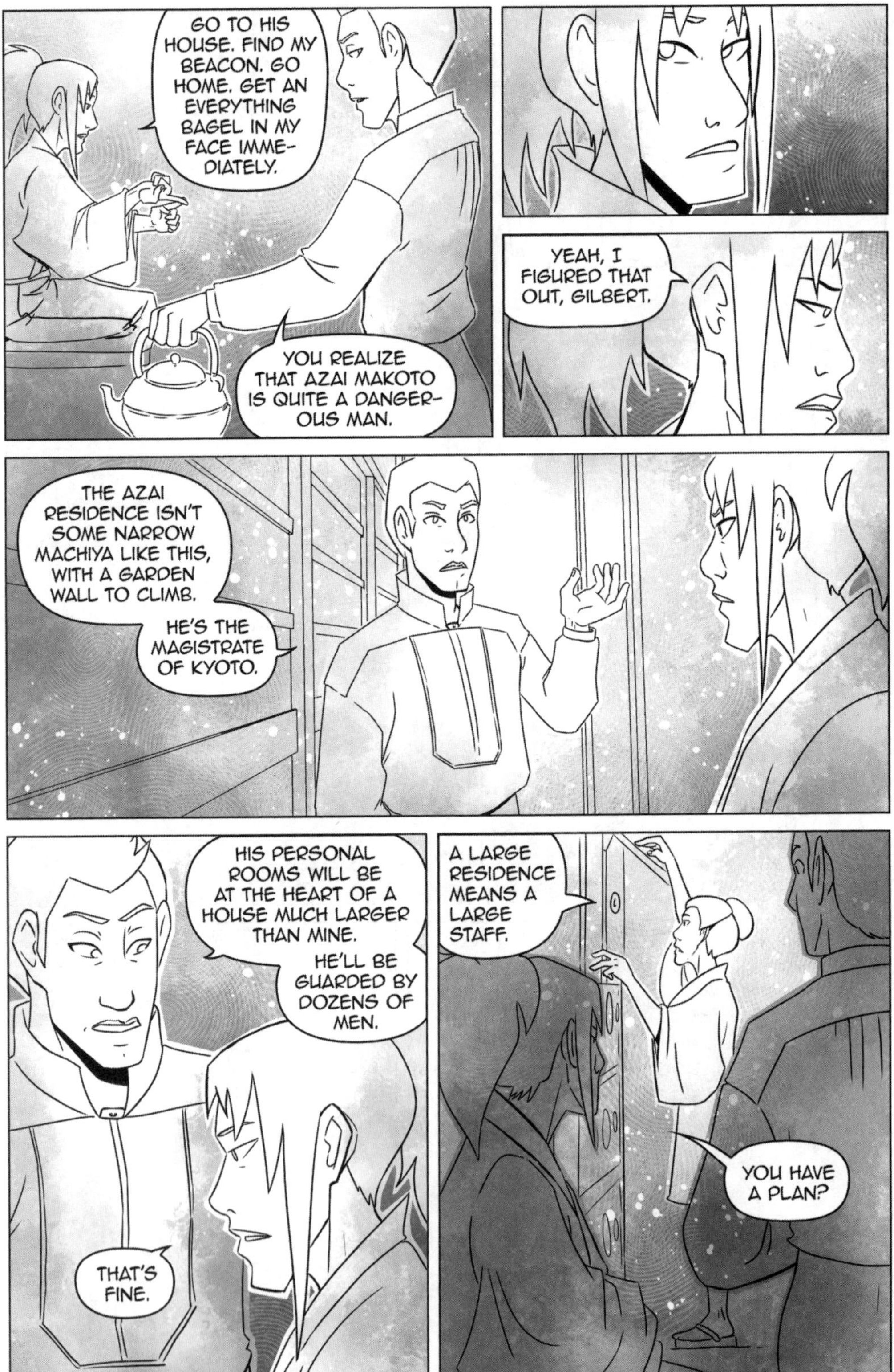
GO TO HIS HOUSE. FIND MY BEACON. GO HOME. GET AN EVERYTHING BAGEL IN MY FACE IMMEDIATELY.
YOU REALIZE THAT AZAI MAKOTO IS QUITE A DANGEROUS MAN.
YEAH, I FIGURED THAT OUT, GILBERT.
THE AZAI RESIDENCE ISN'T SOME NARROW MACHIYA LIKE THIS, WITH A GARDEN WALL TO CLIMB.
HE'S THE MAGISTRATE OF KYOTO.
HIS PERSONAL ROOMS WILL BE AT THE HEART OF A HOUSE MUCH LARGER THAN MINE.
HE'LL BE GUARDED BY DOZENS OF MEN.
THAT'S FINE.
A LARGE RESIDENCE MEANS A LARGE STAFF.
YOU HAVE A PLAN?

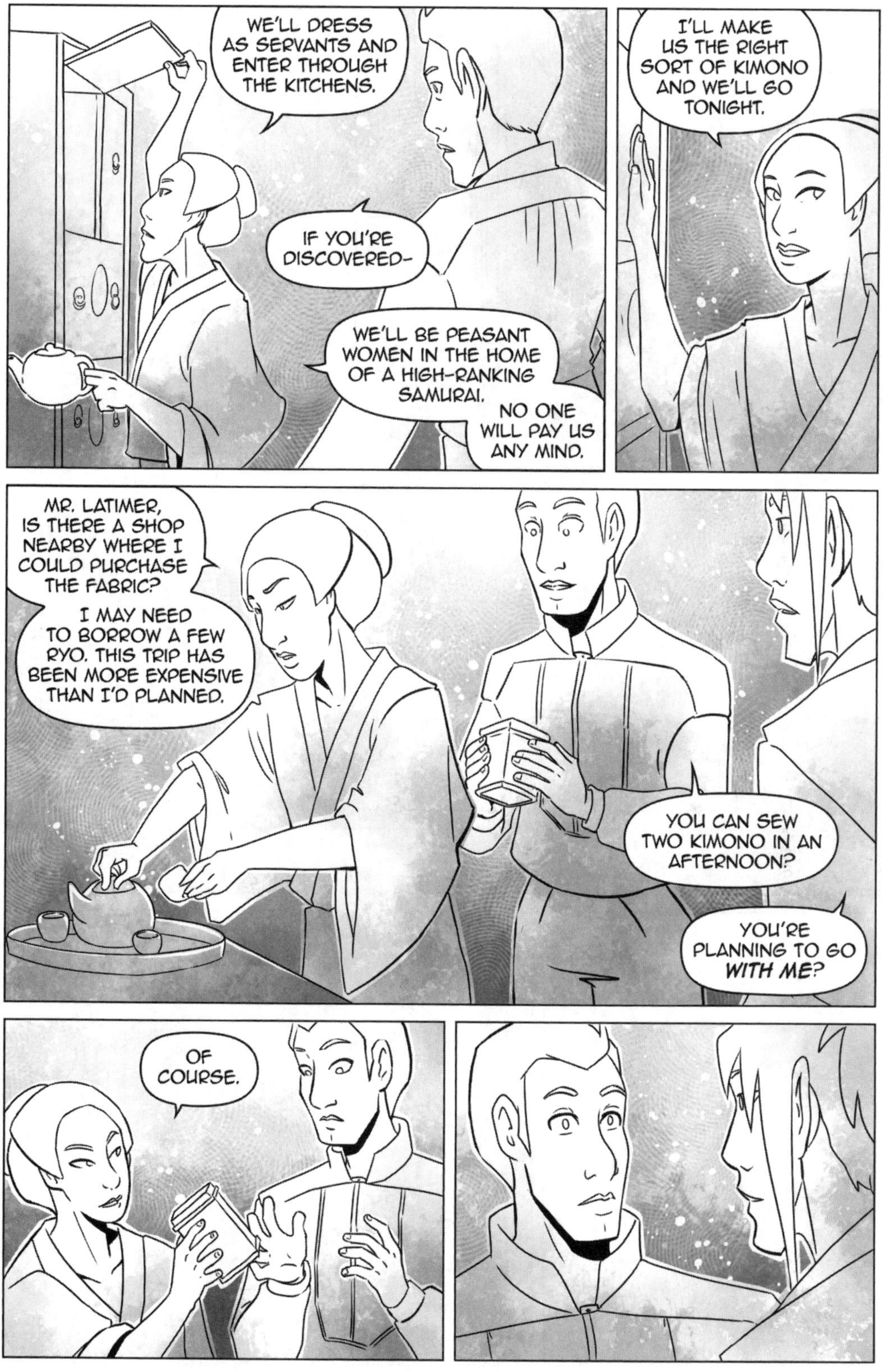
WE'LL DRESS AS SERVANTS AND ENTER THROUGH THE KITCHENS.
IF YOU'RE DISCOVERED-
WE'LL BE PEASANT WOMEN IN THE HOME OF A HIGH-RANKING SAMURAI.
NO ONE WILL PAY US ANY MIND.
I'LL MAKE US THE RIGHT SORT OF KIMONO AND WE'LL GO TONIGHT.
MR. LATIMER, IS THERE A SHOP NEARBY WHERE I COULD PURCHASE THE FABRIC?
I MAY NEED TO BORROW A FEW RYO. THIS TRIP HAS BEEN MORE EXPENSIVE THAN I'D PLANNED.
YOU CAN SEW TWO KIMONO IN AN AFTERNOON?
YOU'RE PLANNING TO GO *WITH ME*?
OF COURSE.

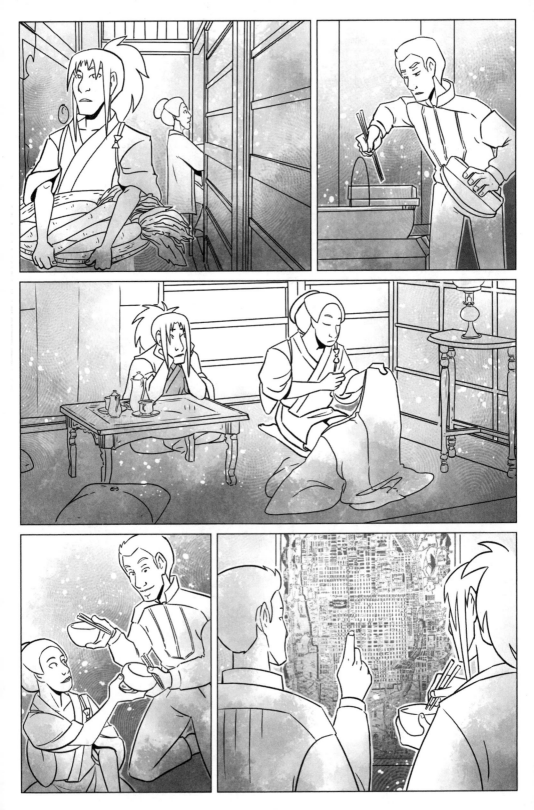

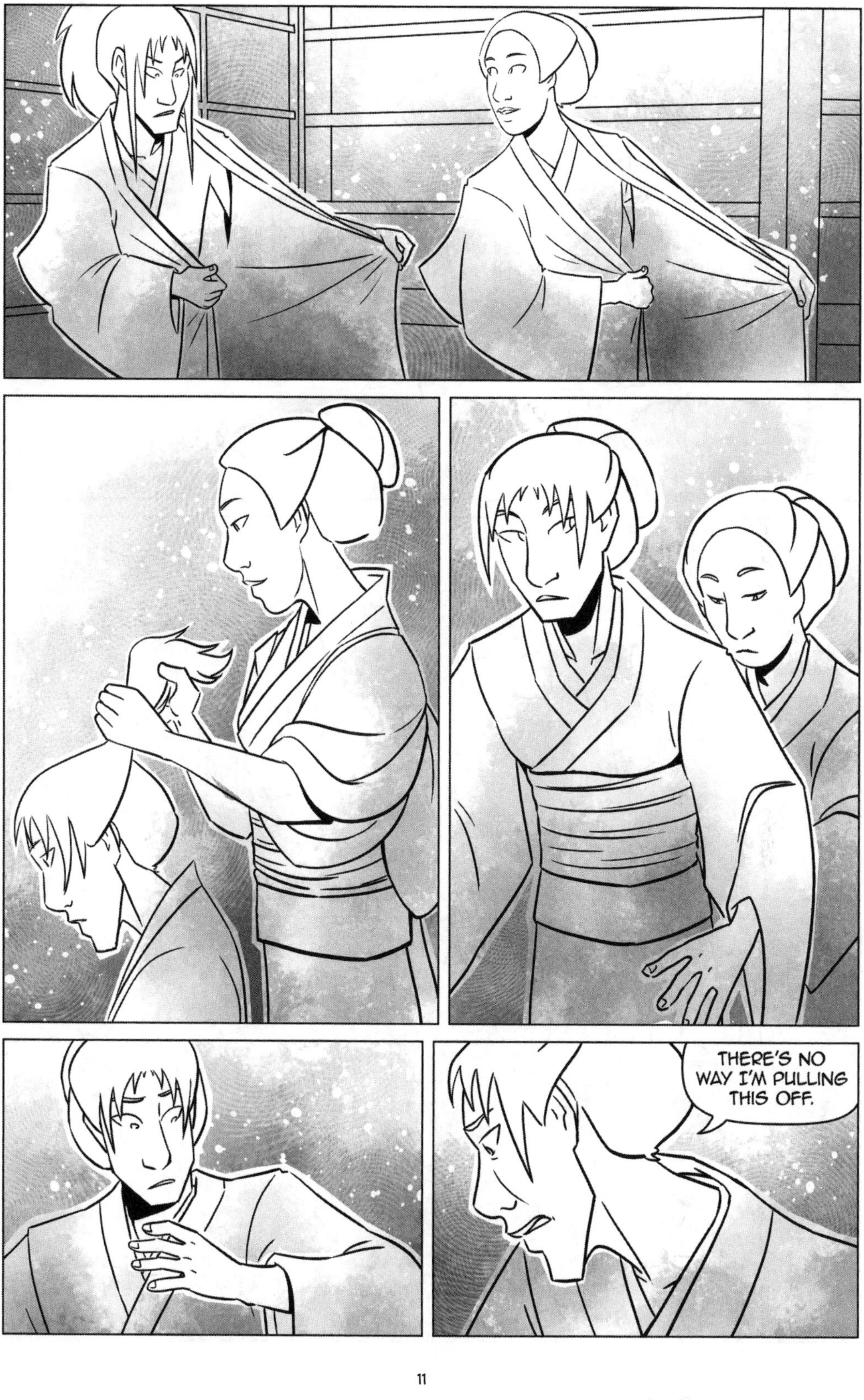
THERE'S NO WAY I'M PULLING THIS OFF.

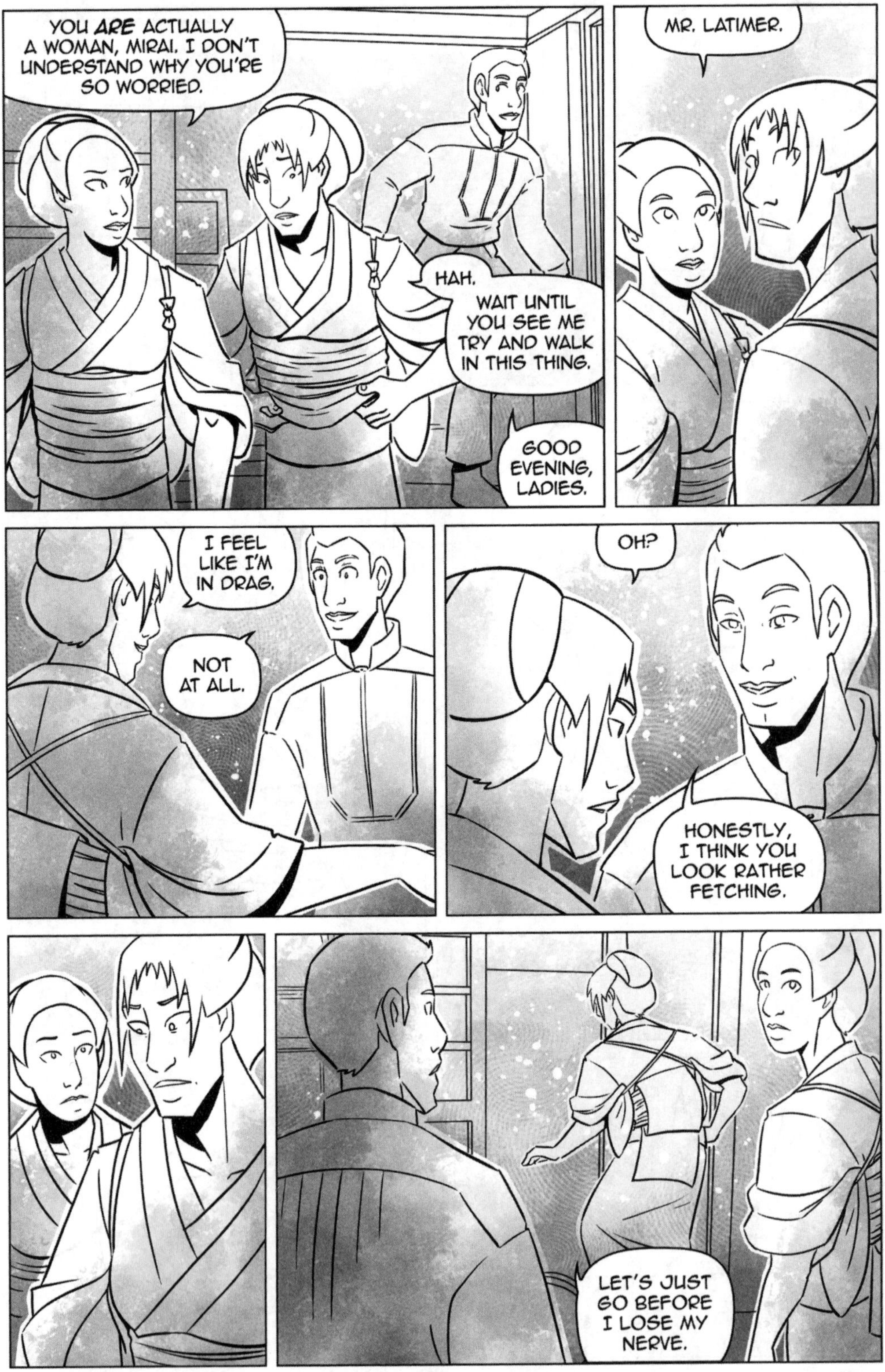

YOU ARE ACTUALLY A WOMAN, MIRAI. I DON'T UNDERSTAND WHY YOU'RE SO WORRIED.
HAH.
WAIT UNTIL YOU SEE ME TRY AND WALK IN THIS THING.
GOOD EVENING, LADIES.
MR. LATIMER.
I FEEL LIKE I'M IN DRAG.
NOT AT ALL.
OH?
HONESTLY, I THINK YOU LOOK RATHER FETCHING.
LET'S JUST GO BEFORE I LOSE MY NERVE.

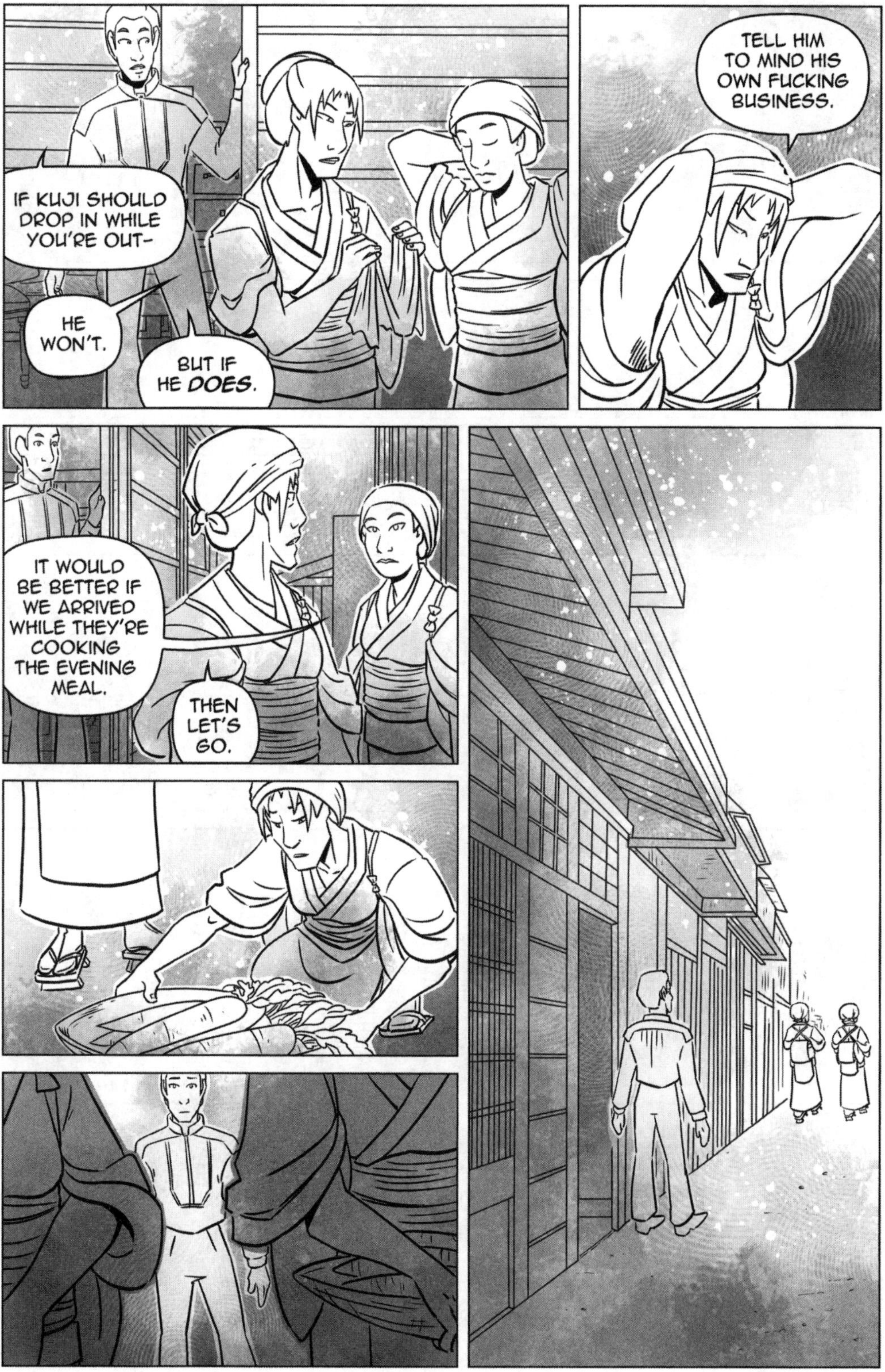
IF KUJI SHOULD DROP IN WHILE YOU'RE OUT-
HE WON'T.
BUT IF HE *DOES*.
TELL HIM TO MIND HIS OWN FUCKING BUSINESS.
IT WOULD BE BETTER IF WE ARRIVED WHILE THEY'RE COOKING THE EVENING MEAL.
THEN LET'S GO.

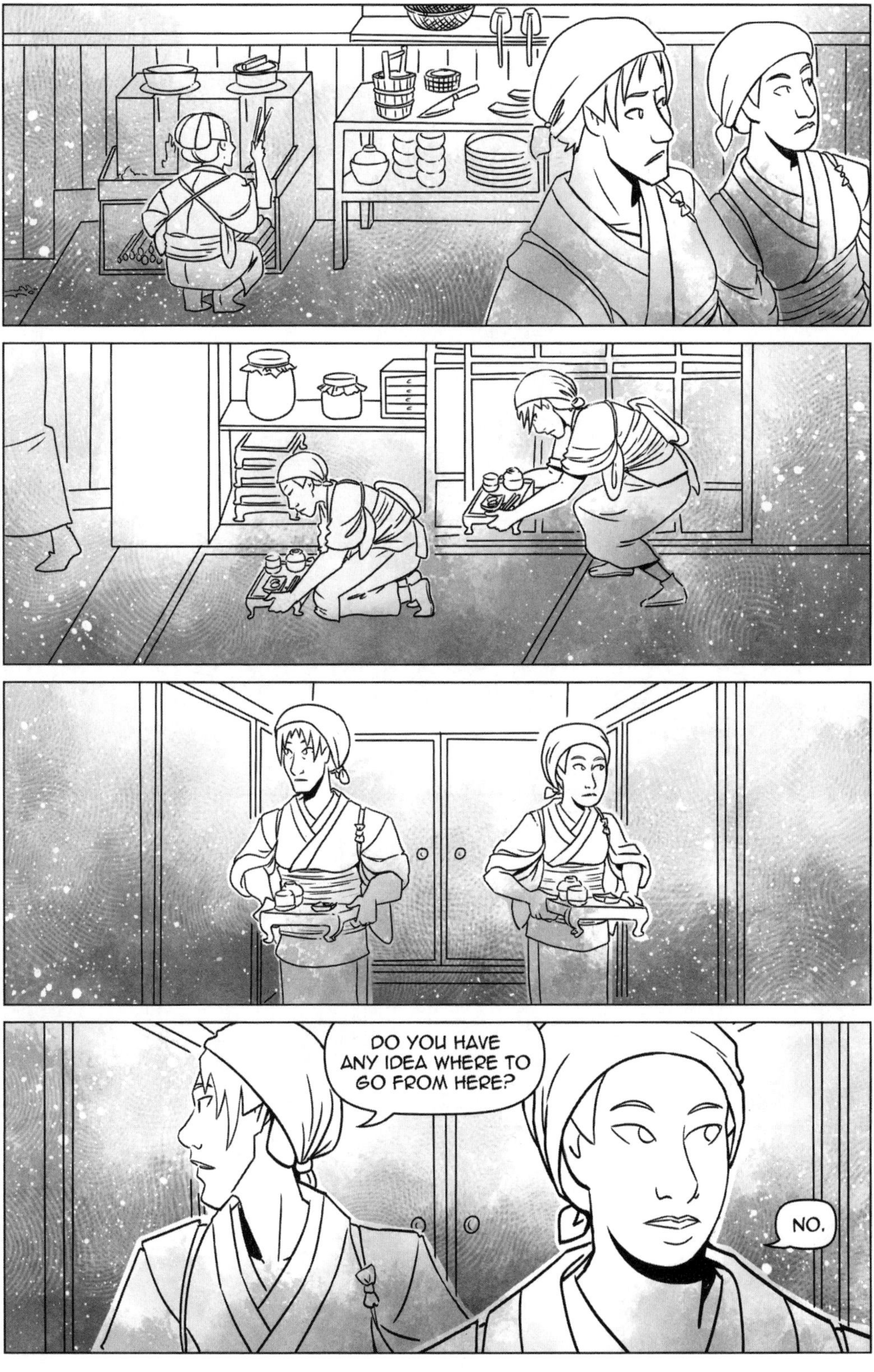
DO YOU HAVE ANY IDEA WHERE TO GO FROM HERE?
NO.

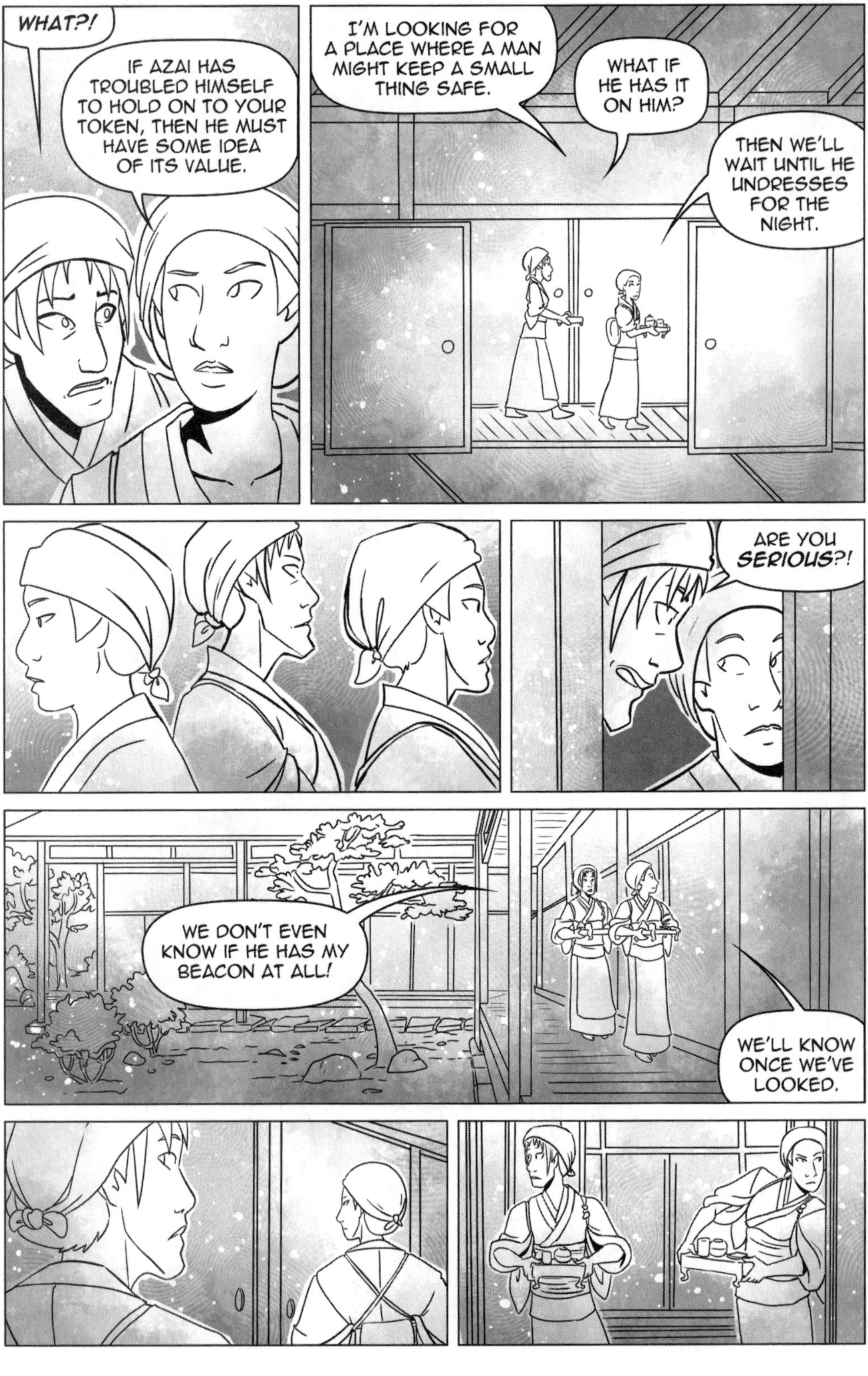
WHAT?!
IF AZAI HAS TROUBLED HIMSELF TO HOLD ON TO YOUR TOKEN, THEN HE MUST HAVE SOME IDEA OF ITS VALUE.
I'M LOOKING FOR A PLACE WHERE A MAN MIGHT KEEP A SMALL THING SAFE.
WHAT IF HE HAS IT ON HIM?
THEN WE'LL WAIT UNTIL HE UNDRESSES FOR THE NIGHT.
ARE YOU SERIOUS?!
WE DON'T EVEN KNOW IF HE HAS MY BEACON AT ALL!
WE'LL KNOW ONCE WE'VE LOOKED.

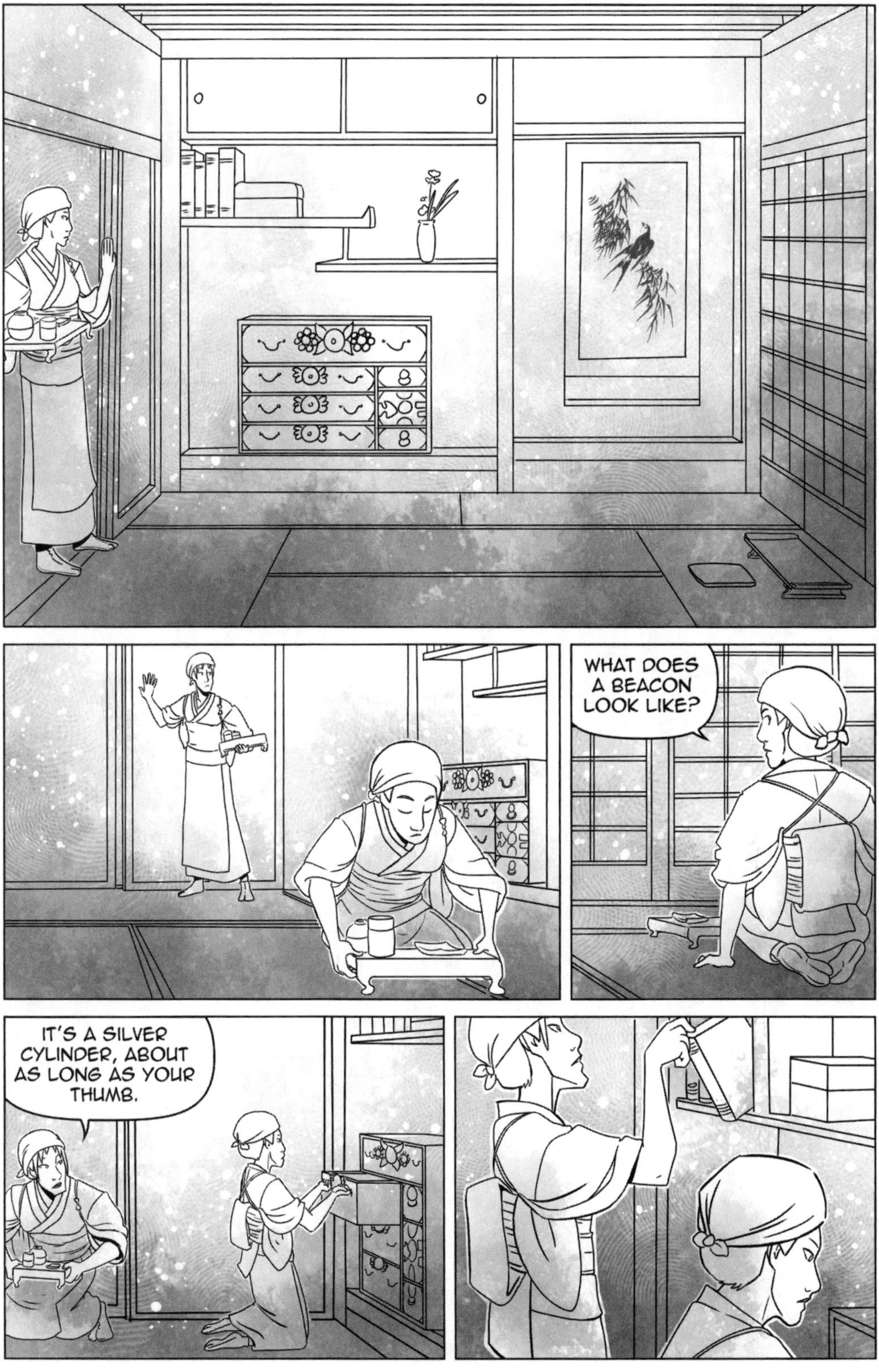
WHAT DOES A BEACON LOOK LIKE?
IT'S A SILVER CYLINDER, ABOUT AS LONG AS YOUR THUMB.

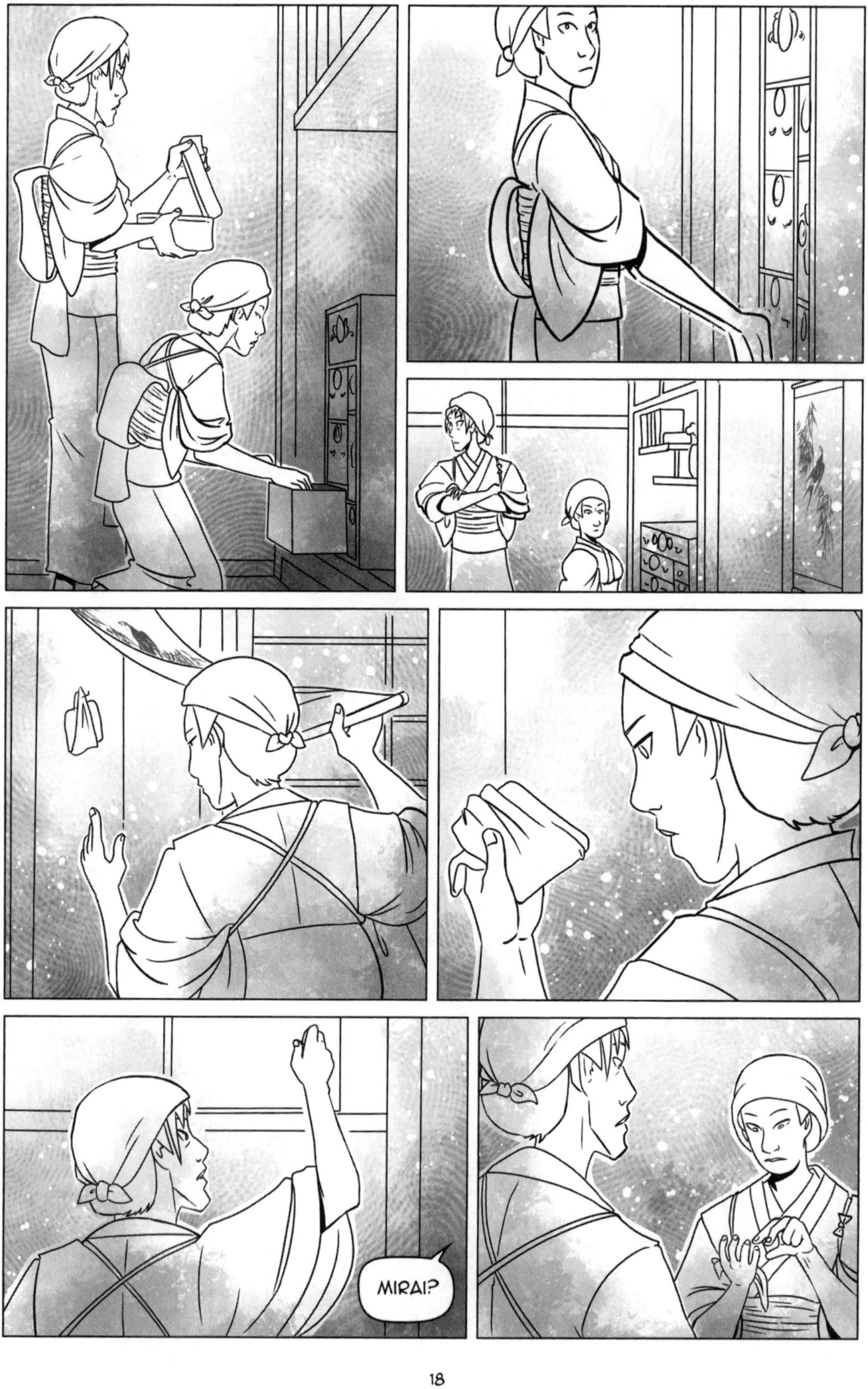
MIRAI?

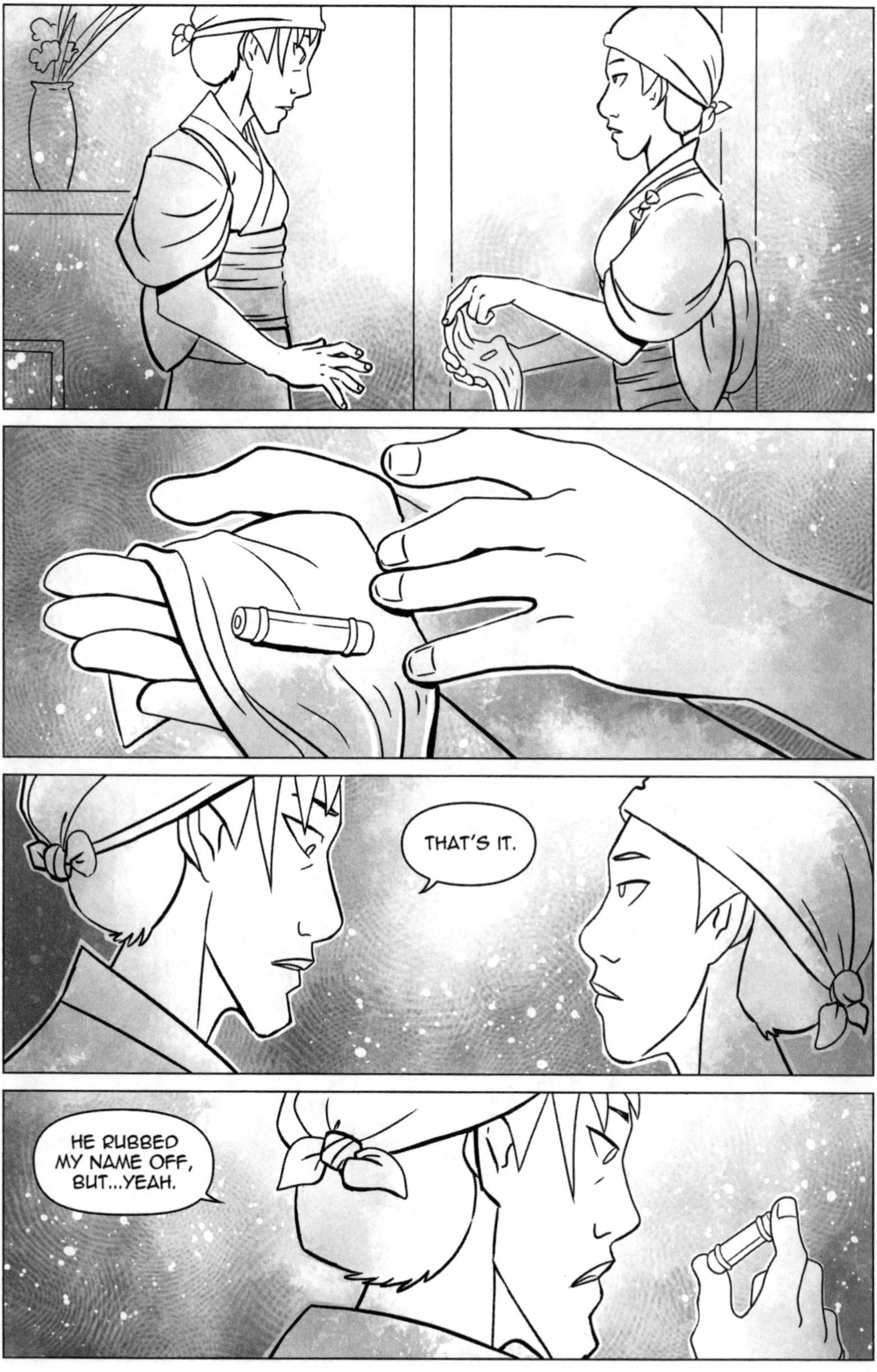
THAT'S IT.
HE RUBBED MY NAME OFF, BUT...YEAH.

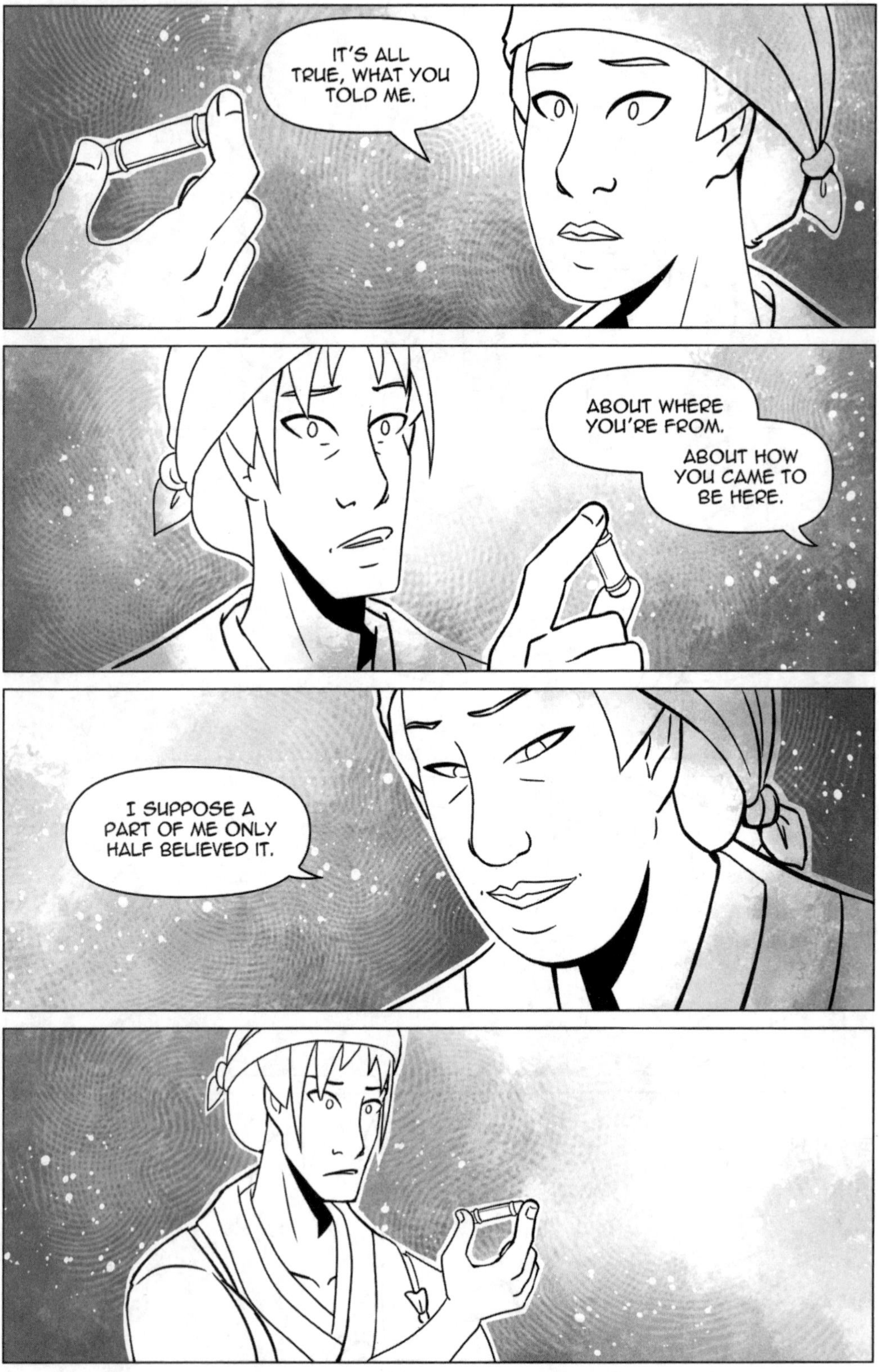
IT'S ALL TRUE, WHAT YOU TOLD ME.
ABOUT WHERE YOU'RE FROM.
ABOUT HOW YOU CAME TO BE HERE.
I SUPPOSE A PART OF ME ONLY HALF BELIEVED IT.

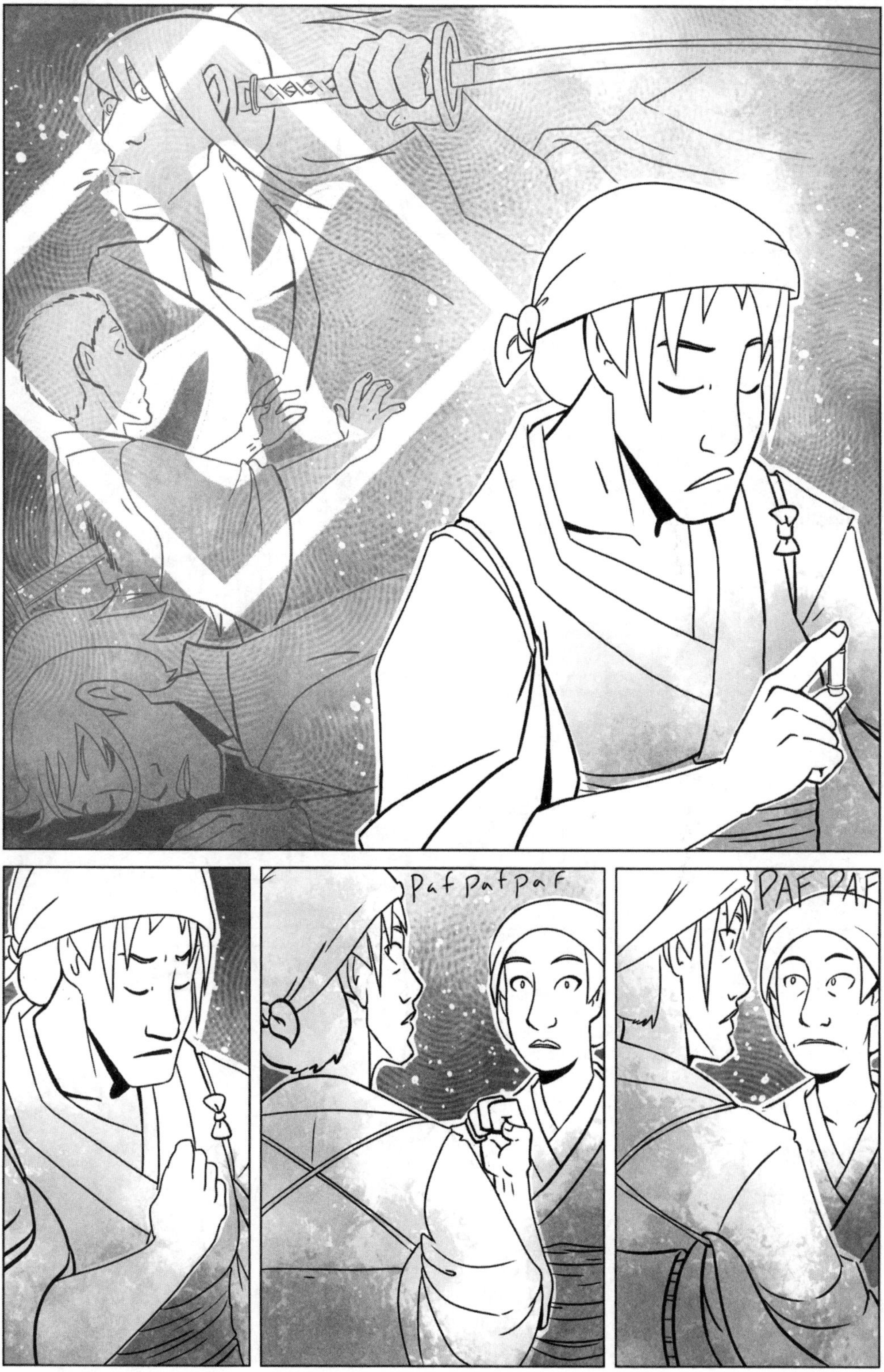
Paf paf paf
PAF PAF

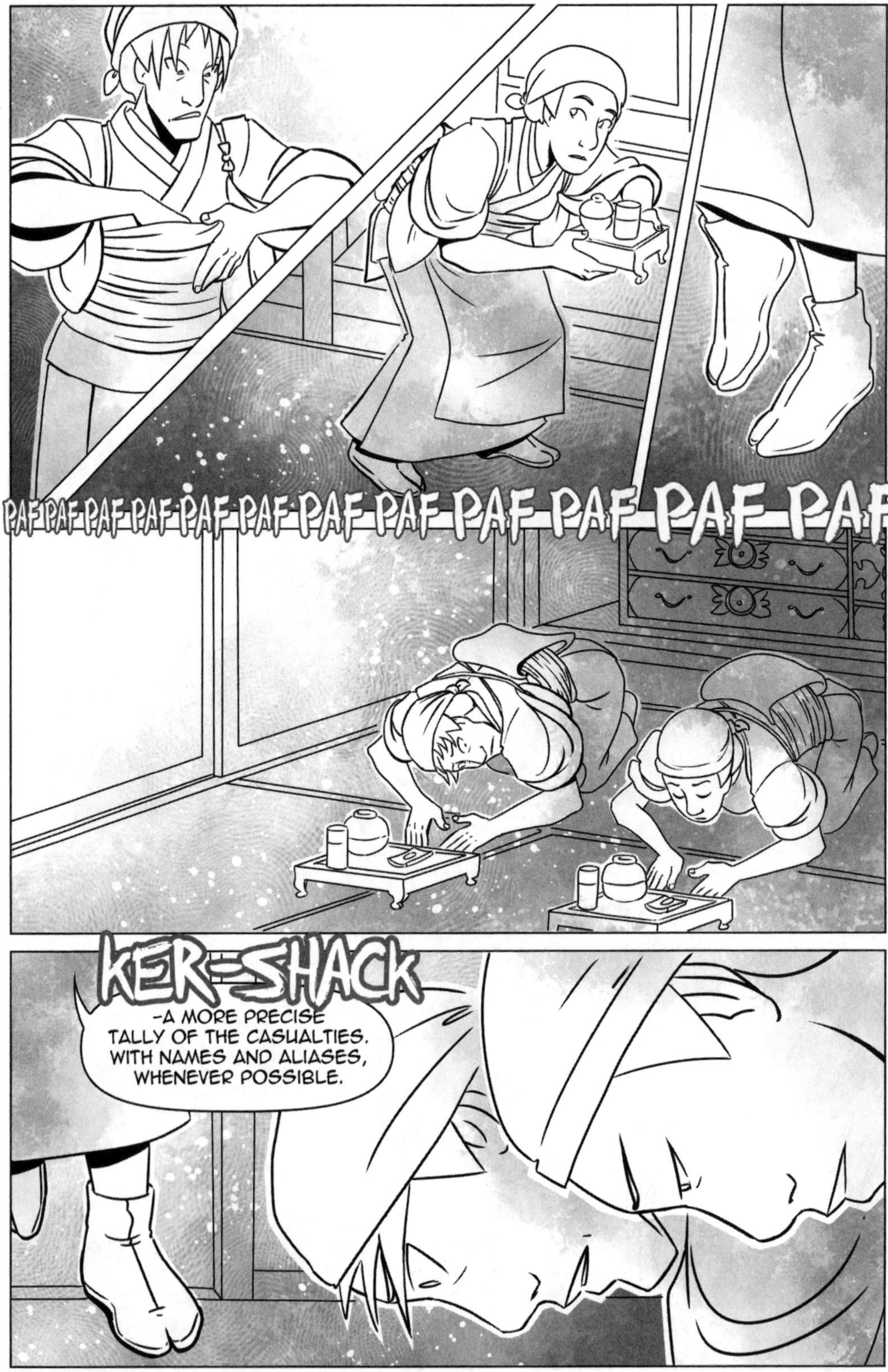
PAF PAF PAF PAF PAF PAF PAF PAF PAF PAF PAF PAF
KER-SHACK
-A MORE PRECISE TALLY OF THE CASUALTIES. WITH NAMES AND ALIASES, WHENEVER POSSIBLE.

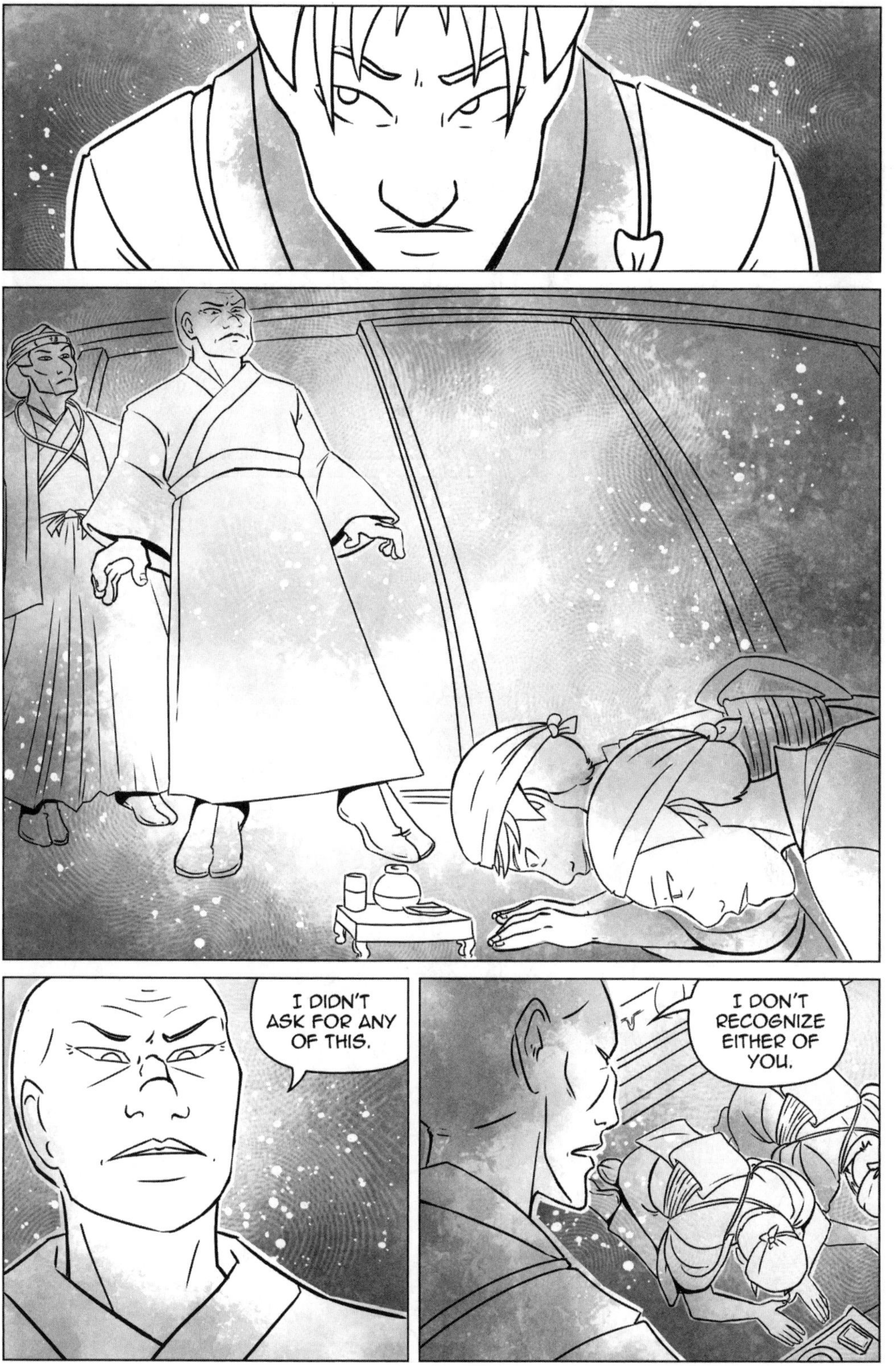
I DIDN'T ASK FOR ANY OF THIS.
I DON'T RECOGNIZE EITHER OF YOU.

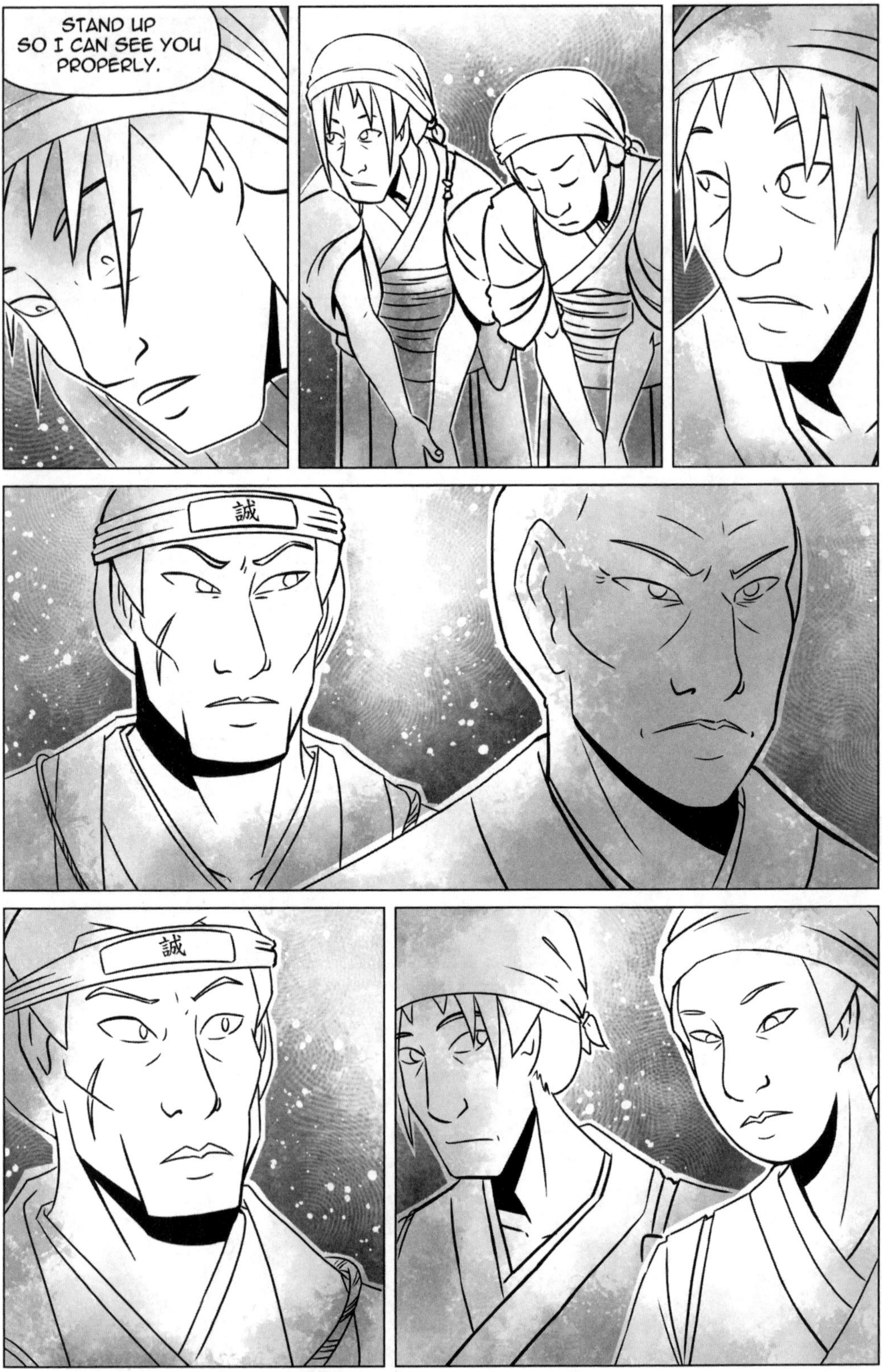
STAND UP SO I CAN SEE YOU PROPERLY.
誠
誠

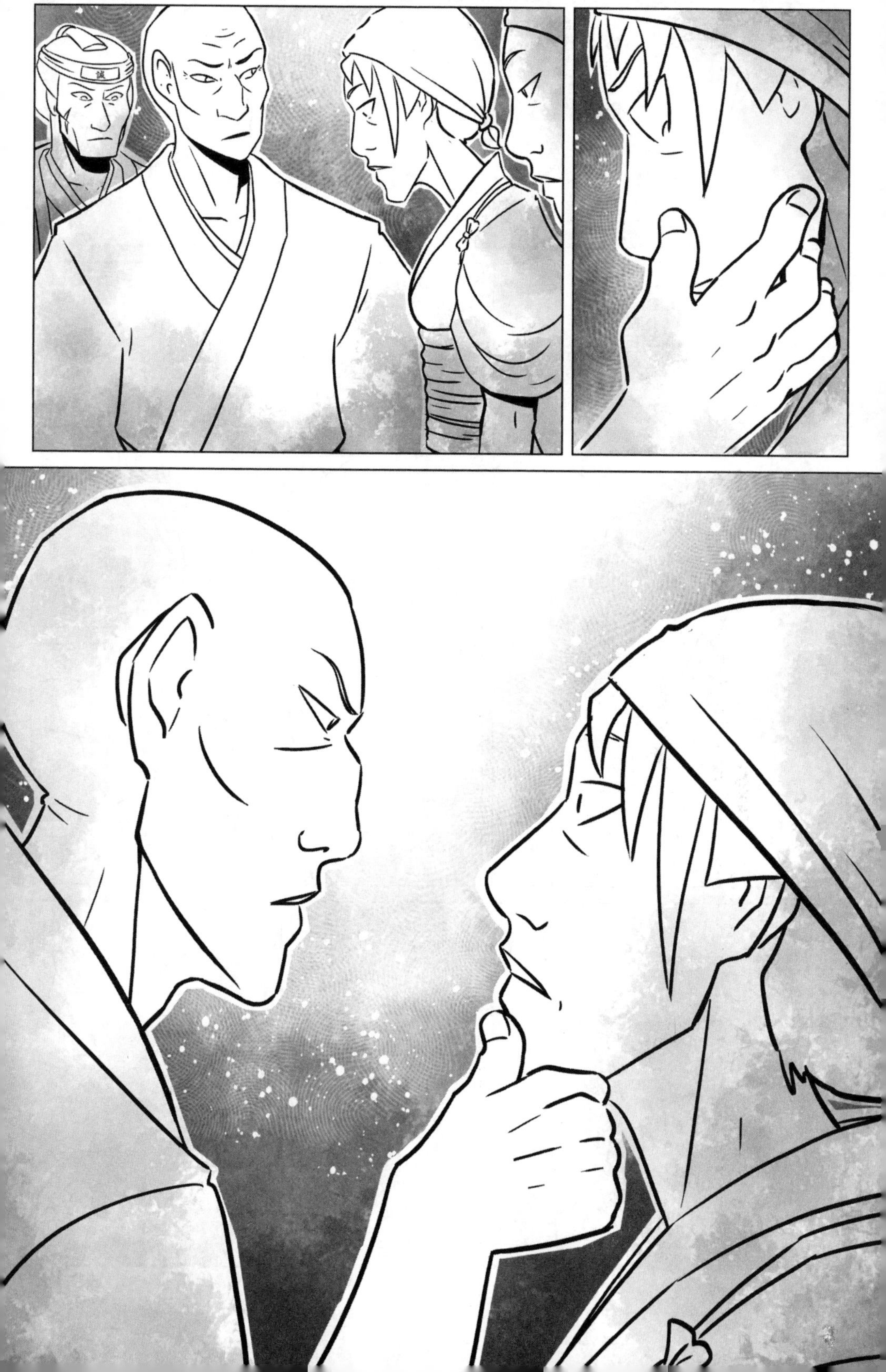

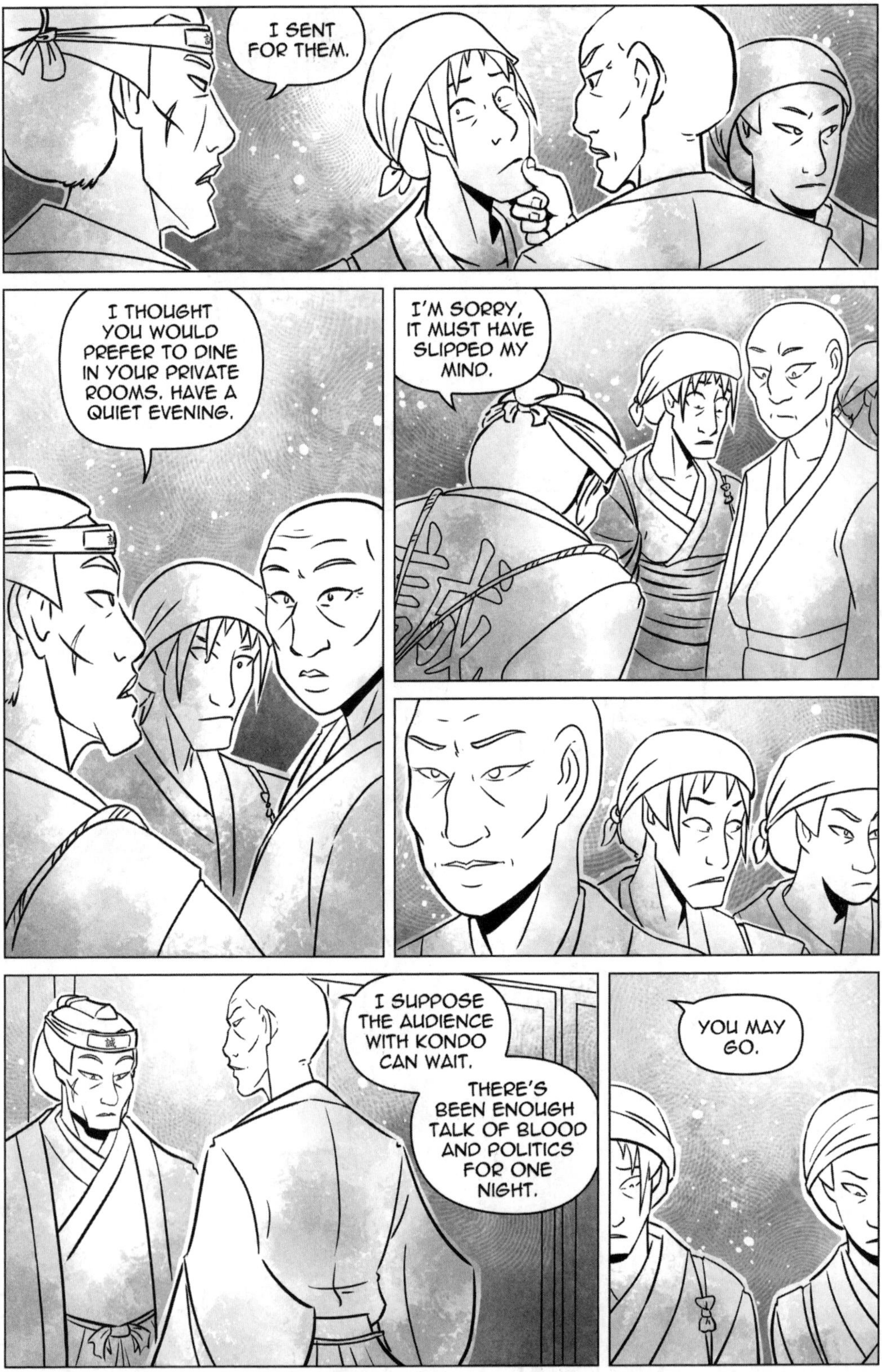
I SENT FOR THEM.
I THOUGHT YOU WOULD PREFER TO DINE IN YOUR PRIVATE ROOMS. HAVE A QUIET EVENING.
I'M SORRY, IT MUST HAVE SLIPPED MY MIND.
I SUPPOSE THE AUDIENCE WITH KONDO CAN WAIT.
THERE'S BEEN ENOUGH TALK OF BLOOD AND POLITICS FOR ONE NIGHT.
YOU MAY GO.

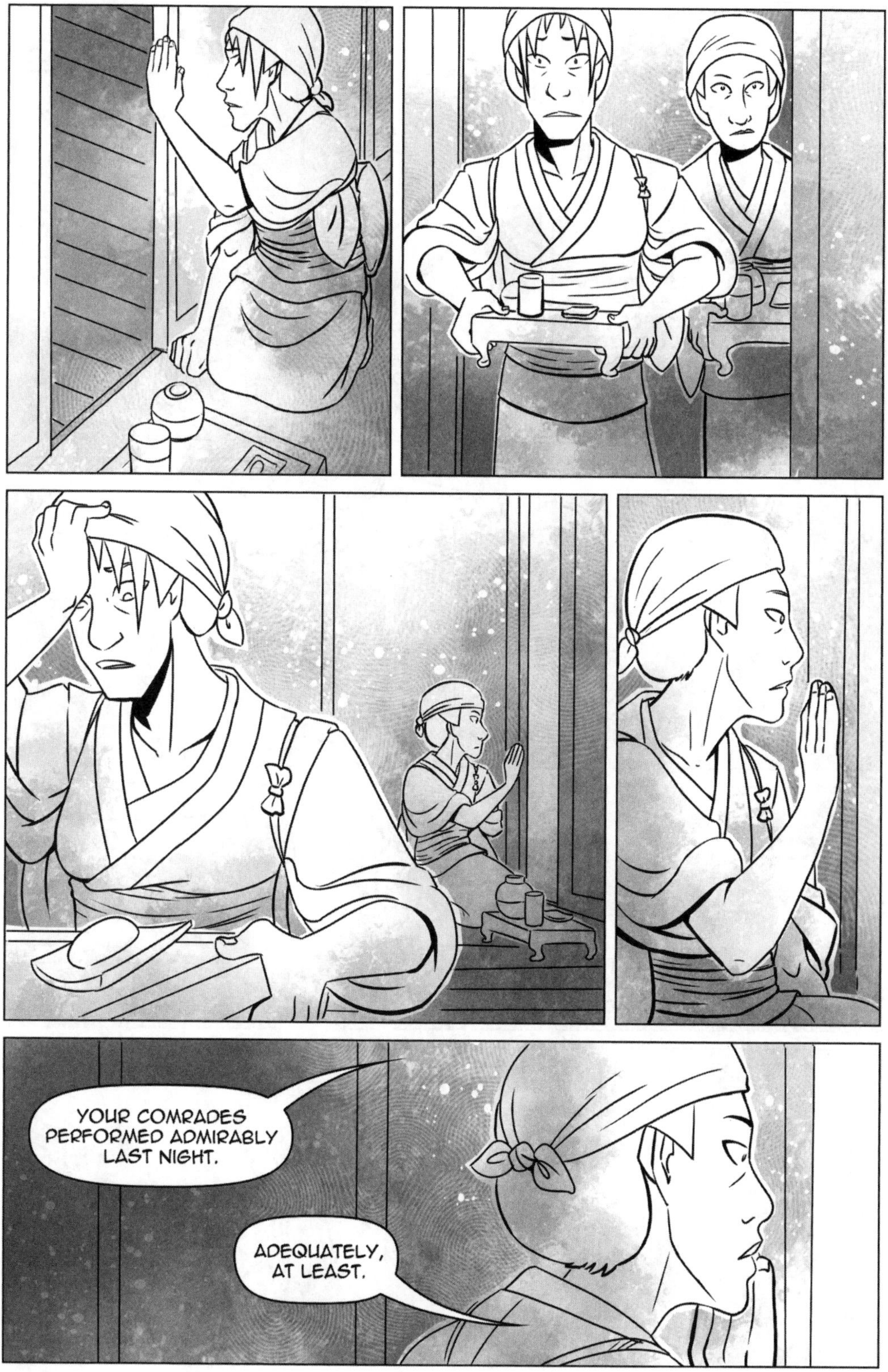
YOUR COMRADES PERFORMED ADMIRABLY LAST NIGHT.
ADEQUATELY, AT LEAST.

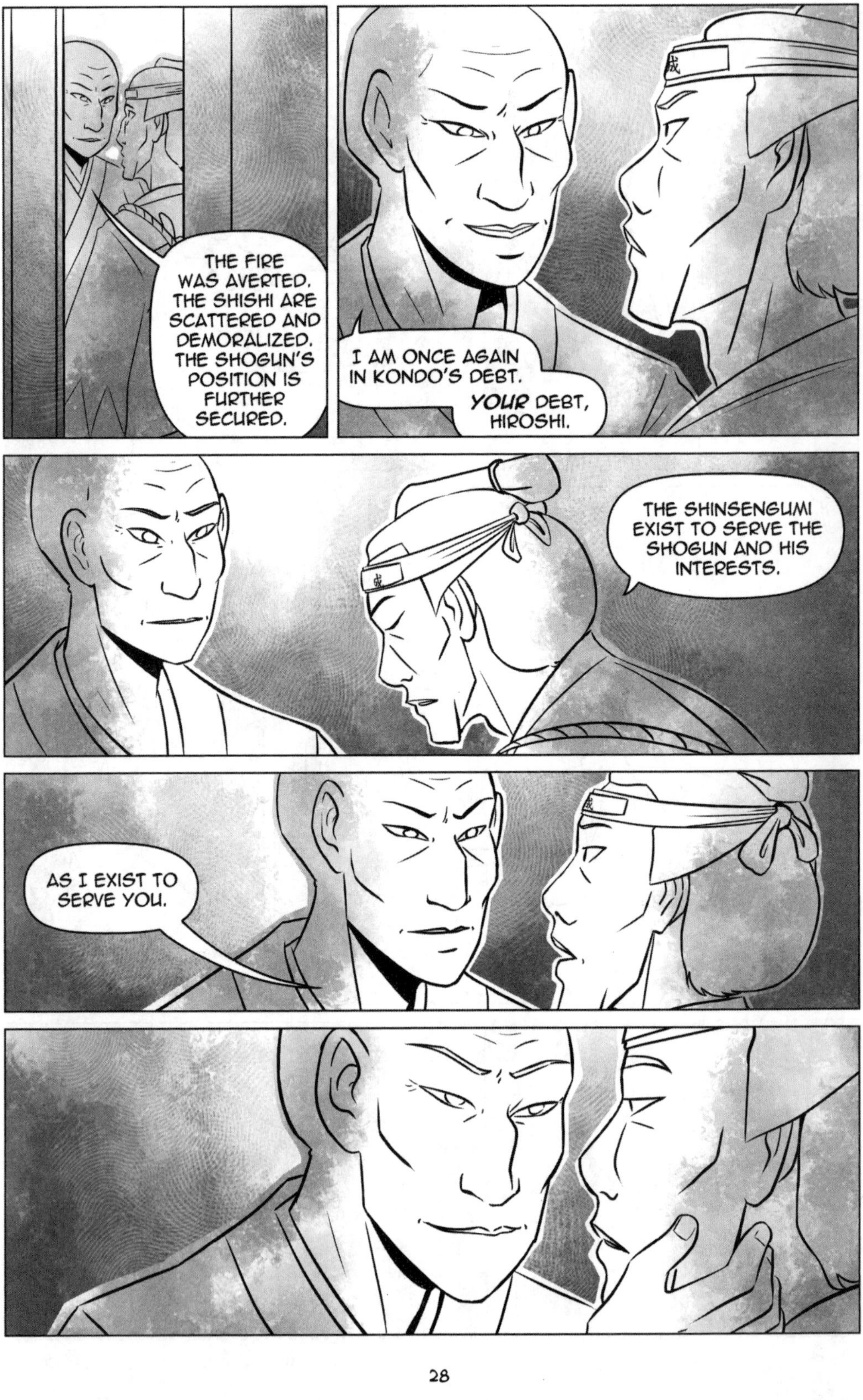
THE FIRE WAS AVERTED. THE SHISHI ARE SCATTERED AND DEMORALIZED. THE SHOGUN'S POSITION IS FURTHER SECURED.
I AM ONCE AGAIN IN KONDO'S DEBT.
*YOUR* DEBT, HIROSHI.
THE SHINSENGUMI EXIST TO SERVE THE SHOGUN AND HIS INTERESTS.
AS I EXIST TO SERVE YOU.

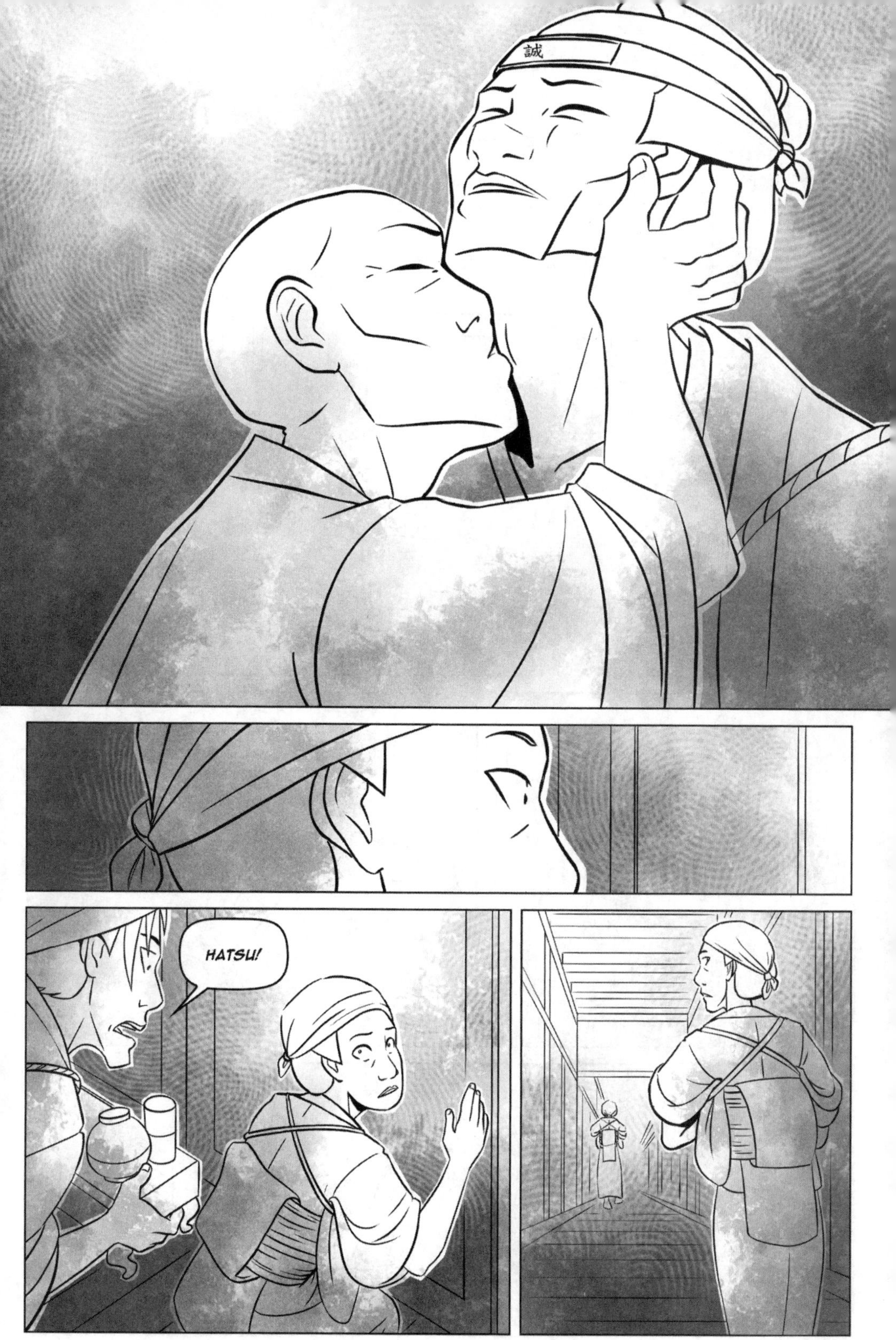
誠
HATSU!

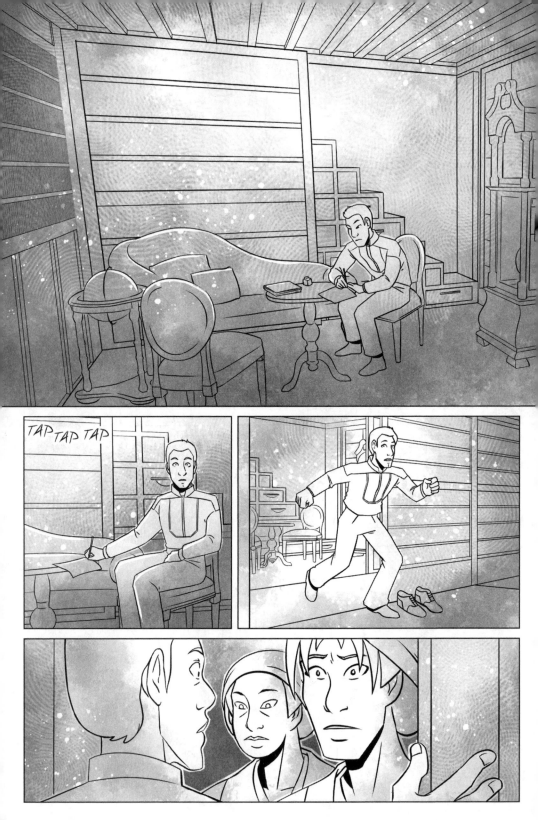

TAP TAP TAP

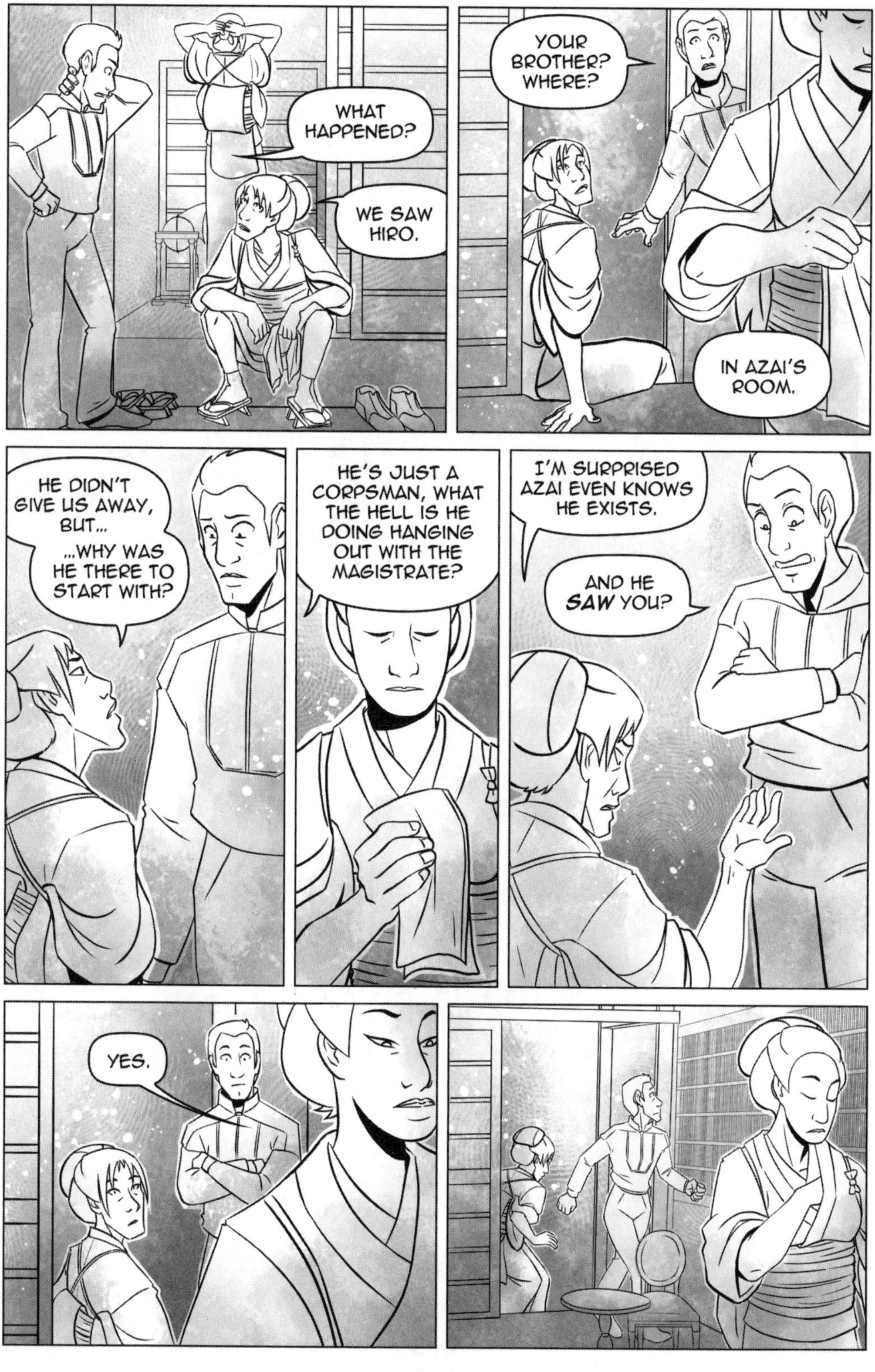
WHAT HAPPENED?
WE SAW HIRO.
YOUR BROTHER? WHERE?
IN AZAI'S ROOM.
HE DIDN'T GIVE US AWAY, BUT...
...WHY WAS HE THERE TO START WITH?
HE'S JUST A CORPSMAN, WHAT THE HELL IS HE DOING HANGING OUT WITH THE MAGISTRATE?
I'M SURPRISED AZAI EVEN KNOWS HE EXISTS.
AND HE *SAW* YOU?
YES.

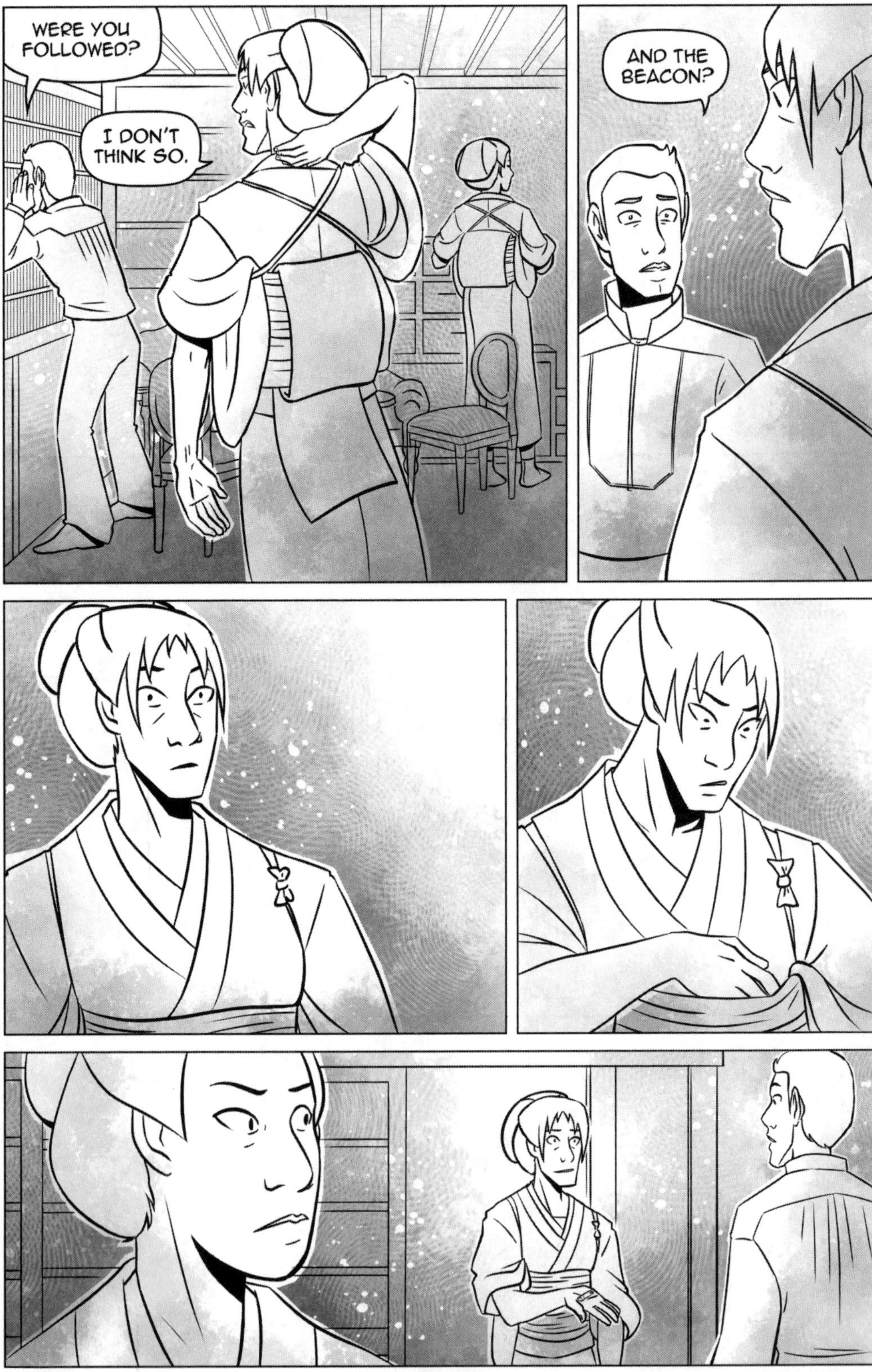
WERE YOU FOLLOWED?
I DON'T THINK SO.
AND THE BEACON?

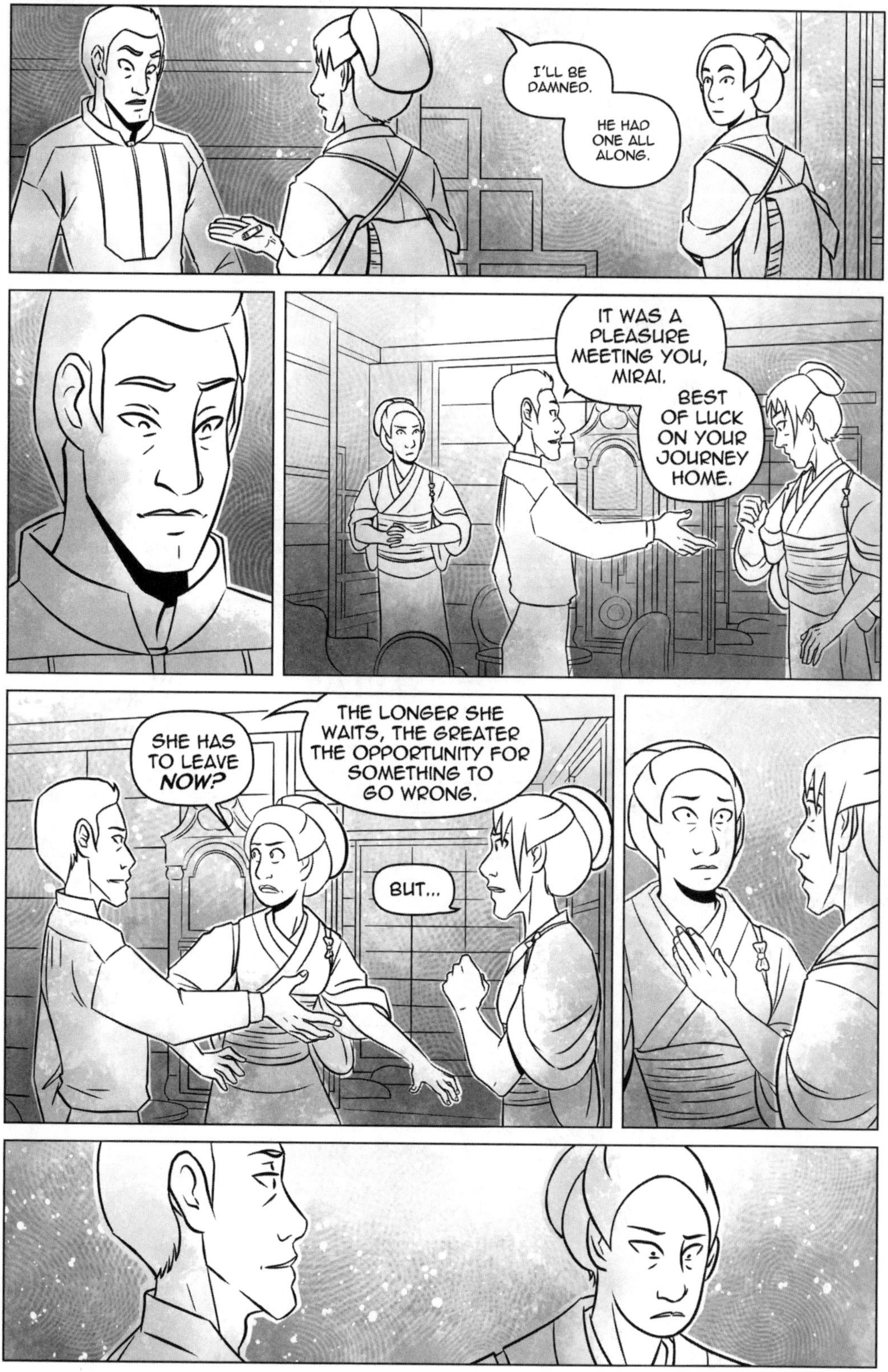
I'LL BE DAMNED.
HE HAD ONE ALL ALONG.
IT WAS A PLEASURE MEETING YOU, MIRAI.
BEST OF LUCK ON YOUR JOURNEY HOME.
SHE HAS TO LEAVE *NOW?*
THE LONGER SHE WAITS, THE GREATER THE OPPORTUNITY FOR SOMETHING TO GO WRONG.
BUT...

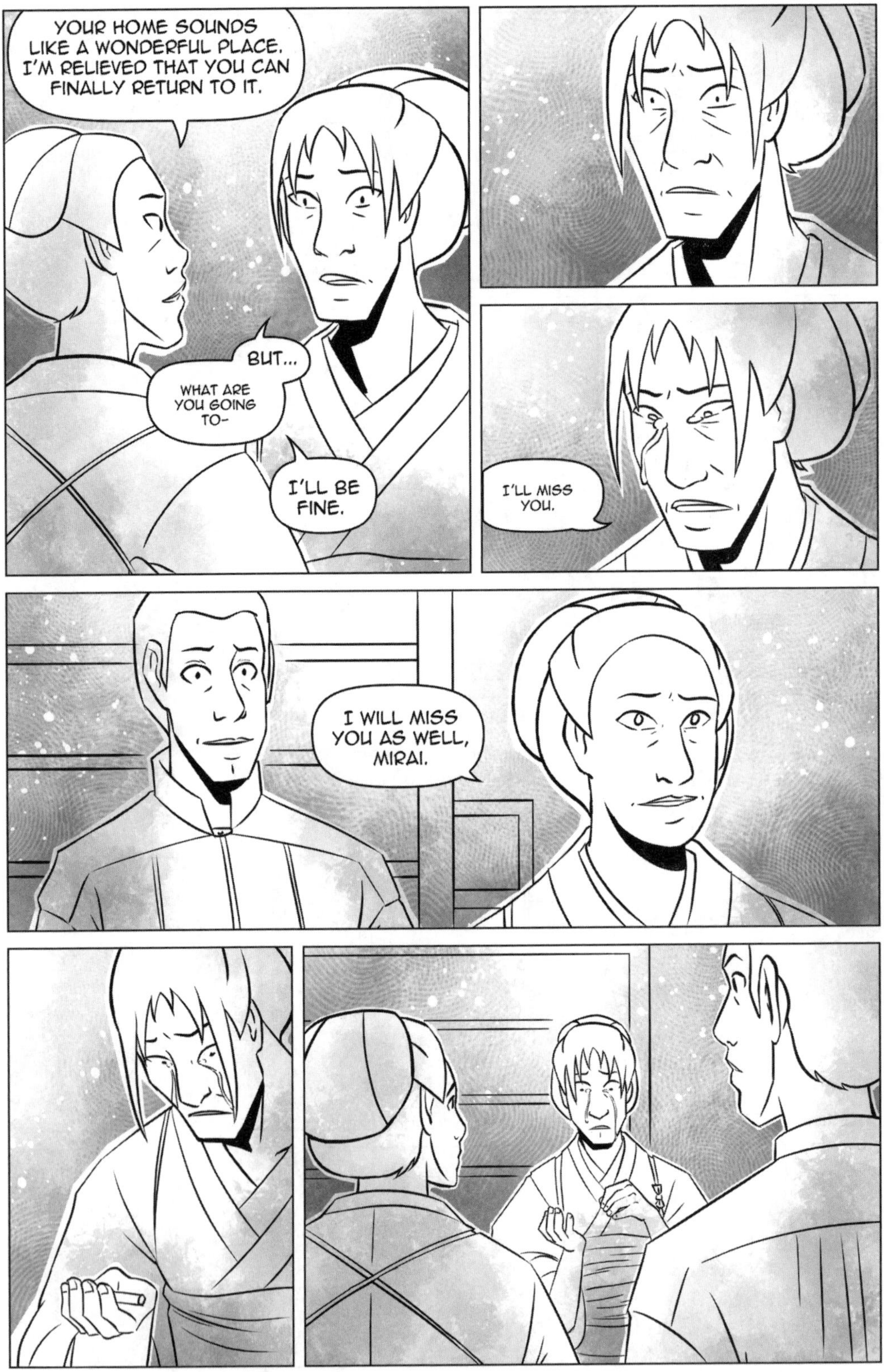
YOUR HOME SOUNDS LIKE A WONDERFUL PLACE. I'M RELIEVED THAT YOU CAN FINALLY RETURN TO IT.
BUT...
WHAT ARE YOU GOING TO-
I'LL BE FINE.
I'LL MISS YOU.
I WILL MISS YOU AS WELL, MIRAI.

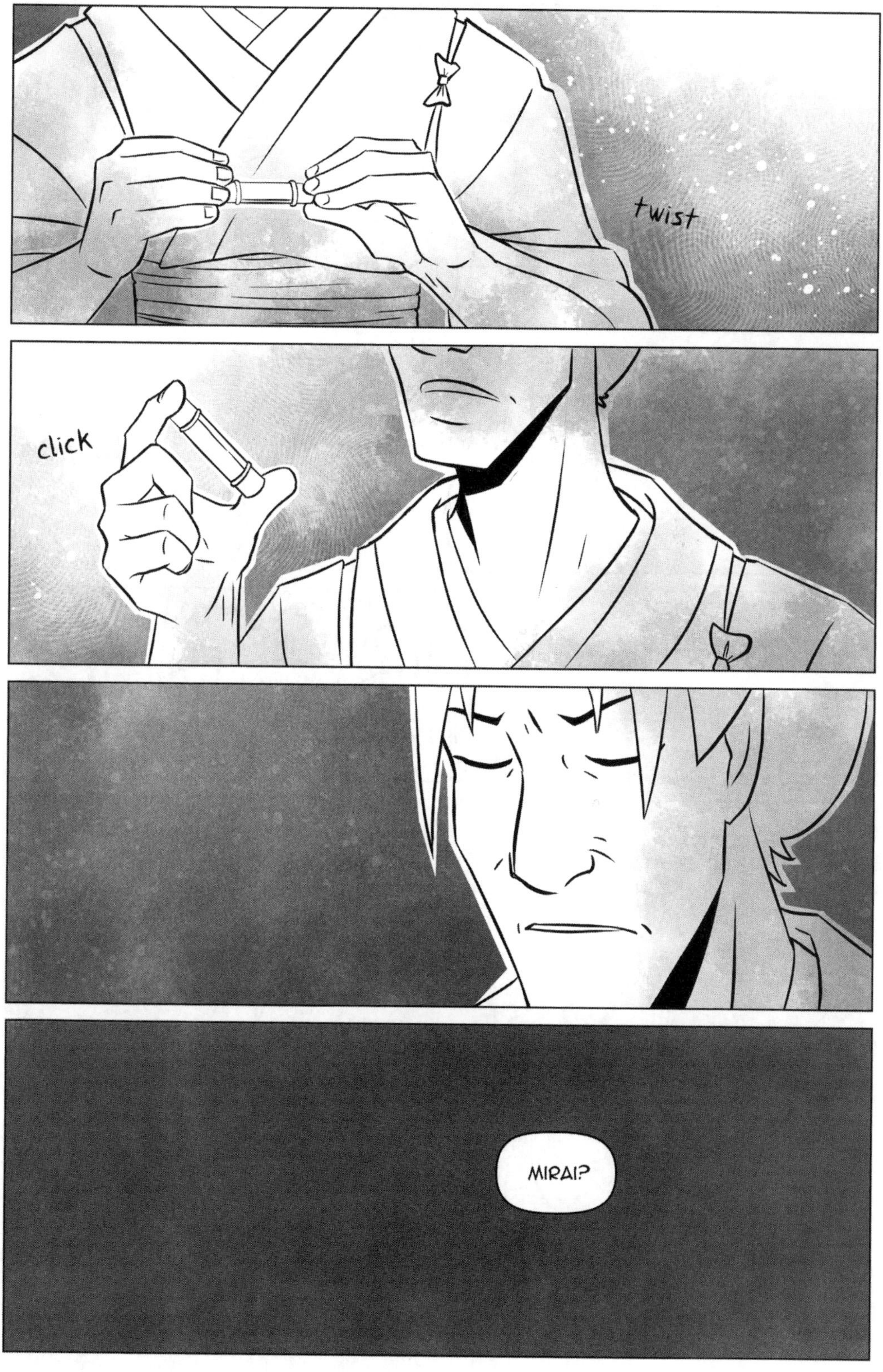
twist
click
MIRAI?

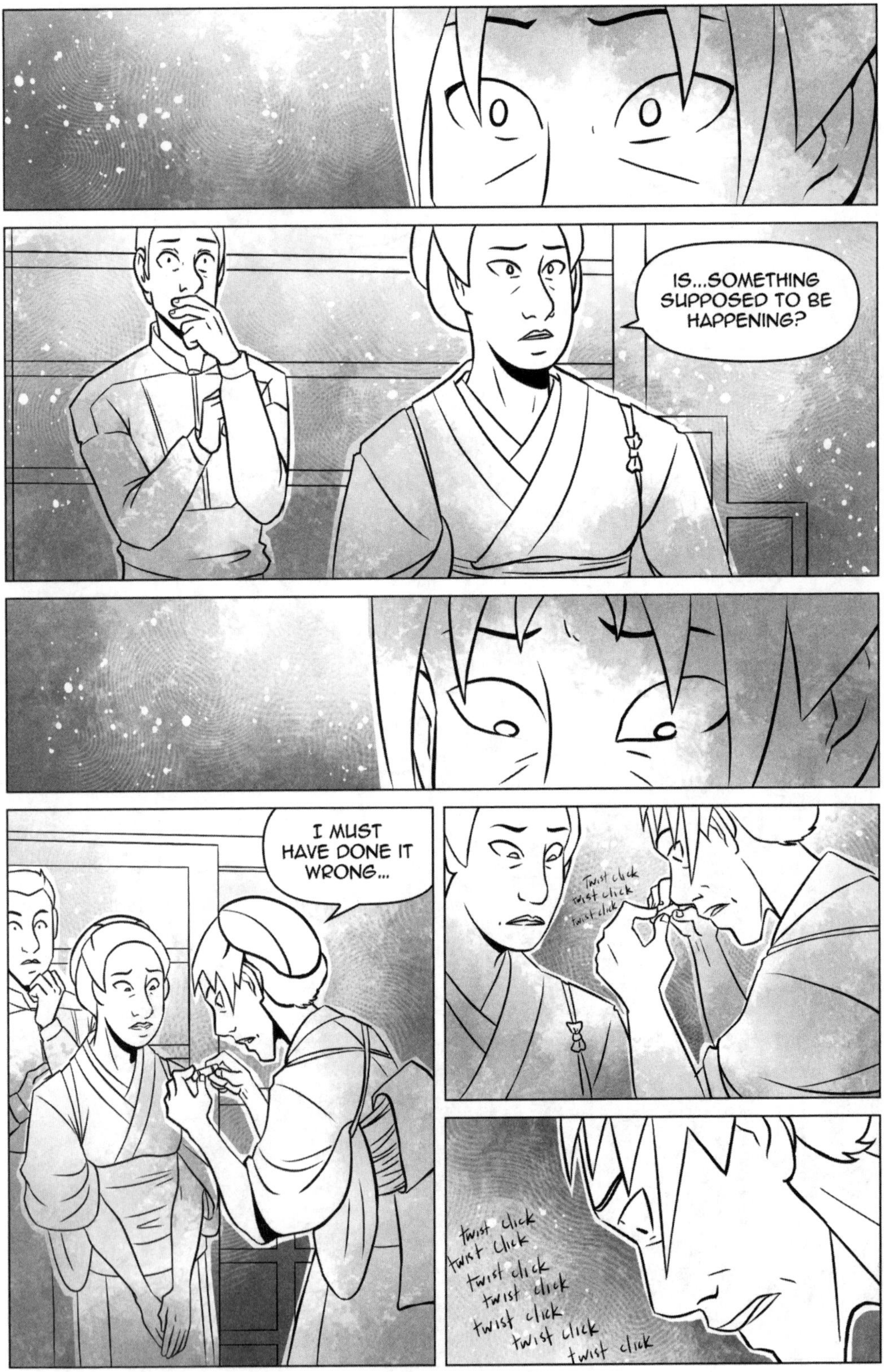
IS...SOMETHING SUPPOSED TO BE HAPPENING?
I MUST HAVE DONE IT WRONG...
twist click
twist click
twist click
twist click
twist click
twist click
twist click
twist click
twist click
twist click

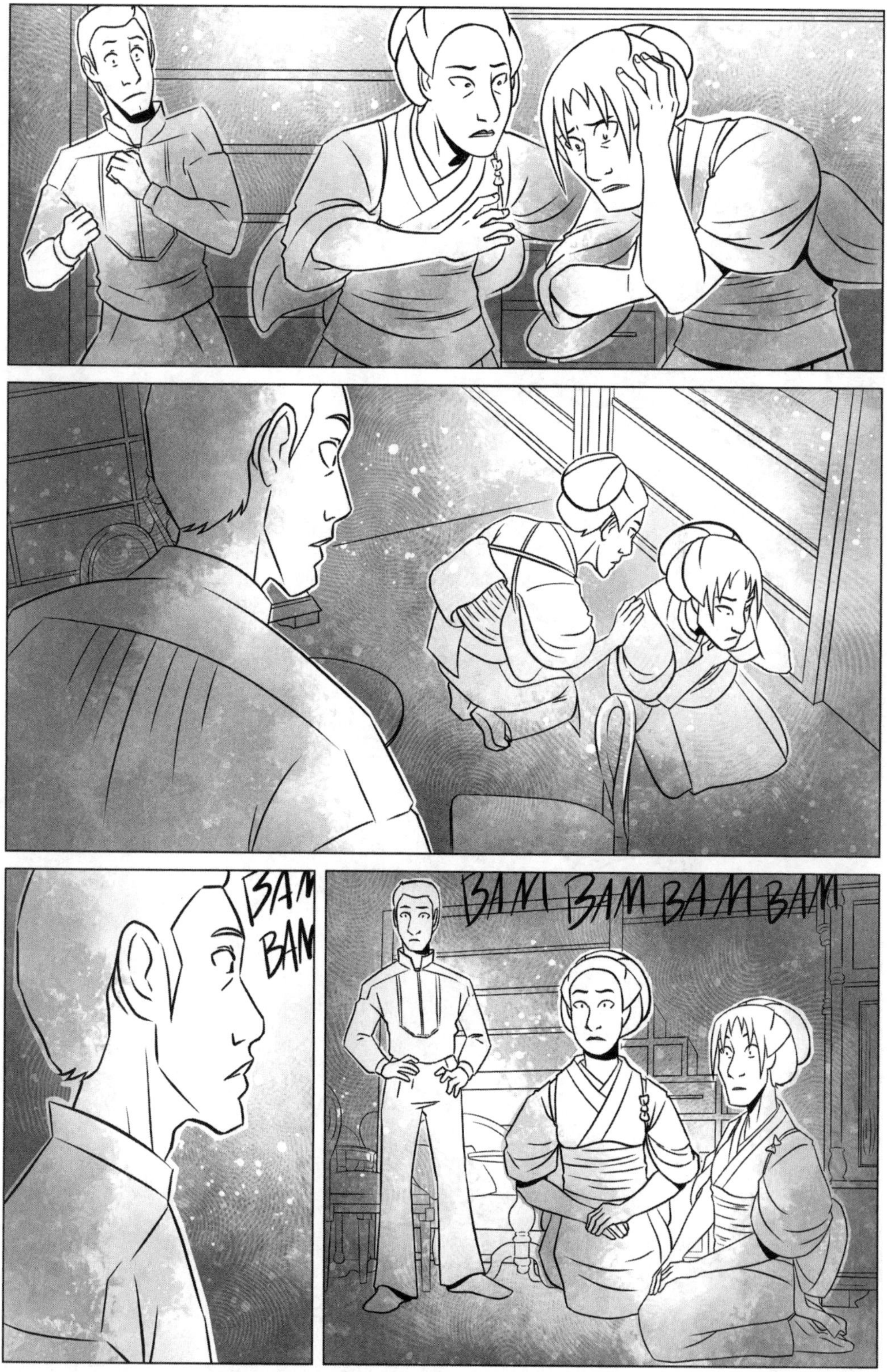
BAM
BAM
BAM BAM BAM BAM

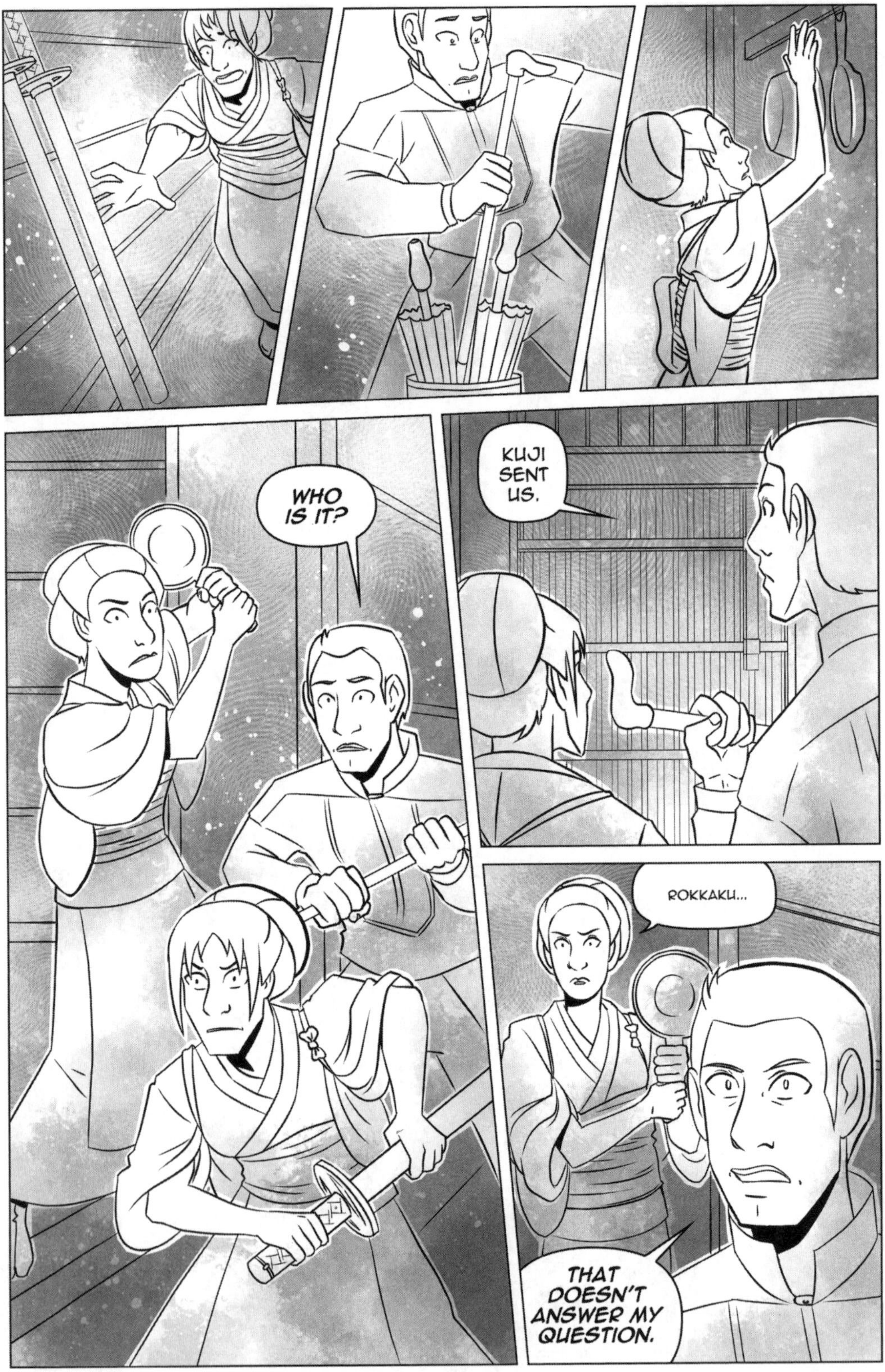
WHO IS IT?
KUJI SENT US.
ROKKAKU...
THAT DOESN'T ANSWER MY QUESTION.

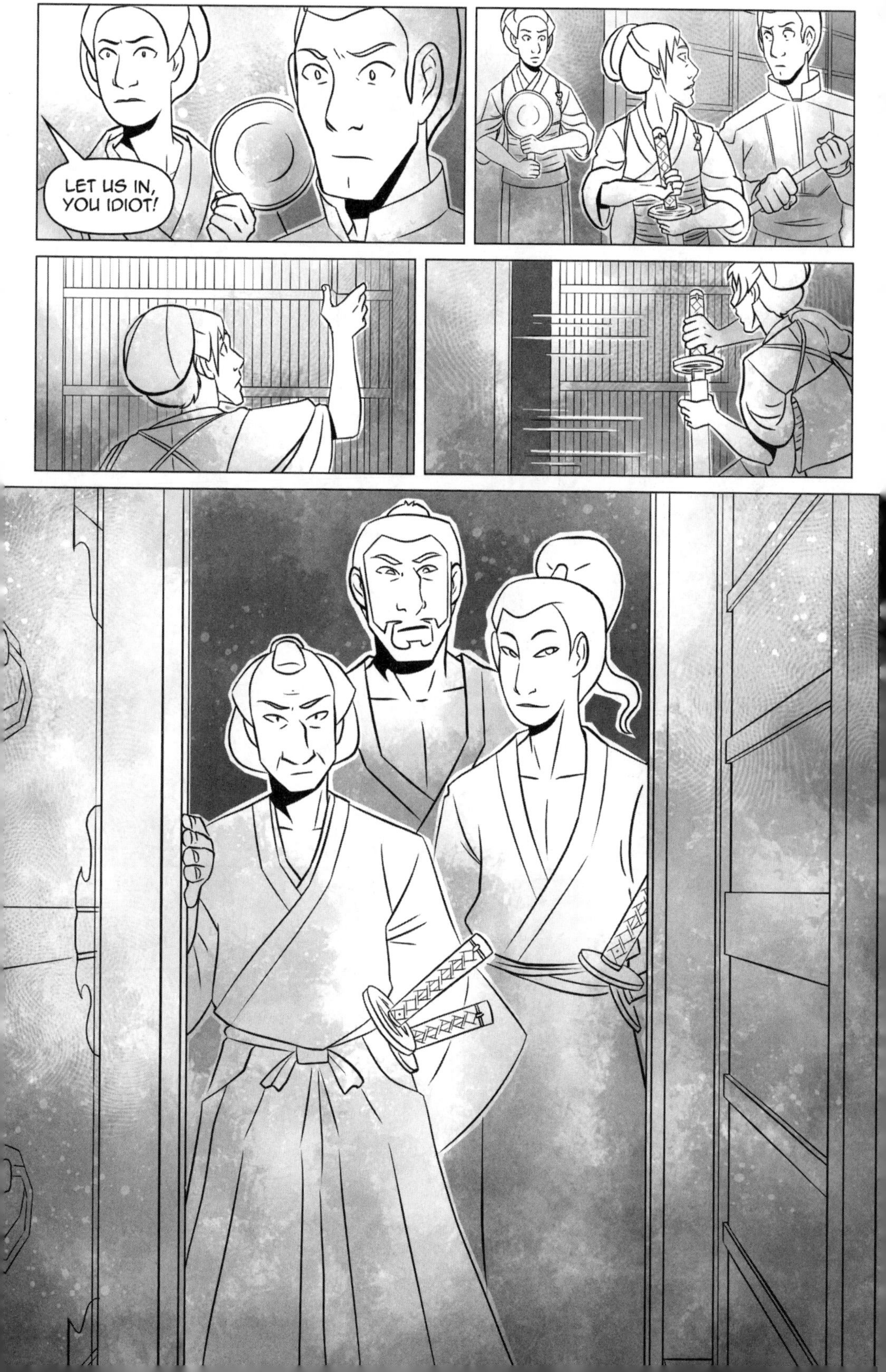
LET US IN, YOU IDIOT!

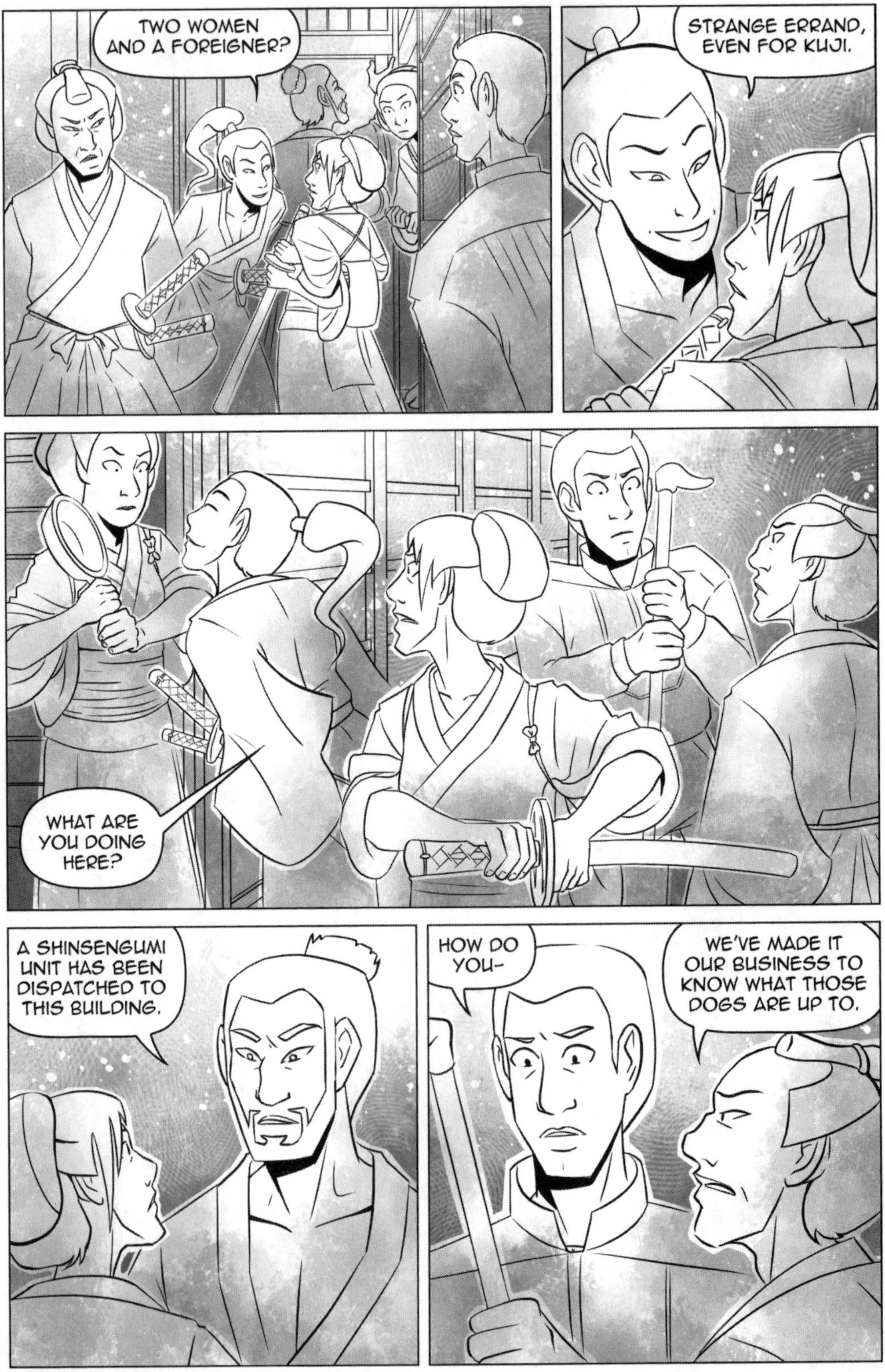
TWO WOMEN AND A FOREIGNER?
STRANGE ERRAND, EVEN FOR KUJI.
WHAT ARE YOU DOING HERE?
A SHINSENGUMI UNIT HAS BEEN DISPATCHED TO THIS BUILDING.
HOW DO YOU-
WE'VE MADE IT OUR BUSINESS TO KNOW WHAT THOSE DOGS ARE UP TO.

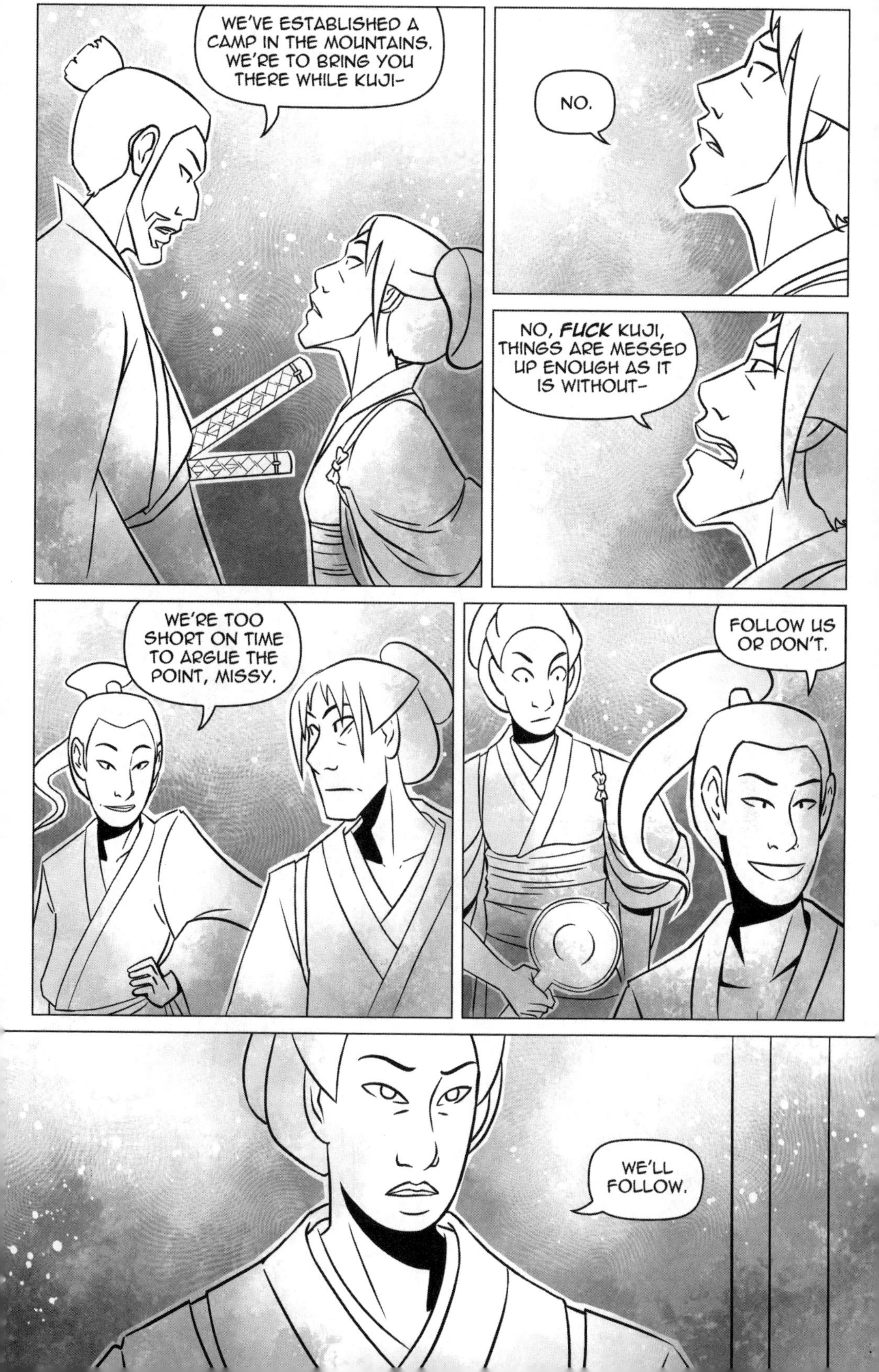
WE'VE ESTABLISHED A CAMP IN THE MOUNTAINS. WE'RE TO BRING YOU THERE WHILE KUJI-
NO.
NO, FUCK KUJI, THINGS ARE MESSED UP ENOUGH AS IT IS WITHOUT-
WE'RE TOO SHORT ON TIME TO ARGUE THE POINT, MISSY.
FOLLOW US OR DON'T.
WE'LL FOLLOW.

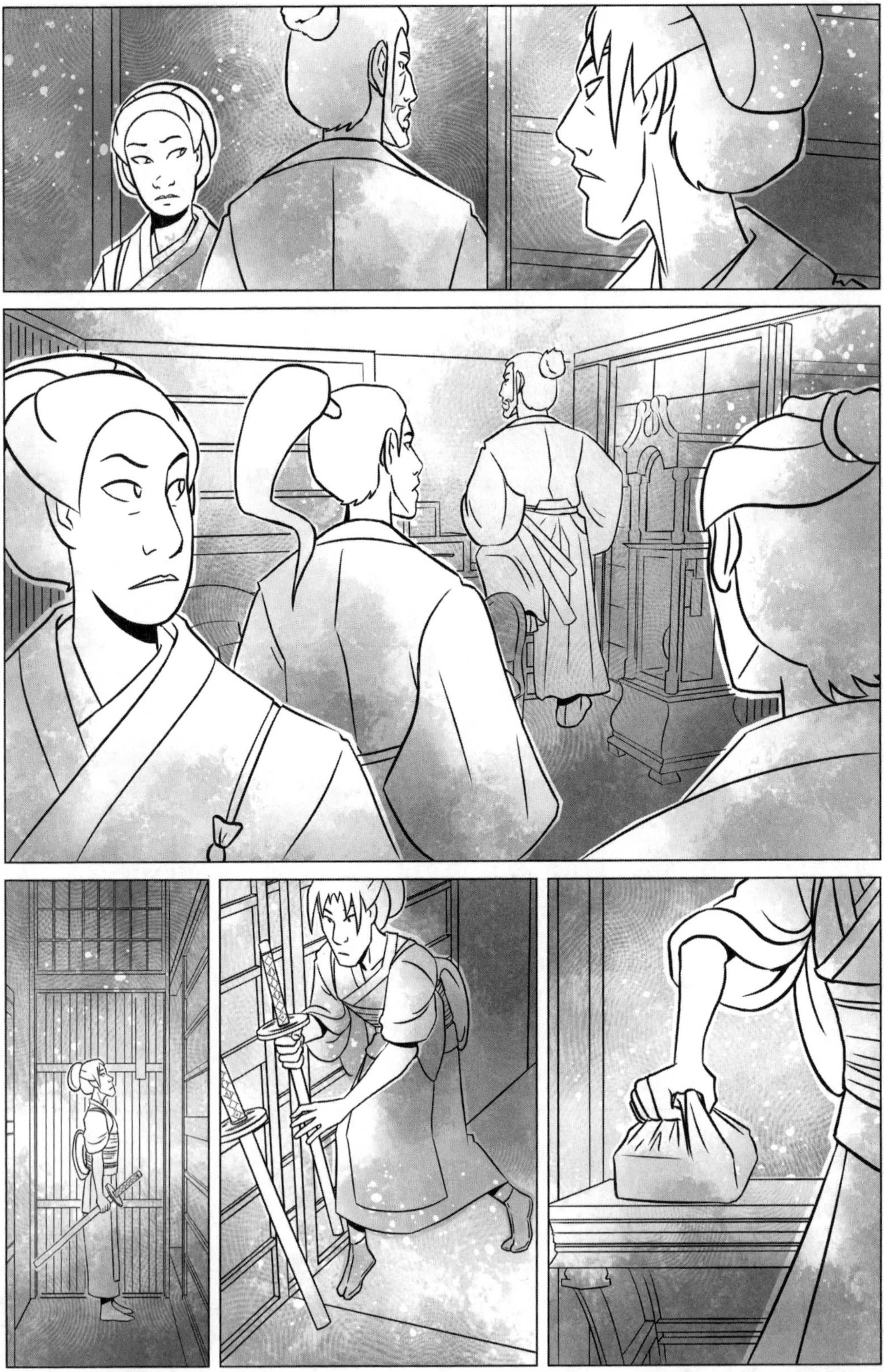

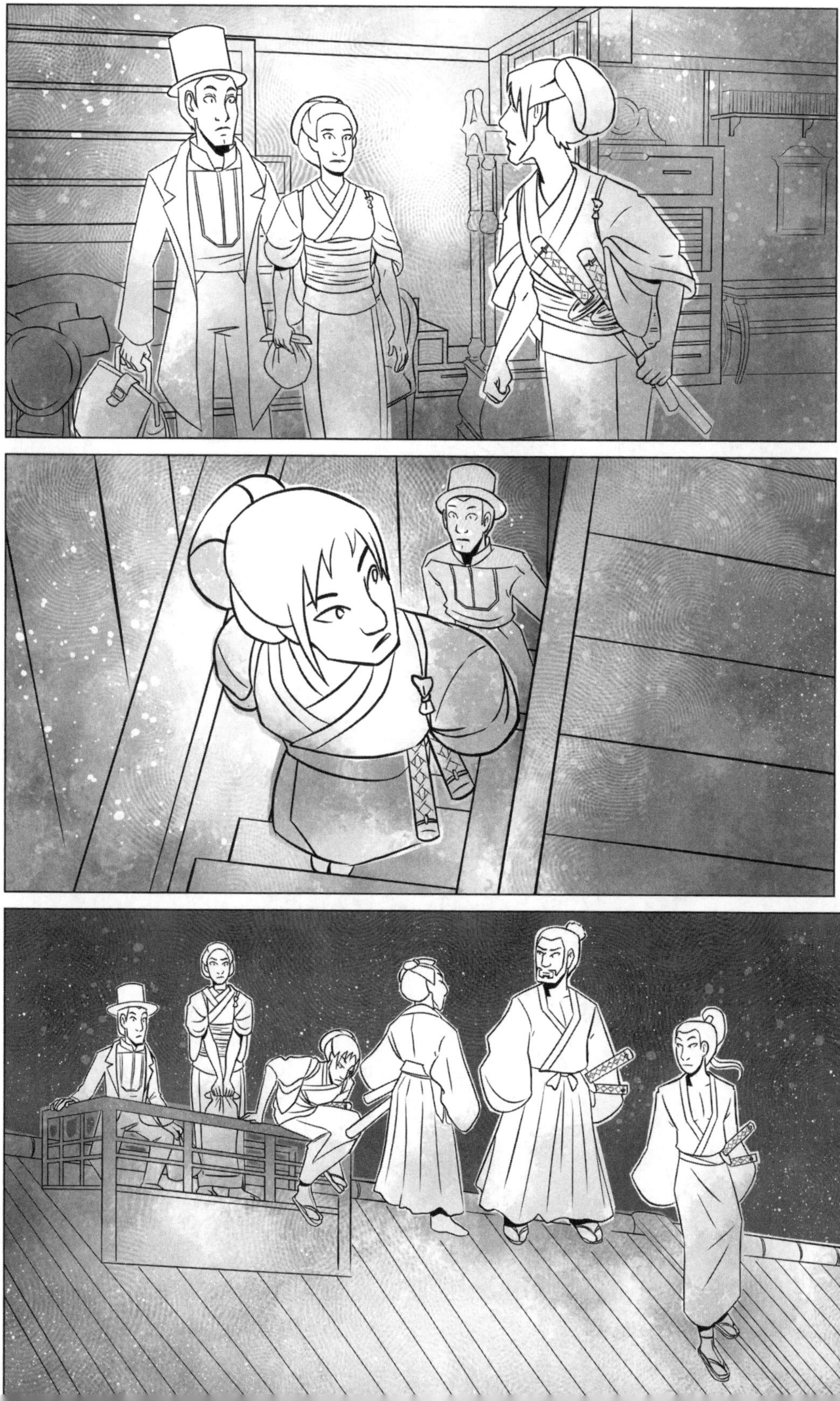

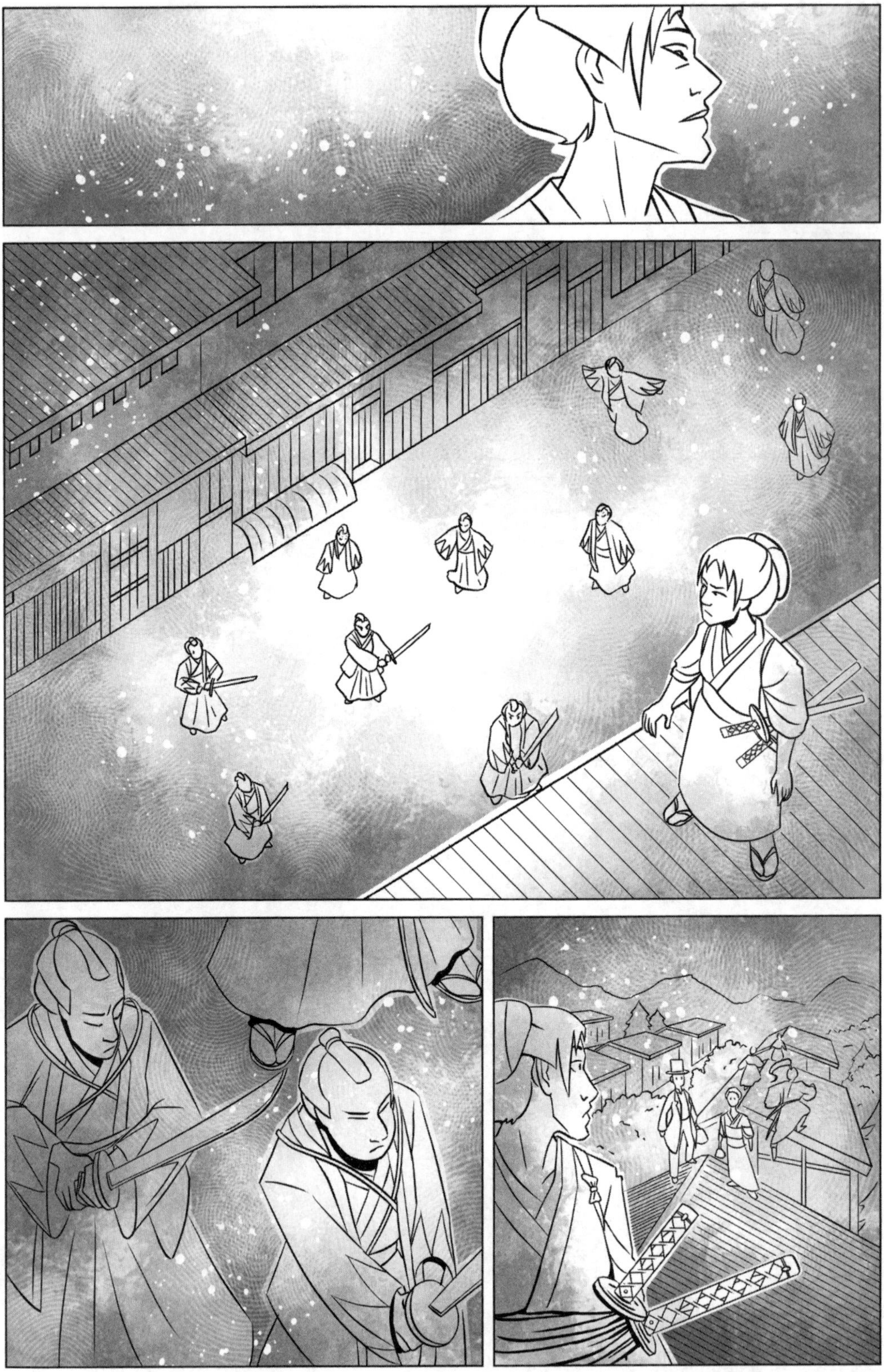

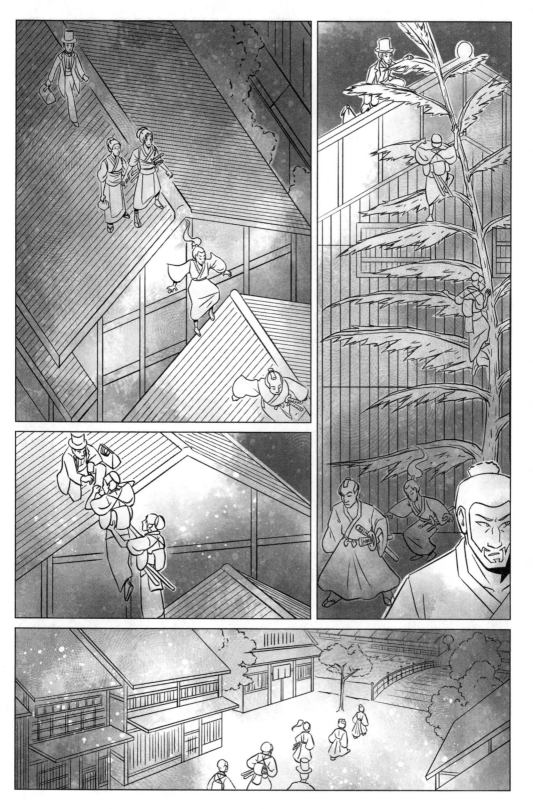

45

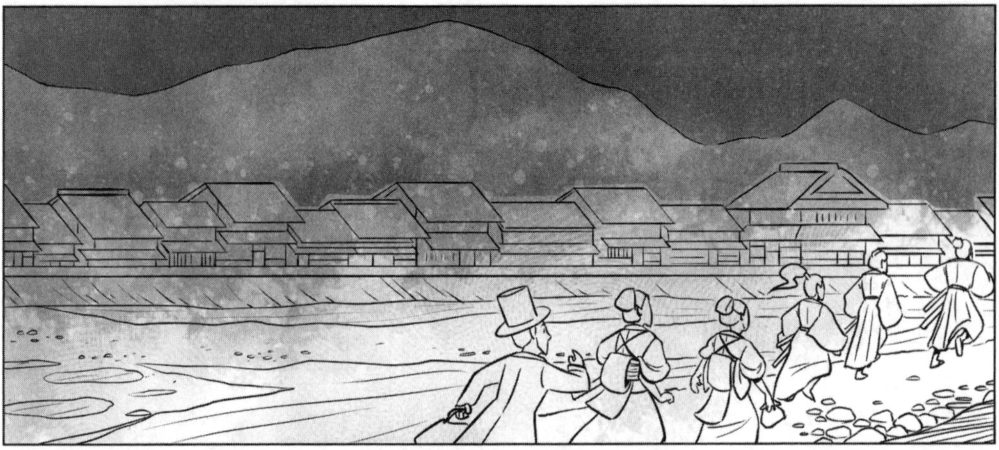

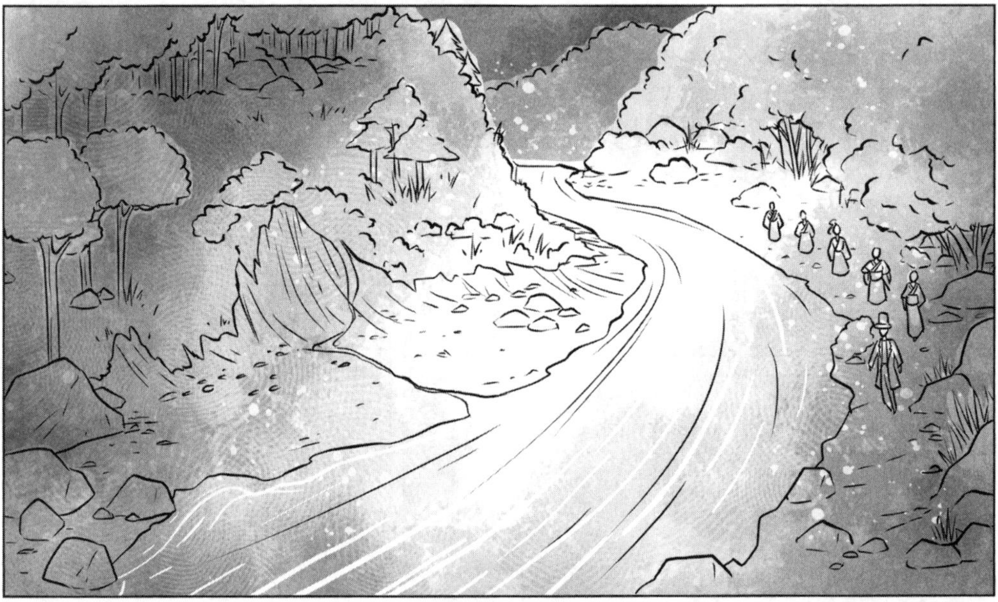

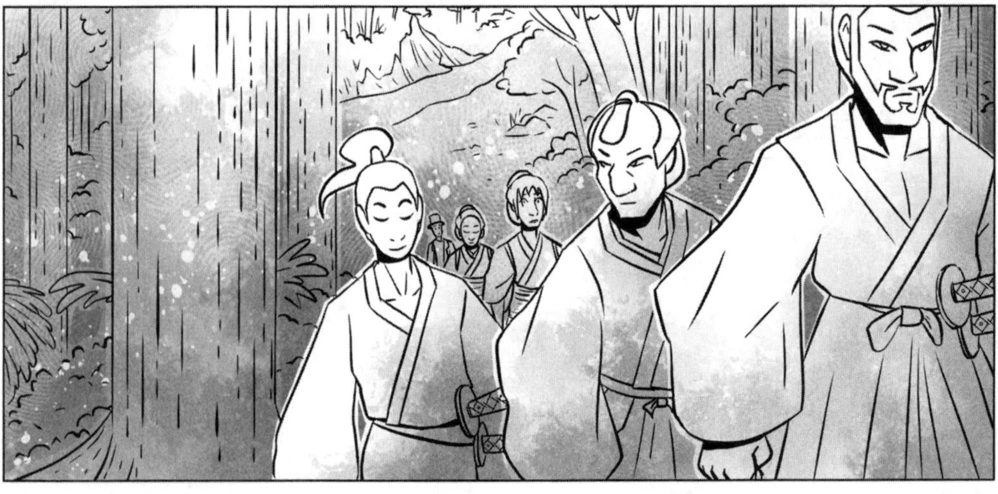

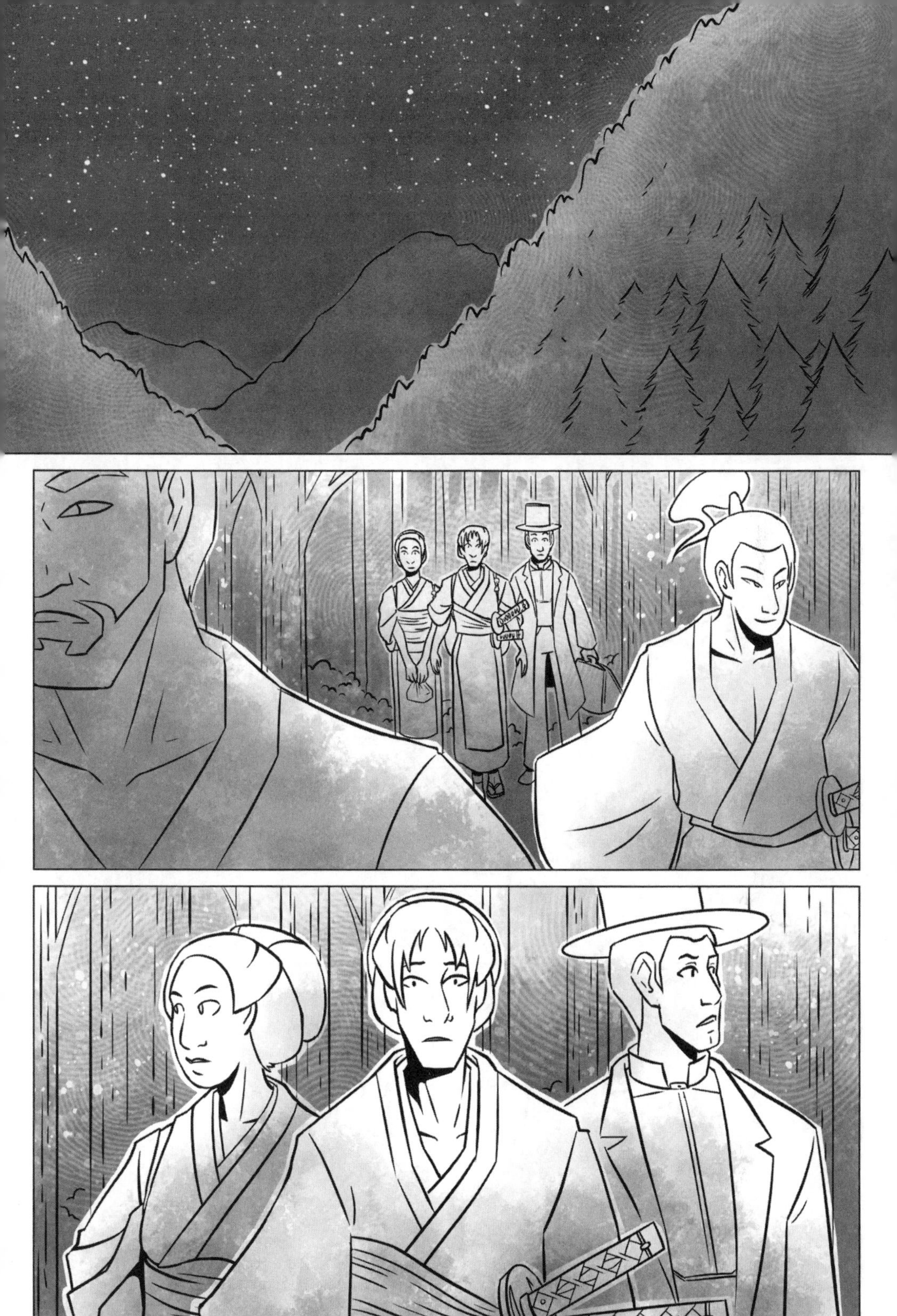

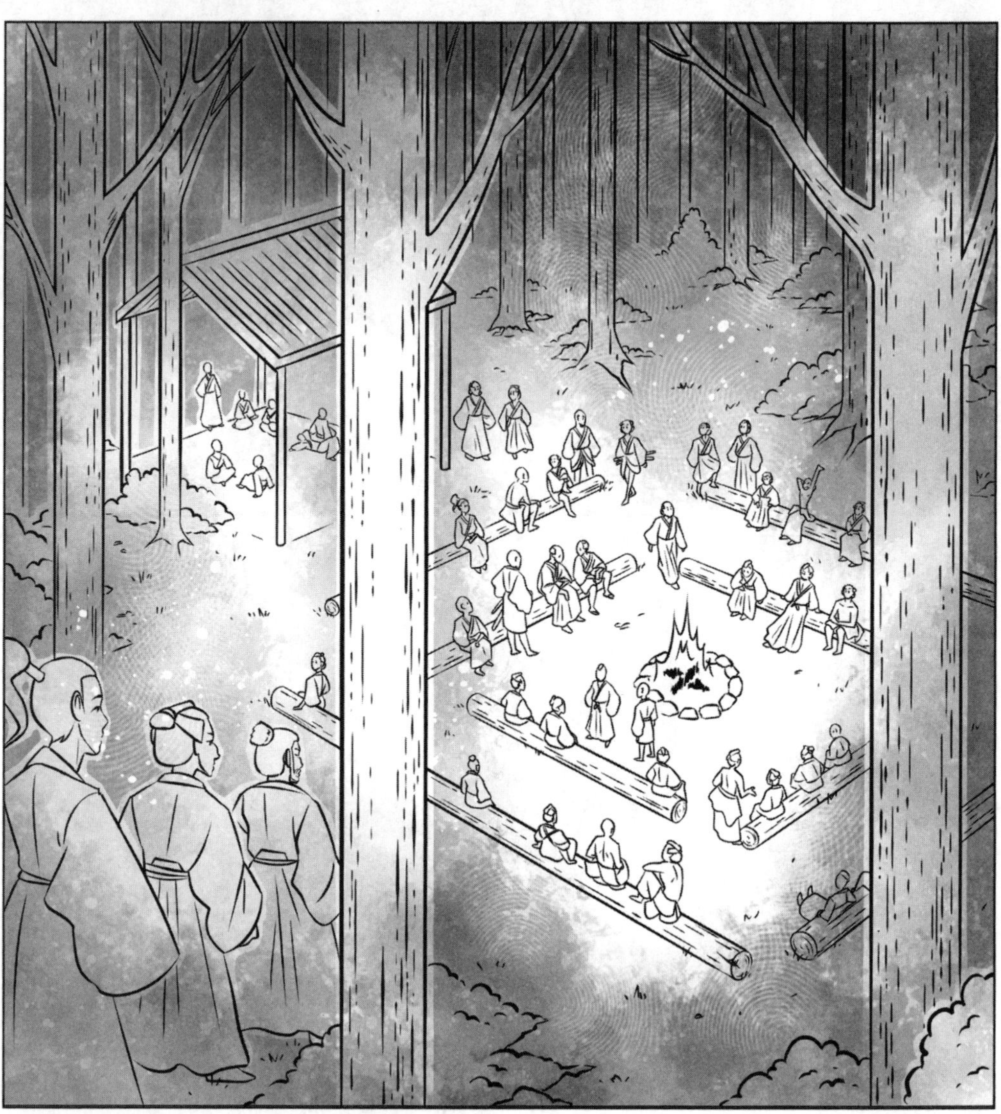

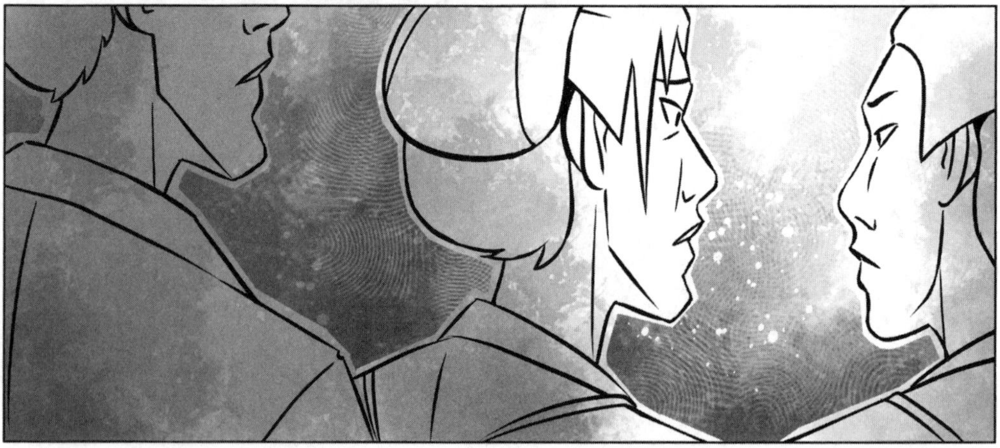

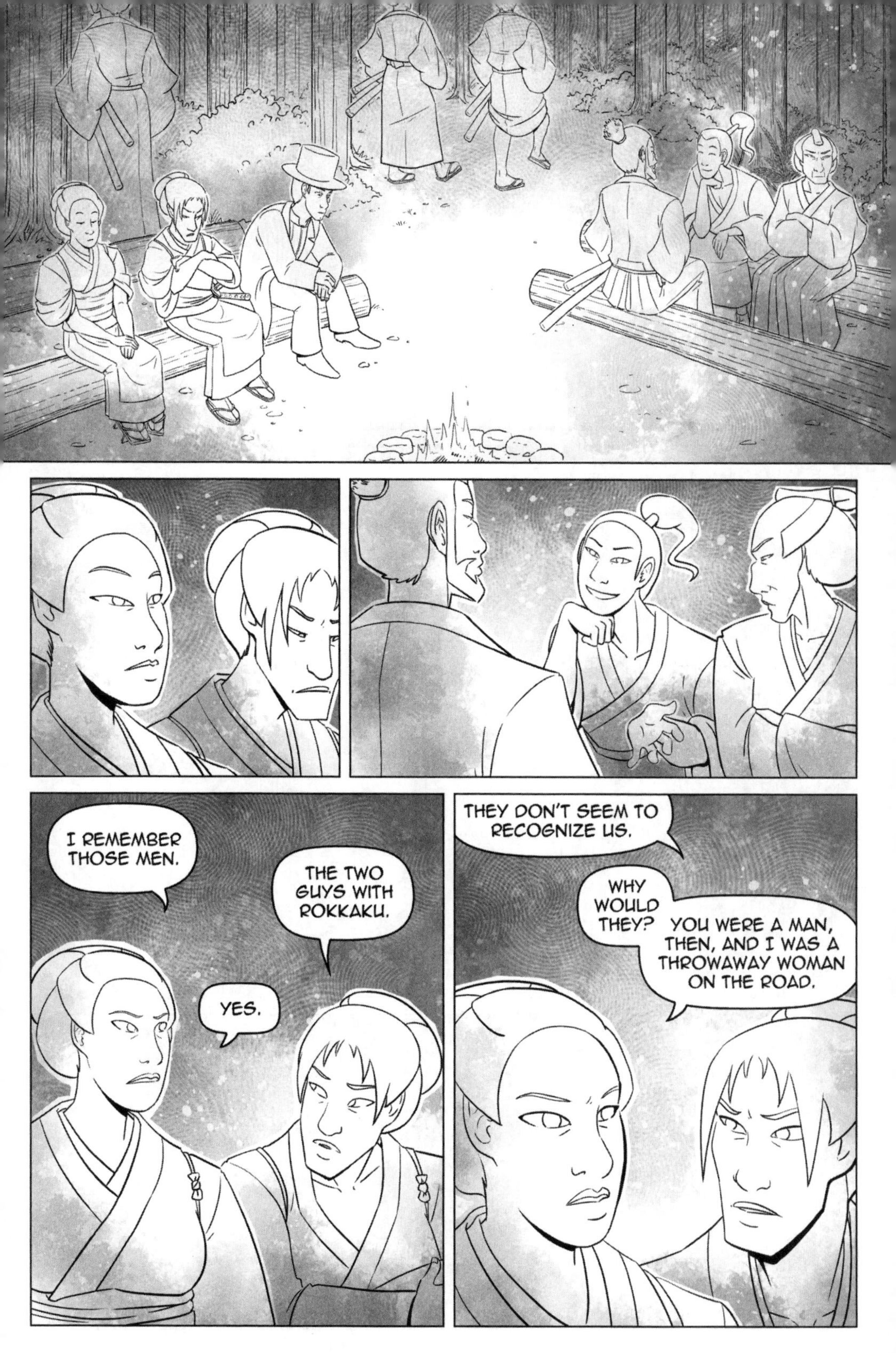
I REMEMBER THOSE MEN.
THE TWO GUYS WITH ROKKAKU.
YES.
THEY DON'T SEEM TO RECOGNIZE US.
WHY WOULD THEY?
YOU WERE A MAN, THEN, AND I WAS A THROWAWAY WOMAN ON THE ROAD.

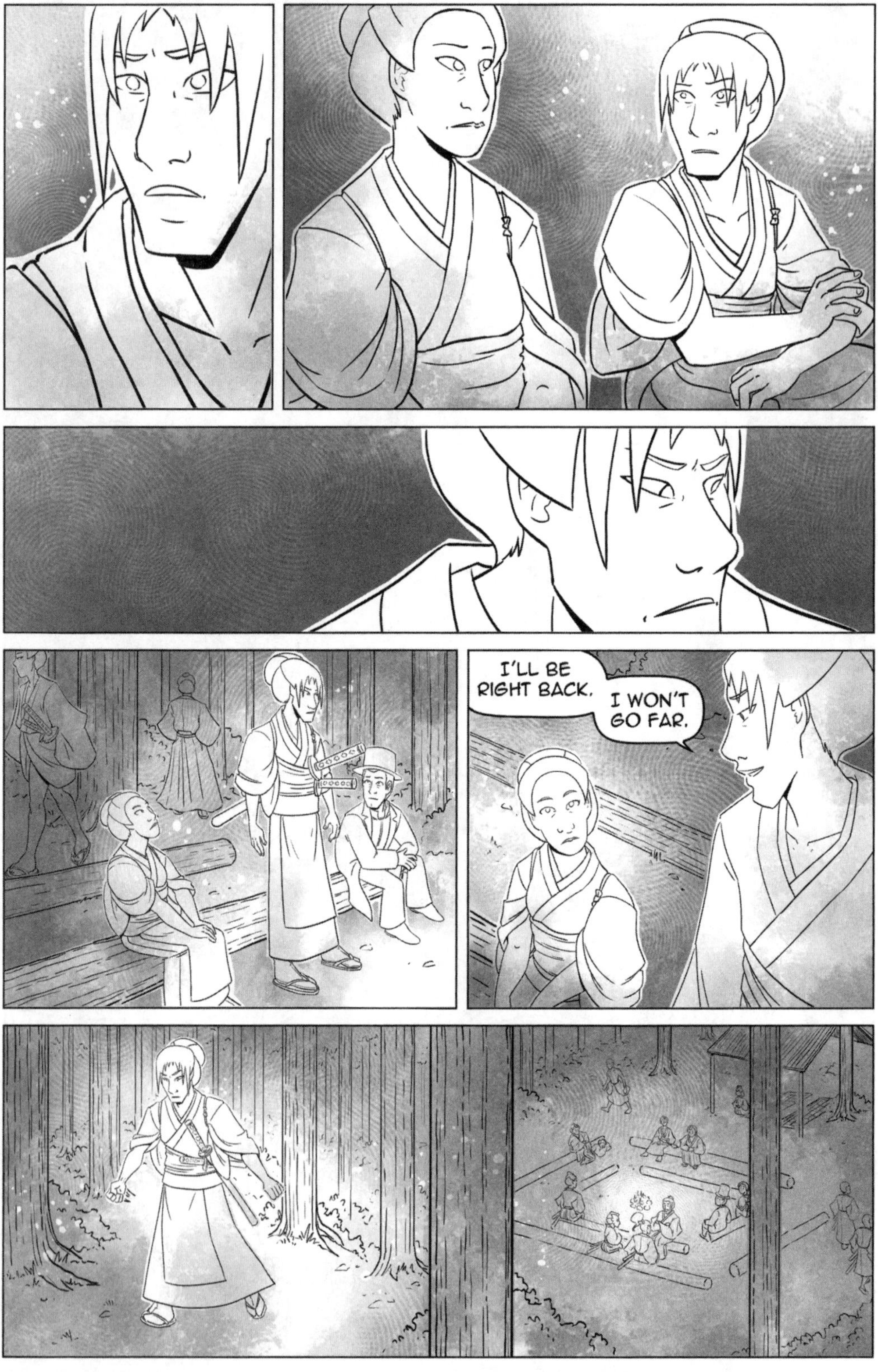
I'LL BE RIGHT BACK.
I WON'T GO FAR.

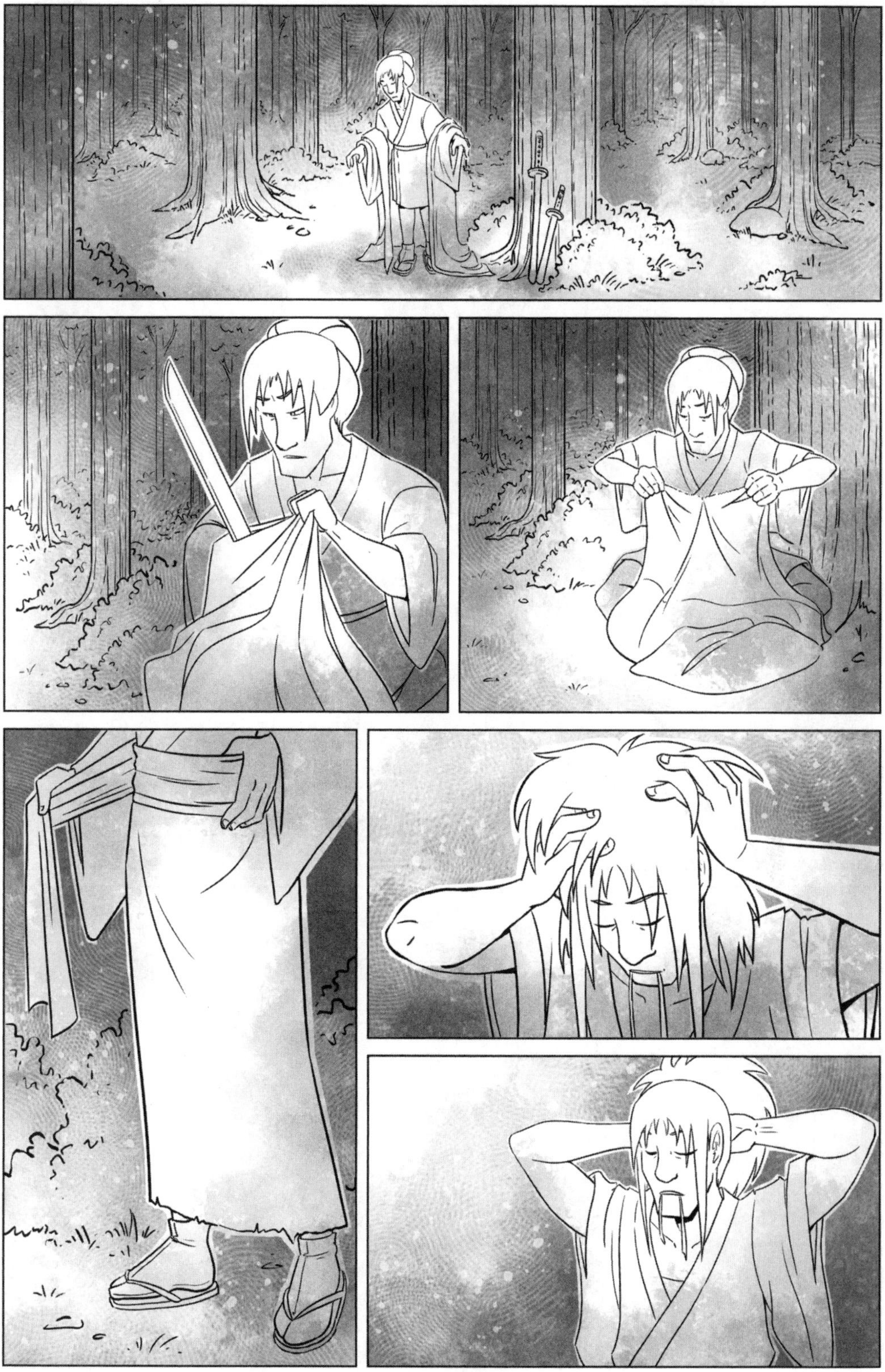

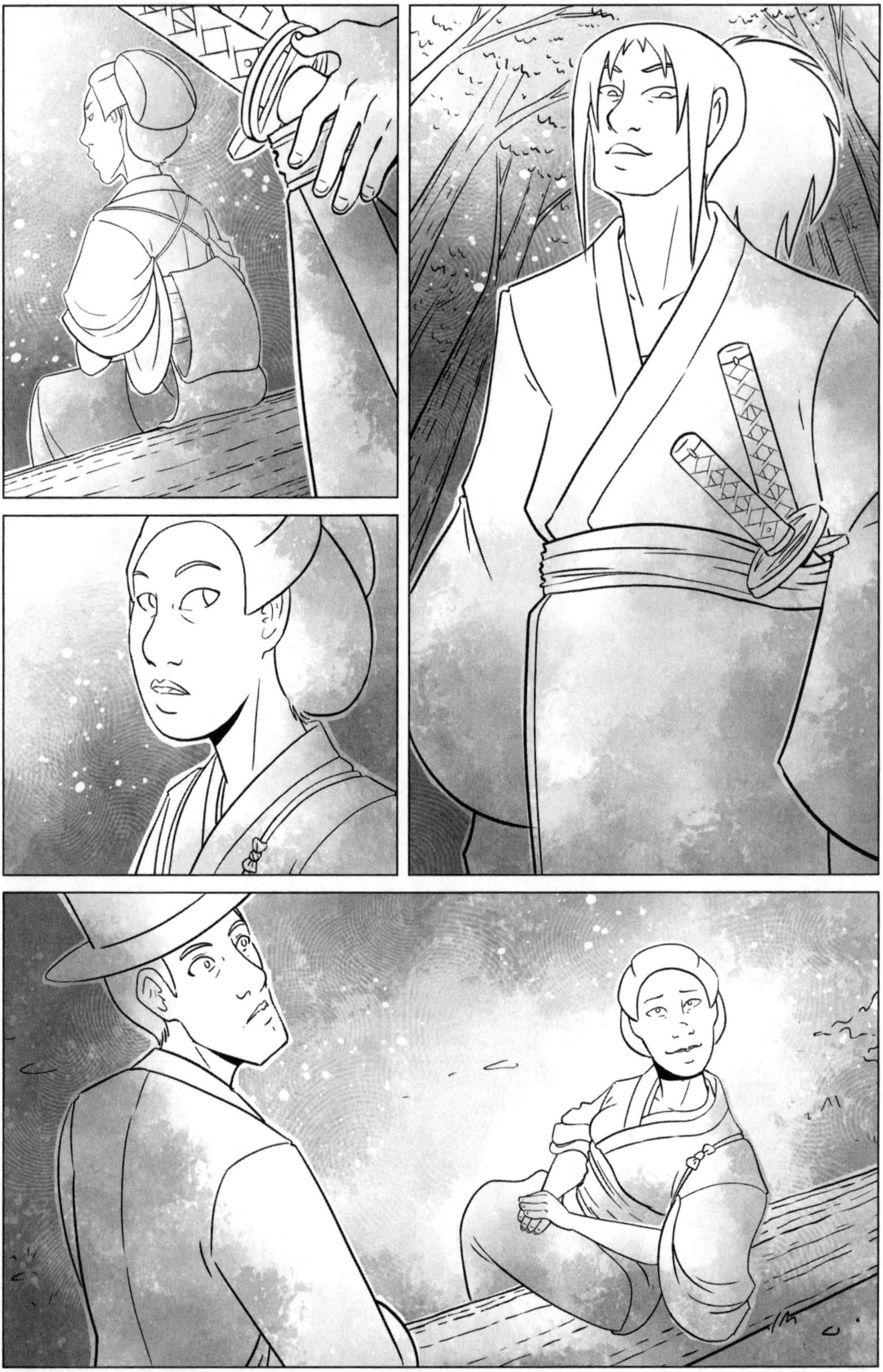

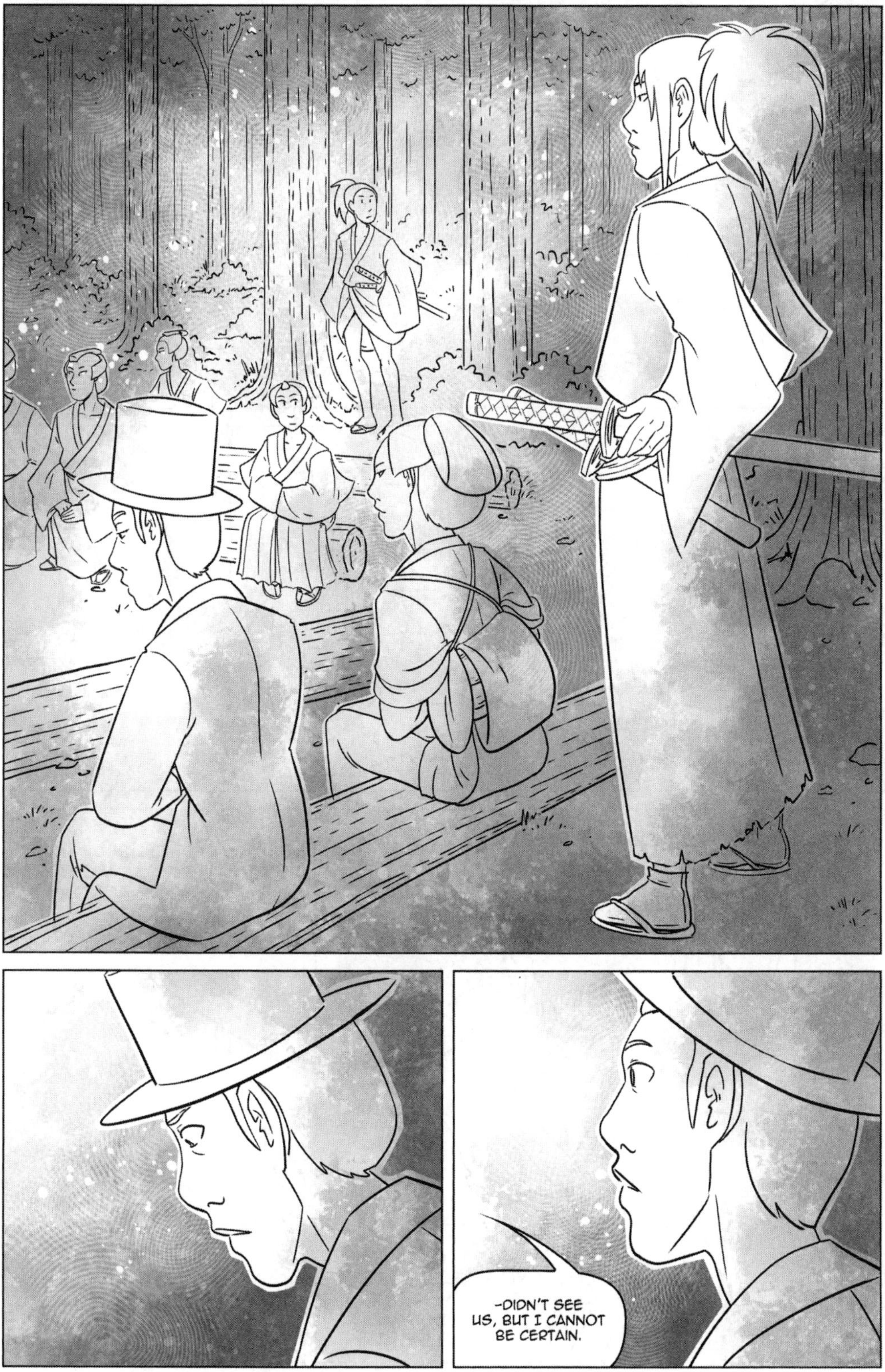
-DIDN'T SEE US, BUT I CANNOT BE CERTAIN.

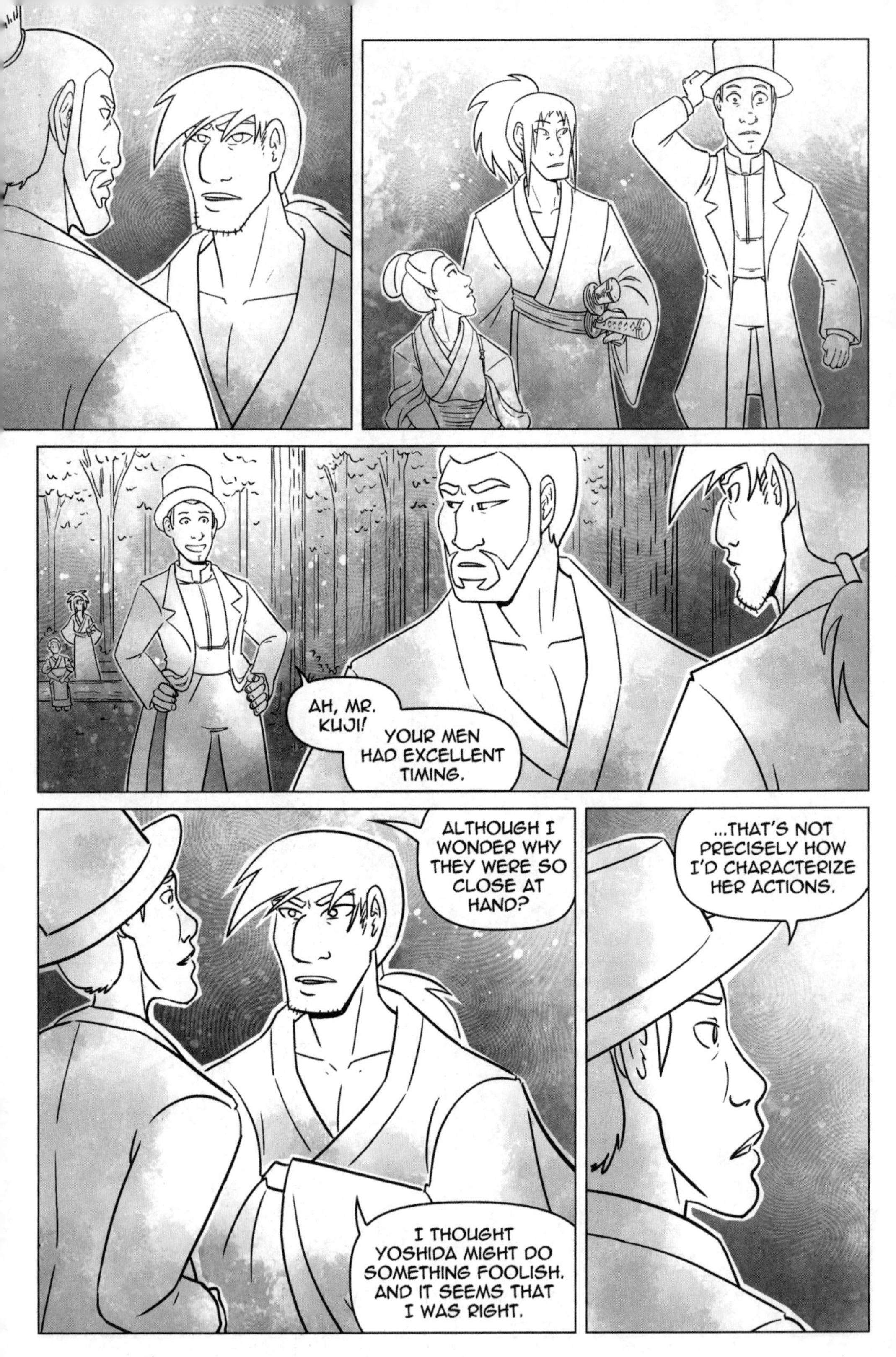
AH, MR. KUJI!
YOUR MEN HAD EXCELLENT TIMING.
ALTHOUGH I WONDER WHY THEY WERE SO CLOSE AT HAND?
I THOUGHT YOSHIDA MIGHT DO SOMETHING FOOLISH. AND IT SEEMS THAT I WAS RIGHT.
...THAT'S NOT PRECISELY HOW I'D CHARACTERIZE HER ACTIONS.

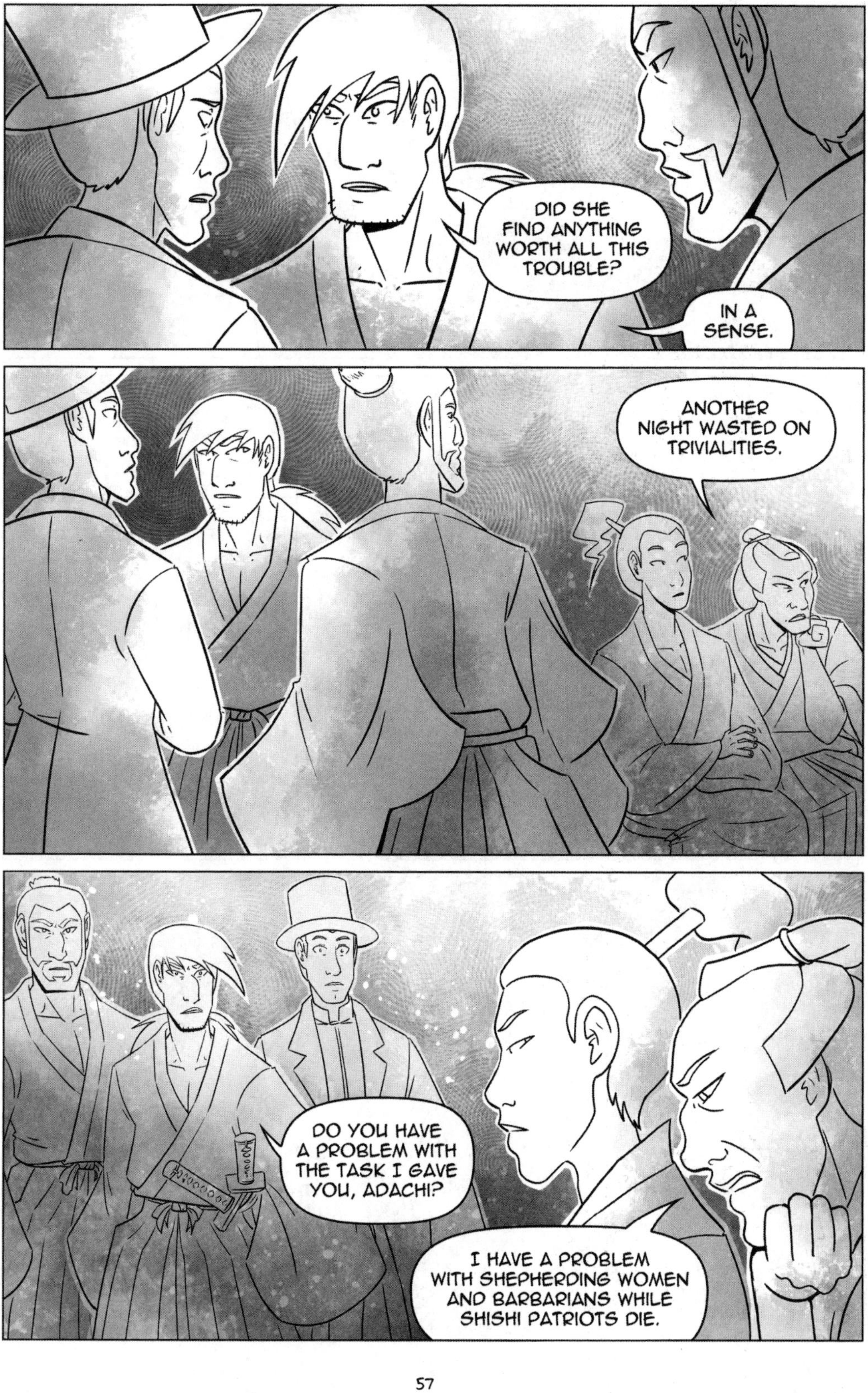
DID SHE FIND ANYTHING WORTH ALL THIS TROUBLE?
IN A SENSE.
ANOTHER NIGHT WASTED ON TRIVIALITIES.
DO YOU HAVE A PROBLEM WITH THE TASK I GAVE YOU, ADACHI?
I HAVE A PROBLEM WITH SHEPHERDING WOMEN AND BARBARIANS WHILE SHISHI PATRIOTS DIE.

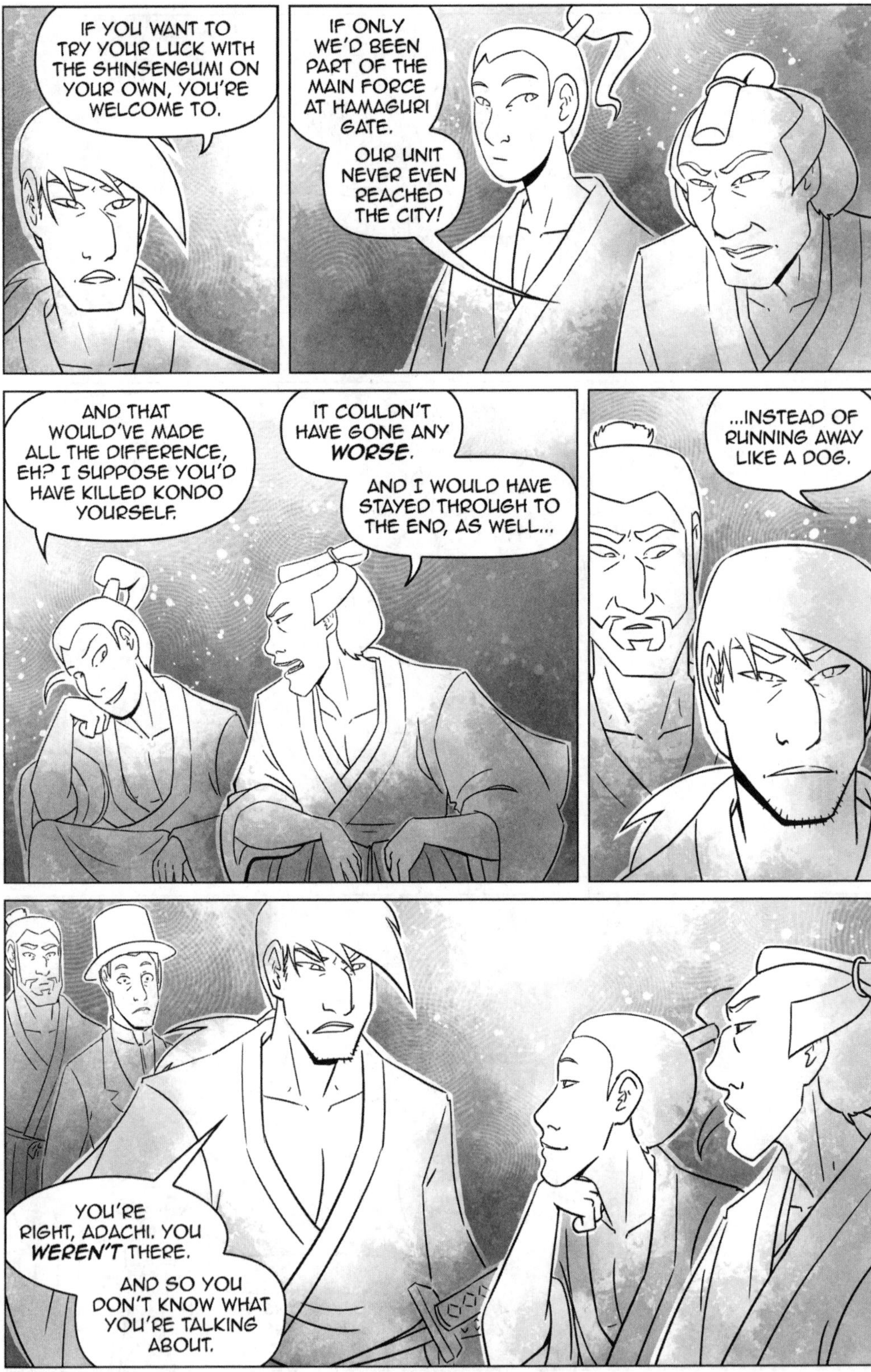
IF YOU WANT TO TRY YOUR LUCK WITH THE SHINSENGUMI ON YOUR OWN, YOU'RE WELCOME TO.
IF ONLY WE'D BEEN PART OF THE MAIN FORCE AT HAMAGURI GATE.
OUR UNIT NEVER EVEN REACHED THE CITY!
AND THAT WOULD'VE MADE ALL THE DIFFERENCE, EH? I SUPPOSE YOU'D HAVE KILLED KONDO YOURSELF.
IT COULDN'T HAVE GONE ANY ***WORSE***.
AND I WOULD HAVE STAYED THROUGH TO THE END, AS WELL...
...INSTEAD OF RUNNING AWAY LIKE A DOG.
YOU'RE RIGHT, ADACHI. YOU ***WEREN'T*** THERE.
AND SO YOU DON'T KNOW WHAT YOU'RE TALKING ABOUT.

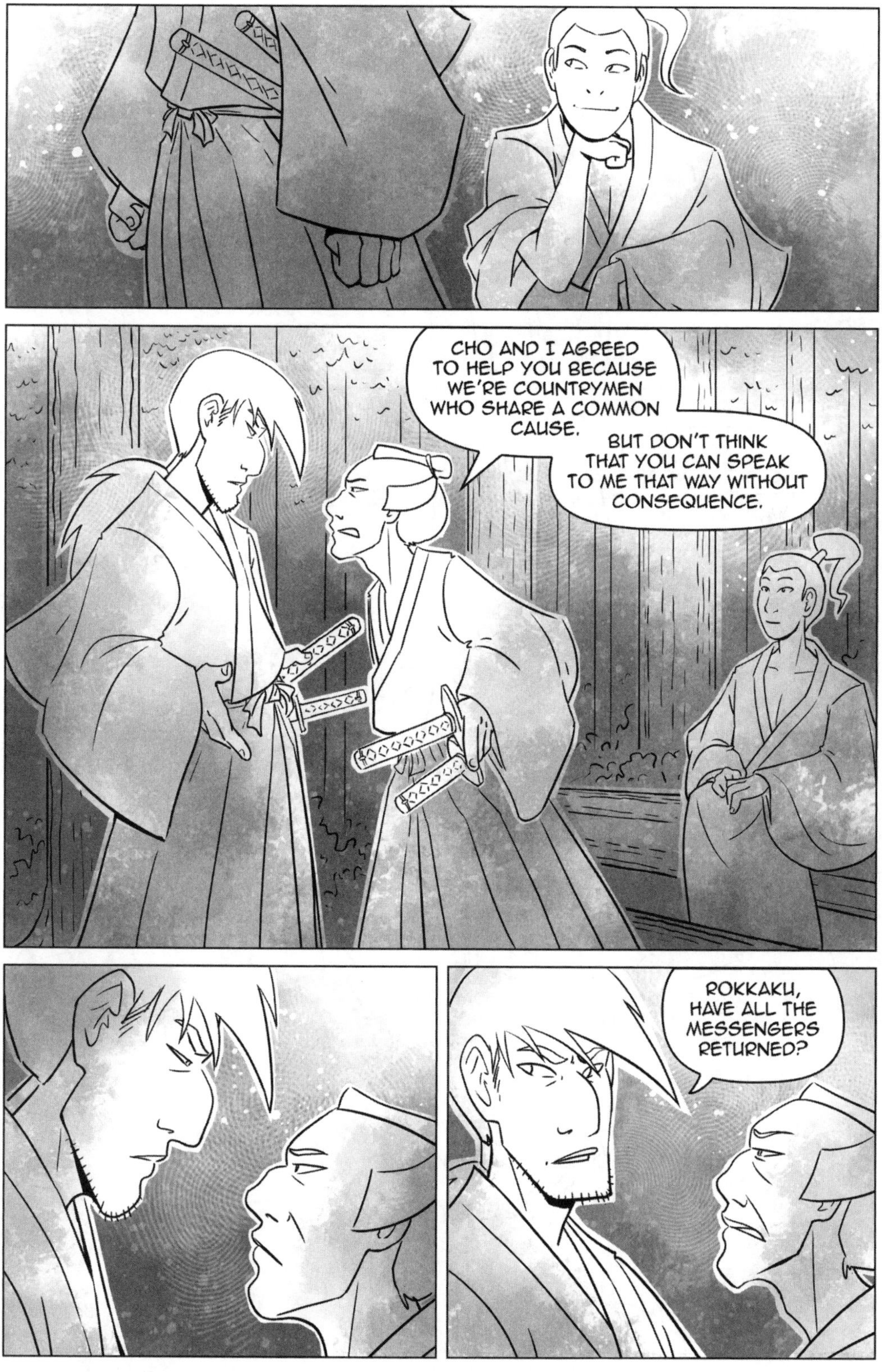
CHO AND I AGREED TO HELP YOU BECAUSE WE'RE COUNTRYMEN WHO SHARE A COMMON CAUSE.
BUT DON'T THINK THAT YOU CAN SPEAK TO ME THAT WAY WITHOUT CONSEQUENCE.
ROKKAKU, HAVE ALL THE MESSENGERS RETURNED?

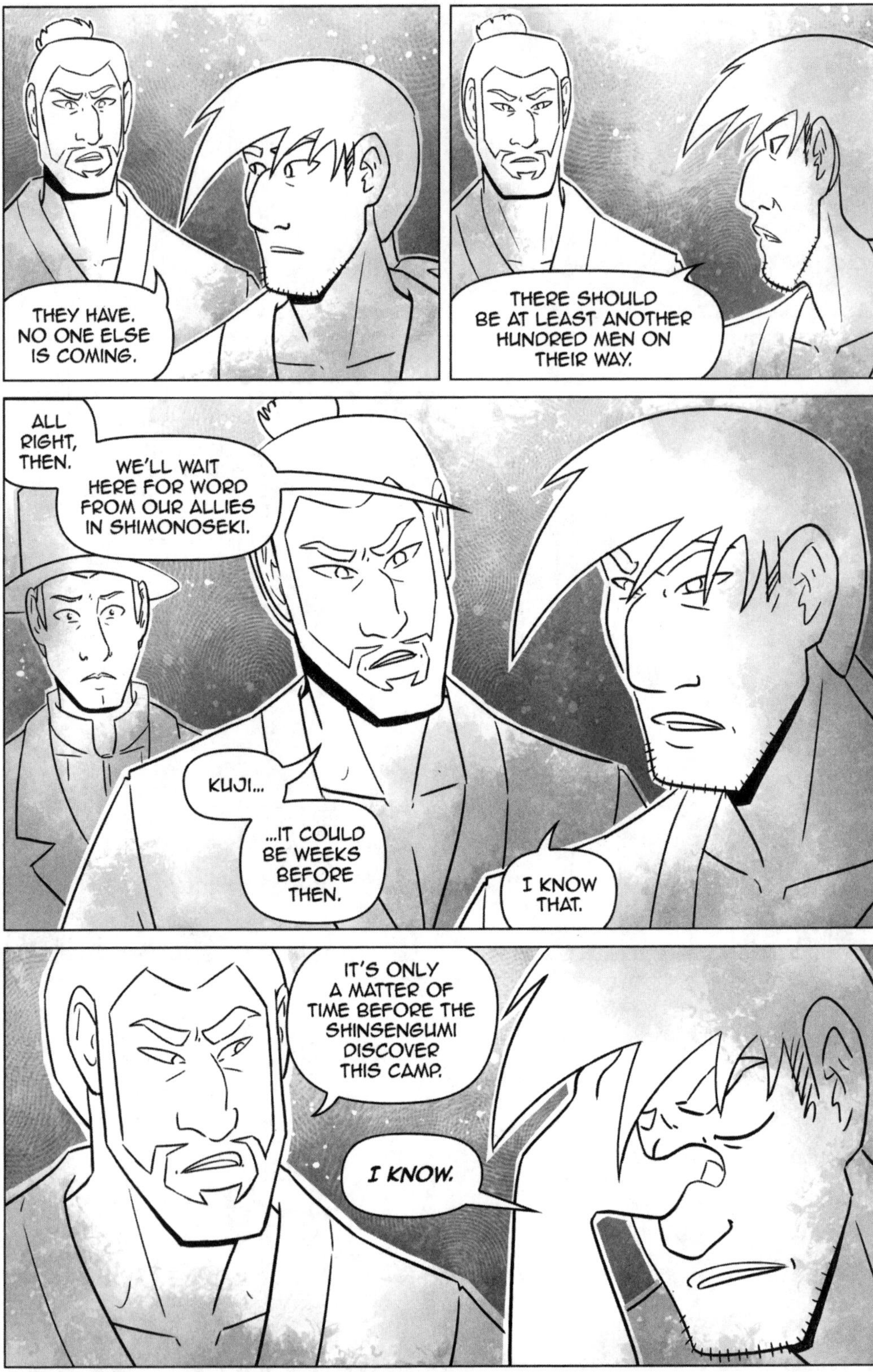
THEY HAVE. NO ONE ELSE IS COMING.
THERE SHOULD BE AT LEAST ANOTHER HUNDRED MEN ON THEIR WAY.
ALL RIGHT, THEN.
WE'LL WAIT HERE FOR WORD FROM OUR ALLIES IN SHIMONOSEKI.
KUJI...
...IT COULD BE WEEKS BEFORE THEN.
I KNOW THAT.
IT'S ONLY A MATTER OF TIME BEFORE THE SHINSENGUMI DISCOVER THIS CAMP.
*I KNOW.*

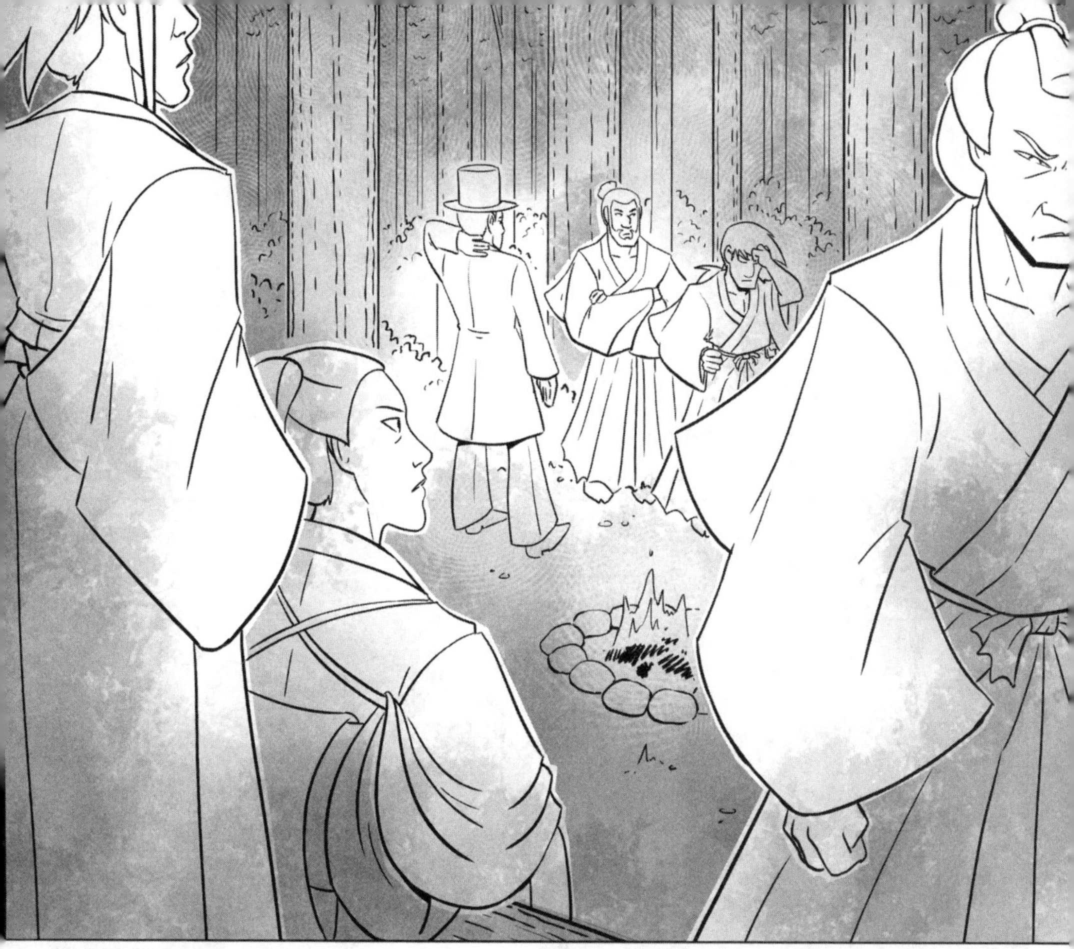

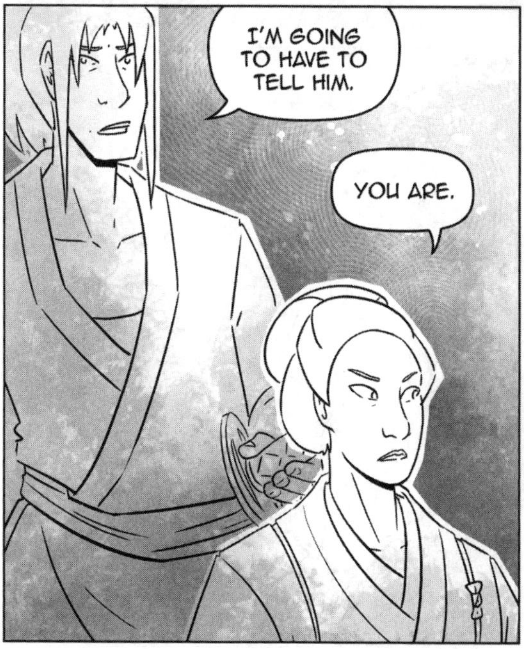
I'M GOING TO HAVE TO TELL HIM.
YOU ARE.

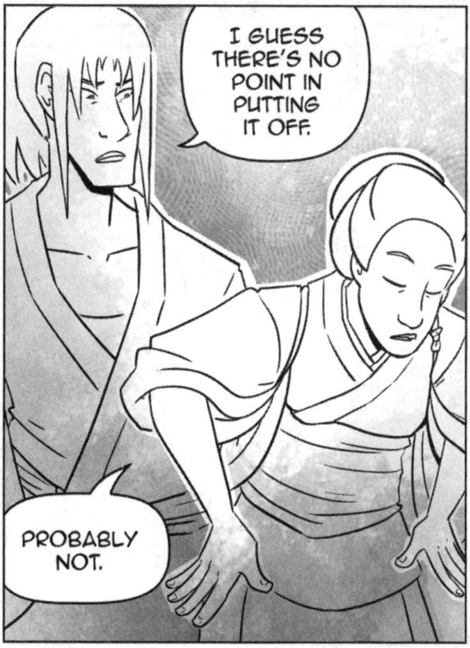
I GUESS THERE'S NO POINT IN PUTTING IT OFF.
PROBABLY NOT.

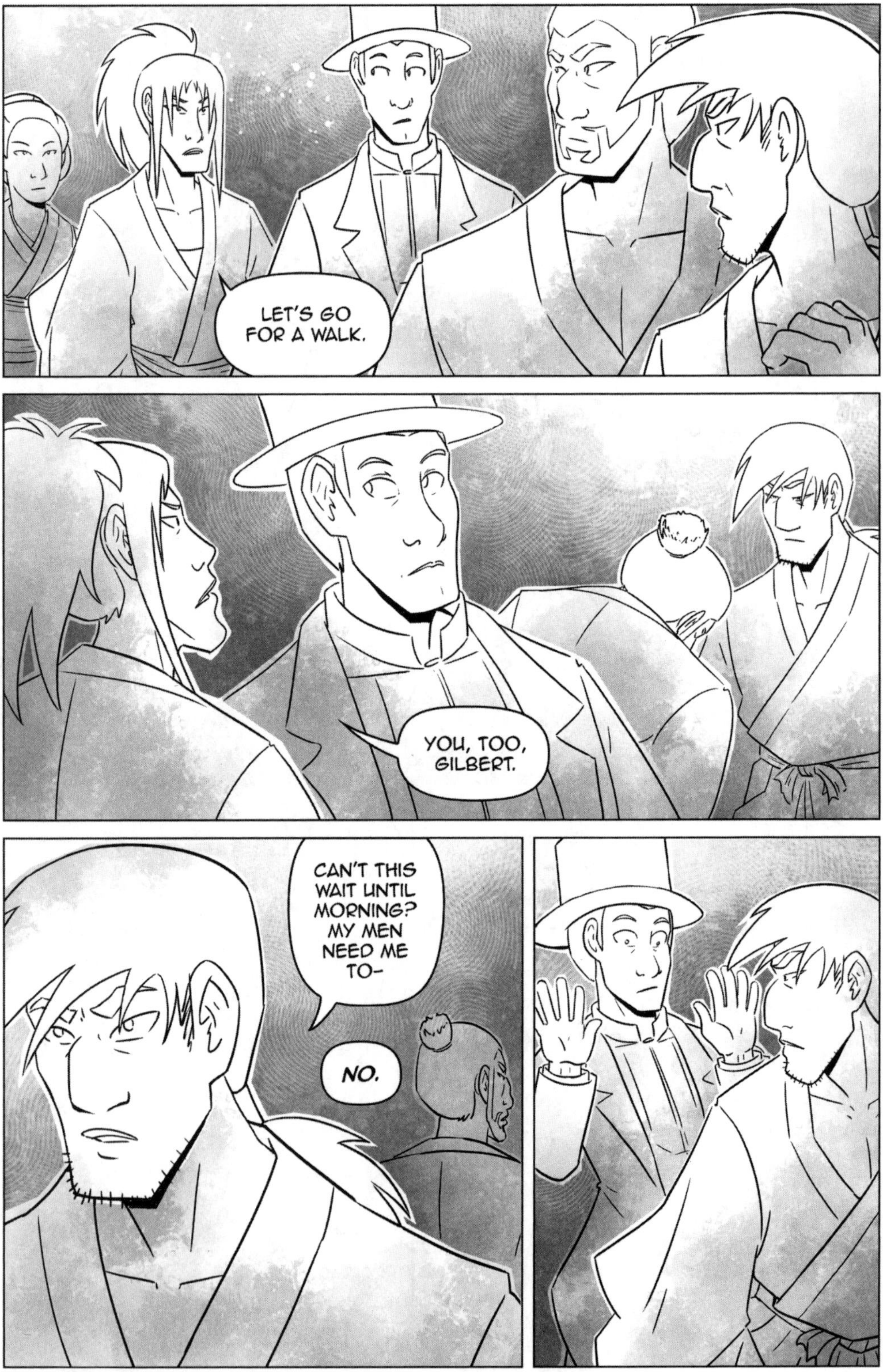
LET'S GO FOR A WALK.
YOU, TOO, GILBERT.
CAN'T THIS WAIT UNTIL MORNING? MY MEN NEED ME TO-
NO.

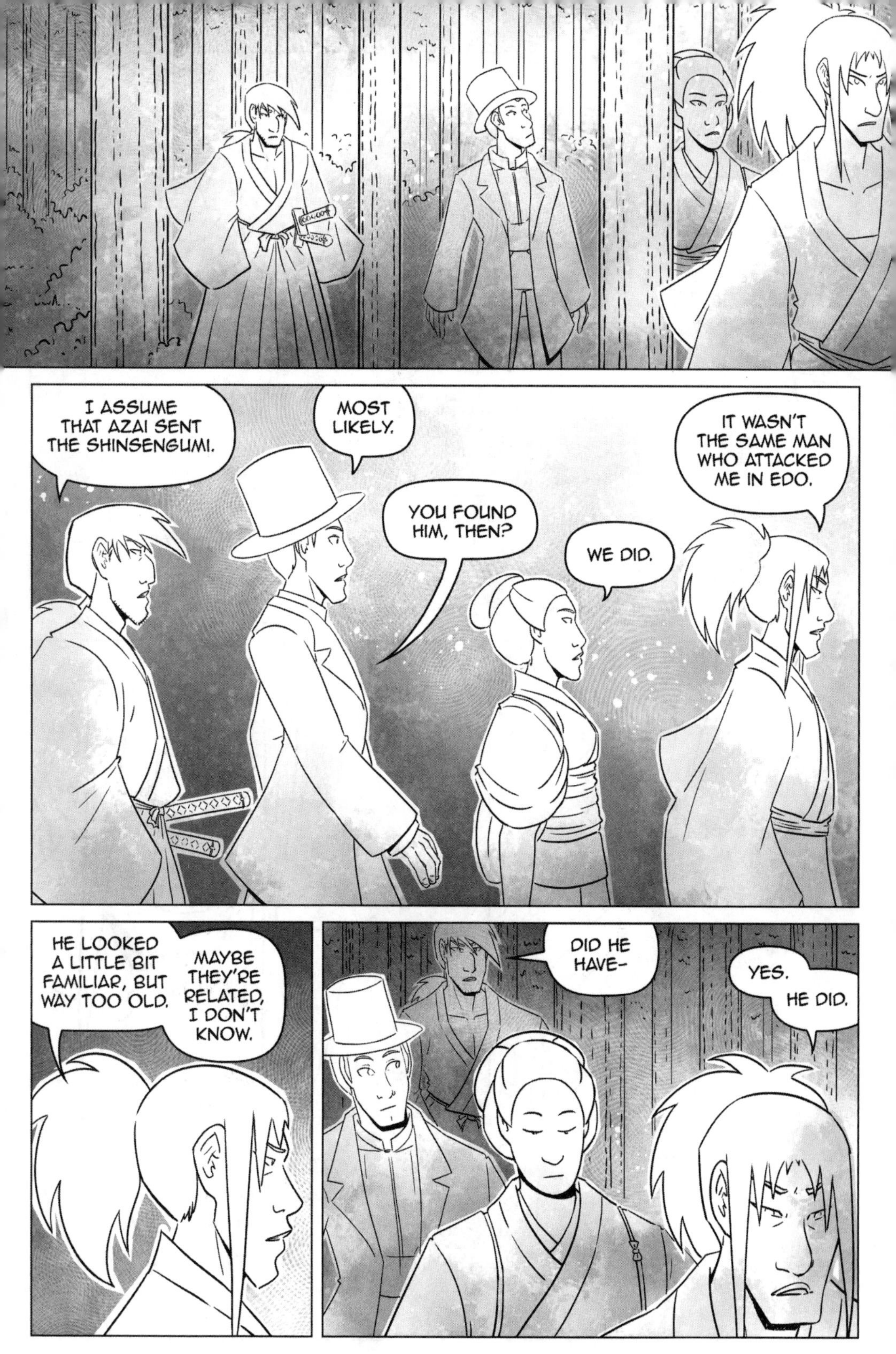

I ASSUME THAT AZAI SENT THE SHINSENGUMI.
MOST LIKELY.
YOU FOUND HIM, THEN?
WE DID.
IT WASN'T THE SAME MAN WHO ATTACKED ME IN EDO.
HE LOOKED A LITTLE BIT FAMILIAR, BUT WAY TOO OLD.
MAYBE THEY'RE RELATED, I DON'T KNOW.
DID HE HAVE-
YES.
HE DID.

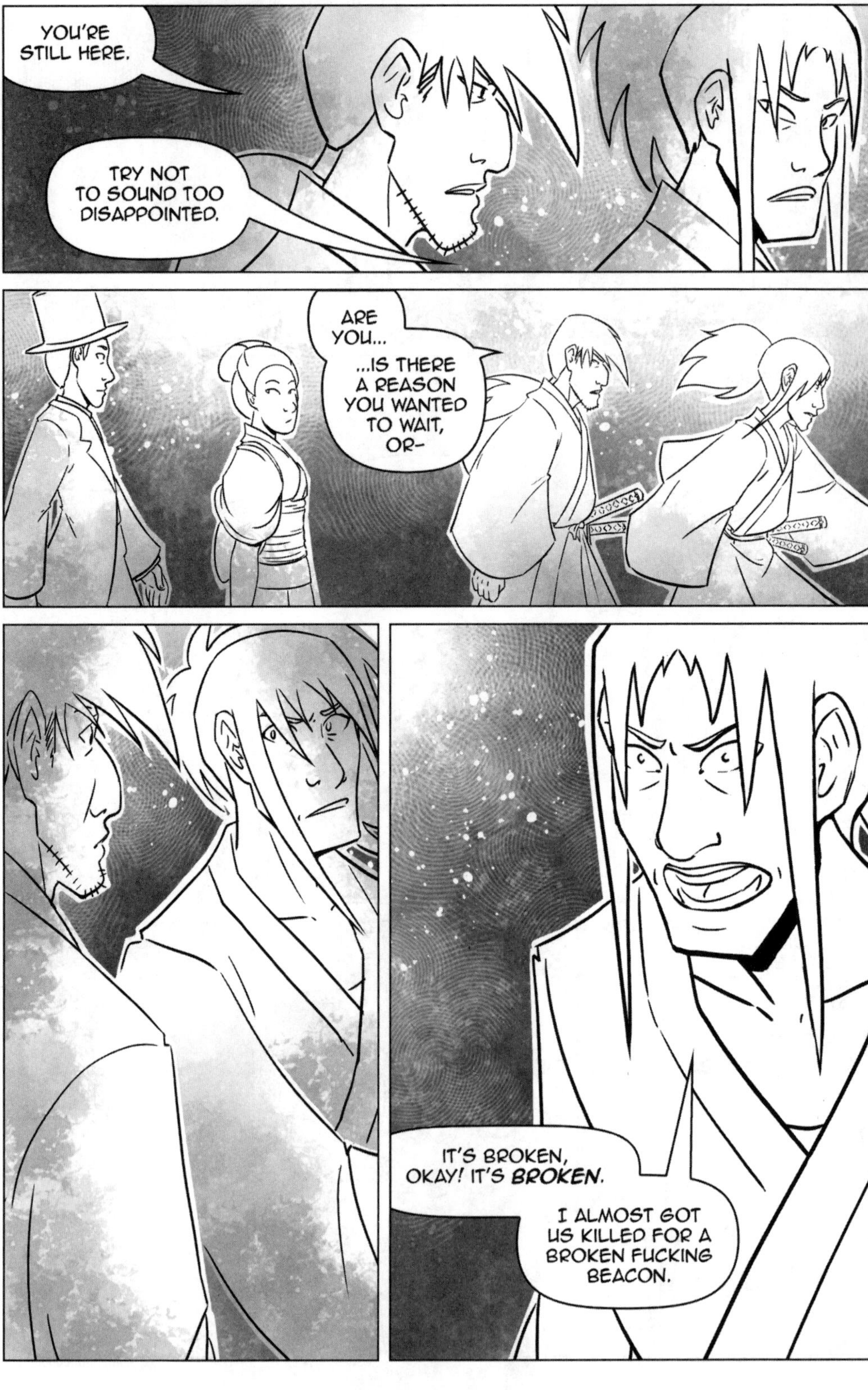
YOU'RE STILL HERE.
TRY NOT TO SOUND TOO DISAPPOINTED.
ARE YOU... ...IS THERE A REASON YOU WANTED TO WAIT, OR-
IT'S BROKEN, OKAY! IT'S **BROKEN**.
I ALMOST GOT US KILLED FOR A BROKEN FUCKING BEACON.

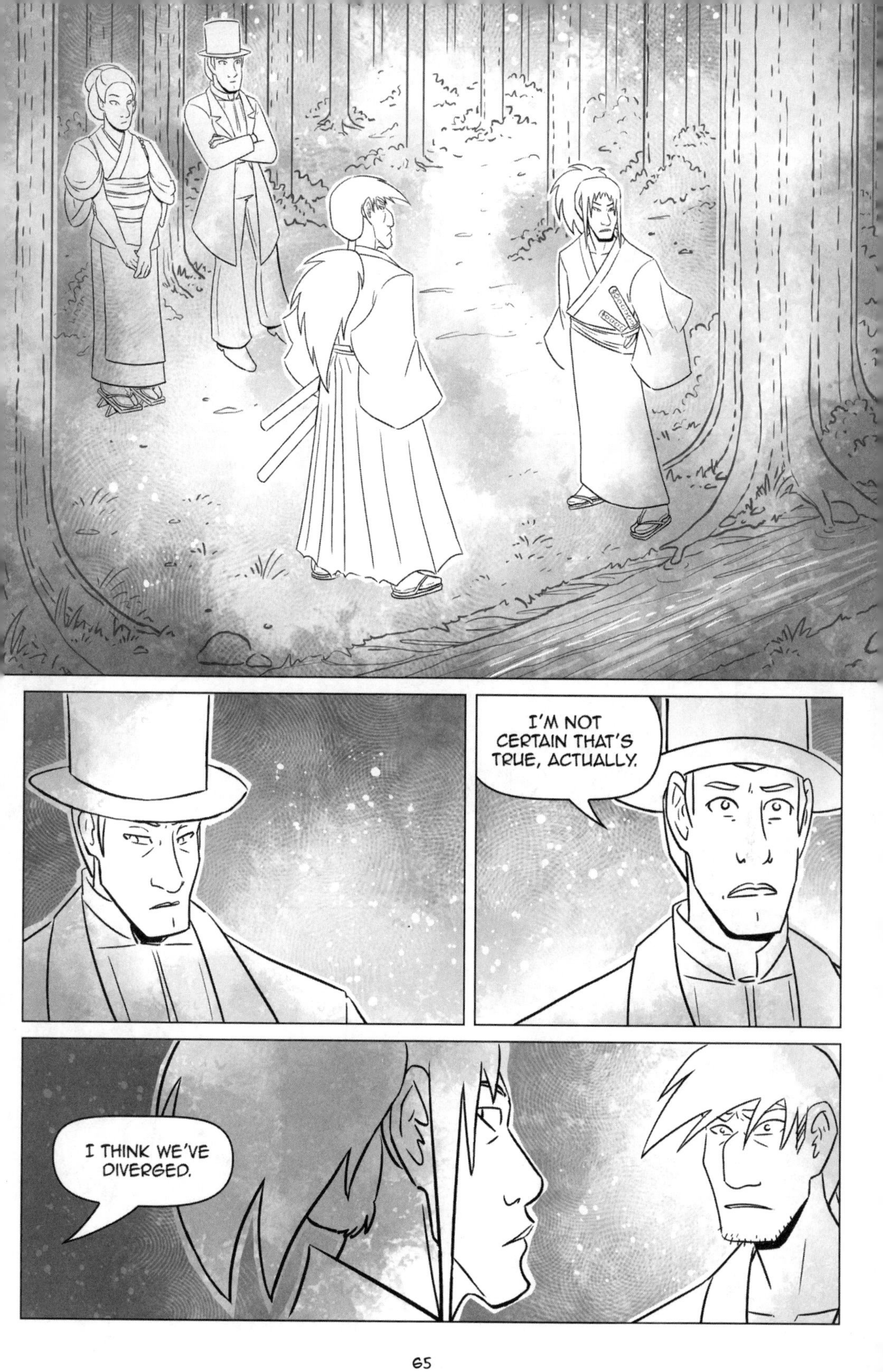
I'M NOT CERTAIN THAT'S TRUE, ACTUALLY.
I THINK WE'VE DIVERGED.

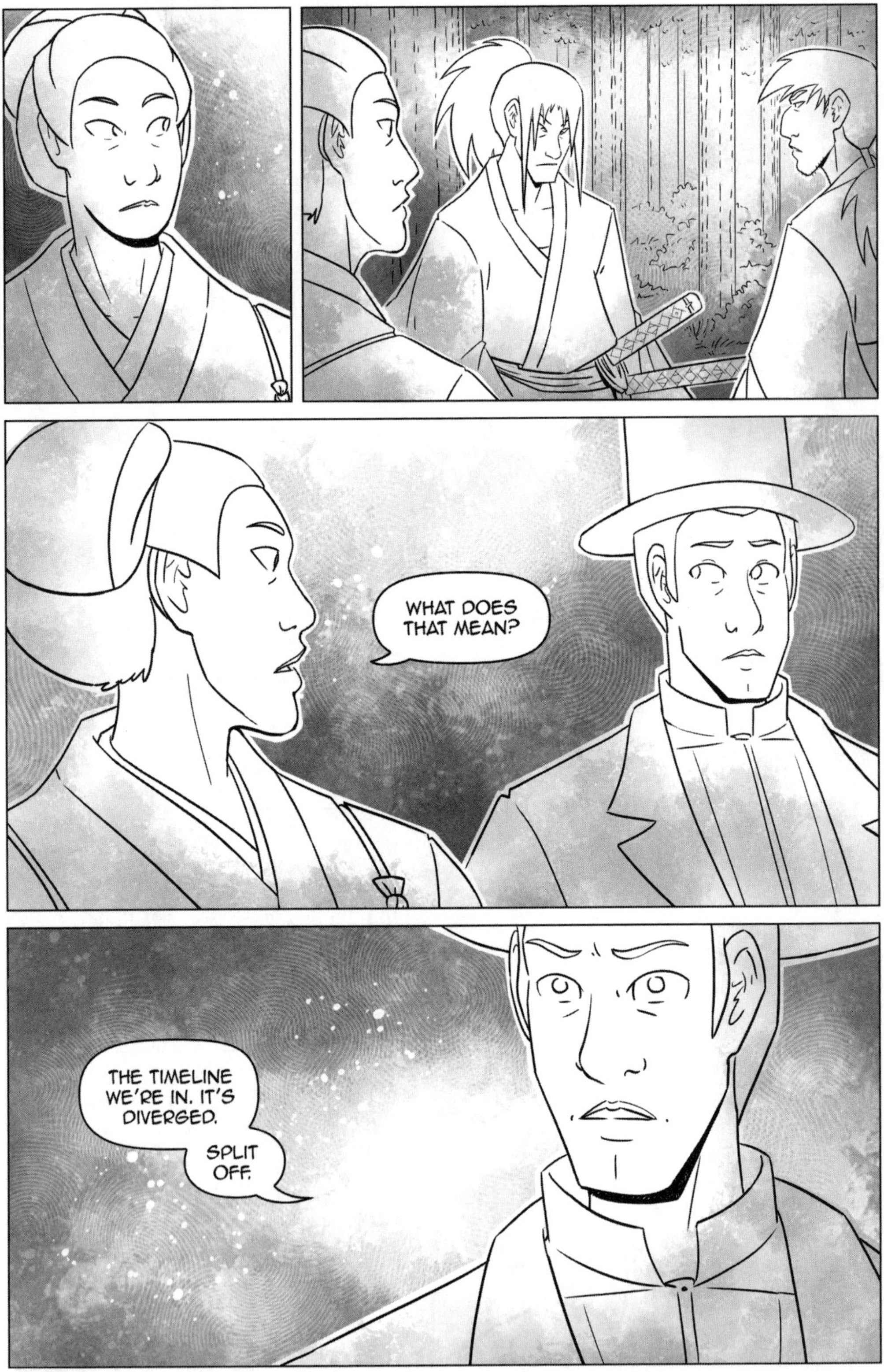
WHAT DOES THAT MEAN?
THE TIMELINE WE'RE IN. IT'S DIVERGED.
SPLIT OFF.

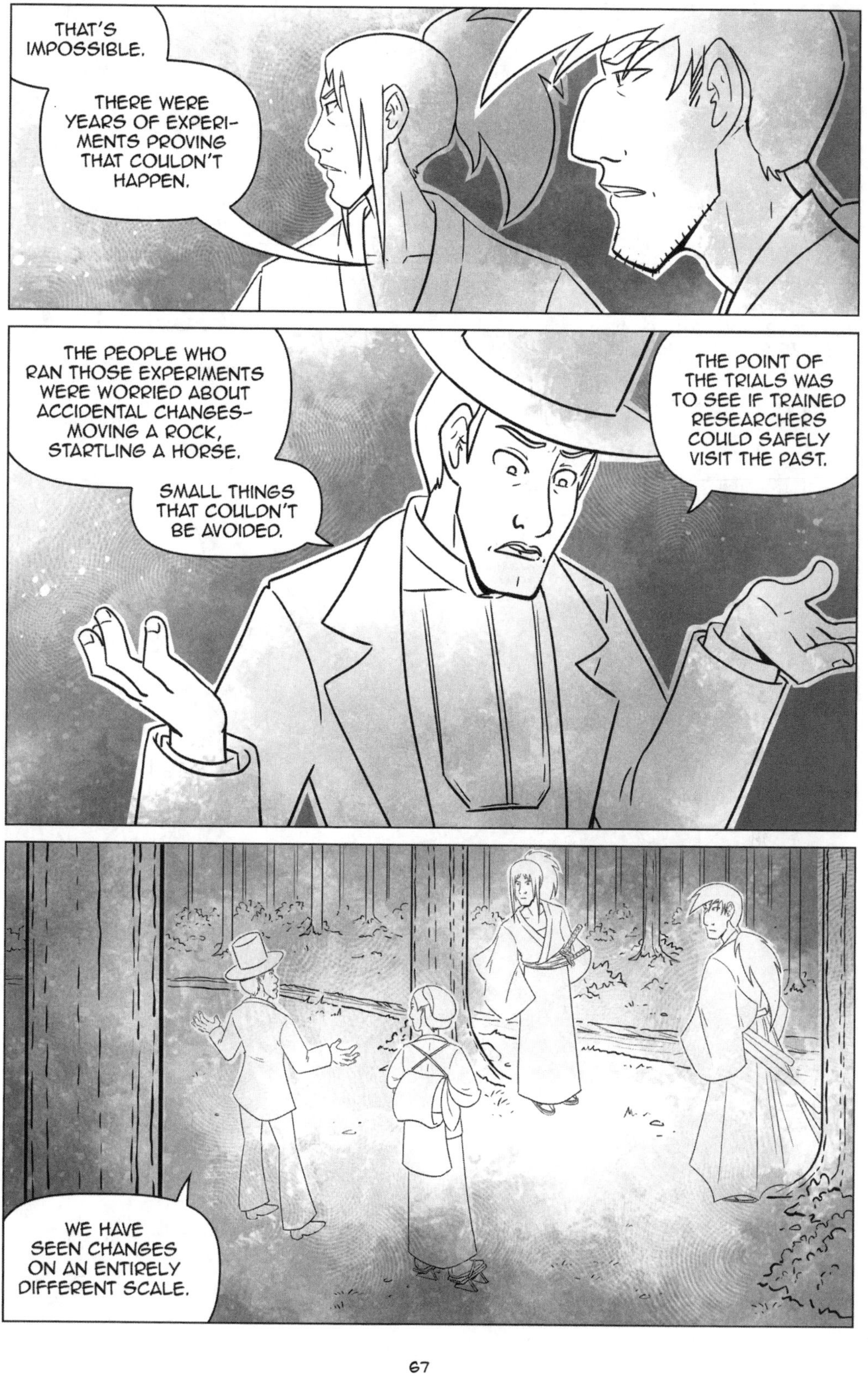
THAT'S IMPOSSIBLE.
THERE WERE YEARS OF EXPERI-MENTS PROVING THAT COULDN'T HAPPEN.
THE PEOPLE WHO RAN THOSE EXPERIMENTS WERE WORRIED ABOUT ACCIDENTAL CHANGES- MOVING A ROCK, STARTLING A HORSE.
SMALL THINGS THAT COULDN'T BE AVOIDED.
THE POINT OF THE TRIALS WAS TO SEE IF TRAINED RESEARCHERS COULD SAFELY VISIT THE PAST.
WE HAVE SEEN CHANGES ON AN ENTIRELY DIFFERENT SCALE.

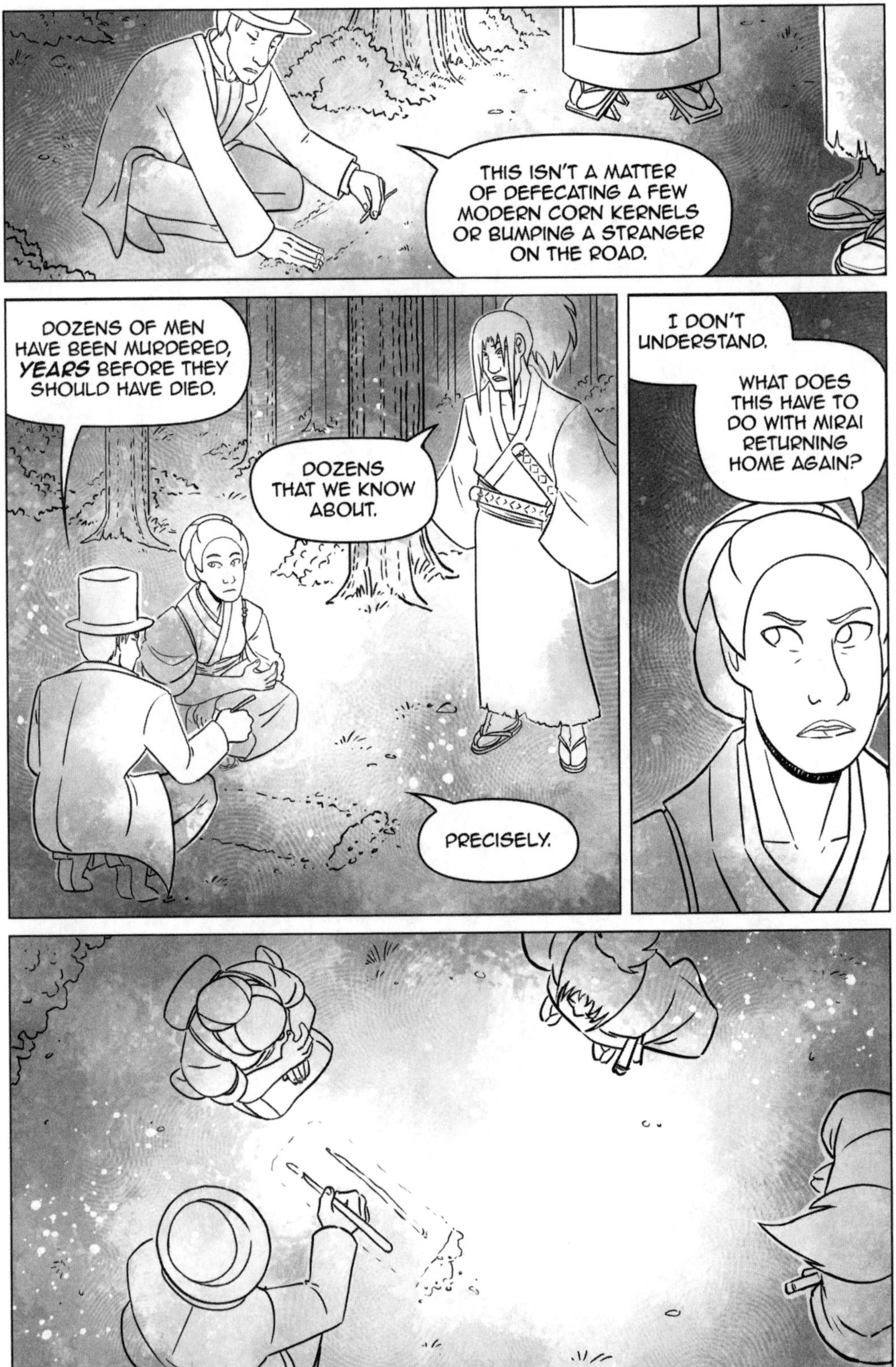
THIS ISN'T A MATTER OF DEFECATING A FEW MODERN CORN KERNELS OR BUMPING A STRANGER ON THE ROAD.
DOZENS OF MEN HAVE BEEN MURDERED, *YEARS* BEFORE THEY SHOULD HAVE DIED.
DOZENS THAT WE KNOW ABOUT.
PRECISELY.
I DON'T UNDERSTAND.
WHAT DOES THIS HAVE TO DO WITH MIRAI RETURNING HOME AGAIN?

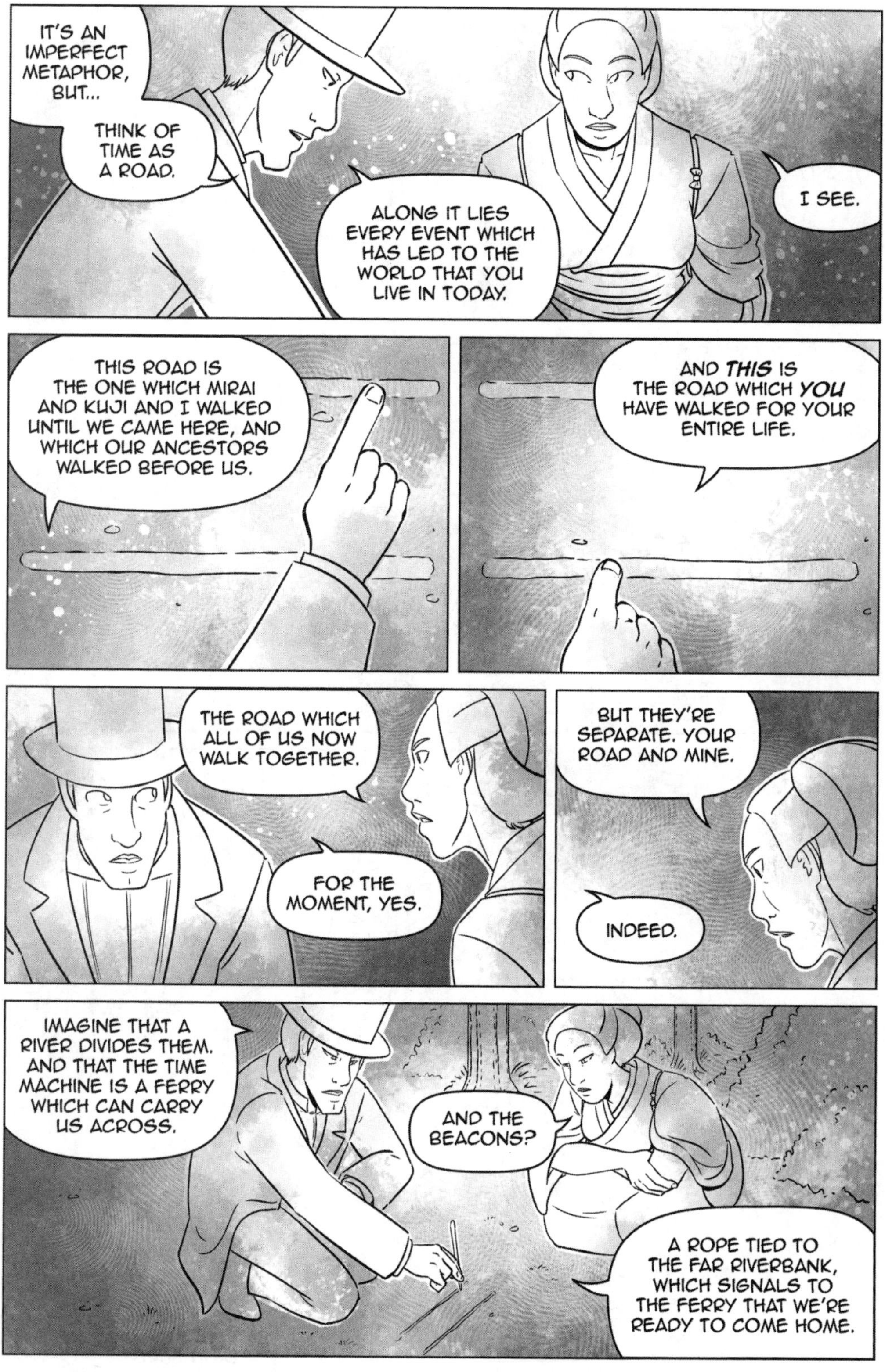
IT'S AN IMPERFECT METAPHOR, BUT...
THINK OF TIME AS A ROAD.
ALONG IT LIES EVERY EVENT WHICH HAS LED TO THE WORLD THAT YOU LIVE IN TODAY.
I SEE.
THIS ROAD IS THE ONE WHICH MIRAI AND KUJI AND I WALKED UNTIL WE CAME HERE, AND WHICH OUR ANCESTORS WALKED BEFORE US.
AND *THIS* IS THE ROAD WHICH *YOU* HAVE WALKED FOR YOUR ENTIRE LIFE.
THE ROAD WHICH ALL OF US NOW WALK TOGETHER.
FOR THE MOMENT, YES.
BUT THEY'RE SEPARATE. YOUR ROAD AND MINE.
INDEED.
IMAGINE THAT A RIVER DIVIDES THEM. AND THAT THE TIME MACHINE IS A FERRY WHICH CAN CARRY US ACROSS.
AND THE BEACONS?
A ROPE TIED TO THE FAR RIVERBANK, WHICH SIGNALS TO THE FERRY THAT WE'RE READY TO COME HOME.

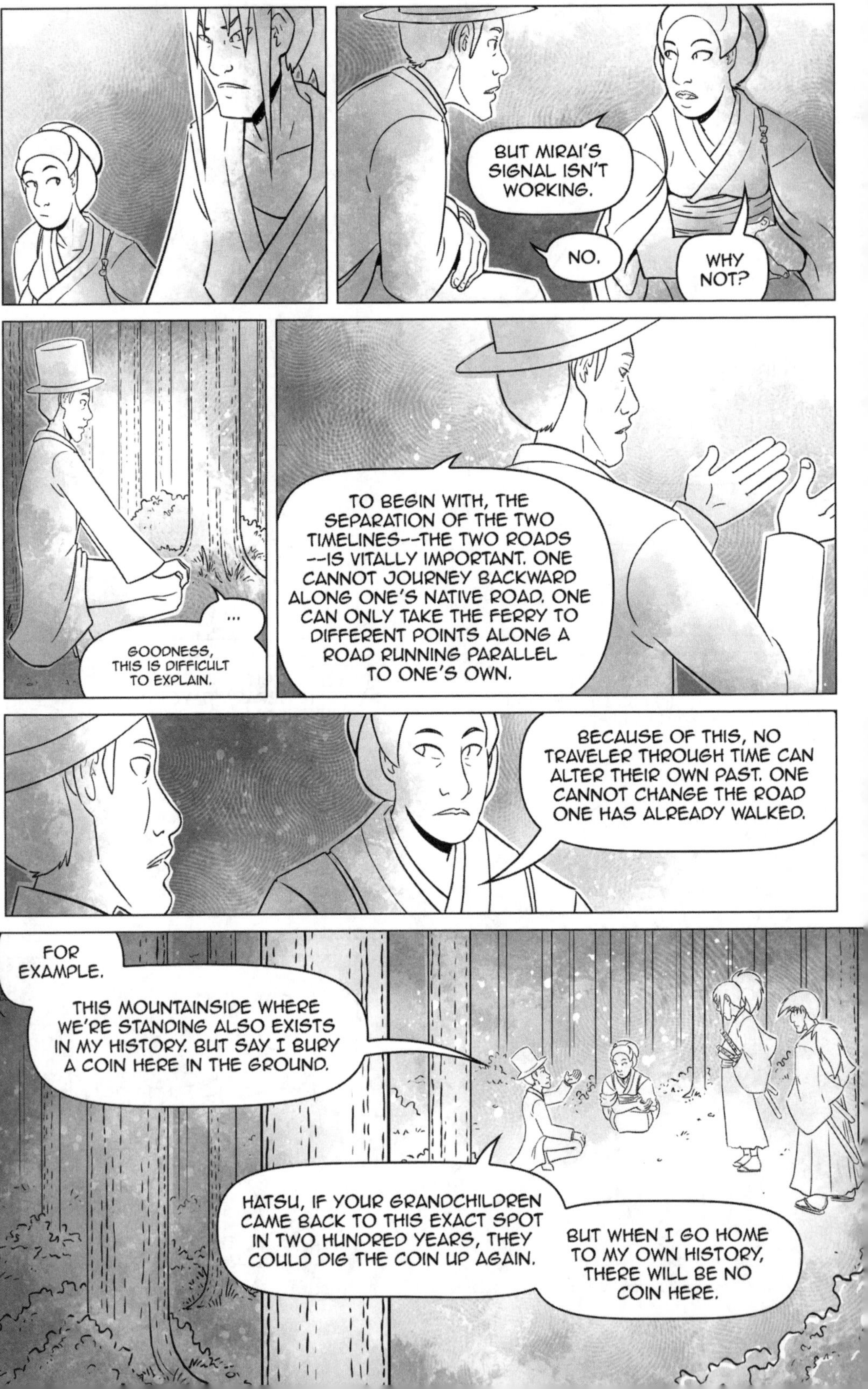

BUT MIRAI'S SIGNAL ISN'T WORKING.
NO.
WHY NOT?
TO BEGIN WITH, THE SEPARATION OF THE TWO TIMELINES--THE TWO ROADS --IS VITALLY IMPORTANT. ONE CANNOT JOURNEY BACKWARD ALONG ONE'S NATIVE ROAD. ONE CAN ONLY TAKE THE FERRY TO DIFFERENT POINTS ALONG A ROAD RUNNING PARALLEL TO ONE'S OWN.
...
GOODNESS, THIS IS DIFFICULT TO EXPLAIN.
BECAUSE OF THIS, NO TRAVELER THROUGH TIME CAN ALTER THEIR OWN PAST. ONE CANNOT CHANGE THE ROAD ONE HAS ALREADY WALKED.
FOR EXAMPLE.
THIS MOUNTAINSIDE WHERE WE'RE STANDING ALSO EXISTS IN MY HISTORY. BUT SAY I BURY A COIN HERE IN THE GROUND.
HATSU, IF YOUR GRANDCHILDREN CAME BACK TO THIS EXACT SPOT IN TWO HUNDRED YEARS, THEY COULD DIG THE COIN UP AGAIN.
BUT WHEN I GO HOME TO MY OWN HISTORY, THERE WILL BE NO COIN HERE.

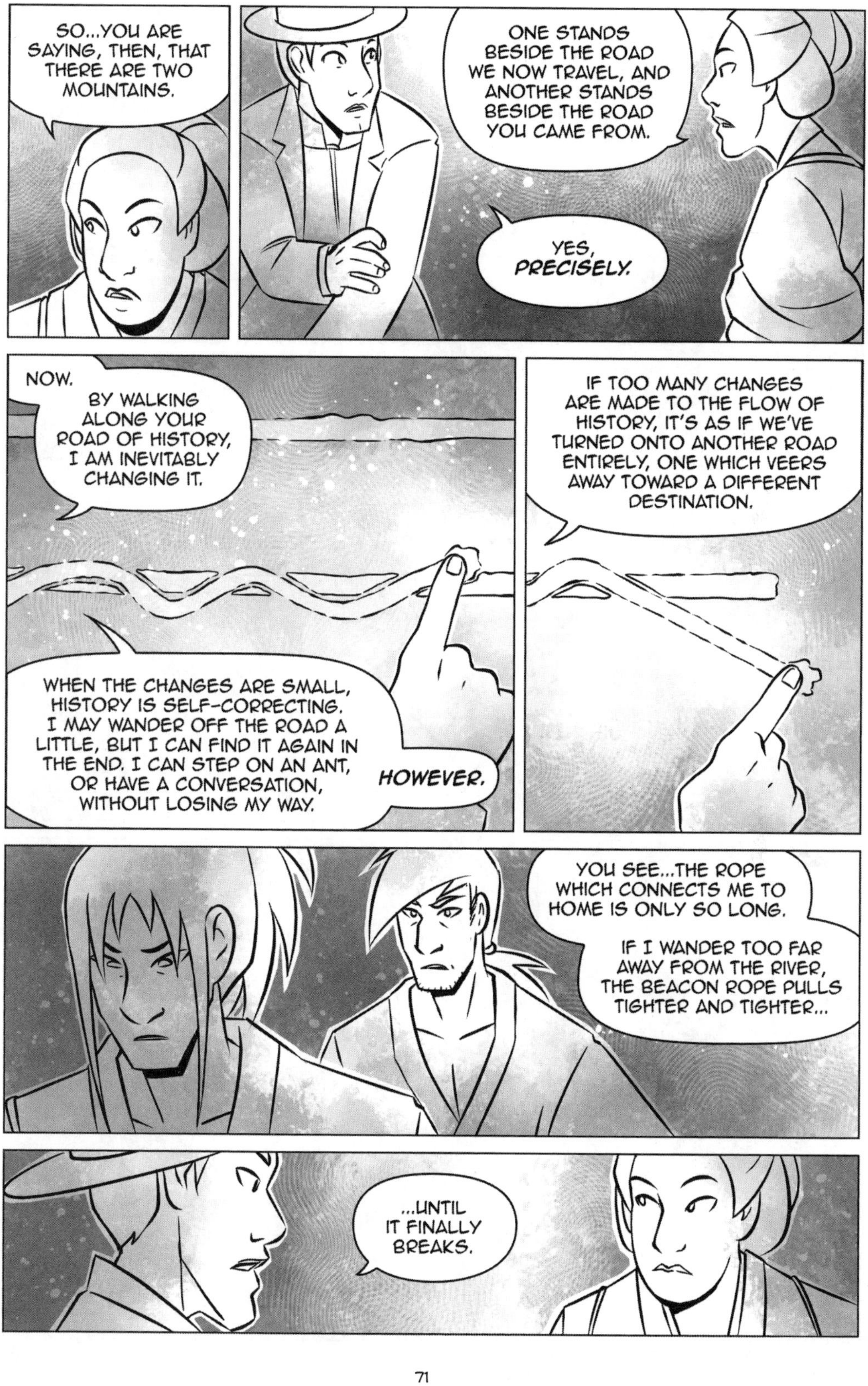
SO...YOU ARE SAYING, THEN, THAT THERE ARE TWO MOUNTAINS.
ONE STANDS BESIDE THE ROAD WE NOW TRAVEL, AND ANOTHER STANDS BESIDE THE ROAD YOU CAME FROM.
YES, *PRECISELY.*
NOW.
BY WALKING ALONG YOUR ROAD OF HISTORY, I AM INEVITABLY CHANGING IT.
WHEN THE CHANGES ARE SMALL, HISTORY IS SELF-CORRECTING. I MAY WANDER OFF THE ROAD A LITTLE, BUT I CAN FIND IT AGAIN IN THE END. I CAN STEP ON AN ANT, OR HAVE A CONVERSATION, WITHOUT LOSING MY WAY.
*HOWEVER.*
IF TOO MANY CHANGES ARE MADE TO THE FLOW OF HISTORY, IT'S AS IF WE'VE TURNED ONTO ANOTHER ROAD ENTIRELY, ONE WHICH VEERS AWAY TOWARD A DIFFERENT DESTINATION.
YOU SEE...THE ROPE WHICH CONNECTS ME TO HOME IS ONLY SO LONG.
IF I WANDER TOO FAR AWAY FROM THE RIVER, THE BEACON ROPE PULLS TIGHTER AND TIGHTER...
...UNTIL IT FINALLY BREAKS.

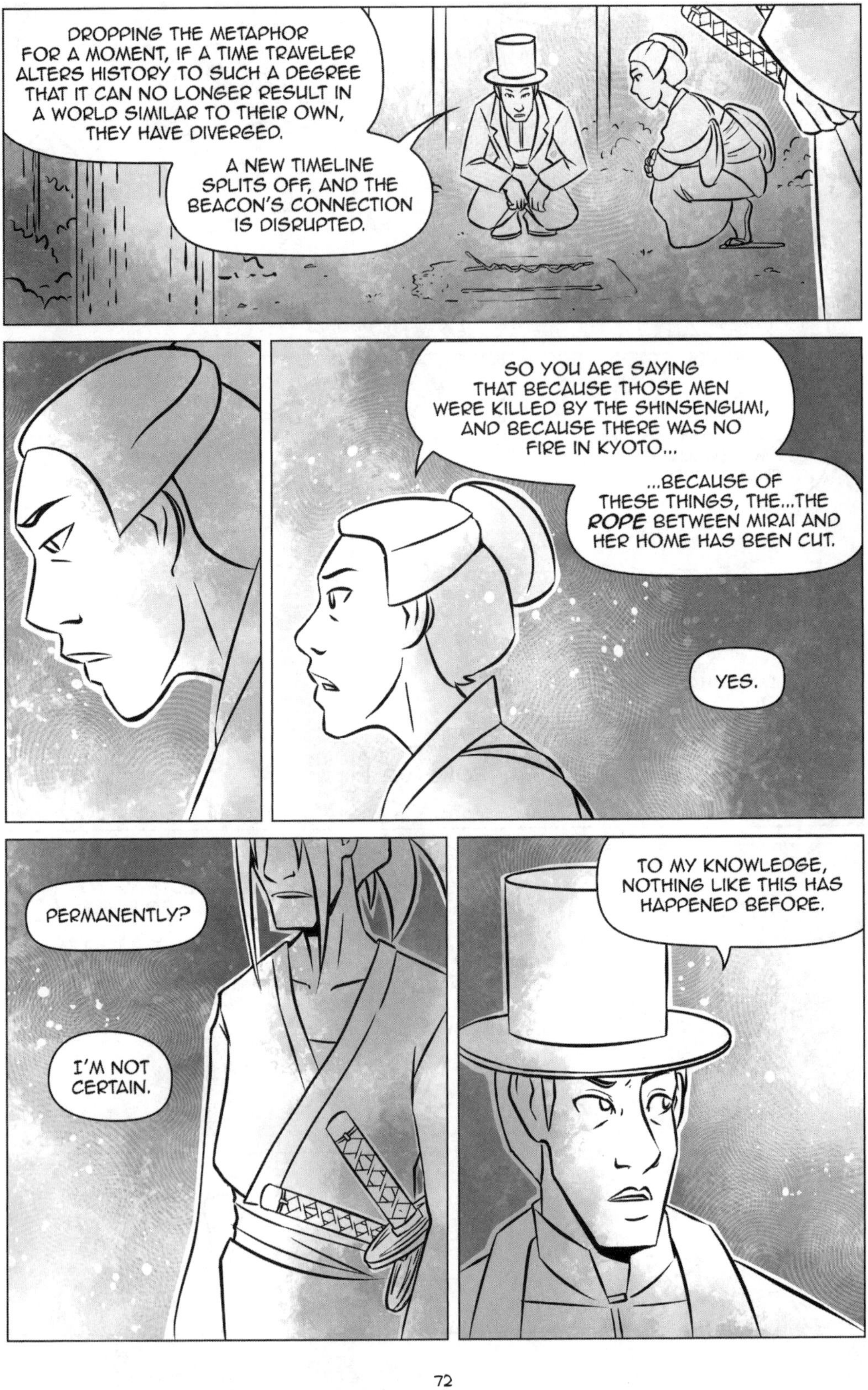
DROPPING THE METAPHOR FOR A MOMENT, IF A TIME TRAVELER ALTERS HISTORY TO SUCH A DEGREE THAT IT CAN NO LONGER RESULT IN A WORLD SIMILAR TO THEIR OWN, THEY HAVE DIVERGED.
A NEW TIMELINE SPLITS OFF, AND THE BEACON'S CONNECTION IS DISRUPTED.
SO YOU ARE SAYING THAT BECAUSE THOSE MEN WERE KILLED BY THE SHINSENGUMI, AND BECAUSE THERE WAS NO FIRE IN KYOTO...
...BECAUSE OF THESE THINGS, THE...THE *ROPE* BETWEEN MIRAI AND HER HOME HAS BEEN CUT.
YES.
PERMANENTLY?
I'M NOT CERTAIN.
TO MY KNOWLEDGE, NOTHING LIKE THIS HAS HAPPENED BEFORE.

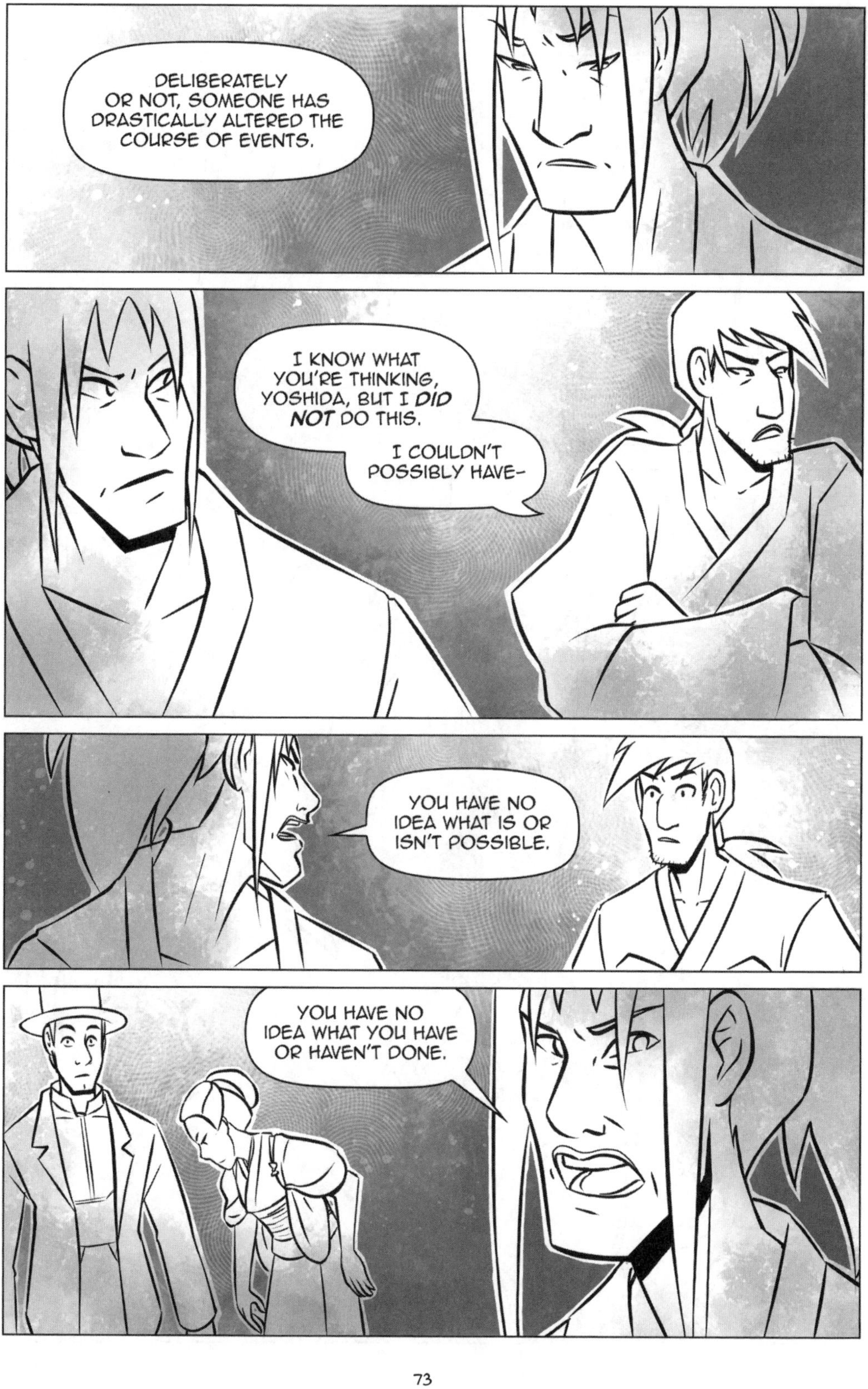
DELIBERATELY OR NOT, SOMEONE HAS DRASTICALLY ALTERED THE COURSE OF EVENTS.
I KNOW WHAT YOU'RE THINKING, YOSHIDA, BUT I *DID NOT* DO THIS.
I COULDN'T POSSIBLY HAVE-
YOU HAVE NO IDEA WHAT IS OR ISN'T POSSIBLE.
YOU HAVE NO IDEA WHAT YOU HAVE OR HAVEN'T DONE.

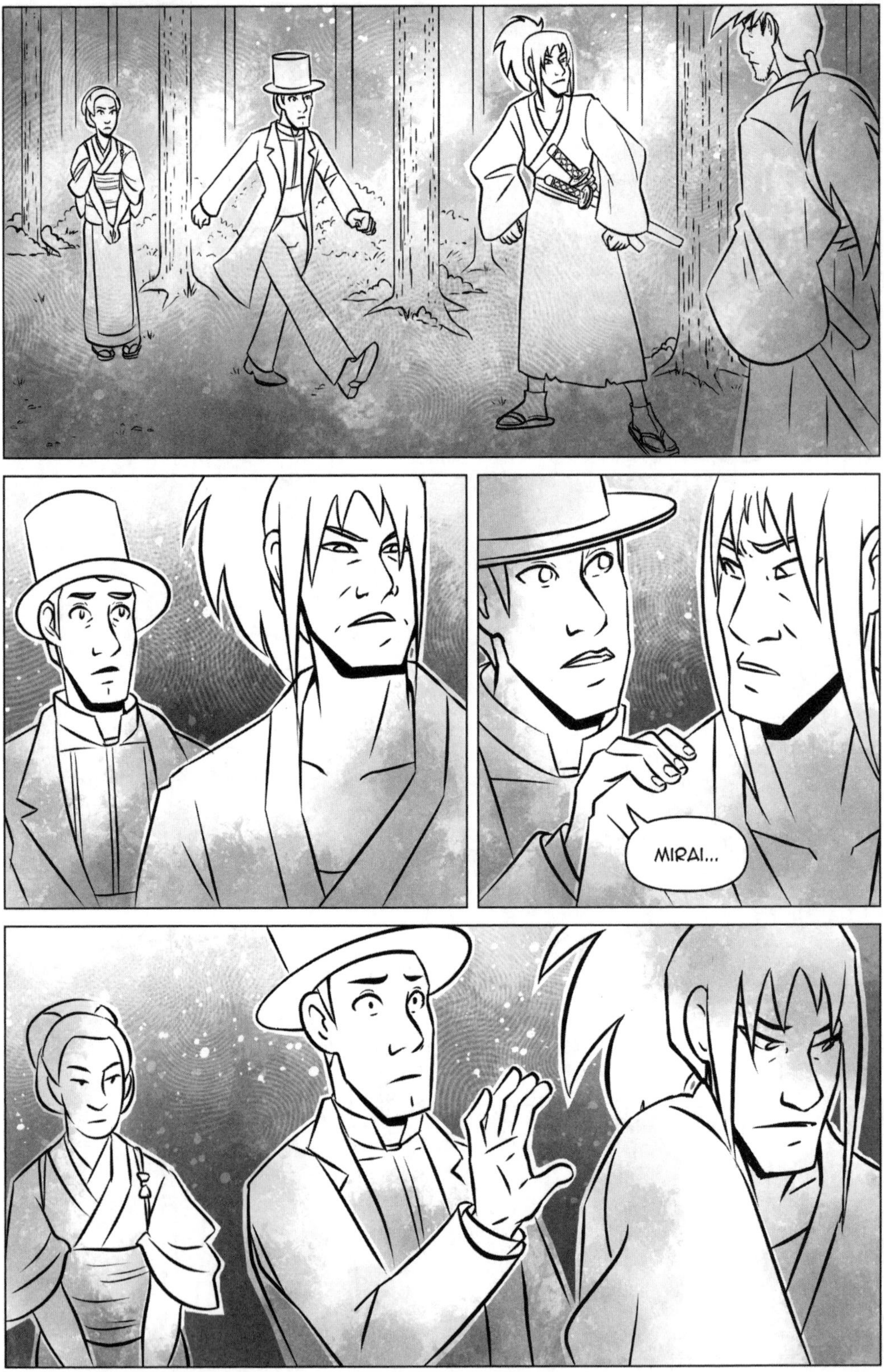
MIRAI...

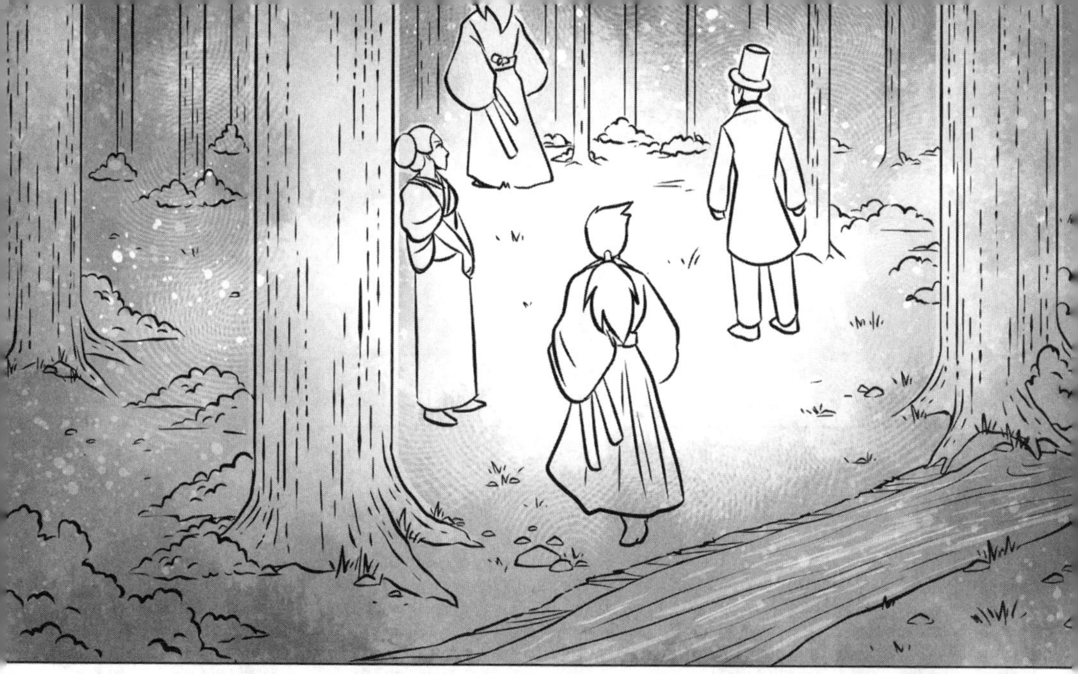

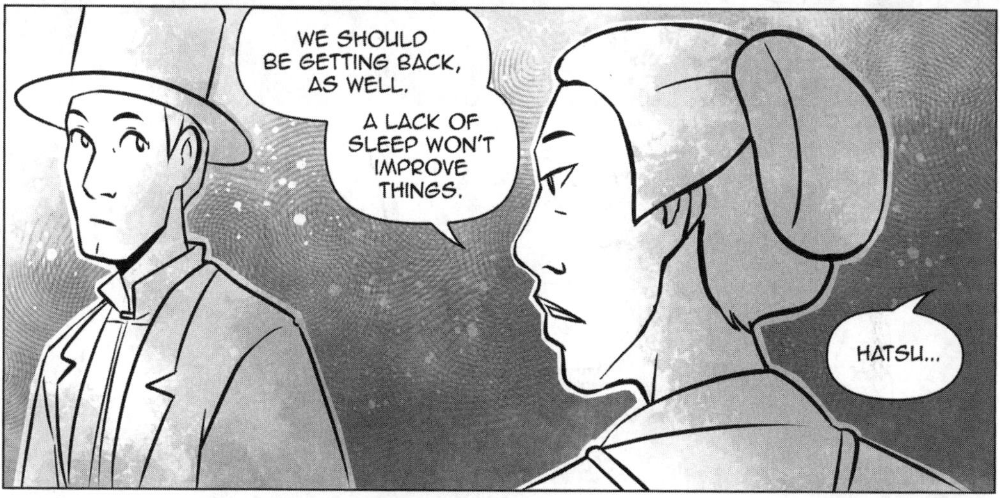
WE SHOULD BE GETTING BACK, AS WELL.
A LACK OF SLEEP WON'T IMPROVE THINGS.
HATSU...

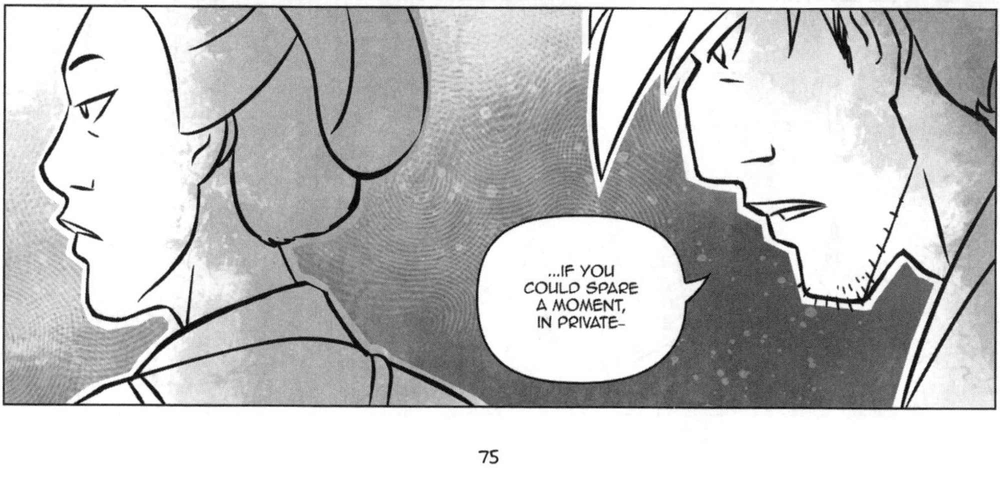
...IF YOU COULD SPARE A MOMENT, IN PRIVATE-

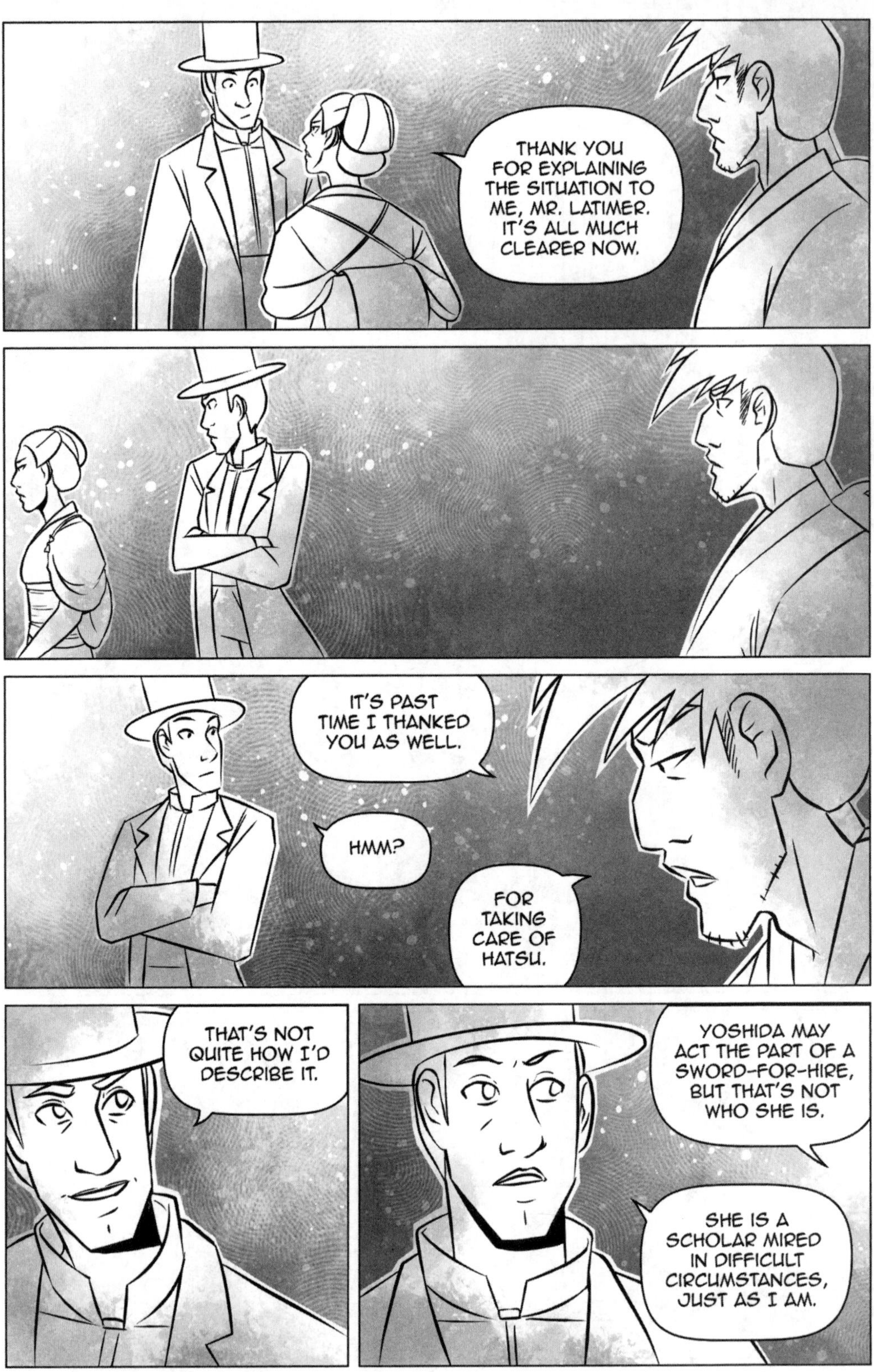
THANK YOU FOR EXPLAINING THE SITUATION TO ME, MR. LATIMER. IT'S ALL MUCH CLEARER NOW.
IT'S PAST TIME I THANKED YOU AS WELL.
HMM?
FOR TAKING CARE OF HATSU.
THAT'S NOT QUITE HOW I'D DESCRIBE IT.
YOSHIDA MAY ACT THE PART OF A SWORD-FOR-HIRE, BUT THAT'S NOT WHO SHE IS.
SHE IS A SCHOLAR MIRED IN DIFFICULT CIRCUMSTANCES, JUST AS I AM.

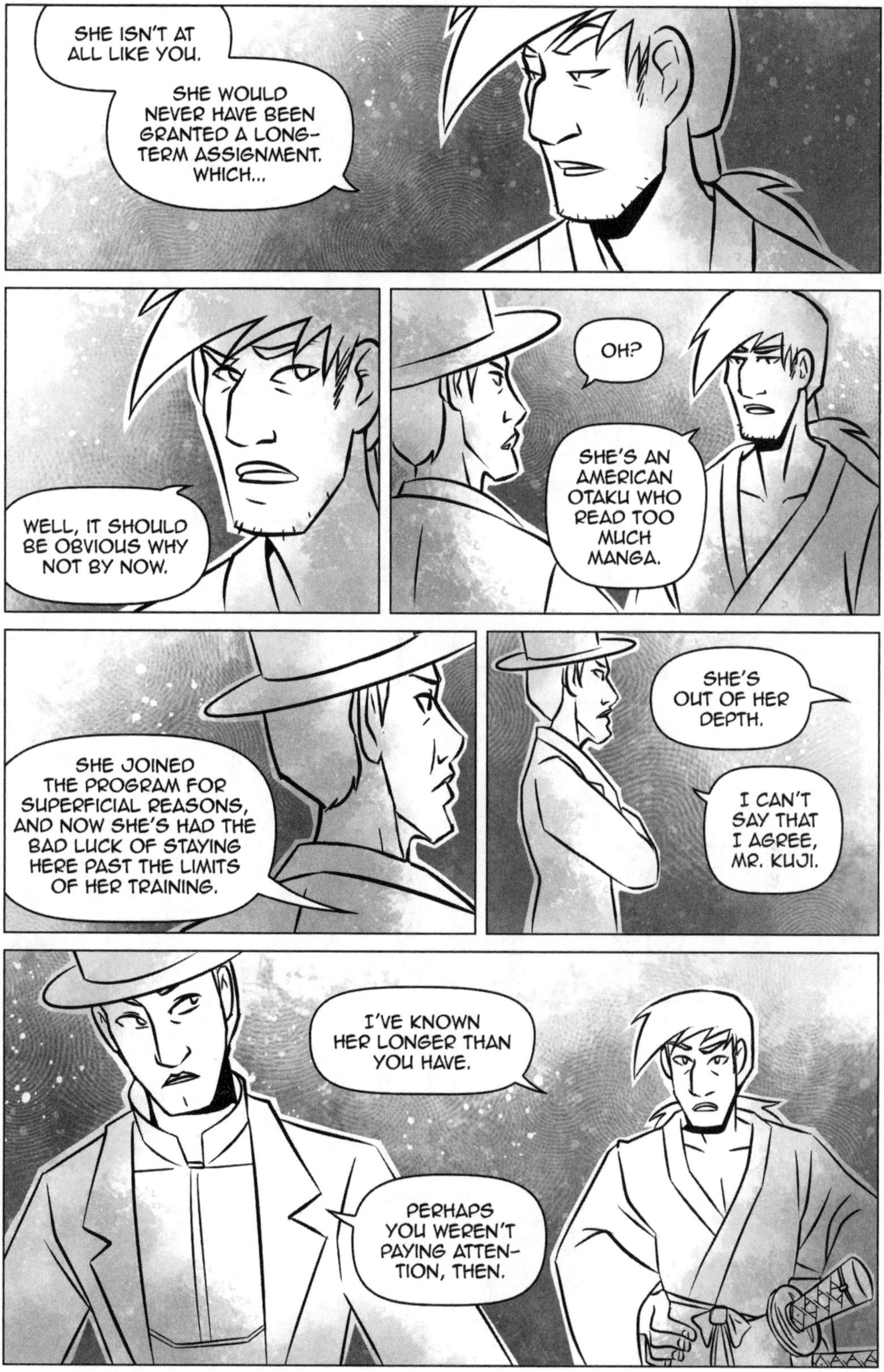
SHE ISN'T AT ALL LIKE YOU.
SHE WOULD NEVER HAVE BEEN GRANTED A LONG-TERM ASSIGNMENT. WHICH...
WELL, IT SHOULD BE OBVIOUS WHY NOT BY NOW.
OH?
SHE'S AN AMERICAN OTAKU WHO READ TOO MUCH MANGA.
SHE JOINED THE PROGRAM FOR SUPERFICIAL REASONS, AND NOW SHE'S HAD THE BAD LUCK OF STAYING HERE PAST THE LIMITS OF HER TRAINING.
SHE'S OUT OF HER DEPTH.
I CAN'T SAY THAT I AGREE, MR. KUJI.
I'VE KNOWN HER LONGER THAN YOU HAVE.
PERHAPS YOU WEREN'T PAYING ATTEN-TION, THEN.

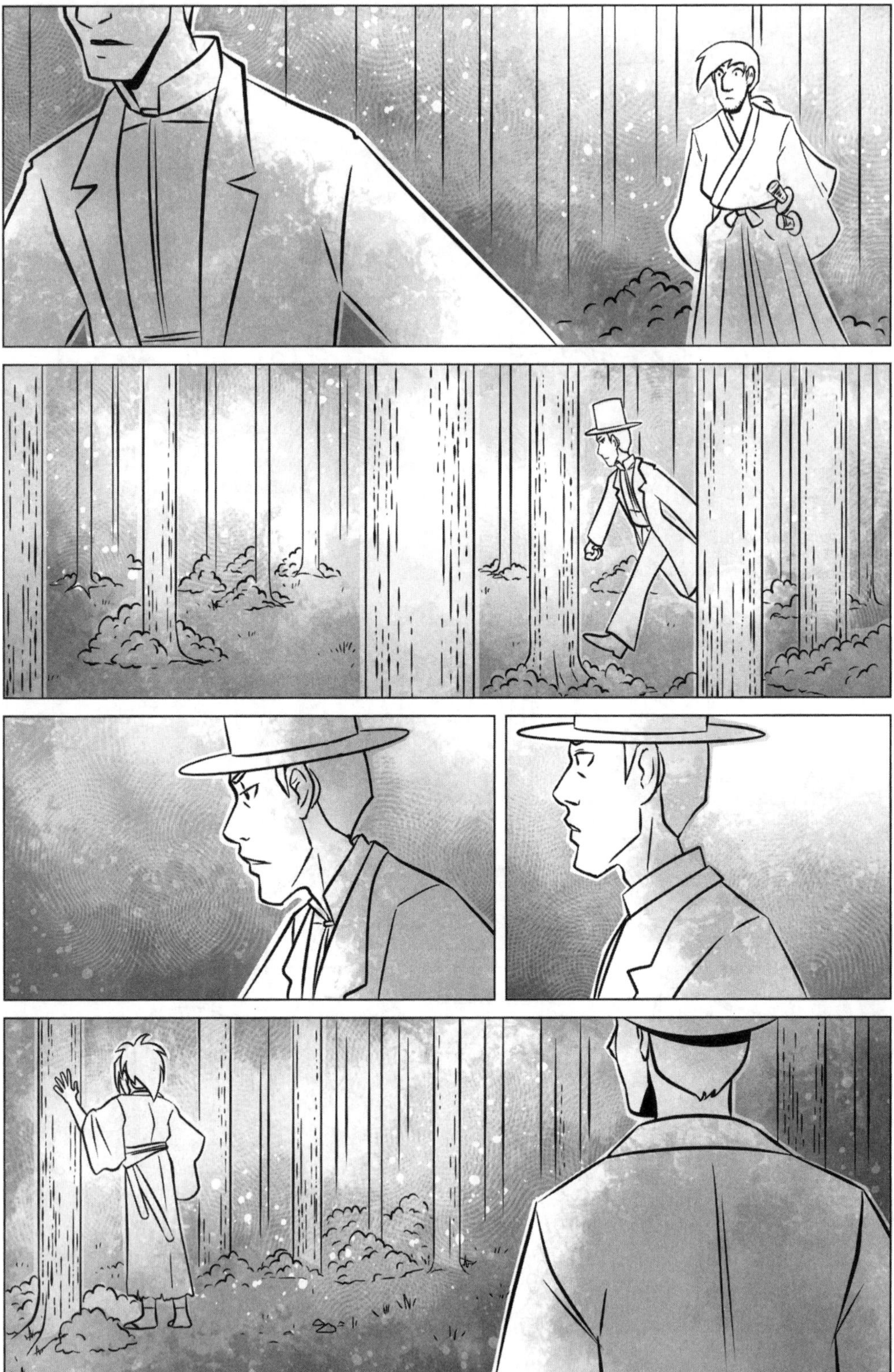

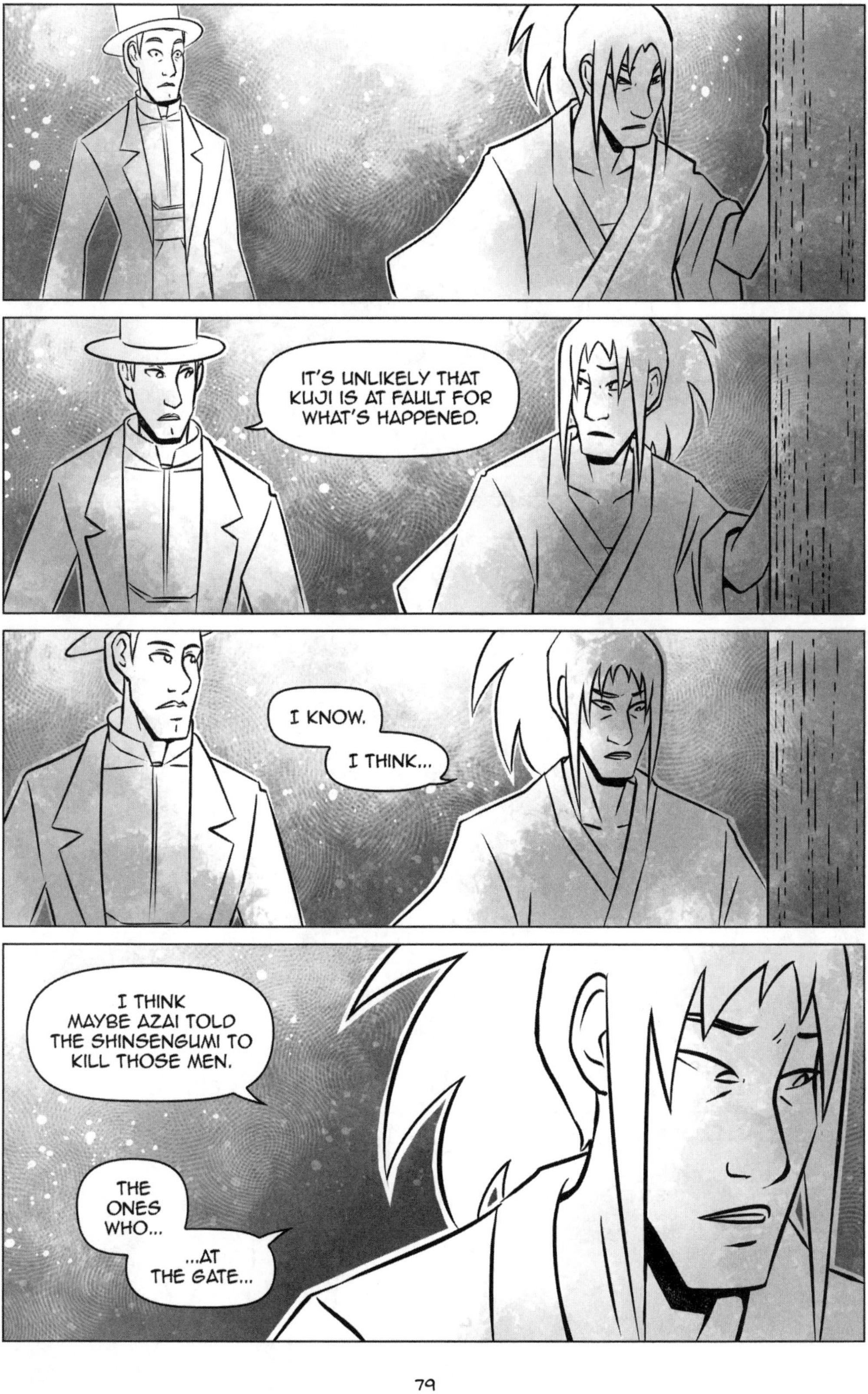
IT'S UNLIKELY THAT KUJI IS AT FAULT FOR WHAT'S HAPPENED.
I KNOW.
I THINK...
I THINK MAYBE AZAI TOLD THE SHINSENGUMI TO KILL THOSE MEN.
THE ONES WHO...
...AT THE GATE...

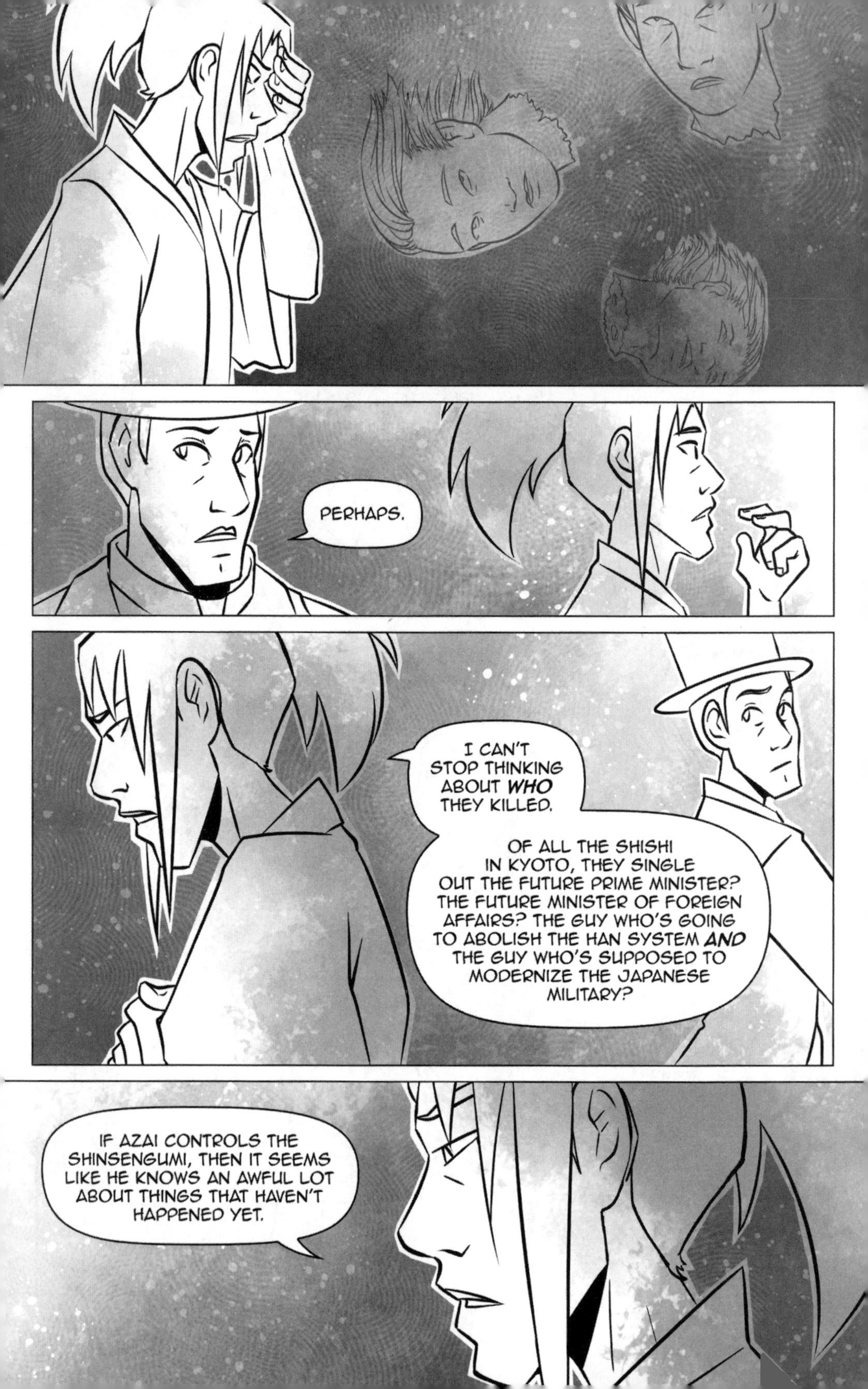
PERHAPS.
I CAN'T STOP THINKING ABOUT *WHO* THEY KILLED.
OF ALL THE SHISHI IN KYOTO, THEY SINGLE OUT THE FUTURE PRIME MINISTER? THE FUTURE MINISTER OF FOREIGN AFFAIRS? THE GUY WHO'S GOING TO ABOLISH THE HAN SYSTEM *AND* THE GUY WHO'S SUPPOSED TO MODERNIZE THE JAPANESE MILITARY?
IF AZAI CONTROLS THE SHINSENGUMI, THEN IT SEEMS LIKE HE KNOWS AN AWFUL LOT ABOUT THINGS THAT HAVEN'T HAPPENED YET.

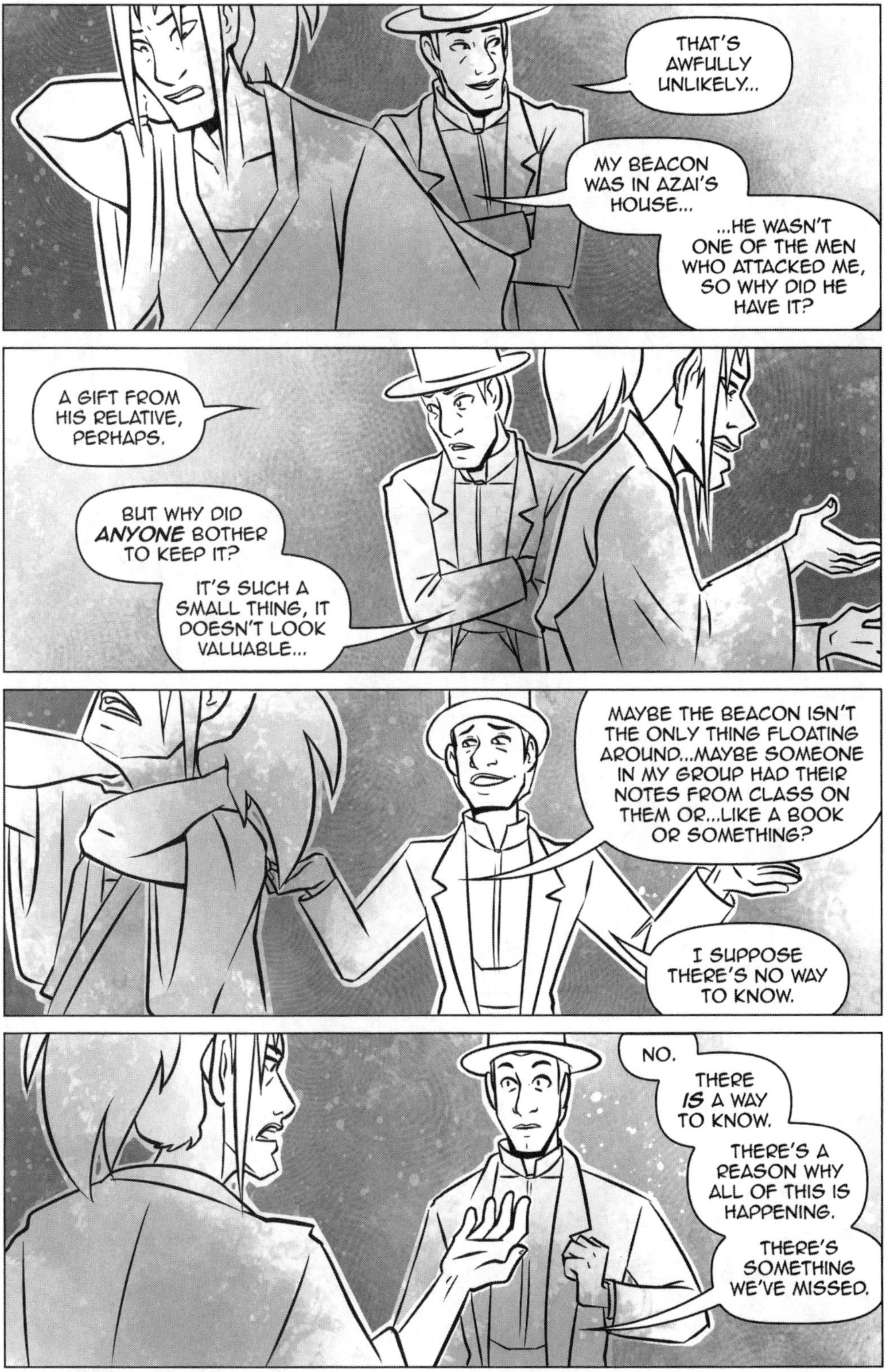
THAT'S AWFULLY UNLIKELY...
MY BEACON WAS IN AZAI'S HOUSE...
...HE WASN'T ONE OF THE MEN WHO ATTACKED ME, SO WHY DID HE HAVE IT?
A GIFT FROM HIS RELATIVE, PERHAPS.
BUT WHY DID ANYONE BOTHER TO KEEP IT?
IT'S SUCH A SMALL THING, IT DOESN'T LOOK VALUABLE...
MAYBE THE BEACON ISN'T THE ONLY THING FLOATING AROUND...MAYBE SOMEONE IN MY GROUP HAD THEIR NOTES FROM CLASS ON THEM OR...LIKE A BOOK OR SOMETHING?
I SUPPOSE THERE'S NO WAY TO KNOW.
NO.
THERE IS A WAY TO KNOW.
THERE'S A REASON WHY ALL OF THIS IS HAPPENING.
THERE'S SOMETHING WE'VE MISSED.

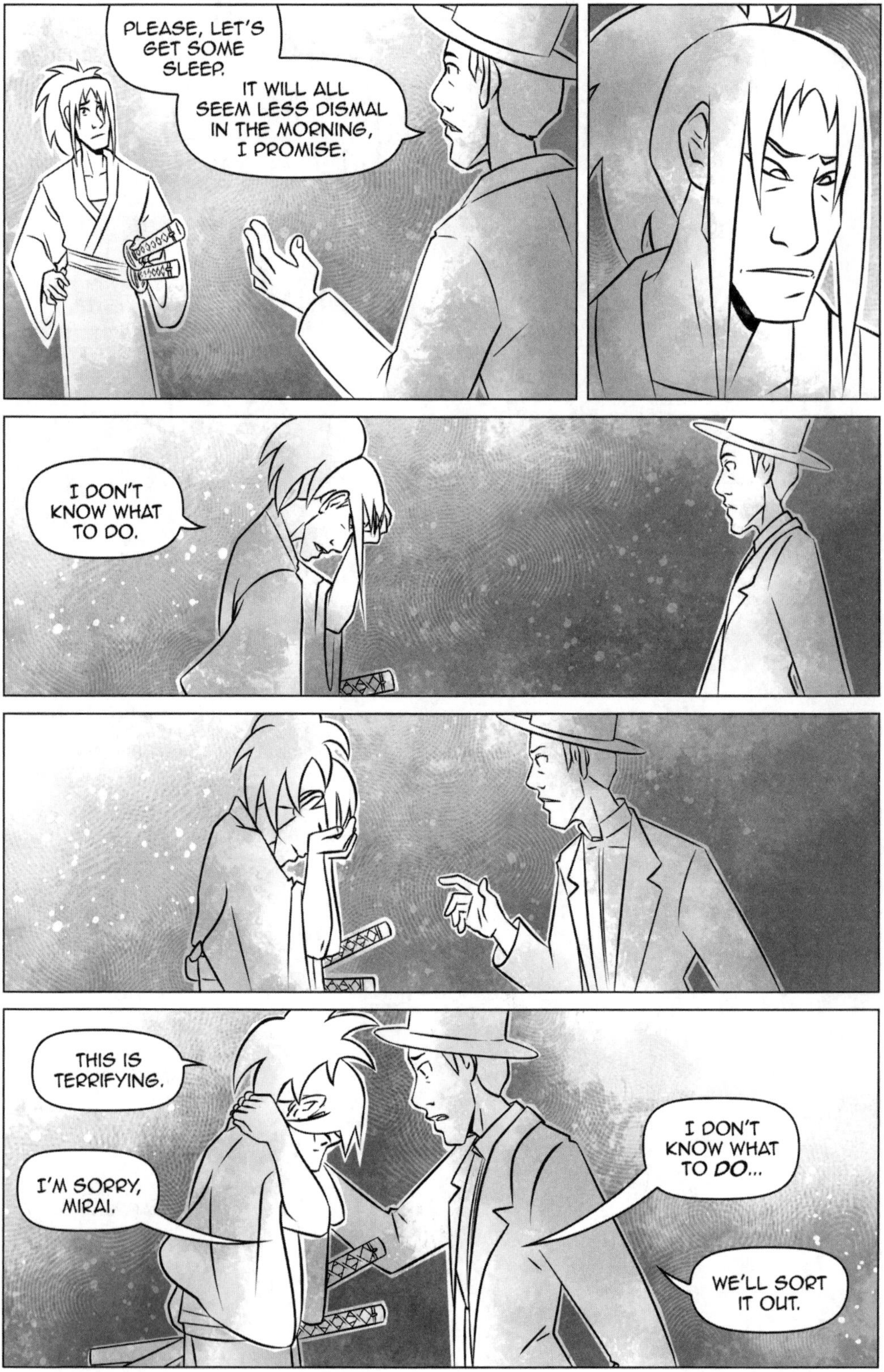
PLEASE, LET'S GET SOME SLEEP.
IT WILL ALL SEEM LESS DISMAL IN THE MORNING, I PROMISE.
I DON'T KNOW WHAT TO DO.
THIS IS TERRIFYING.
I'M SORRY, MIRAI.
I DON'T KNOW WHAT TO *DO*...
WE'LL SORT IT OUT.

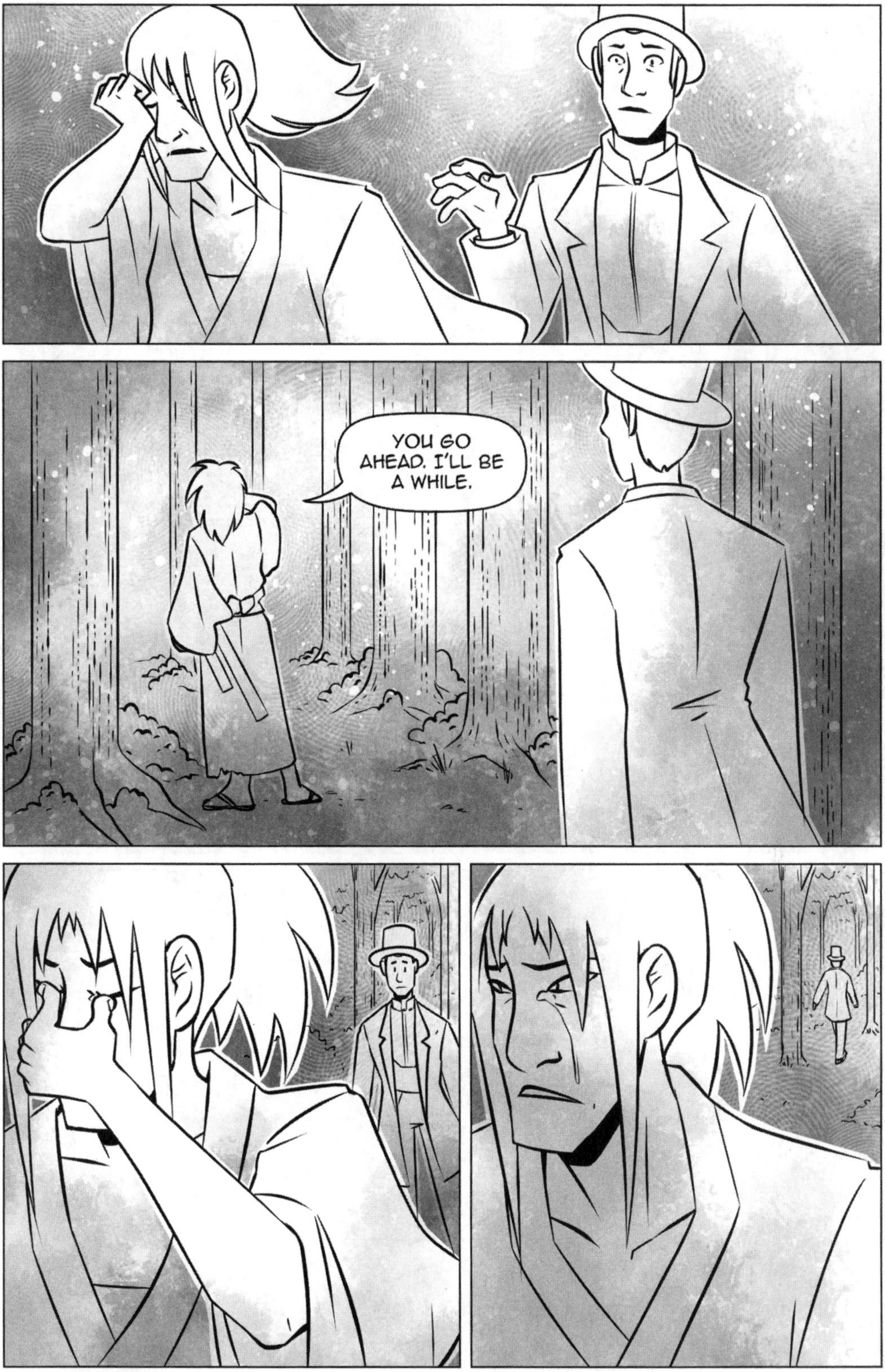
YOU GO AHEAD. I'LL BE A WHILE.

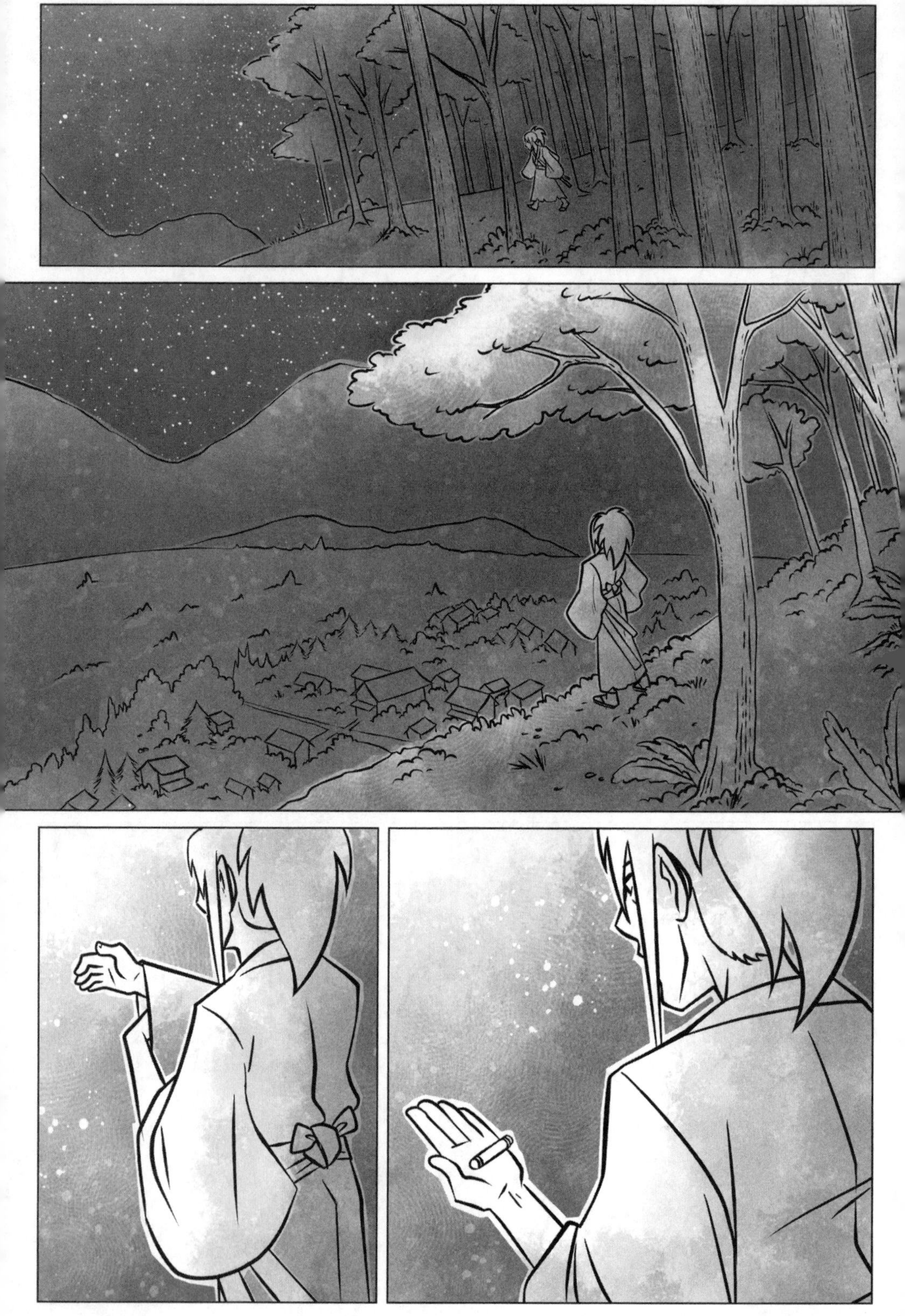

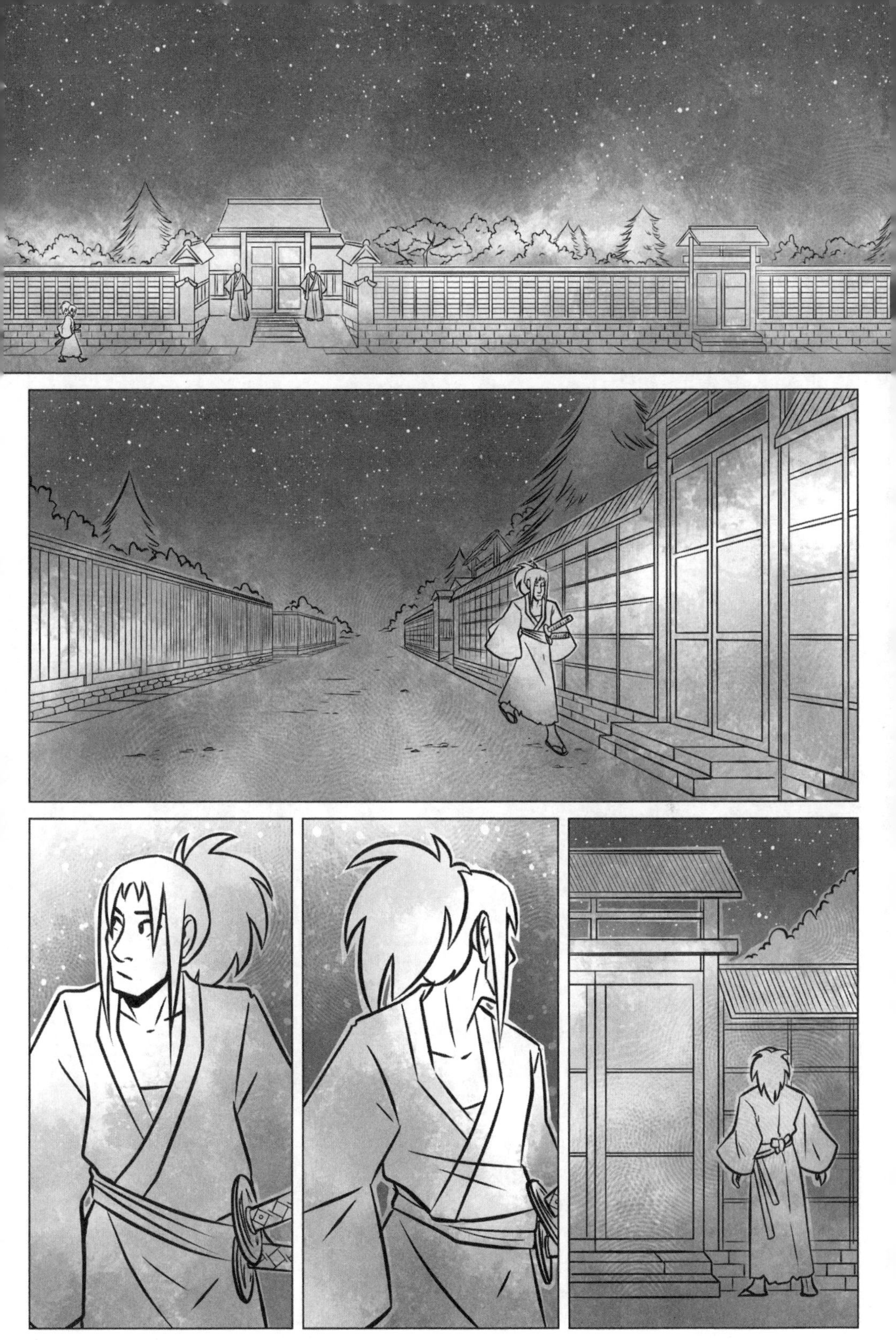

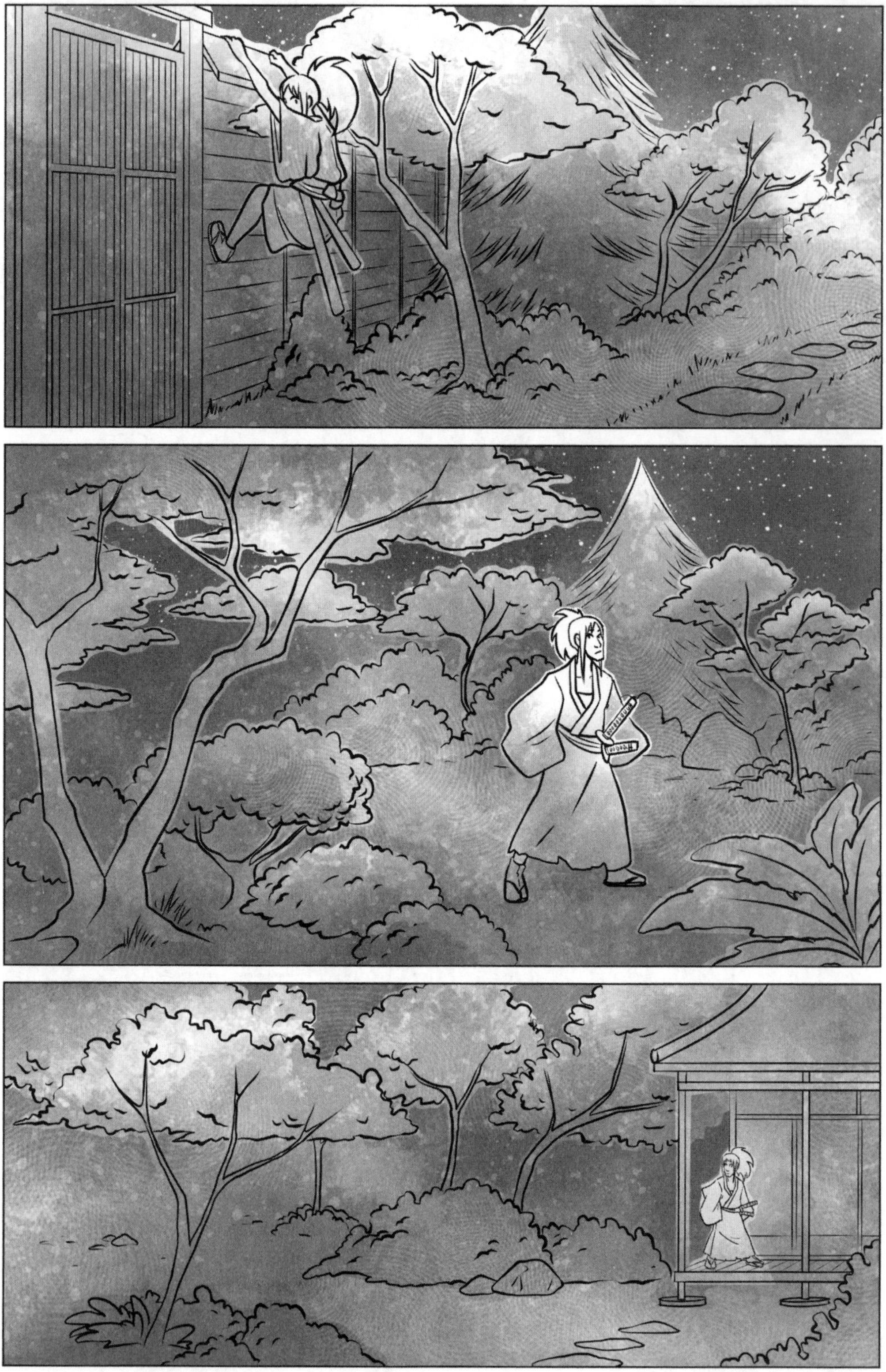

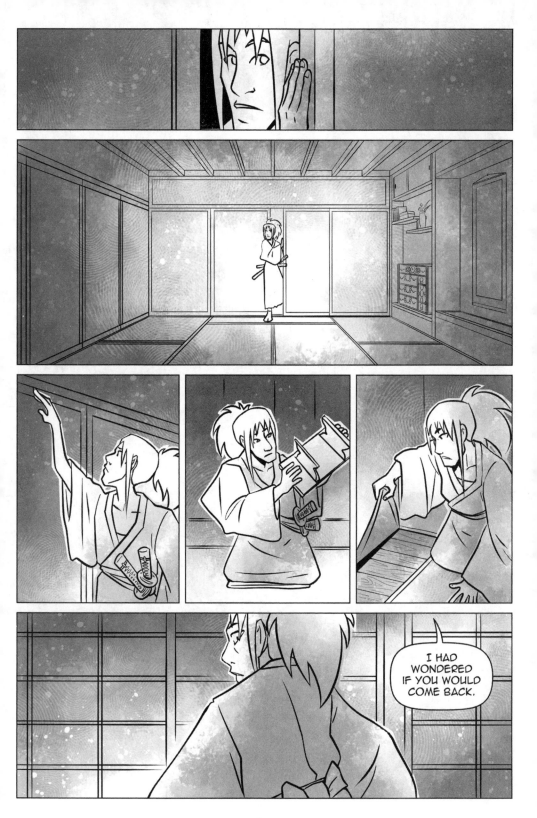

I HAD WONDERED IF YOU WOULD COME BACK.

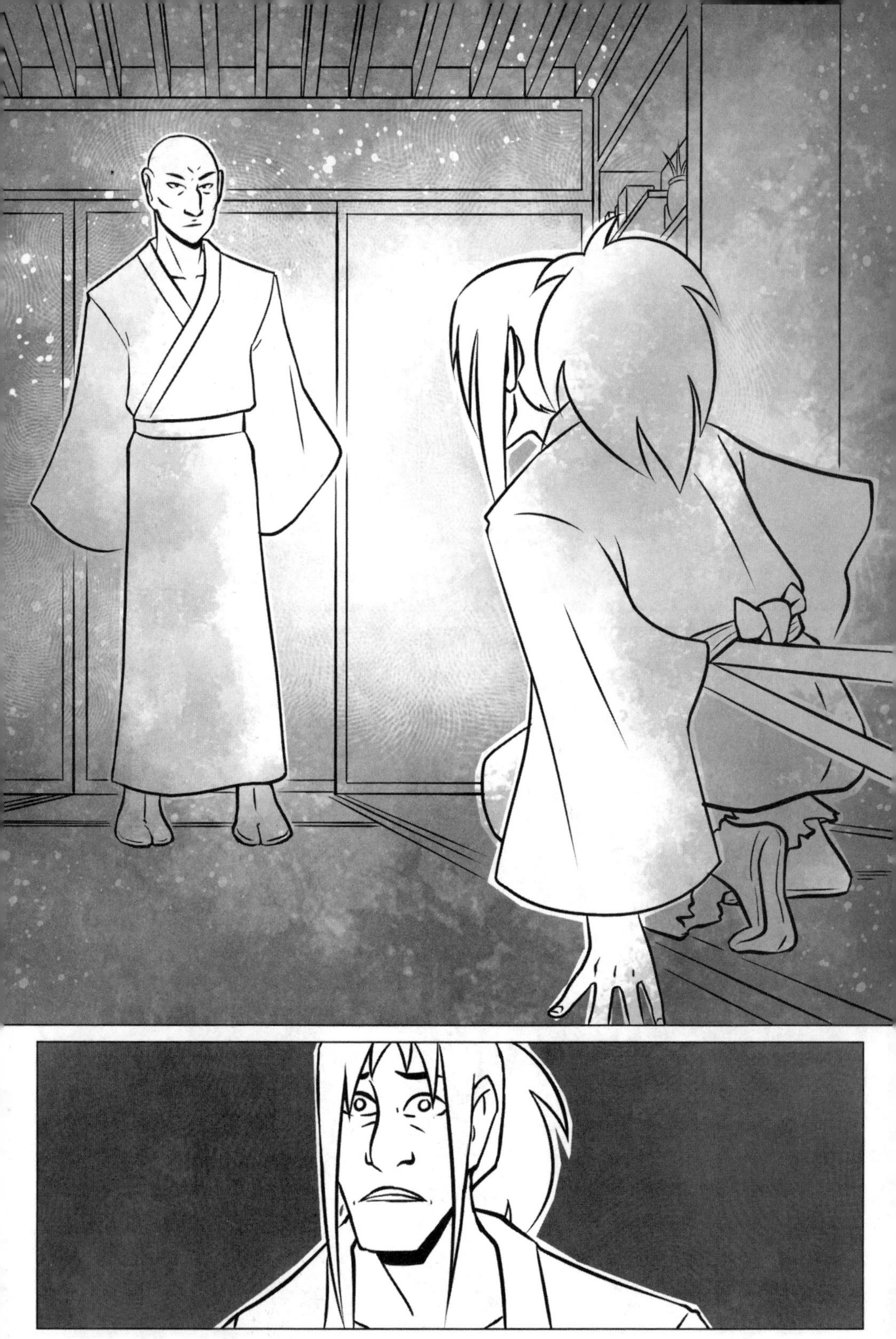

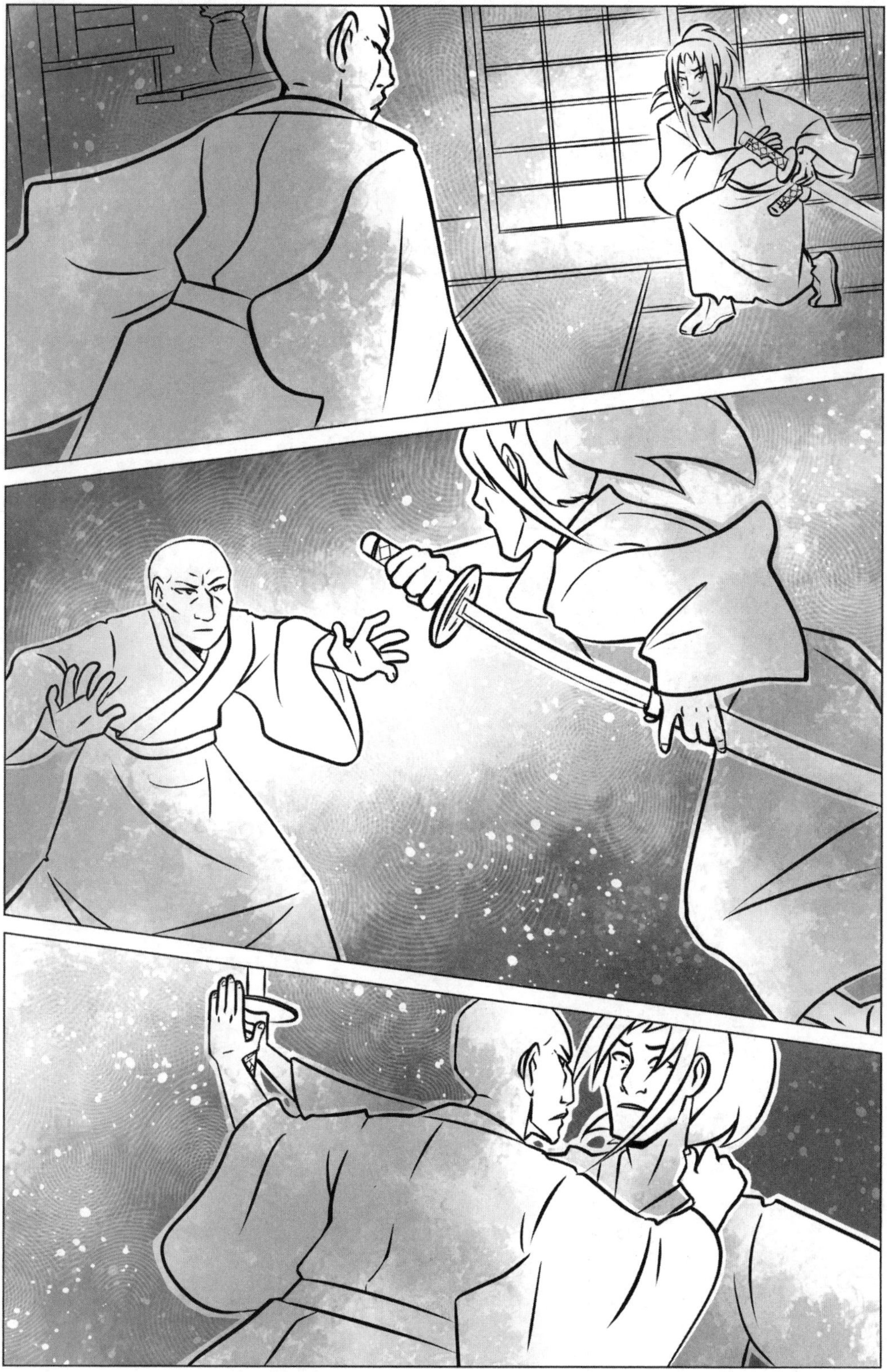

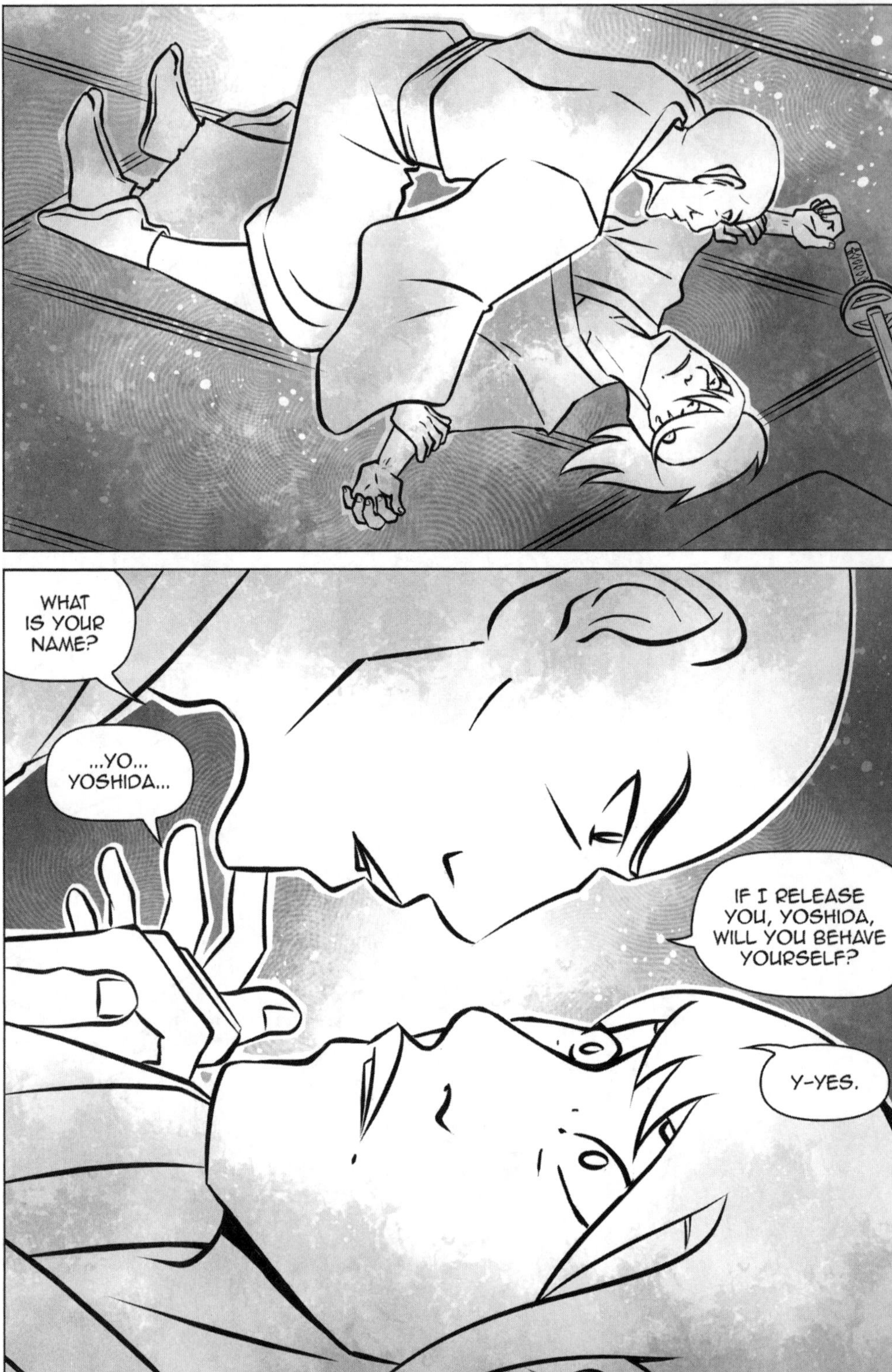
WHAT IS YOUR NAME?
...YO... YOSHIDA...
IF I RELEASE YOU, YOSHIDA, WILL YOU BEHAVE YOURSELF?
Y-YES.

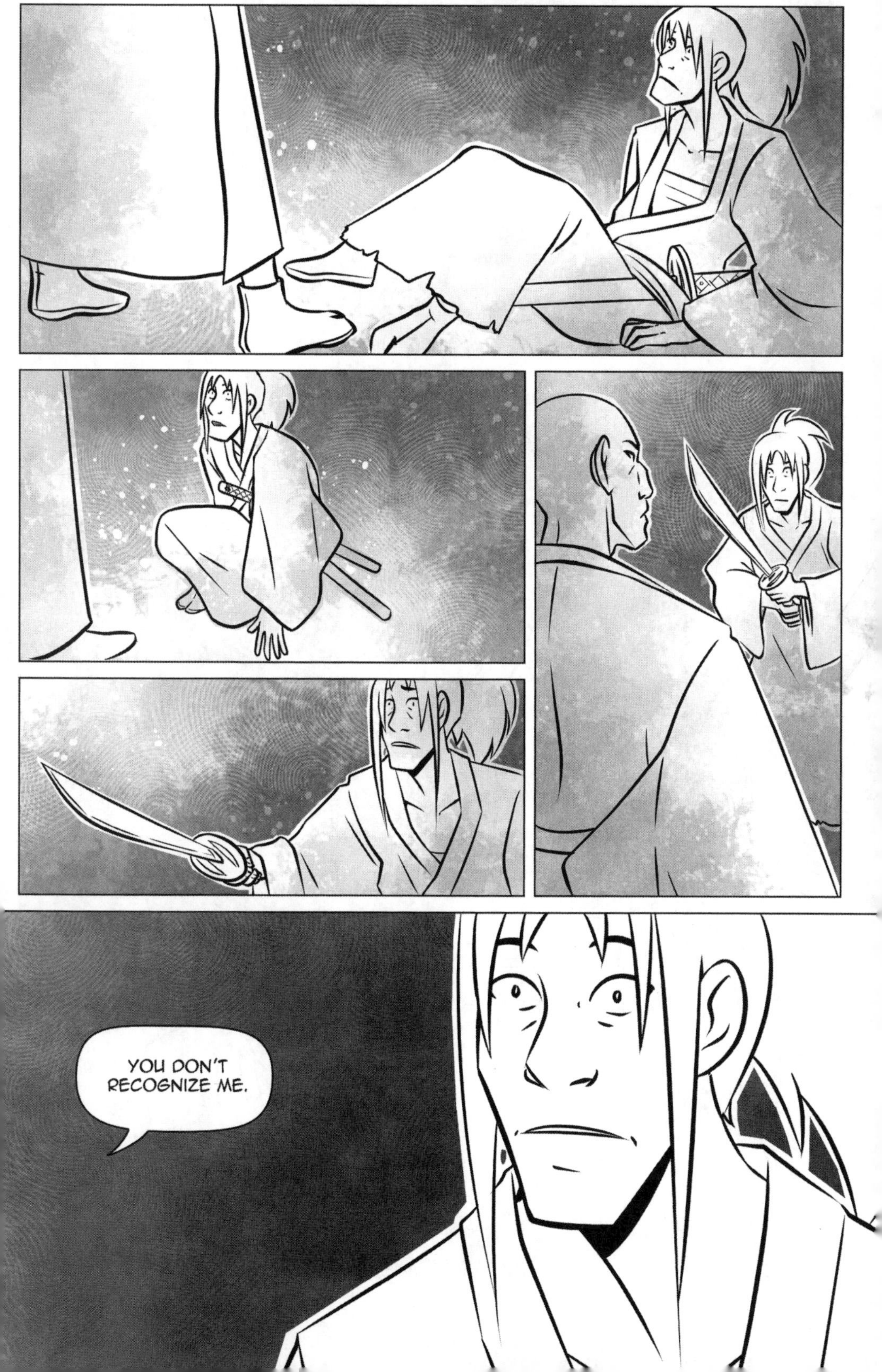
YOU DON'T RECOGNIZE ME.

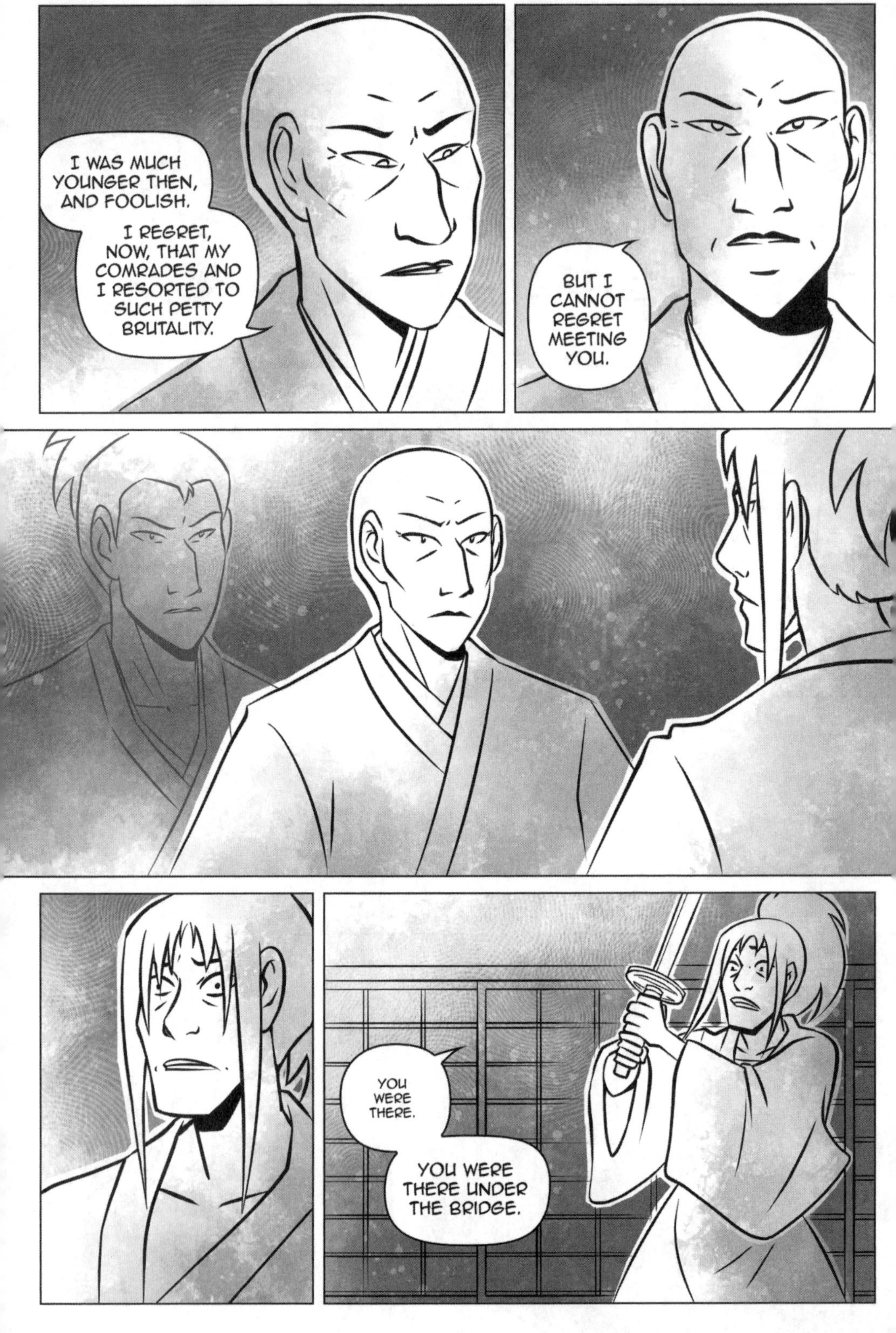
I WAS MUCH YOUNGER THEN, AND FOOLISH.
I REGRET, NOW, THAT MY COMRADES AND I RESORTED TO SUCH PETTY BRUTALITY.
BUT I CANNOT REGRET MEETING YOU.
YOU WERE THERE.
YOU WERE THERE UNDER THE BRIDGE.

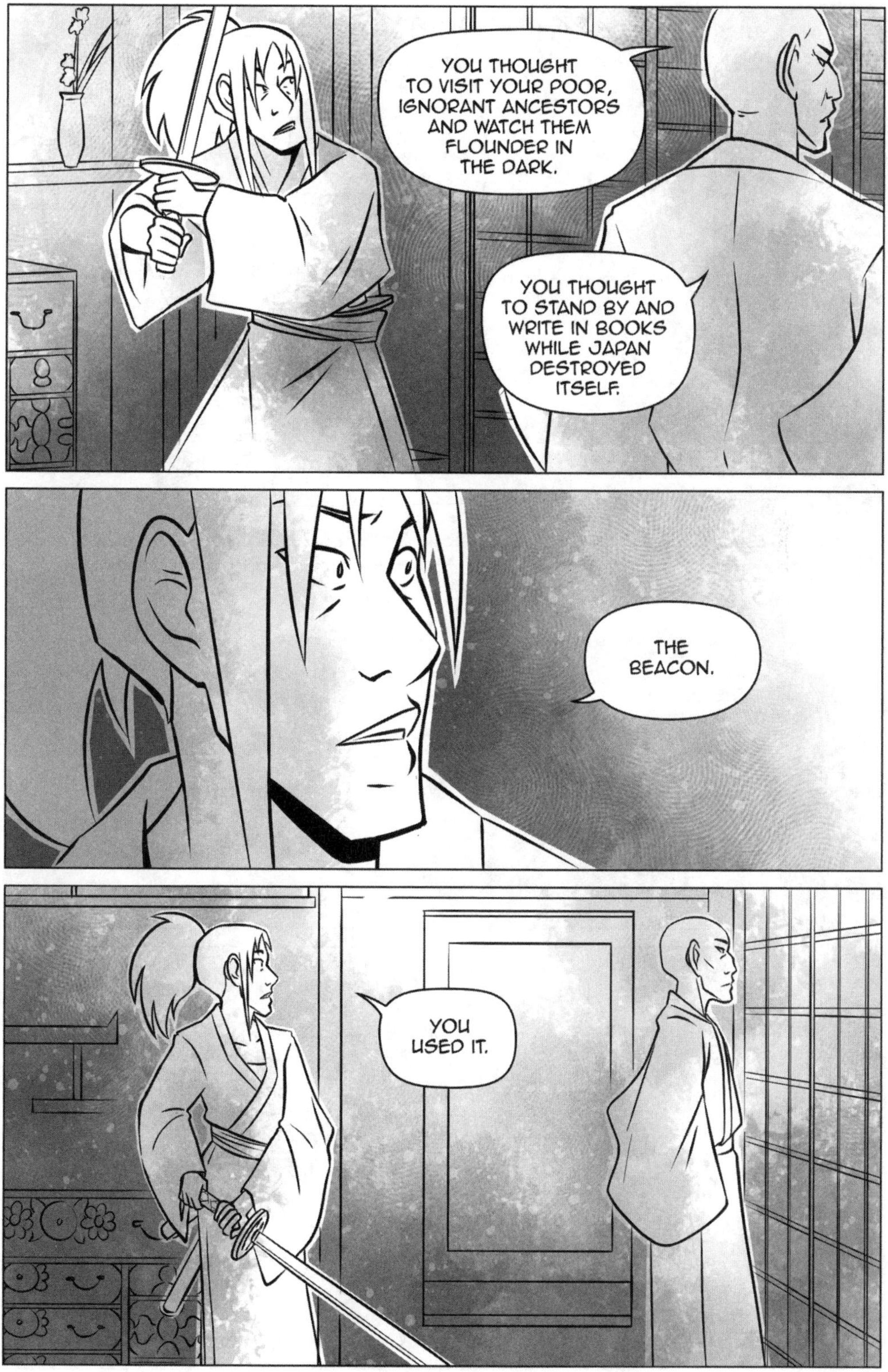
YOU THOUGHT TO VISIT YOUR POOR, IGNORANT ANCESTORS AND WATCH THEM FLOUNDER IN THE DARK.
YOU THOUGHT TO STAND BY AND WRITE IN BOOKS WHILE JAPAN DESTROYED ITSELF.
THE BEACON.
YOU USED IT.

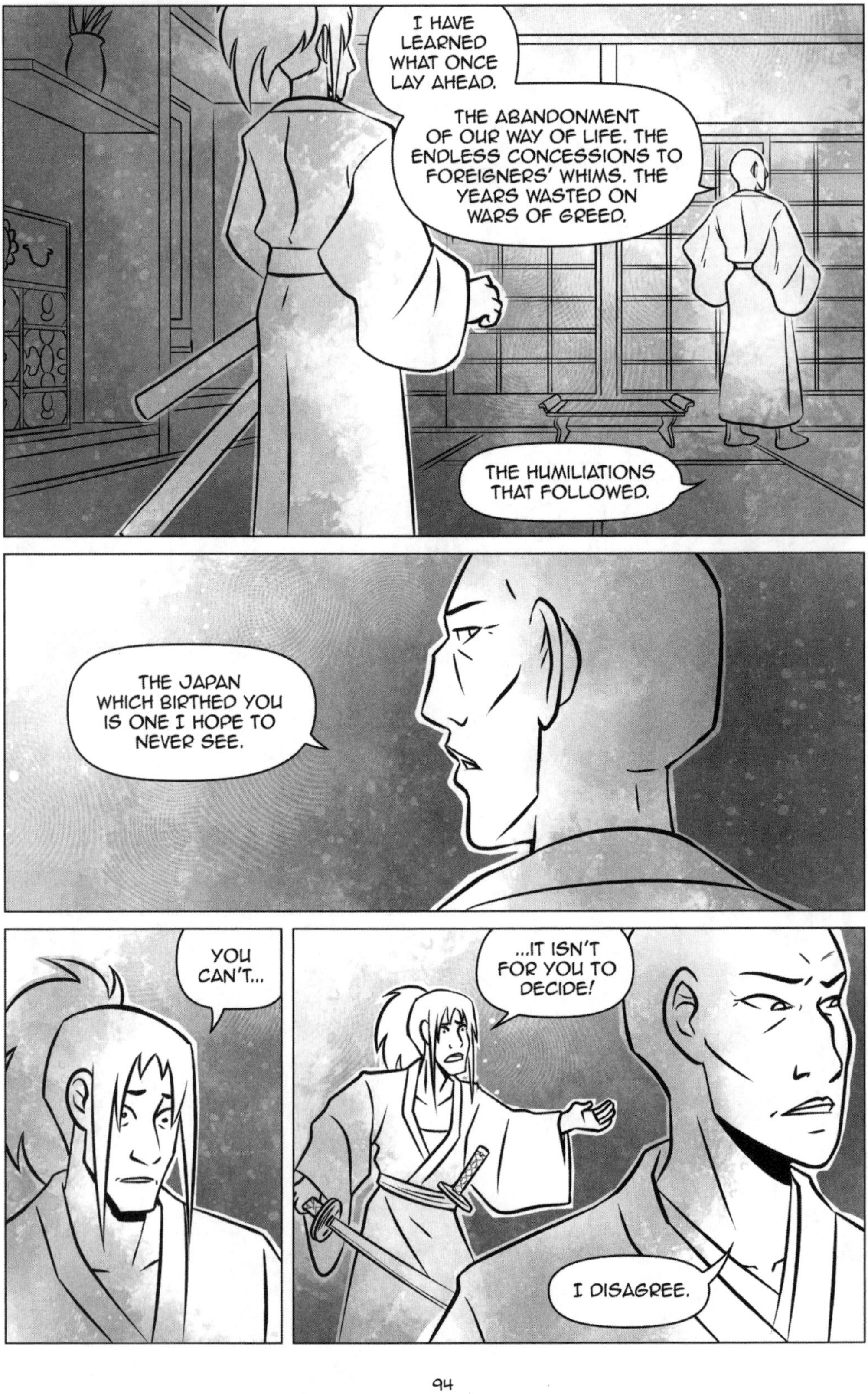
I HAVE LEARNED WHAT ONCE LAY AHEAD.
THE ABANDONMENT OF OUR WAY OF LIFE. THE ENDLESS CONCESSIONS TO FOREIGNERS' WHIMS. THE YEARS WASTED ON WARS OF GREED.
THE HUMILIATIONS THAT FOLLOWED.
THE JAPAN WHICH BIRTHED YOU IS ONE I HOPE TO NEVER SEE.
YOU CAN'T...
...IT ISN'T FOR YOU TO DECIDE!
I DISAGREE.

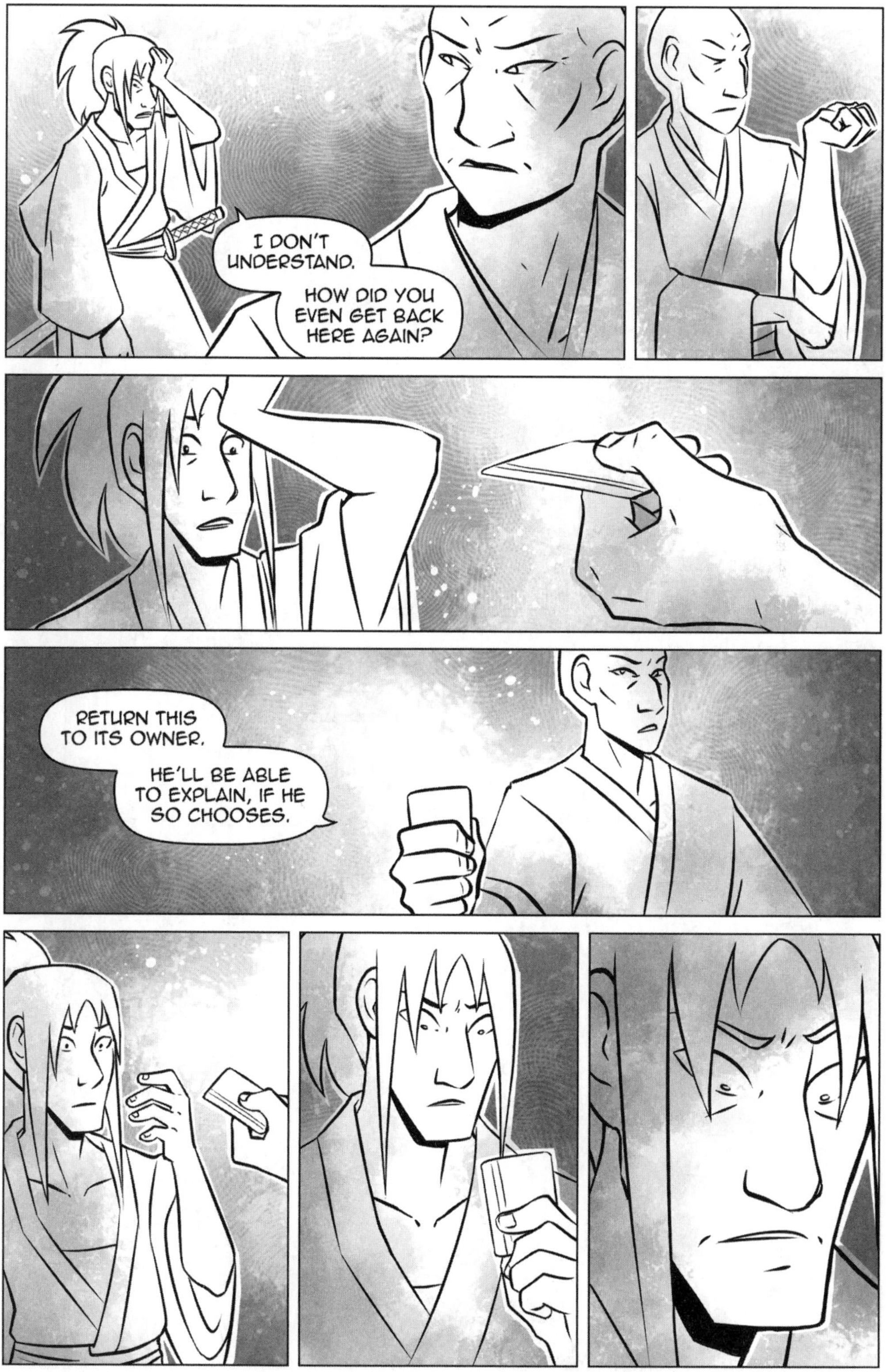
I DON'T UNDERSTAND.
HOW DID YOU EVEN GET BACK HERE AGAIN?
RETURN THIS TO ITS OWNER.
HE'LL BE ABLE TO EXPLAIN, IF HE SO CHOOSES.

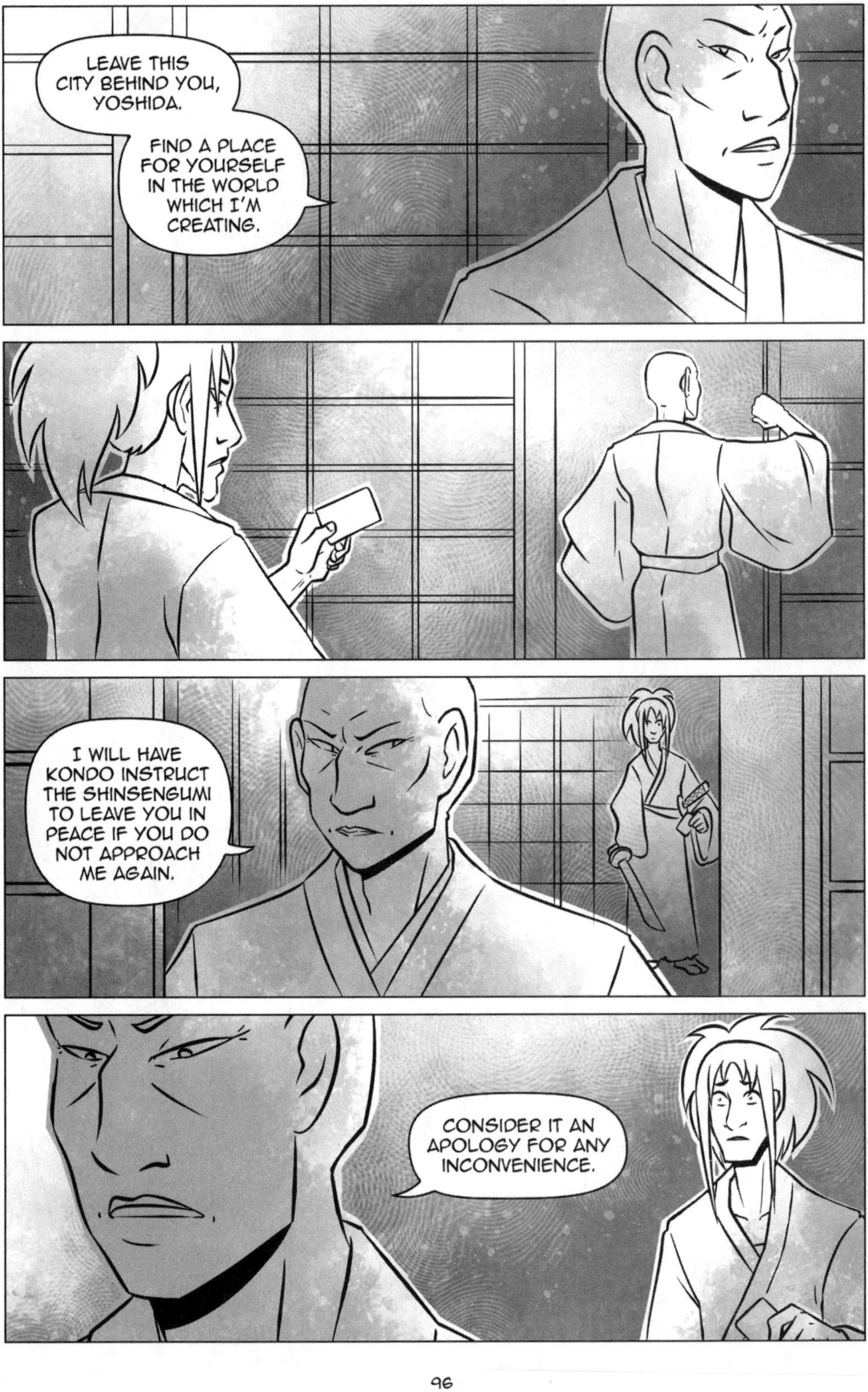
LEAVE THIS CITY BEHIND YOU, YOSHIDA.
FIND A PLACE FOR YOURSELF IN THE WORLD WHICH I'M CREATING.
I WILL HAVE KONDO INSTRUCT THE SHINSENGUMI TO LEAVE YOU IN PEACE IF YOU DO NOT APPROACH ME AGAIN.
CONSIDER IT AN APOLOGY FOR ANY INCONVENIENCE.

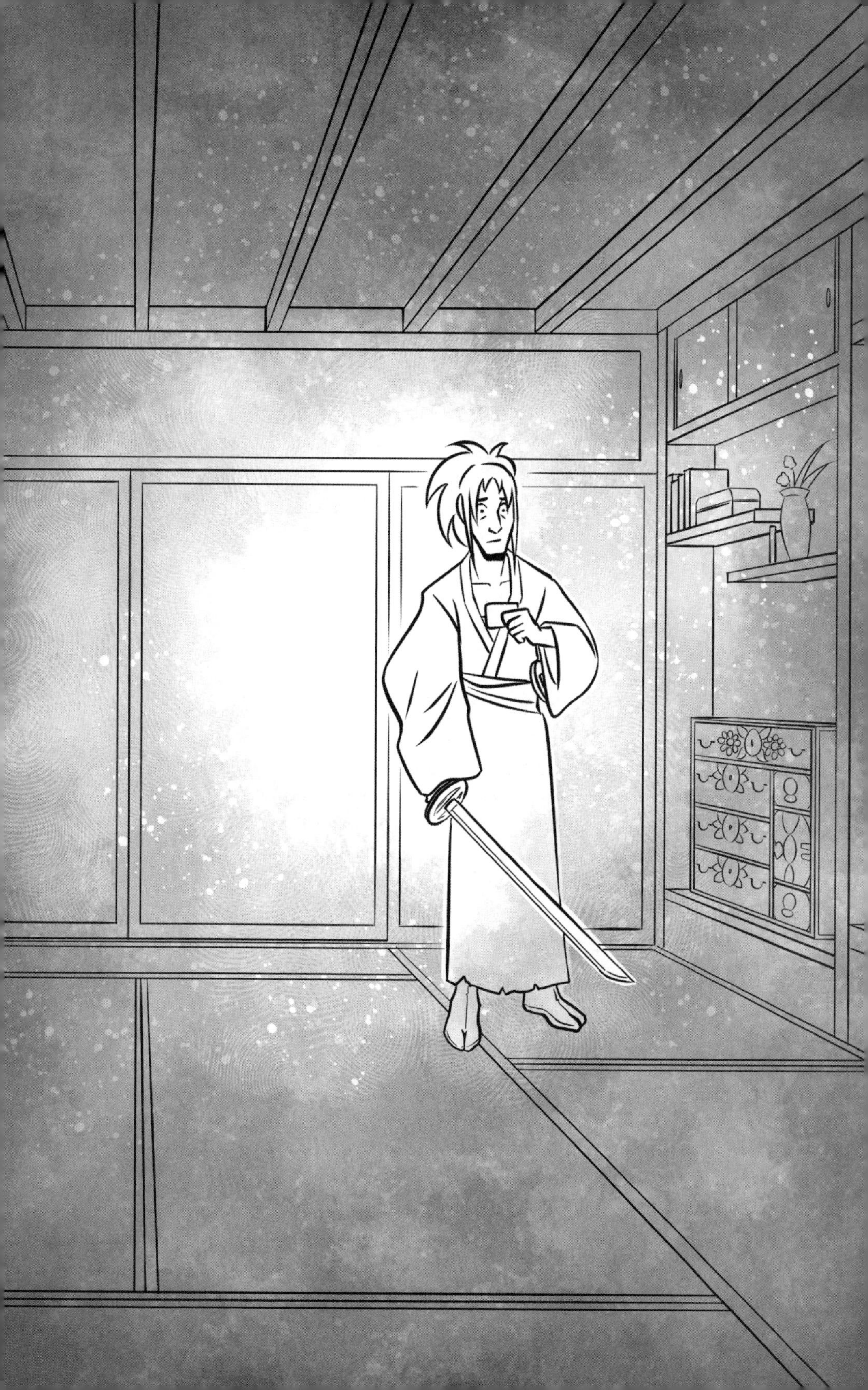

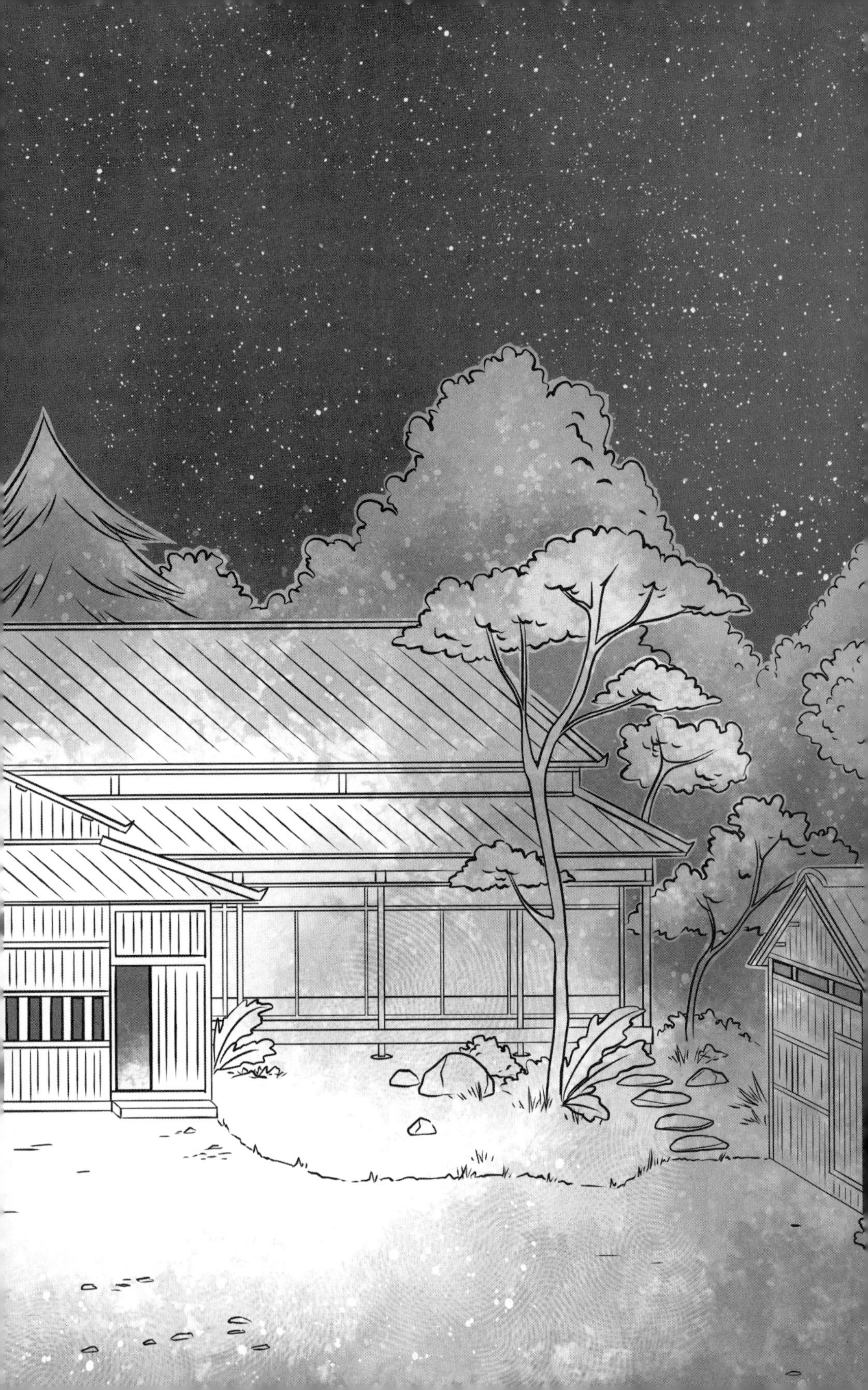

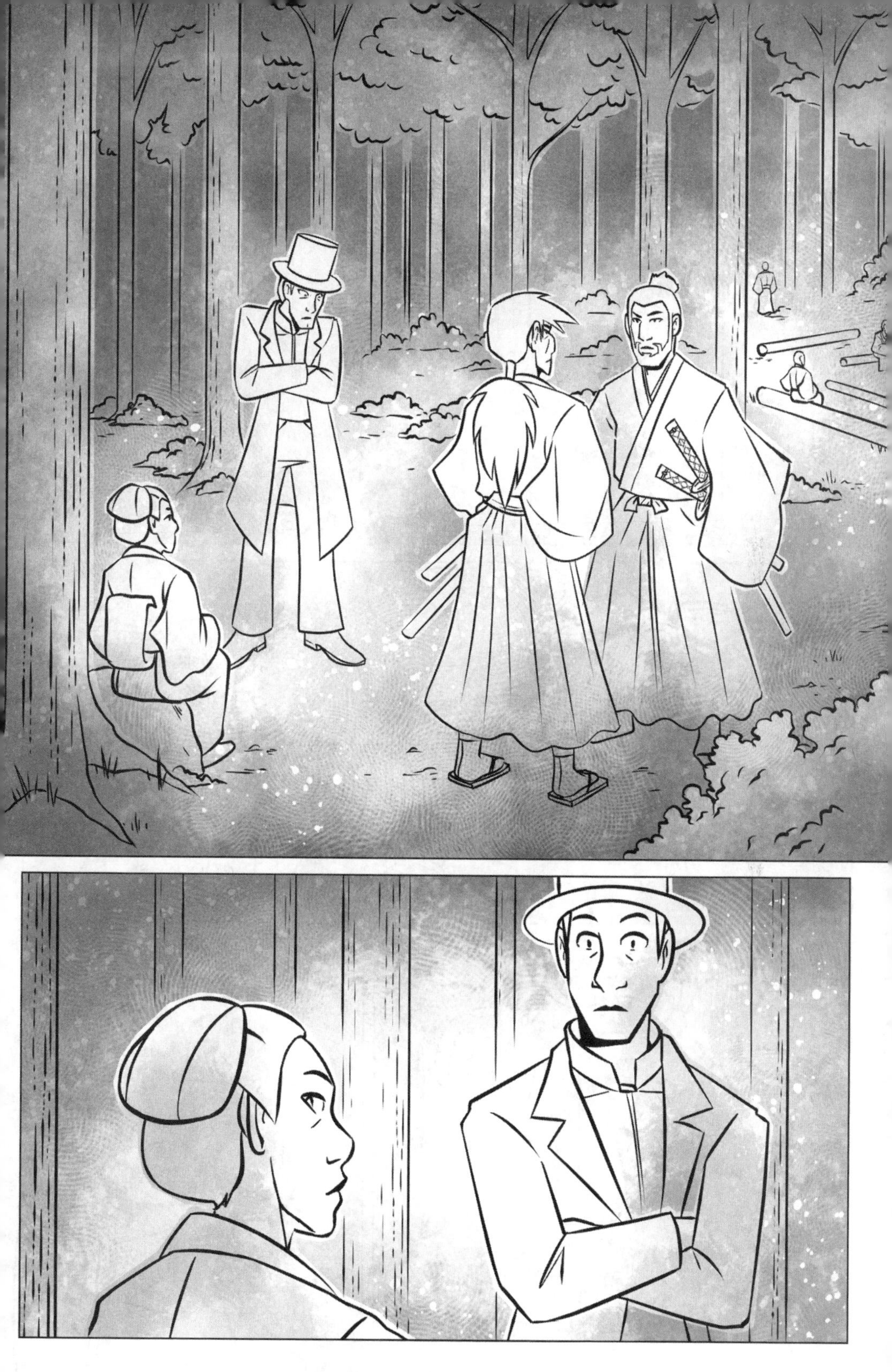

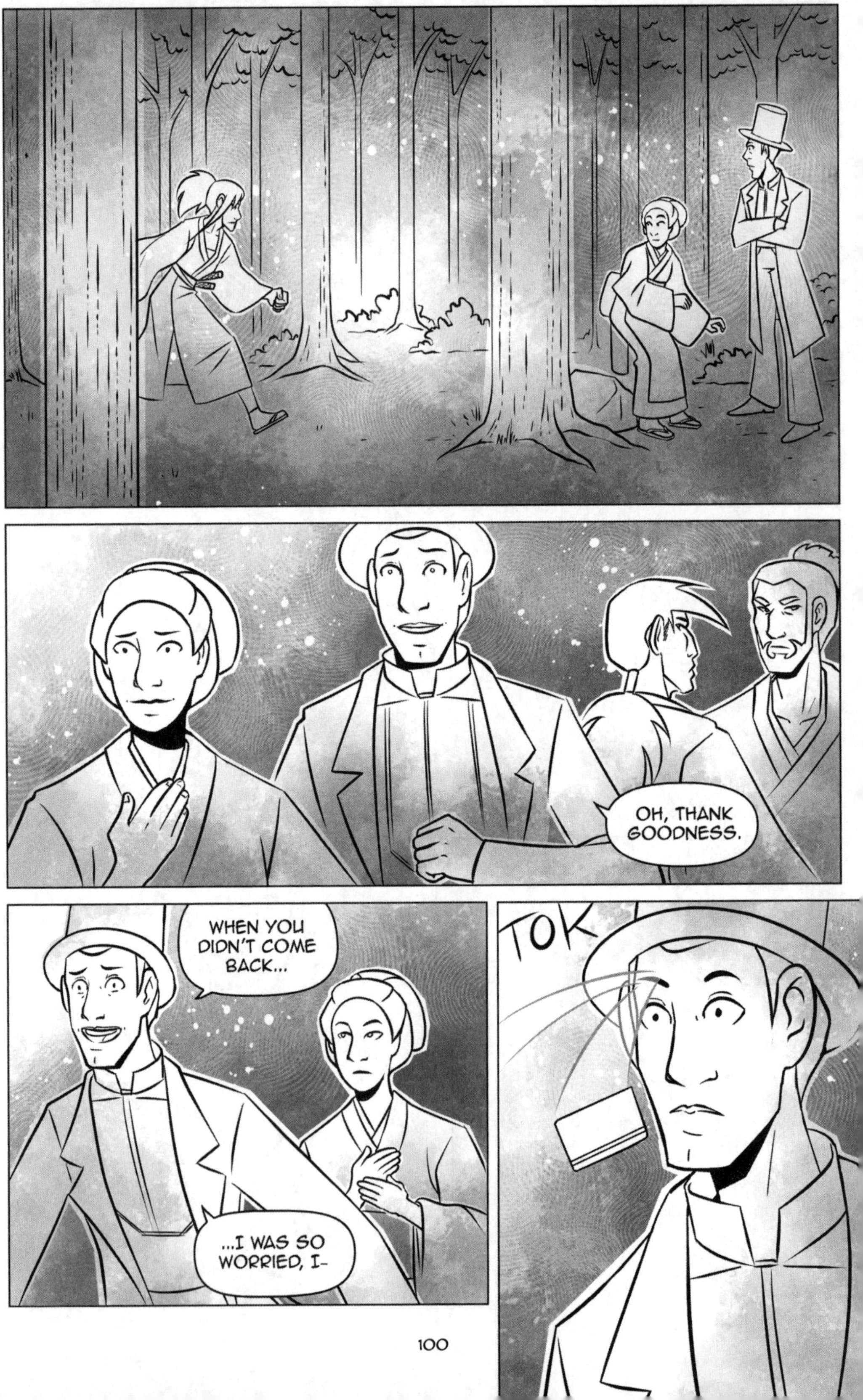
OH, THANK GOODNESS.
WHEN YOU DIDN'T COME BACK...
...I WAS SO WORRIED, I-
TOK

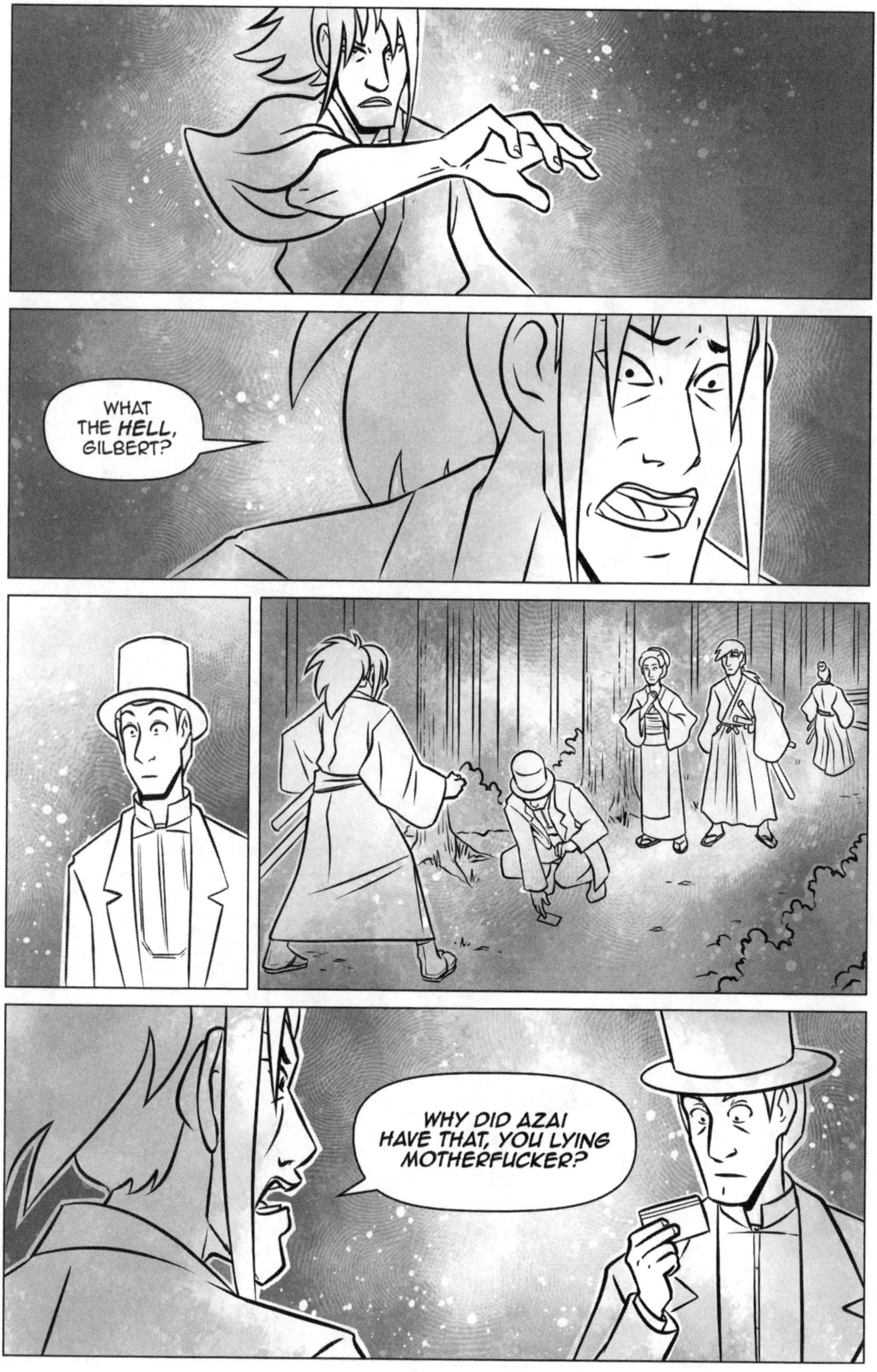
WHAT THE *HELL*, GILBERT?
WHY DID AZAI HAVE THAT, YOU LYING MOTHERFUCKER?

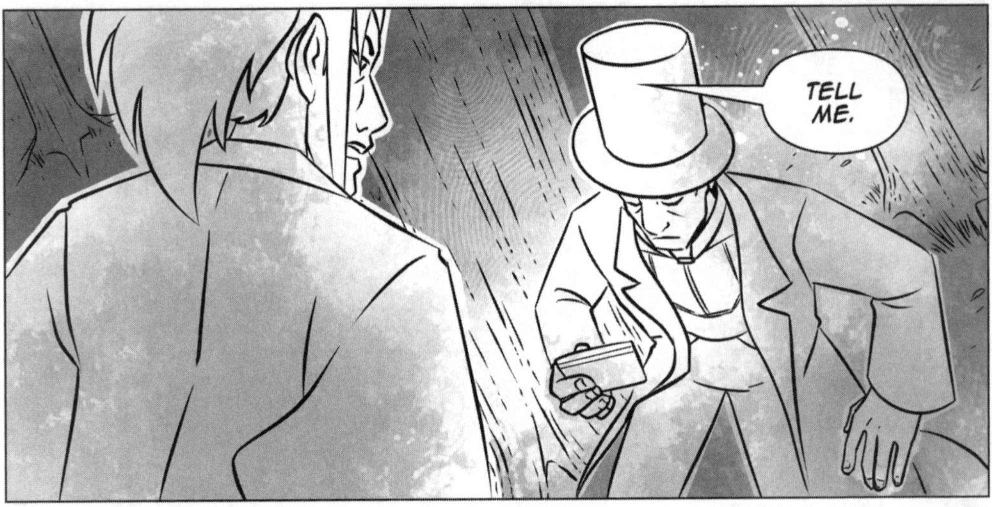
TELL ME.

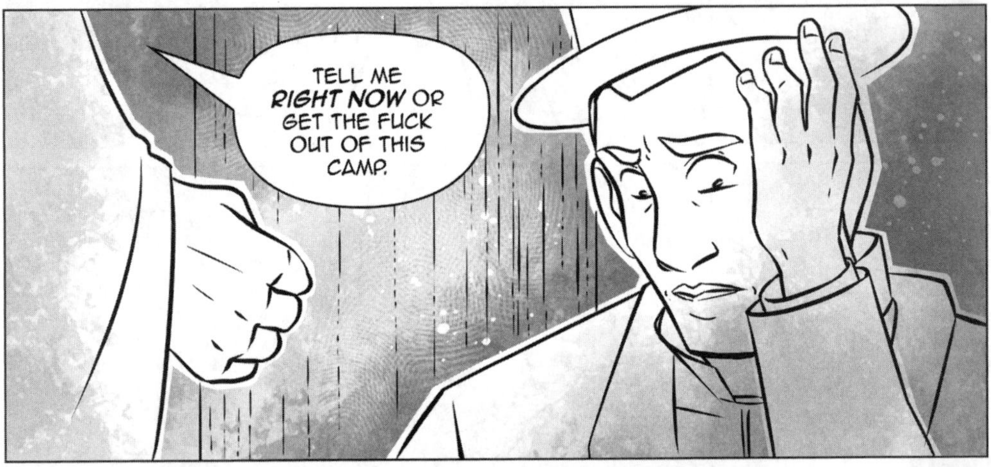
TELL ME RIGHT NOW OR GET THE FUCK OUT OF THIS CAMP.

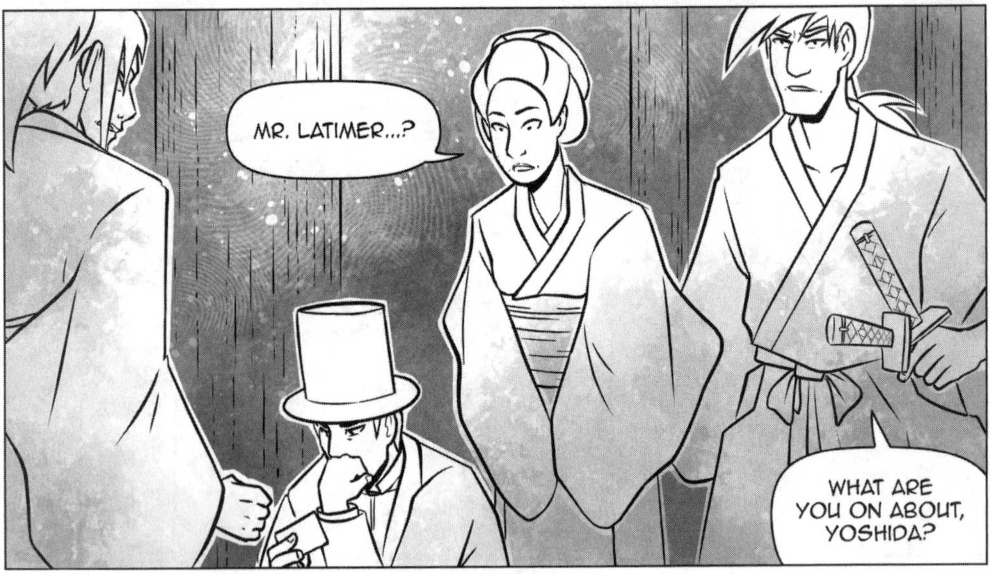
MR. LATIMER...?
WHAT ARE YOU ON ABOUT, YOSHIDA?

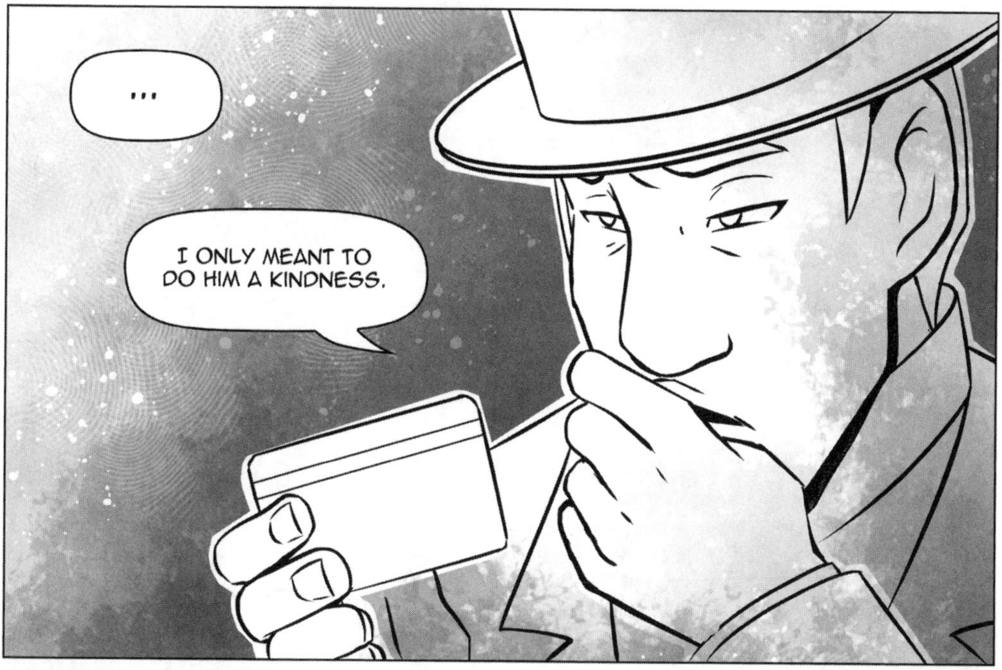
...
I ONLY MEANT TO DO HIM A KINDNESS.

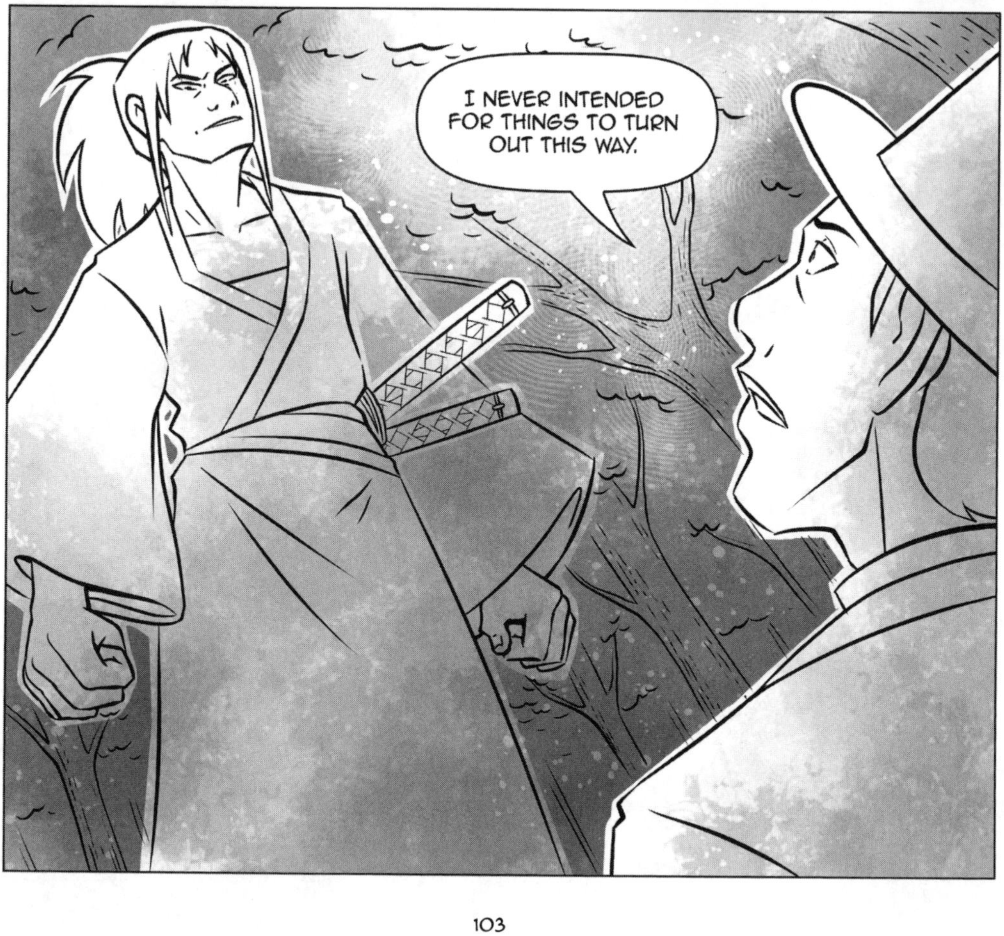
I NEVER INTENDED FOR THINGS TO TURN OUT THIS WAY.

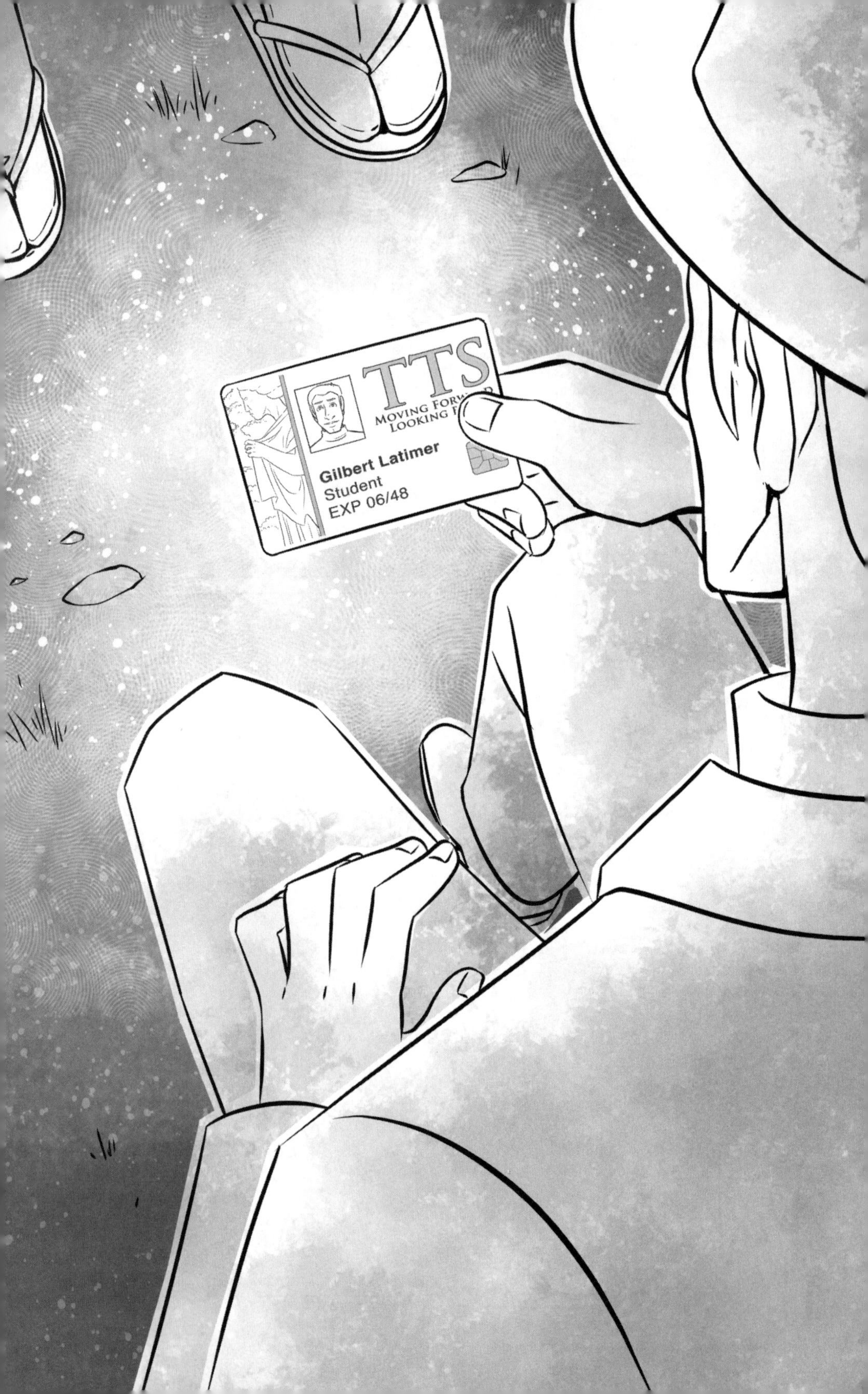
TTS
Gilbert Latimer
Student
EXP 06/48

TTS
MOVING FORWARD
LOOKING BACK
Gilbert Latimer
Student
EXP 06/48

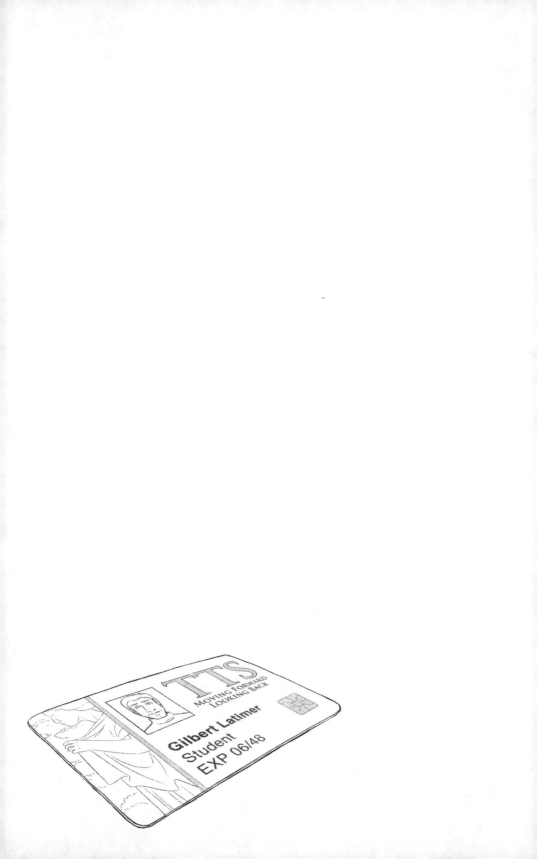

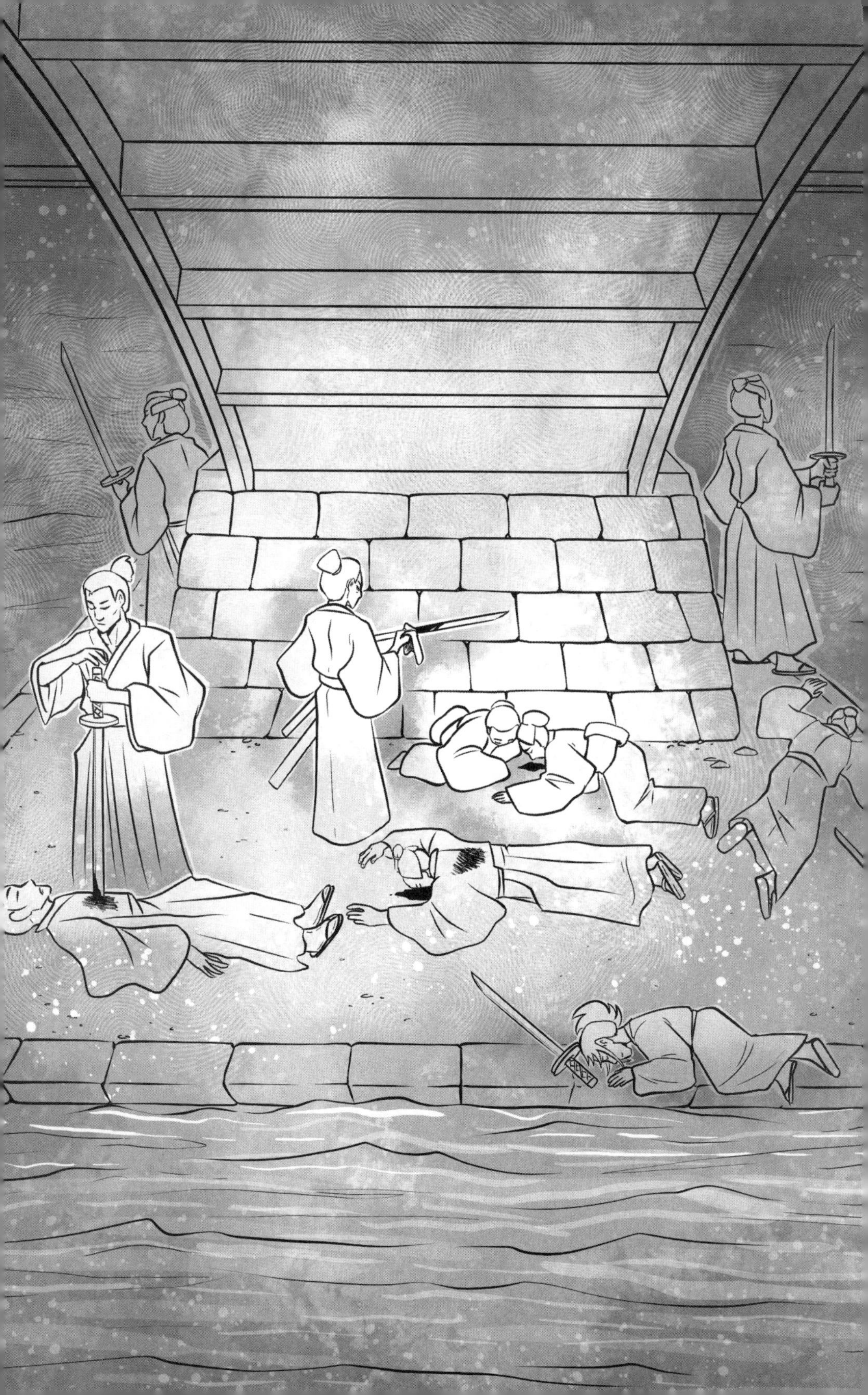

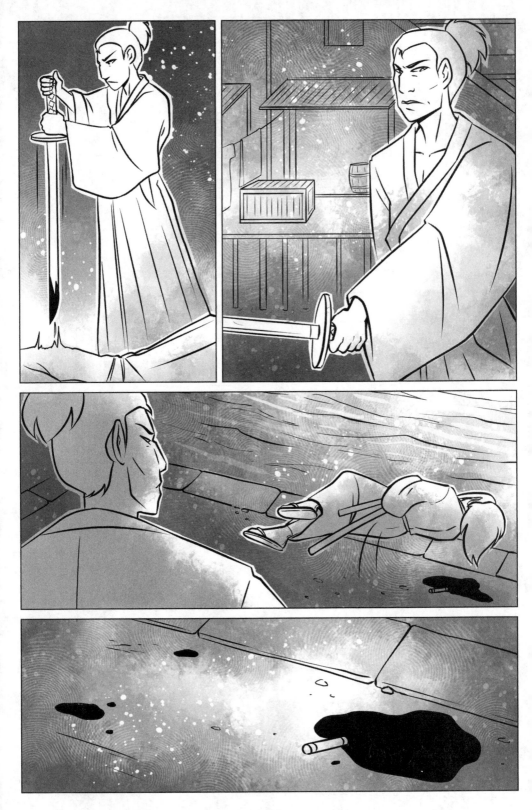

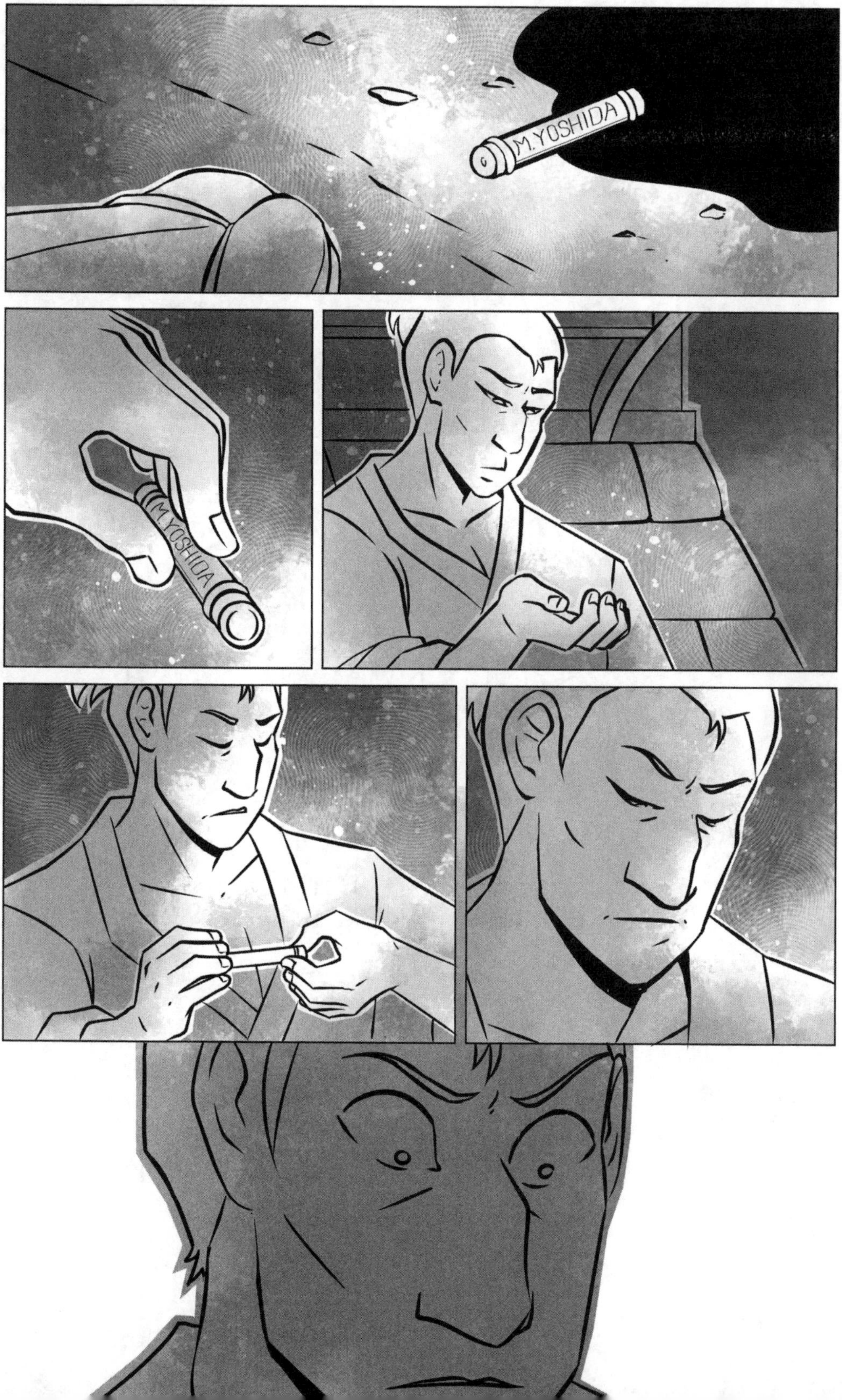
M.YOSHIDA
M.YOSHIDA

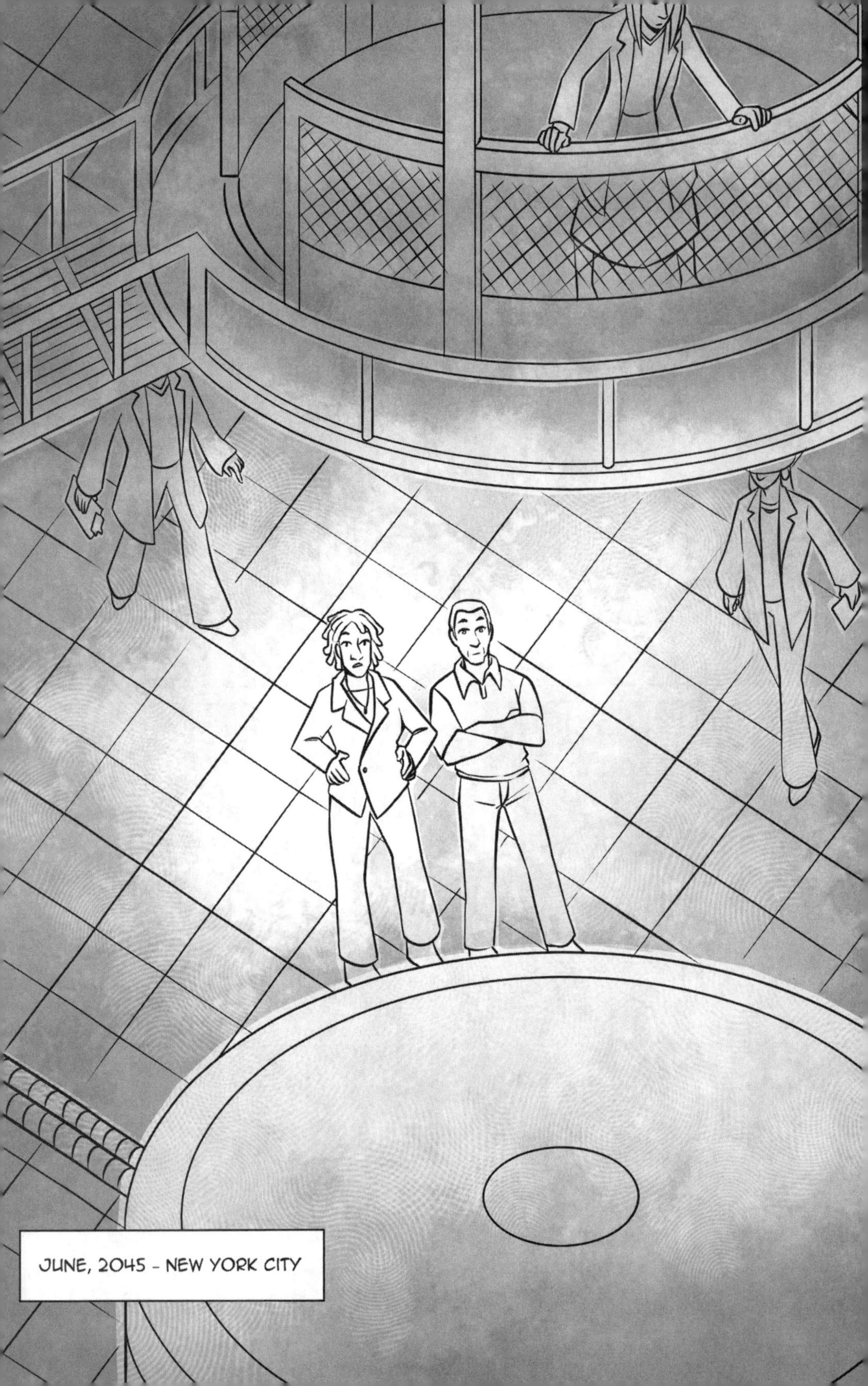
JUNE, 2045 - NEW YORK CITY

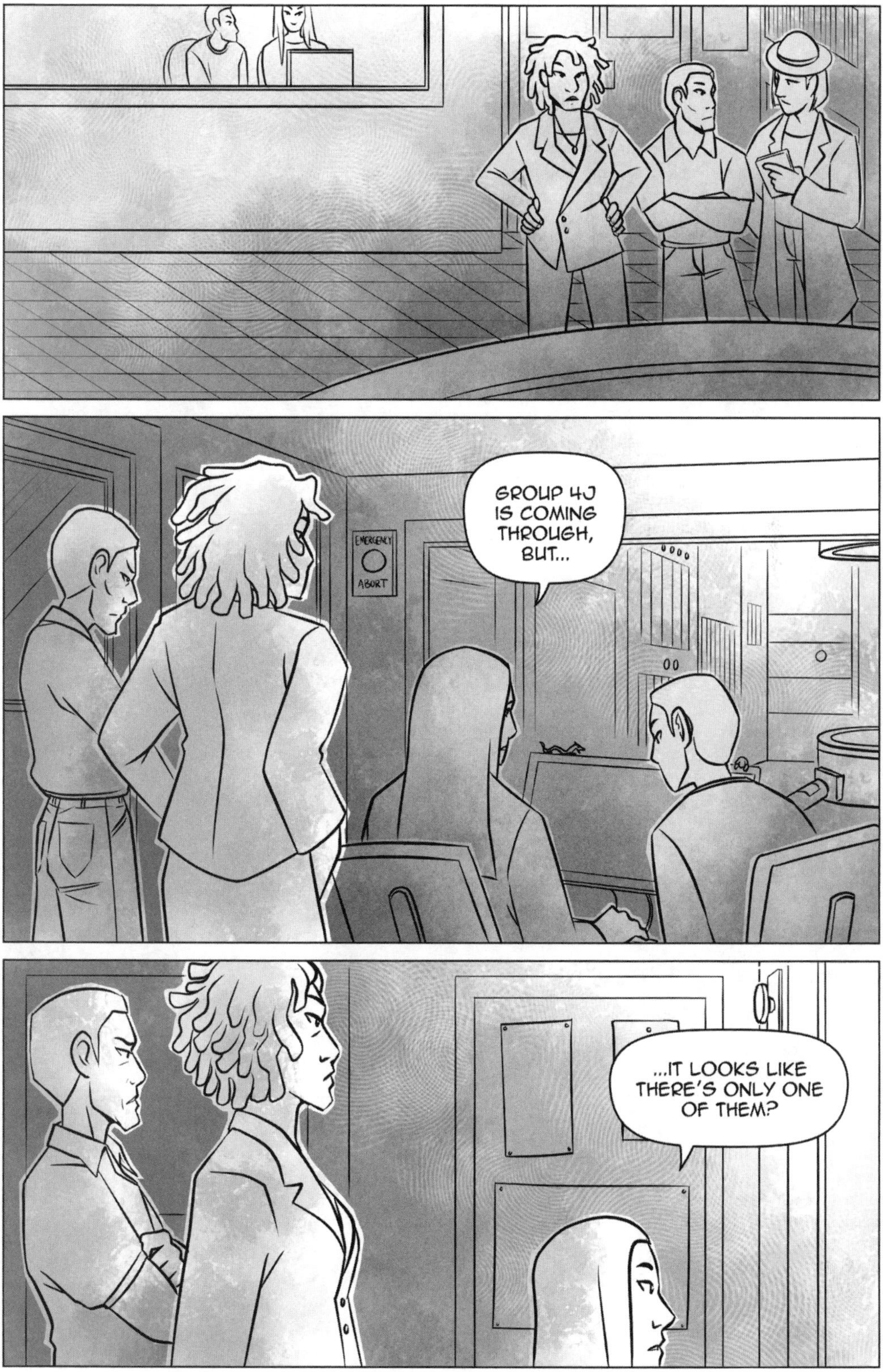
EMERGENCY
ABORT
GROUP 4J IS COMING THROUGH, BUT...
...IT LOOKS LIKE THERE'S ONLY ONE OF THEM?

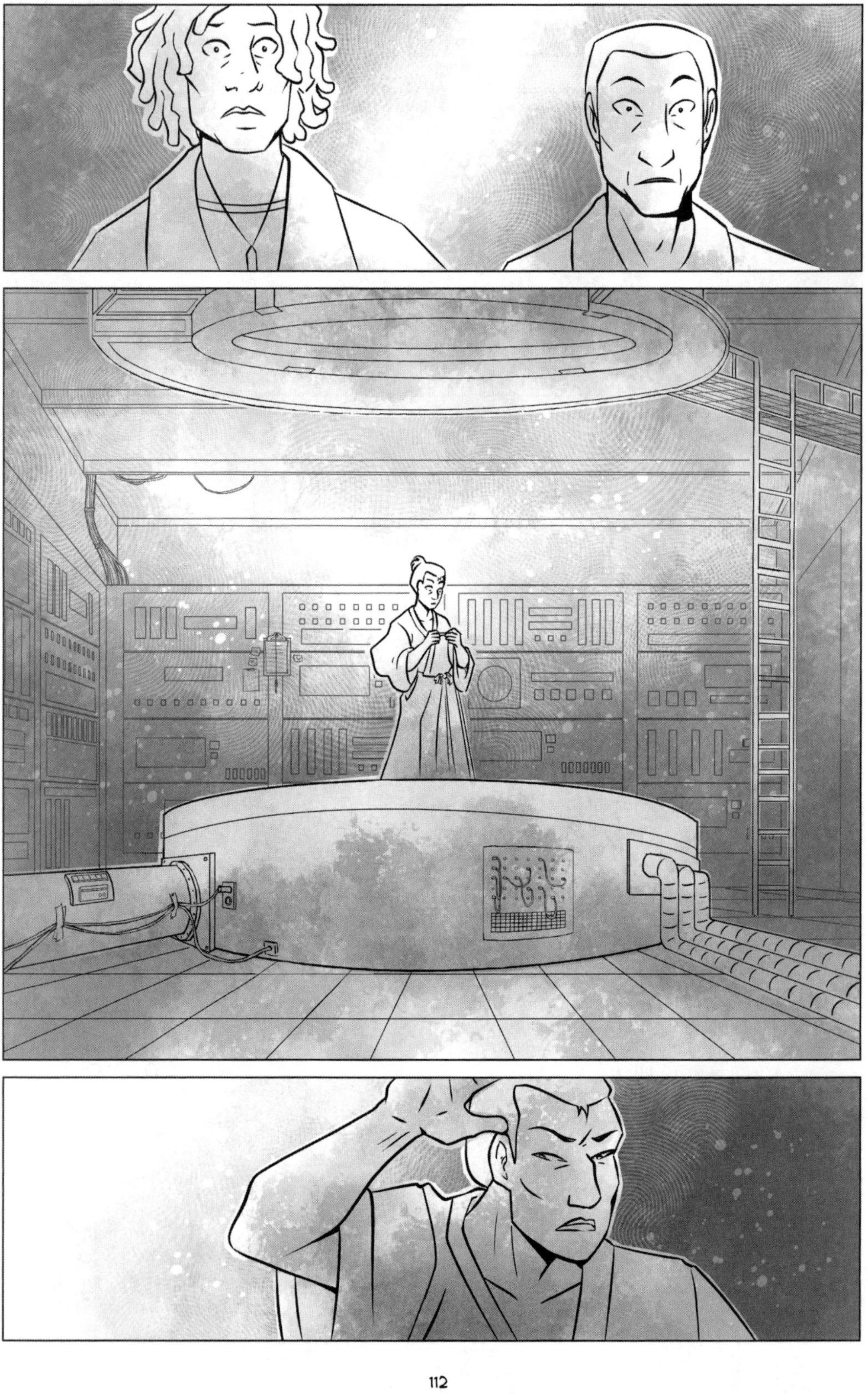

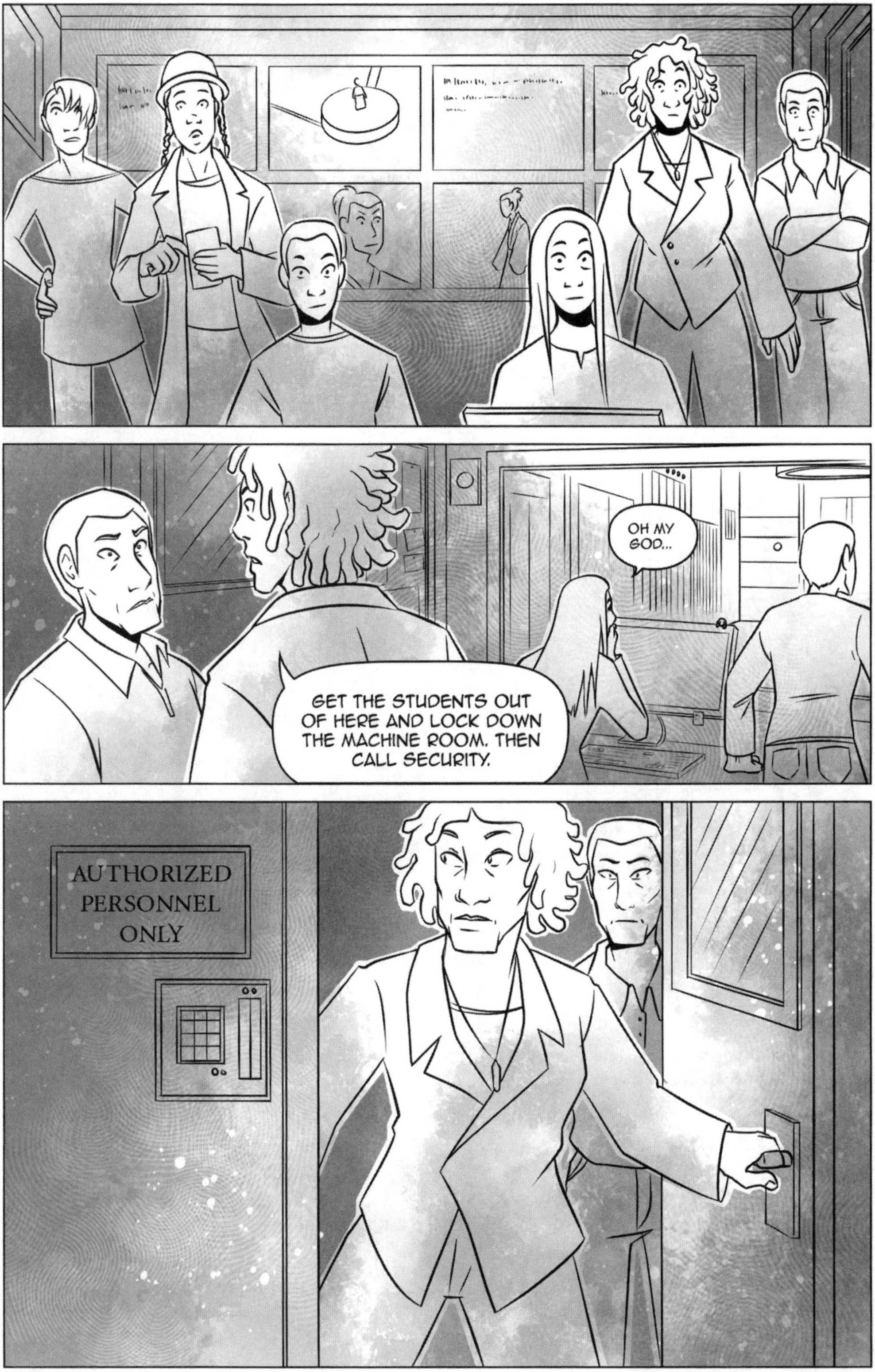
OH MY GOD...
GET THE STUDENTS OUT OF HERE AND LOCK DOWN THE MACHINE ROOM. THEN CALL SECURITY.
AUTHORIZED PERSONNEL ONLY

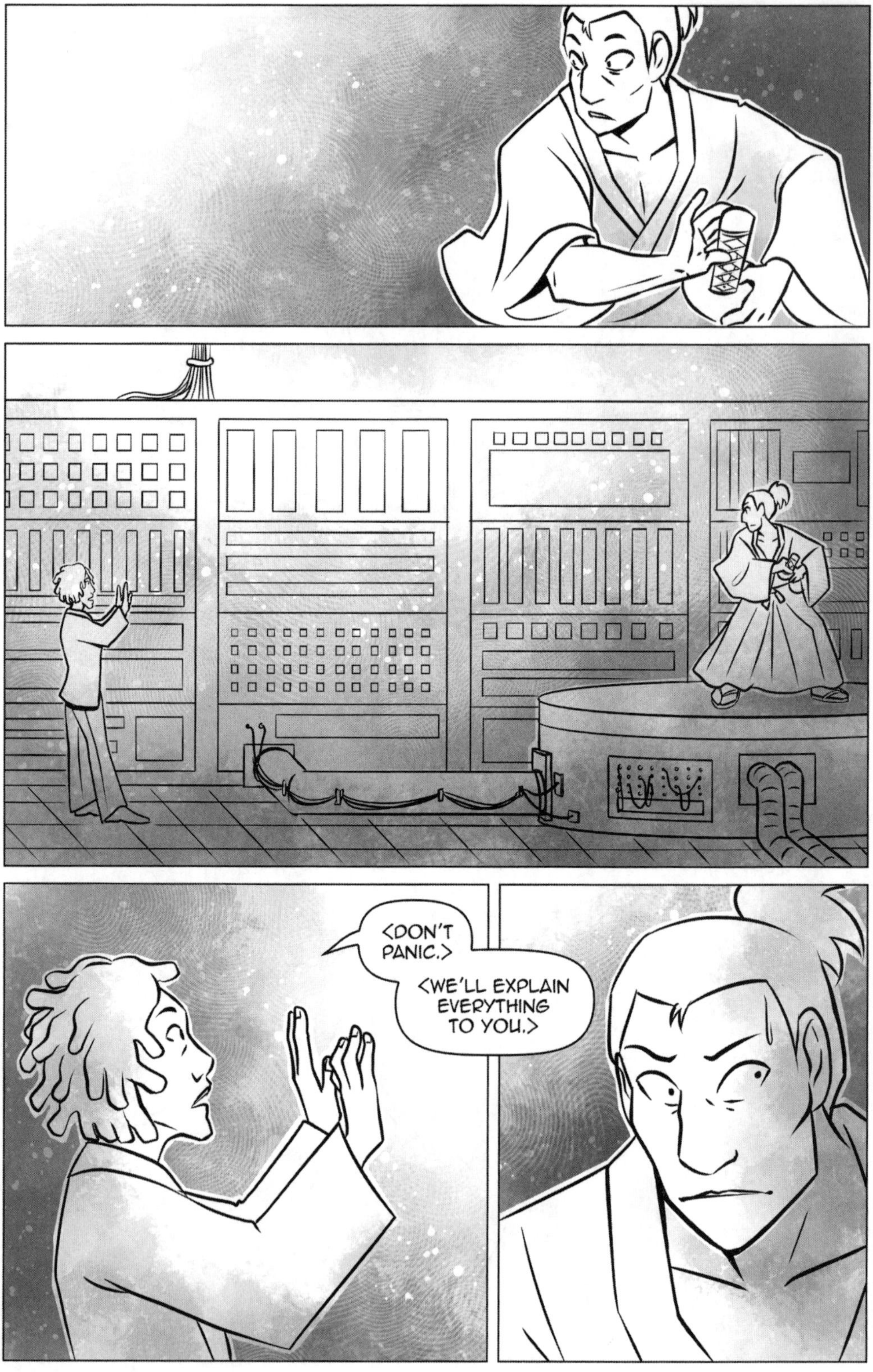
<DON'T PANIC.>
<WE'LL EXPLAIN EVERYTHING TO YOU.>

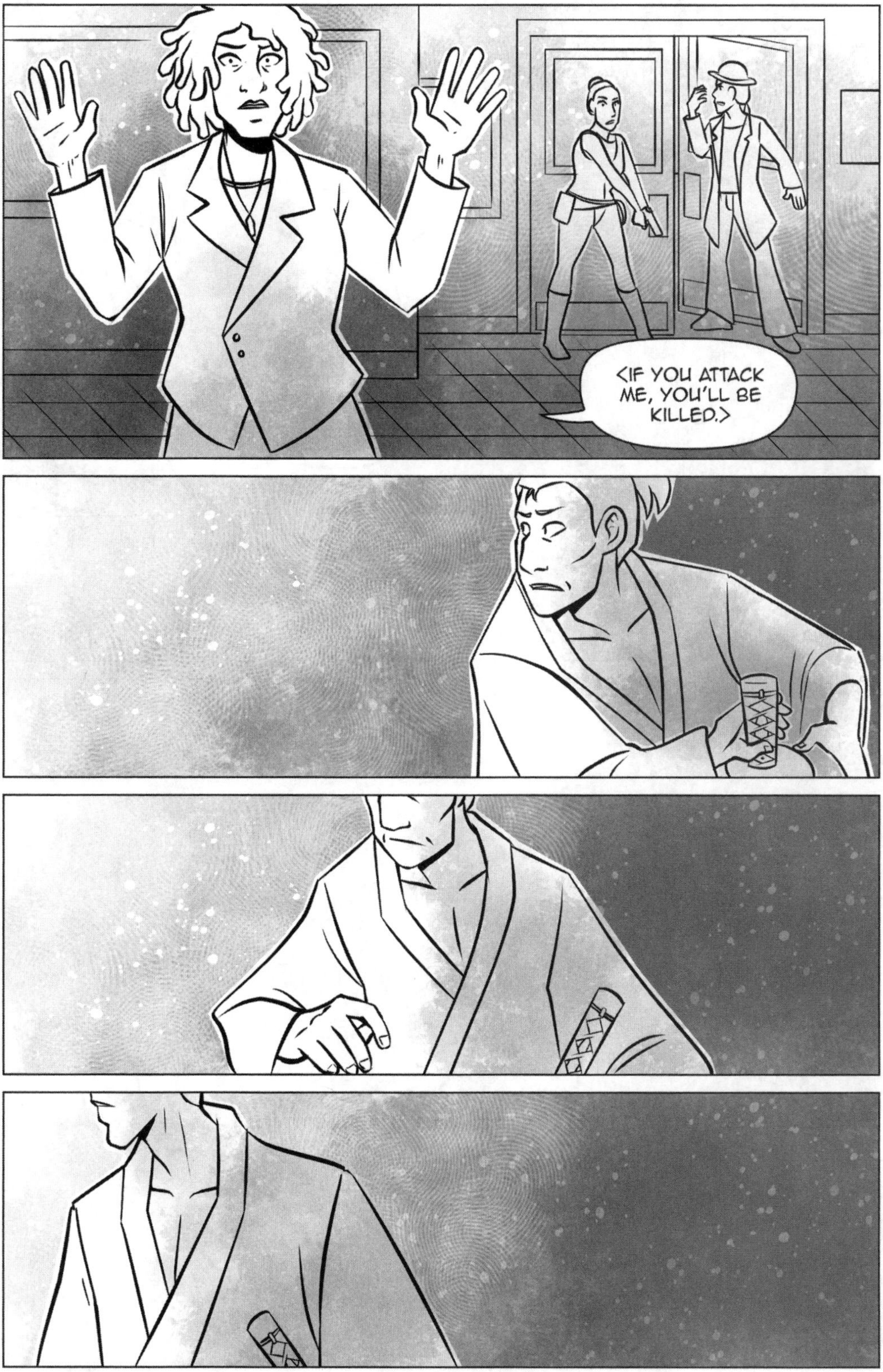
<IF YOU ATTACK ME, YOU'LL BE KILLED.>

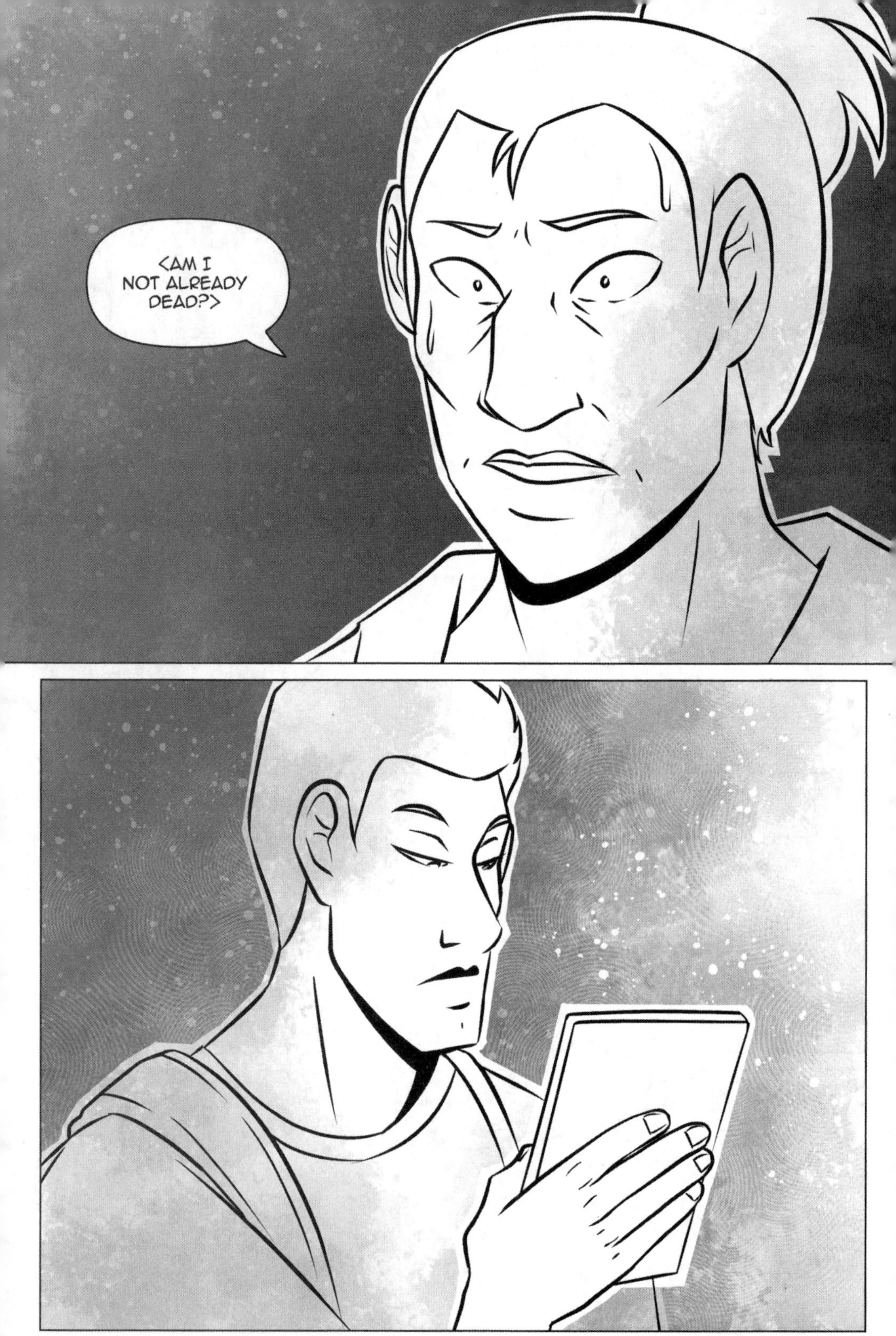
<AM I NOT ALREADY DEAD?>

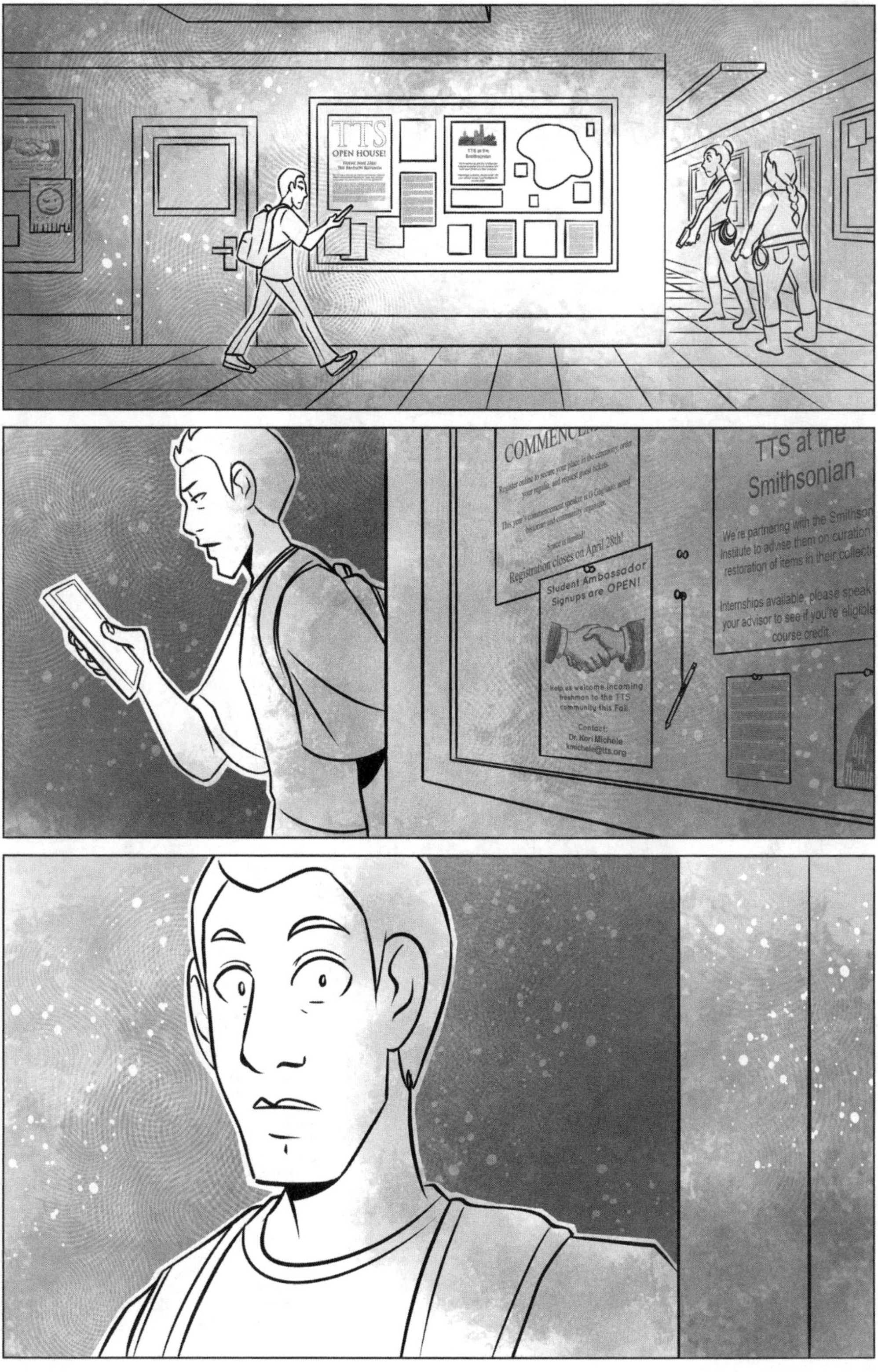
TTS
OPEN HOUSE!
COMMENCE
Register online to secure your place in the ceremony, order your regalia, and request guest tickets.
Space is limited!
Registration closes on April 28th!
Student Ambassador Signups are OPEN!
Help us welcome incoming freshman to the TTS community this Fall.
Contact:
Dr. Kori Michele
kmichele@tts.org
TTS at the Smithsonian
We're partnering with the Smithson
Institute to advise them on curation
restoration of items in their collecti
Internships available, please speak
your advisor to see if you're eligible
course credit.

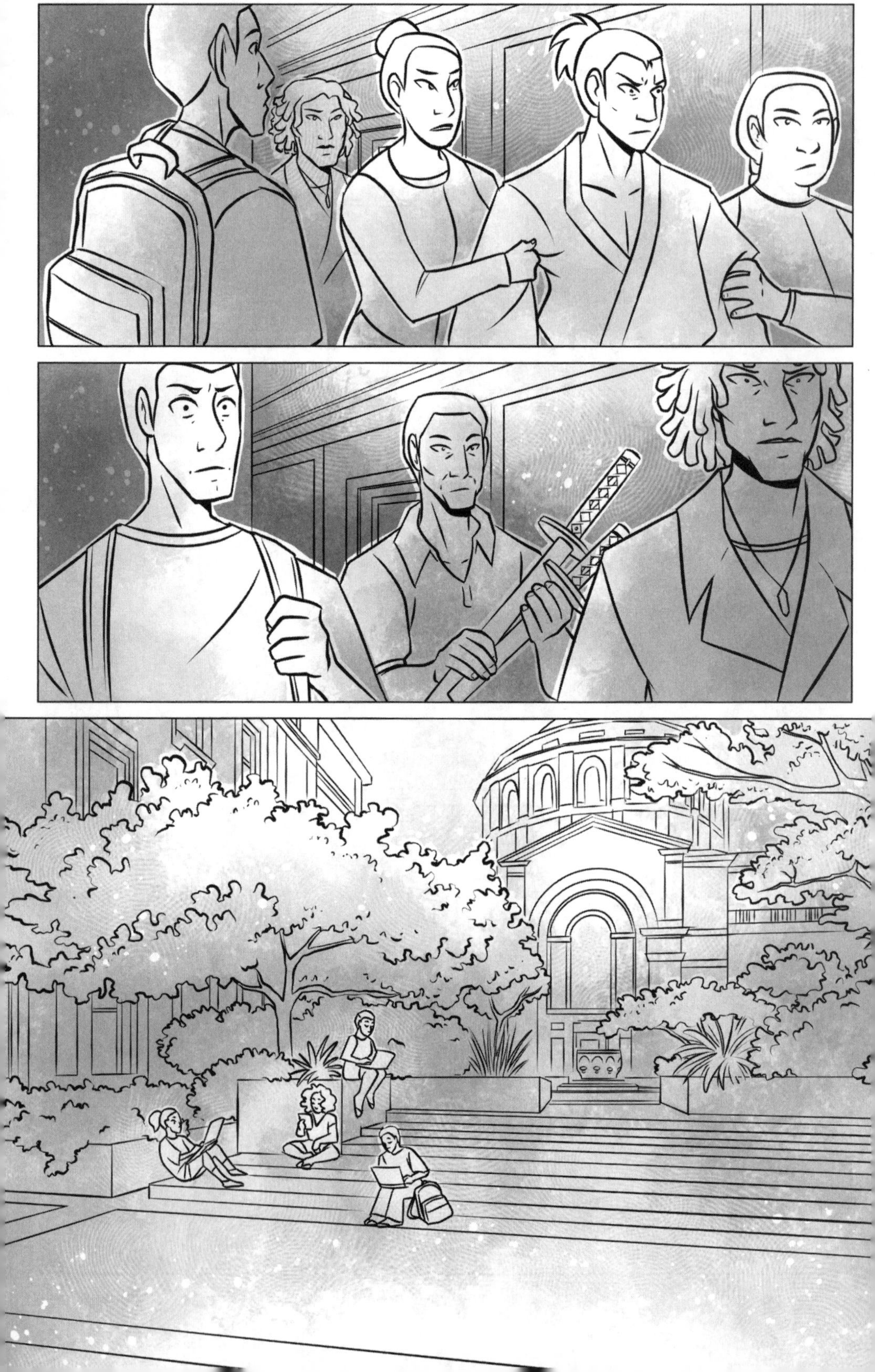

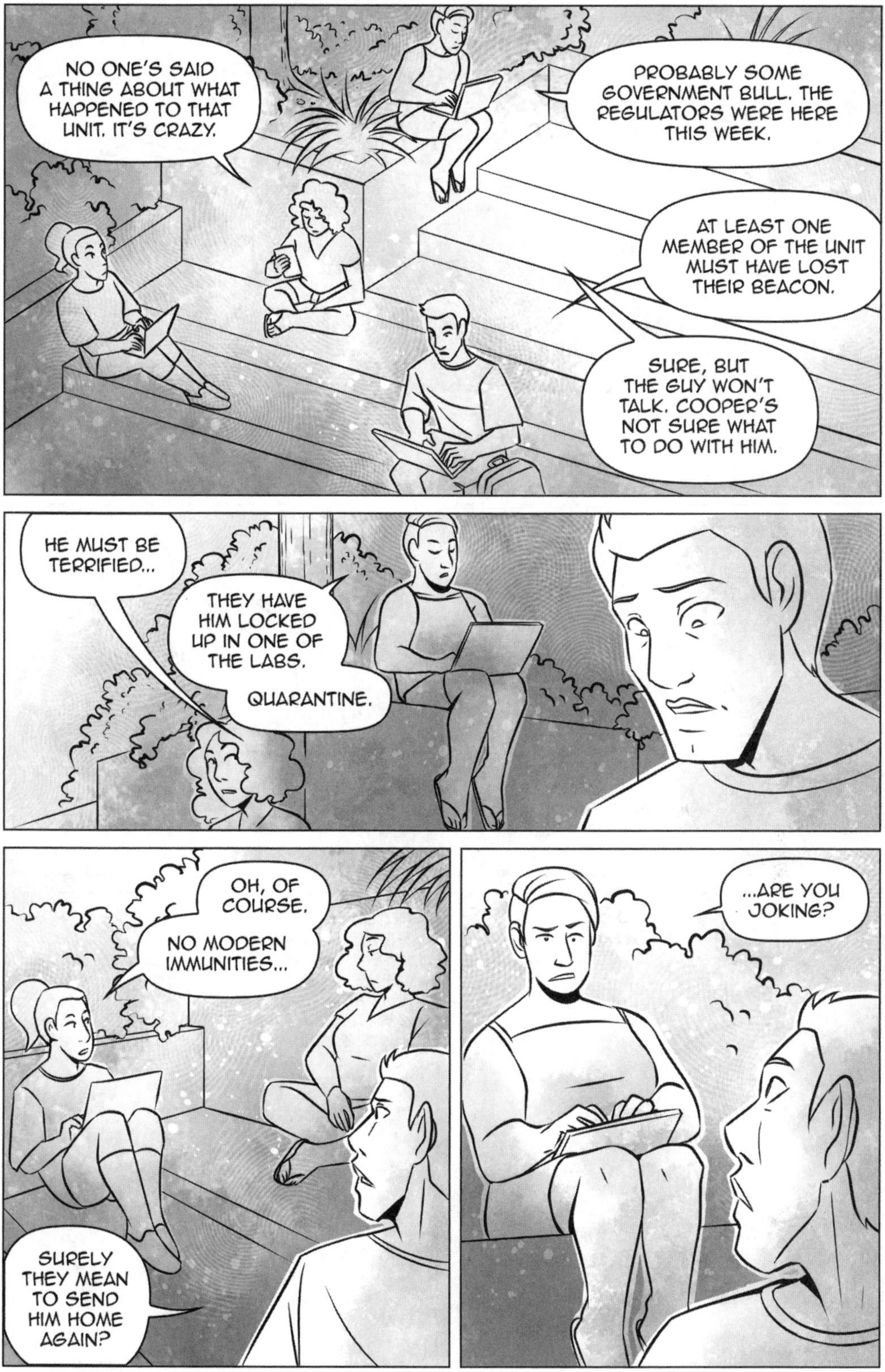
NO ONE'S SAID A THING ABOUT WHAT HAPPENED TO THAT UNIT. IT'S CRAZY.
PROBABLY SOME GOVERNMENT BULL. THE REGULATORS WERE HERE THIS WEEK.
AT LEAST ONE MEMBER OF THE UNIT MUST HAVE LOST THEIR BEACON.
SURE, BUT THE GUY WON'T TALK. COOPER'S NOT SURE WHAT TO DO WITH HIM.
HE MUST BE TERRIFIED...
THEY HAVE HIM LOCKED UP IN ONE OF THE LABS.
QUARANTINE.
OH, OF COURSE.
NO MODERN IMMUNITIES...
SURELY THEY MEAN TO SEND HIM HOME AGAIN?
...ARE YOU JOKING?

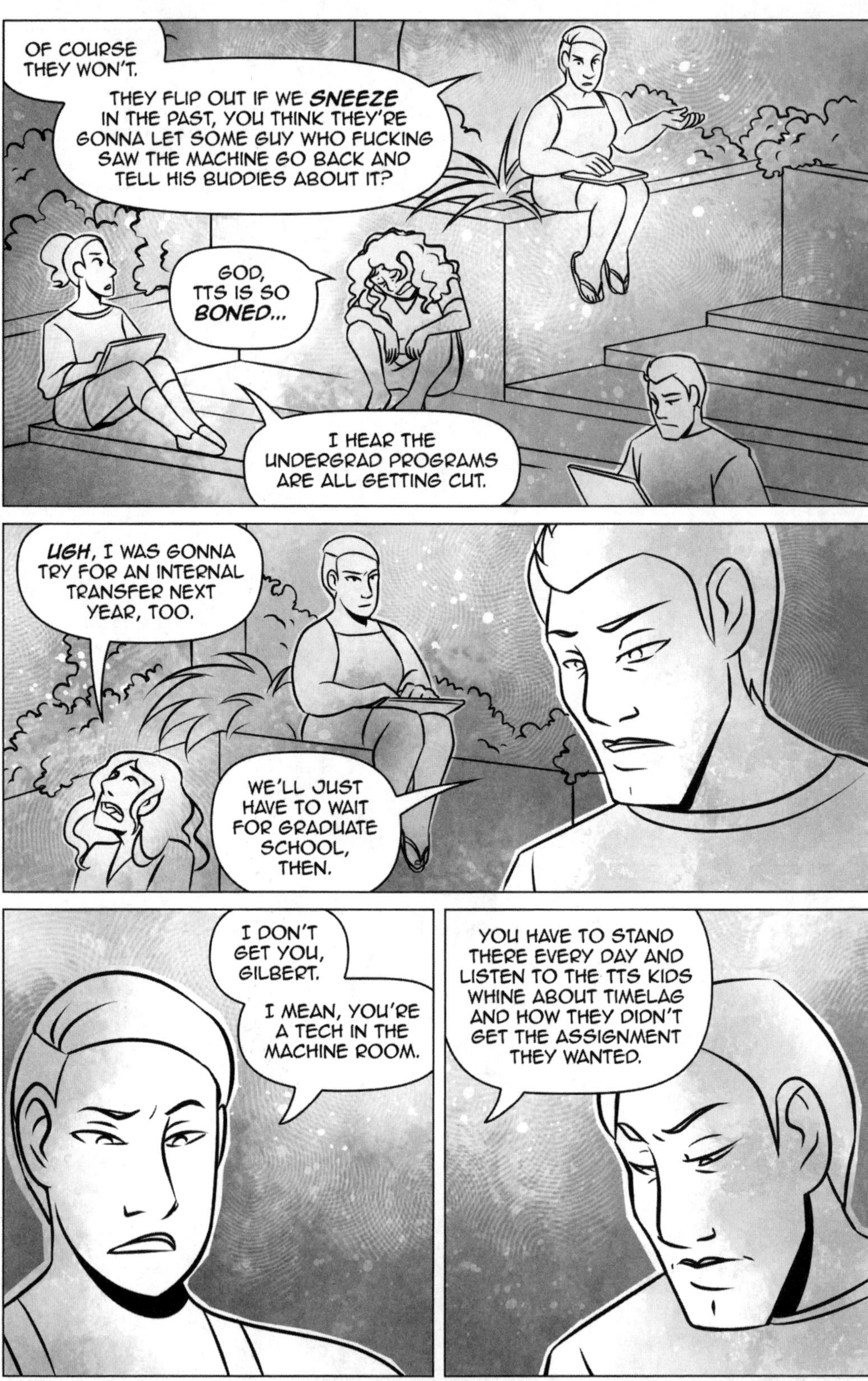
OF COURSE THEY WON'T.
THEY FLIP OUT IF WE **SNEEZE** IN THE PAST, YOU THINK THEY'RE GONNA LET SOME GUY WHO FUCKING SAW THE MACHINE GO BACK AND TELL HIS BUDDIES ABOUT IT?
GOD, TTS IS SO **BONED...**
I HEAR THE UNDERGRAD PROGRAMS ARE ALL GETTING CUT.
**UGH**, I WAS GONNA TRY FOR AN INTERNAL TRANSFER NEXT YEAR, TOO.
WE'LL JUST HAVE TO WAIT FOR GRADUATE SCHOOL, THEN.
I DON'T GET YOU, GILBERT.
I MEAN, YOU'RE A TECH IN THE MACHINE ROOM.
YOU HAVE TO STAND THERE EVERY DAY AND LISTEN TO THE TTS KIDS WHINE ABOUT TIMELAG AND HOW THEY DIDN'T GET THE ASSIGNMENT THEY WANTED.

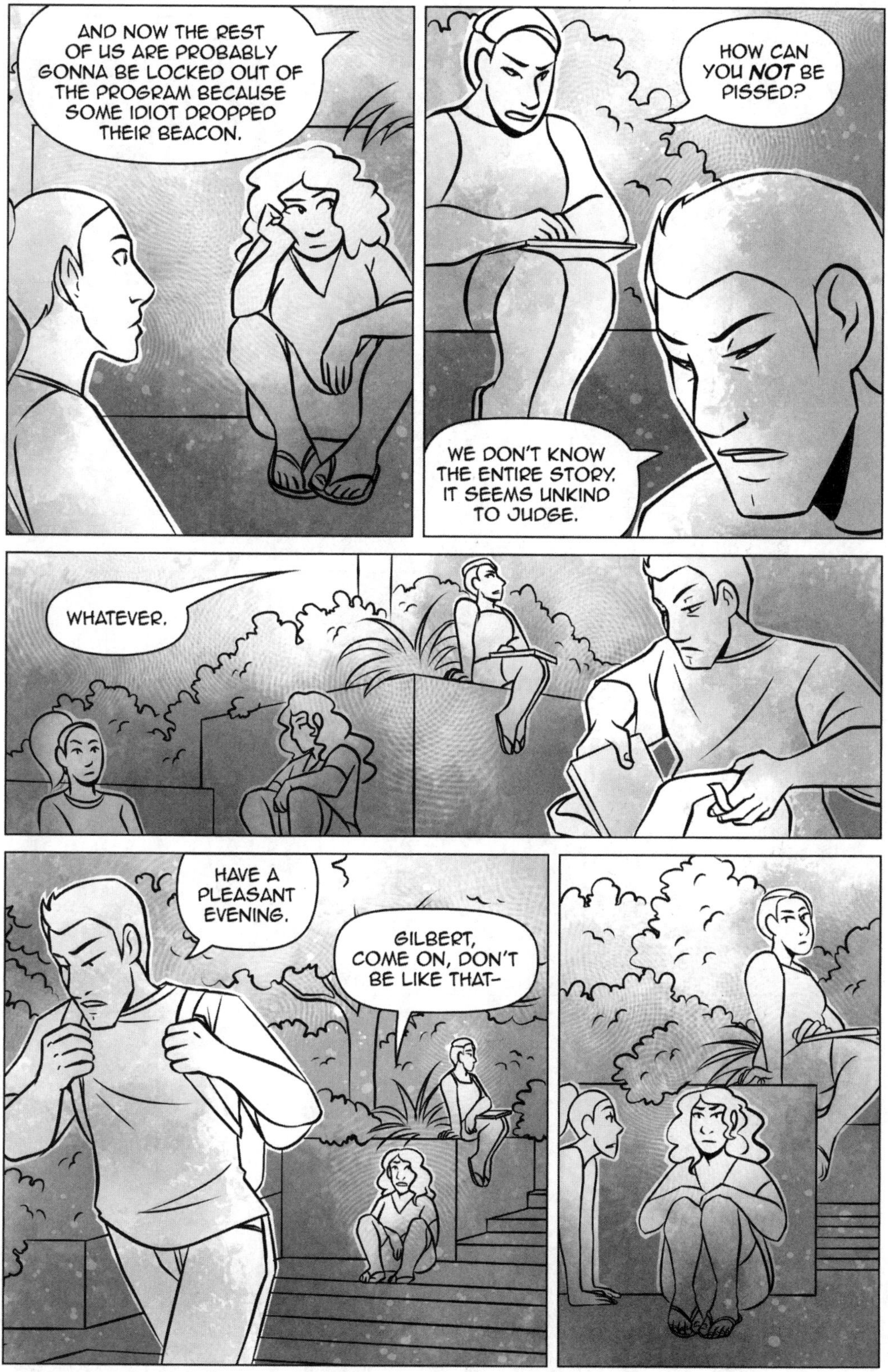
AND NOW THE REST OF US ARE PROBABLY GONNA BE LOCKED OUT OF THE PROGRAM BECAUSE SOME IDIOT DROPPED THEIR BEACON.
HOW CAN YOU **NOT** BE PISSED?
WE DON'T KNOW THE ENTIRE STORY. IT SEEMS UNKIND TO JUDGE.
WHATEVER.
HAVE A PLEASANT EVENING.
GILBERT, COME ON, DON'T BE LIKE THAT-

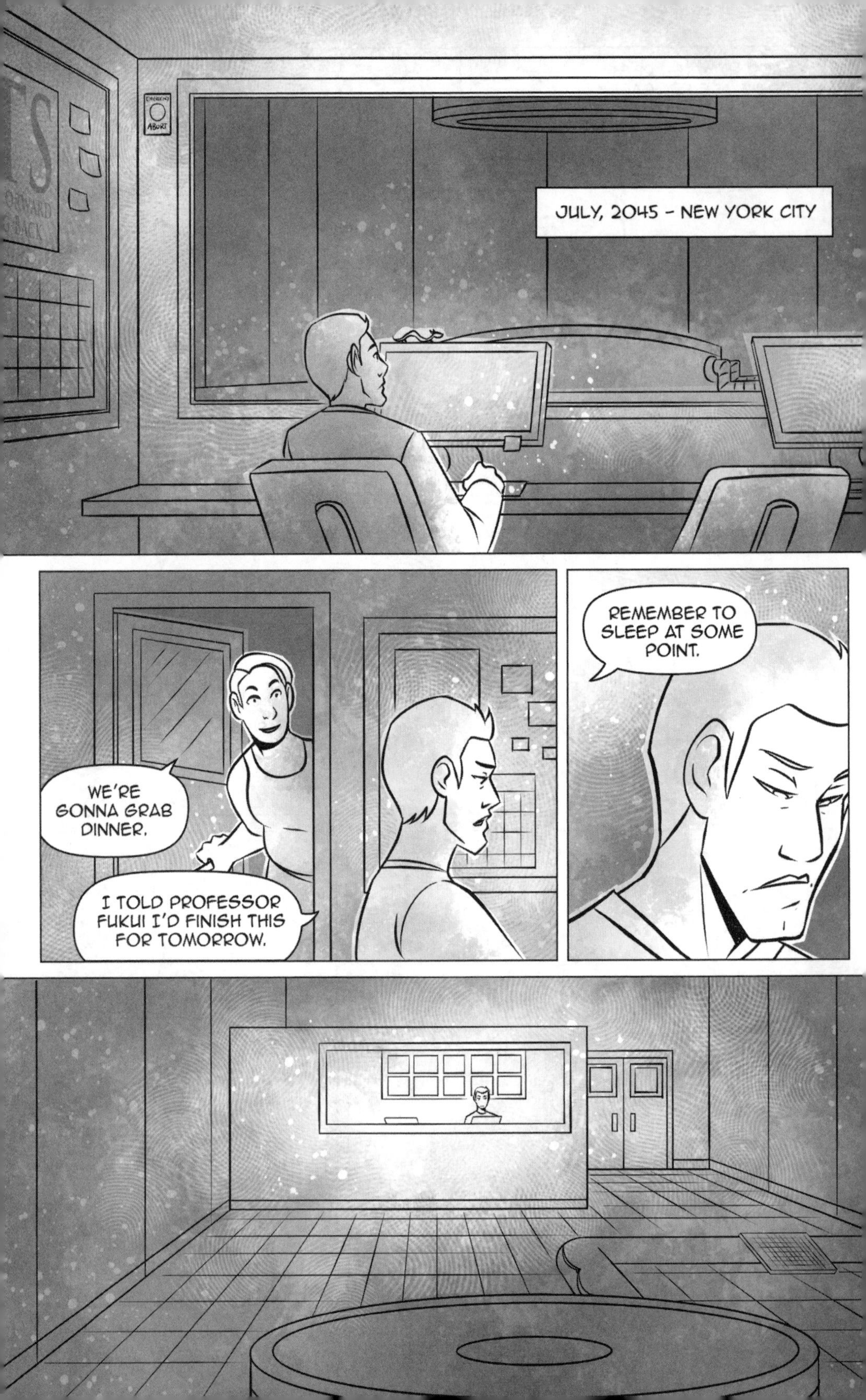
JULY, 2045 – NEW YORK CITY
WE'RE GONNA GRAB DINNER.
I TOLD PROFESSOR FUKUI I'D FINISH THIS FOR TOMORROW.
REMEMBER TO SLEEP AT SOME POINT.

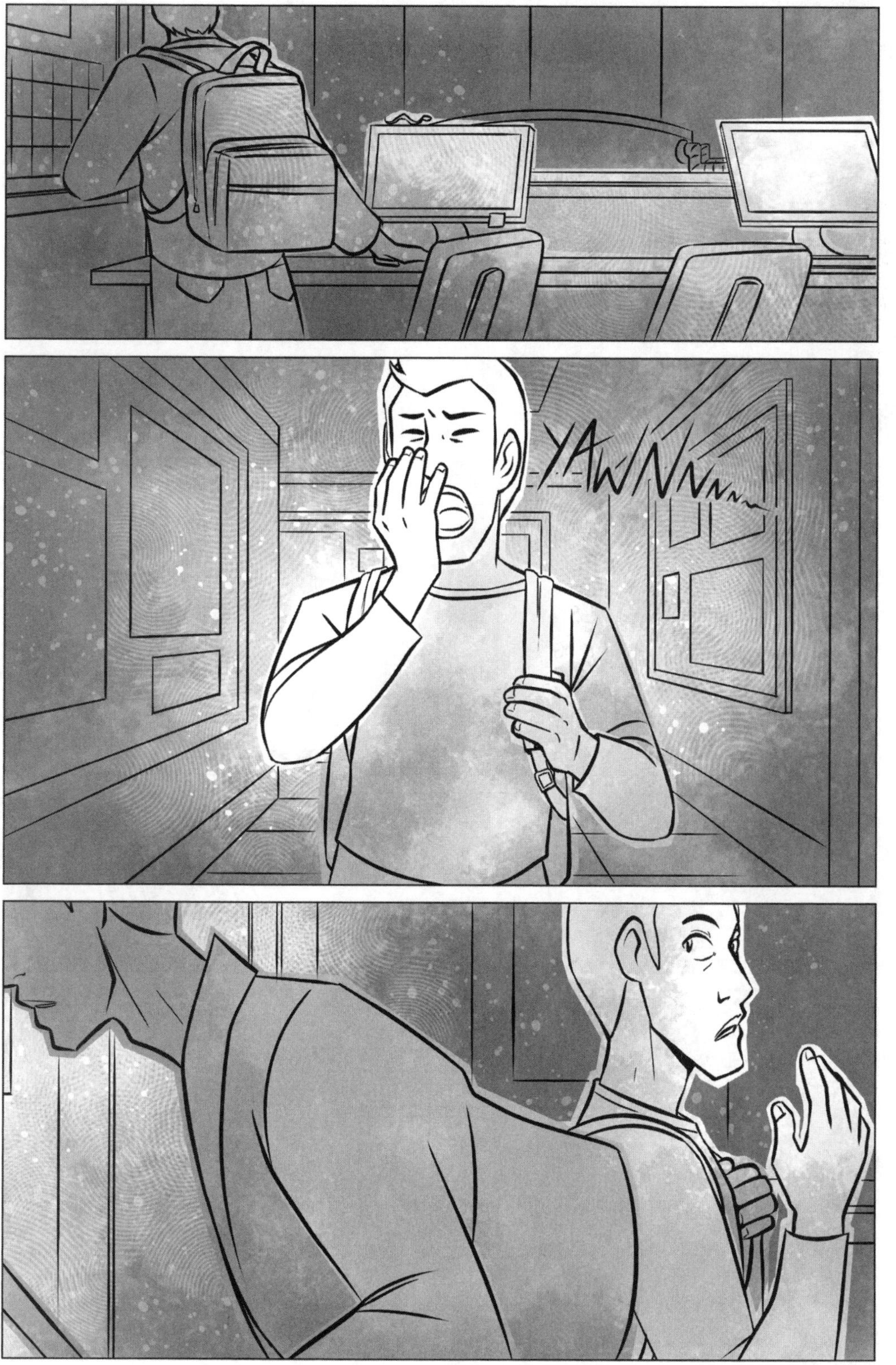
YAWNNnnn

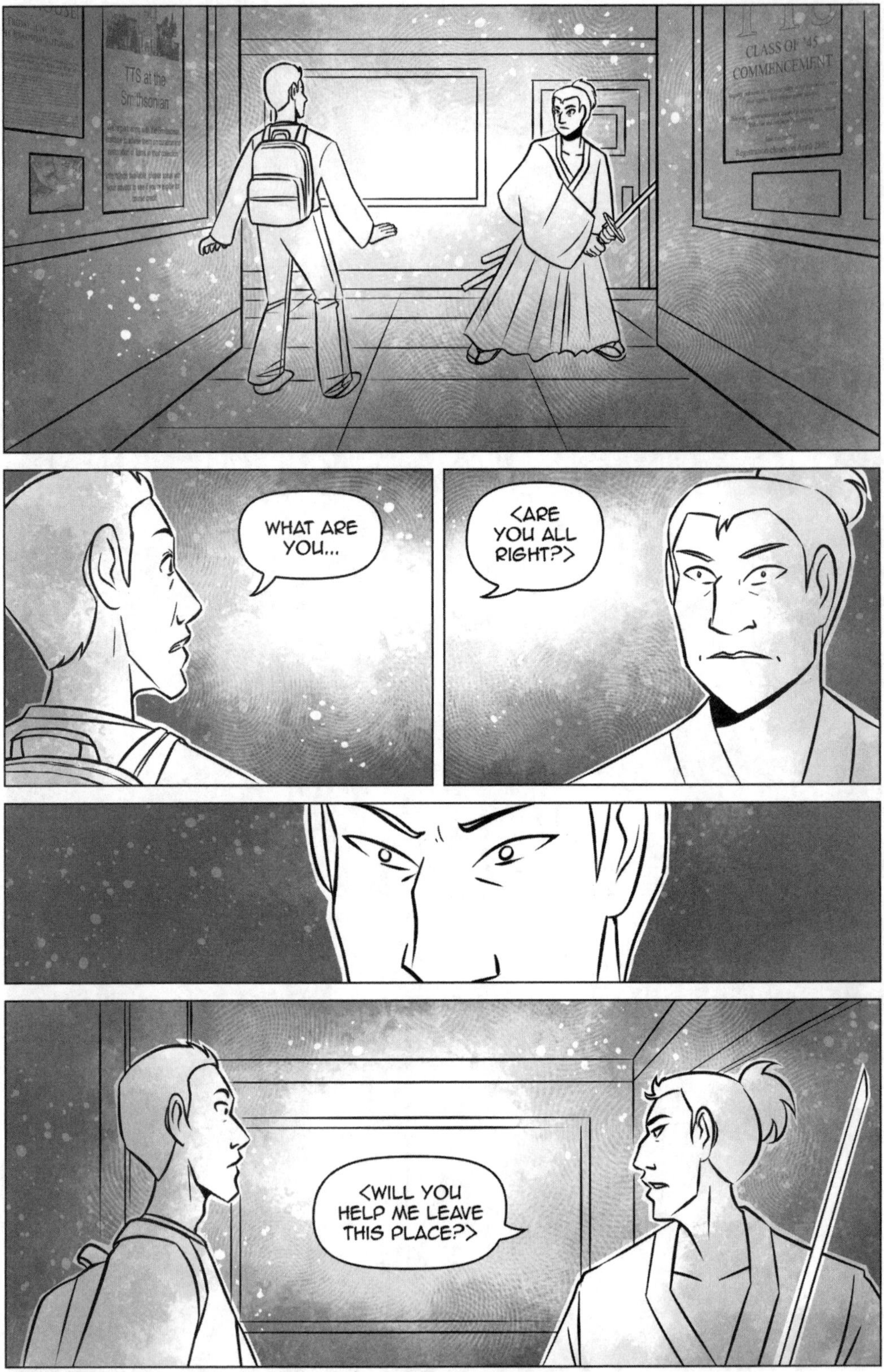
TTS at the Smithsonian
CLASS OF '45 COMMENCEMENT
WHAT ARE YOU...
<ARE YOU ALL RIGHT?>
<WILL YOU HELP ME LEAVE THIS PLACE?>

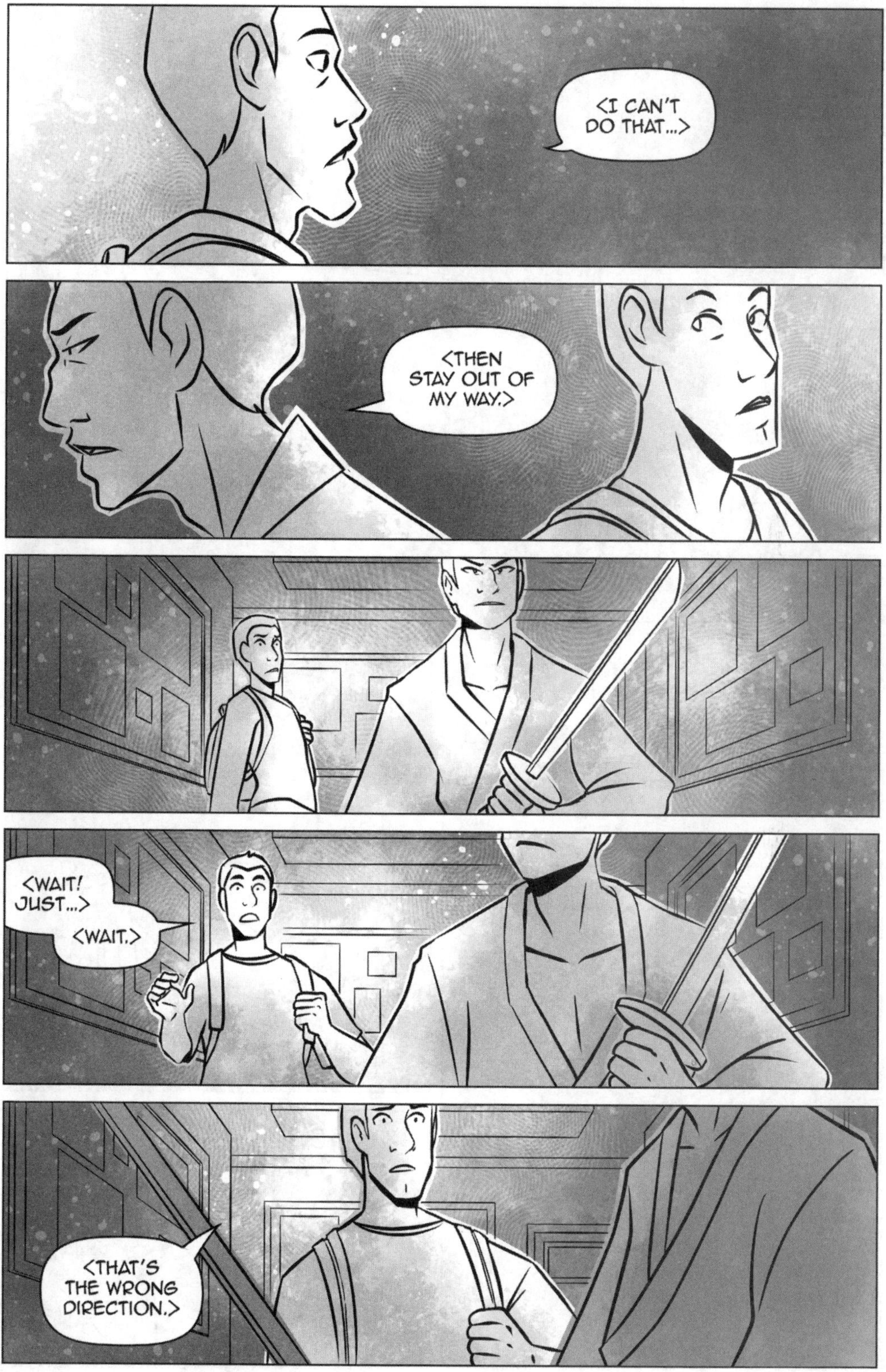
<I CAN'T DO THAT...>
<THEN STAY OUT OF MY WAY.>
<WAIT! JUST...>
<WAIT.>
<THAT'S THE WRONG DIRECTION.>

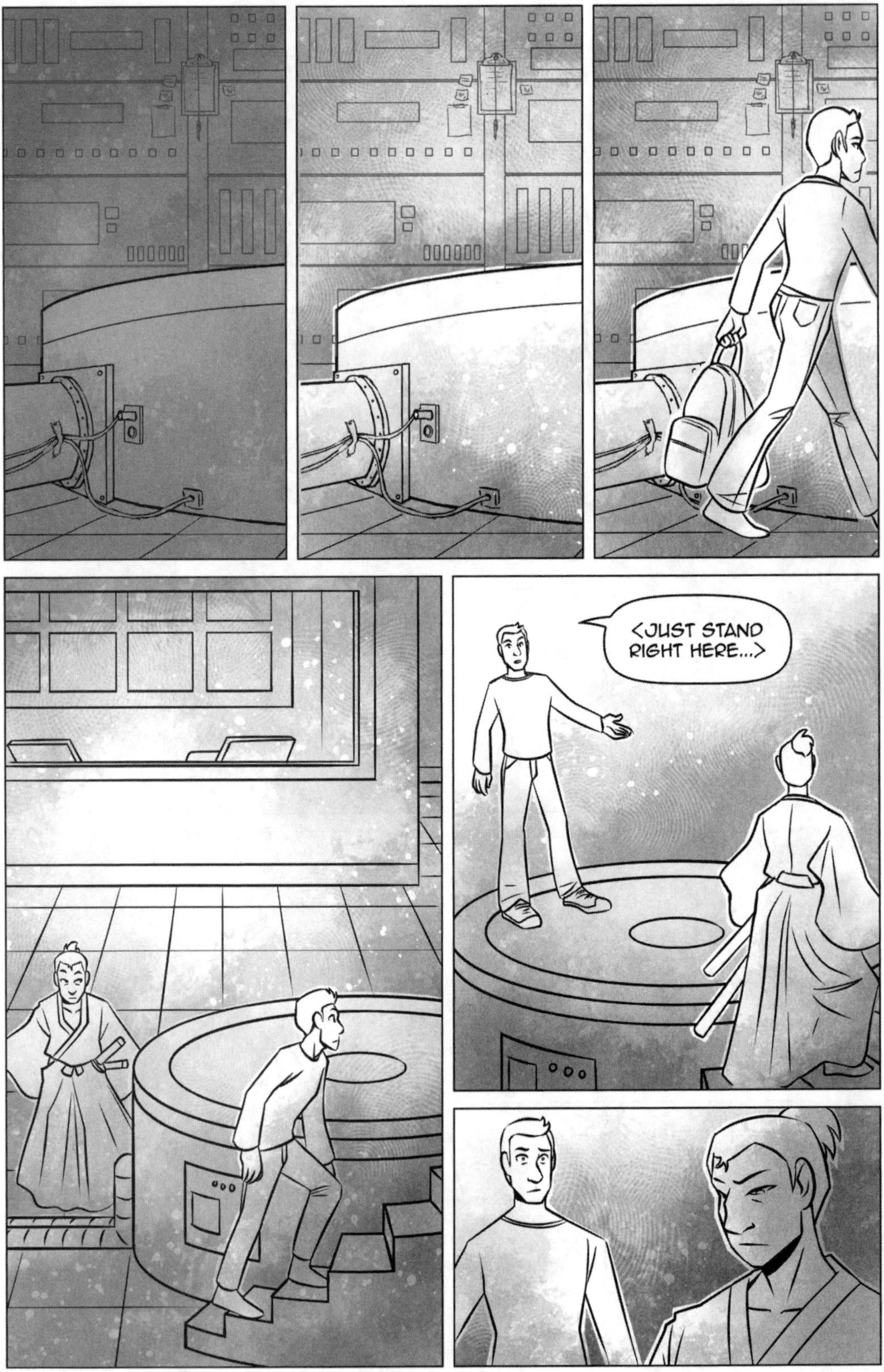
<JUST STAND RIGHT HERE...>

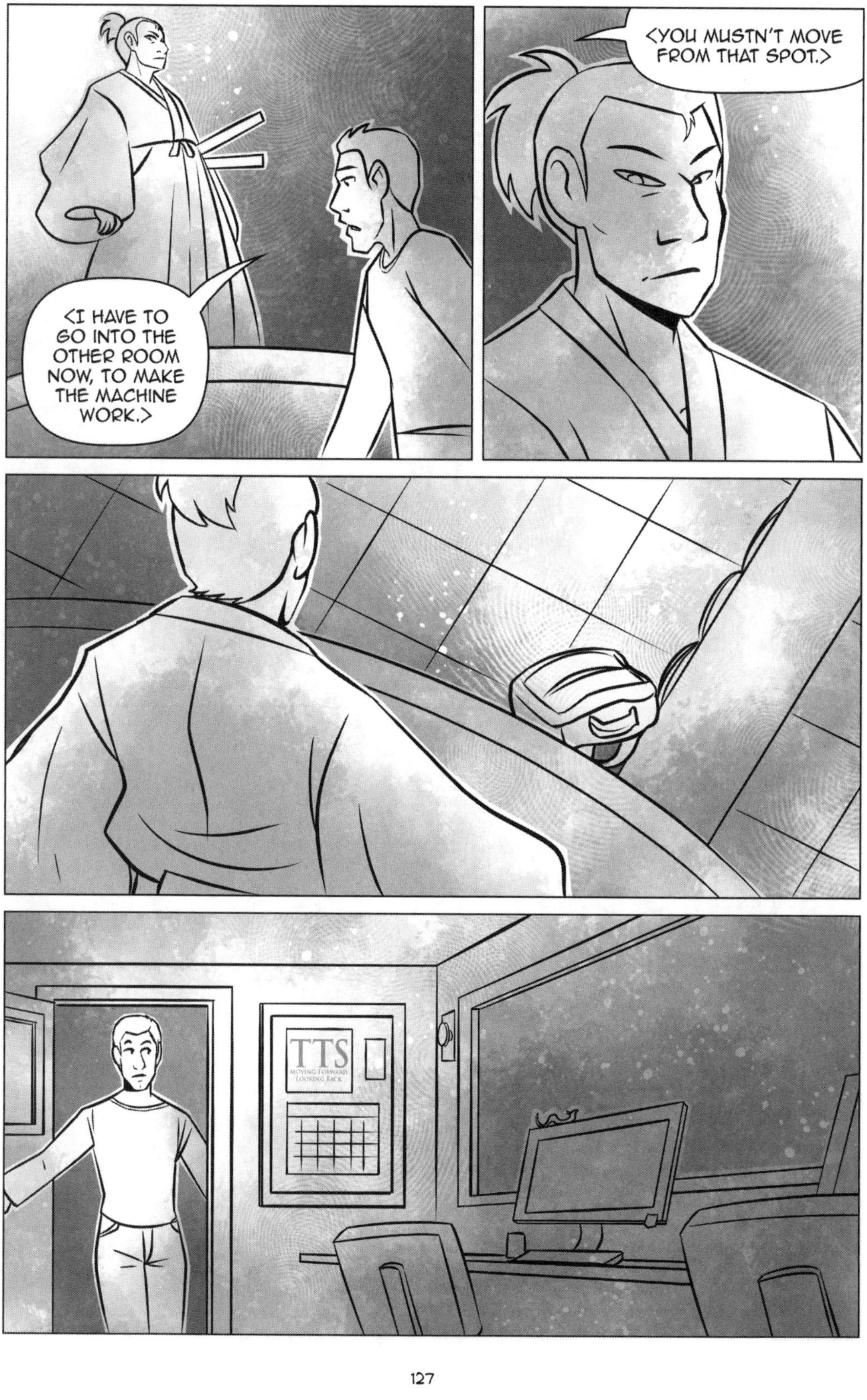
<I HAVE TO GO INTO THE OTHER ROOM NOW, TO MAKE THE MACHINE WORK.>
<YOU MUSTN'T MOVE FROM THAT SPOT.>
TTS
MOVING FORWARD LOOKING BACK

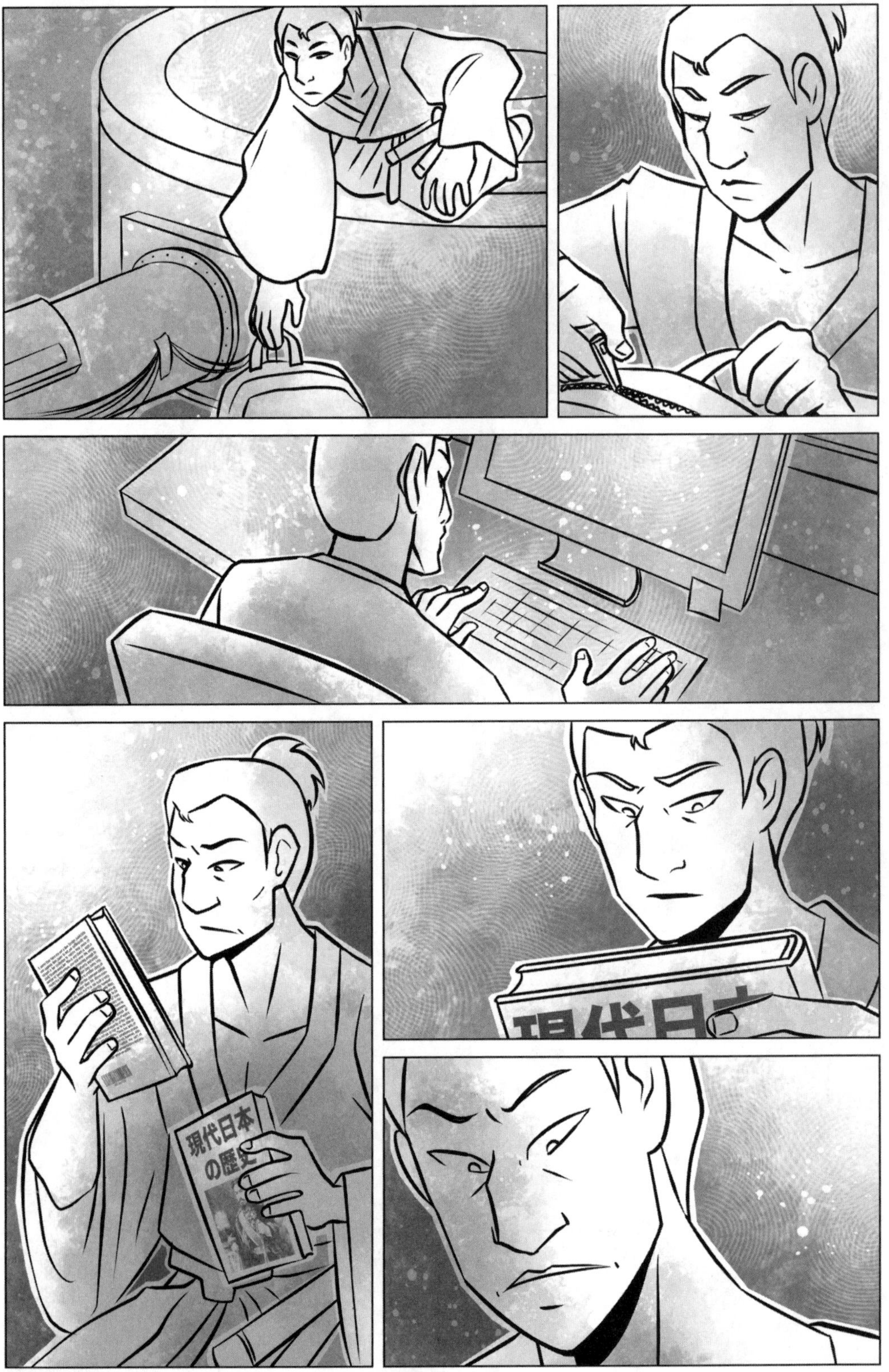
現代日本
の歴史

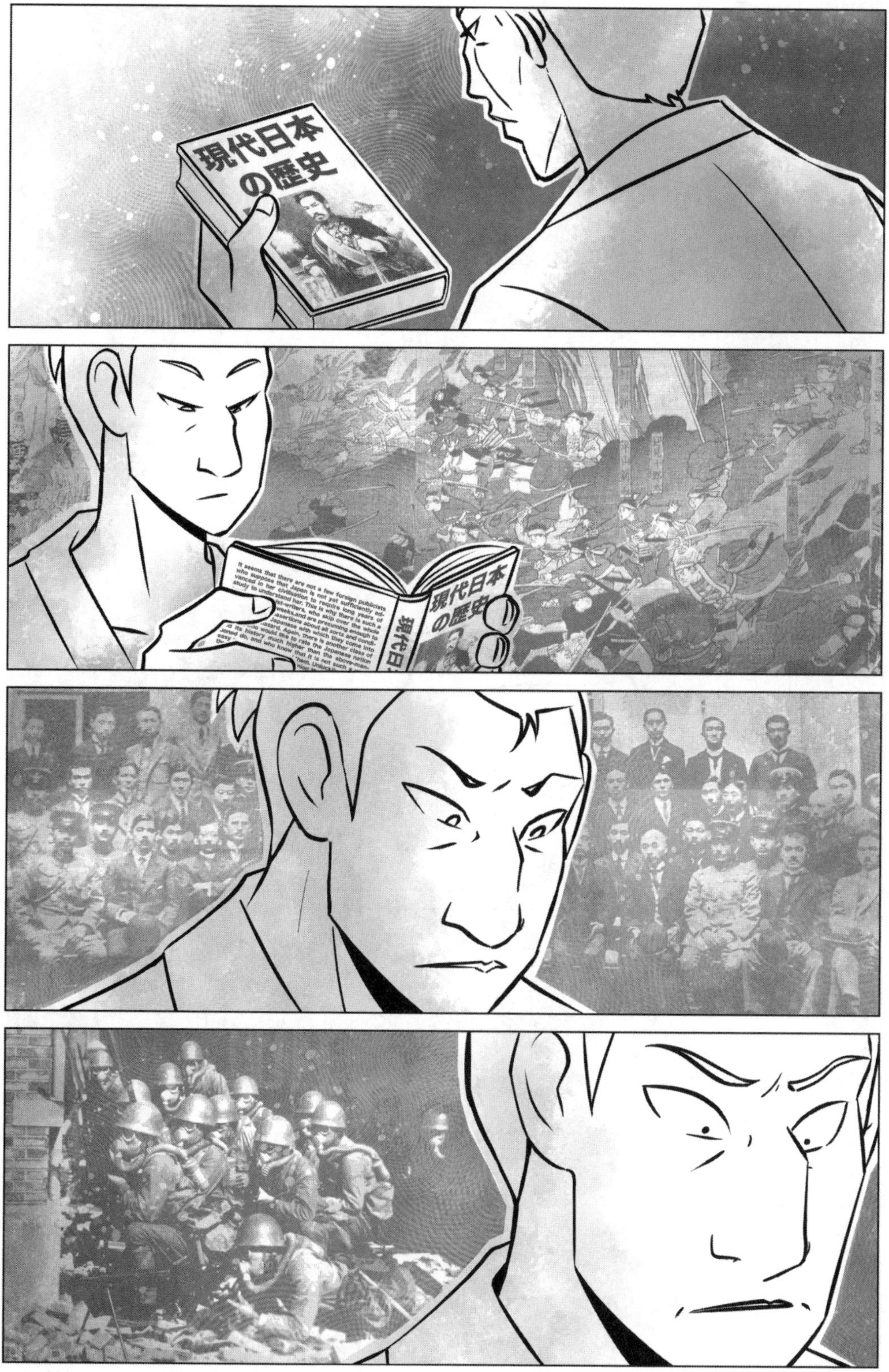
現代日本の歴史
It seems that there are not a few foreign publicists
who suppose that Japan is not yet sufficiently ad-
vanced in her civilisation to require long years of
study to understand her. This is why there is such a
現代日本の歴史

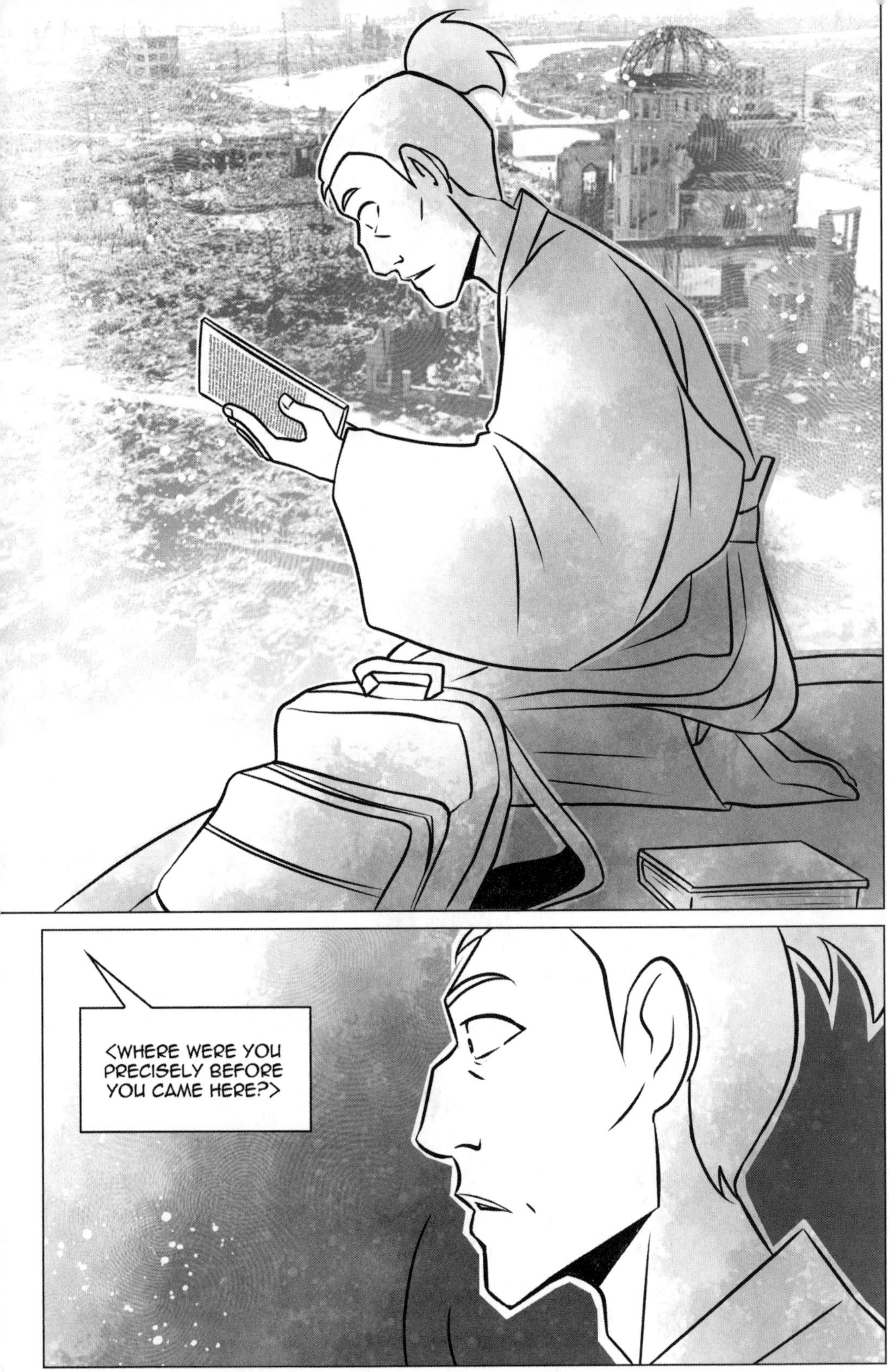
<WHERE WERE YOU PRECISELY BEFORE YOU CAME HERE?>

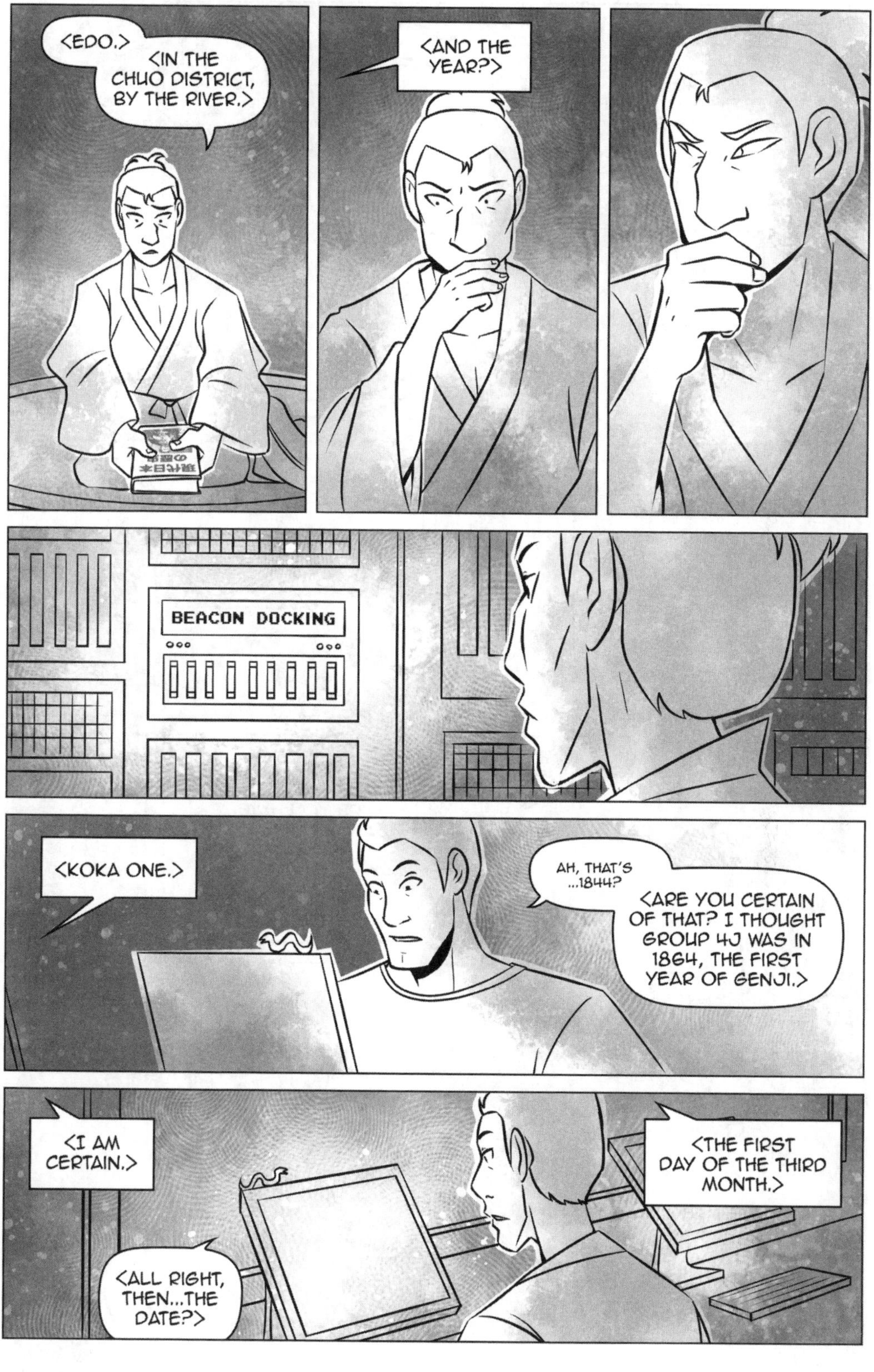
<EDO.>
<IN THE CHUO DISTRICT, BY THE RIVER.>
<AND THE YEAR?>
BEACON DOCKING
<KOKA ONE.>
AH, THAT'S ...1844?
<ARE YOU CERTAIN OF THAT? I THOUGHT GROUP 4J WAS IN 1864, THE FIRST YEAR OF GENJI.>
<I AM CERTAIN.>
<ALL RIGHT, THEN...THE DATE?>
<THE FIRST DAY OF THE THIRD MONTH.>

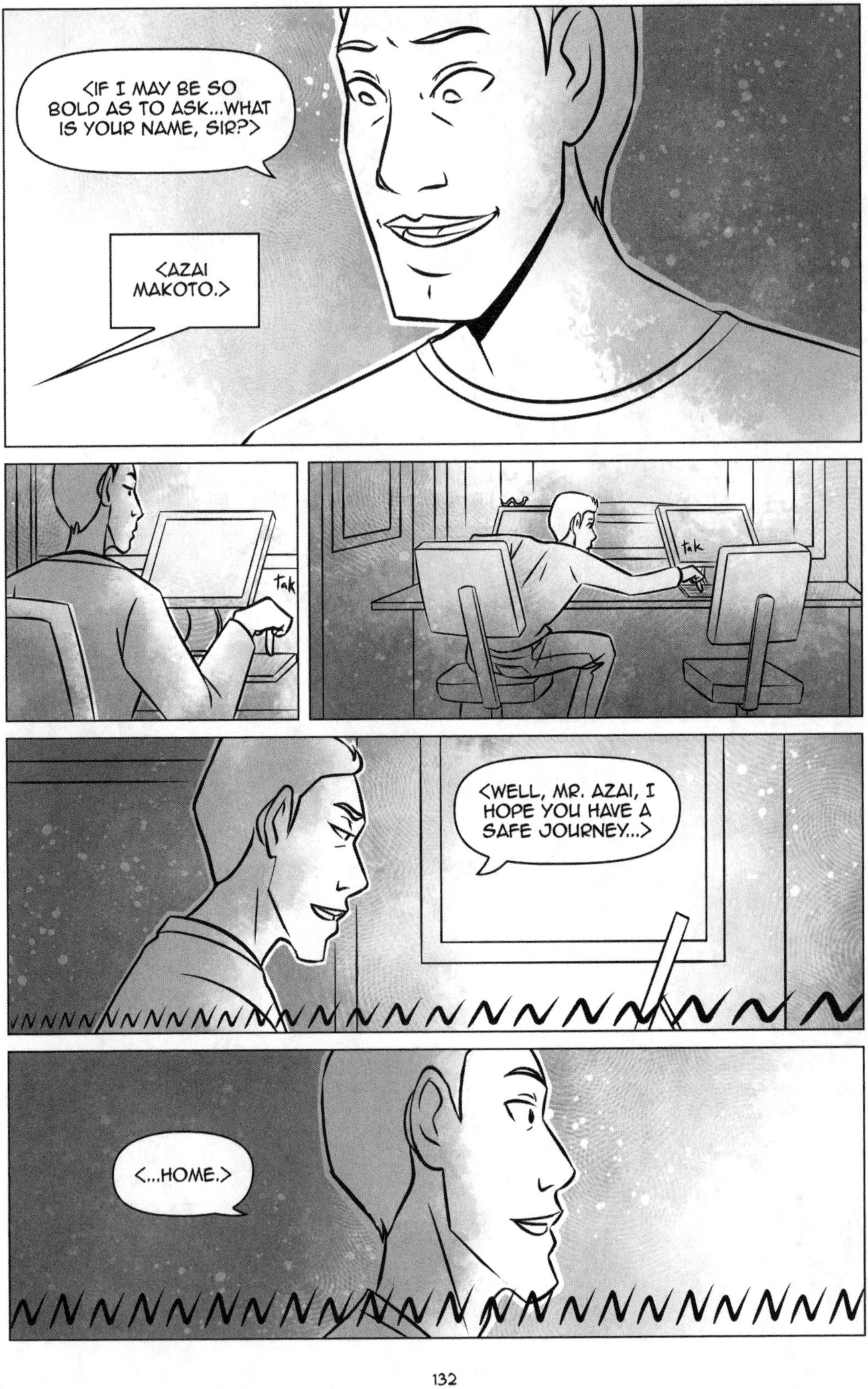
<IF I MAY BE SO BOLD AS TO ASK...WHAT IS YOUR NAME, SIR?>
<AZAI MAKOTO.>
tak
tak
<WELL, MR. AZAI, I HOPE YOU HAVE A SAFE JOURNEY...>
NNNNNNNNNNNNNNNNNNNNNNN
<...HOME.>
NNNNNNNNNNNNNNNNNNNNNNNNNNN

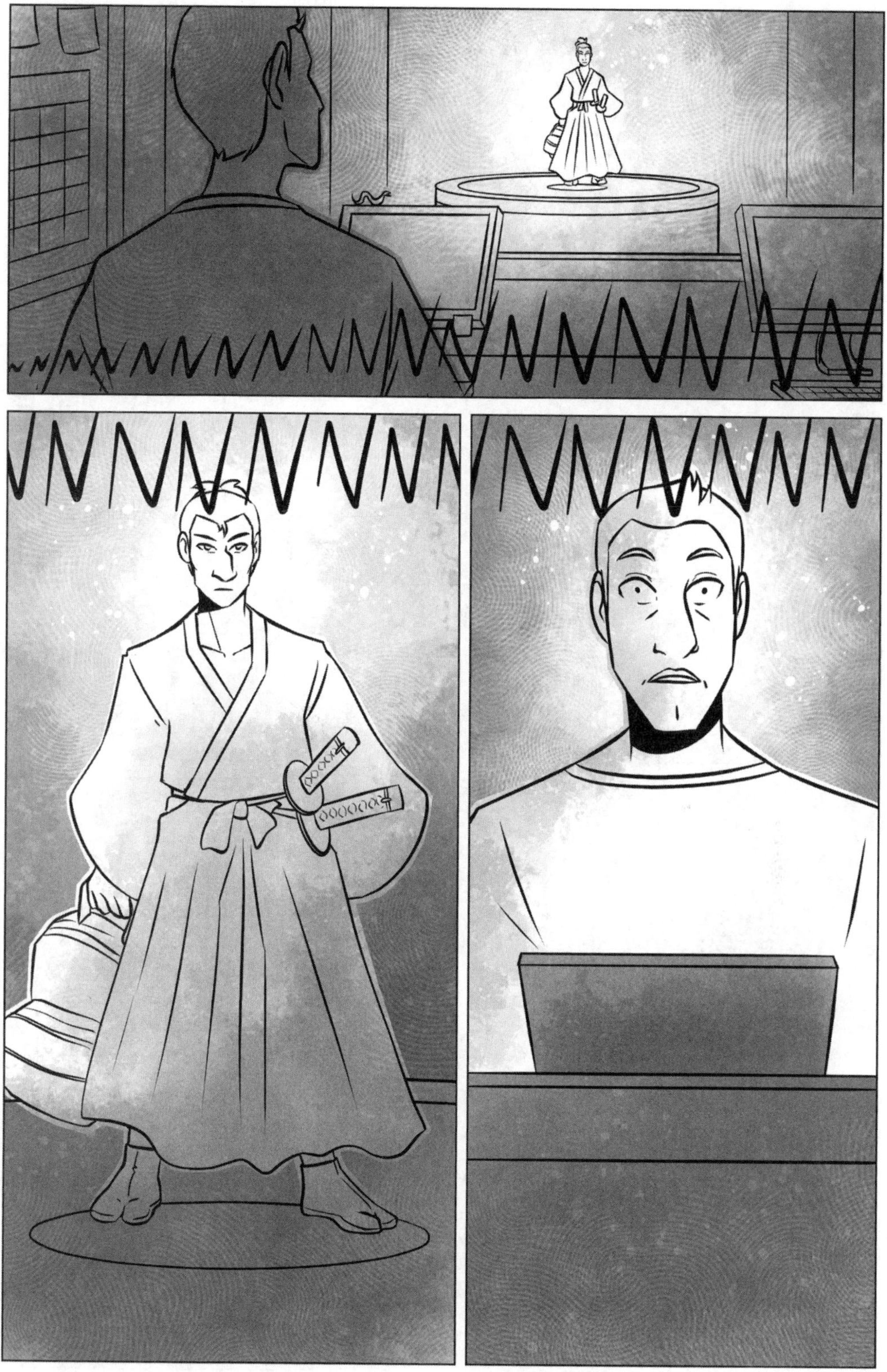

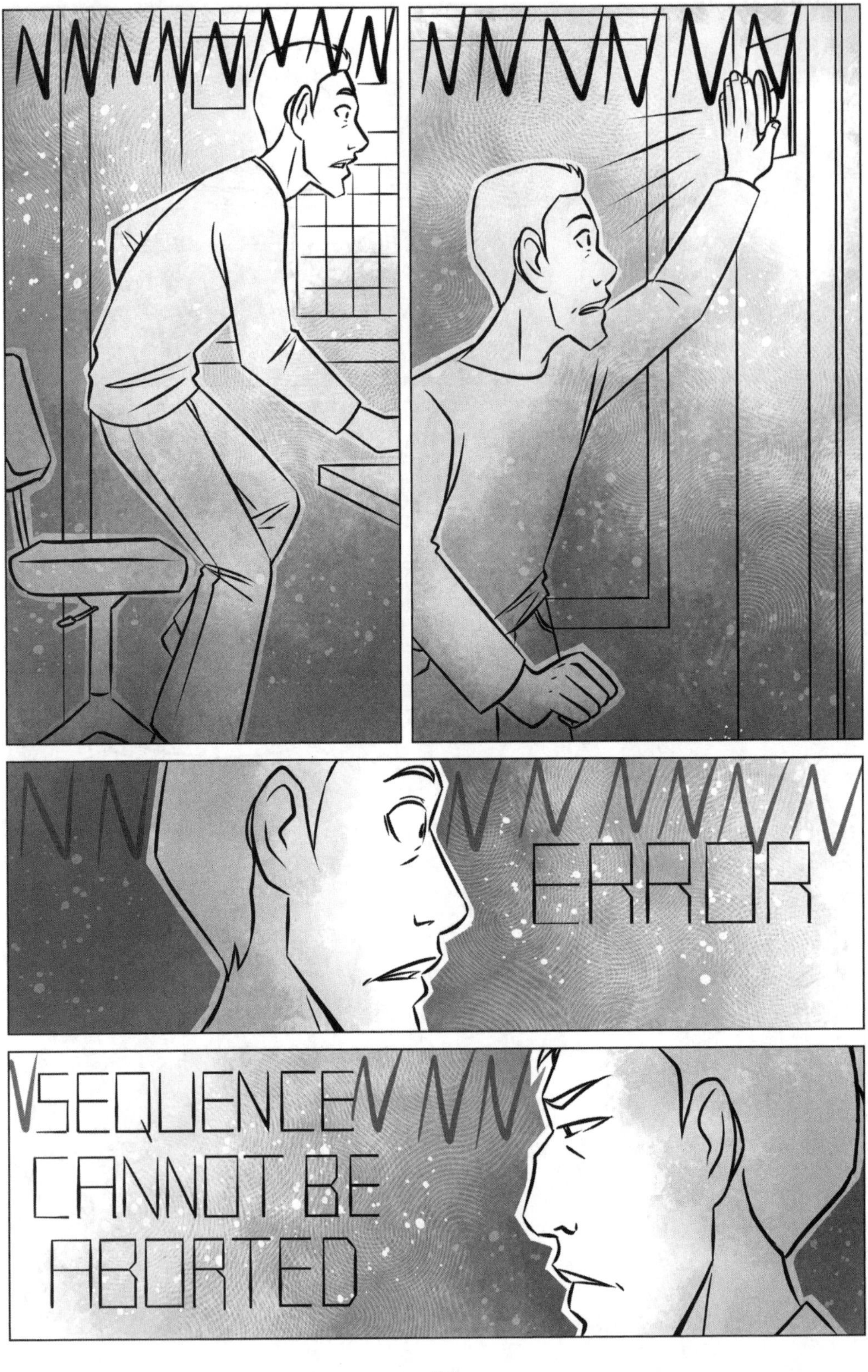
NNNNNNNNN
NNNNNNNN
NN NNNNNNN
ERROR
SEQUENCE CANNOT BE ABORTED

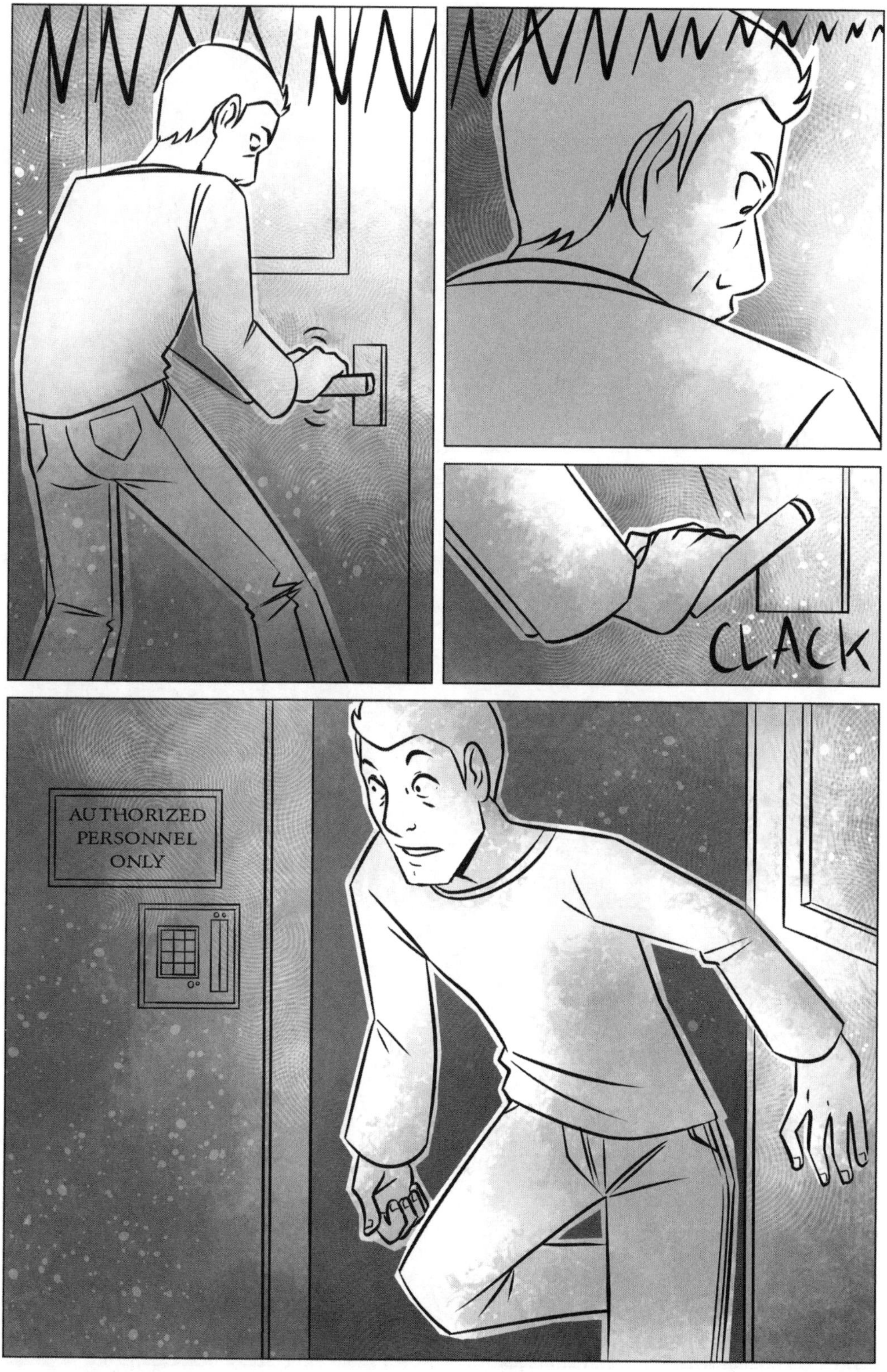
NNNNNNNNNNNNNNNNNNNnnnnnnnn
CLACK
AUTHORIZED PERSONNEL ONLY

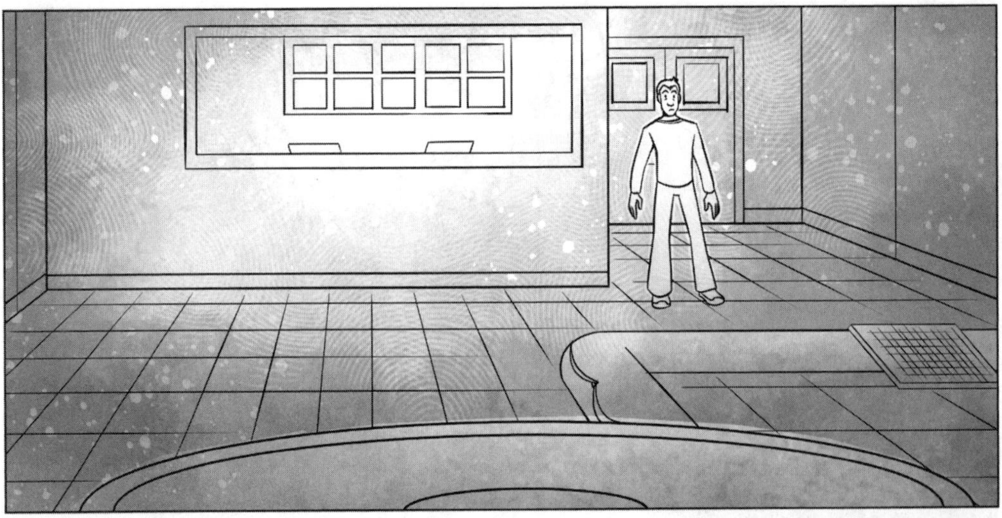

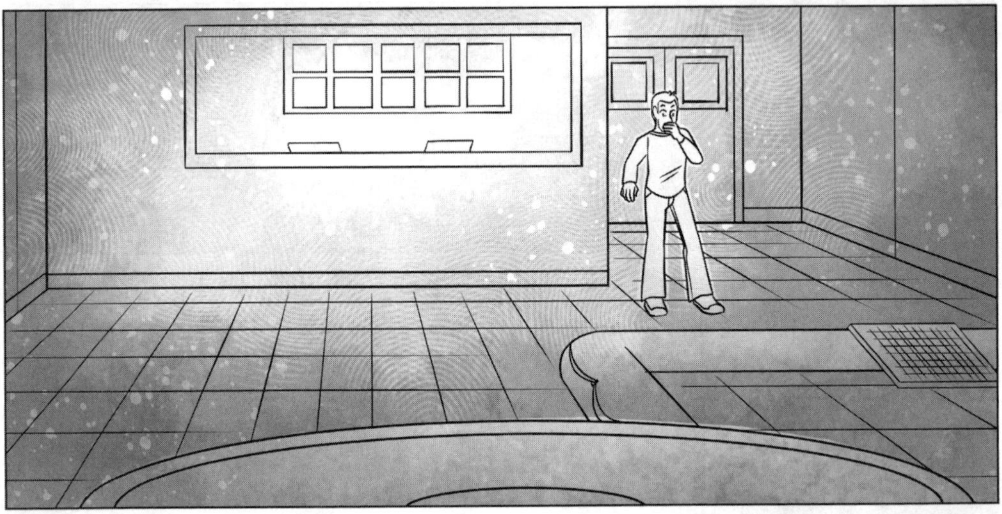

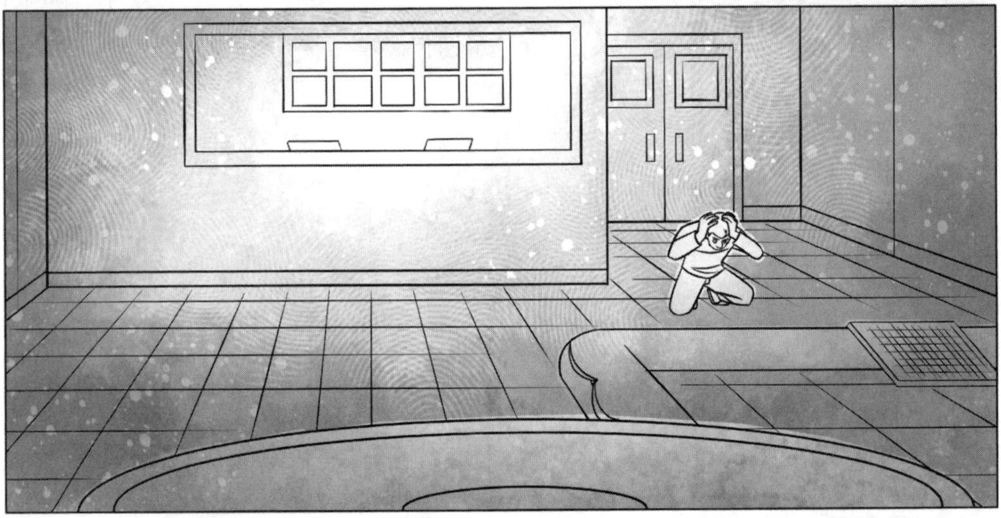

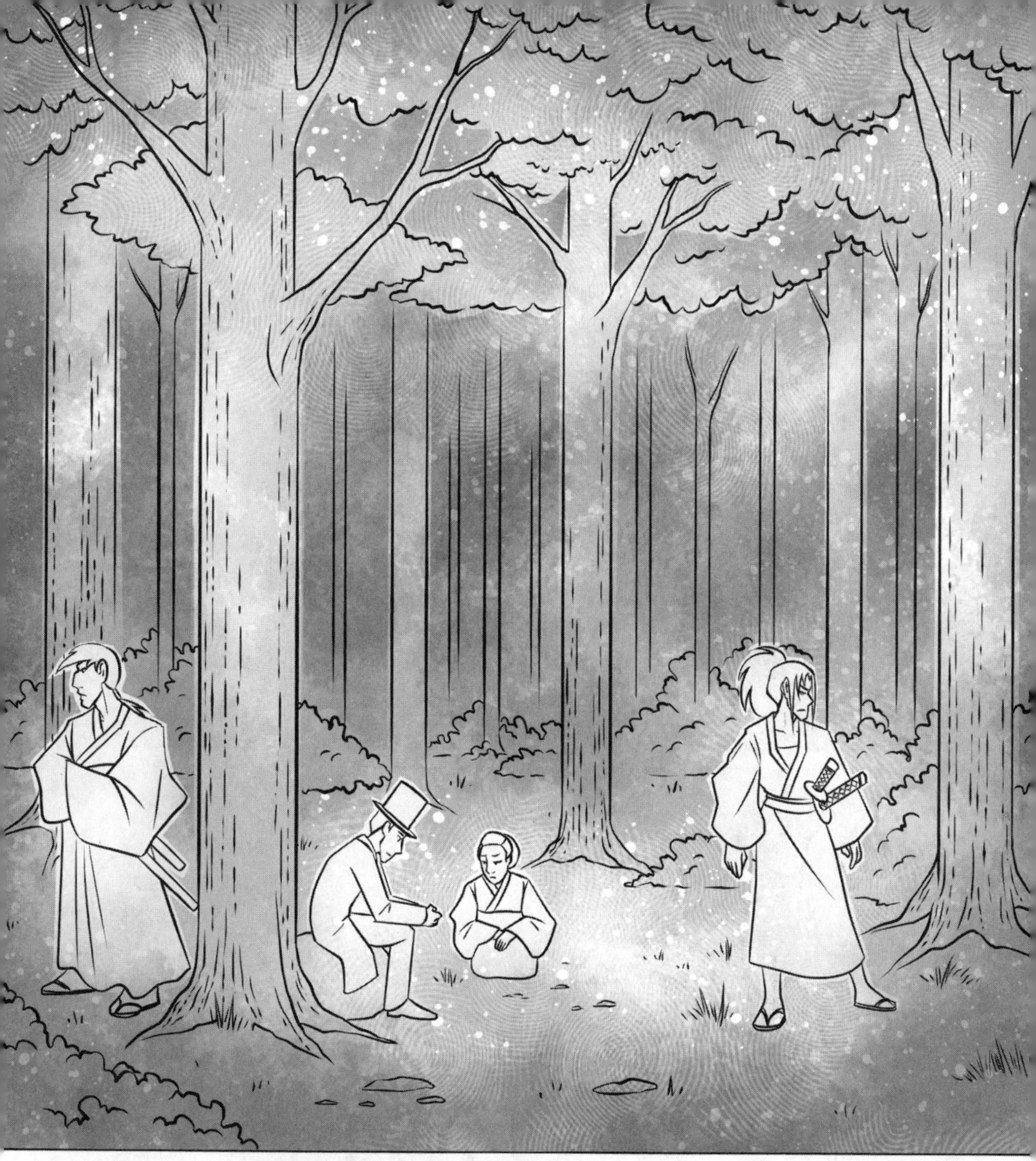

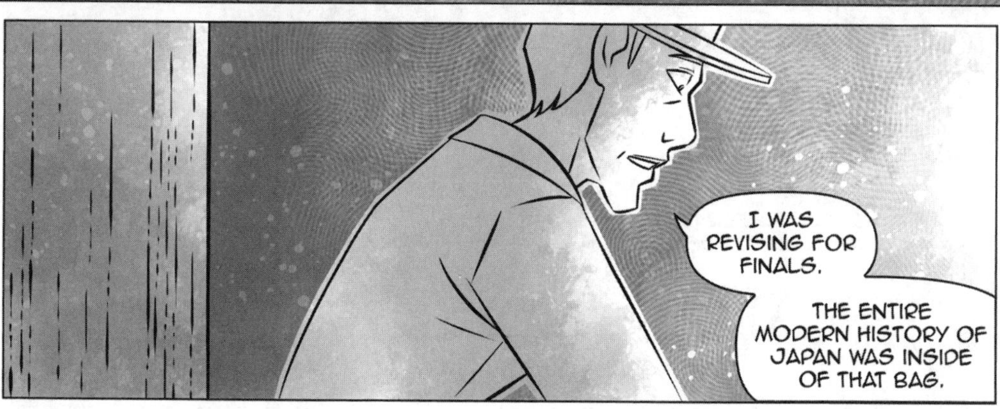
I WAS REVISING FOR FINALS.
THE ENTIRE MODERN HISTORY OF JAPAN WAS INSIDE OF THAT BAG.

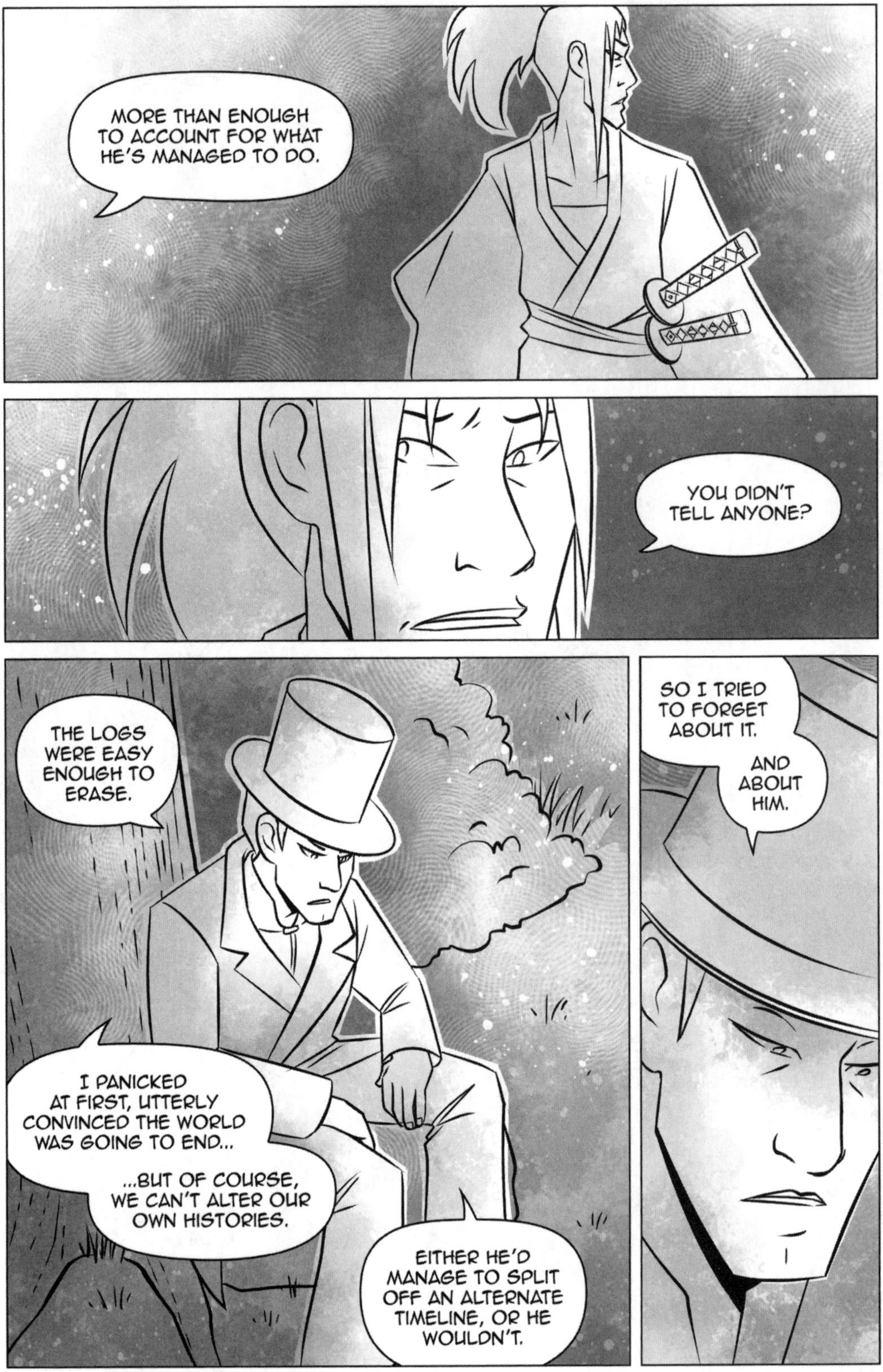
MORE THAN ENOUGH TO ACCOUNT FOR WHAT HE'S MANAGED TO DO.
YOU DIDN'T TELL ANYONE?
THE LOGS WERE EASY ENOUGH TO ERASE.
I PANICKED AT FIRST, UTTERLY CONVINCED THE WORLD WAS GOING TO END...
...BUT OF COURSE, WE CAN'T ALTER OUR OWN HISTORIES.
EITHER HE'D MANAGE TO SPLIT OFF AN ALTERNATE TIMELINE, OR HE WOULDN'T.
SO I TRIED TO FORGET ABOUT IT.
AND ABOUT HIM.

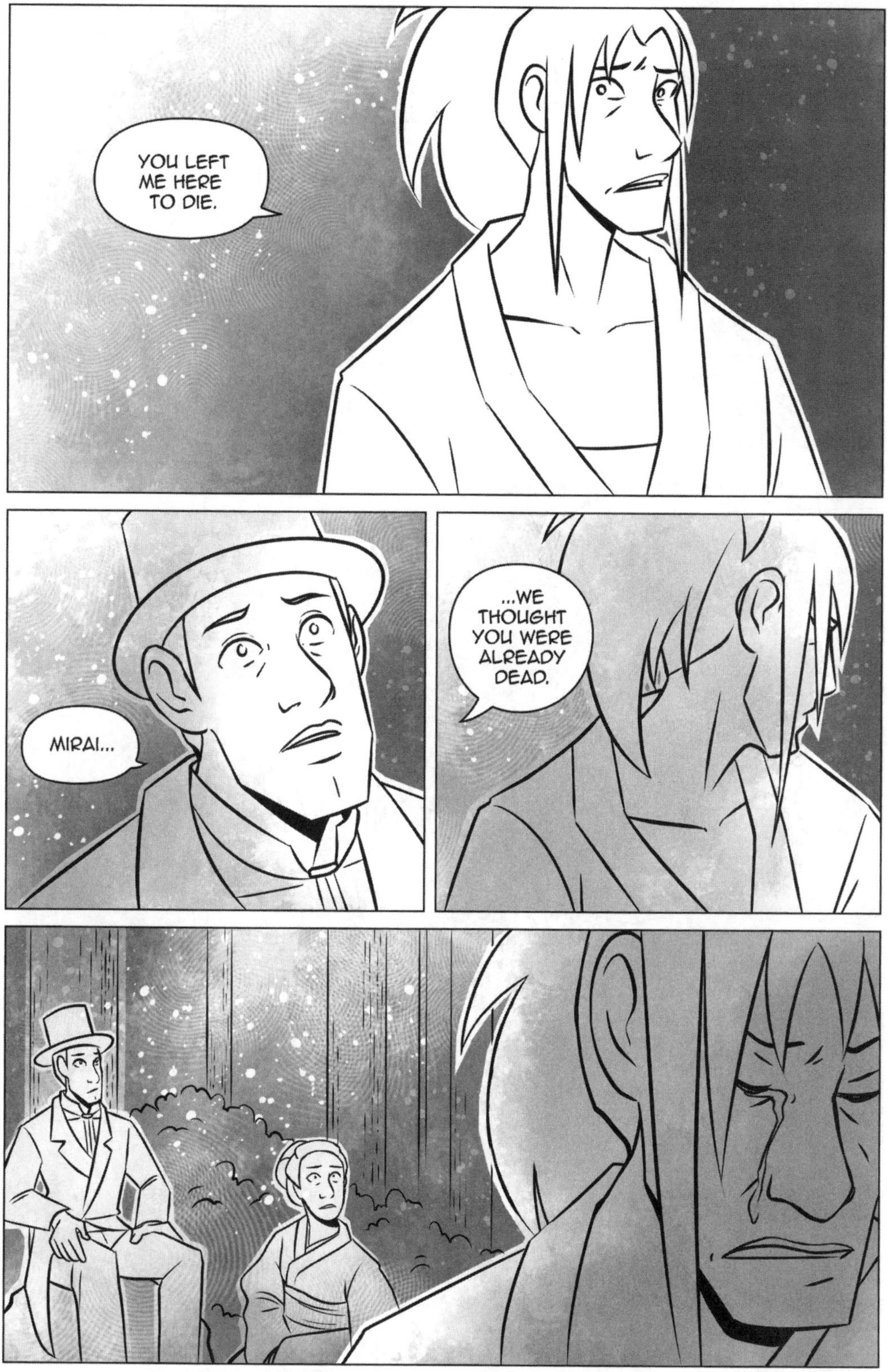
YOU LEFT ME HERE TO DIE.
MIRAI...
...WE THOUGHT YOU WERE ALREADY DEAD.

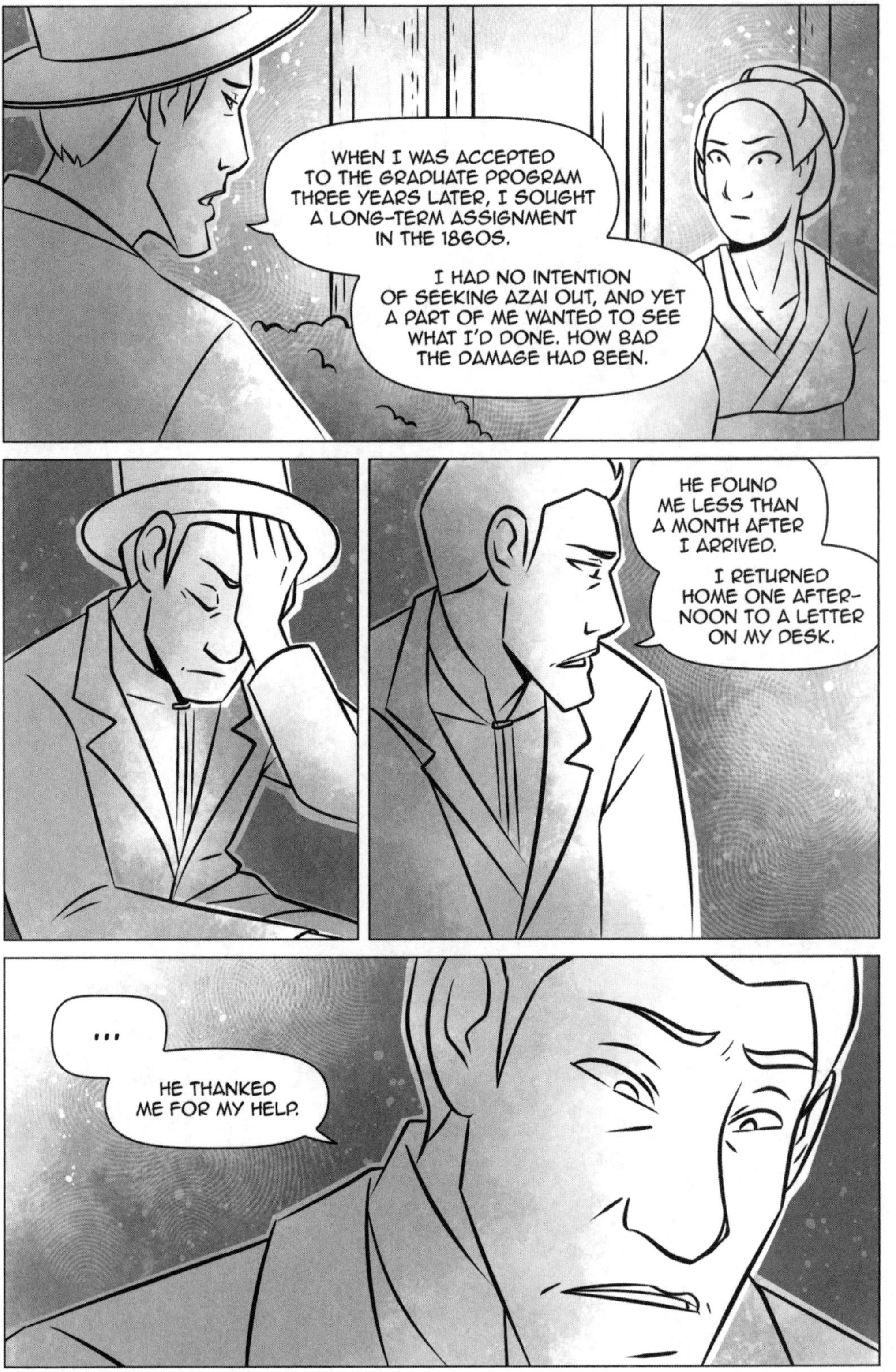
WHEN I WAS ACCEPTED TO THE GRADUATE PROGRAM THREE YEARS LATER, I SOUGHT A LONG-TERM ASSIGNMENT IN THE 1860S.
I HAD NO INTENTION OF SEEKING AZAI OUT, AND YET A PART OF ME WANTED TO SEE WHAT I'D DONE. HOW BAD THE DAMAGE HAD BEEN.
HE FOUND ME LESS THAN A MONTH AFTER I ARRIVED.
I RETURNED HOME ONE AFTER-NOON TO A LETTER ON MY DESK.
...
HE THANKED ME FOR MY HELP.

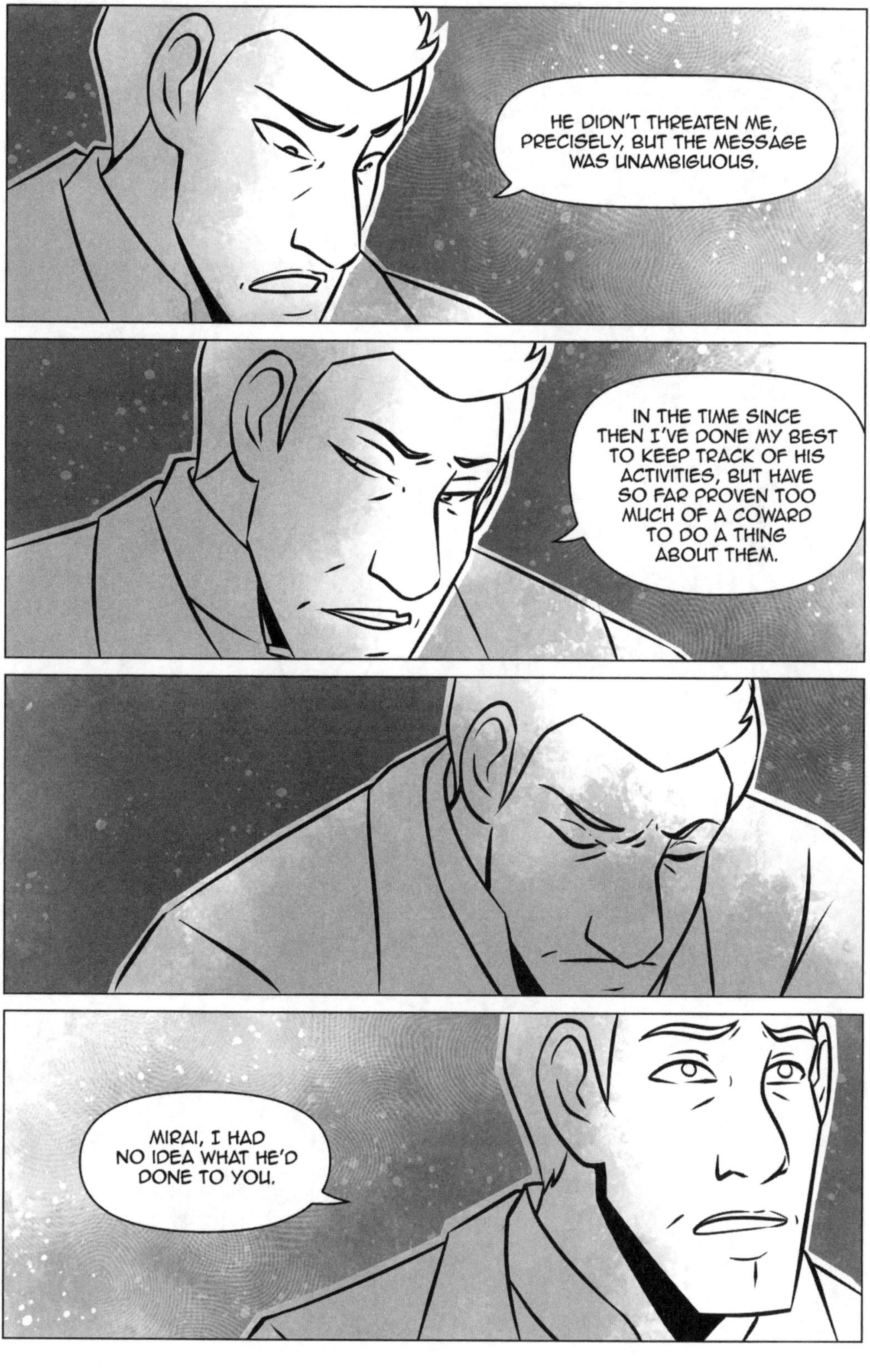
HE DIDN'T THREATEN ME, PRECISELY, BUT THE MESSAGE WAS UNAMBIGUOUS.
IN THE TIME SINCE THEN I'VE DONE MY BEST TO KEEP TRACK OF HIS ACTIVITIES, BUT HAVE SO FAR PROVEN TOO MUCH OF A COWARD TO DO A THING ABOUT THEM.
MIRAI, I HAD NO IDEA WHAT HE'D DONE TO YOU.

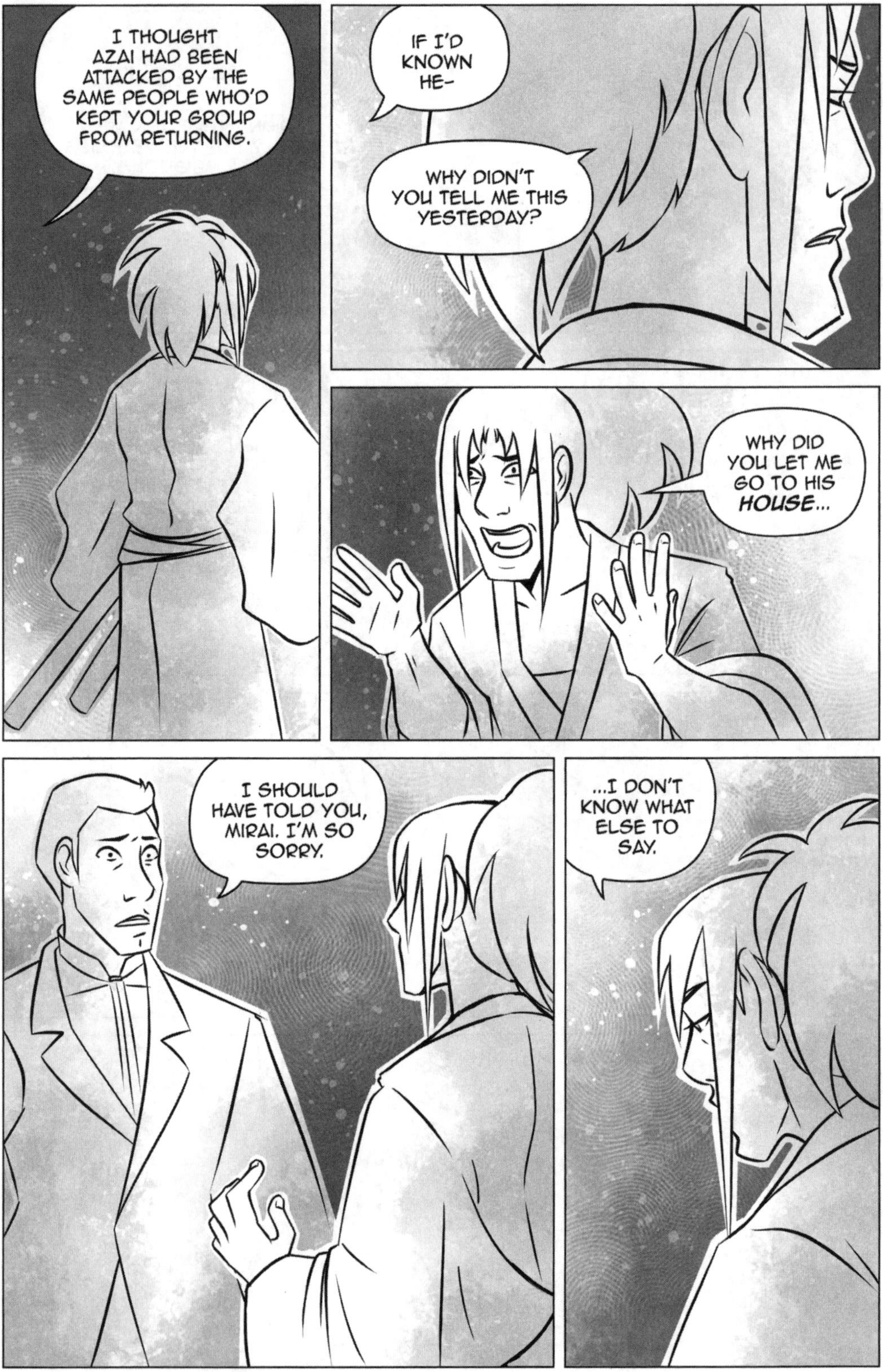

I THOUGHT AZAI HAD BEEN ATTACKED BY THE SAME PEOPLE WHO'D KEPT YOUR GROUP FROM RETURNING.
IF I'D KNOWN HE-
WHY DIDN'T YOU TELL ME THIS YESTERDAY?
WHY DID YOU LET ME GO TO HIS *HOUSE*...
I SHOULD HAVE TOLD YOU, MIRAI. I'M SO SORRY.
...I DON'T KNOW WHAT ELSE TO SAY.

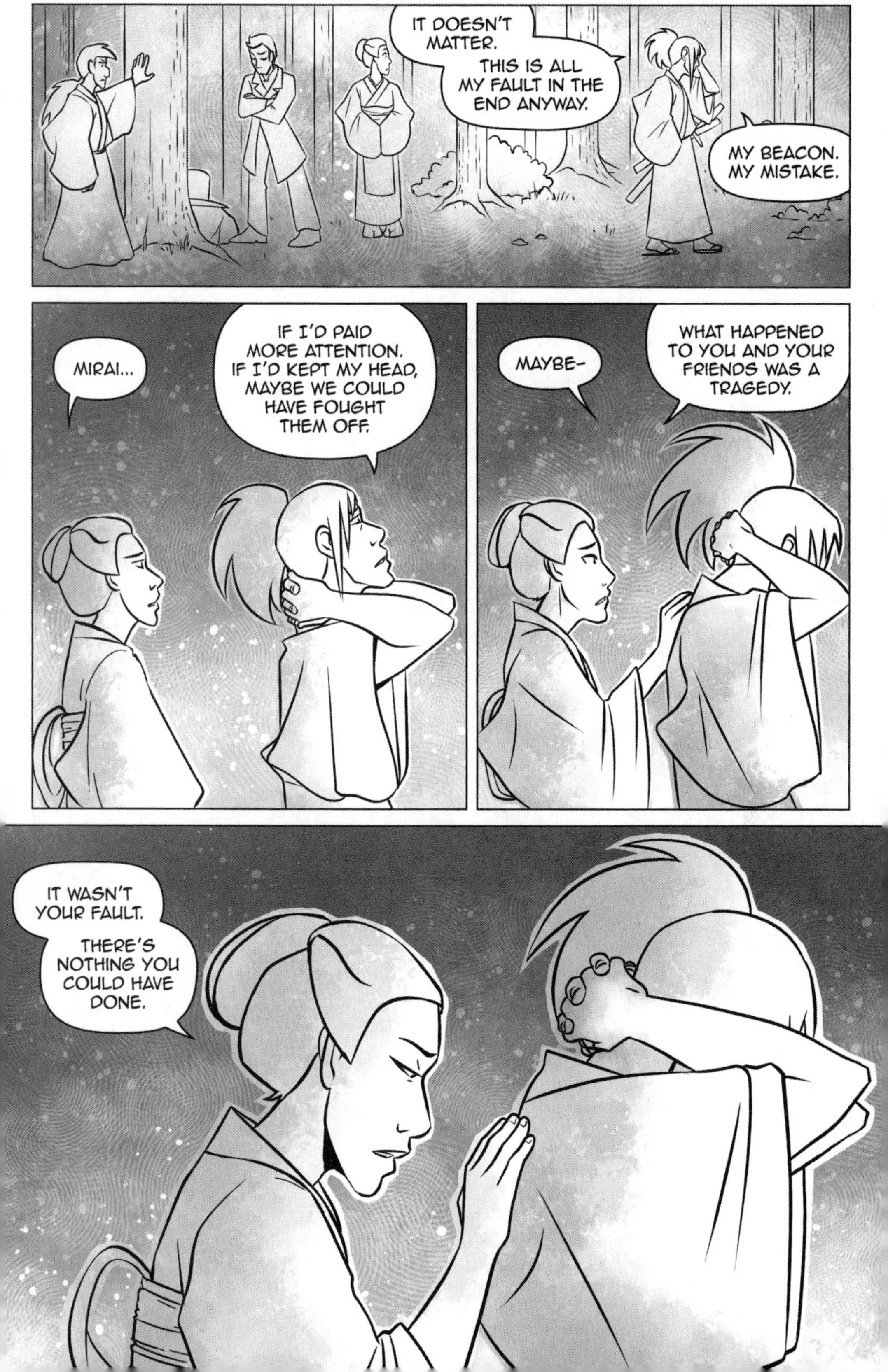
IT DOESN'T MATTER.
THIS IS ALL MY FAULT IN THE END ANYWAY.
MY BEACON. MY MISTAKE.
MIRAI...
IF I'D PAID MORE ATTENTION. IF I'D KEPT MY HEAD, MAYBE WE COULD HAVE FOUGHT THEM OFF.
MAYBE-
WHAT HAPPENED TO YOU AND YOUR FRIENDS WAS A TRAGEDY.
IT WASN'T YOUR FAULT.
THERE'S NOTHING YOU COULD HAVE DONE.

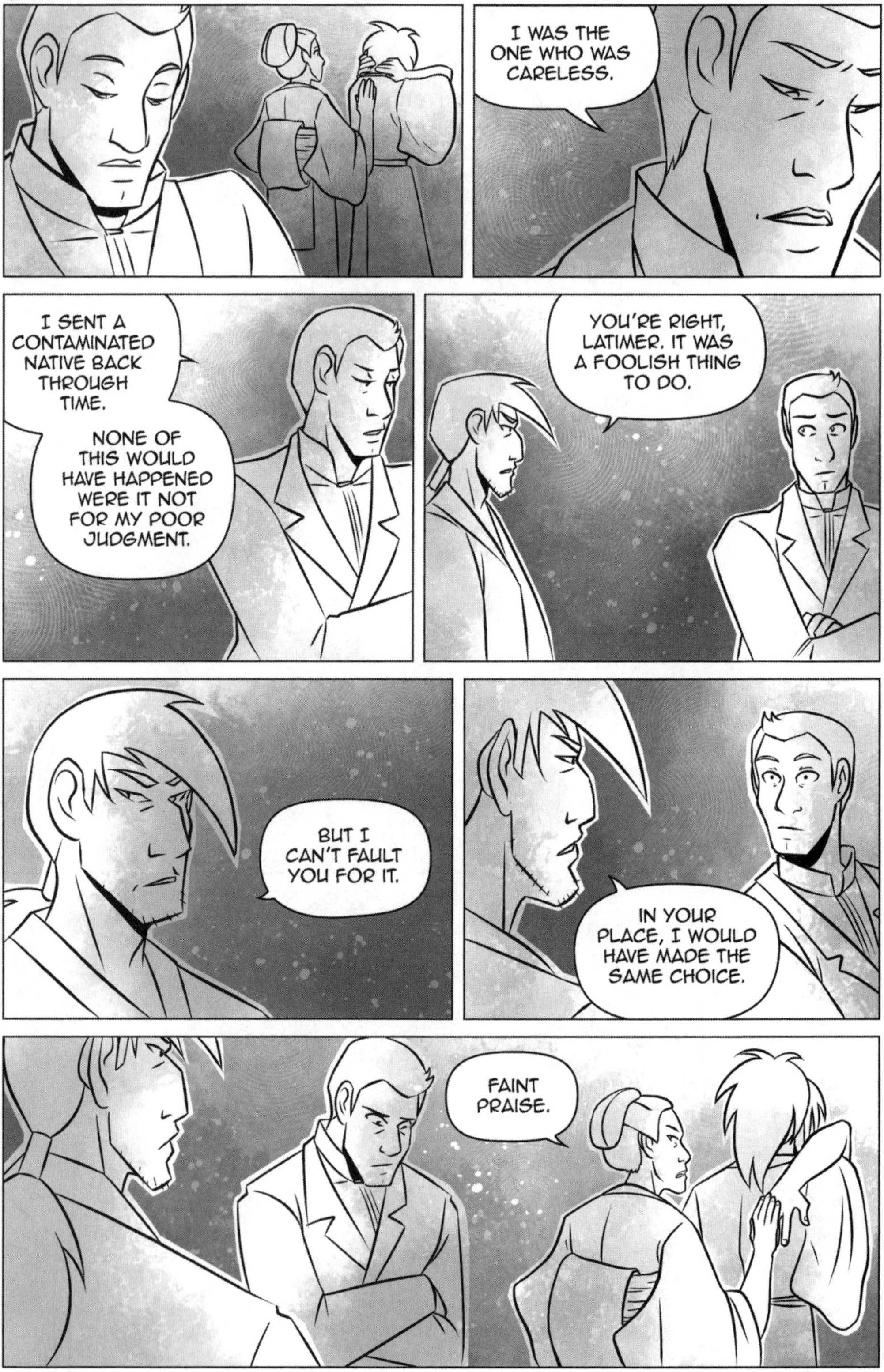
I WAS THE ONE WHO WAS CARELESS.
I SENT A CONTAMINATED NATIVE BACK THROUGH TIME.
NONE OF THIS WOULD HAVE HAPPENED WERE IT NOT FOR MY POOR JUDGMENT.
YOU'RE RIGHT, LATIMER. IT WAS A FOOLISH THING TO DO.
BUT I CAN'T FAULT YOU FOR IT.
IN YOUR PLACE, I WOULD HAVE MADE THE SAME CHOICE.
FAINT PRAISE.

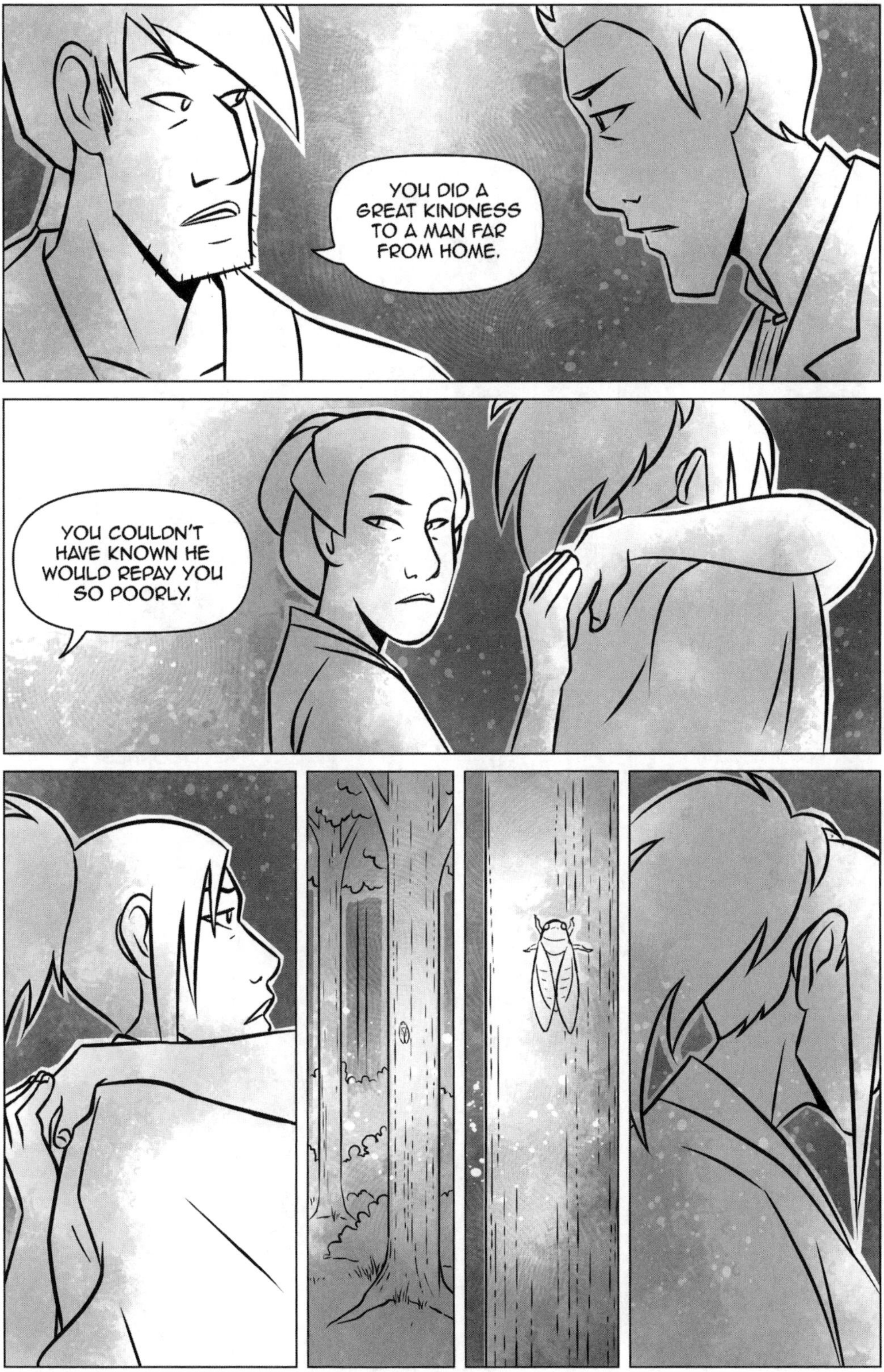
YOU DID A GREAT KINDNESS TO A MAN FAR FROM HOME.
YOU COULDN'T HAVE KNOWN HE WOULD REPAY YOU SO POORLY.

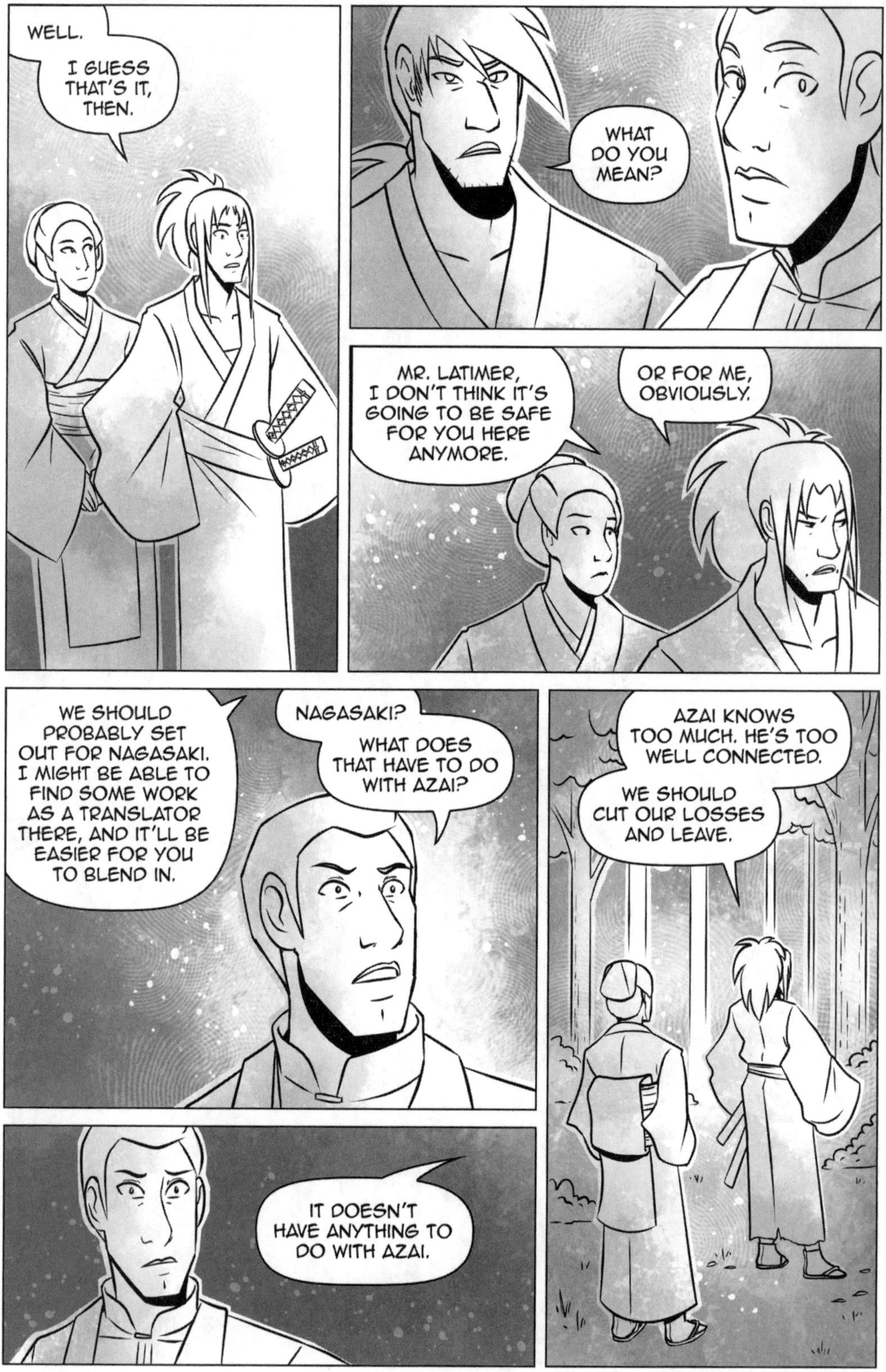
WELL.
I GUESS THAT'S IT, THEN.
WHAT DO YOU MEAN?
MR. LATIMER, I DON'T THINK IT'S GOING TO BE SAFE FOR YOU HERE ANYMORE.
OR FOR ME, OBVIOUSLY.
WE SHOULD PROBABLY SET OUT FOR NAGASAKI. I MIGHT BE ABLE TO FIND SOME WORK AS A TRANSLATOR THERE, AND IT'LL BE EASIER FOR YOU TO BLEND IN.
NAGASAKI?
WHAT DOES THAT HAVE TO DO WITH AZAI?
IT DOESN'T HAVE ANYTHING TO DO WITH AZAI.
AZAI KNOWS TOO MUCH. HE'S TOO WELL CONNECTED.
WE SHOULD CUT OUR LOSSES AND LEAVE.

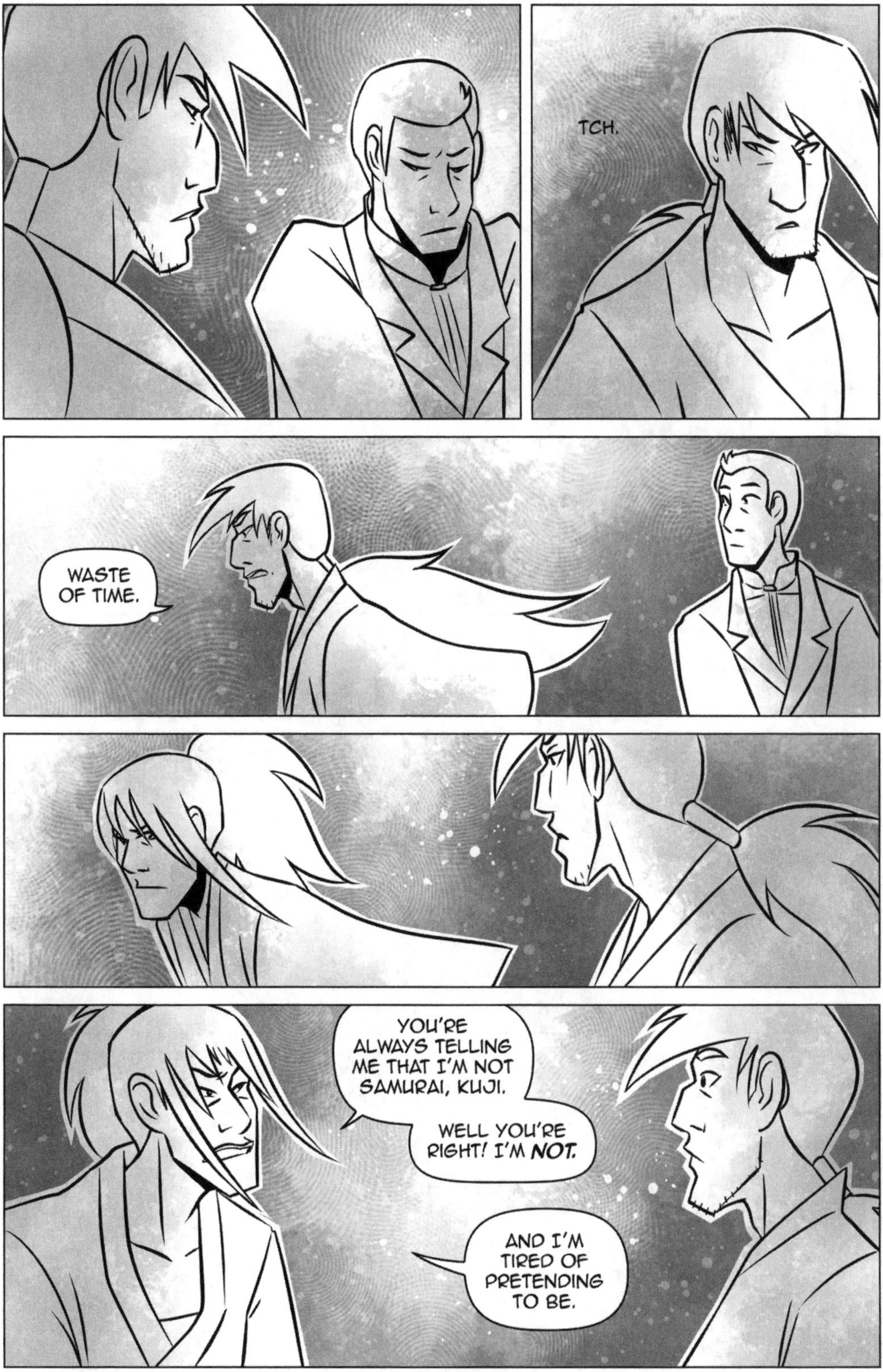
TCH.
WASTE OF TIME.
YOU'RE ALWAYS TELLING ME THAT I'M NOT SAMURAI, KUJI.
WELL YOU'RE RIGHT! I'M ***NOT.***
AND I'M TIRED OF PRETENDING TO BE.

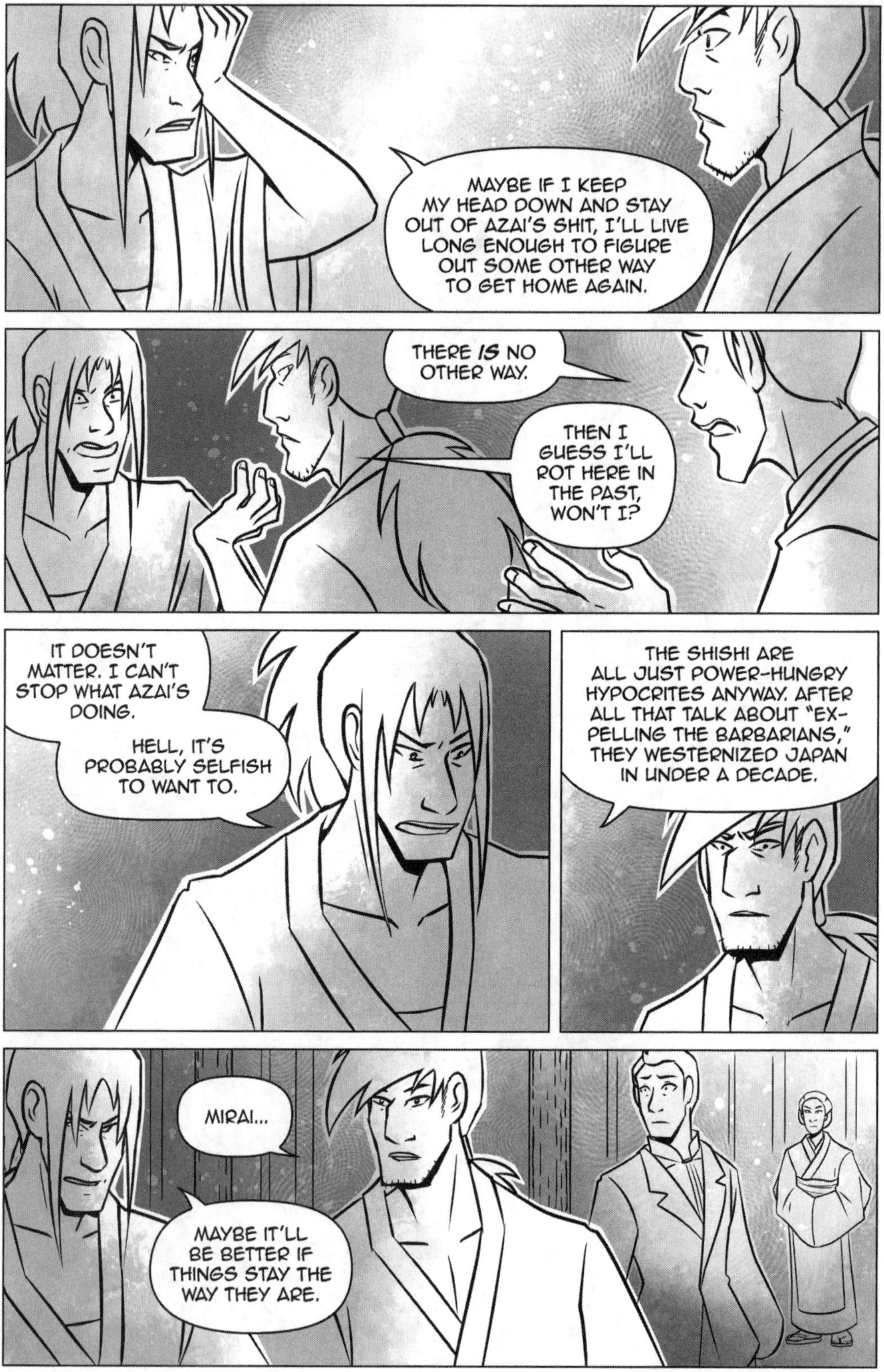
MAYBE IF I KEEP MY HEAD DOWN AND STAY OUT OF AZAI'S SHIT, I'LL LIVE LONG ENOUGH TO FIGURE OUT SOME OTHER WAY TO GET HOME AGAIN.
THERE *IS* NO OTHER WAY.
THEN I GUESS I'LL ROT HERE IN THE PAST, WON'T I?
IT DOESN'T MATTER. I CAN'T STOP WHAT AZAI'S DOING.
HELL, IT'S PROBABLY SELFISH TO WANT TO.
THE SHISHI ARE ALL JUST POWER-HUNGRY HYPOCRITES ANYWAY. AFTER ALL THAT TALK ABOUT "EX-PELLING THE BARBARIANS," THEY WESTERNIZED JAPAN IN UNDER A DECADE.
MIRAI...
MAYBE IT'LL BE BETTER IF THINGS STAY THE WAY THEY ARE.

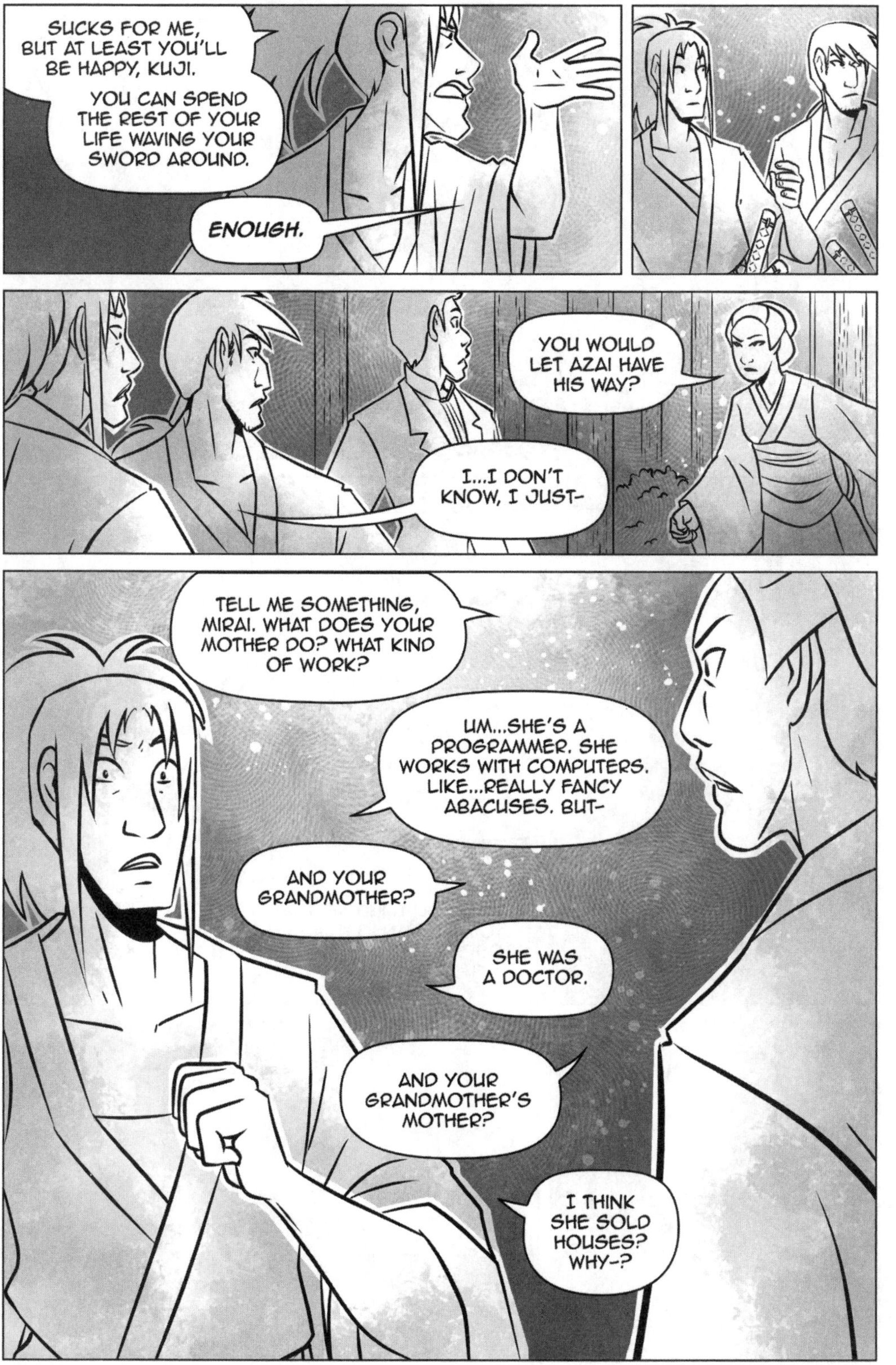
SUCKS FOR ME, BUT AT LEAST YOU'LL BE HAPPY, KUJI.
YOU CAN SPEND THE REST OF YOUR LIFE WAVING YOUR SWORD AROUND.
ENOUGH.
YOU WOULD LET AZAI HAVE HIS WAY?
I...I DON'T KNOW, I JUST-
TELL ME SOMETHING, MIRAI. WHAT DOES YOUR MOTHER DO? WHAT KIND OF WORK?
UM...SHE'S A PROGRAMMER. SHE WORKS WITH COMPUTERS. LIKE...REALLY FANCY ABACUSES. BUT-
AND YOUR GRANDMOTHER?
SHE WAS A DOCTOR.
AND YOUR GRANDMOTHER'S MOTHER?
I THINK SHE SOLD HOUSES? WHY-?

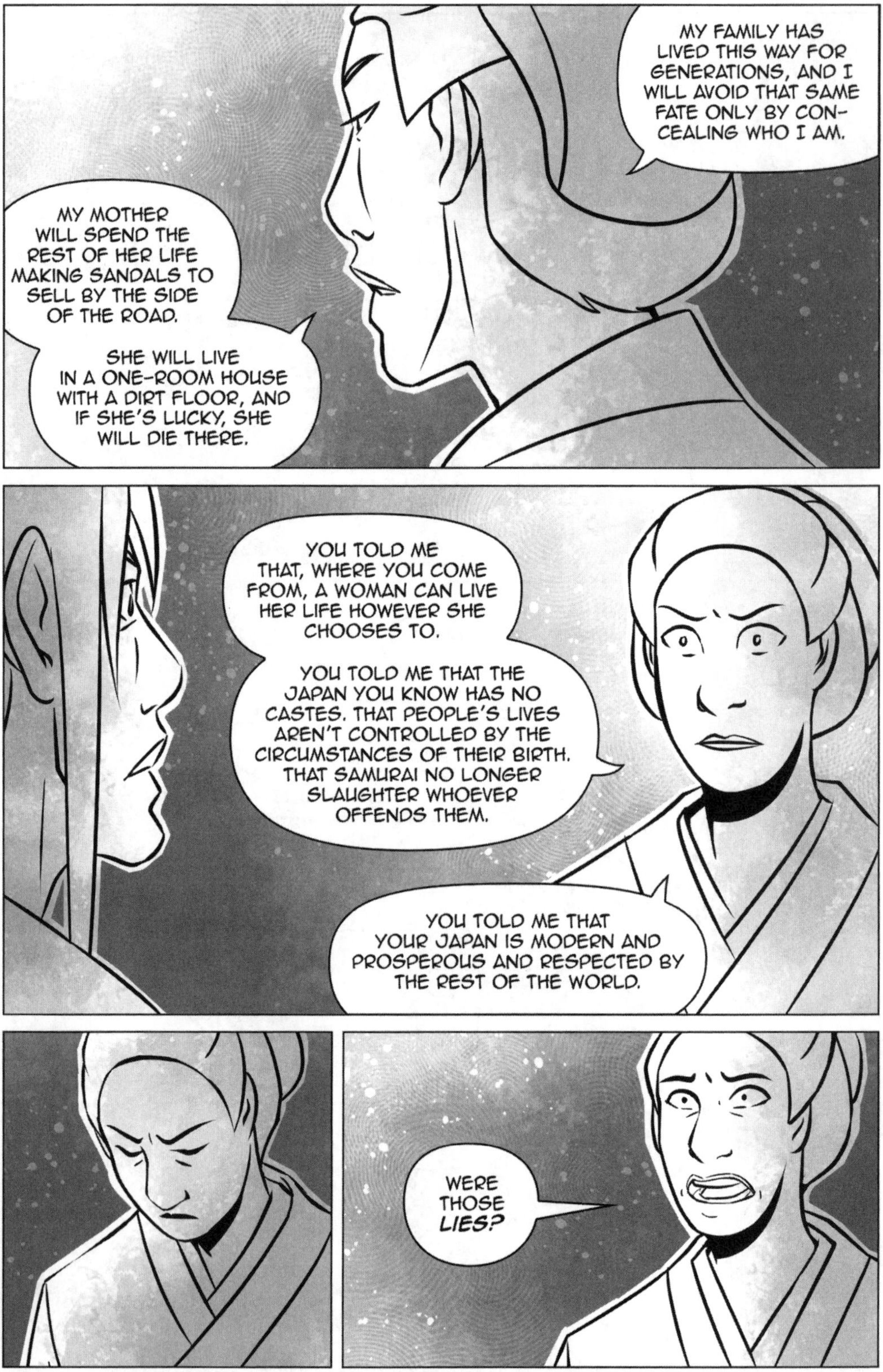
MY MOTHER WILL SPEND THE REST OF HER LIFE MAKING SANDALS TO SELL BY THE SIDE OF THE ROAD.
SHE WILL LIVE IN A ONE-ROOM HOUSE WITH A DIRT FLOOR, AND IF SHE'S LUCKY, SHE WILL DIE THERE.
MY FAMILY HAS LIVED THIS WAY FOR GENERATIONS, AND I WILL AVOID THAT SAME FATE ONLY BY CONCEALING WHO I AM.
YOU TOLD ME THAT, WHERE YOU COME FROM, A WOMAN CAN LIVE HER LIFE HOWEVER SHE CHOOSES TO.
YOU TOLD ME THAT THE JAPAN YOU KNOW HAS NO CASTES. THAT PEOPLE'S LIVES AREN'T CONTROLLED BY THE CIRCUMSTANCES OF THEIR BIRTH. THAT SAMURAI NO LONGER SLAUGHTER WHOEVER OFFENDS THEM.
YOU TOLD ME THAT YOUR JAPAN IS MODERN AND PROSPEROUS AND RESPECTED BY THE REST OF THE WORLD.
WERE THOSE *LIES?*

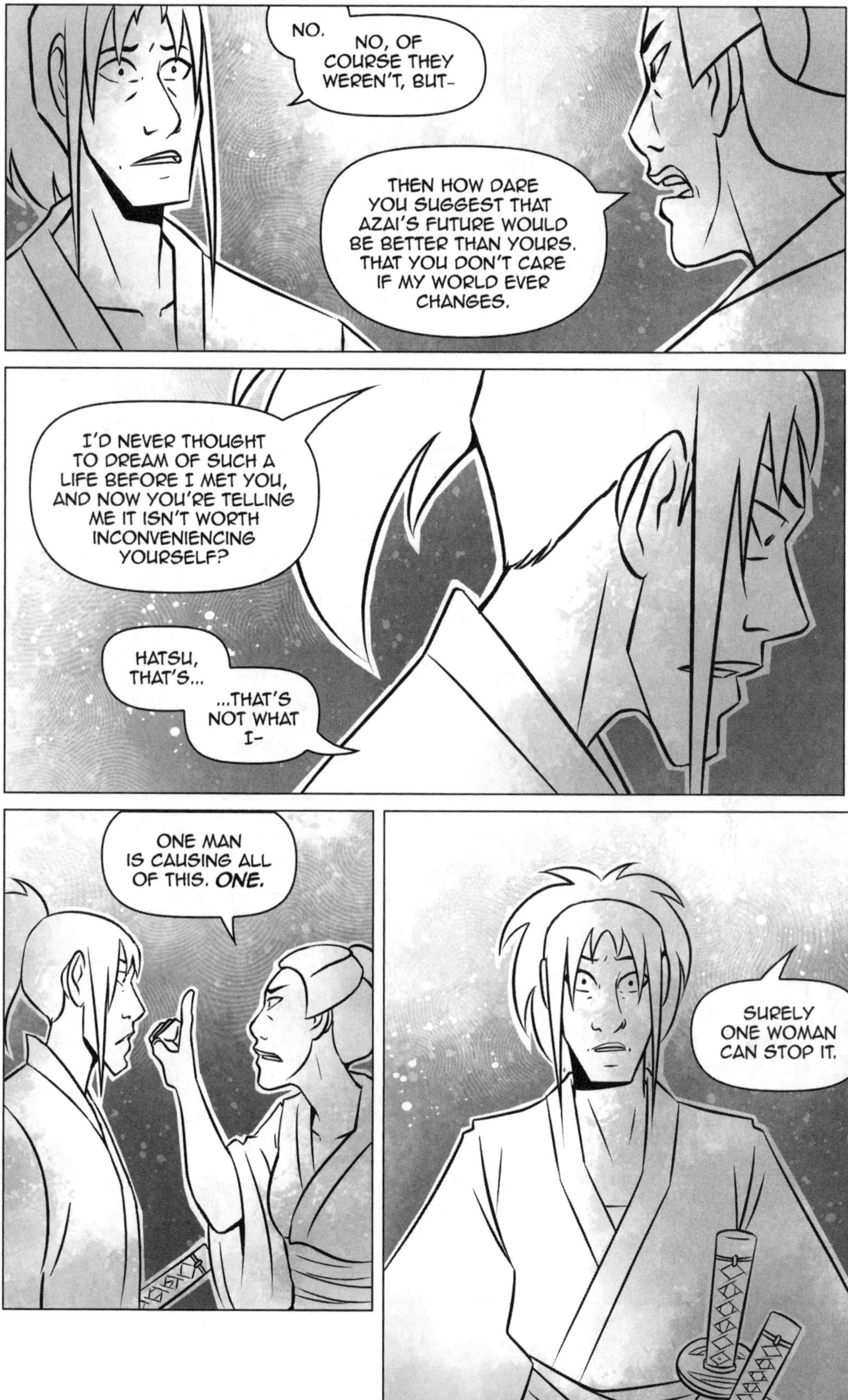
NO.
NO, OF COURSE THEY WEREN'T, BUT-
THEN HOW DARE YOU SUGGEST THAT AZAI'S FUTURE WOULD BE BETTER THAN YOURS. THAT YOU DON'T CARE IF MY WORLD EVER CHANGES.
I'D NEVER THOUGHT TO DREAM OF SUCH A LIFE BEFORE I MET YOU, AND NOW YOU'RE TELLING ME IT ISN'T WORTH INCONVENIENCING YOURSELF?
HATSU, THAT'S...
...THAT'S NOT WHAT I-
ONE MAN IS CAUSING ALL OF THIS. *ONE.*
SURELY ONE WOMAN CAN STOP IT.

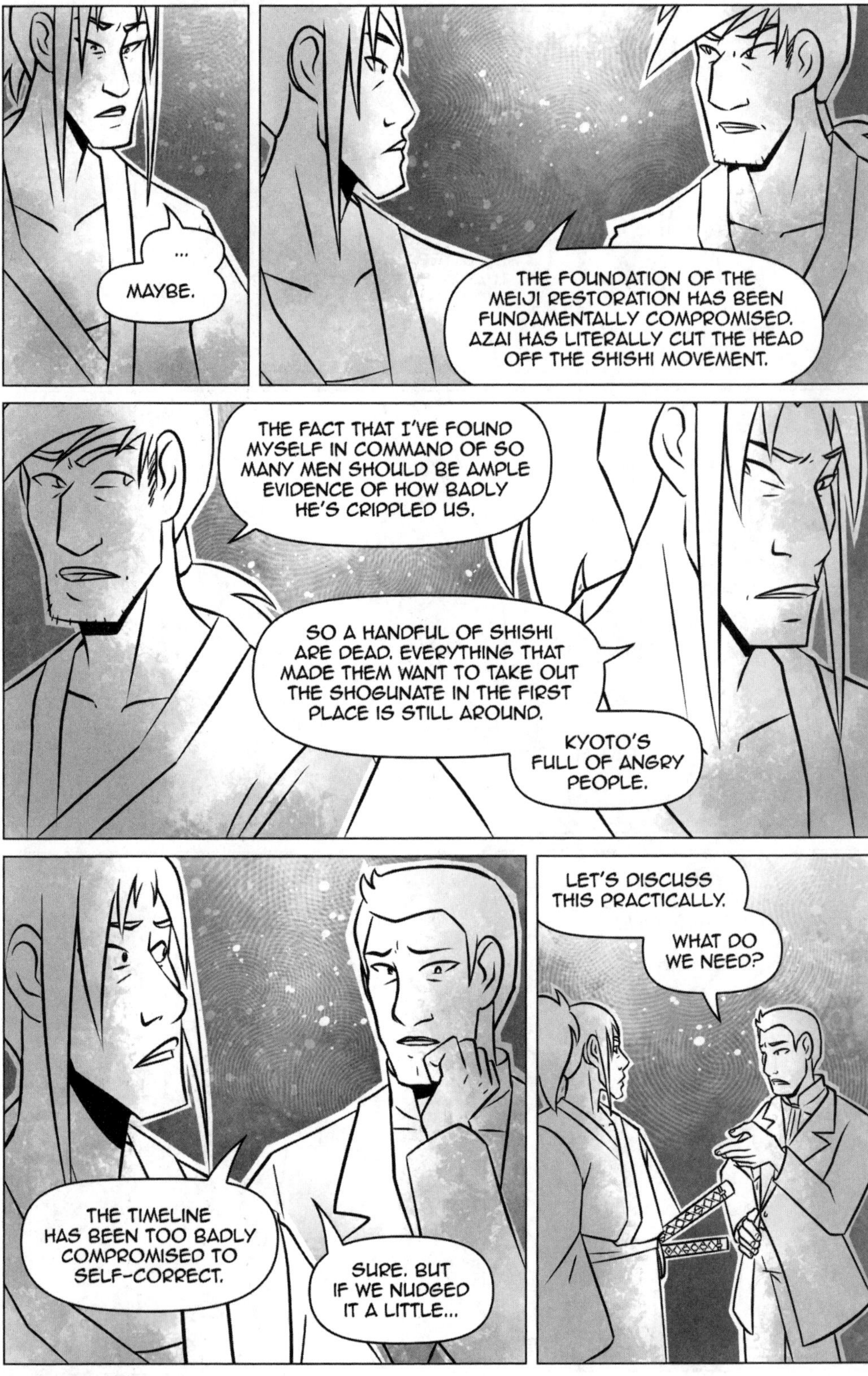
...
MAYBE.
THE FOUNDATION OF THE MEIJI RESTORATION HAS BEEN FUNDAMENTALLY COMPROMISED. AZAI HAS LITERALLY CUT THE HEAD OFF THE SHISHI MOVEMENT.
THE FACT THAT I'VE FOUND MYSELF IN COMMAND OF SO MANY MEN SHOULD BE AMPLE EVIDENCE OF HOW BADLY HE'S CRIPPLED US.
SO A HANDFUL OF SHISHI ARE DEAD. EVERYTHING THAT MADE THEM WANT TO TAKE OUT THE SHOGUNATE IN THE FIRST PLACE IS STILL AROUND.
KYOTO'S FULL OF ANGRY PEOPLE.
THE TIMELINE HAS BEEN TOO BADLY COMPROMISED TO SELF-CORRECT.
SURE. BUT IF WE NUDGED IT A LITTLE...
LET'S DISCUSS THIS PRACTICALLY.
WHAT DO WE NEED?

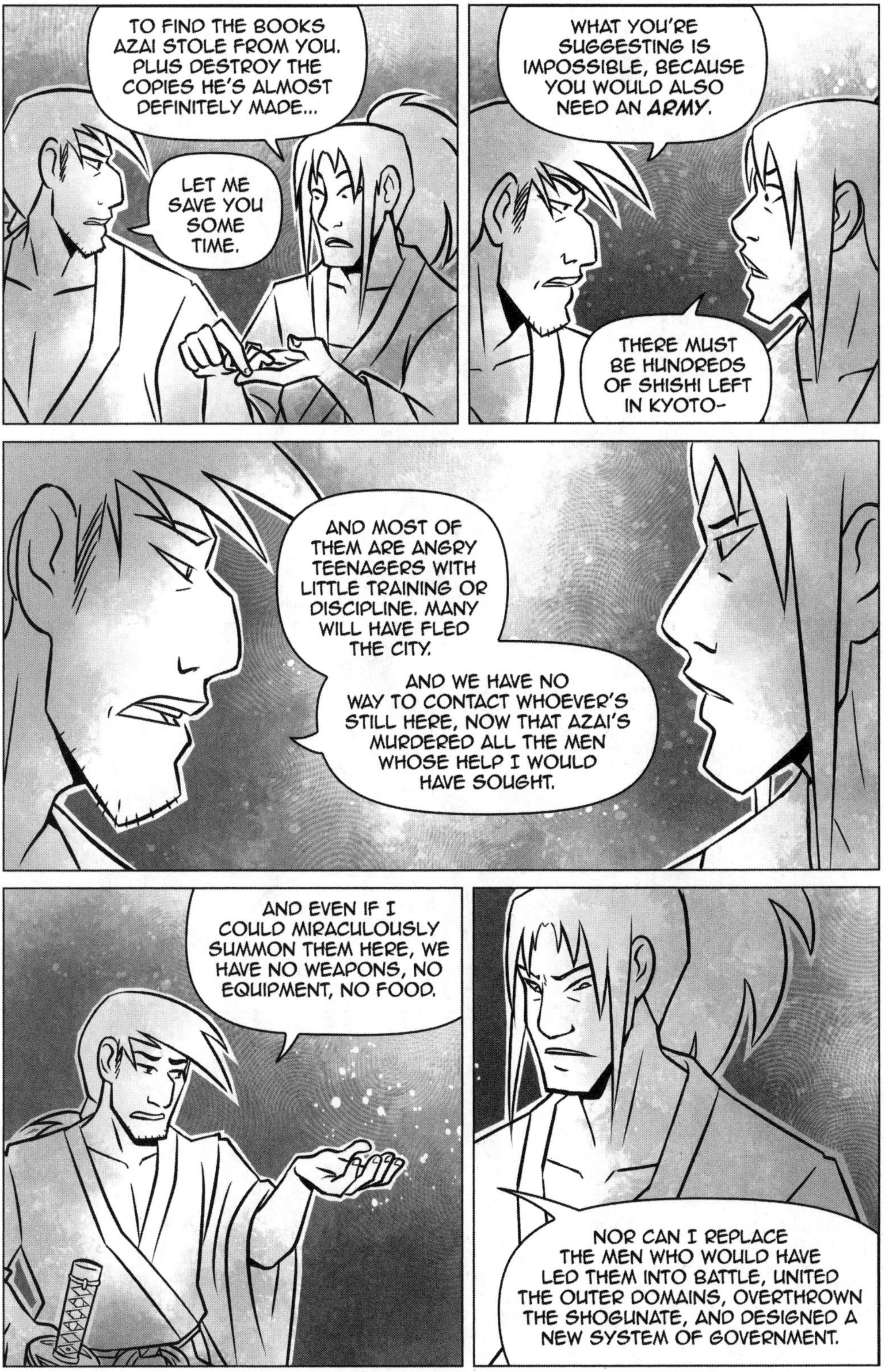
TO FIND THE BOOKS AZAI STOLE FROM YOU. PLUS DESTROY THE COPIES HE'S ALMOST DEFINITELY MADE...
LET ME SAVE YOU SOME TIME.
WHAT YOU'RE SUGGESTING IS IMPOSSIBLE, BECAUSE YOU WOULD ALSO NEED AN *ARMY*.
THERE MUST BE HUNDREDS OF SHISHI LEFT IN KYOTO-
AND MOST OF THEM ARE ANGRY TEENAGERS WITH LITTLE TRAINING OR DISCIPLINE. MANY WILL HAVE FLED THE CITY.
AND WE HAVE NO WAY TO CONTACT WHOEVER'S STILL HERE, NOW THAT AZAI'S MURDERED ALL THE MEN WHOSE HELP I WOULD HAVE SOUGHT.
AND EVEN IF I COULD MIRACULOUSLY SUMMON THEM HERE, WE HAVE NO WEAPONS, NO EQUIPMENT, NO FOOD.
NOR CAN I REPLACE THE MEN WHO WOULD HAVE LED THEM INTO BATTLE, UNITED THE OUTER DOMAINS, OVERTHROWN THE SHOGUNATE, AND DESIGNED A NEW SYSTEM OF GOVERNMENT.

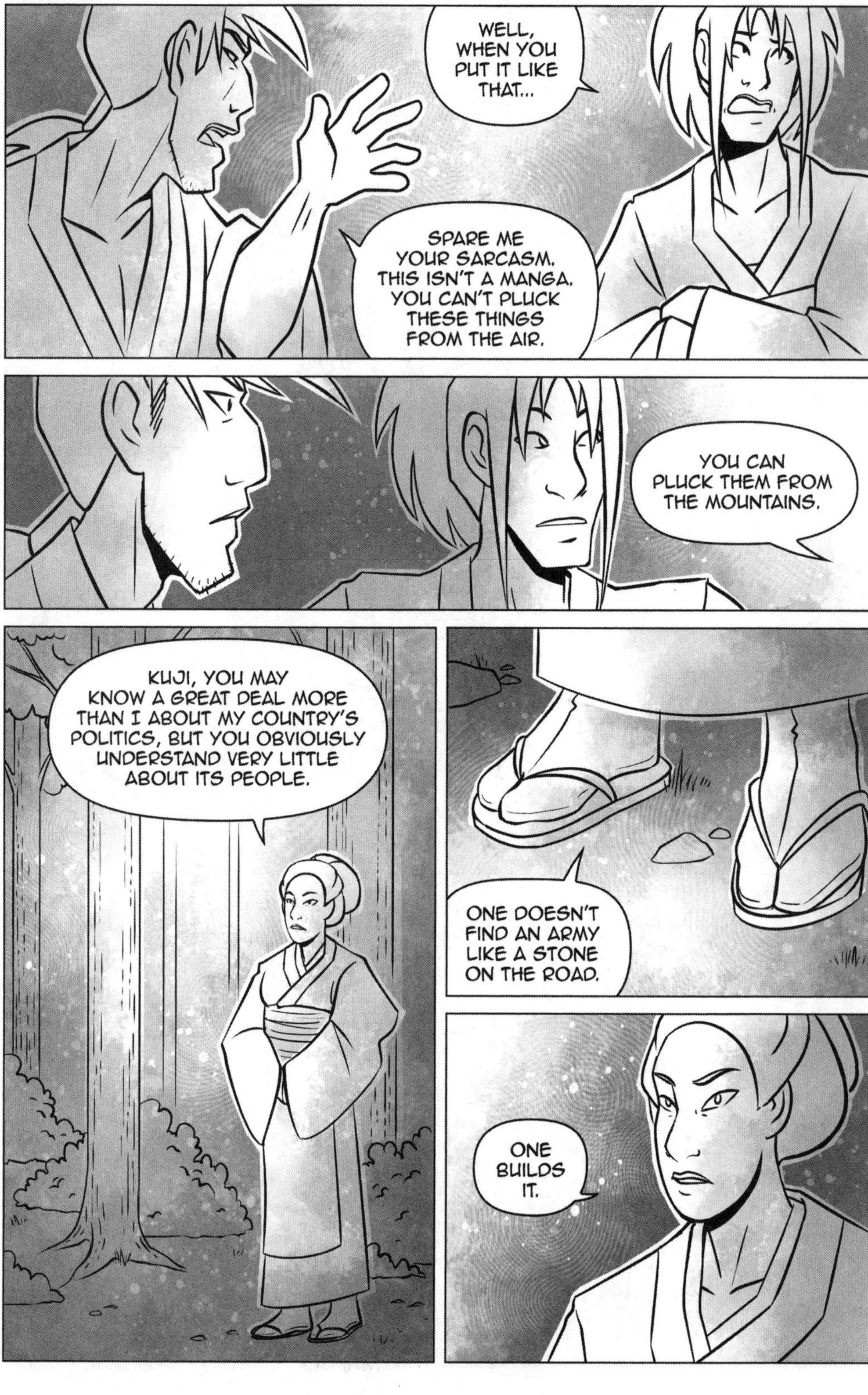
WELL, WHEN YOU PUT IT LIKE THAT...
SPARE ME YOUR SARCASM. THIS ISN'T A MANGA. YOU CAN'T PLUCK THESE THINGS FROM THE AIR.
YOU CAN PLUCK THEM FROM THE MOUNTAINS.
KUJI, YOU MAY KNOW A GREAT DEAL MORE THAN I ABOUT MY COUNTRY'S POLITICS, BUT YOU OBVIOUSLY UNDERSTAND VERY LITTLE ABOUT ITS PEOPLE.
ONE DOESN'T FIND AN ARMY LIKE A STONE ON THE ROAD.
ONE BUILDS IT.

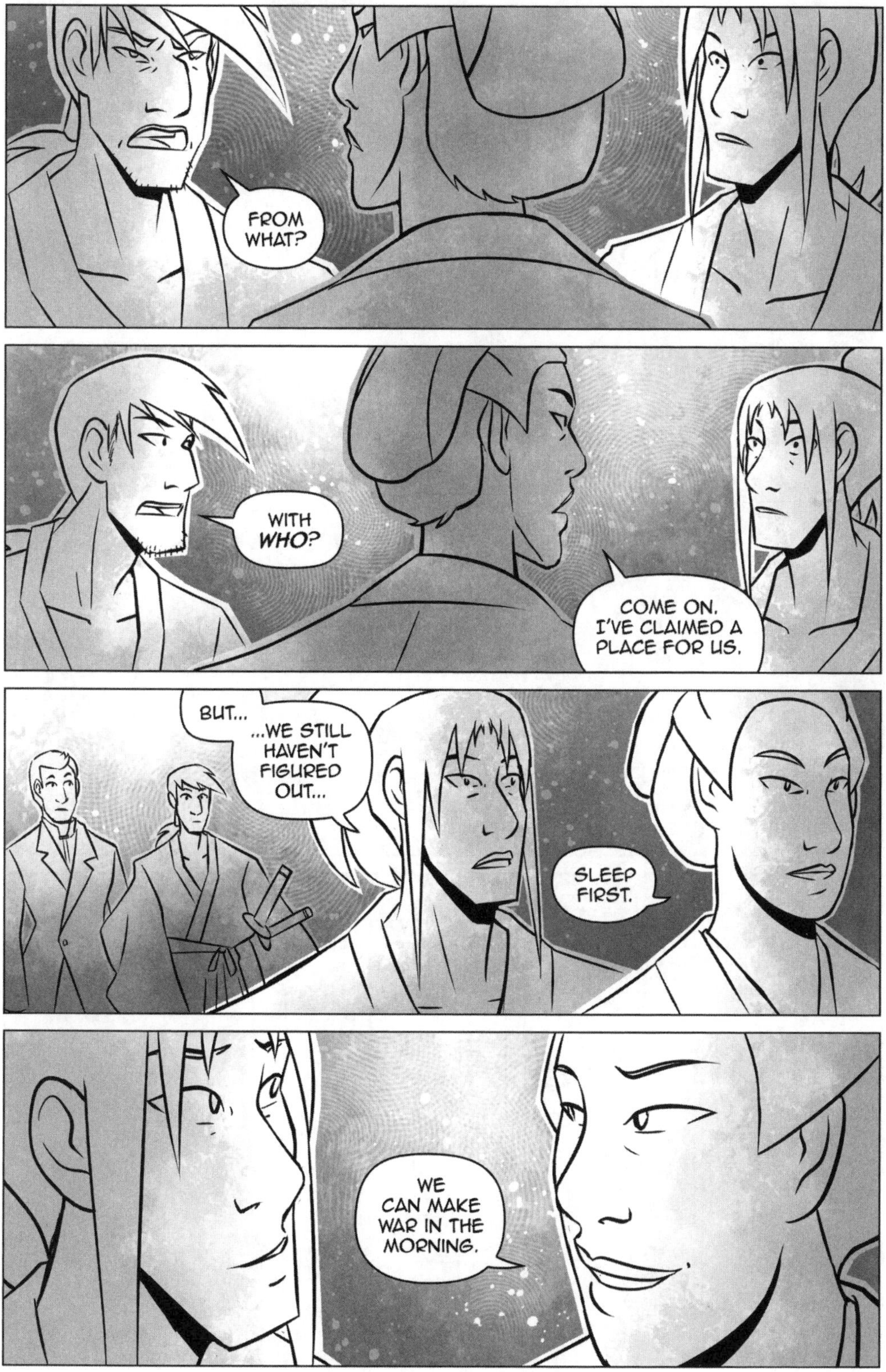
FROM WHAT?
WITH WHO?
COME ON. I'VE CLAIMED A PLACE FOR US.
BUT...
...WE STILL HAVEN'T FIGURED OUT...
SLEEP FIRST.
WE CAN MAKE WAR IN THE MORNING.

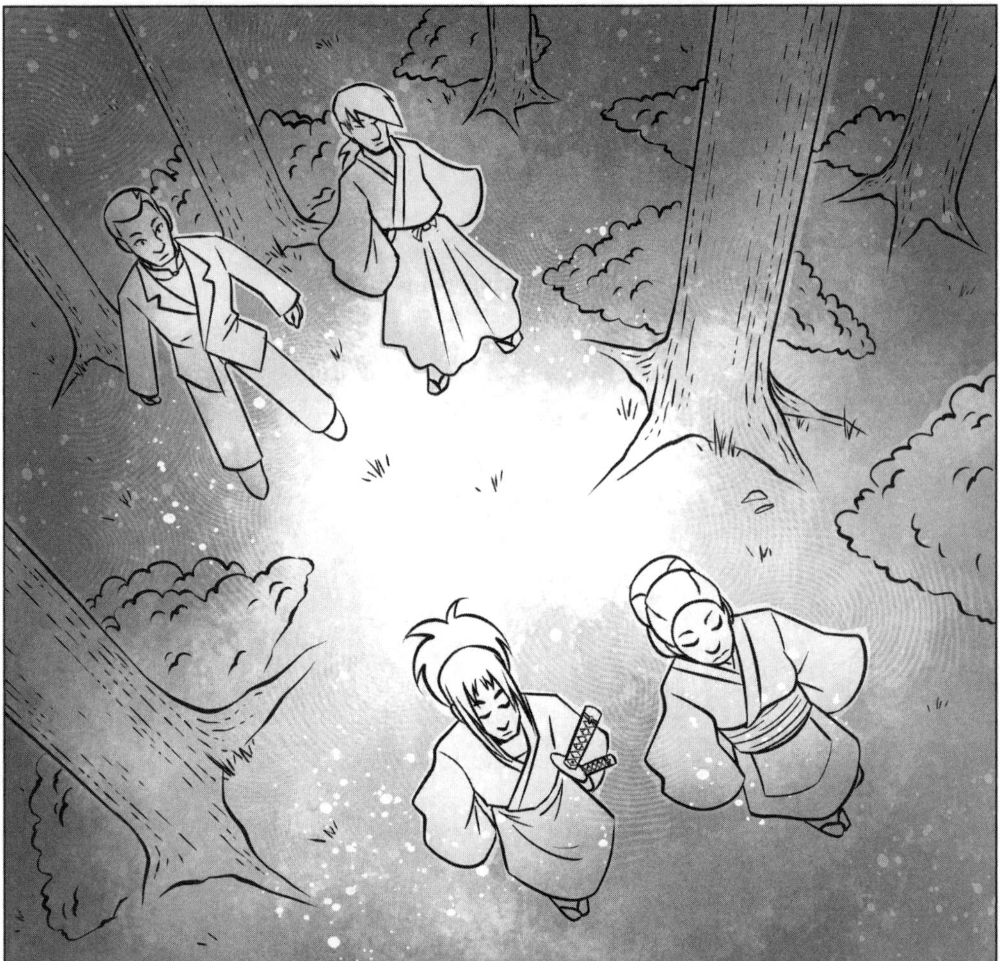

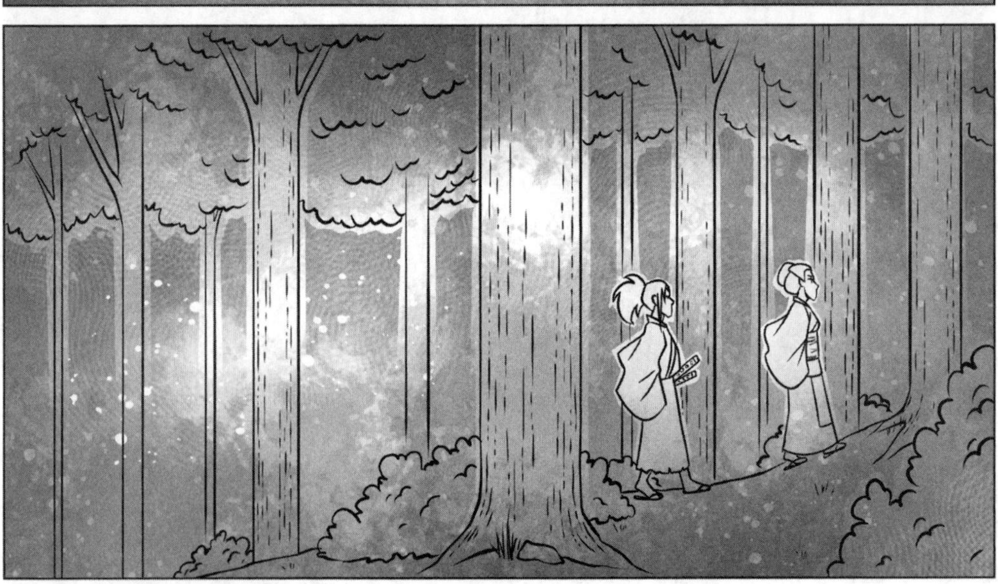

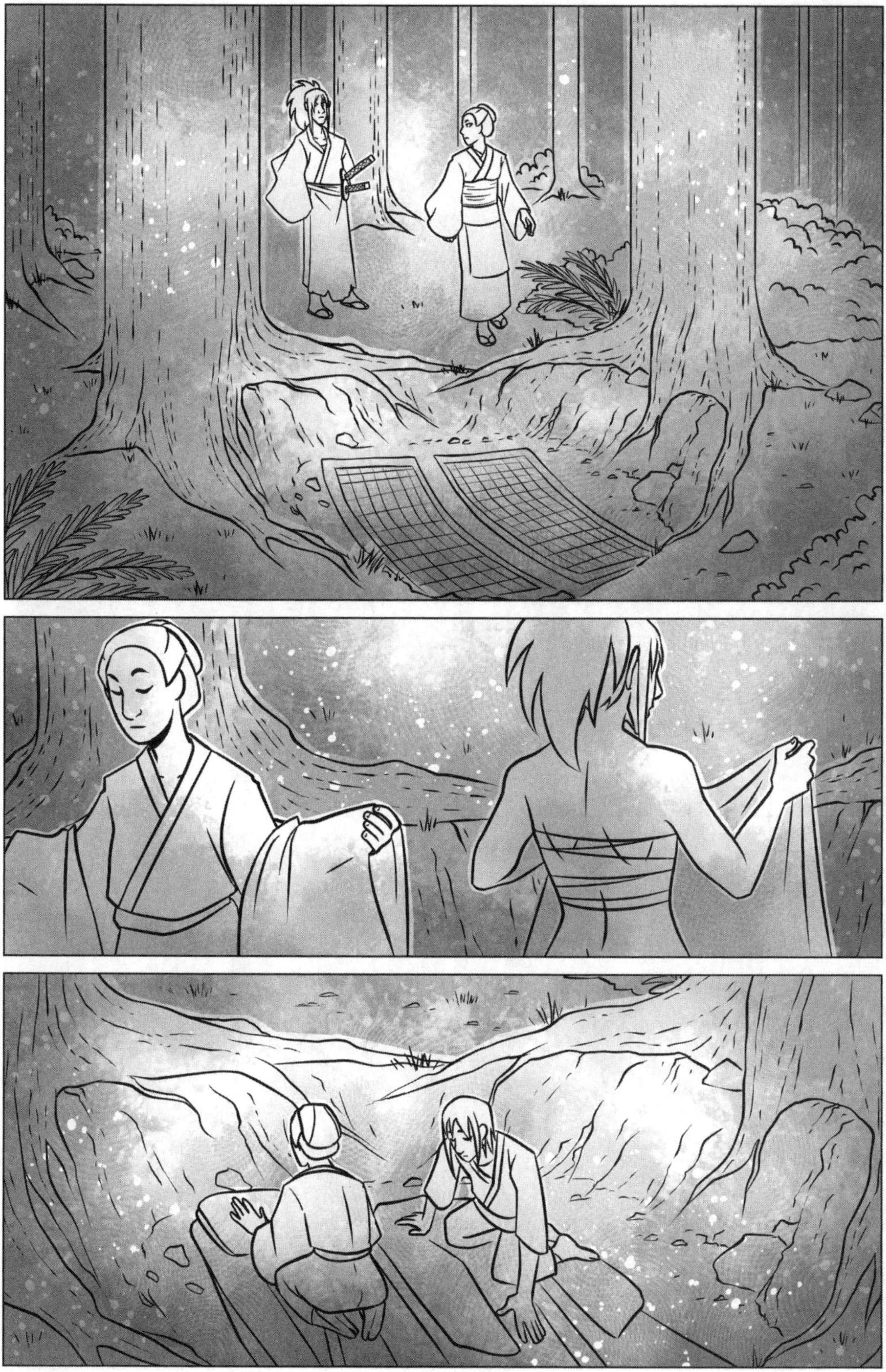

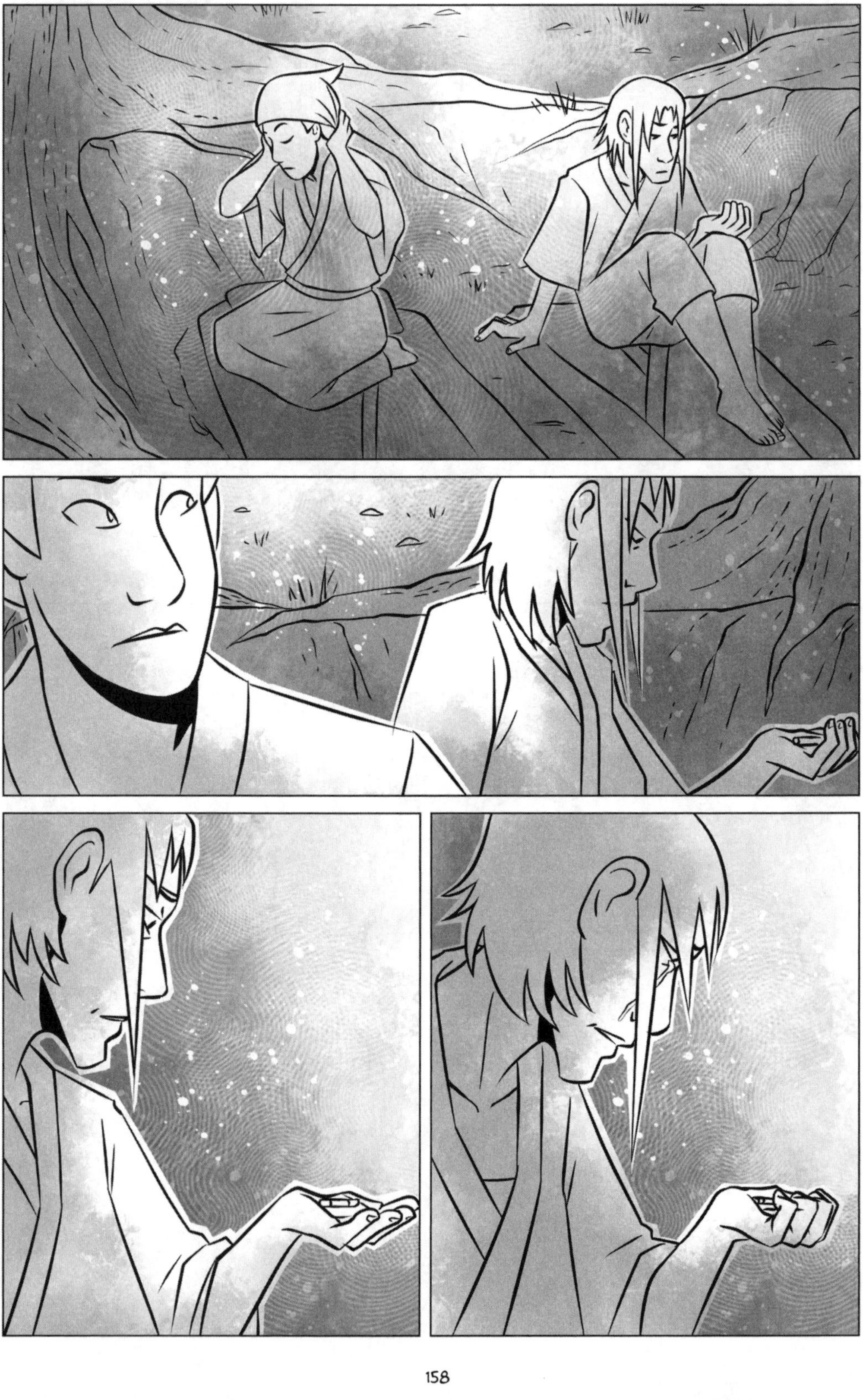

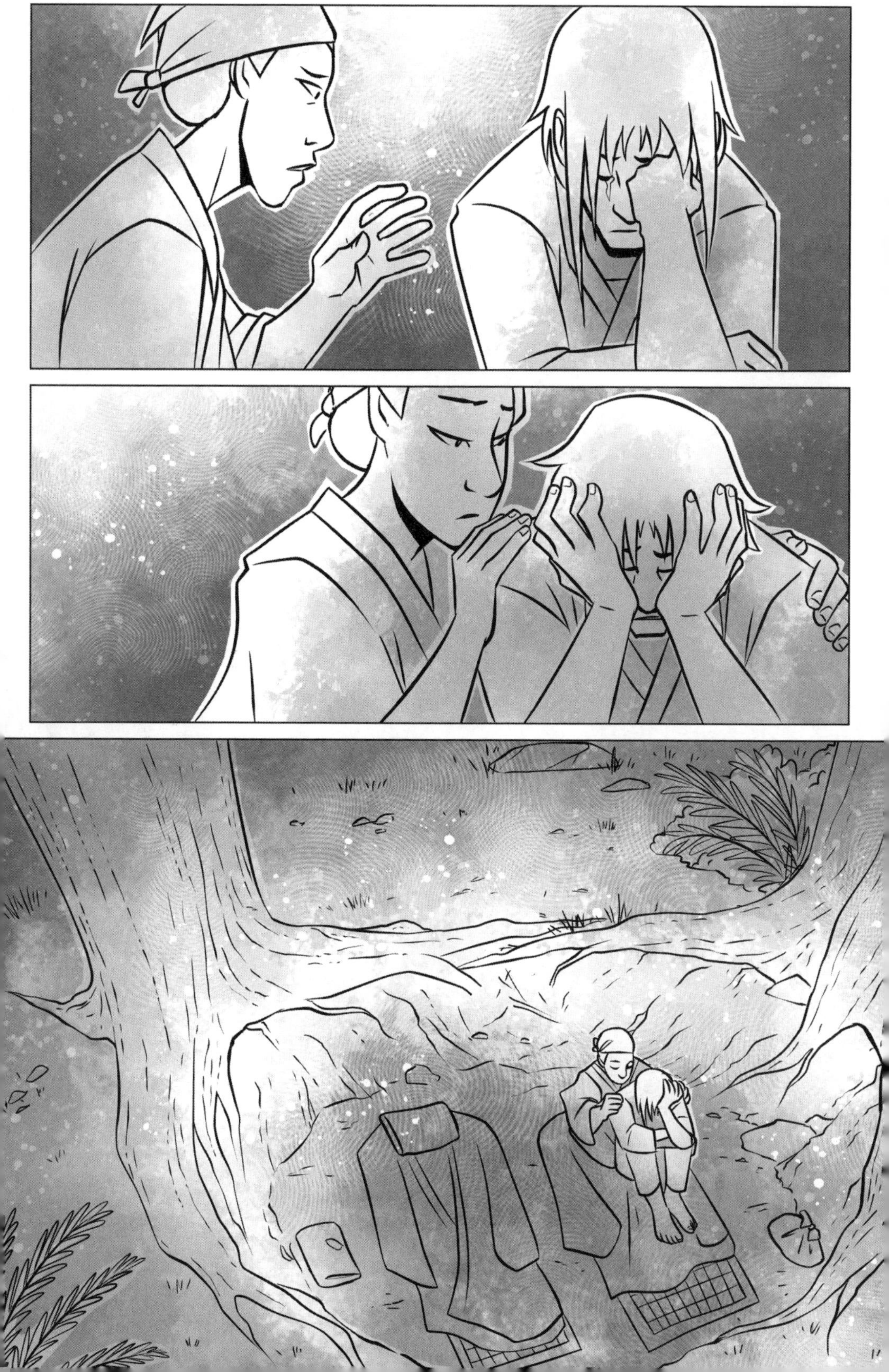

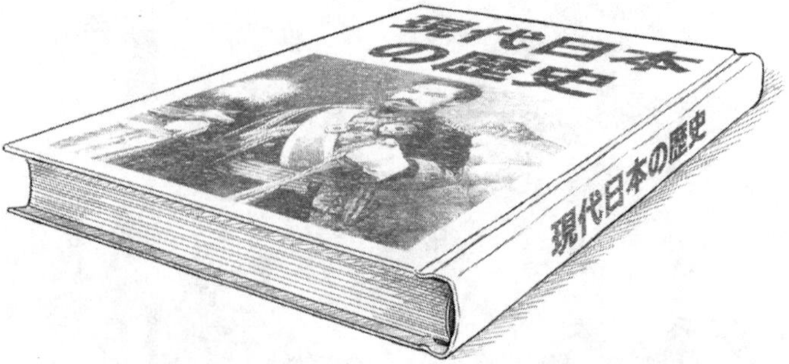
現代日本の歴史
現代日本の歴史

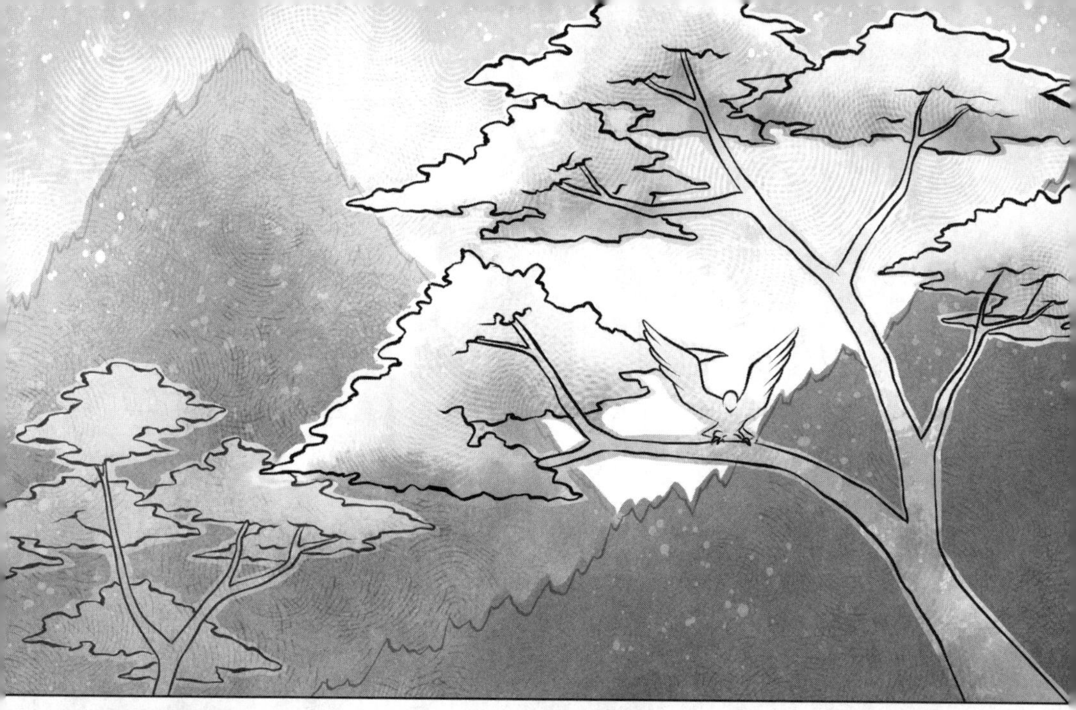
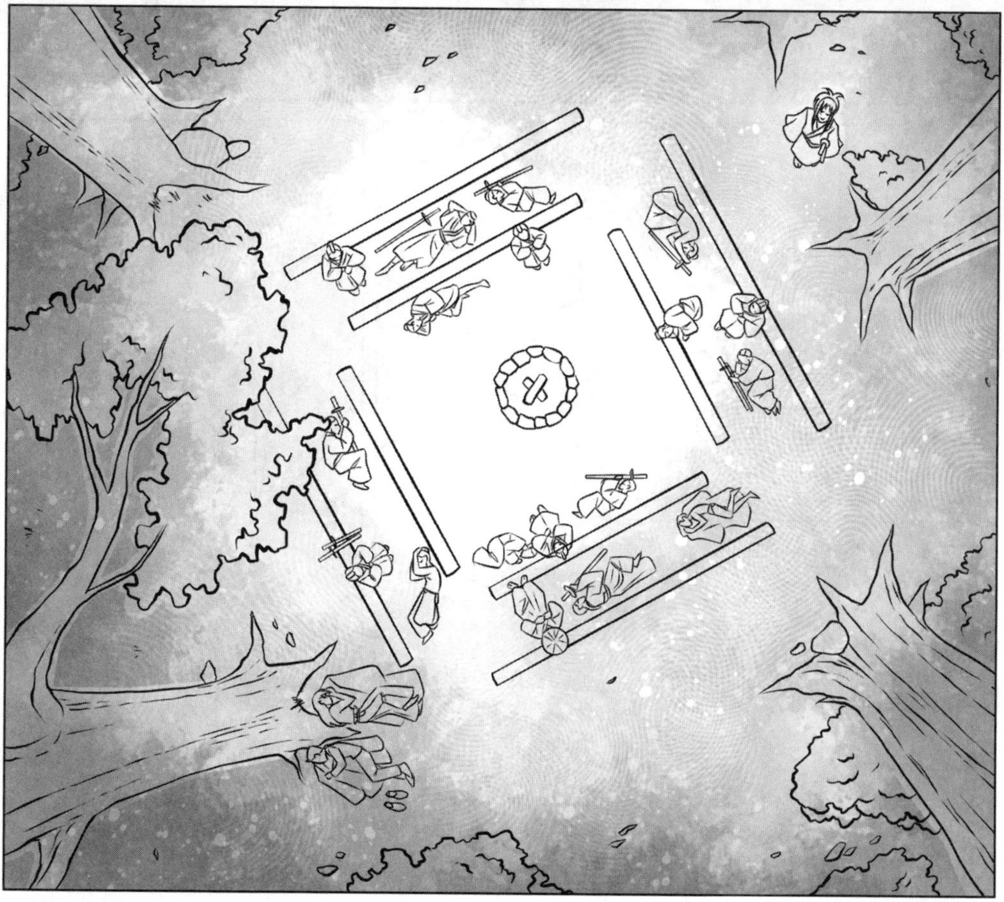

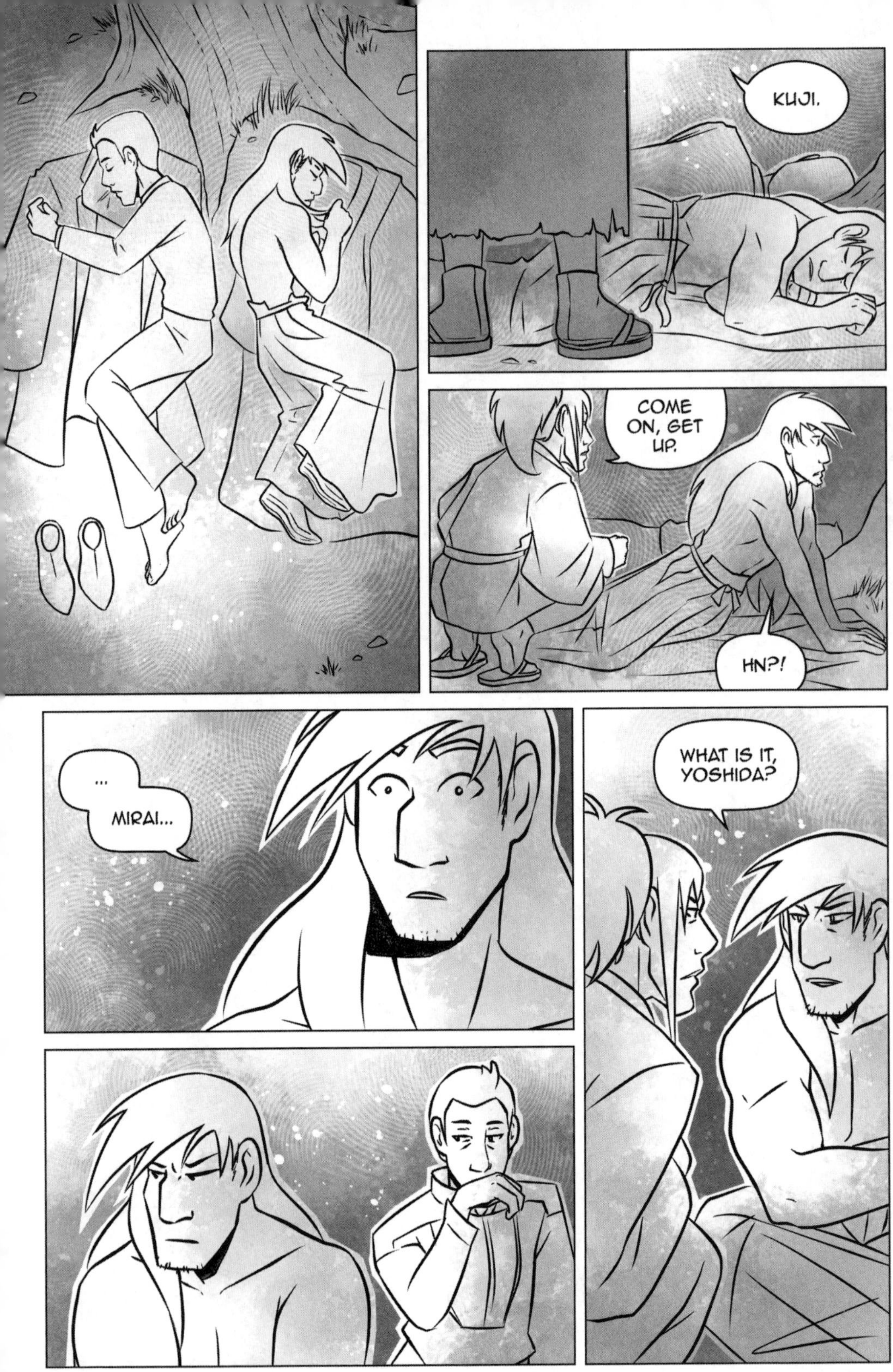
KUJI.
COME ON, GET UP.
HN?!
... MIRAI...
WHAT IS IT, YOSHIDA?

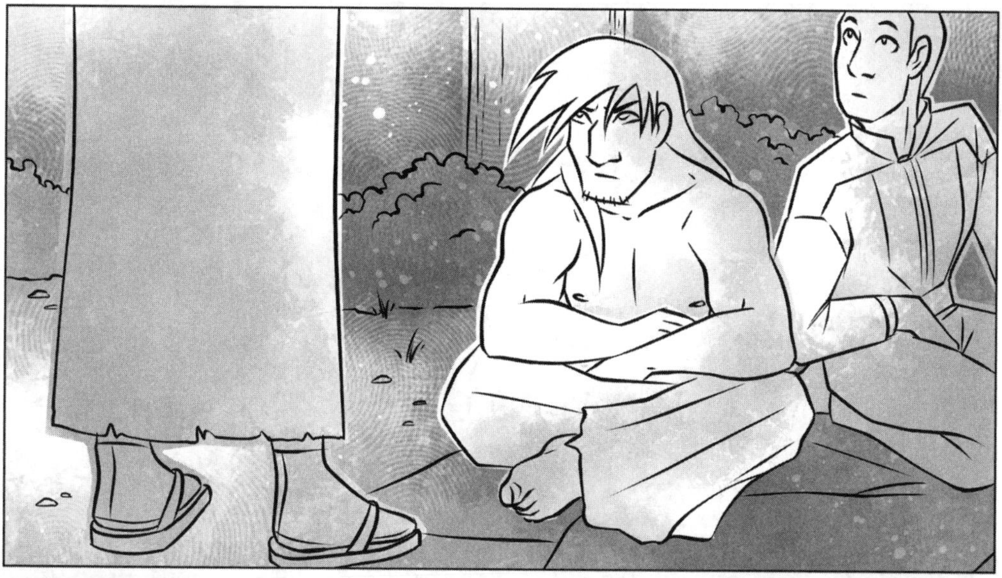

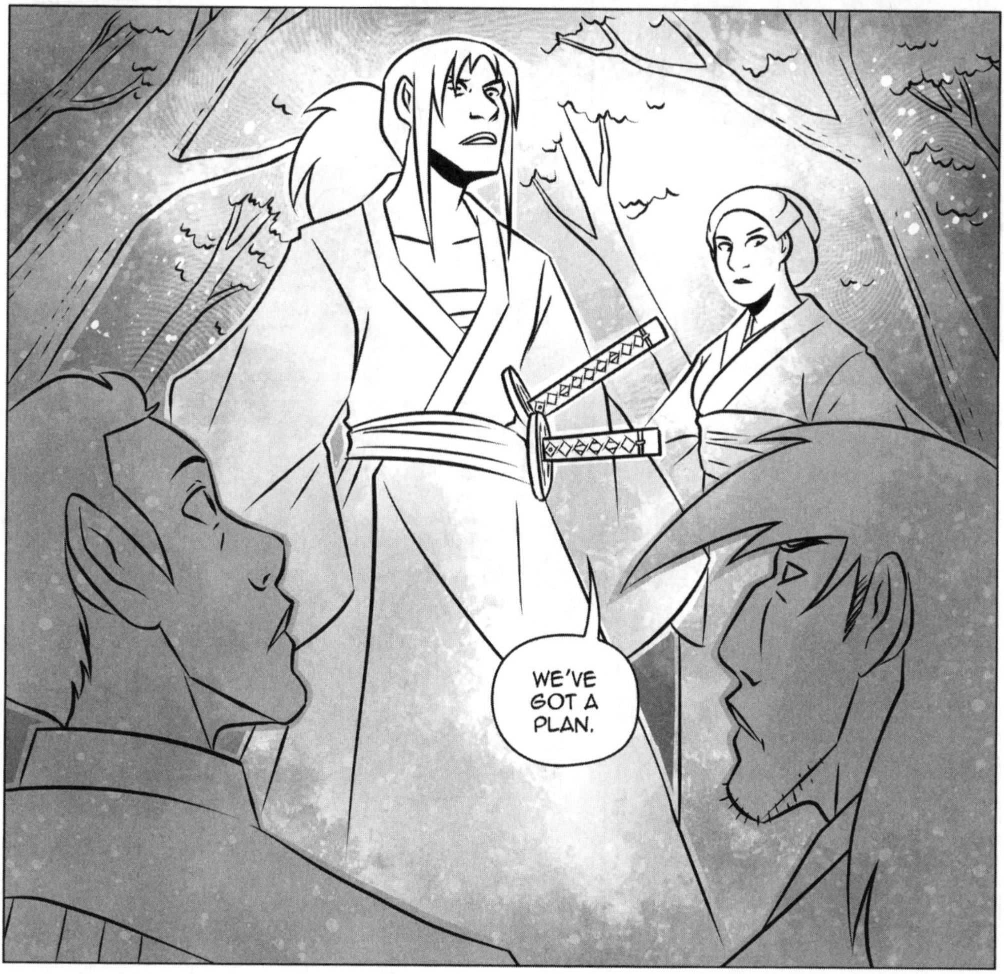
WE'VE GOT A PLAN.

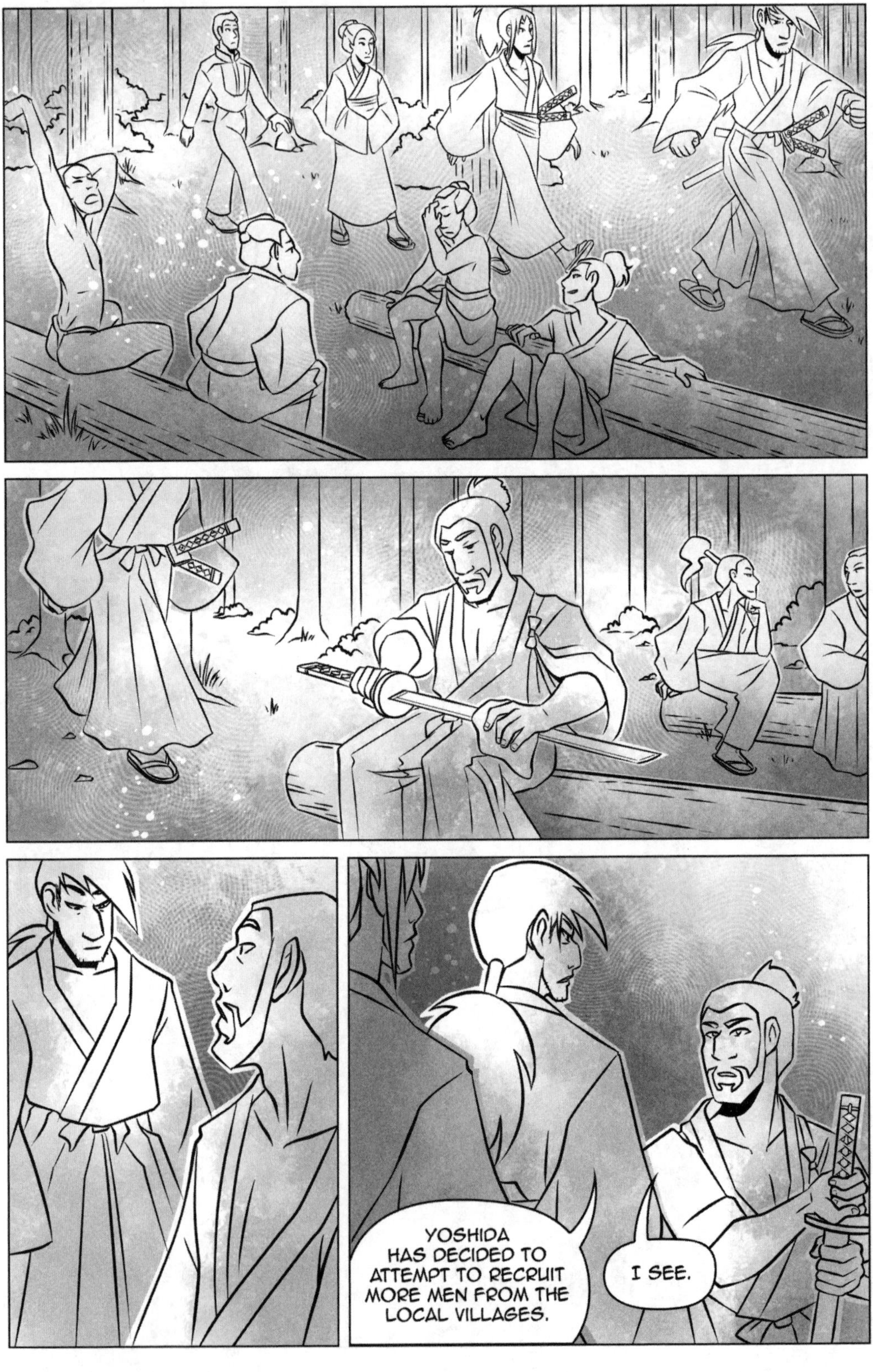
YOSHIDA HAS DECIDED TO ATTEMPT TO RECRUIT MORE MEN FROM THE LOCAL VILLAGES.
I SEE.

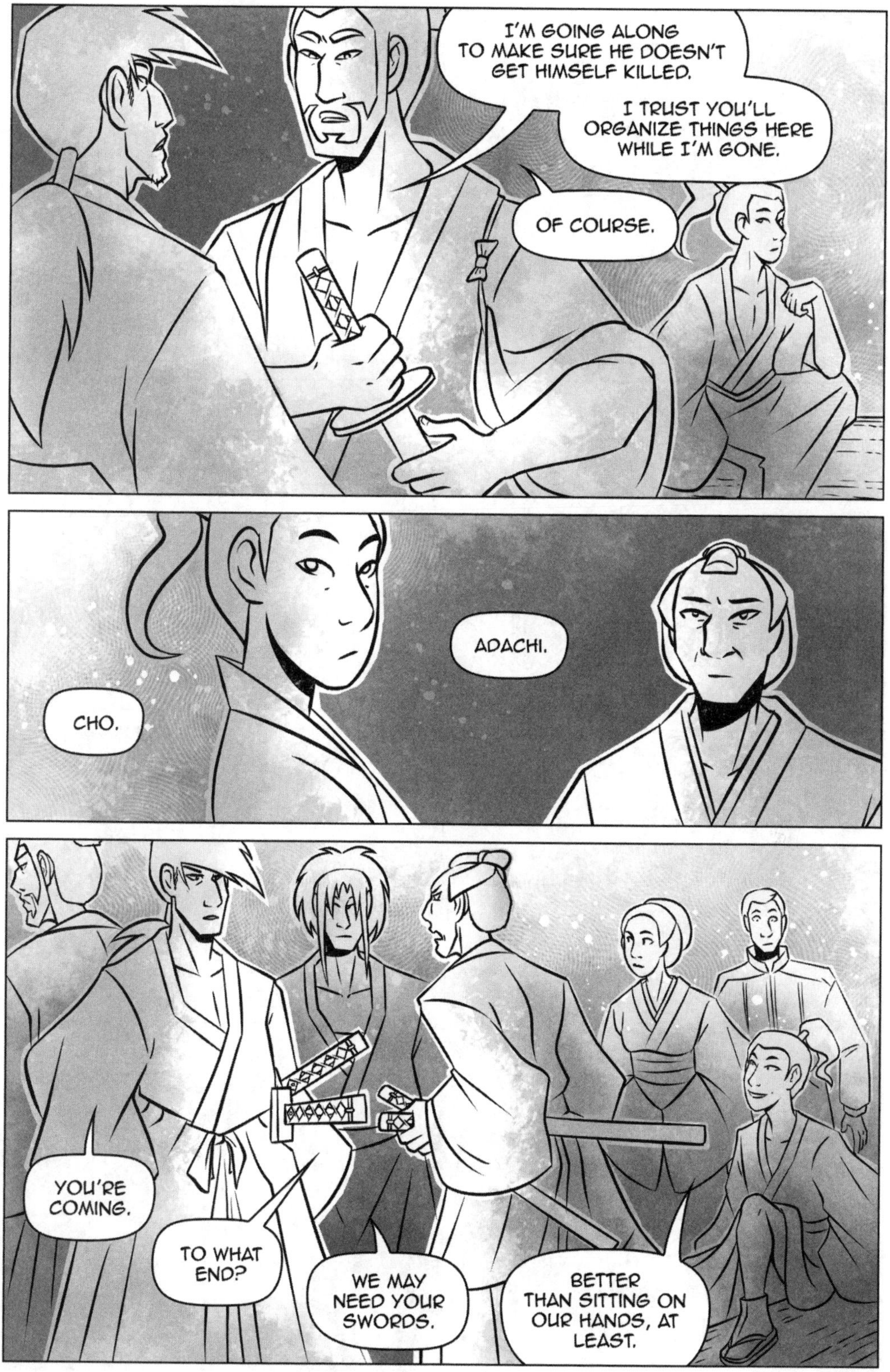
I'M GOING ALONG TO MAKE SURE HE DOESN'T GET HIMSELF KILLED.
I TRUST YOU'LL ORGANIZE THINGS HERE WHILE I'M GONE.
OF COURSE.
ADACHI.
CHO.
YOU'RE COMING.
TO WHAT END?
WE MAY NEED YOUR SWORDS.
BETTER THAN SITTING ON OUR HANDS, AT LEAST.

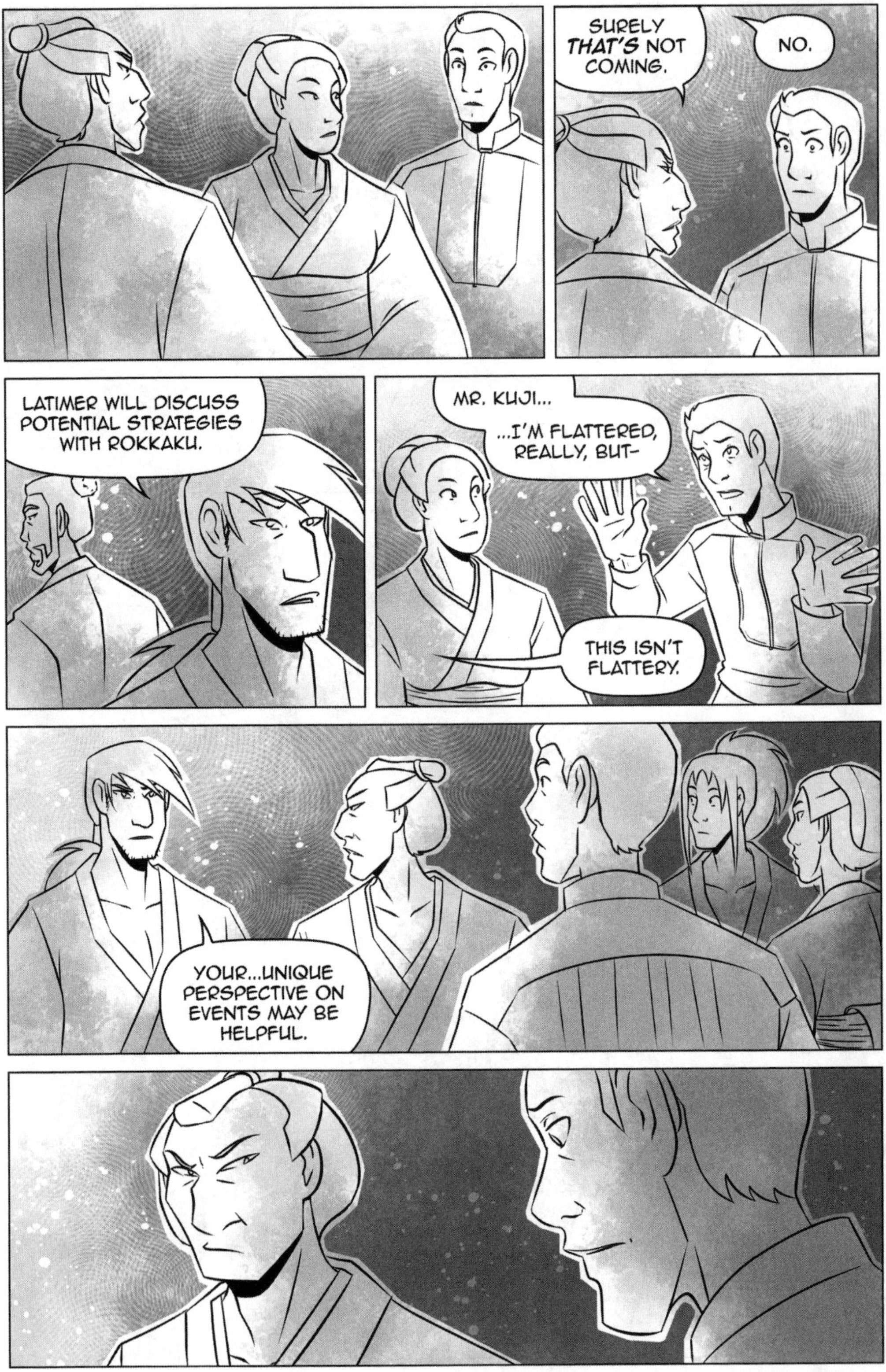
SURELY THAT'S NOT COMING.
NO.
LATIMER WILL DISCUSS POTENTIAL STRATEGIES WITH ROKKAKU.
MR. KUJI...
...I'M FLATTERED, REALLY, BUT-
THIS ISN'T FLATTERY.
YOUR...UNIQUE PERSPECTIVE ON EVENTS MAY BE HELPFUL.

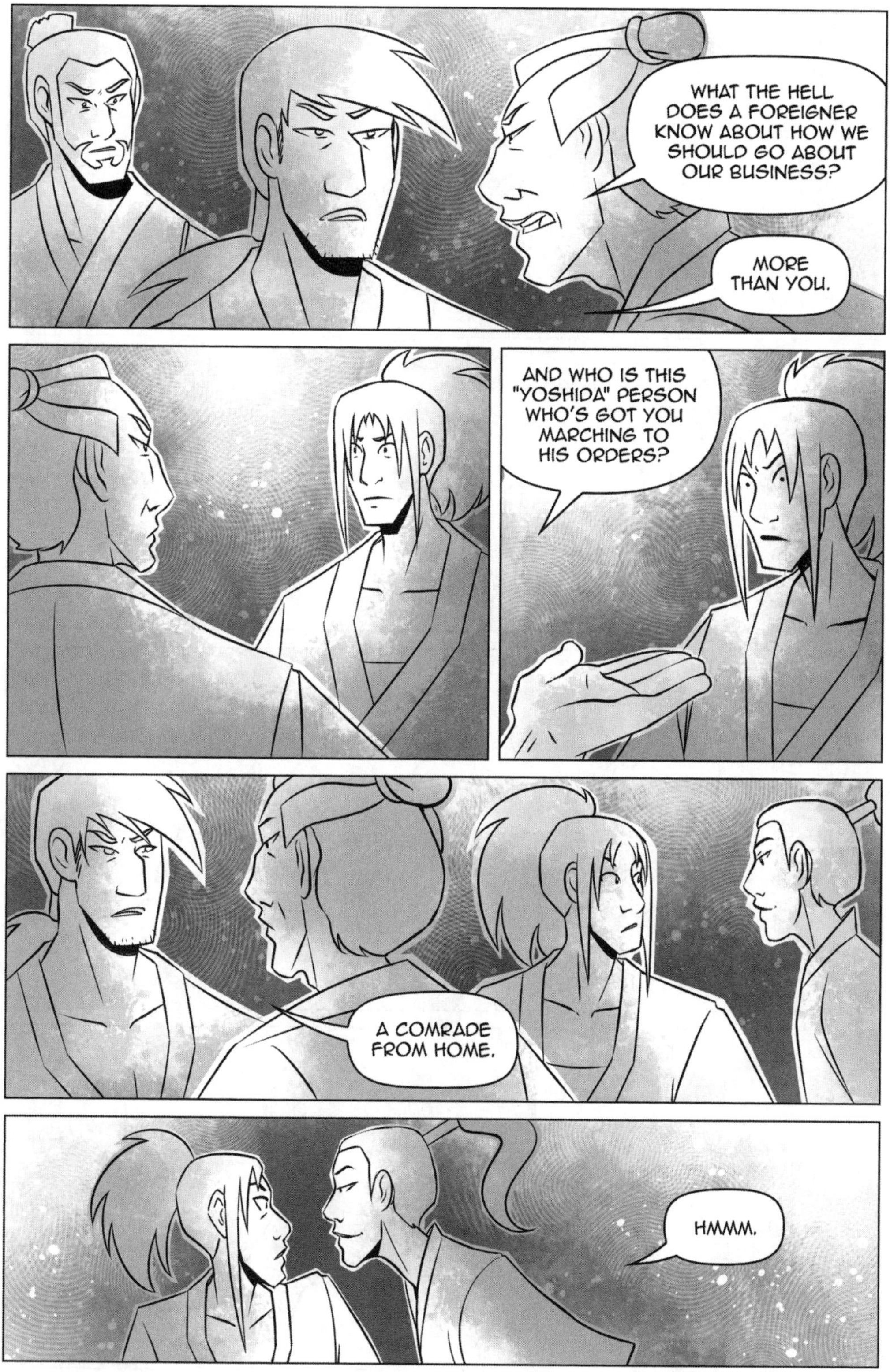
WHAT THE HELL DOES A FOREIGNER KNOW ABOUT HOW WE SHOULD GO ABOUT OUR BUSINESS?
MORE THAN YOU.
AND WHO IS THIS "YOSHIDA" PERSON WHO'S GOT YOU MARCHING TO HIS ORDERS?
A COMRADE FROM HOME.
HMMM.

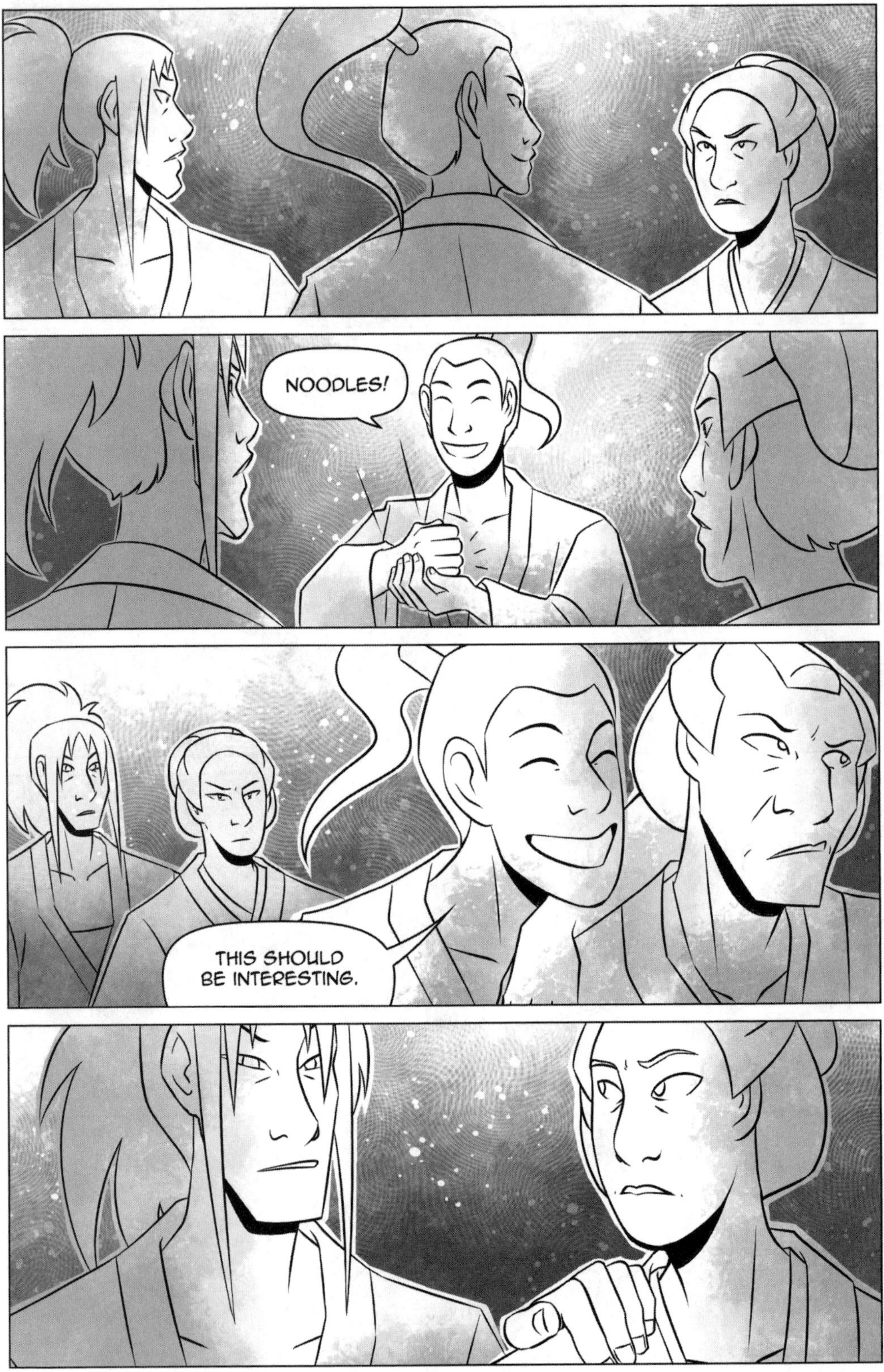
NOODLES!
THIS SHOULD BE INTERESTING.

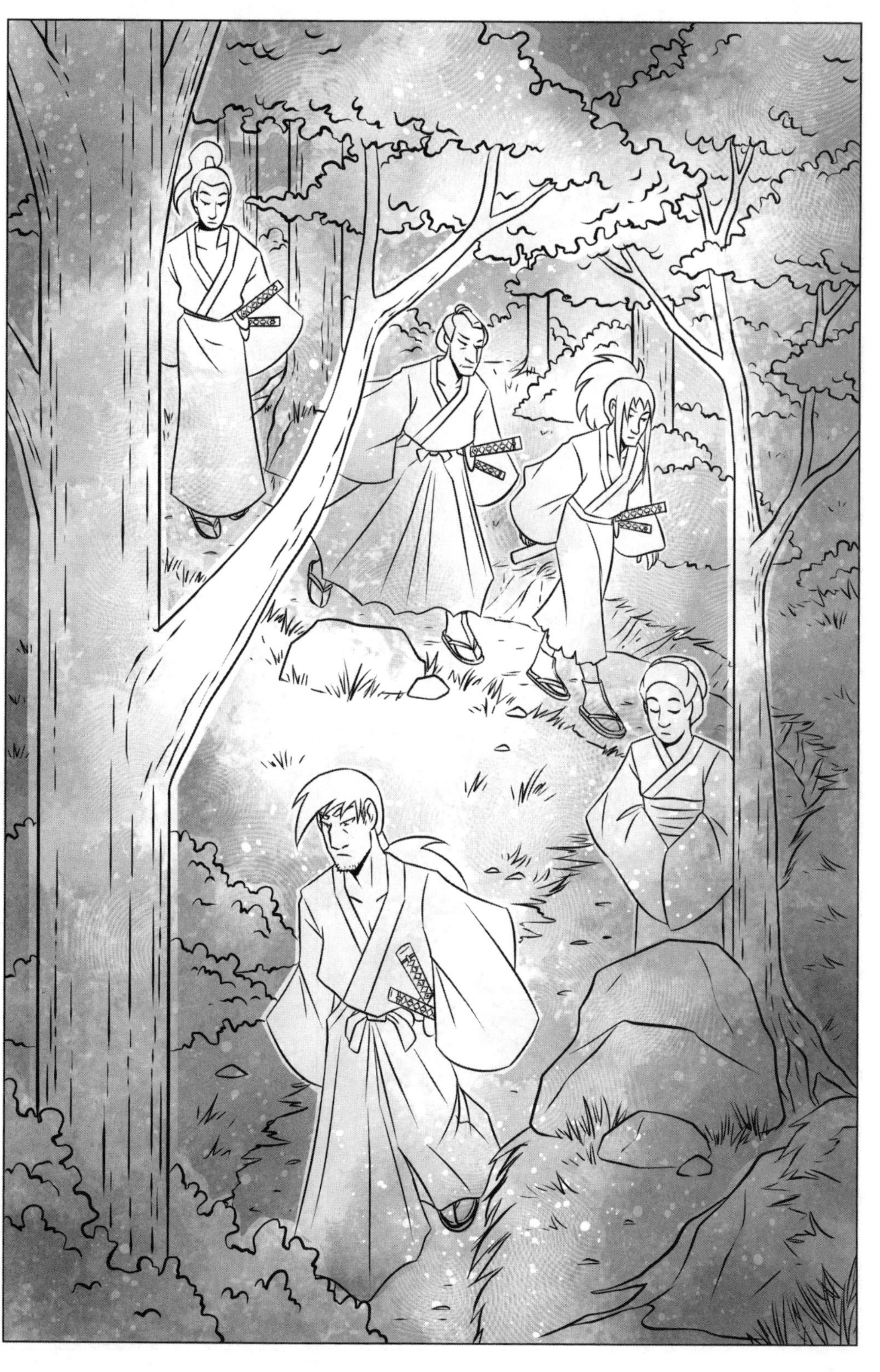

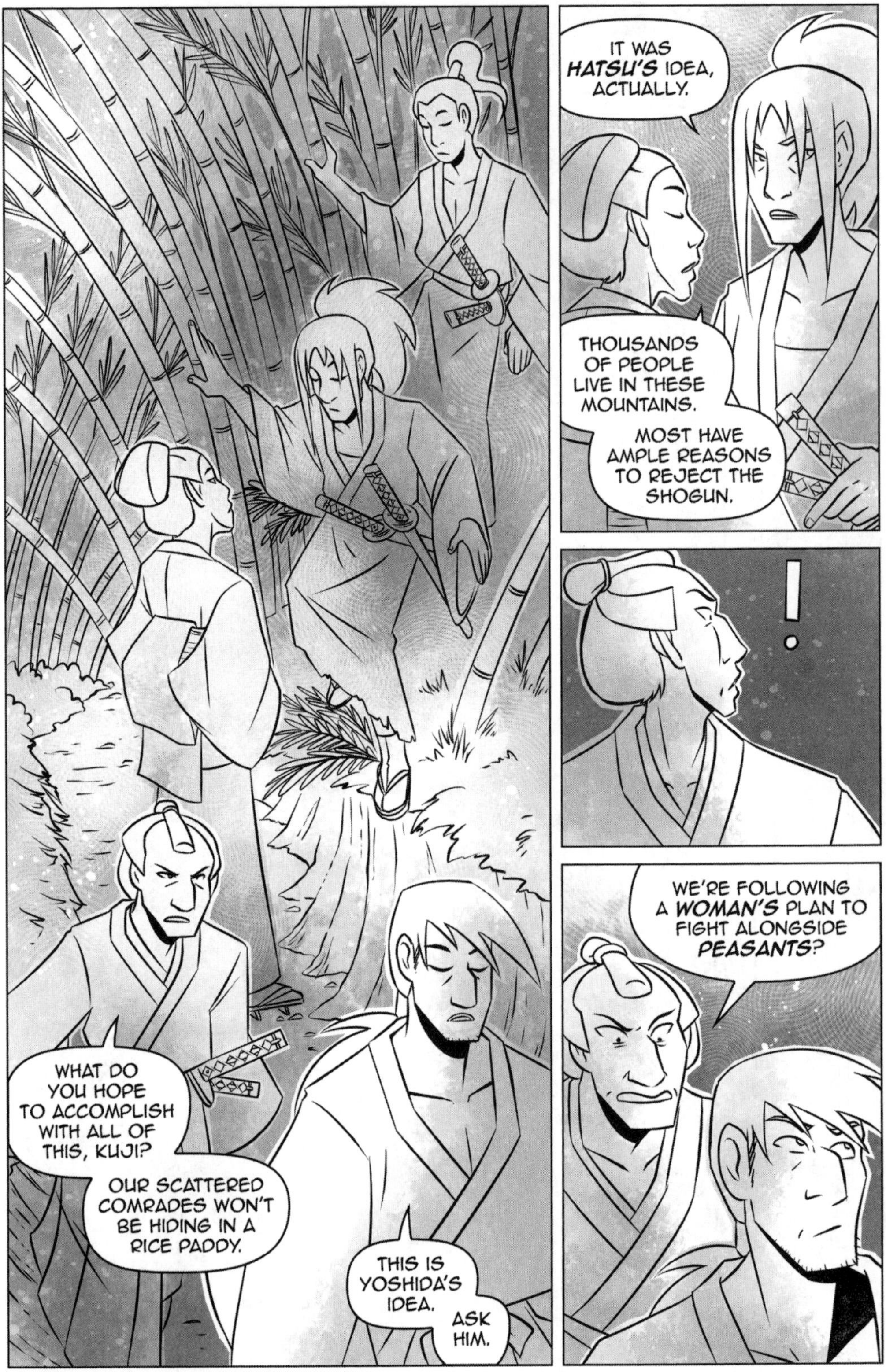
WHAT DO YOU HOPE TO ACCOMPLISH WITH ALL OF THIS, KUJI?
OUR SCATTERED COMRADES WON'T BE HIDING IN A RICE PADDY.
THIS IS YOSHIDA'S IDEA.
ASK HIM.
IT WAS **HATSU'S** IDEA, ACTUALLY.
THOUSANDS OF PEOPLE LIVE IN THESE MOUNTAINS.
MOST HAVE AMPLE REASONS TO REJECT THE SHOGUN.
!
WE'RE FOLLOWING A **WOMAN'S** PLAN TO FIGHT ALONGSIDE **PEASANTS**?

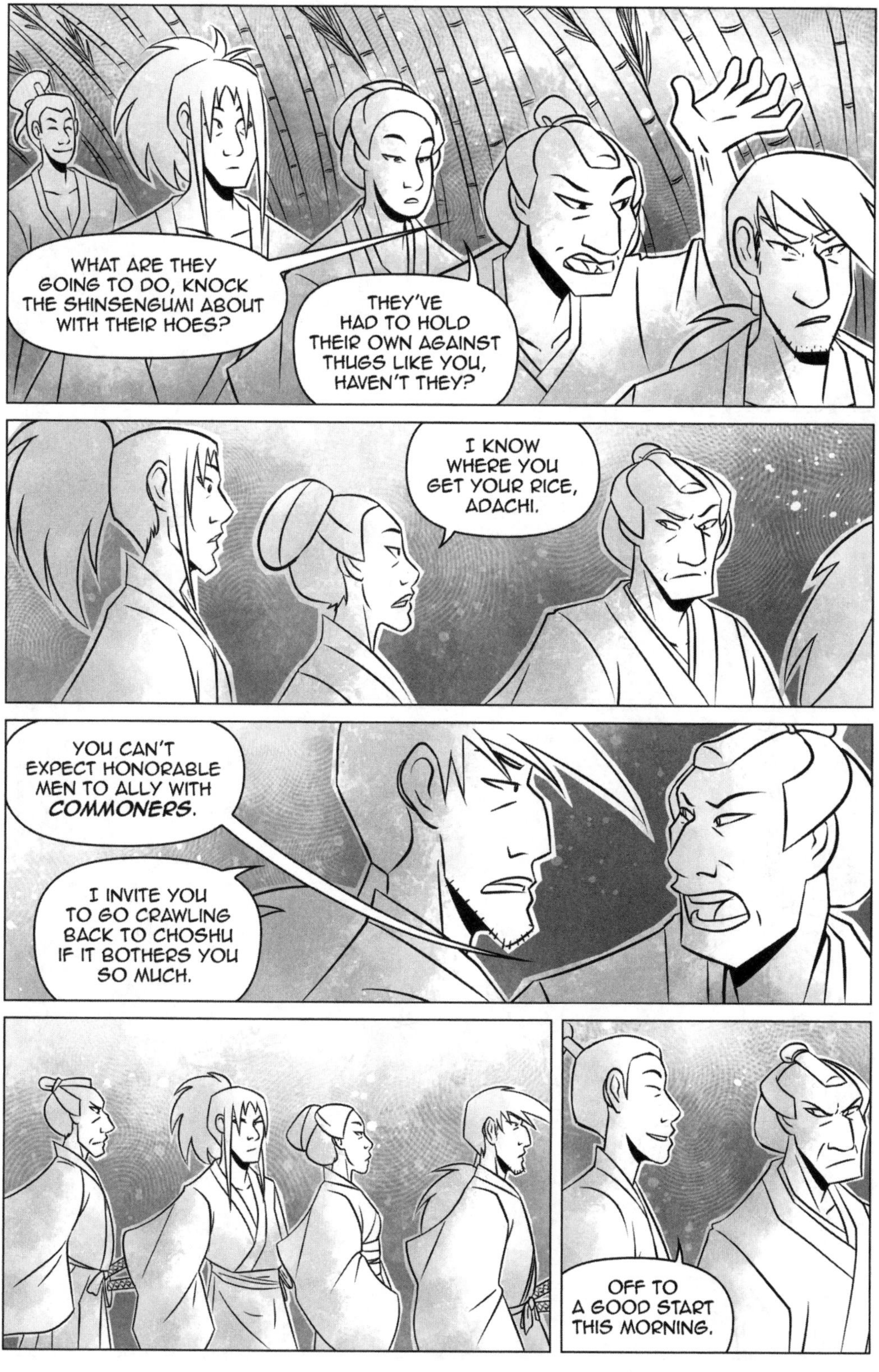
WHAT ARE THEY GOING TO DO, KNOCK THE SHINSENGUMI ABOUT WITH THEIR HOES?
THEY'VE HAD TO HOLD THEIR OWN AGAINST THUGS LIKE YOU, HAVEN'T THEY?
I KNOW WHERE YOU GET YOUR RICE, ADACHI.
YOU CAN'T EXPECT HONORABLE MEN TO ALLY WITH ***COMMONERS***.
I INVITE YOU TO GO CRAWLING BACK TO CHOSHU IF IT BOTHERS YOU SO MUCH.
OFF TO A GOOD START THIS MORNING.

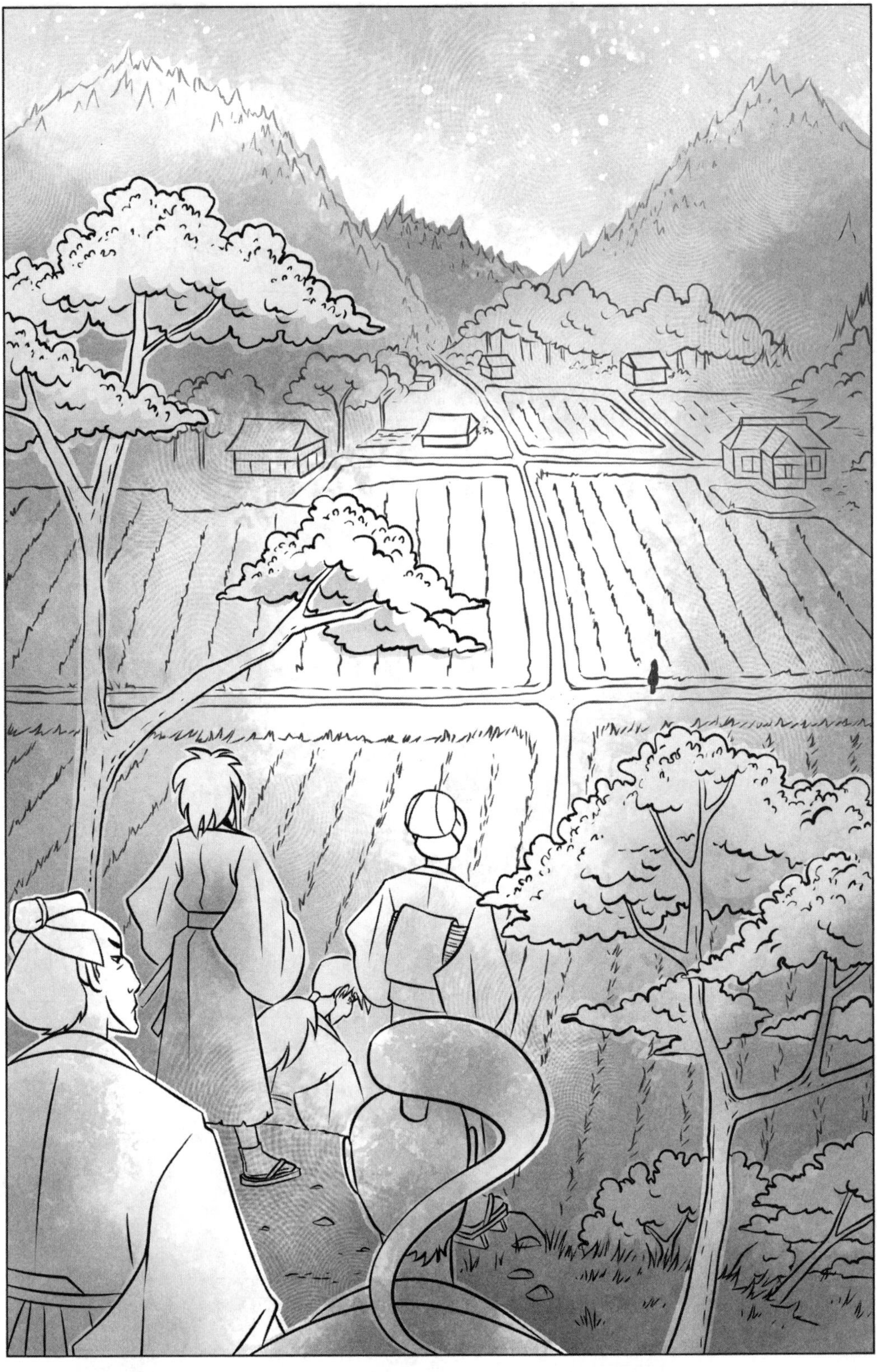

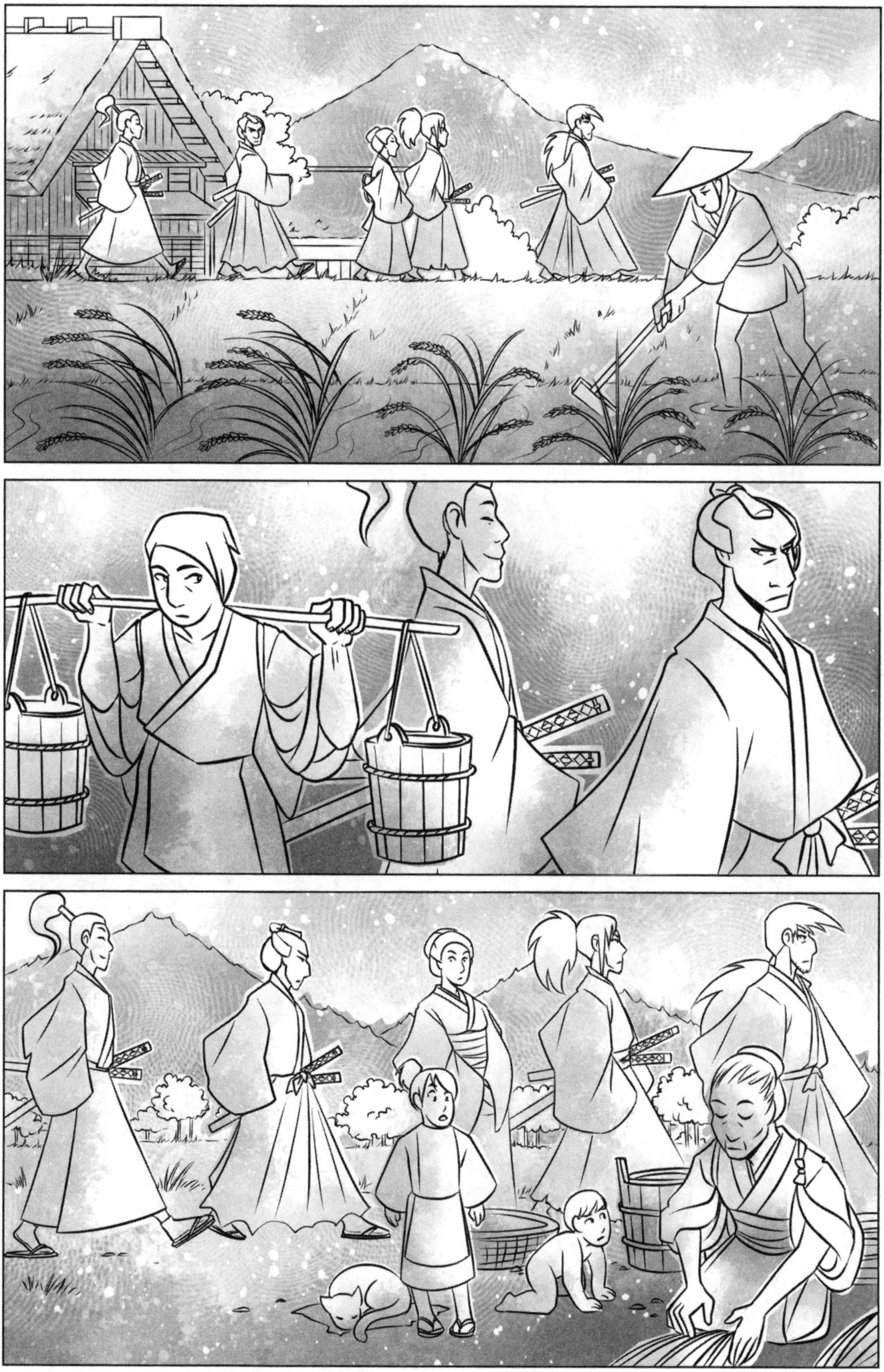

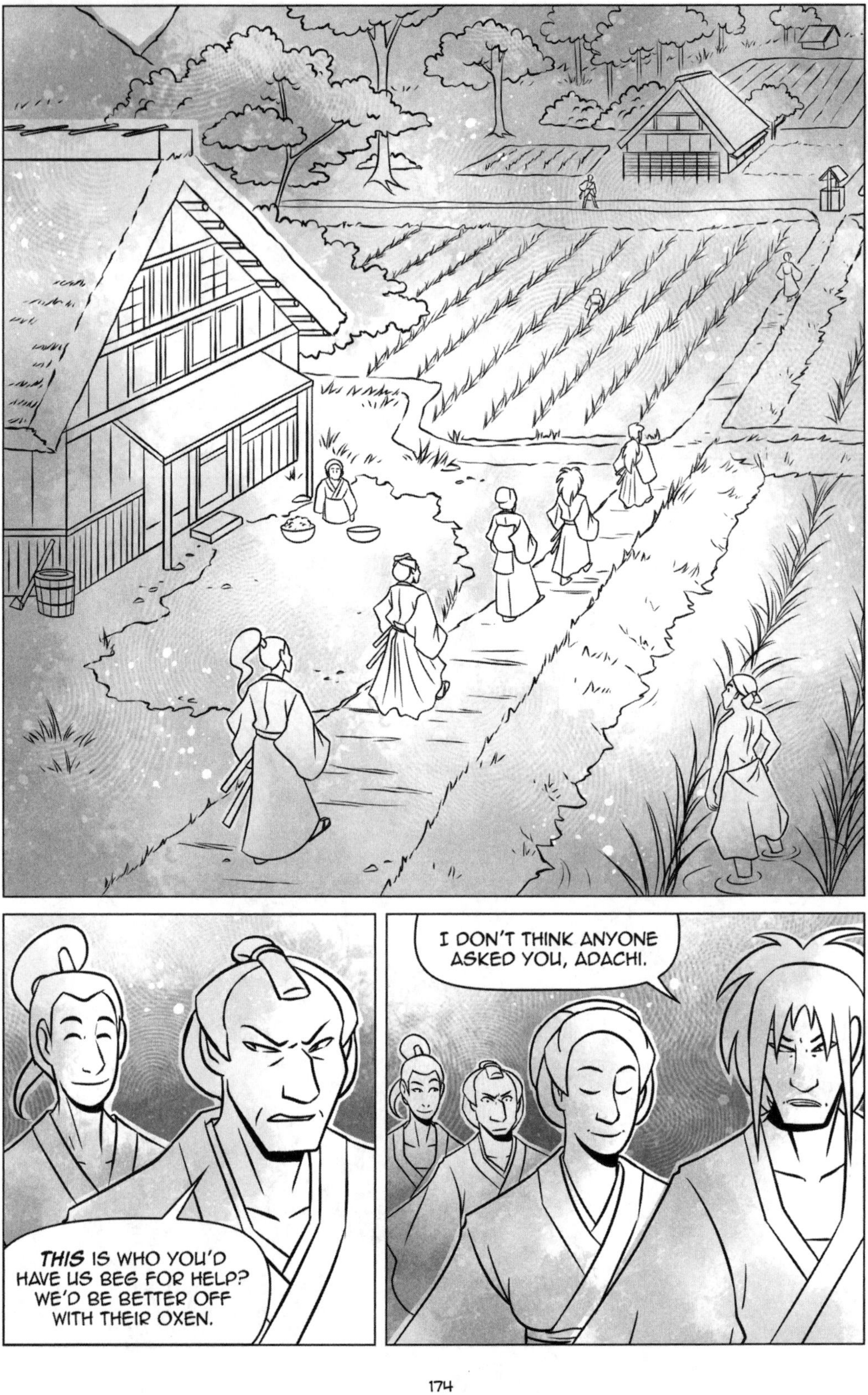
THIS IS WHO YOU'D HAVE US BEG FOR HELP? WE'D BE BETTER OFF WITH THEIR OXEN.
I DON'T THINK ANYONE ASKED YOU, ADACHI.

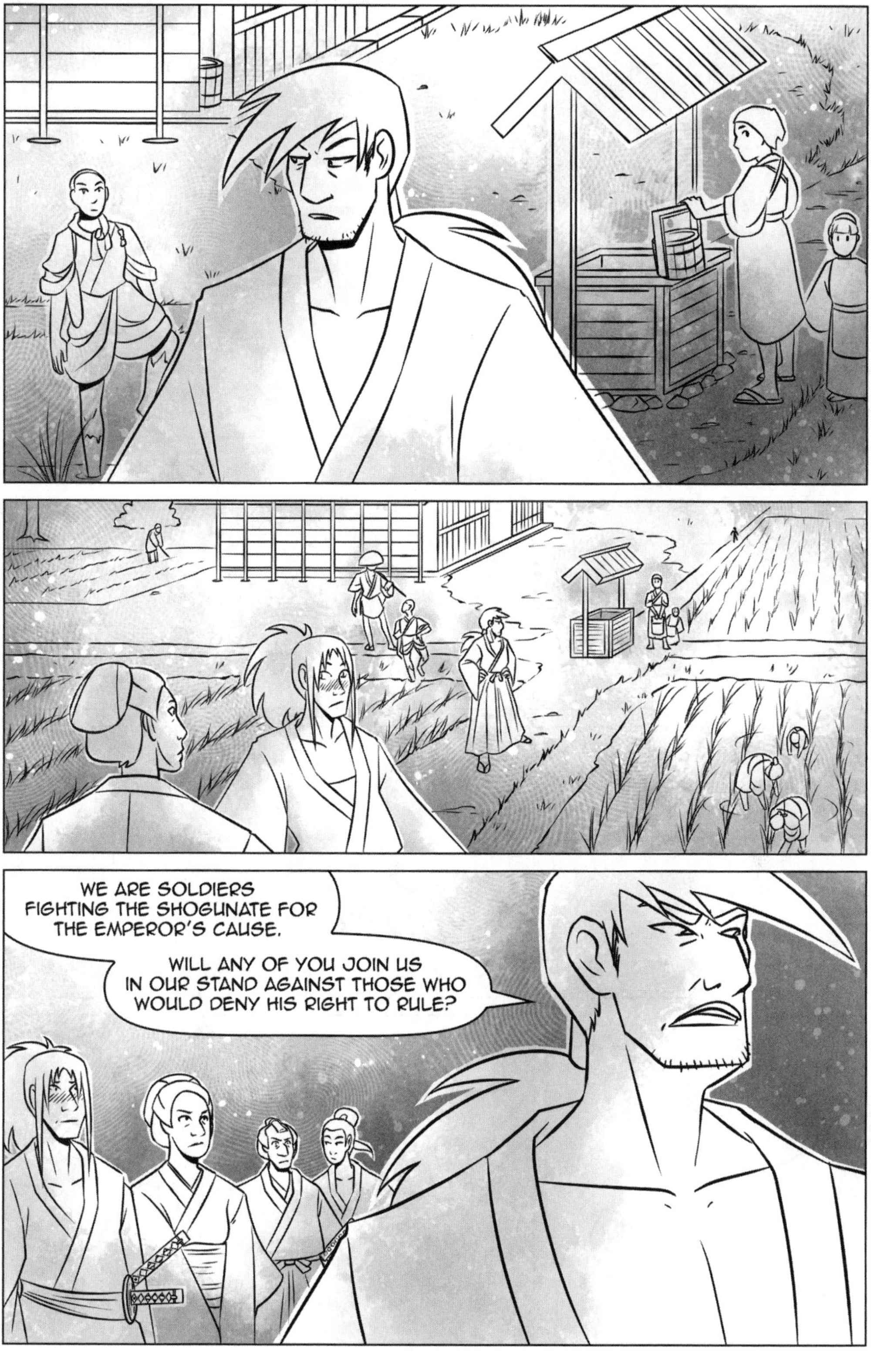
WE ARE SOLDIERS FIGHTING THE SHOGUNATE FOR THE EMPEROR'S CAUSE.
WILL ANY OF YOU JOIN US IN OUR STAND AGAINST THOSE WHO WOULD DENY HIS RIGHT TO RULE?

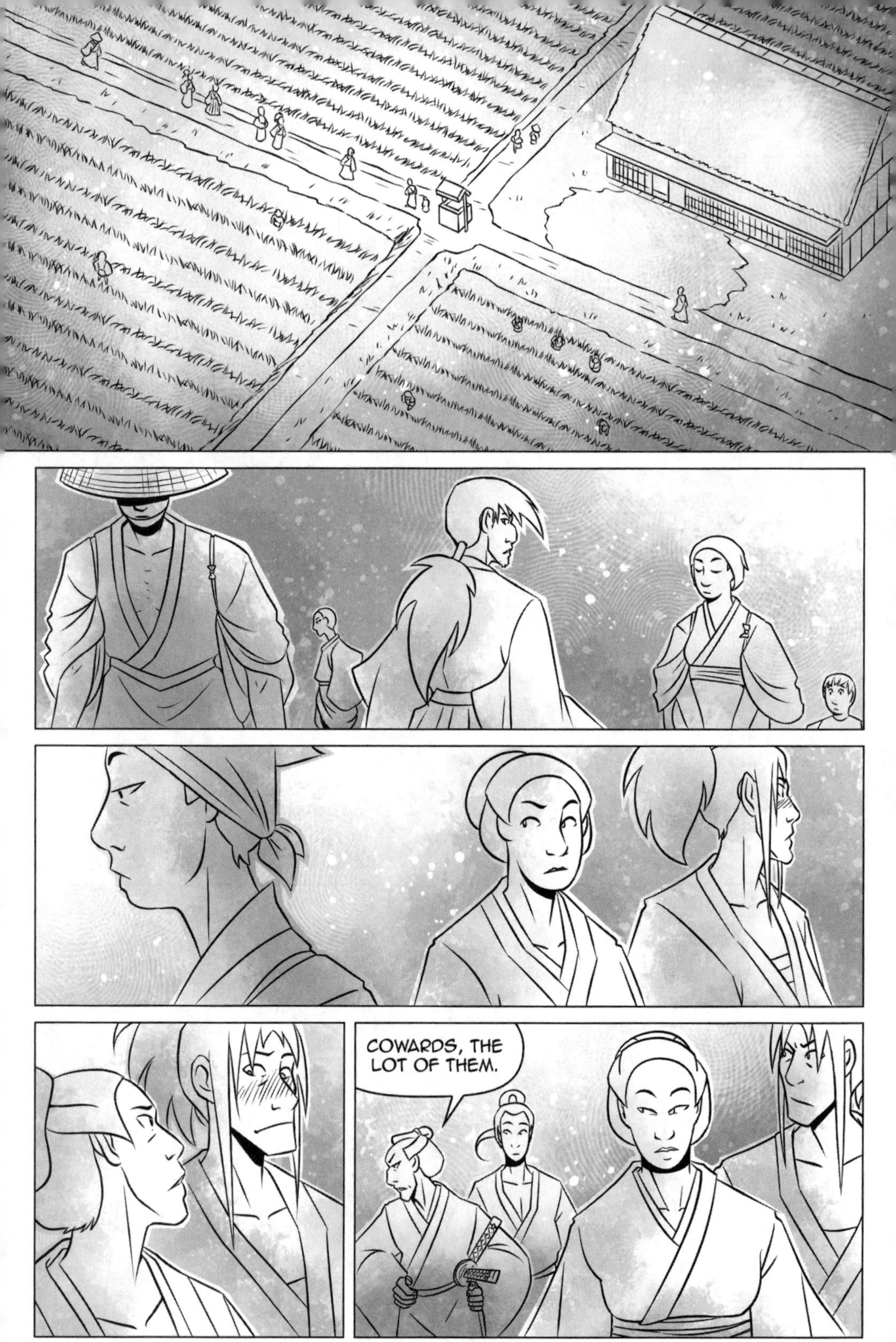
COWARDS, THE LOT OF THEM.

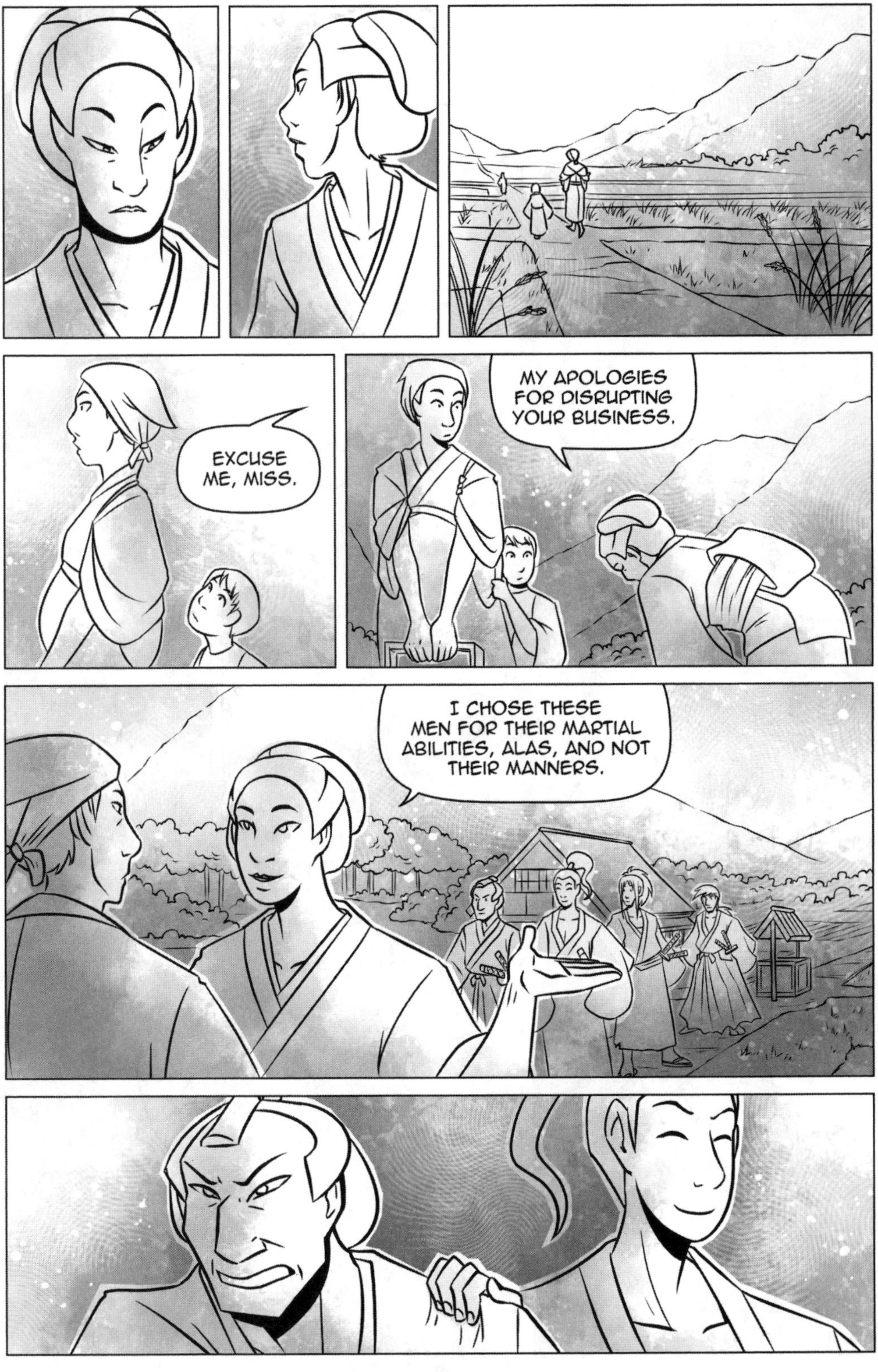
EXCUSE ME, MISS.
MY APOLOGIES FOR DISRUPTING YOUR BUSINESS.
I CHOSE THESE MEN FOR THEIR MARTIAL ABILITIES, ALAS, AND NOT THEIR MANNERS.

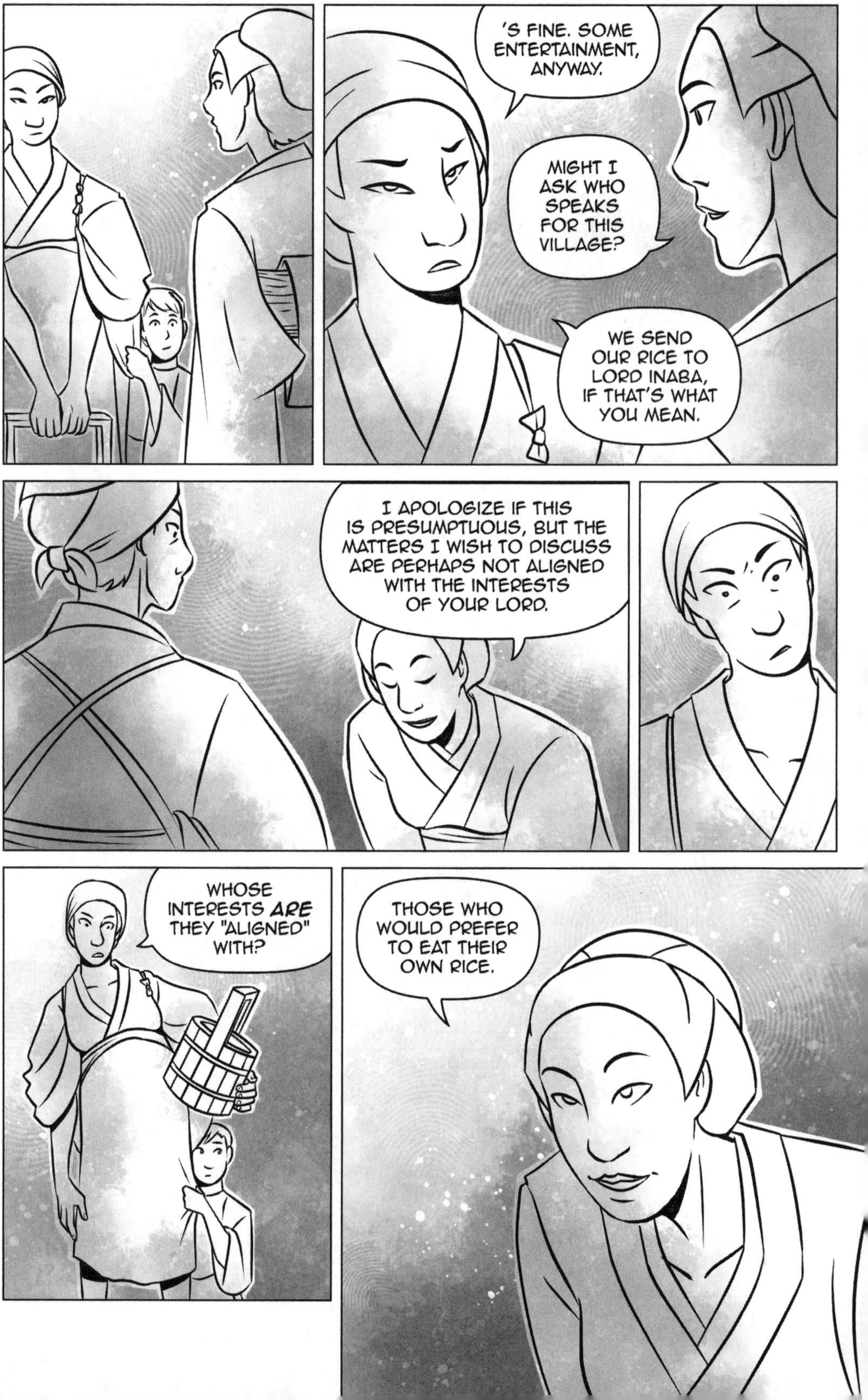
'S FINE. SOME ENTERTAINMENT, ANYWAY.
MIGHT I ASK WHO SPEAKS FOR THIS VILLAGE?
WE SEND OUR RICE TO LORD INABA, IF THAT'S WHAT YOU MEAN.
I APOLOGIZE IF THIS IS PRESUMPTUOUS, BUT THE MATTERS I WISH TO DISCUSS ARE PERHAPS NOT ALIGNED WITH THE INTERESTS OF YOUR LORD.
WHOSE INTERESTS *ARE* THEY "ALIGNED" WITH?
THOSE WHO WOULD PREFER TO EAT THEIR OWN RICE.

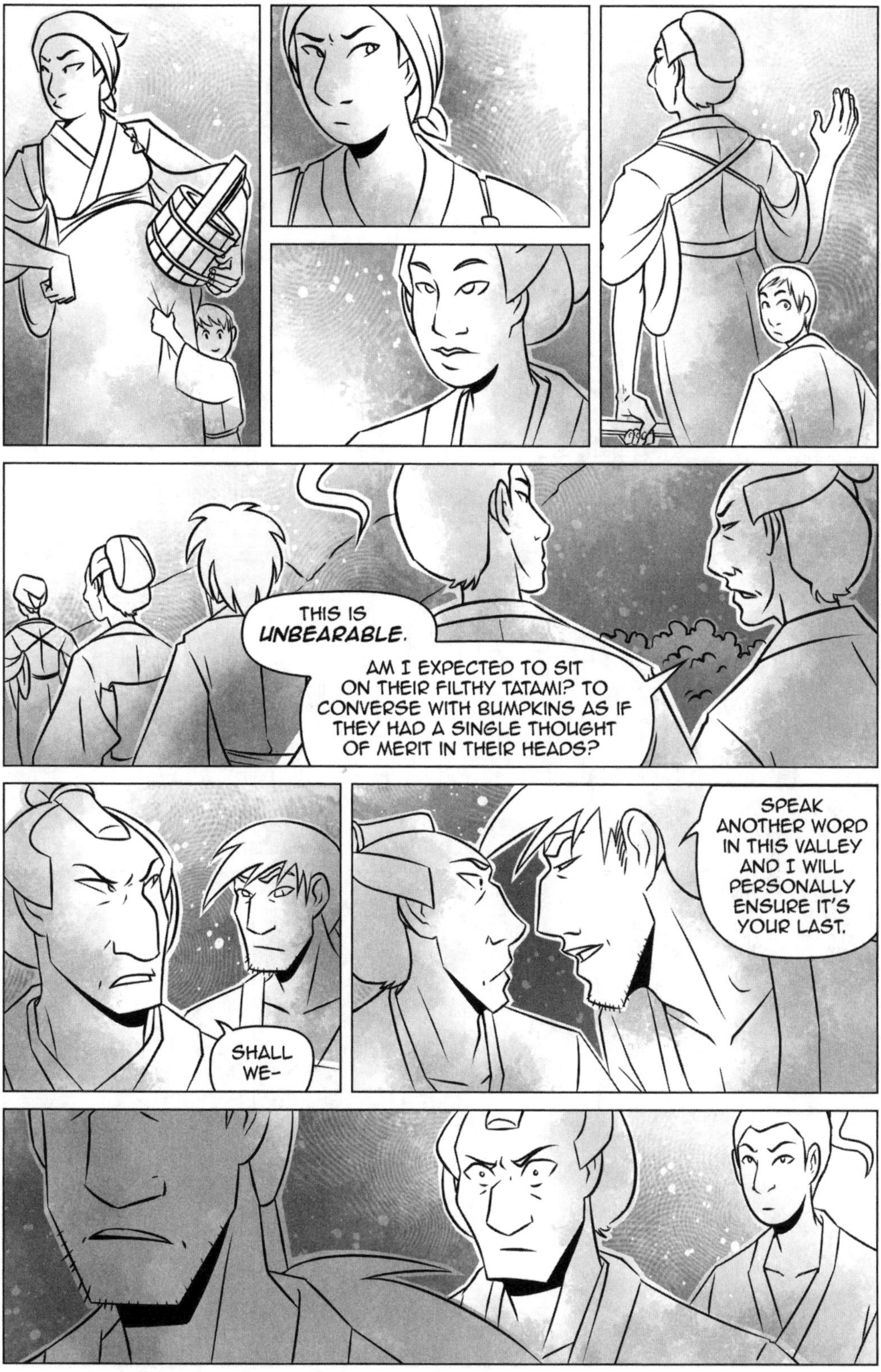
THIS IS UNBEARABLE.
AM I EXPECTED TO SIT ON THEIR FILTHY TATAMI? TO CONVERSE WITH BUMPKINS AS IF THEY HAD A SINGLE THOUGHT OF MERIT IN THEIR HEADS?
SHALL WE-
SPEAK ANOTHER WORD IN THIS VALLEY AND I WILL PERSONALLY ENSURE IT'S YOUR LAST.

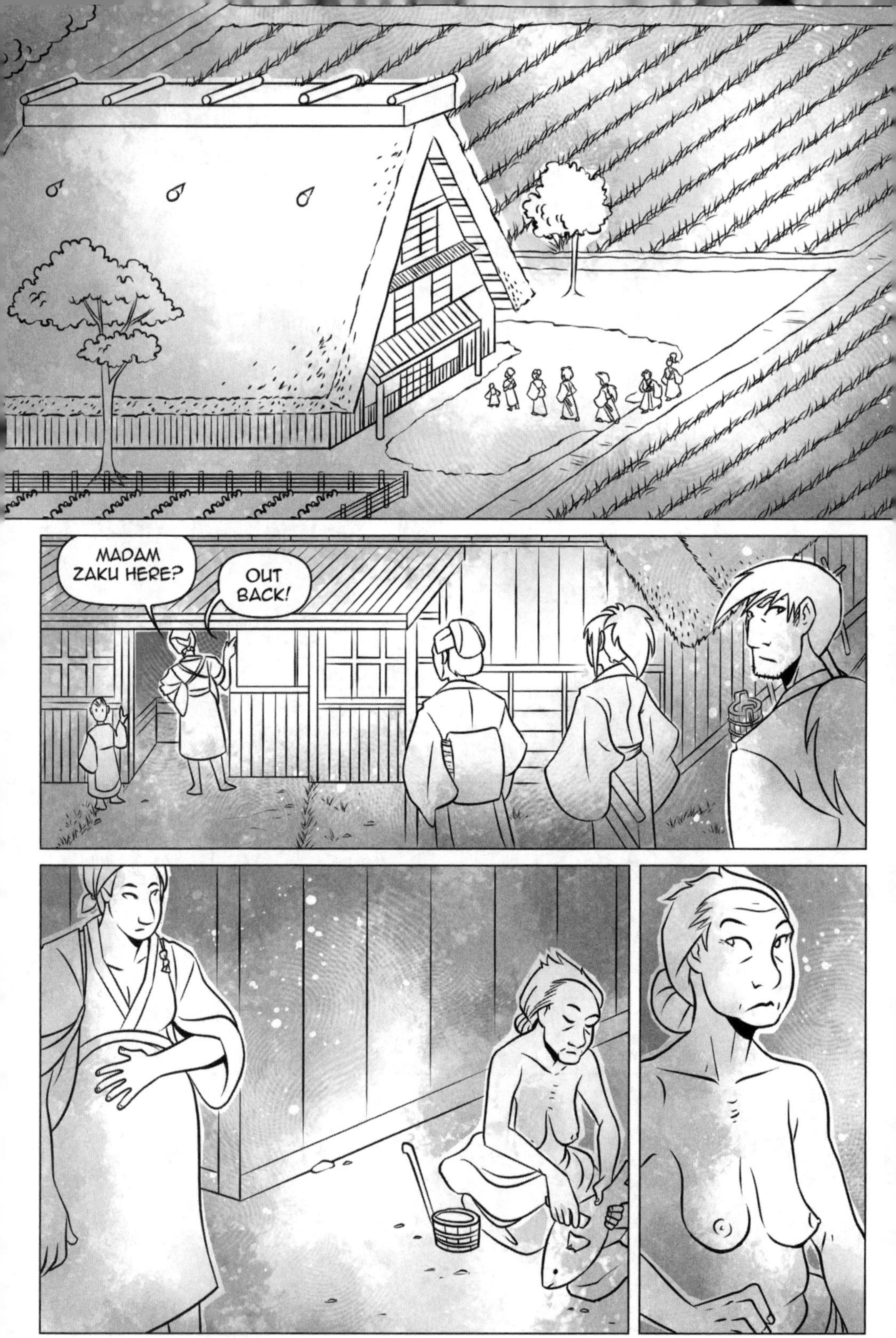
MADAM ZAKU HERE?
OUT BACK!

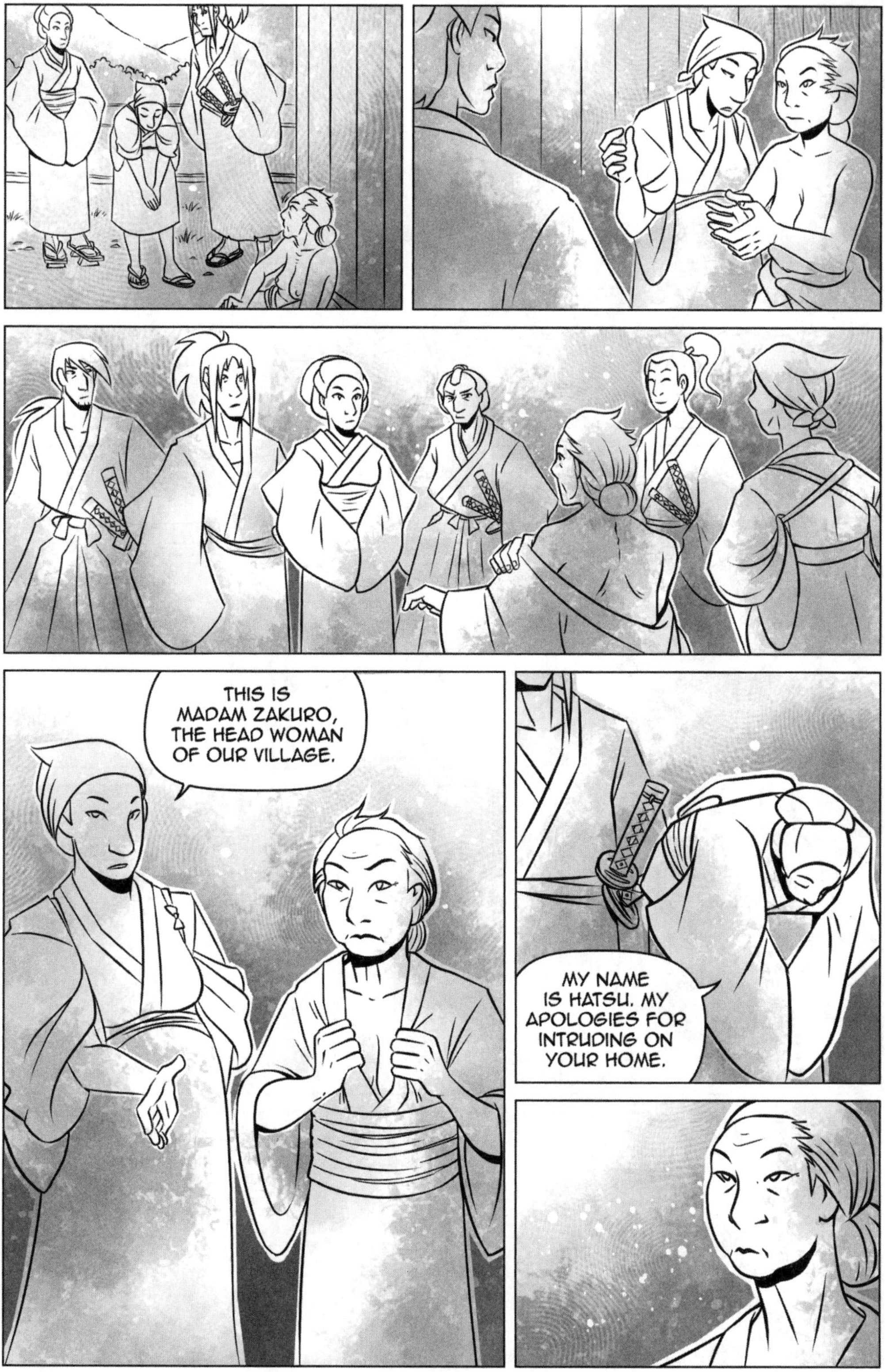
THIS IS MADAM ZAKURO, THE HEAD WOMAN OF OUR VILLAGE.
MY NAME IS HATSU. MY APOLOGIES FOR INTRUDING ON YOUR HOME.

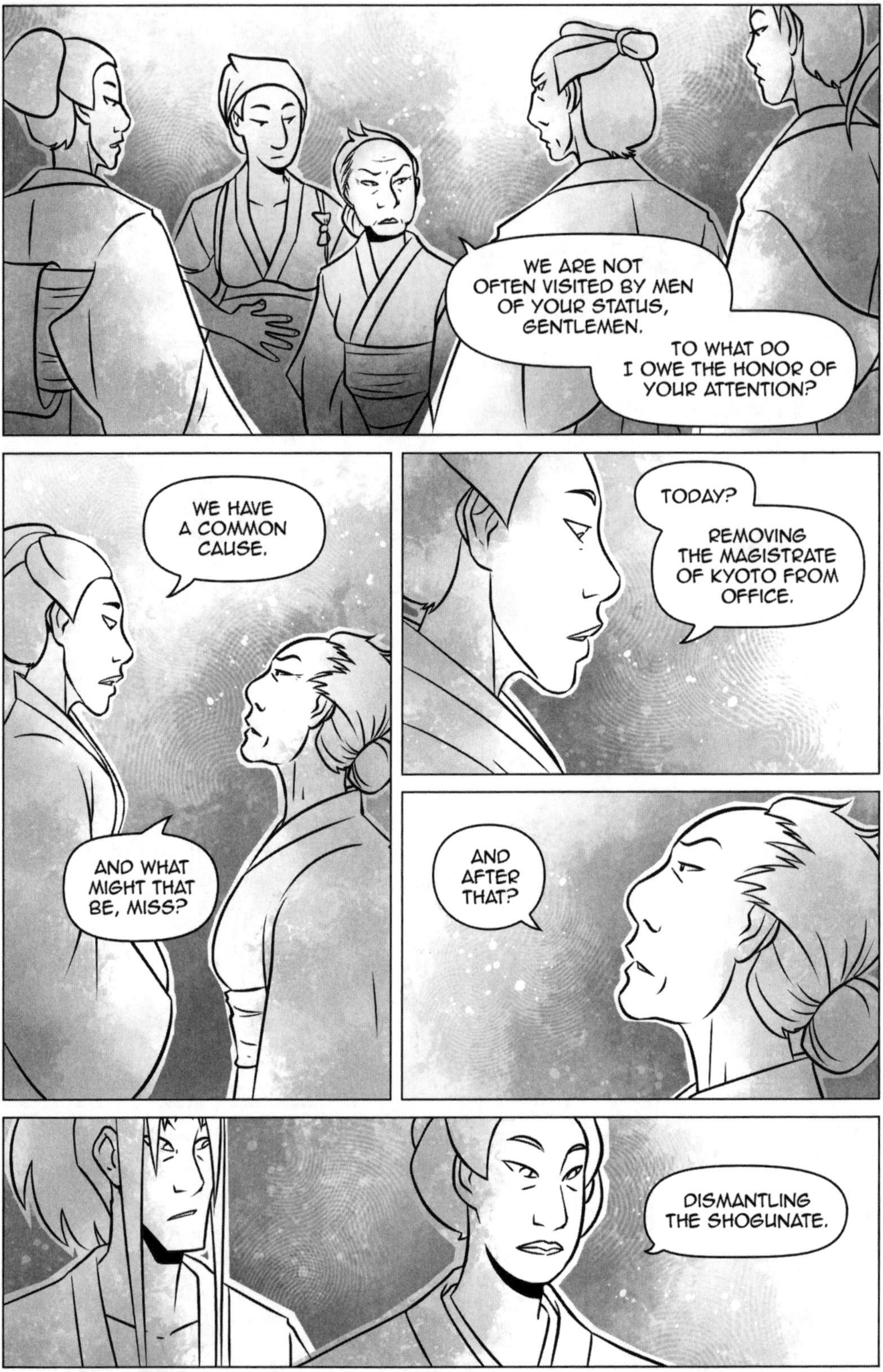
WE ARE NOT OFTEN VISITED BY MEN OF YOUR STATUS, GENTLEMEN.
TO WHAT DO I OWE THE HONOR OF YOUR ATTENTION?
WE HAVE A COMMON CAUSE.
AND WHAT MIGHT THAT BE, MISS?
TODAY?
REMOVING THE MAGISTRATE OF KYOTO FROM OFFICE.
AND AFTER THAT?
DISMANTLING THE SHOGUNATE.

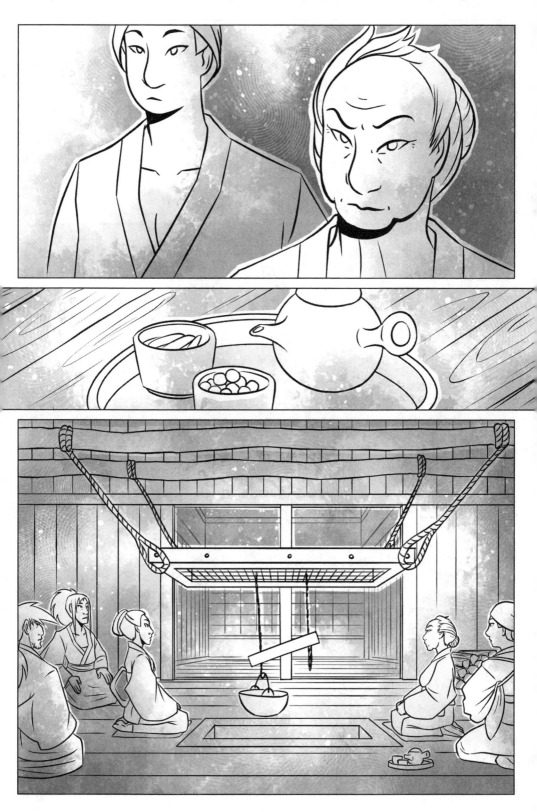

183

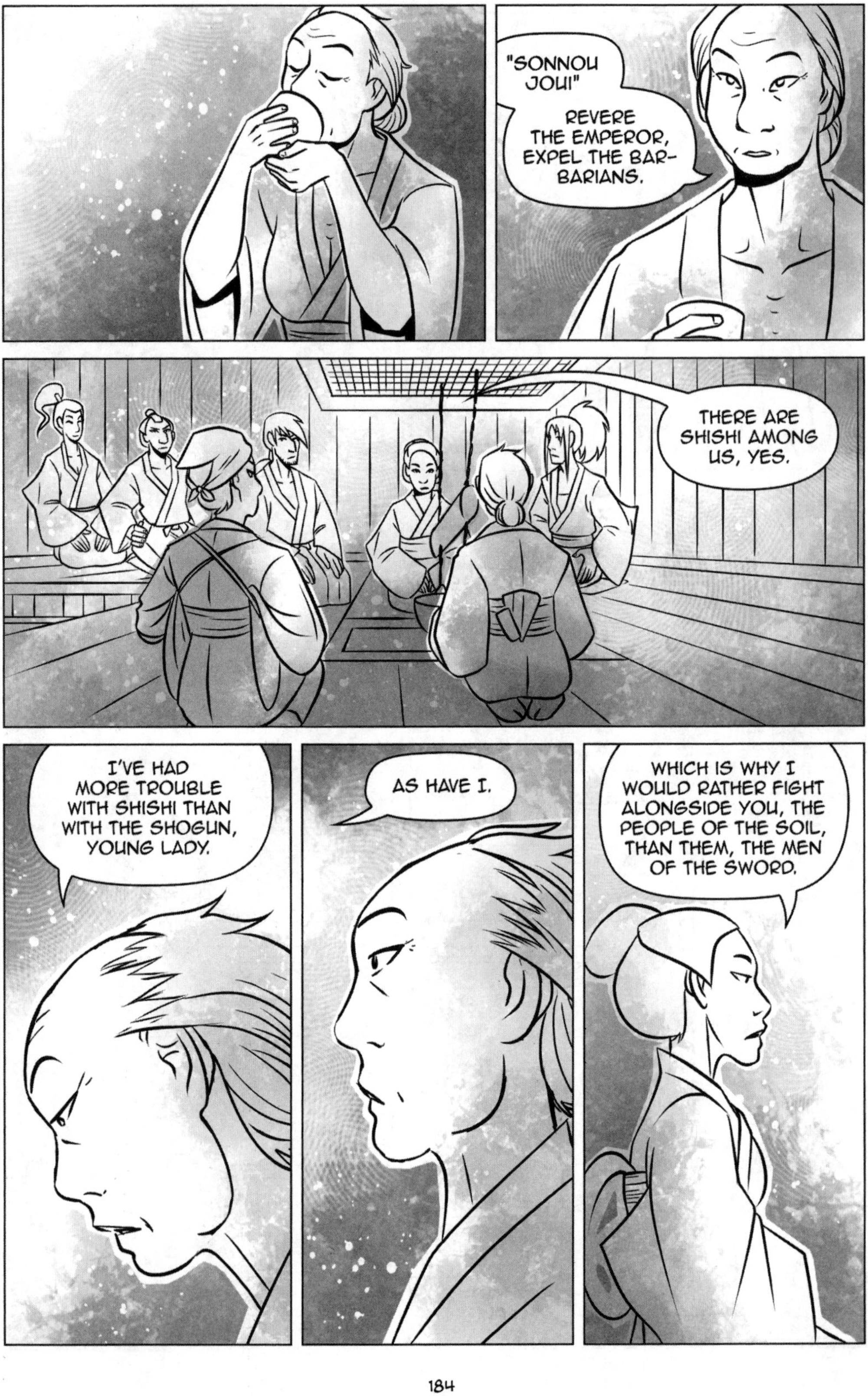
"SONNOU JOUI"
REVERE THE EMPEROR, EXPEL THE BAR-BARIANS.
THERE ARE SHISHI AMONG US, YES.
I'VE HAD MORE TROUBLE WITH SHISHI THAN WITH THE SHOGUN, YOUNG LADY.
AS HAVE I.
WHICH IS WHY I WOULD RATHER FIGHT ALONGSIDE YOU, THE PEOPLE OF THE SOIL, THAN THEM, THE MEN OF THE SWORD.

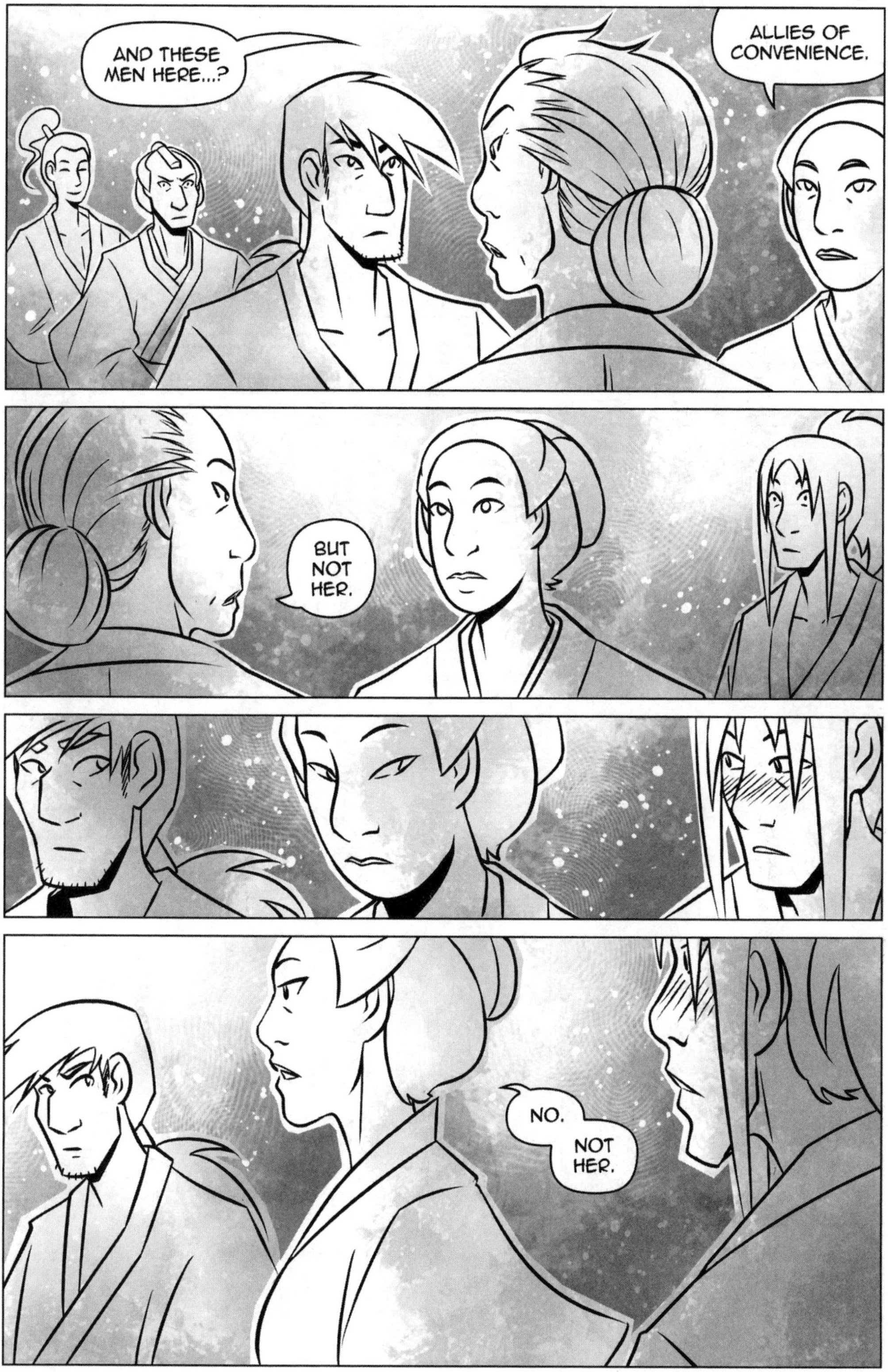
AND THESE MEN HERE...?
ALLIES OF CONVENIENCE.
BUT NOT HER.
NO.
NOT HER.

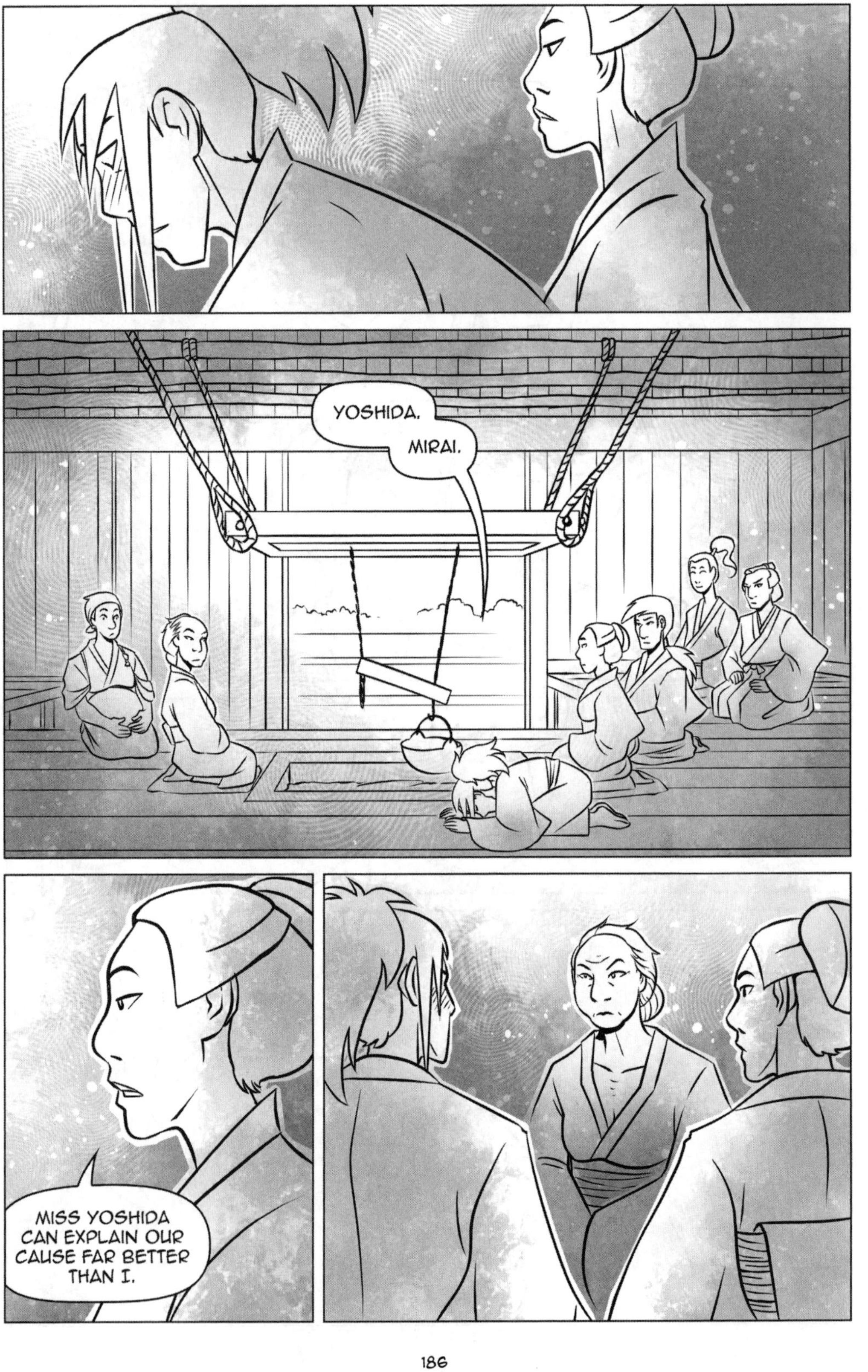
YOSHIDA.
MIRAI.
MISS YOSHIDA CAN EXPLAIN OUR CAUSE FAR BETTER THAN I.

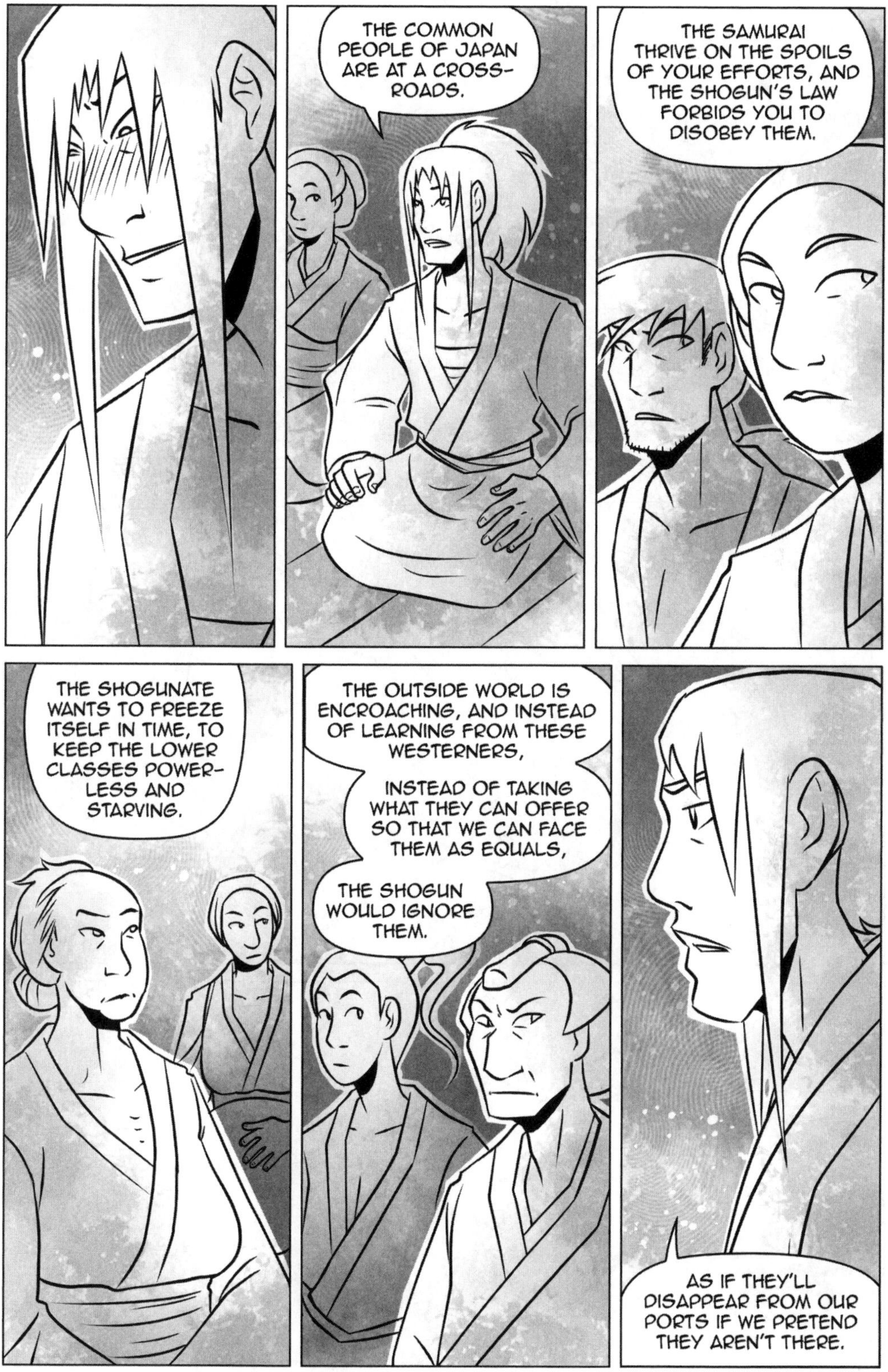
THE COMMON PEOPLE OF JAPAN ARE AT A CROSS-ROADS.
THE SAMURAI THRIVE ON THE SPOILS OF YOUR EFFORTS, AND THE SHOGUN'S LAW FORBIDS YOU TO DISOBEY THEM.
THE SHOGUNATE WANTS TO FREEZE ITSELF IN TIME, TO KEEP THE LOWER CLASSES POWER-LESS AND STARVING.
THE OUTSIDE WORLD IS ENCROACHING, AND INSTEAD OF LEARNING FROM THESE WESTERNERS,
INSTEAD OF TAKING WHAT THEY CAN OFFER SO THAT WE CAN FACE THEM AS EQUALS,
THE SHOGUN WOULD IGNORE THEM.
AS IF THEY'LL DISAPPEAR FROM OUR PORTS IF WE PRETEND THEY AREN'T THERE.

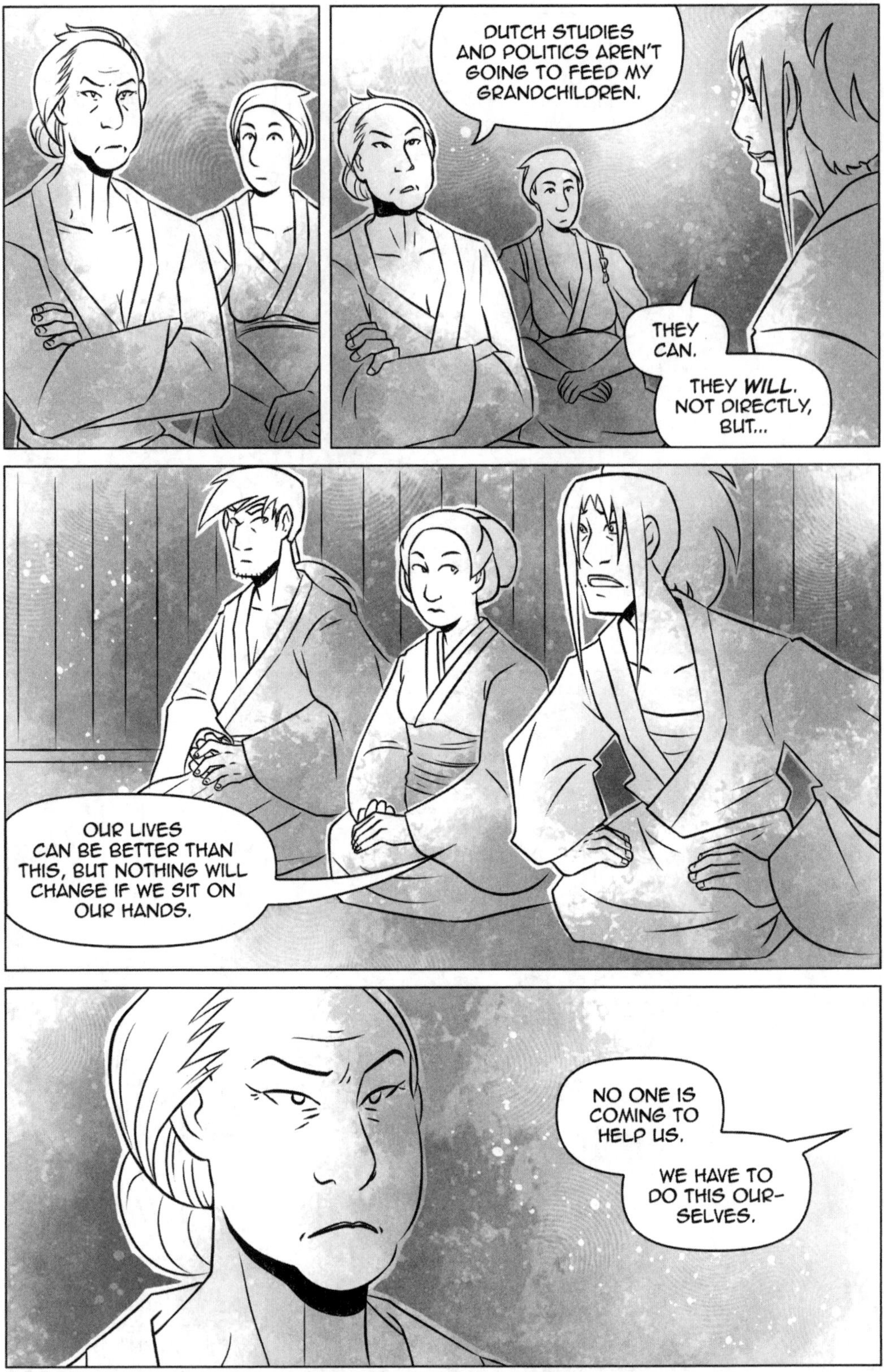
DUTCH STUDIES AND POLITICS AREN'T GOING TO FEED MY GRANDCHILDREN.
THEY CAN.
THEY *WILL*. NOT DIRECTLY, BUT...
OUR LIVES CAN BE BETTER THAN THIS, BUT NOTHING WILL CHANGE IF WE SIT ON OUR HANDS.
NO ONE IS COMING TO HELP US.
WE HAVE TO DO THIS OUR-SELVES.

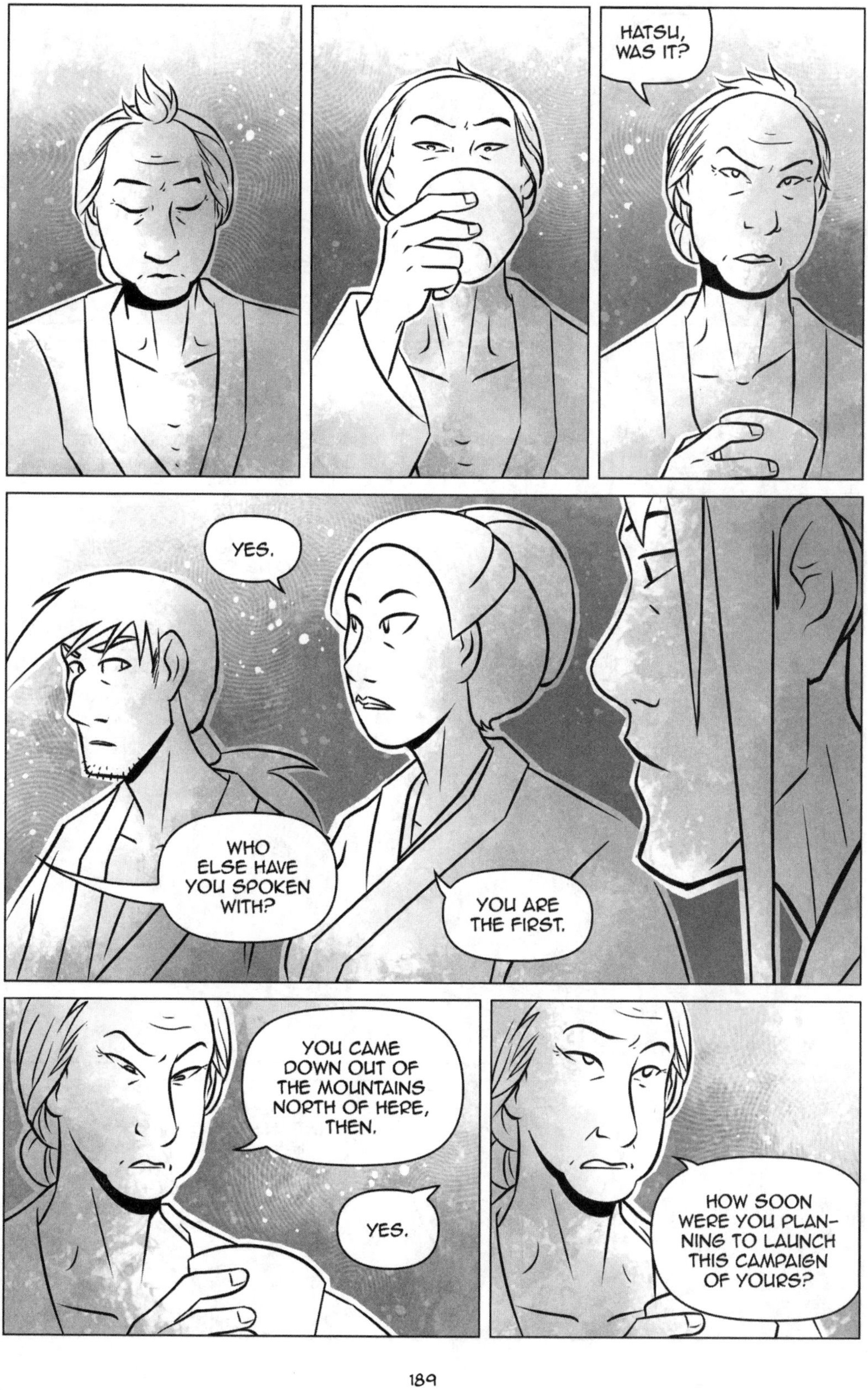
HATSU, WAS IT?
YES.
WHO ELSE HAVE YOU SPOKEN WITH?
YOU ARE THE FIRST.
YOU CAME DOWN OUT OF THE MOUNTAINS NORTH OF HERE, THEN.
YES.
HOW SOON WERE YOU PLAN-NING TO LAUNCH THIS CAMPAIGN OF YOURS?

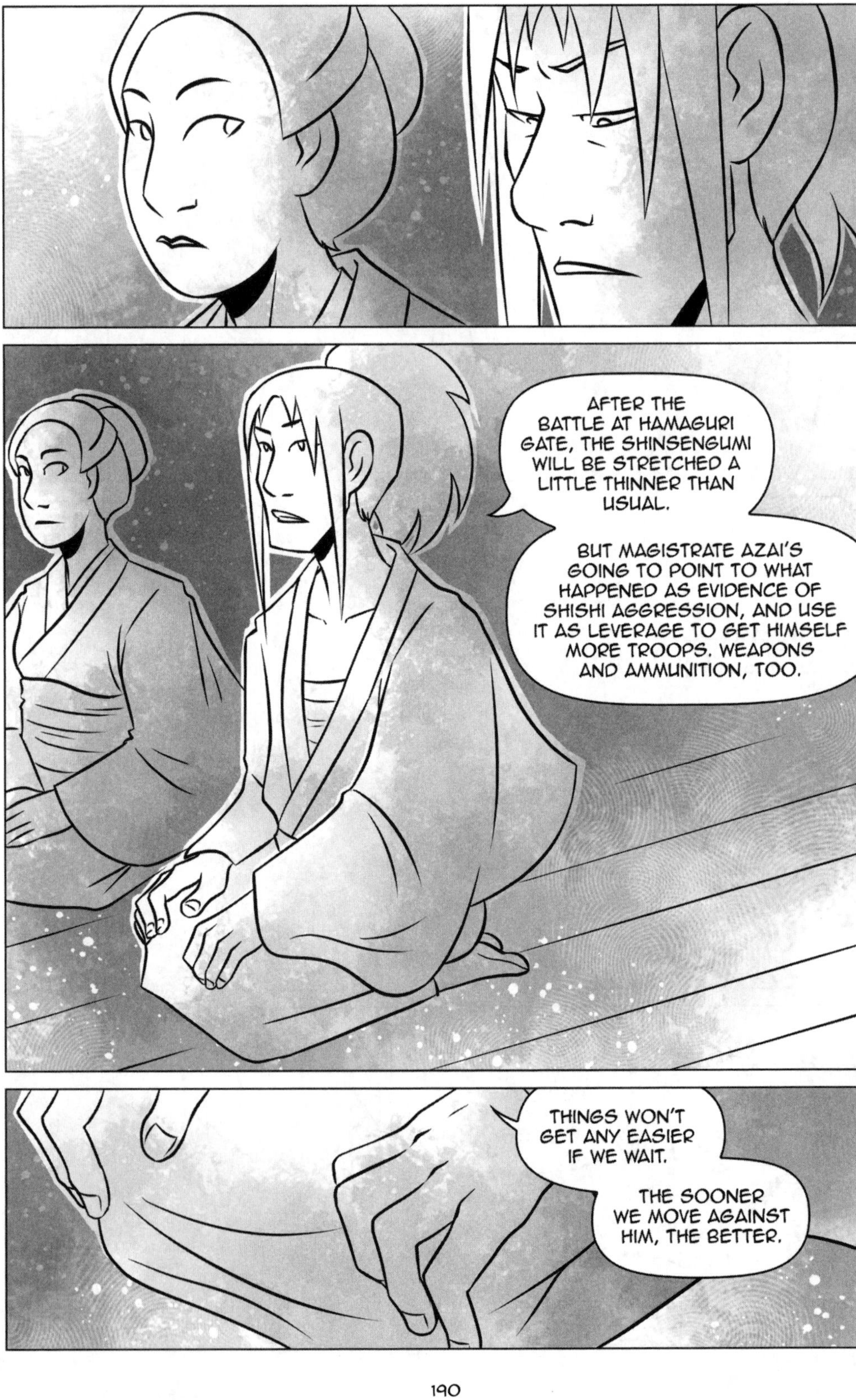
AFTER THE BATTLE AT HAMAGURI GATE, THE SHINSENGUMI WILL BE STRETCHED A LITTLE THINNER THAN USUAL.
BUT MAGISTRATE AZAI'S GOING TO POINT TO WHAT HAPPENED AS EVIDENCE OF SHISHI AGGRESSION, AND USE IT AS LEVERAGE TO GET HIMSELF MORE TROOPS. WEAPONS AND AMMUNITION, TOO.
THINGS WON'T GET ANY EASIER IF WE WAIT.
THE SOONER WE MOVE AGAINST HIM, THE BETTER.

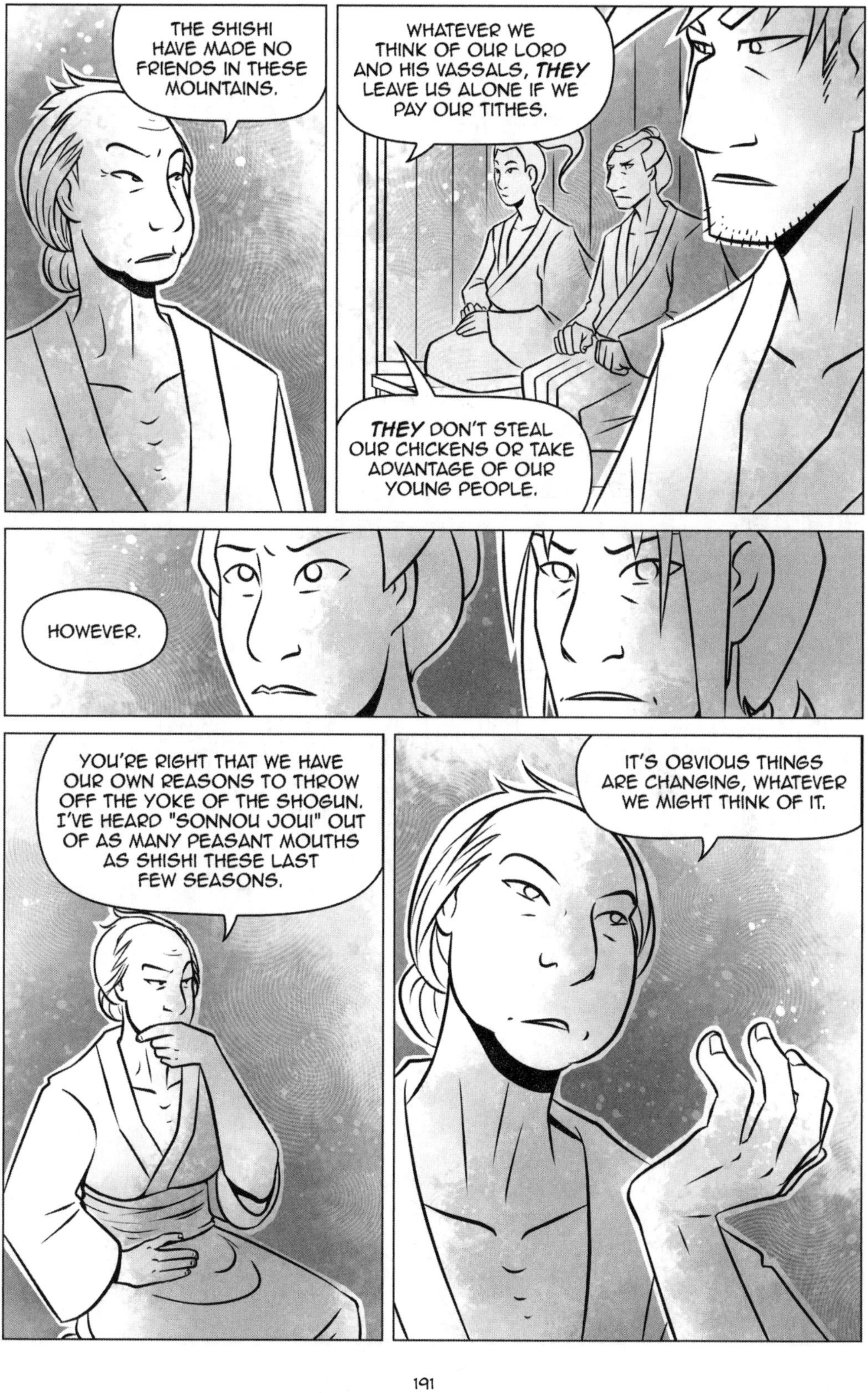
THE SHISHI HAVE MADE NO FRIENDS IN THESE MOUNTAINS.
WHATEVER WE THINK OF OUR LORD AND HIS VASSALS, *THEY* LEAVE US ALONE IF WE PAY OUR TITHES.
*THEY* DON'T STEAL OUR CHICKENS OR TAKE ADVANTAGE OF OUR YOUNG PEOPLE.
HOWEVER.
YOU'RE RIGHT THAT WE HAVE OUR OWN REASONS TO THROW OFF THE YOKE OF THE SHOGUN. I'VE HEARD "SONNOU JOUI" OUT OF AS MANY PEASANT MOUTHS AS SHISHI THESE LAST FEW SEASONS.
IT'S OBVIOUS THINGS ARE CHANGING, WHATEVER WE MIGHT THINK OF IT.

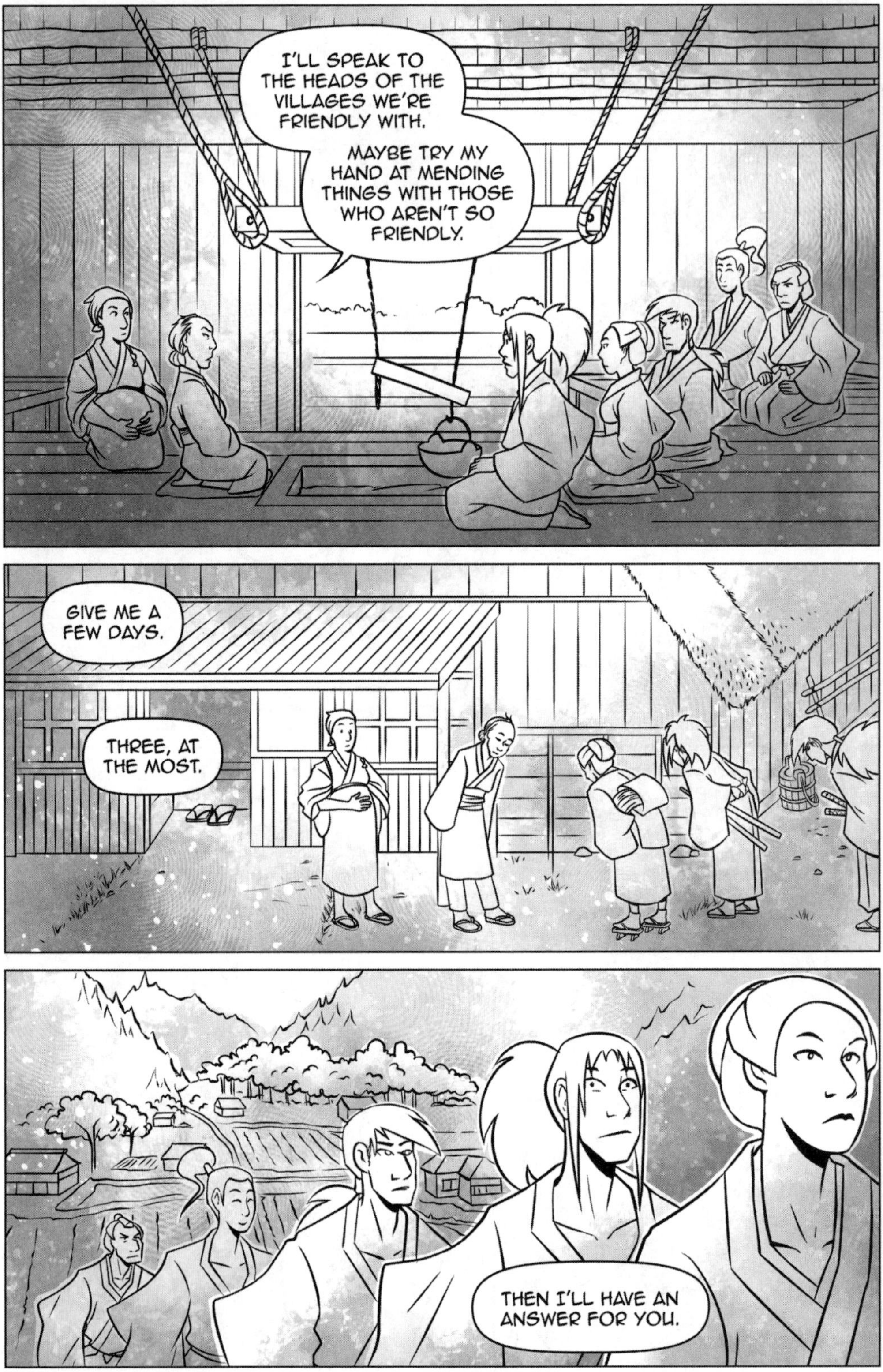
I'LL SPEAK TO THE HEADS OF THE VILLAGES WE'RE FRIENDLY WITH.
MAYBE TRY MY HAND AT MENDING THINGS WITH THOSE WHO AREN'T SO FRIENDLY.
GIVE ME A FEW DAYS.
THREE, AT THE MOST.
THEN I'LL HAVE AN ANSWER FOR YOU.

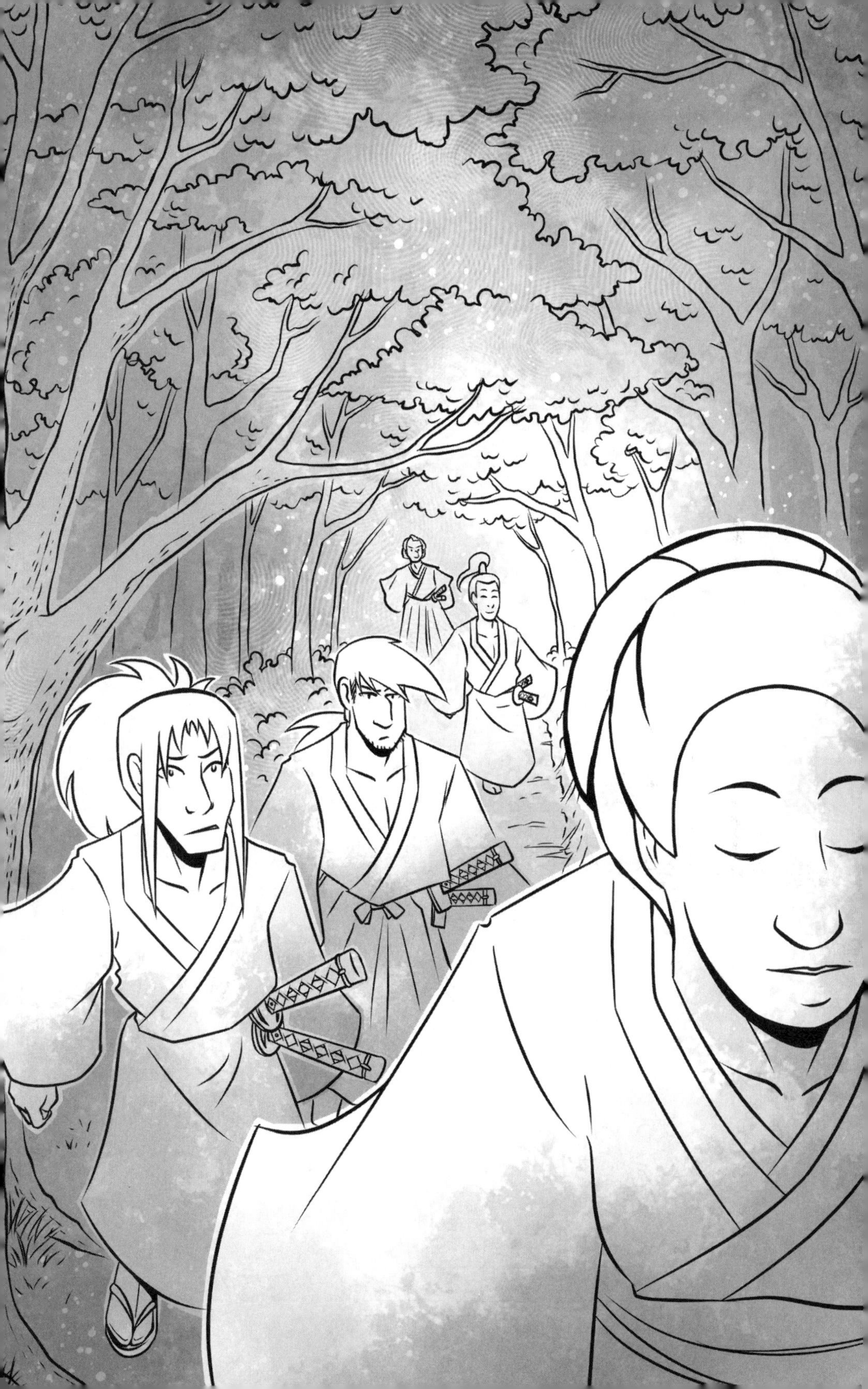

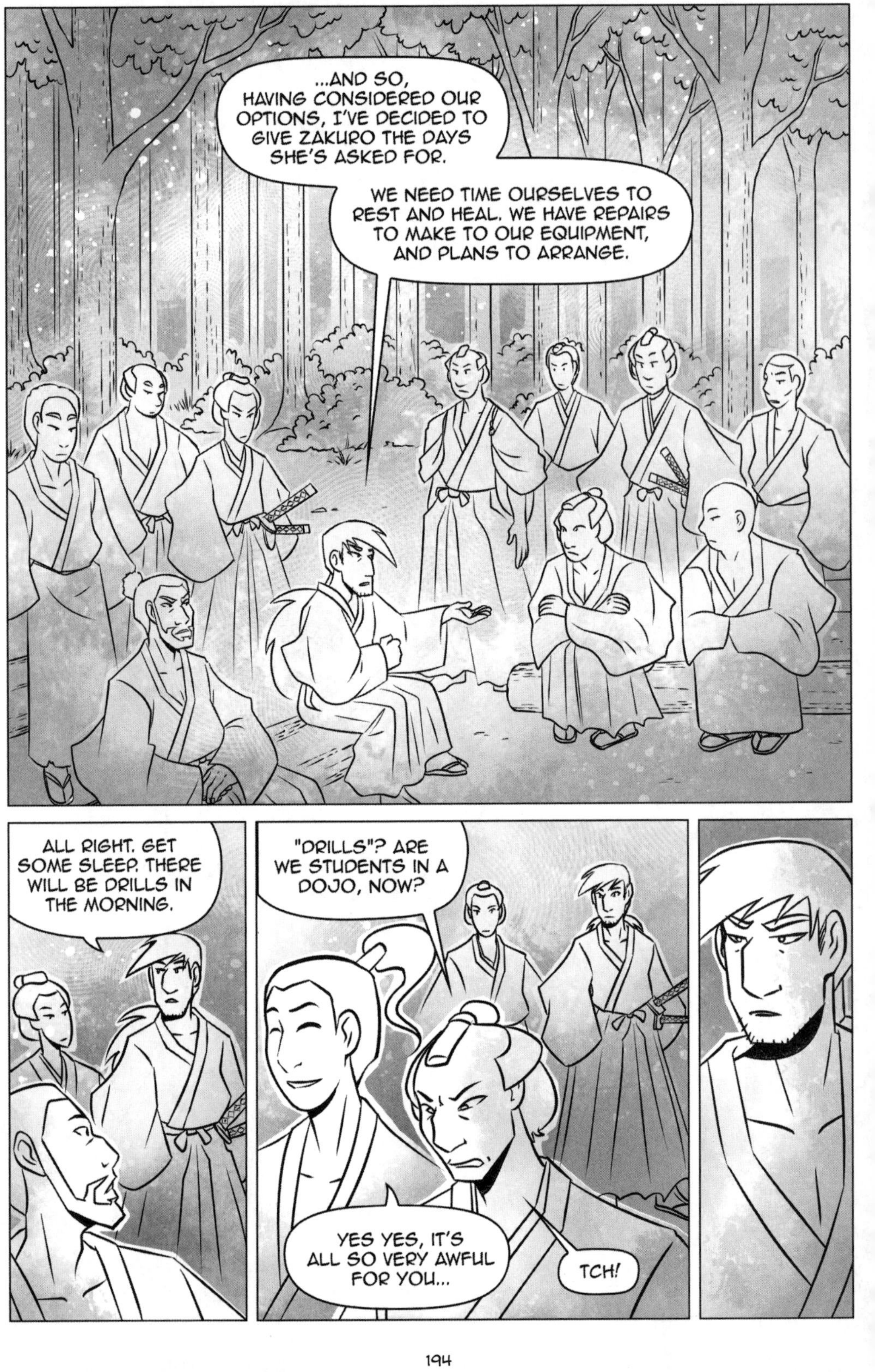
...AND SO, HAVING CONSIDERED OUR OPTIONS, I'VE DECIDED TO GIVE ZAKURO THE DAYS SHE'S ASKED FOR.
WE NEED TIME OURSELVES TO REST AND HEAL. WE HAVE REPAIRS TO MAKE TO OUR EQUIPMENT, AND PLANS TO ARRANGE.
ALL RIGHT. GET SOME SLEEP. THERE WILL BE DRILLS IN THE MORNING.
"DRILLS"? ARE WE STUDENTS IN A DOJO, NOW?
YES YES, IT'S ALL SO VERY AWFUL FOR YOU...
TCH!

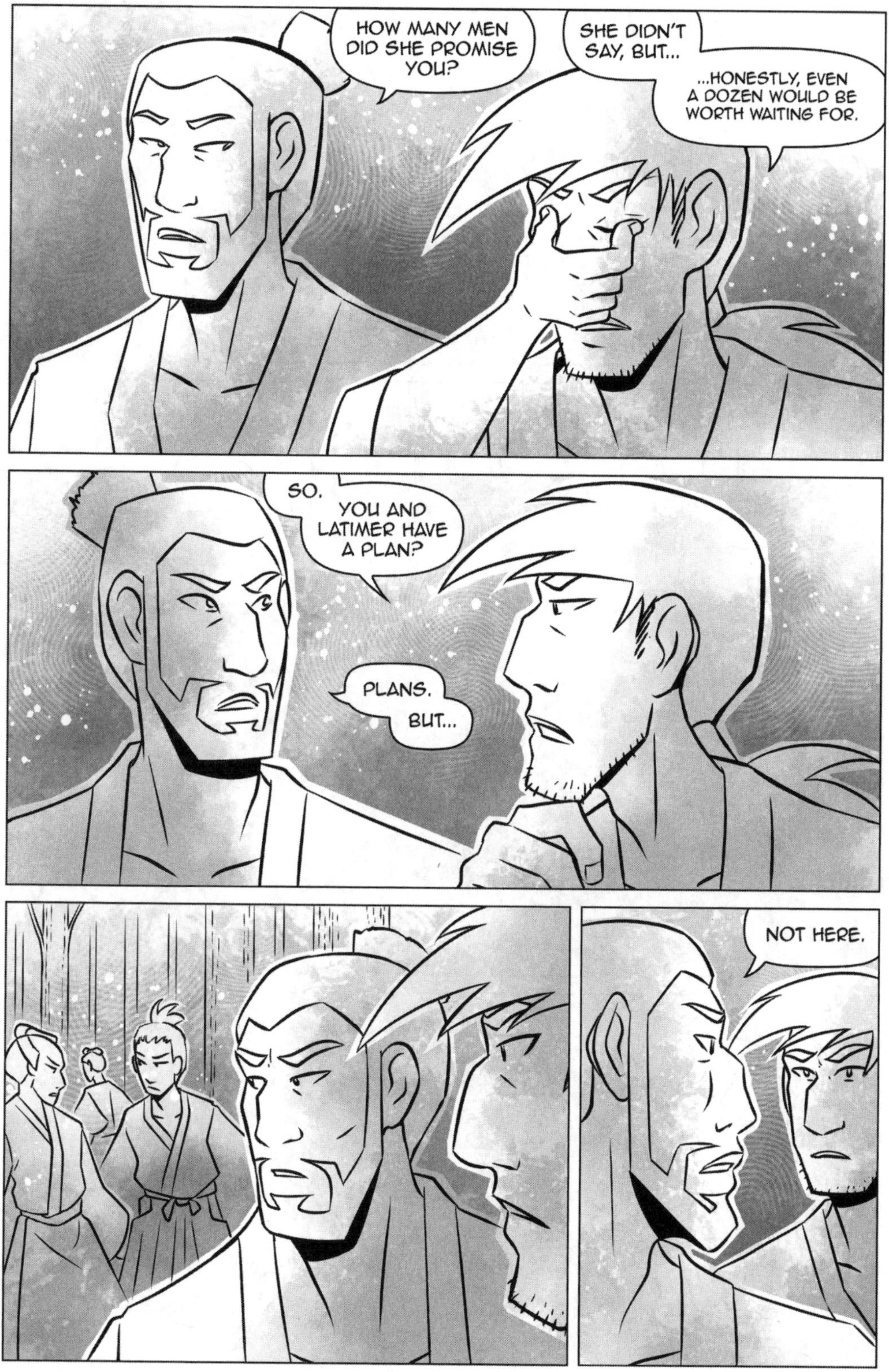
HOW MANY MEN DID SHE PROMISE YOU?
SHE DIDN'T SAY, BUT...
...HONESTLY, EVEN A DOZEN WOULD BE WORTH WAITING FOR.
SO.
YOU AND LATIMER HAVE A PLAN?
PLANS.
BUT...
NOT HERE.

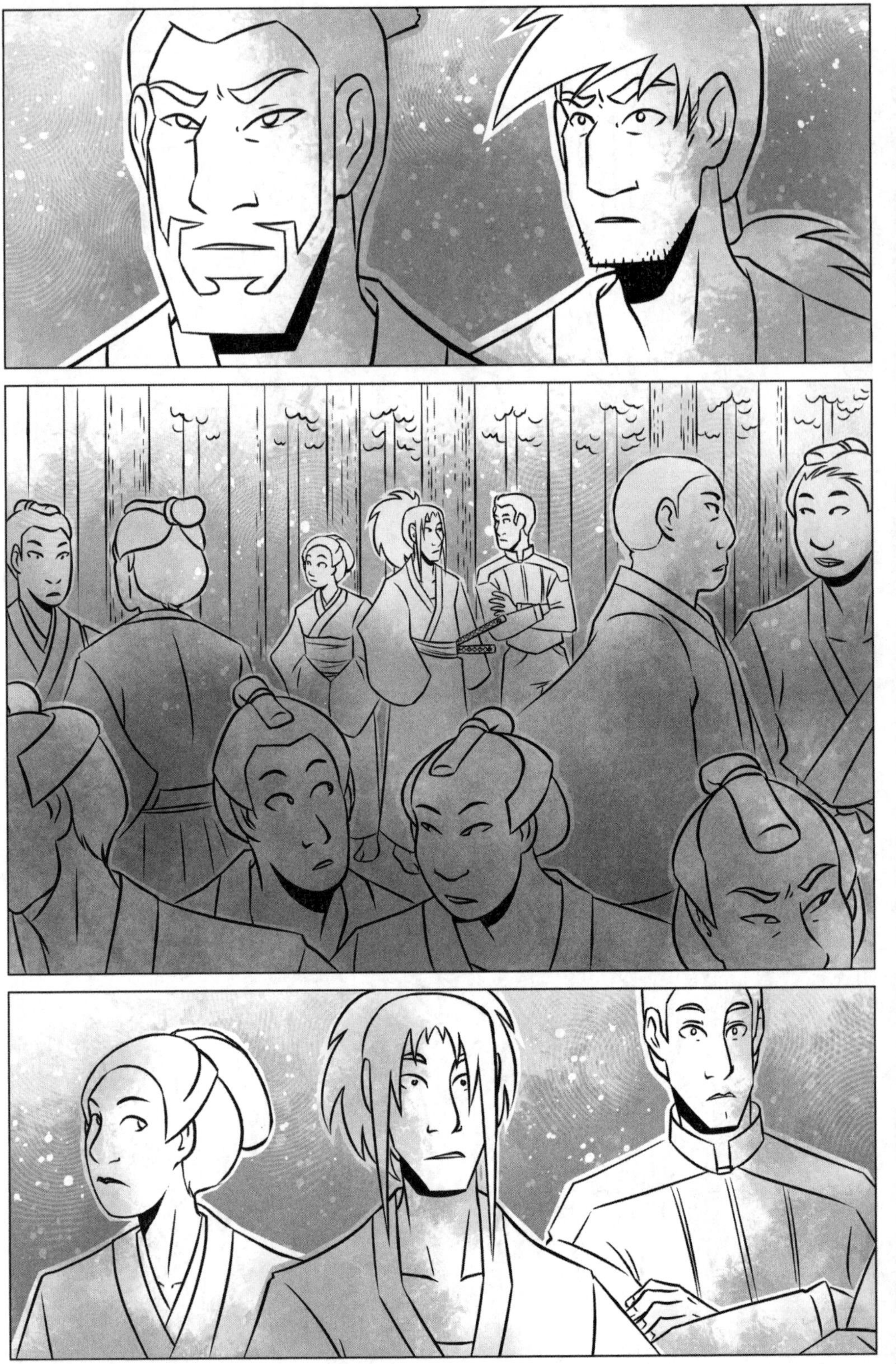

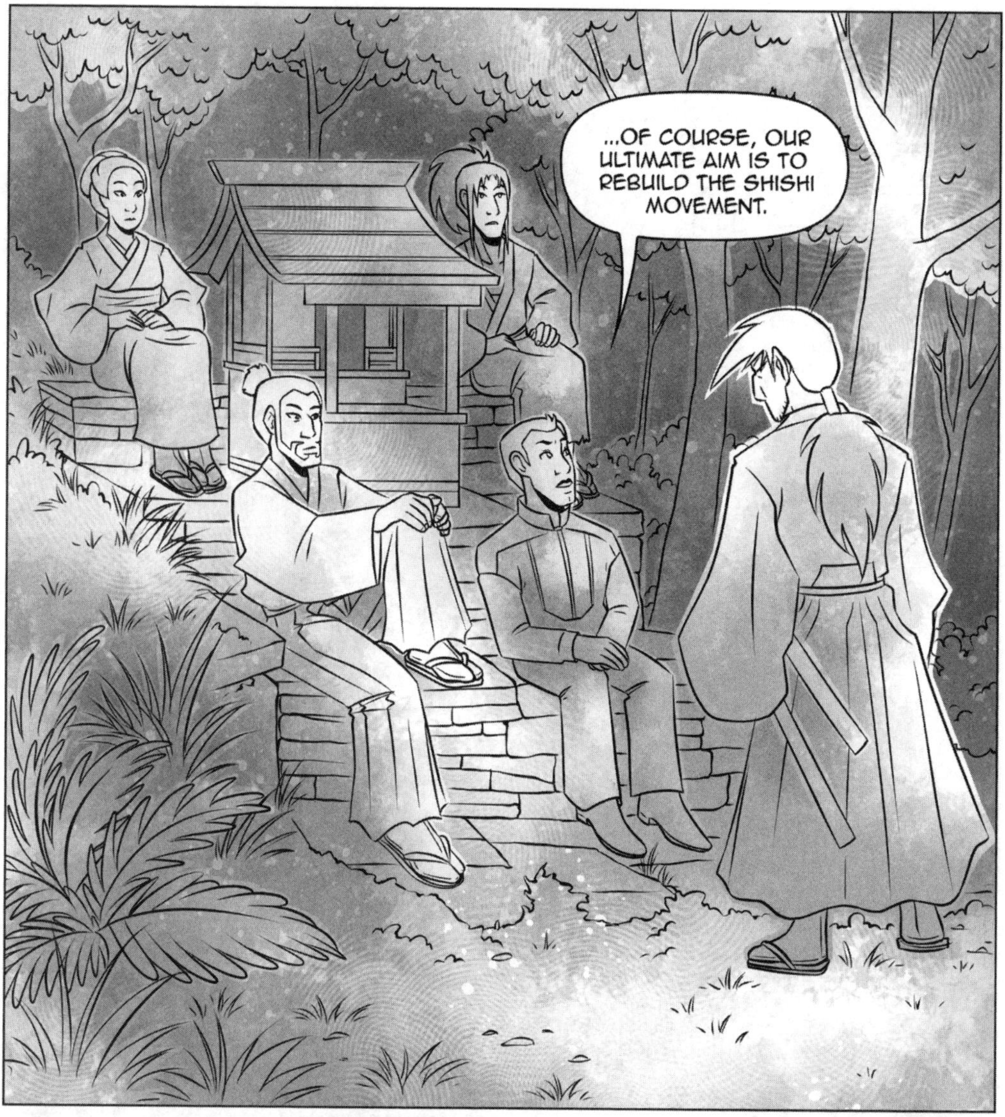
...OF COURSE, OUR ULTIMATE AIM IS TO REBUILD THE SHISHI MOVEMENT.

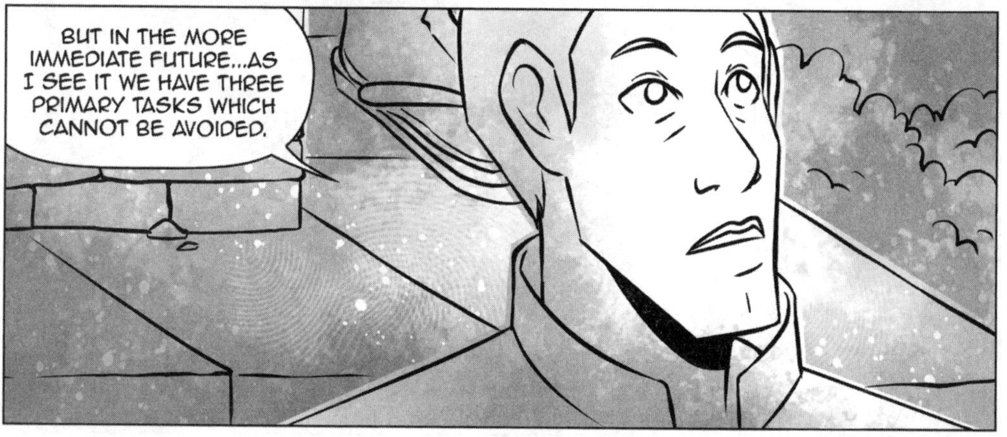
BUT IN THE MORE IMMEDIATE FUTURE...AS I SEE IT WE HAVE THREE PRIMARY TASKS WHICH CANNOT BE AVOIDED.

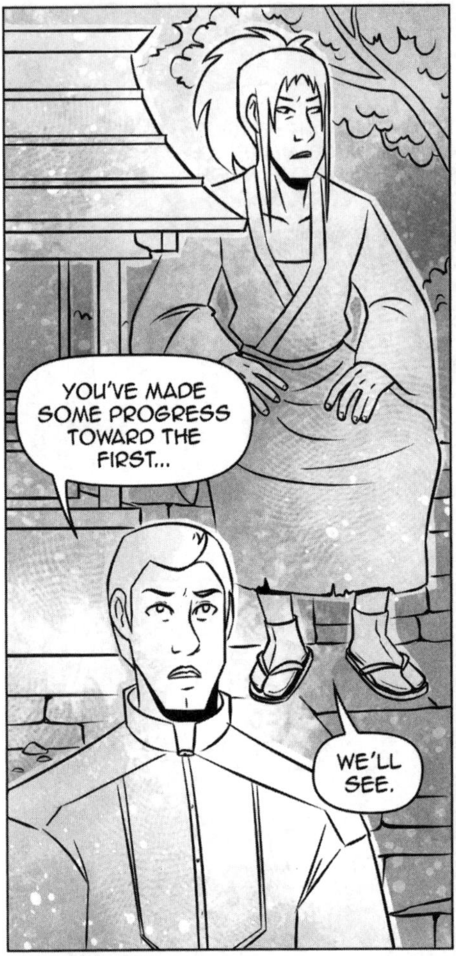
YOU'VE MADE SOME PROGRESS TOWARD THE FIRST...
WE'LL SEE.

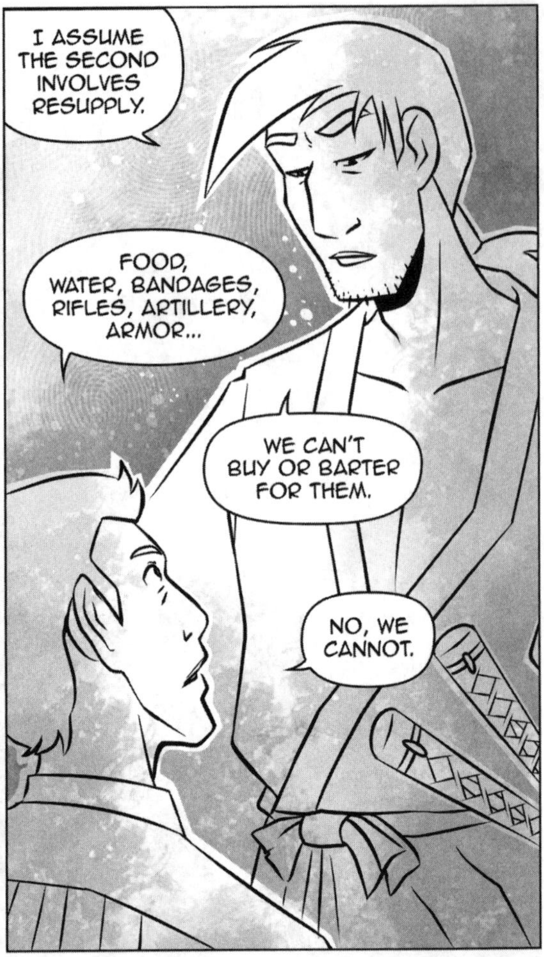
I ASSUME THE SECOND INVOLVES RESUPPLY.
FOOD, WATER, BANDAGES, RIFLES, ARTILLERY, ARMOR...
WE CAN'T BUY OR BARTER FOR THEM.
NO, WE CANNOT.

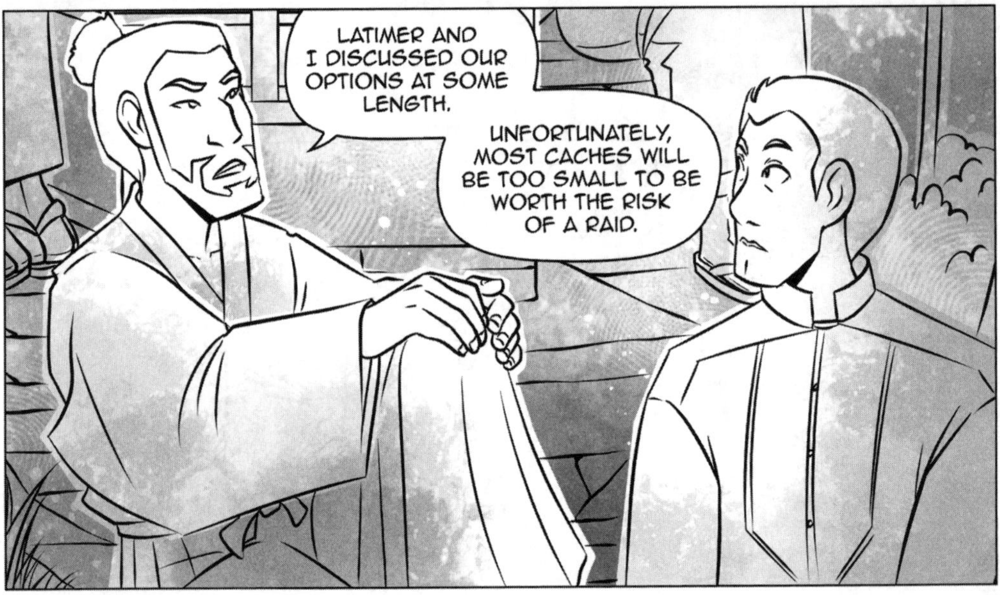
LATIMER AND I DISCUSSED OUR OPTIONS AT SOME LENGTH.
UNFORTUNATELY, MOST CACHES WILL BE TOO SMALL TO BE WORTH THE RISK OF A RAID.

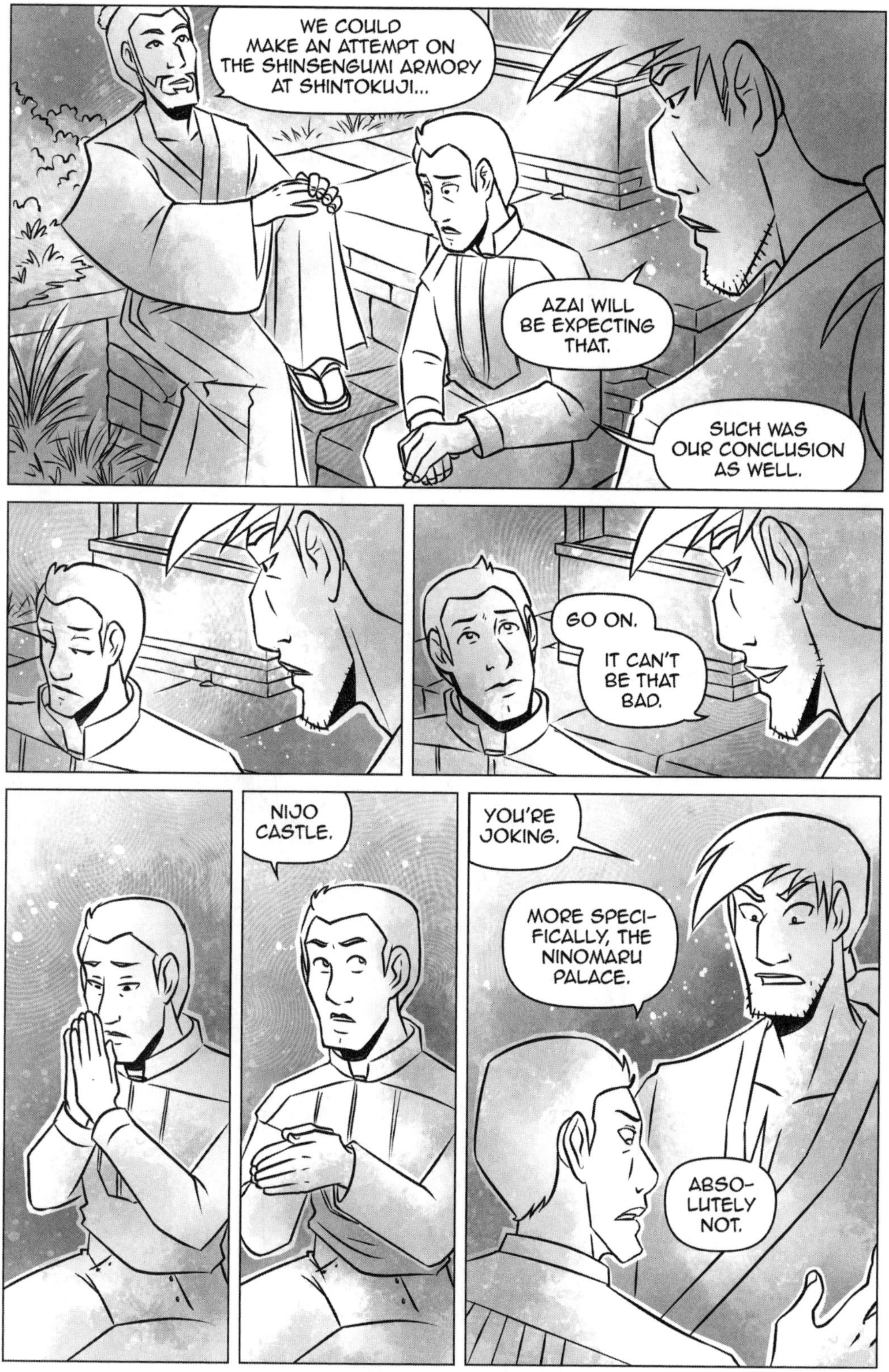
WE COULD MAKE AN ATTEMPT ON THE SHINSENGUMI ARMORY AT SHINTOKUJI...
AZAI WILL BE EXPECTING THAT.
SUCH WAS OUR CONCLUSION AS WELL.
GO ON.
IT CAN'T BE THAT BAD.
NIJO CASTLE.
YOU'RE JOKING.
MORE SPECI-FICALLY, THE NINOMARU PALACE.
ABSO-LUTELY NOT.

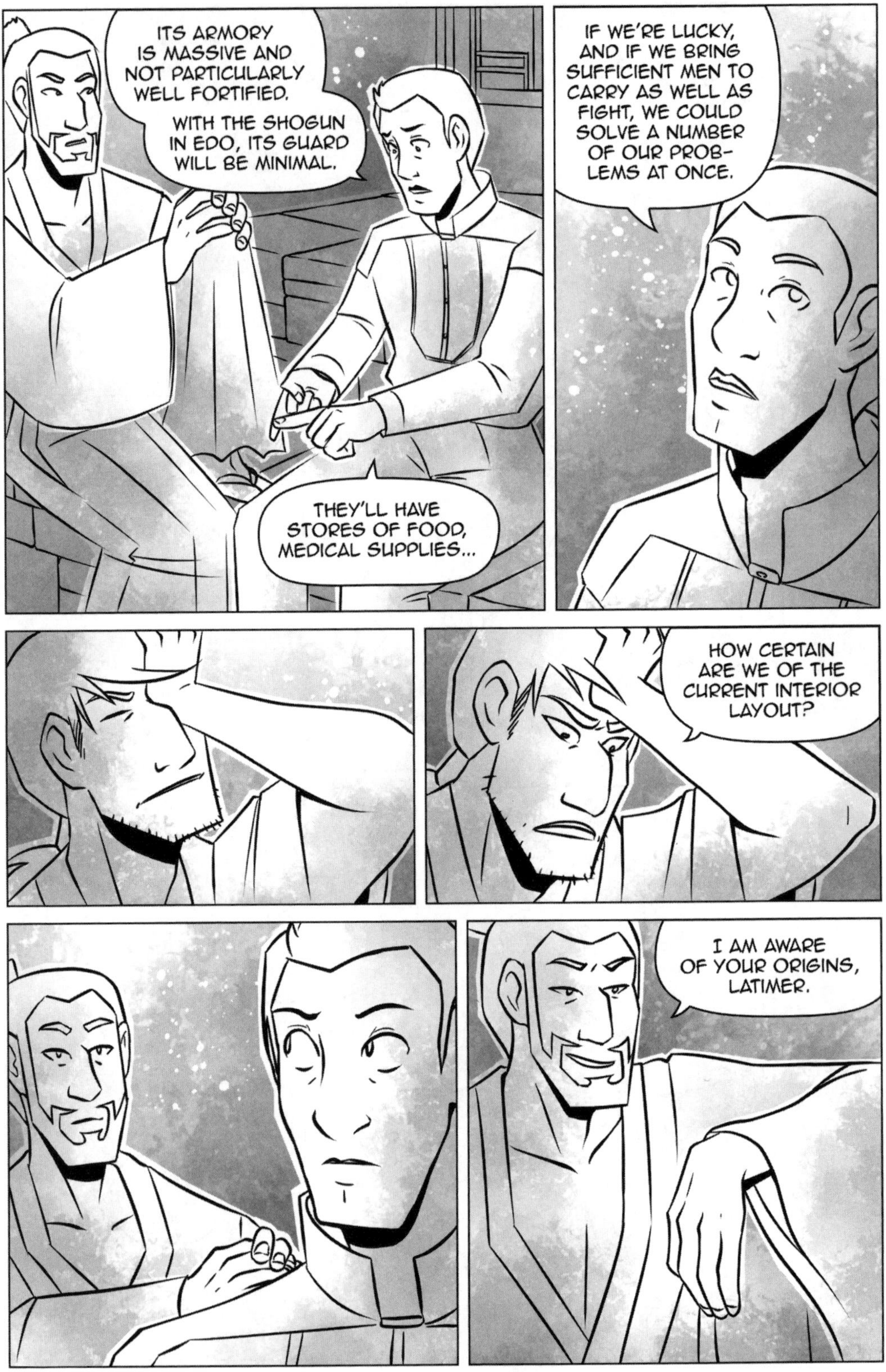
ITS ARMORY IS MASSIVE AND NOT PARTICULARLY WELL FORTIFIED.
WITH THE SHOGUN IN EDO, ITS GUARD WILL BE MINIMAL.
THEY'LL HAVE STORES OF FOOD, MEDICAL SUPPLIES...
IF WE'RE LUCKY, AND IF WE BRING SUFFICIENT MEN TO CARRY AS WELL AS FIGHT, WE COULD SOLVE A NUMBER OF OUR PROB-LEMS AT ONCE.
HOW CERTAIN ARE WE OF THE CURRENT INTERIOR LAYOUT?
I AM AWARE OF YOUR ORIGINS, LATIMER.

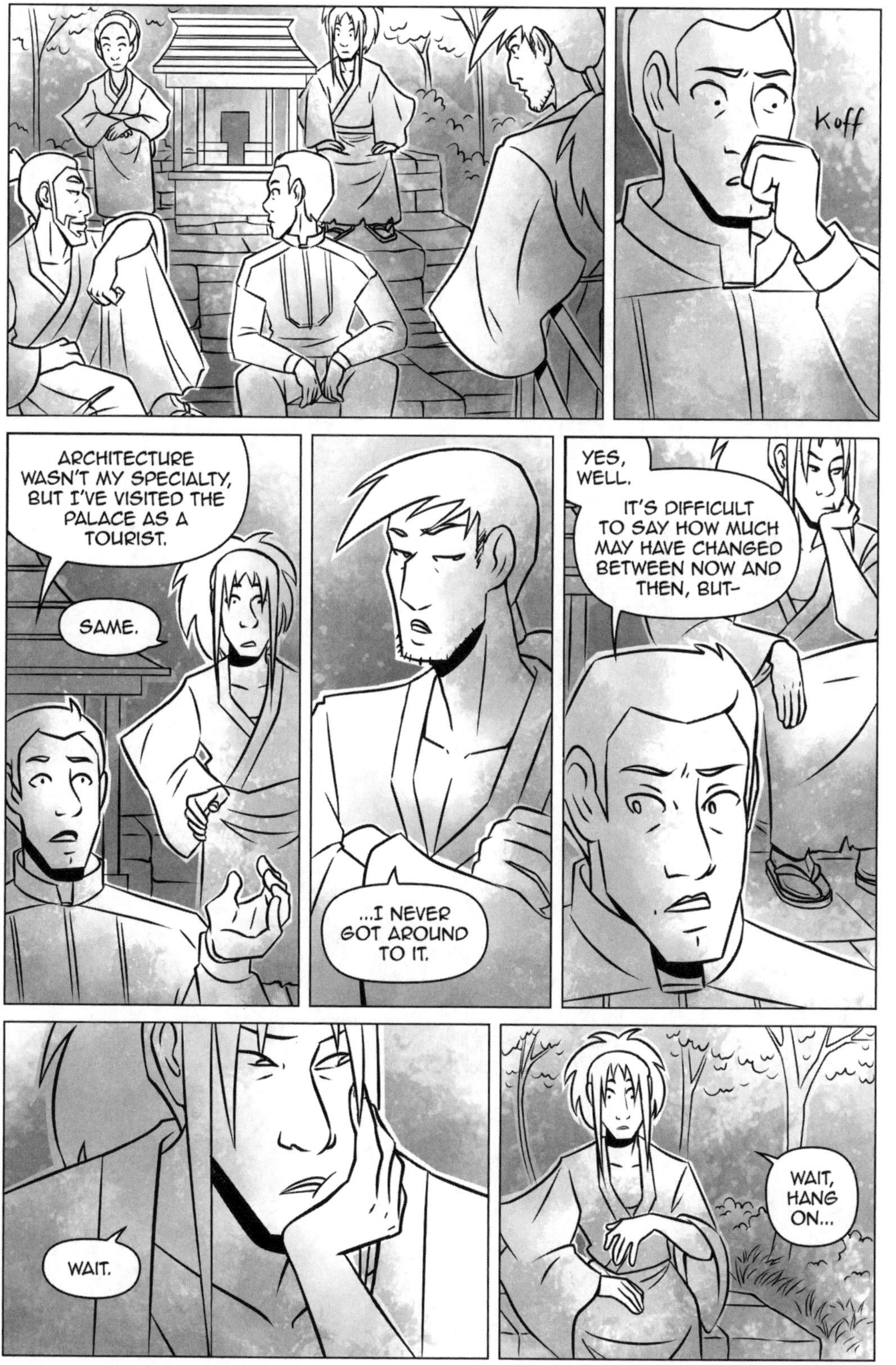
Koff
ARCHITECTURE WASN'T MY SPECIALTY, BUT I'VE VISITED THE PALACE AS A TOURIST.
SAME.
...I NEVER GOT AROUND TO IT.
YES, WELL.
IT'S DIFFICULT TO SAY HOW MUCH MAY HAVE CHANGED BETWEEN NOW AND THEN, BUT-
WAIT.
WAIT, HANG ON...

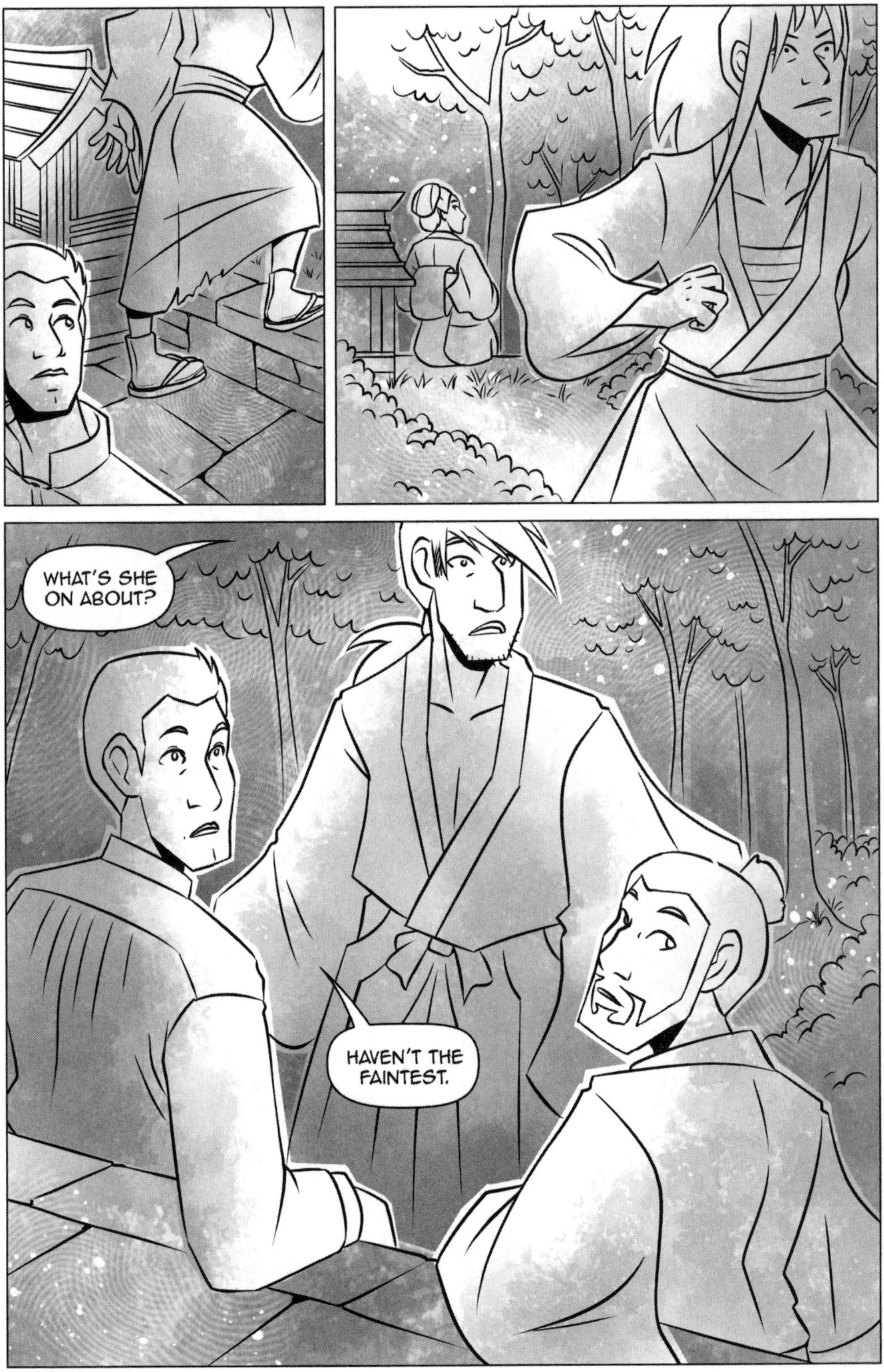
WHAT'S SHE ON ABOUT?
HAVEN'T THE FAINTEST.

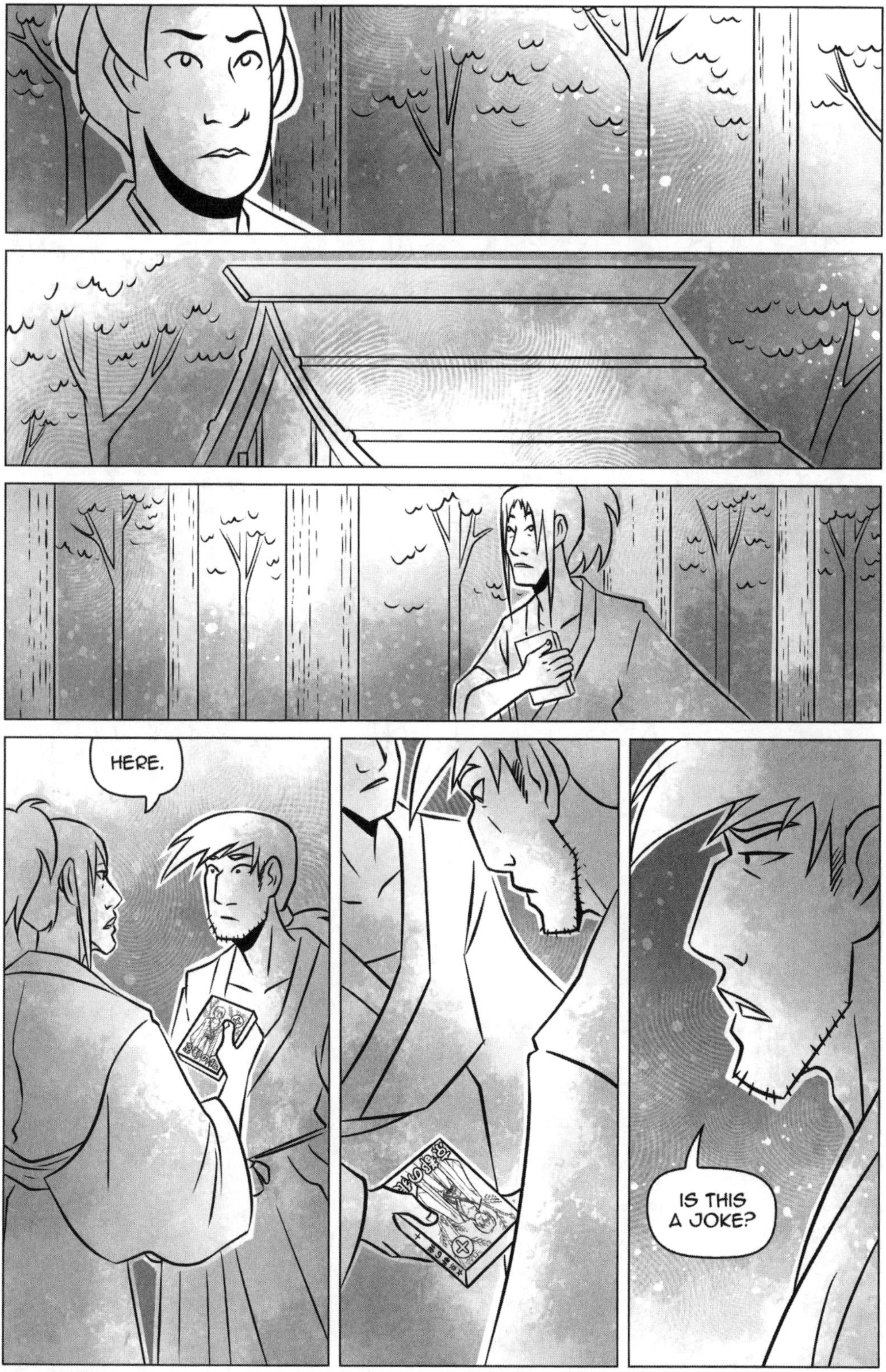
HERE.
IS THIS A JOKE?

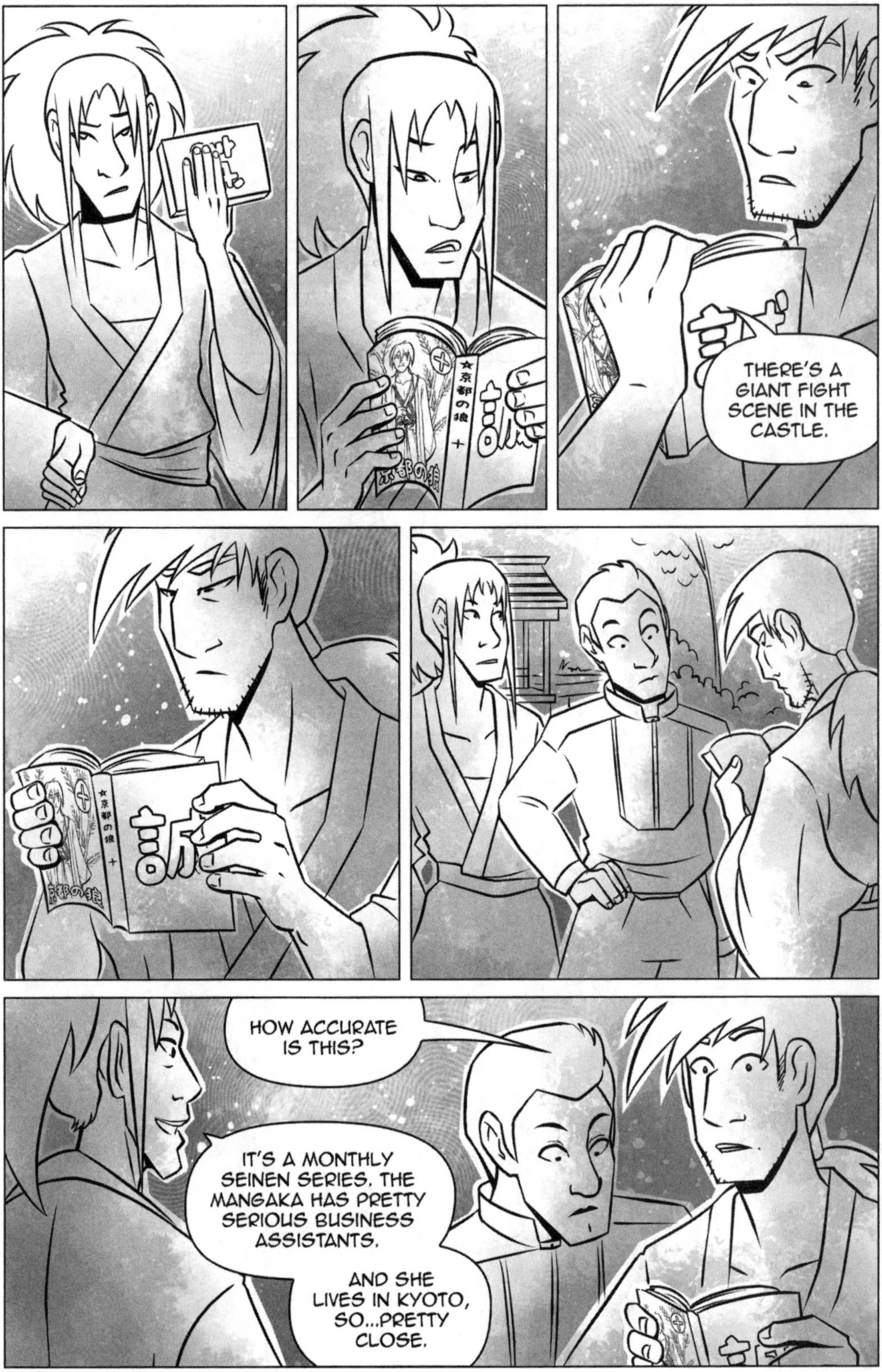
京都の狼
THERE'S A GIANT FIGHT SCENE IN THE CASTLE.
HOW ACCURATE IS THIS?
IT'S A MONTHLY SEINEN SERIES. THE MANGAKA HAS PRETTY SERIOUS BUSINESS ASSISTANTS.
AND SHE LIVES IN KYOTO, SO...PRETTY CLOSE.

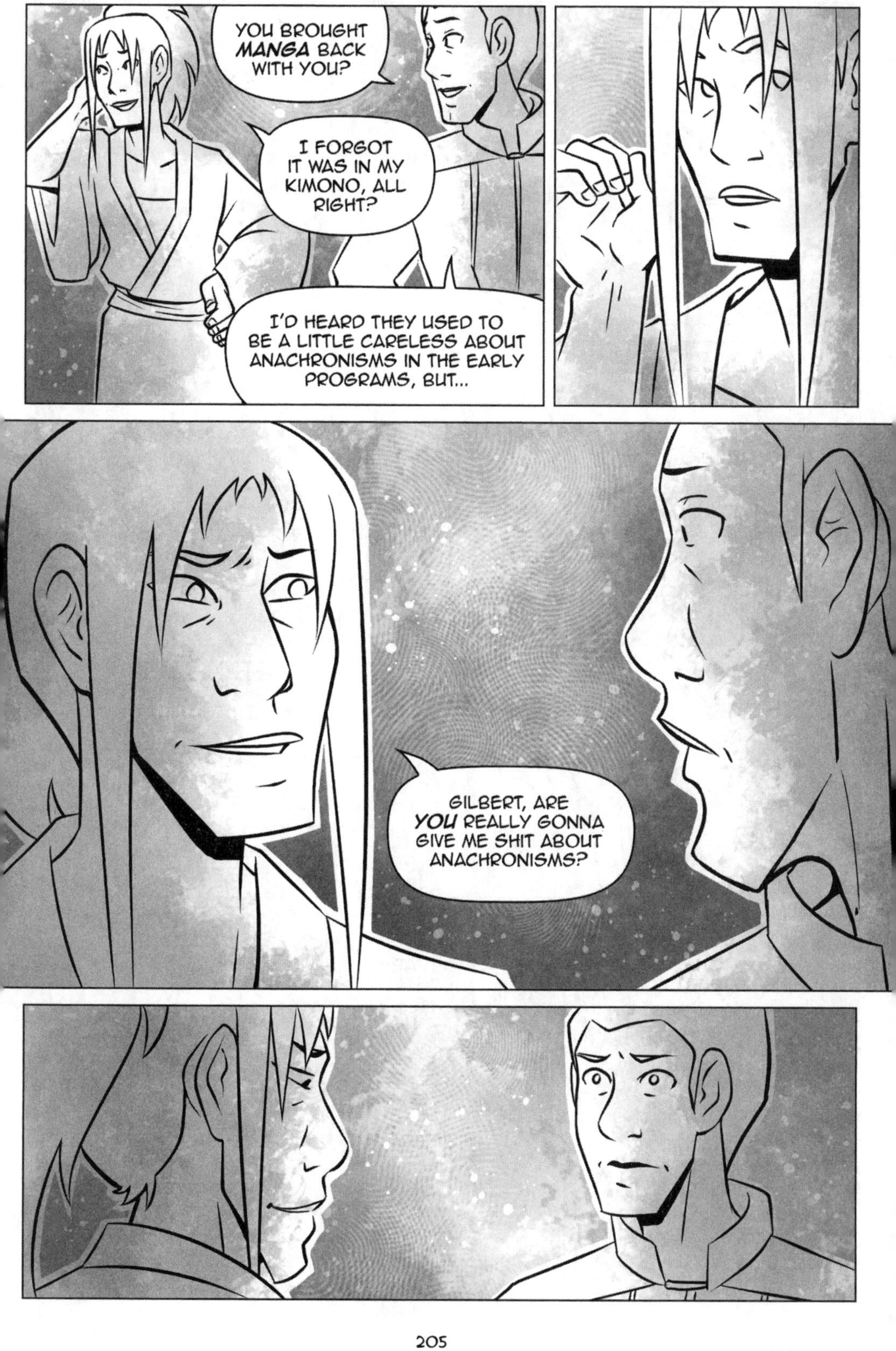
YOU BROUGHT MANGA BACK WITH YOU?
I FORGOT IT WAS IN MY KIMONO, ALL RIGHT?
I'D HEARD THEY USED TO BE A LITTLE CARELESS ABOUT ANACHRONISMS IN THE EARLY PROGRAMS, BUT...
GILBERT, ARE YOU REALLY GONNA GIVE ME SHIT ABOUT ANACHRONISMS?

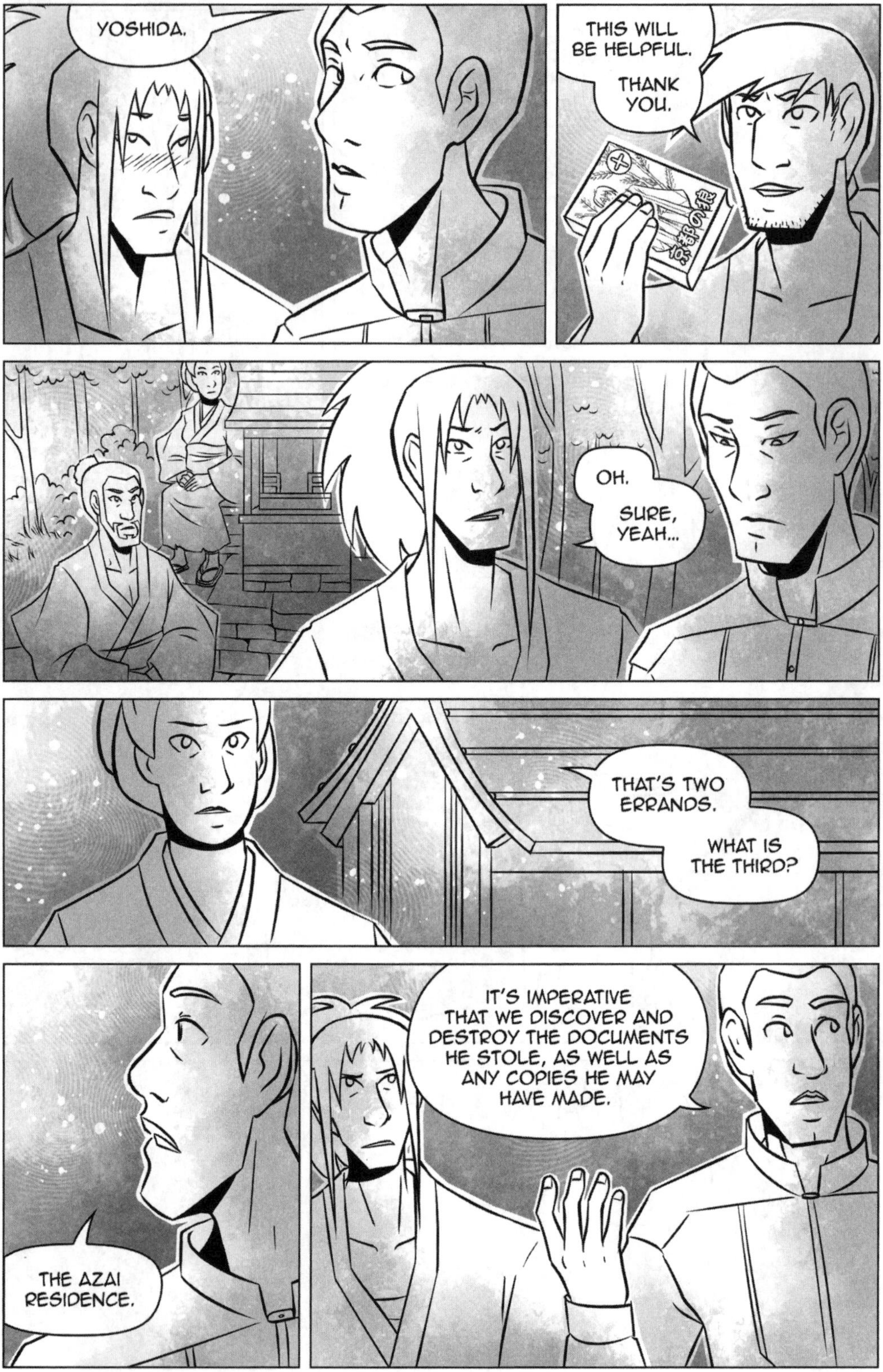
YOSHIDA.
THIS WILL BE HELPFUL.
THANK YOU.
OH.
SURE, YEAH...
THAT'S TWO ERRANDS.
WHAT IS THE THIRD?
THE AZAI RESIDENCE.
IT'S IMPERATIVE THAT WE DISCOVER AND DESTROY THE DOCUMENTS HE STOLE, AS WELL AS ANY COPIES HE MAY HAVE MADE.

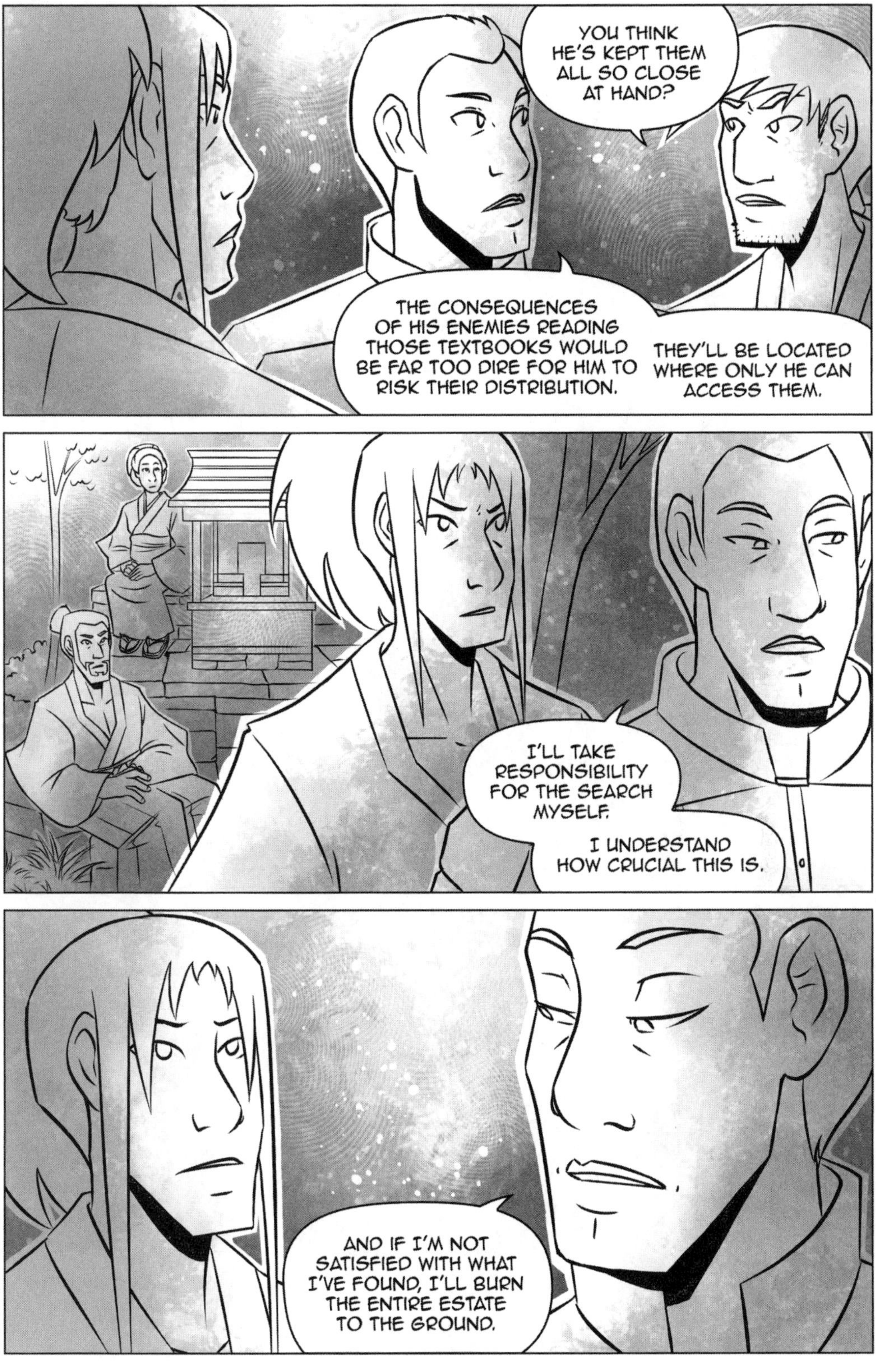
YOU THINK HE'S KEPT THEM ALL SO CLOSE AT HAND?
THE CONSEQUENCES OF HIS ENEMIES READING THOSE TEXTBOOKS WOULD BE FAR TOO DIRE FOR HIM TO RISK THEIR DISTRIBUTION.
THEY'LL BE LOCATED WHERE ONLY HE CAN ACCESS THEM.
I'LL TAKE RESPONSIBILITY FOR THE SEARCH MYSELF.
I UNDERSTAND HOW CRUCIAL THIS IS.
AND IF I'M NOT SATISFIED WITH WHAT I'VE FOUND, I'LL BURN THE ENTIRE ESTATE TO THE GROUND.

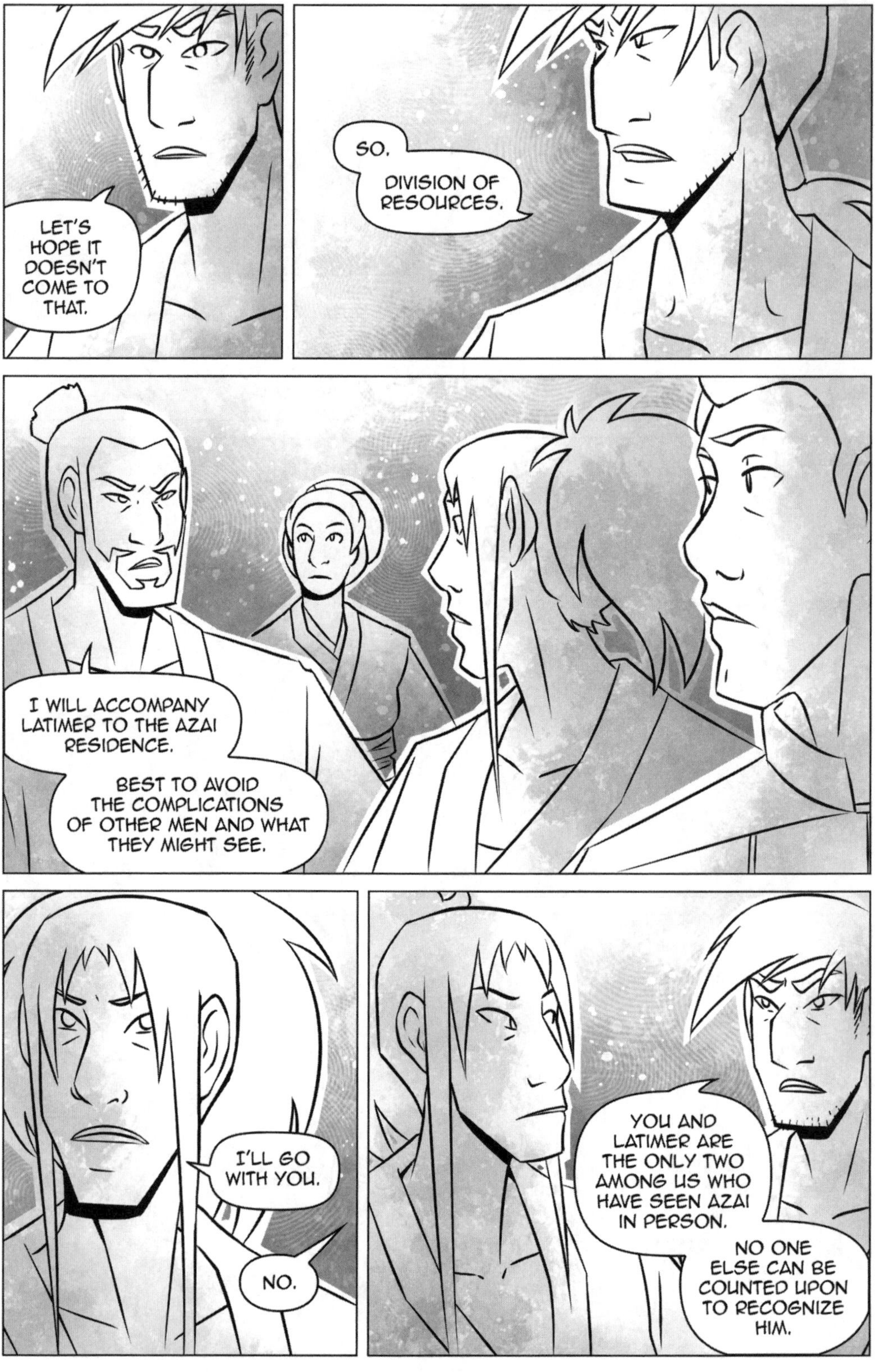
LET'S HOPE IT DOESN'T COME TO THAT.
SO.
DIVISION OF RESOURCES.
I WILL ACCOMPANY LATIMER TO THE AZAI RESIDENCE.
BEST TO AVOID THE COMPLICATIONS OF OTHER MEN AND WHAT THEY MIGHT SEE.
I'LL GO WITH YOU.
NO.
YOU AND LATIMER ARE THE ONLY TWO AMONG US WHO HAVE SEEN AZAI IN PERSON.
NO ONE ELSE CAN BE COUNTED UPON TO RECOGNIZE HIM.

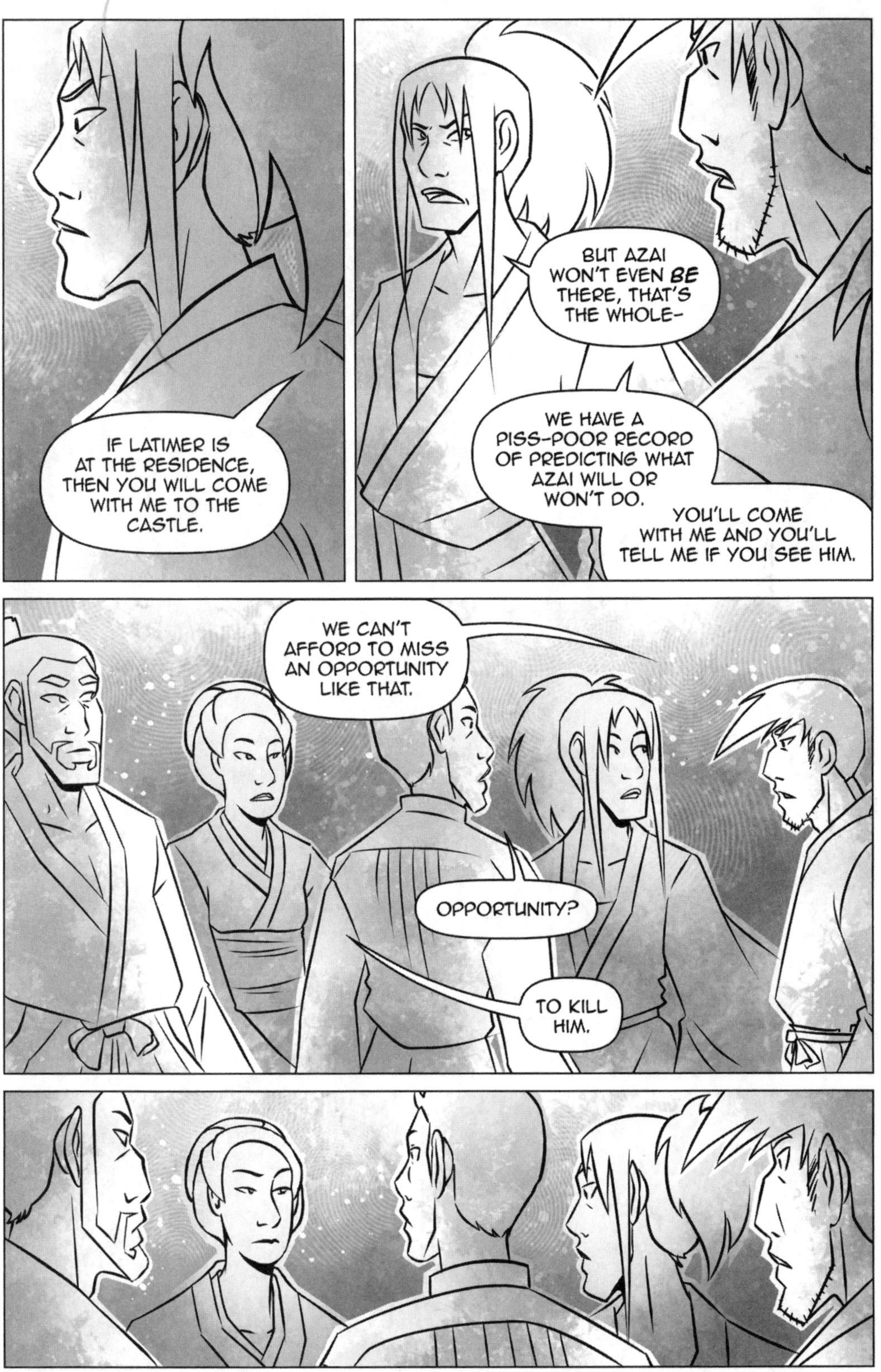
IF LATIMER IS AT THE RESIDENCE, THEN YOU WILL COME WITH ME TO THE CASTLE.
BUT AZAI WON'T EVEN **BE** THERE, THAT'S THE WHOLE-
WE HAVE A PISS-POOR RECORD OF PREDICTING WHAT AZAI WILL OR WON'T DO.
YOU'LL COME WITH ME AND YOU'LL TELL ME IF YOU SEE HIM.
WE CAN'T AFFORD TO MISS AN OPPORTUNITY LIKE THAT.
OPPORTUNITY?
TO KILL HIM.

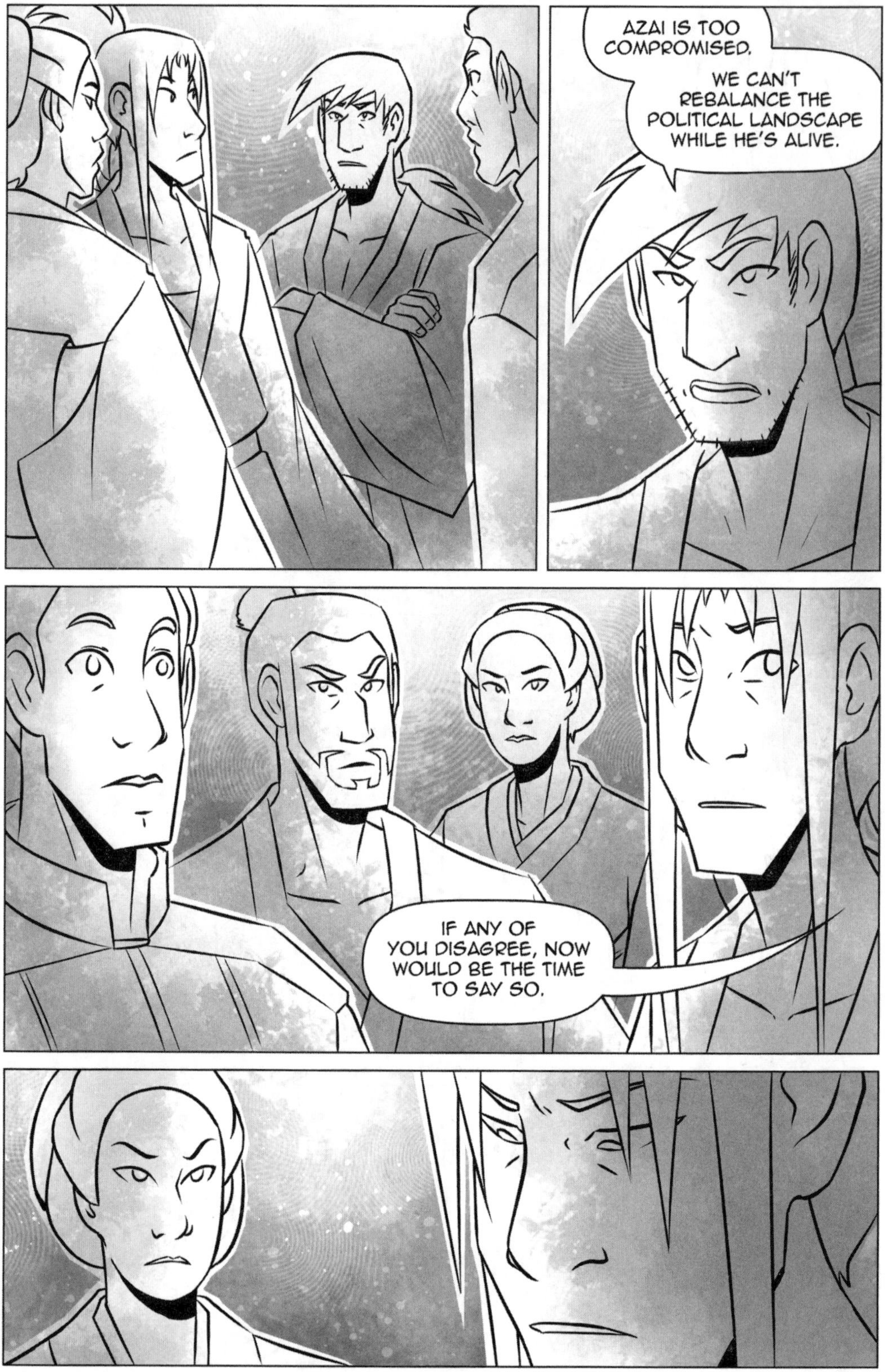
AZAI IS TOO COMPROMISED.
WE CAN'T REBALANCE THE POLITICAL LANDSCAPE WHILE HE'S ALIVE.
IF ANY OF YOU DISAGREE, NOW WOULD BE THE TIME TO SAY SO.

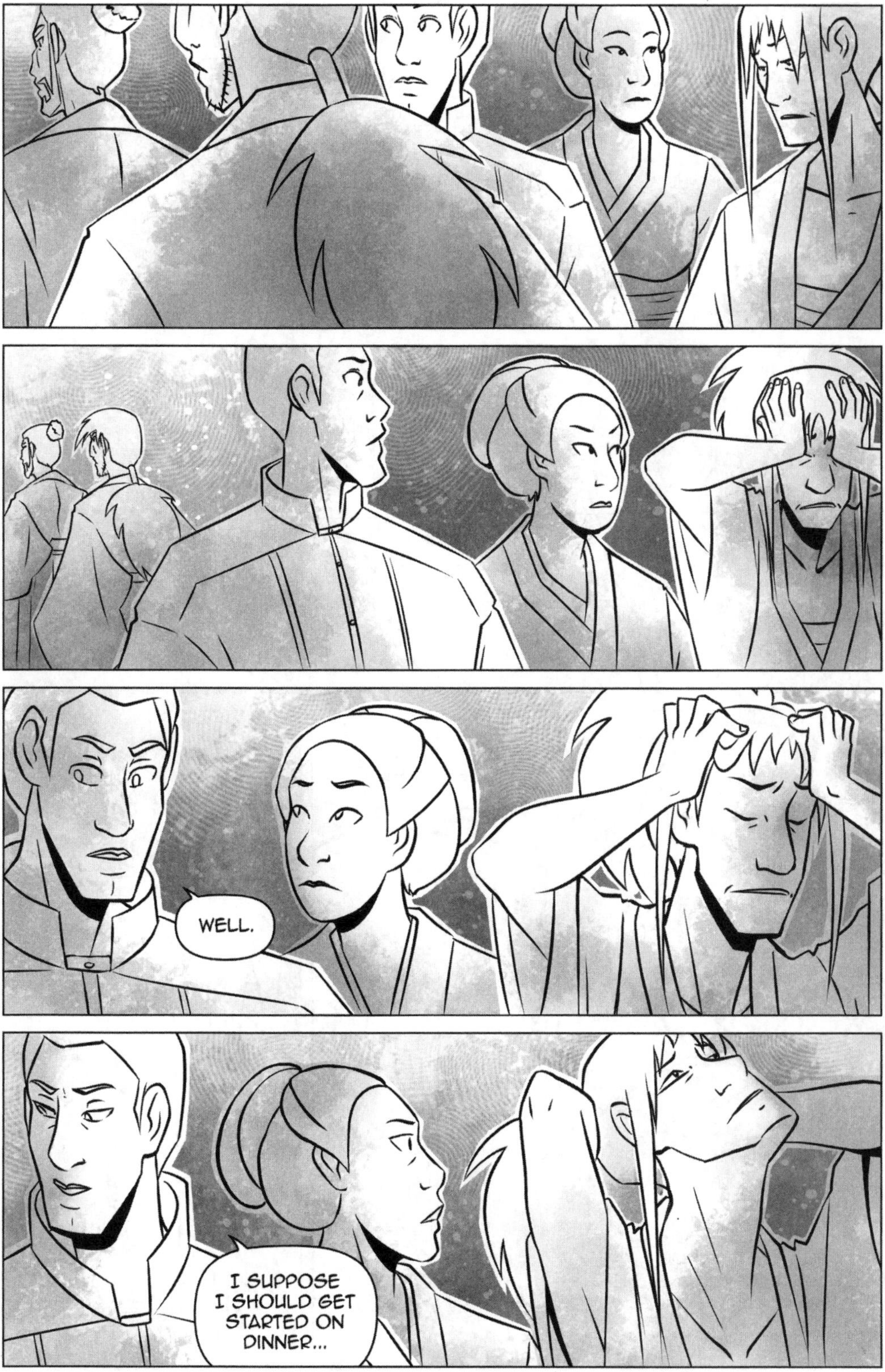
WELL.
I SUPPOSE I SHOULD GET STARTED ON DINNER...

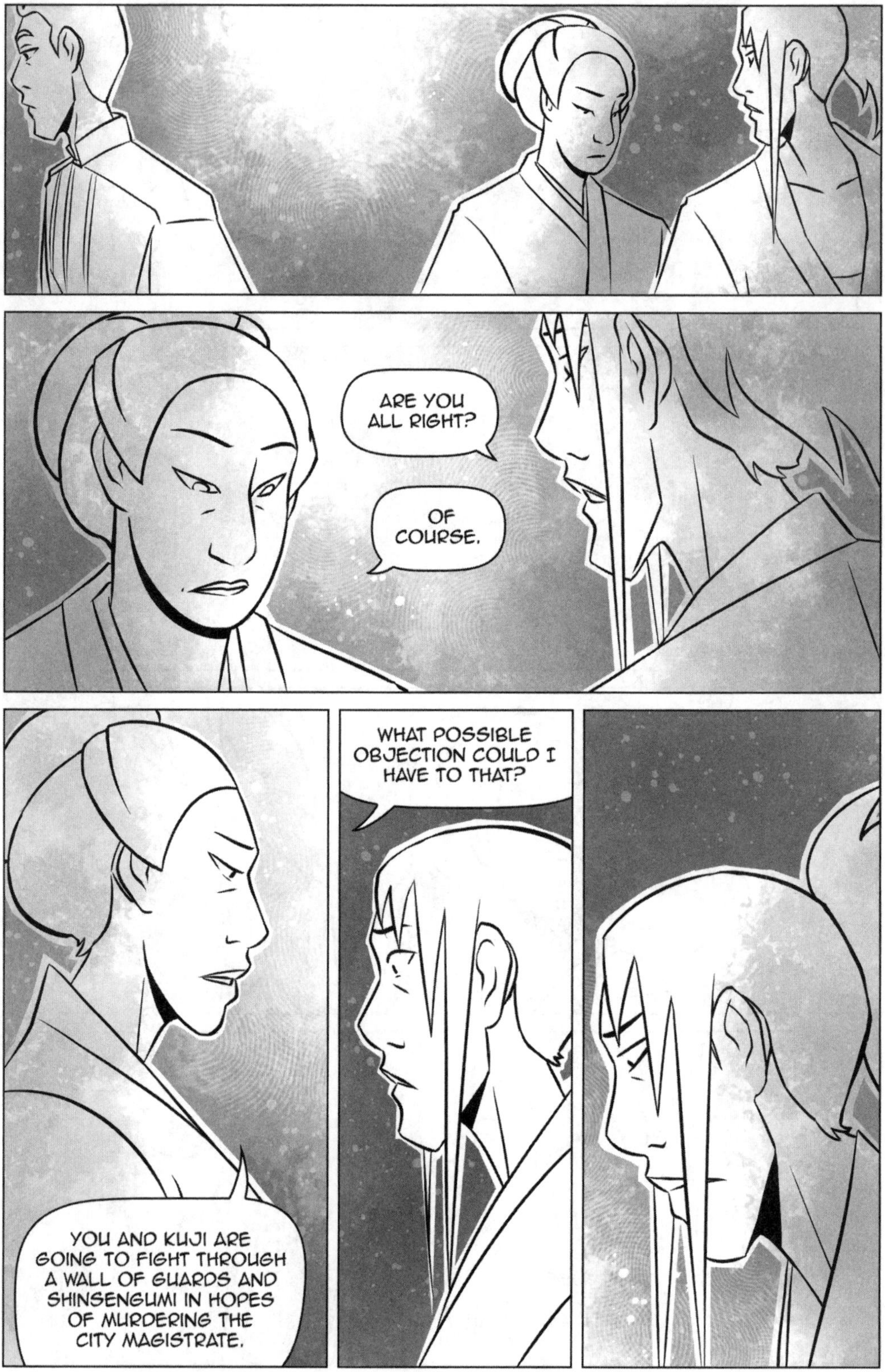
ARE YOU ALL RIGHT?
OF COURSE.
YOU AND KUJI ARE GOING TO FIGHT THROUGH A WALL OF GUARDS AND SHINSENGUMI IN HOPES OF MURDERING THE CITY MAGISTRATE.
WHAT POSSIBLE OBJECTION COULD I HAVE TO THAT?

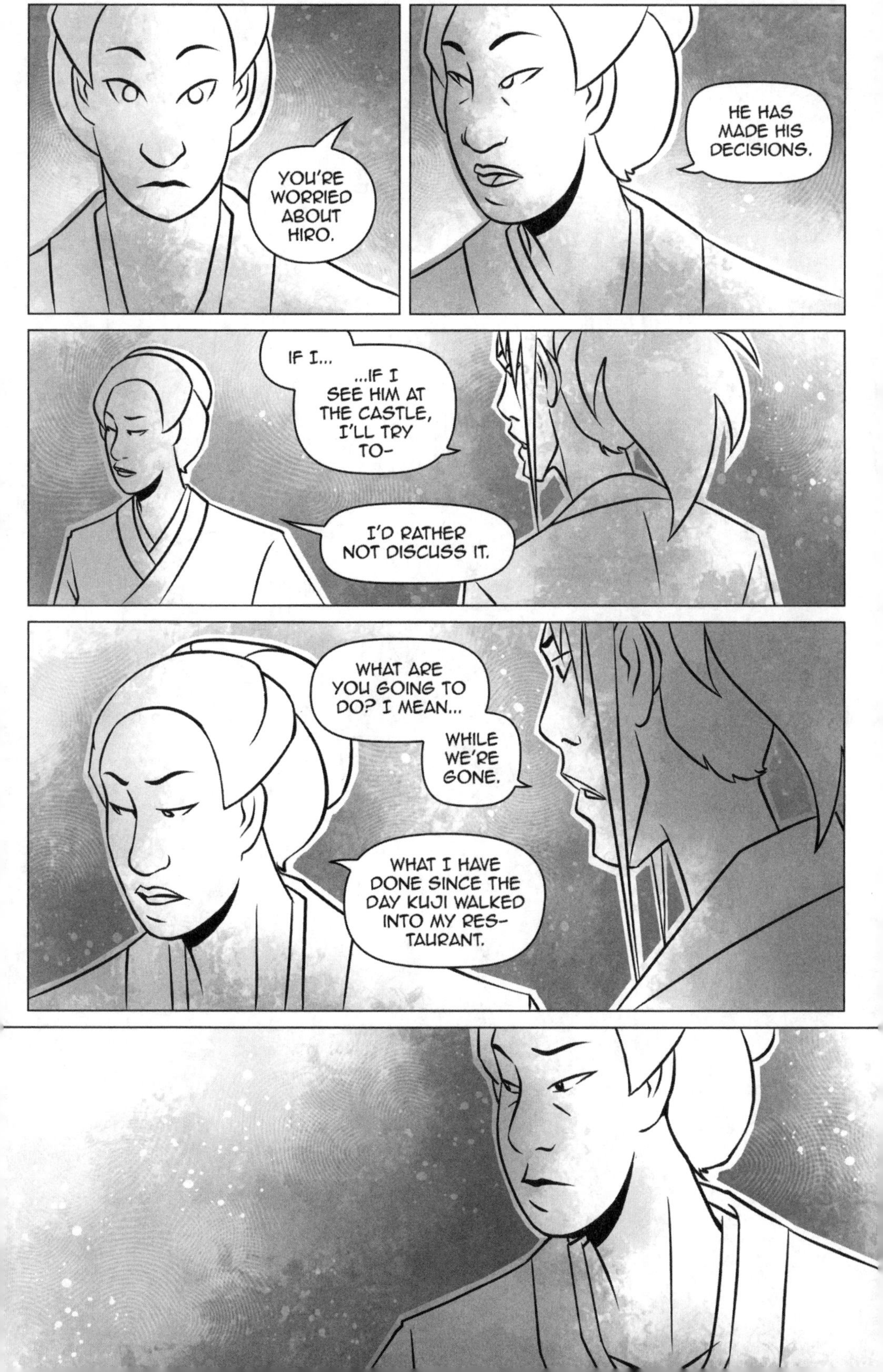
YOU'RE WORRIED ABOUT HIRO.
HE HAS MADE HIS DECISIONS.
IF I...
...IF I SEE HIM AT THE CASTLE, I'LL TRY TO-
I'D RATHER NOT DISCUSS IT.
WHAT ARE YOU GOING TO DO? I MEAN...
WHILE WE'RE GONE.
WHAT I HAVE DONE SINCE THE DAY KUJI WALKED INTO MY RES-TAURANT.

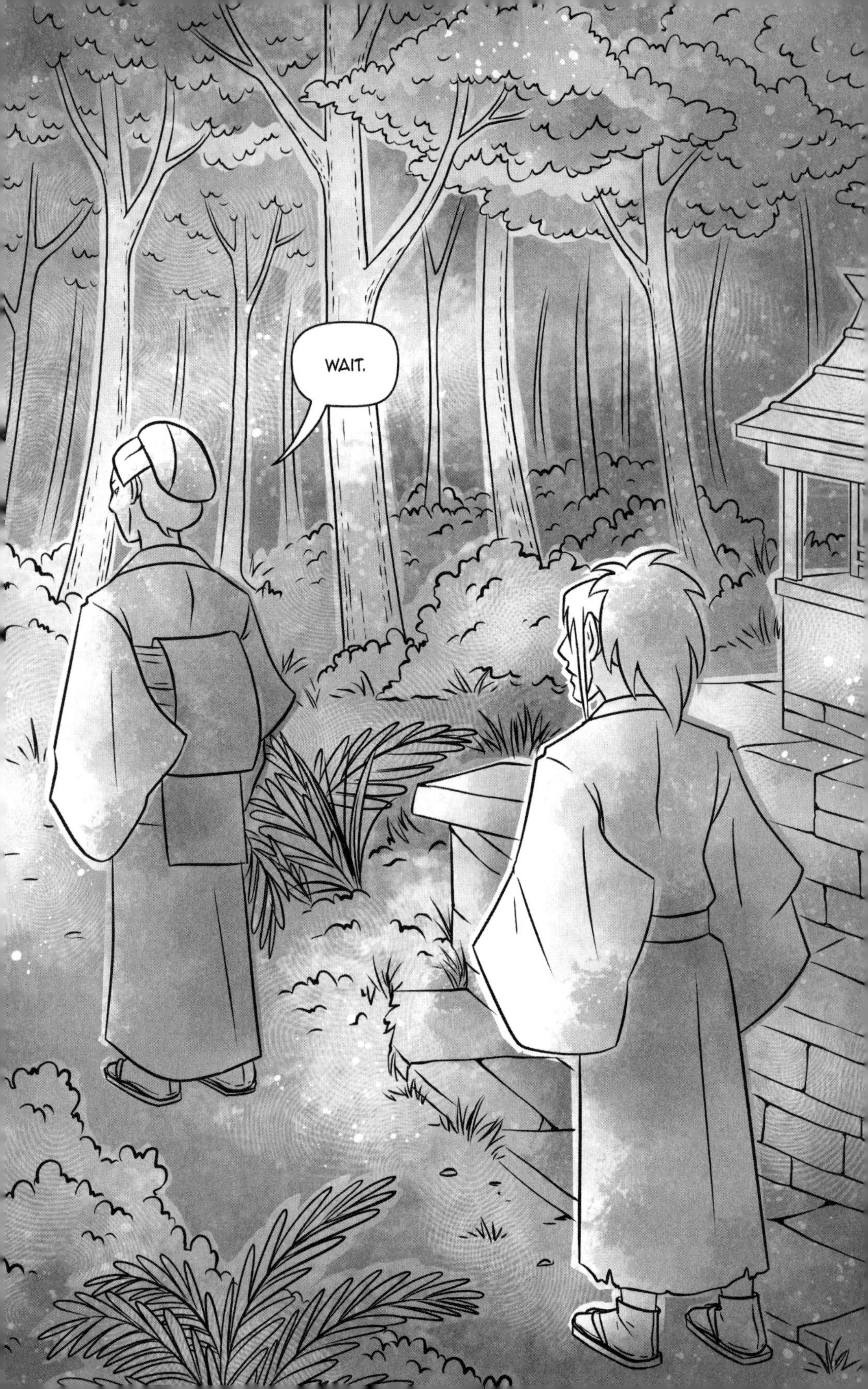
WAIT.

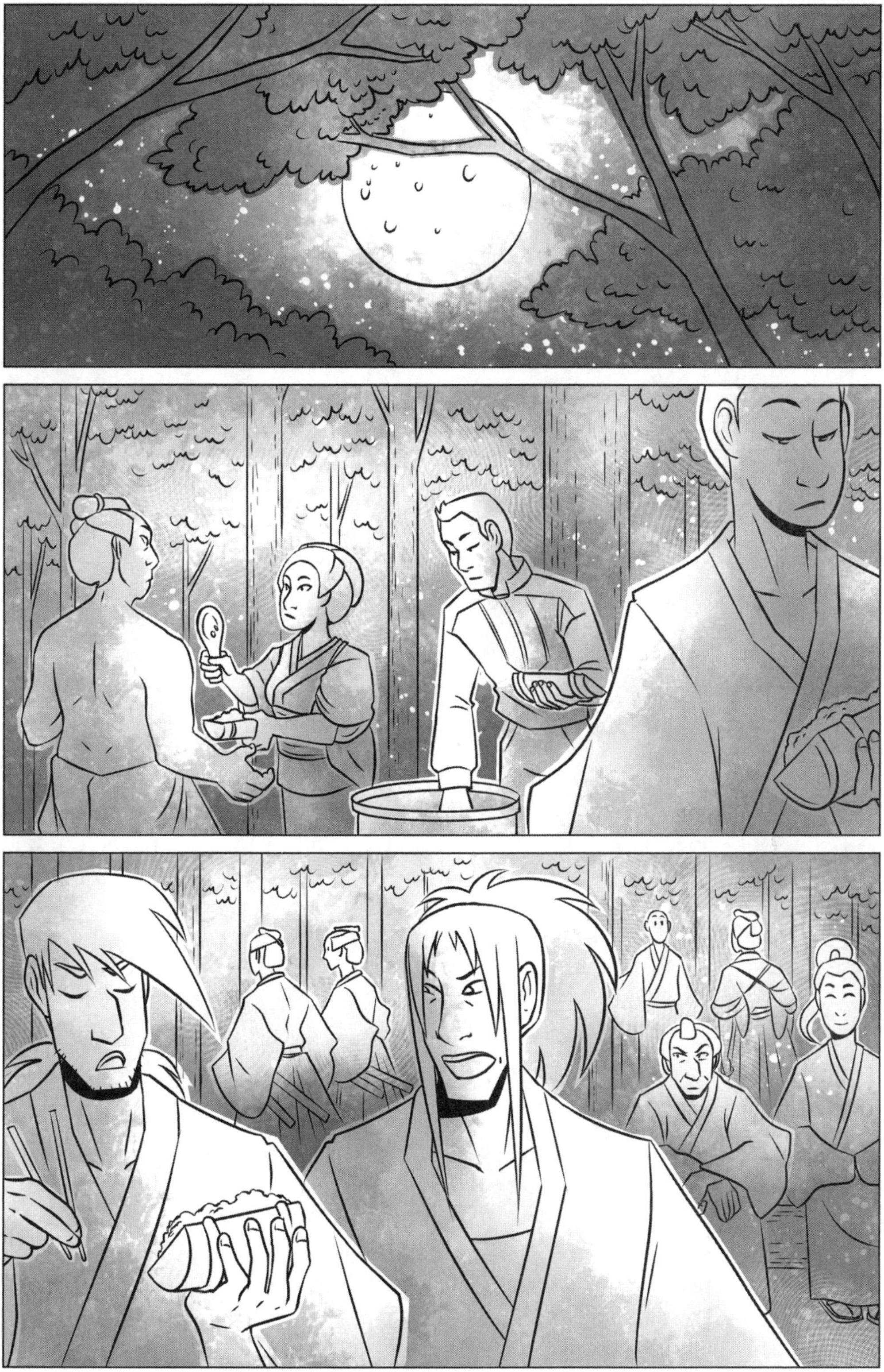

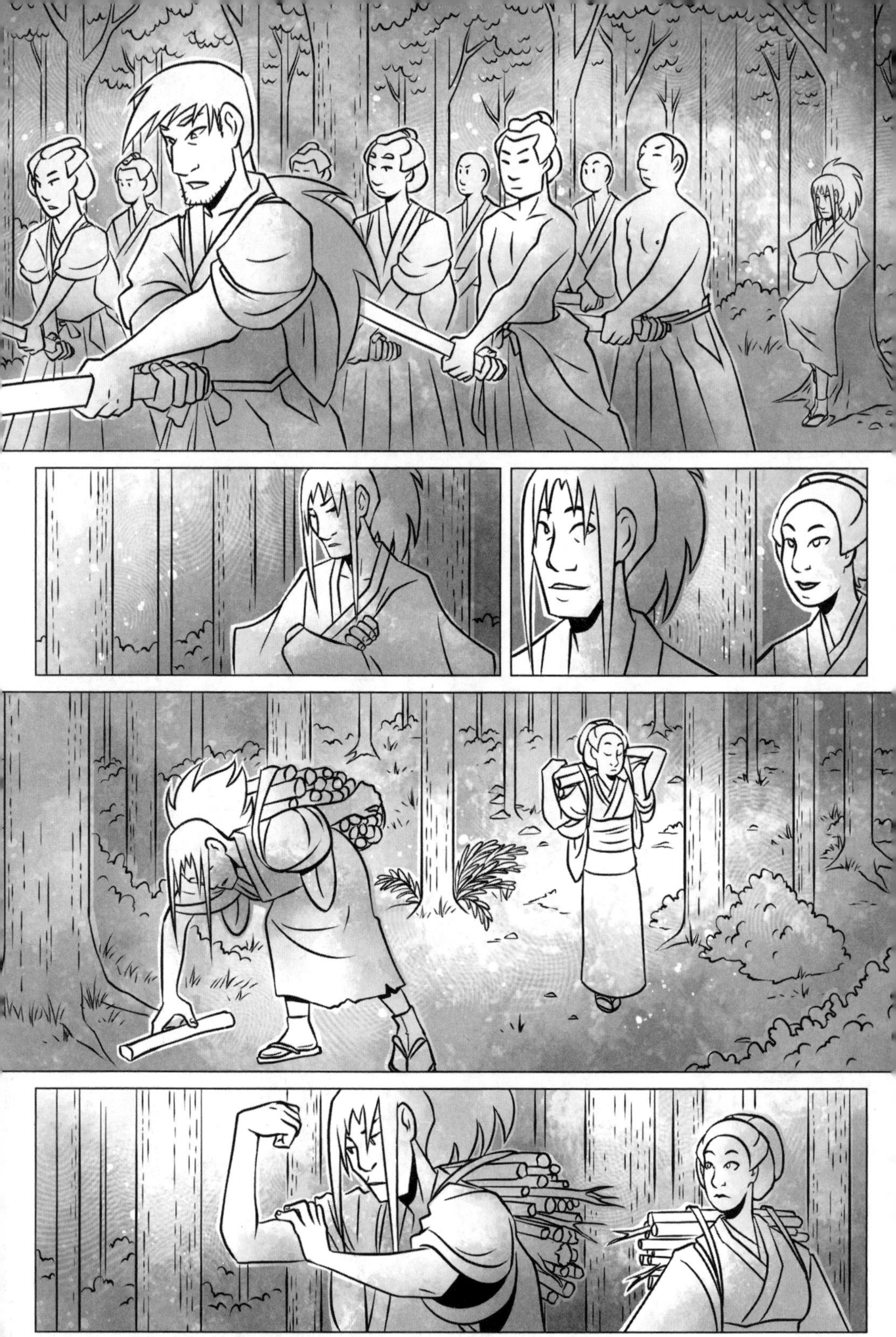

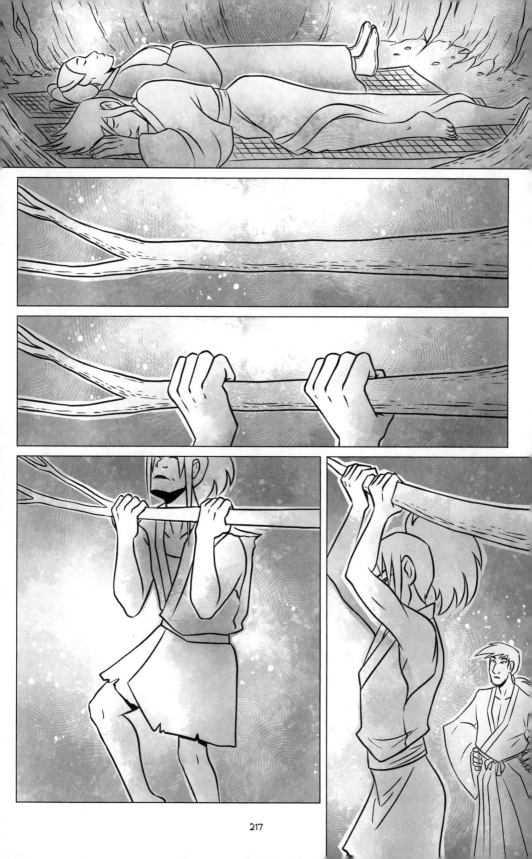

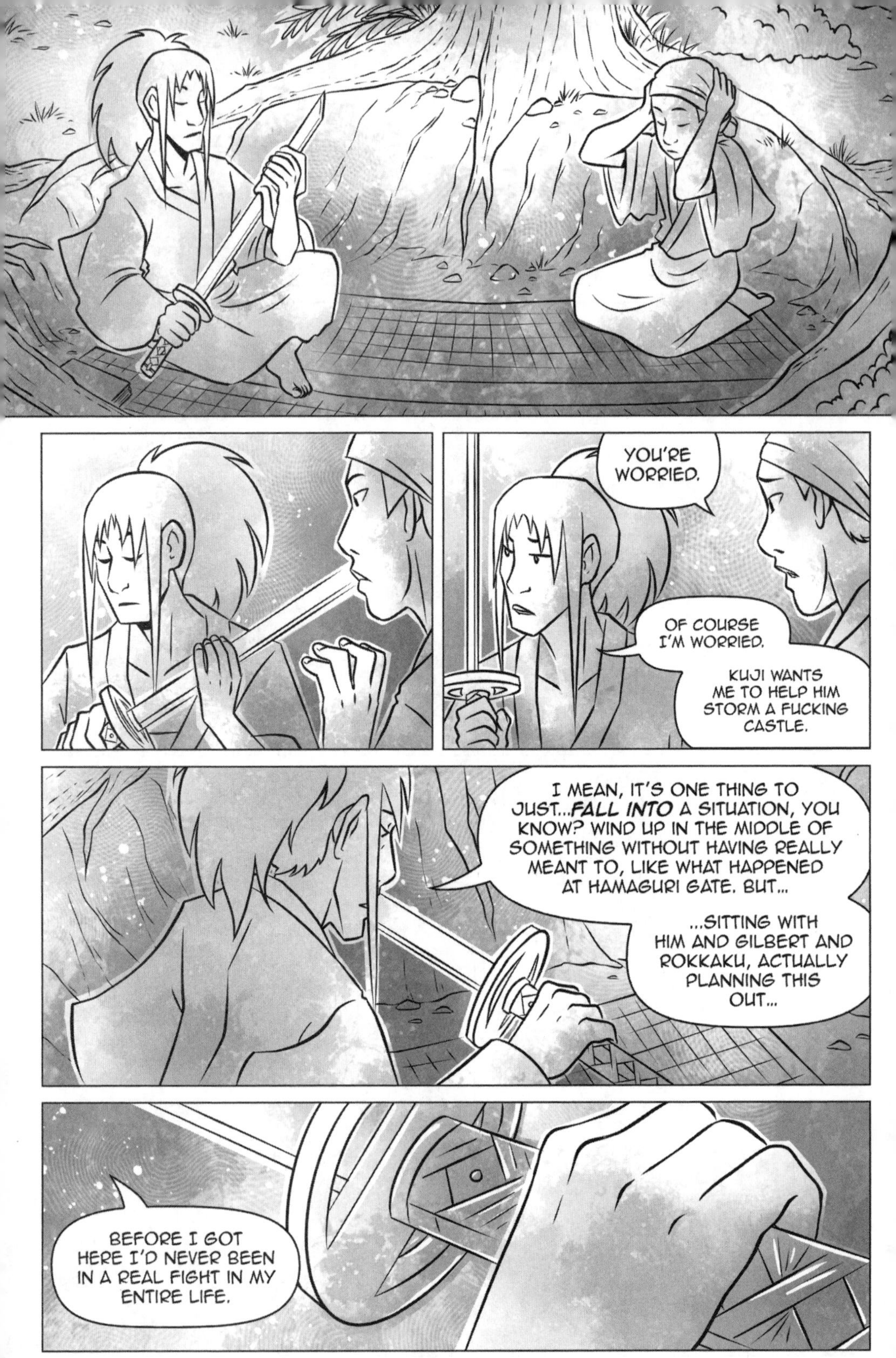
YOU'RE WORRIED.
OF COURSE I'M WORRIED.
KUJI WANTS ME TO HELP HIM STORM A FUCKING CASTLE.
I MEAN, IT'S ONE THING TO JUST...*FALL INTO* A SITUATION, YOU KNOW? WIND UP IN THE MIDDLE OF SOMETHING WITHOUT HAVING REALLY MEANT TO, LIKE WHAT HAPPENED AT HAMAGURI GATE. BUT...
...SITTING WITH HIM AND GILBERT AND ROKKAKU, ACTUALLY PLANNING THIS OUT...
BEFORE I GOT HERE I'D NEVER BEEN IN A REAL FIGHT IN MY ENTIRE LIFE.

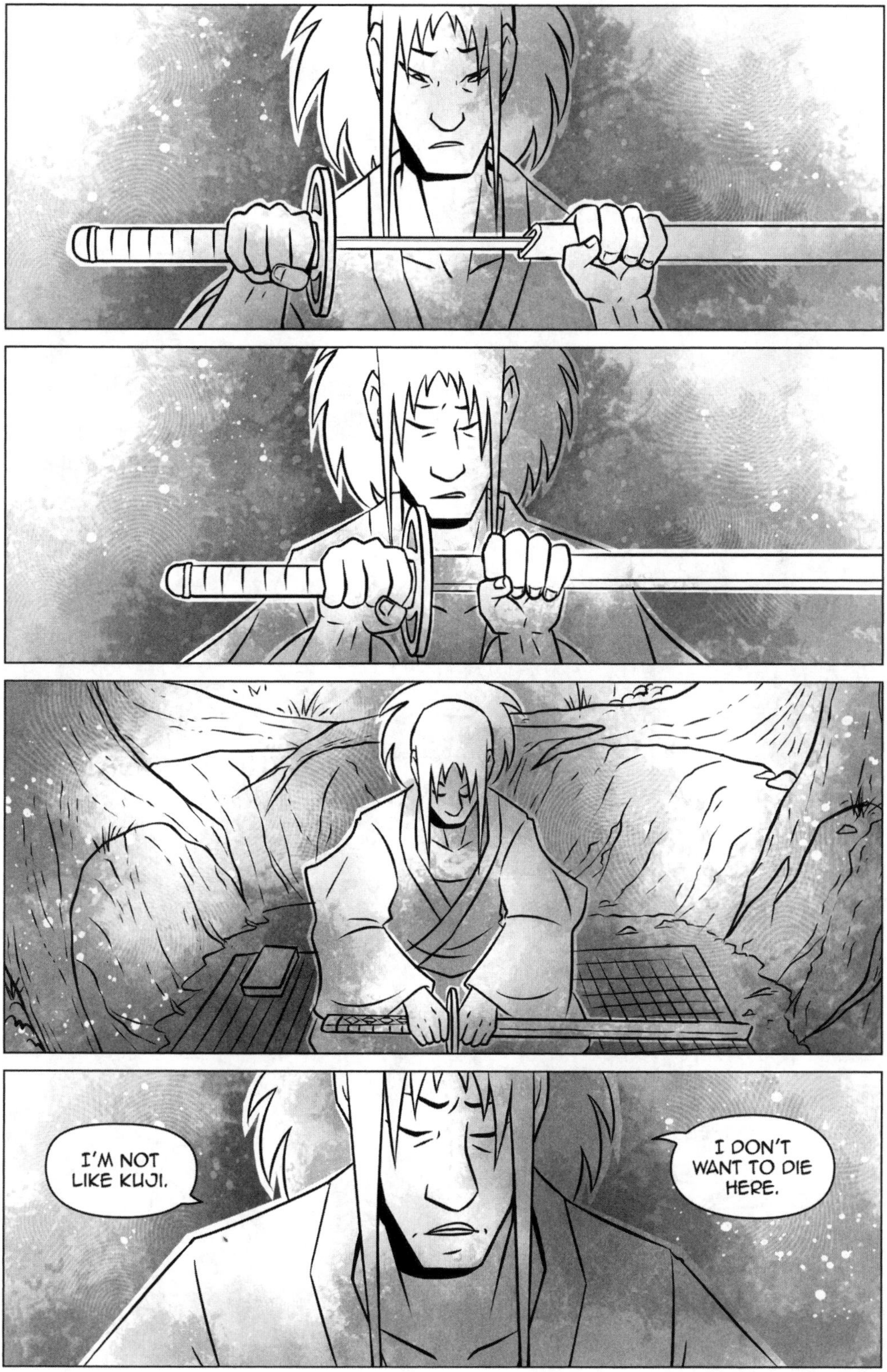
I'M NOT LIKE KUJI.
I DON'T WANT TO DIE HERE.

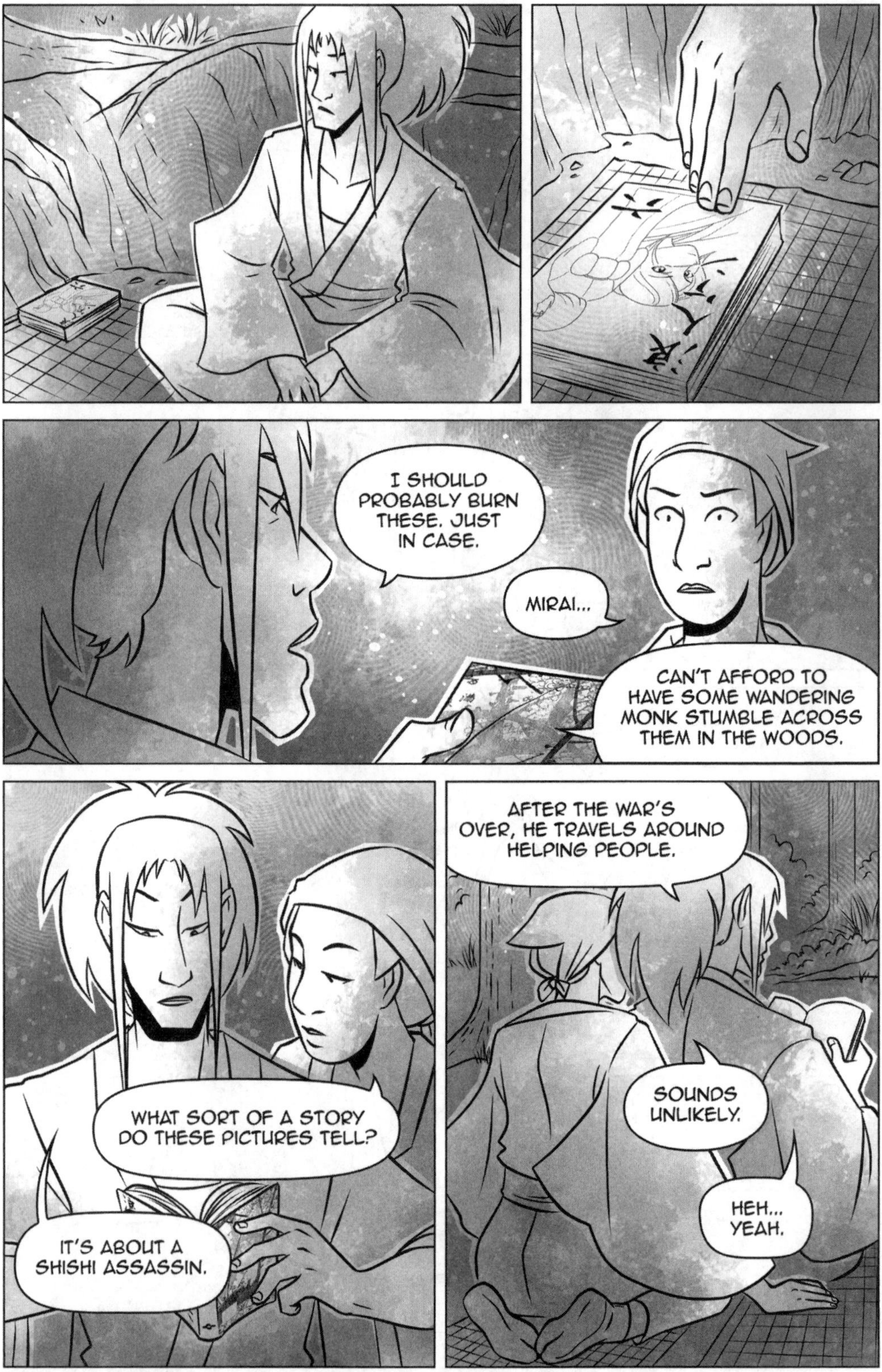
I SHOULD PROBABLY BURN THESE. JUST IN CASE.
MIRAI...
CAN'T AFFORD TO HAVE SOME WANDERING MONK STUMBLE ACROSS THEM IN THE WOODS.
WHAT SORT OF A STORY DO THESE PICTURES TELL?
IT'S ABOUT A SHISHI ASSASSIN.
AFTER THE WAR'S OVER, HE TRAVELS AROUND HELPING PEOPLE.
SOUNDS UNLIKELY.
HEH... YEAH.

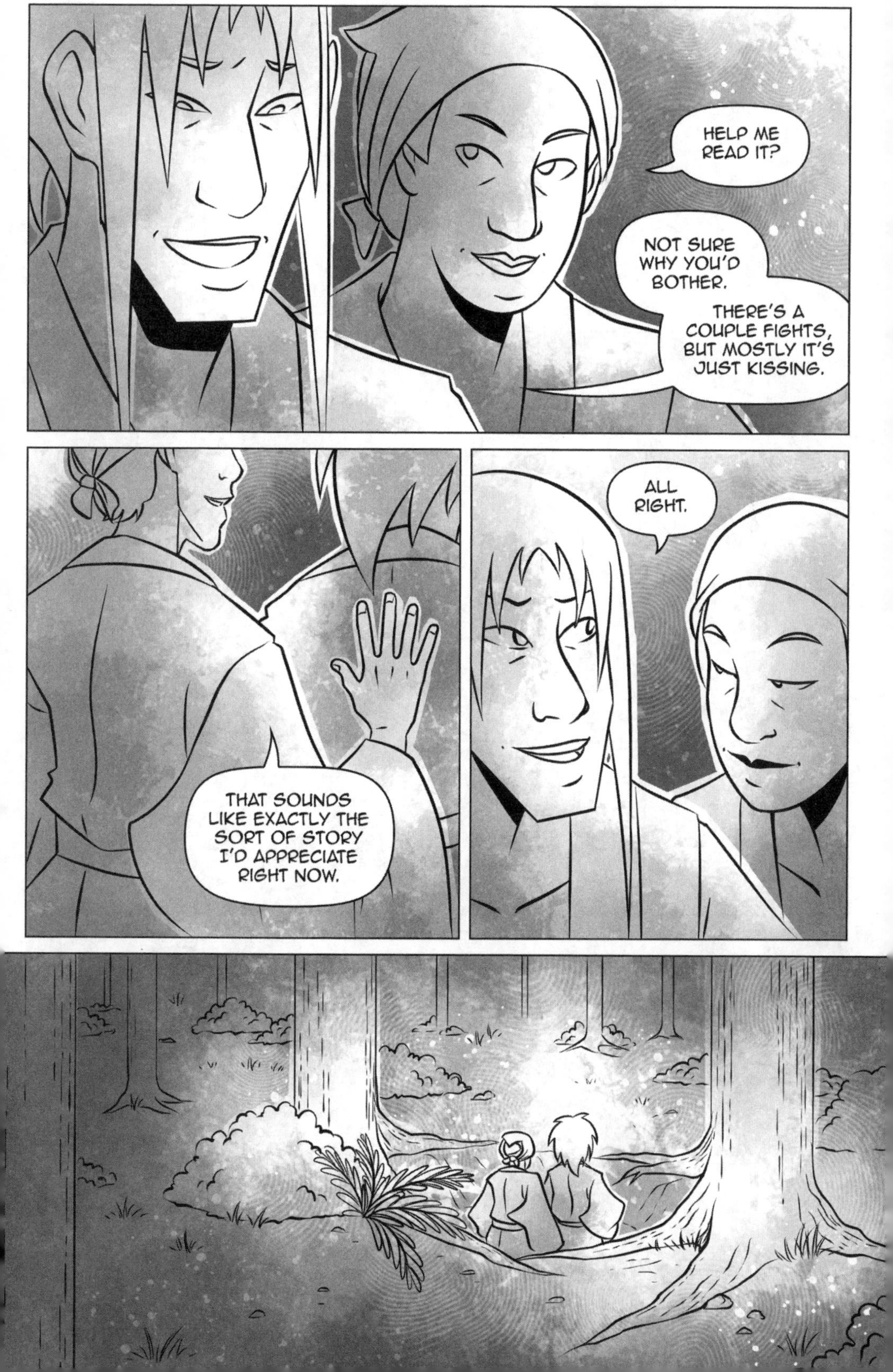
HELP ME READ IT?
NOT SURE WHY YOU'D BOTHER.
THERE'S A COUPLE FIGHTS, BUT MOSTLY IT'S JUST KISSING.
THAT SOUNDS LIKE EXACTLY THE SORT OF STORY I'D APPRECIATE RIGHT NOW.
ALL RIGHT.

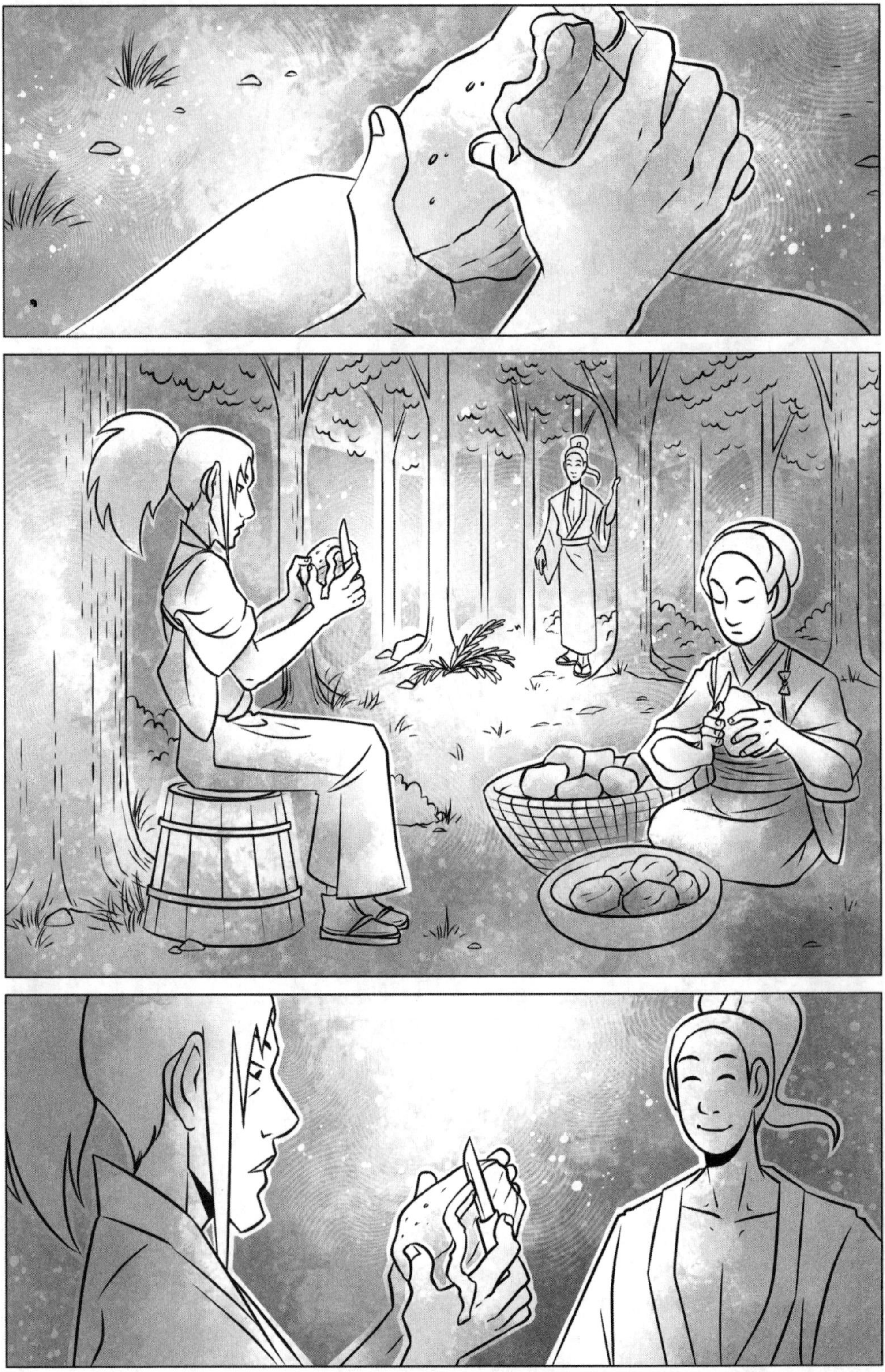

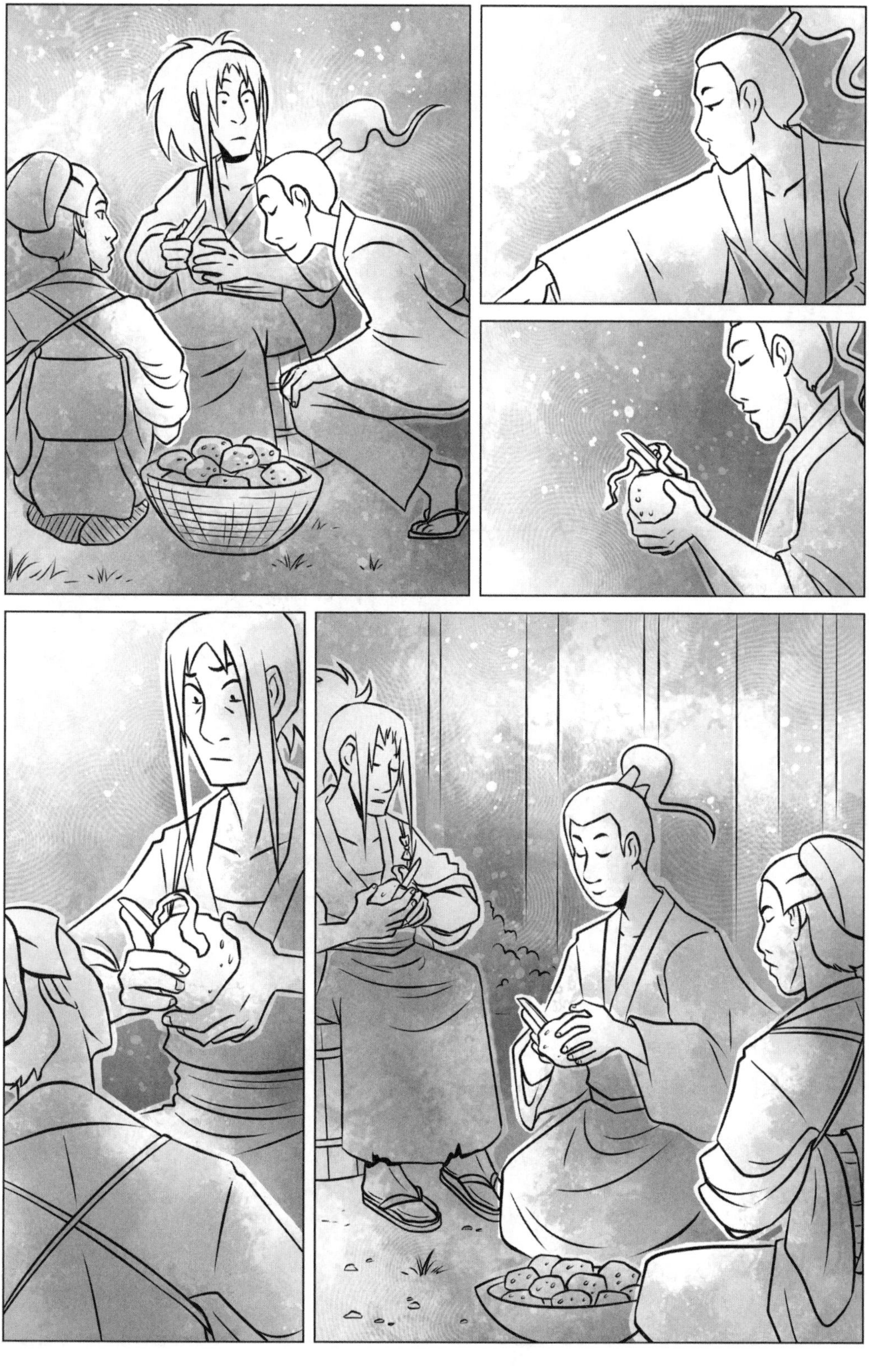

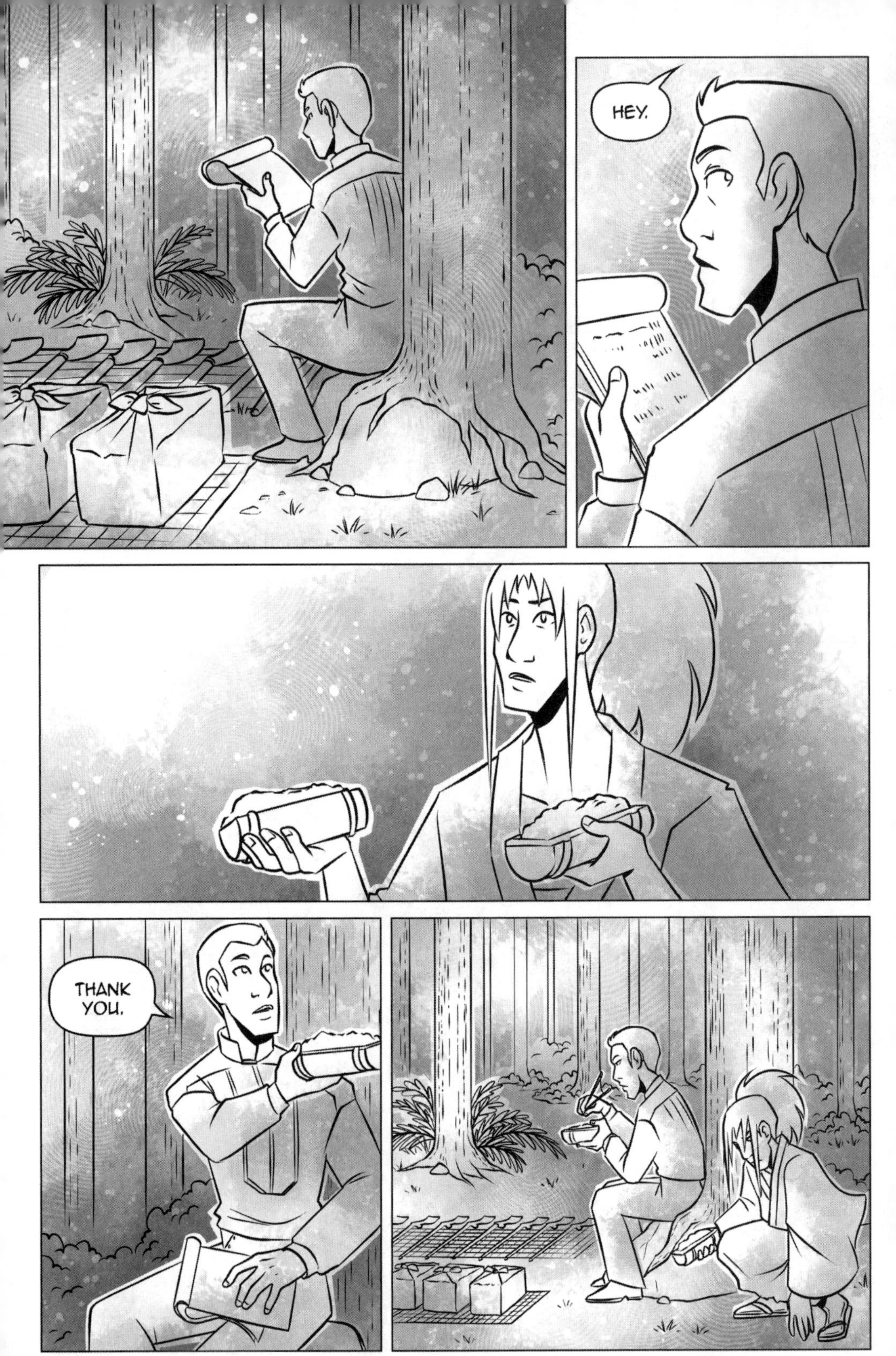
HEY.
THANK YOU.

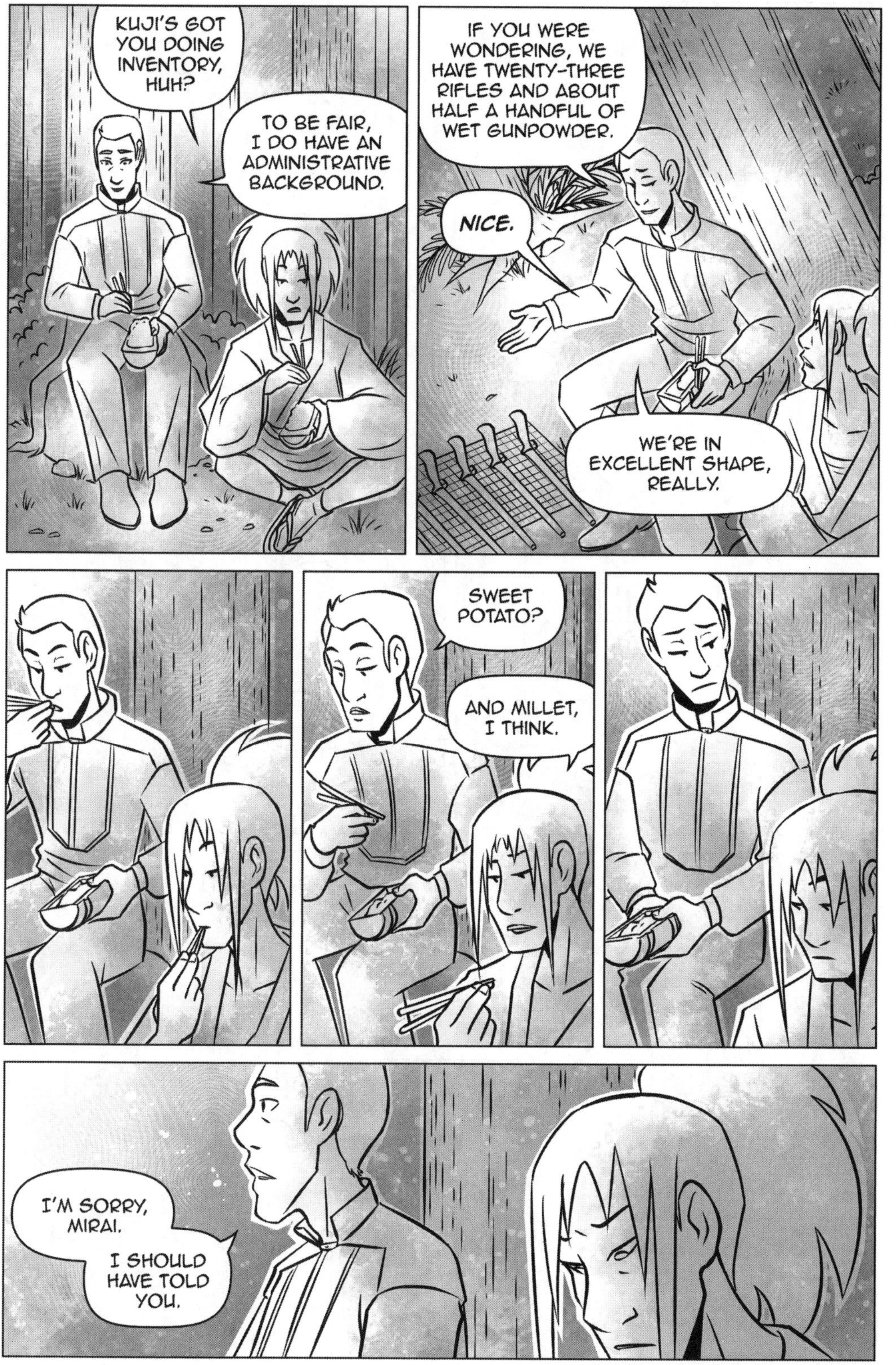
KUJI'S GOT YOU DOING INVENTORY, HUH?
TO BE FAIR, I DO HAVE AN ADMINISTRATIVE BACKGROUND.
IF YOU WERE WONDERING, WE HAVE TWENTY-THREE RIFLES AND ABOUT HALF A HANDFUL OF WET GUNPOWDER.
NICE.
WE'RE IN EXCELLENT SHAPE, REALLY.
SWEET POTATO?
AND MILLET, I THINK.
I'M SORRY, MIRAI.
I SHOULD HAVE TOLD YOU.

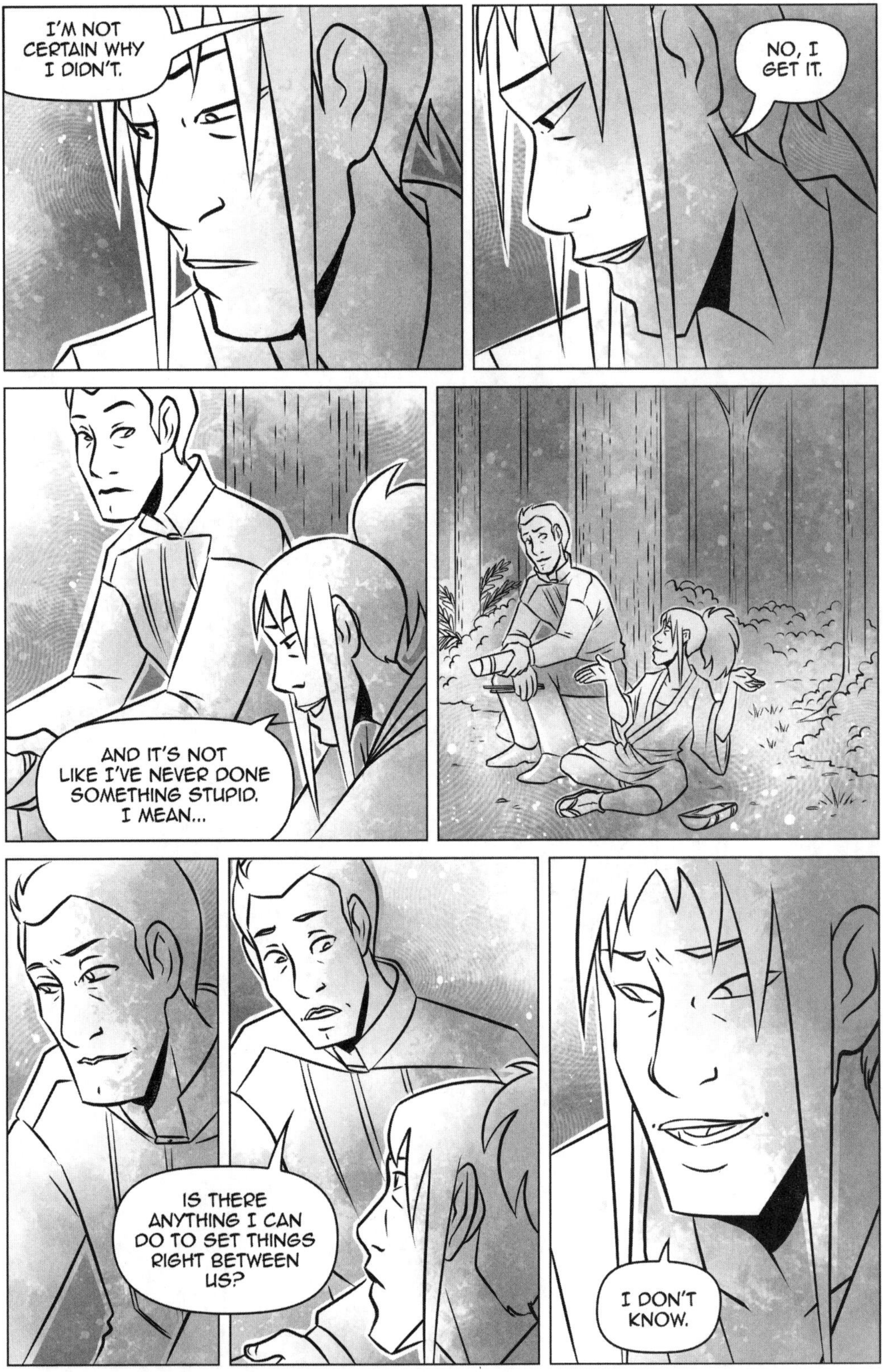
I'M NOT CERTAIN WHY I DIDN'T.
NO, I GET IT.
AND IT'S NOT LIKE I'VE NEVER DONE SOMETHING STUPID. I MEAN...
IS THERE ANYTHING I CAN DO TO SET THINGS RIGHT BETWEEN US?
I DON'T KNOW.

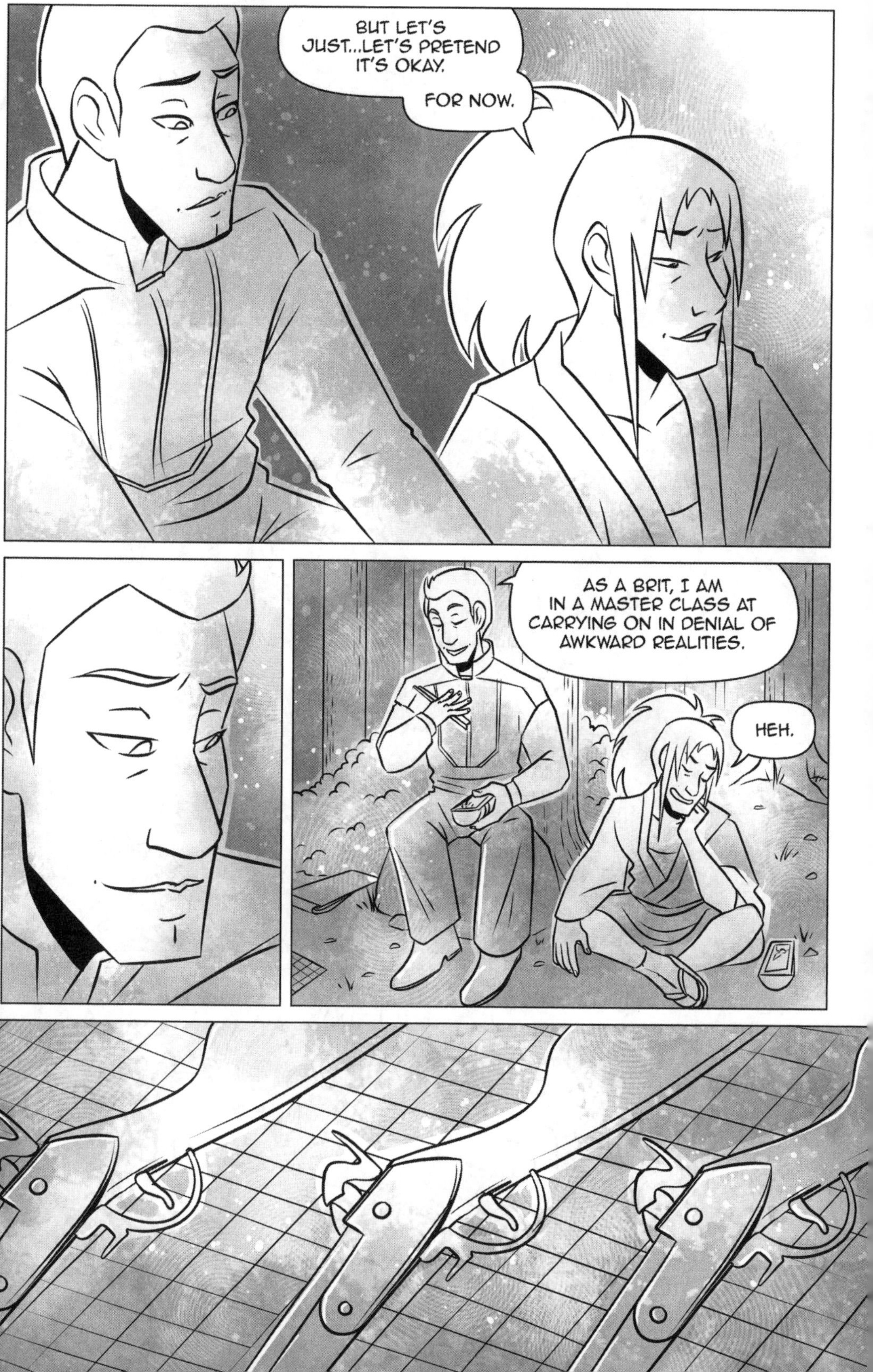
BUT LET'S JUST...LET'S PRETEND IT'S OKAY.
FOR NOW.
AS A BRIT, I AM IN A MASTER CLASS AT CARRYING ON IN DENIAL OF AWKWARD REALITIES.
HEH.

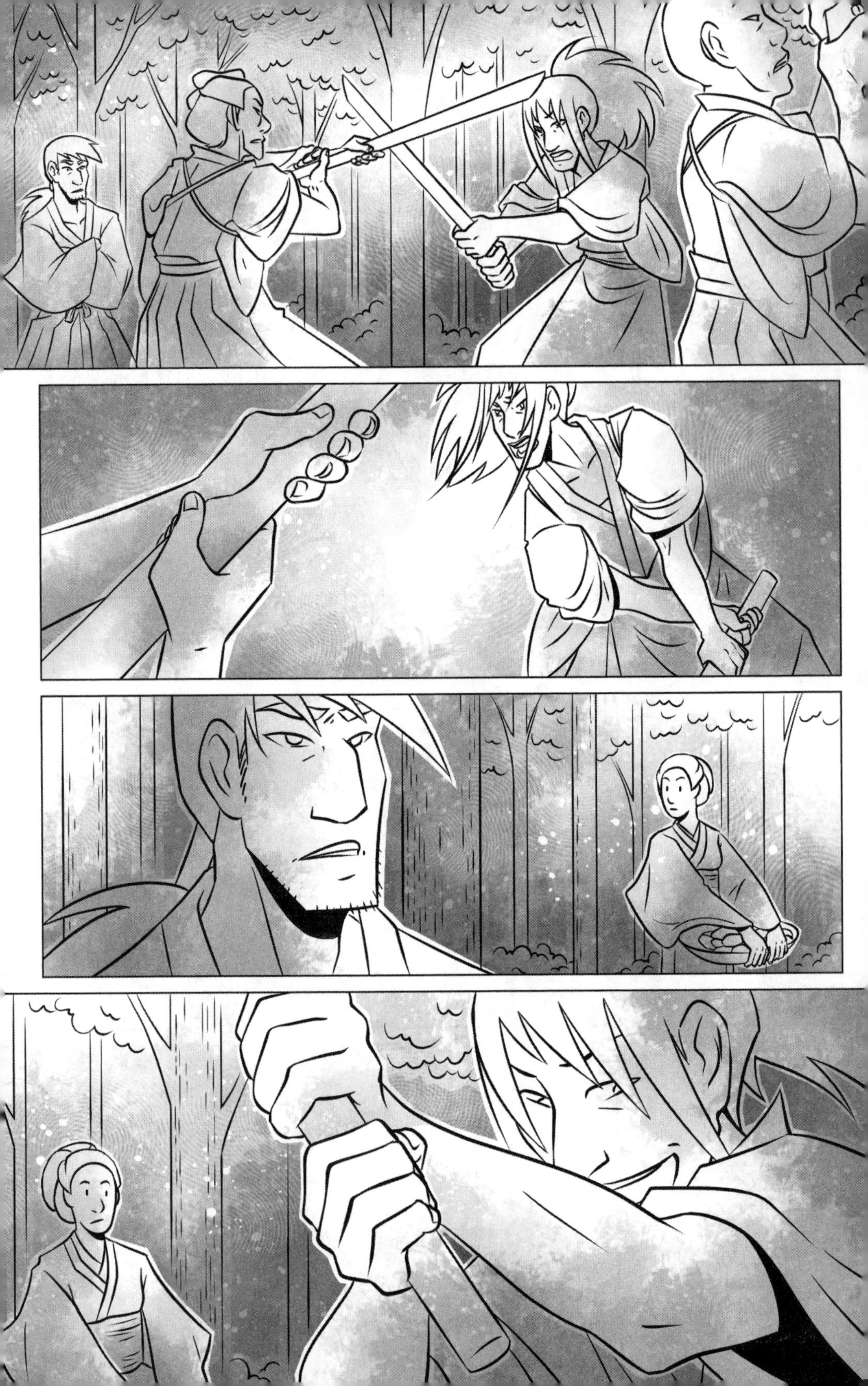

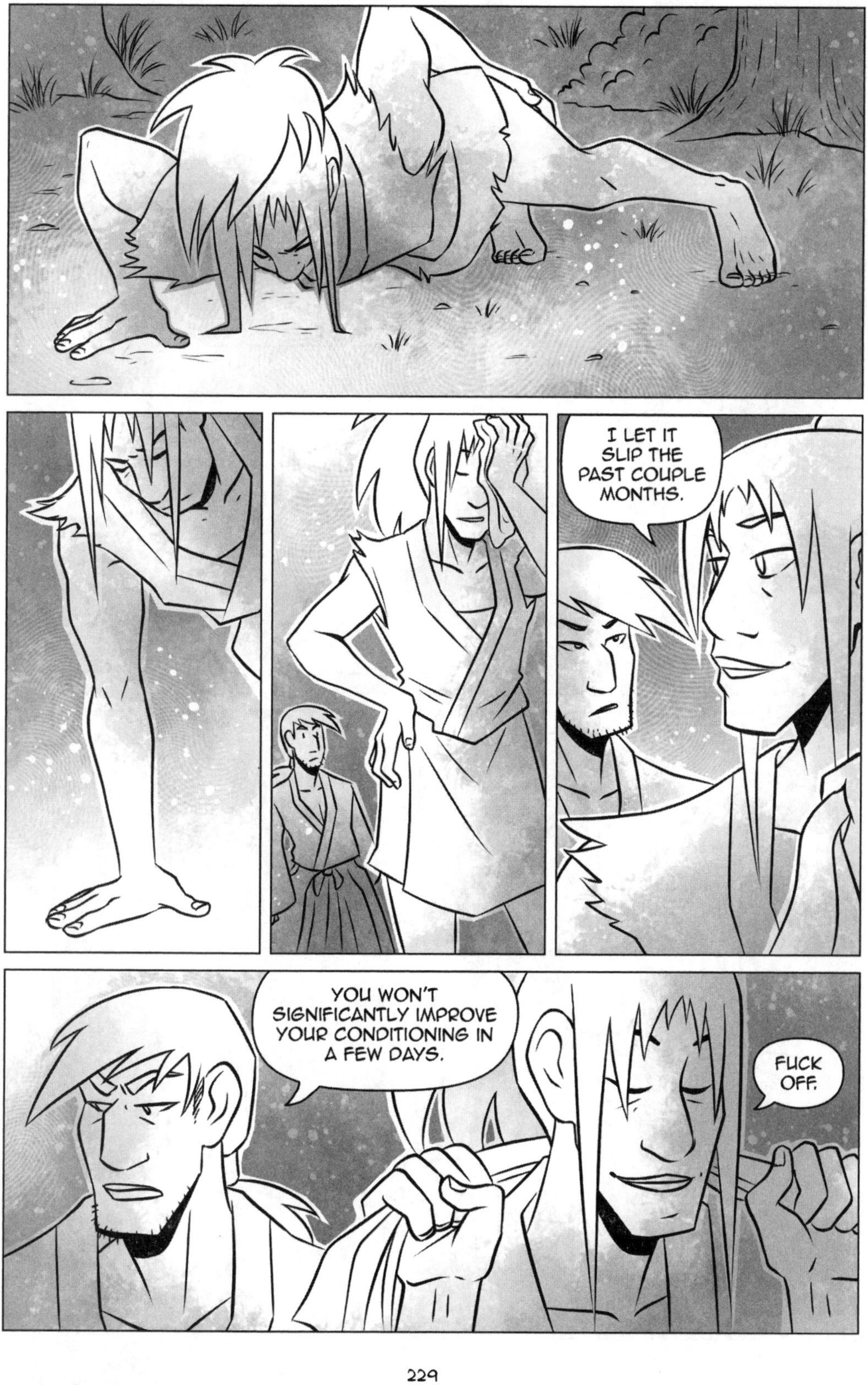
I LET IT SLIP THE PAST COUPLE MONTHS.
YOU WON'T SIGNIFICANTLY IMPROVE YOUR CONDITIONING IN A FEW DAYS.
FUCK OFF.

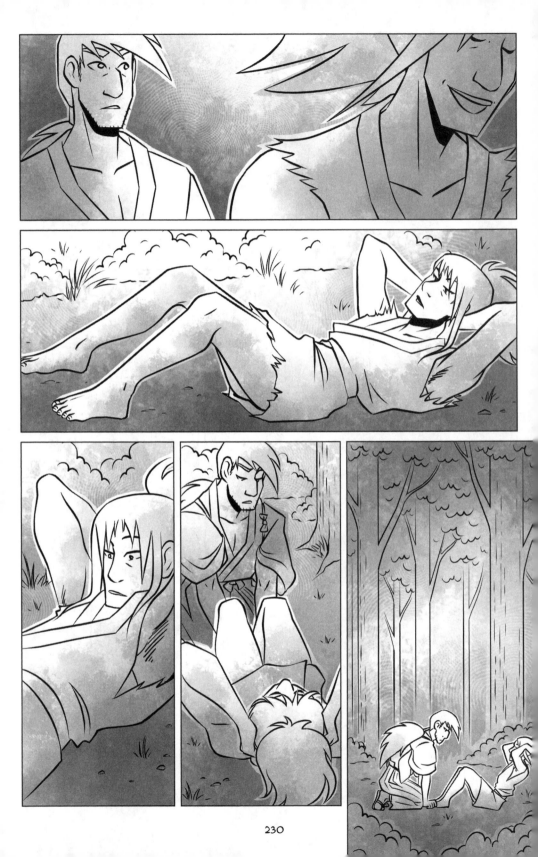

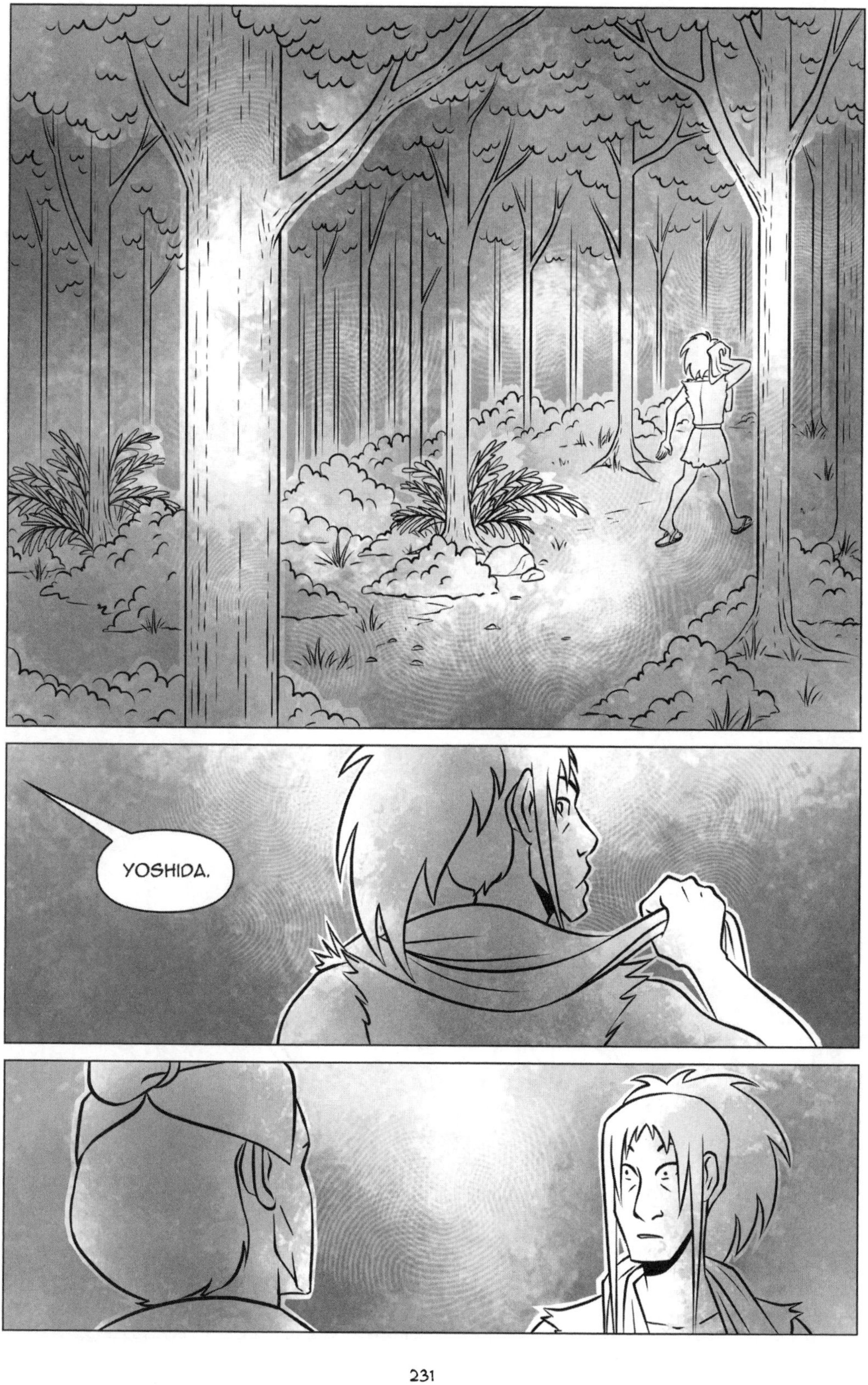
YOSHIDA.

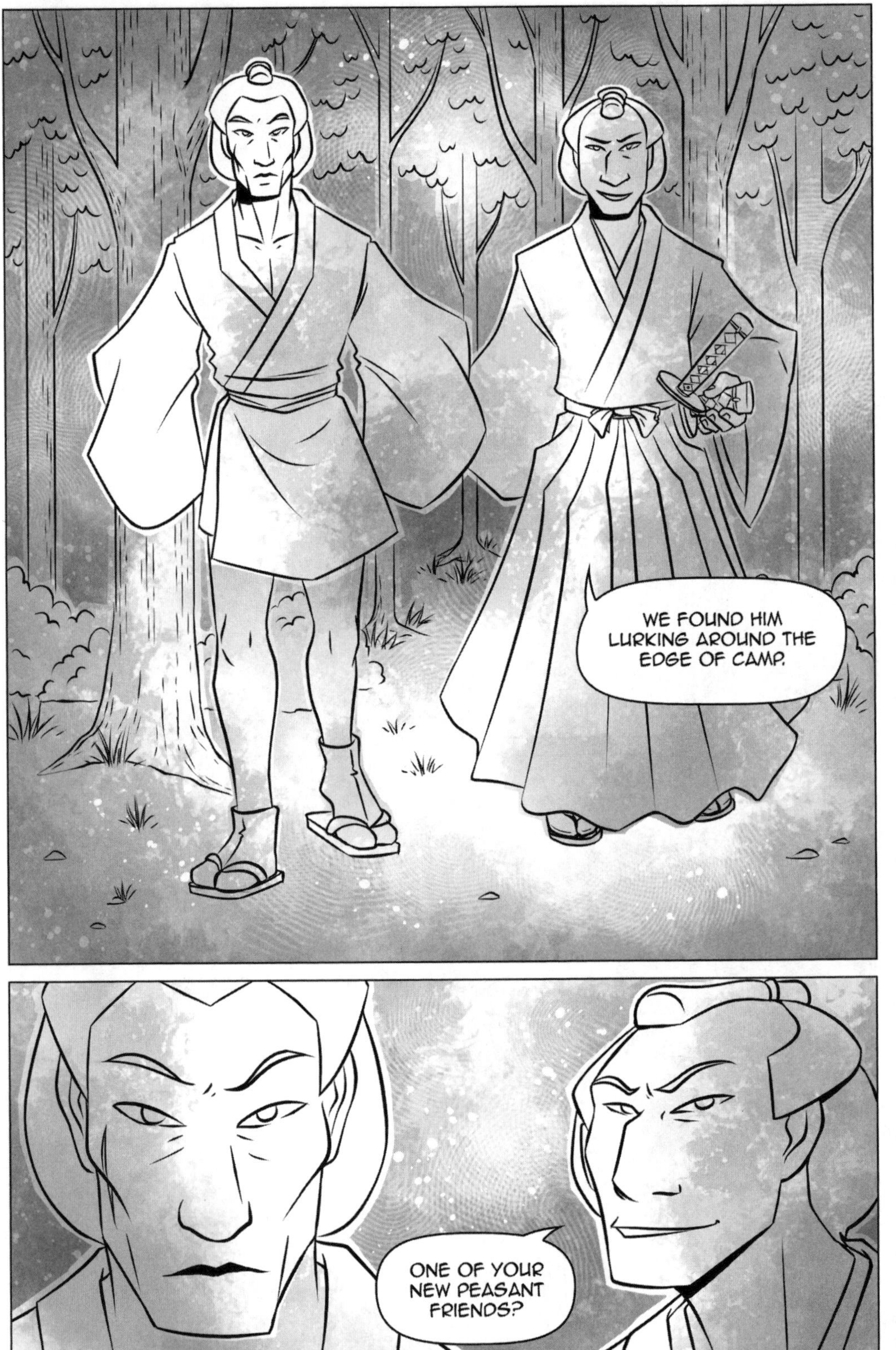
WE FOUND HIM LURKING AROUND THE EDGE OF CAMP.
ONE OF YOUR NEW PEASANT FRIENDS?

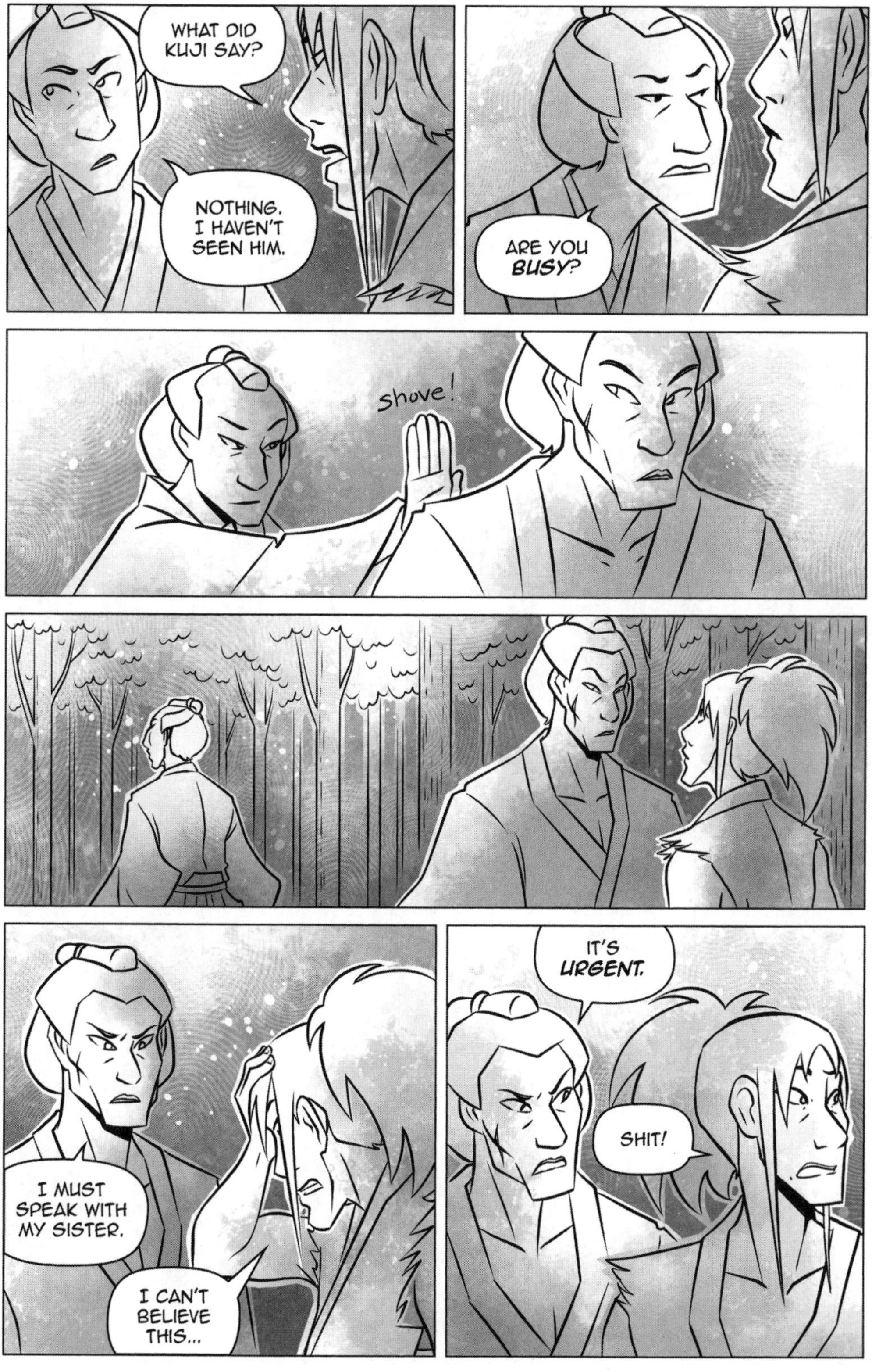
WHAT DID KUJI SAY?
NOTHING. I HAVEN'T SEEN HIM.
ARE YOU BUSY?
shove!
I MUST SPEAK WITH MY SISTER.
I CAN'T BELIEVE THIS...
IT'S URGENT.
SHIT!

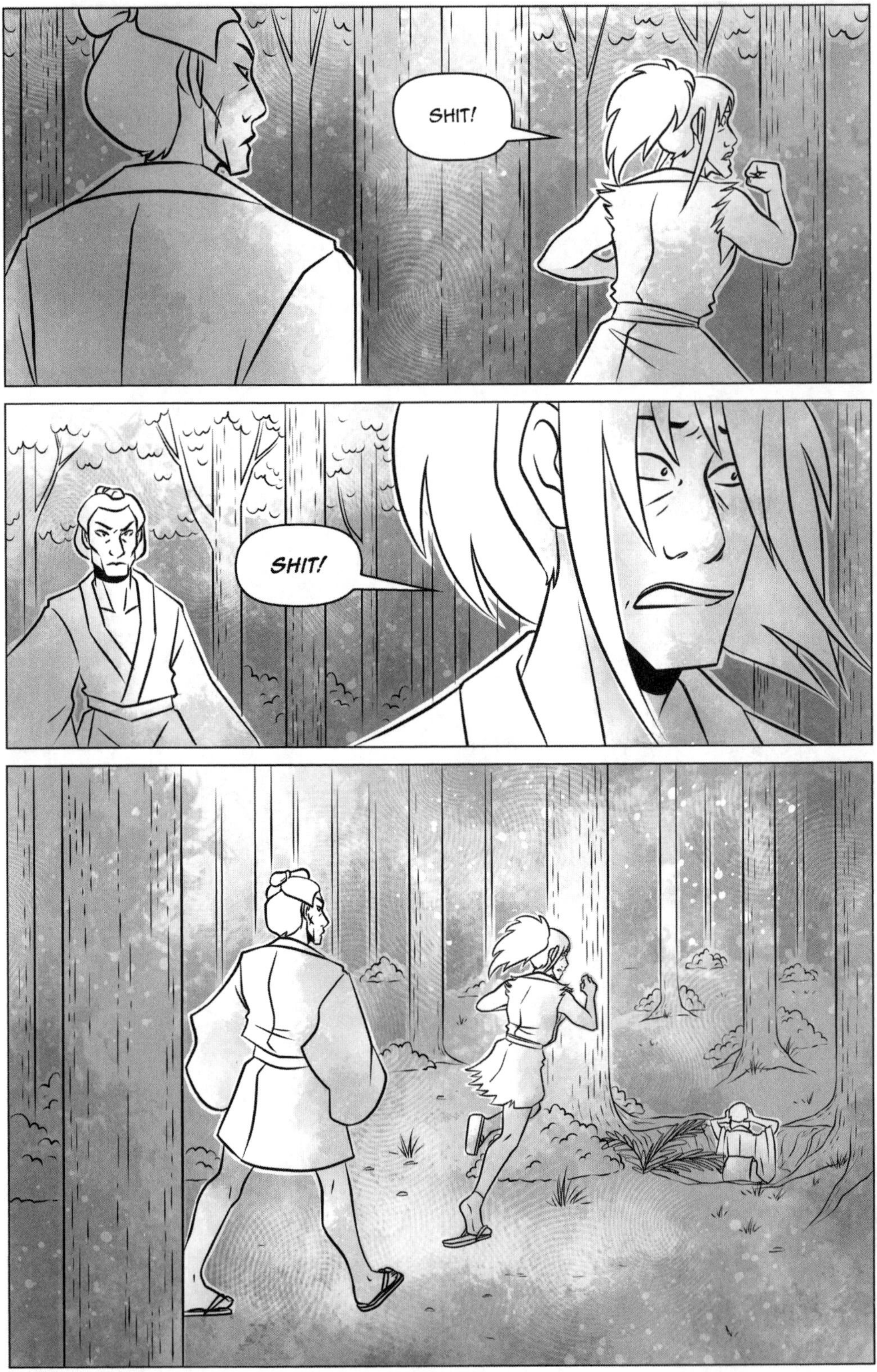
SHIT!
SHIT!

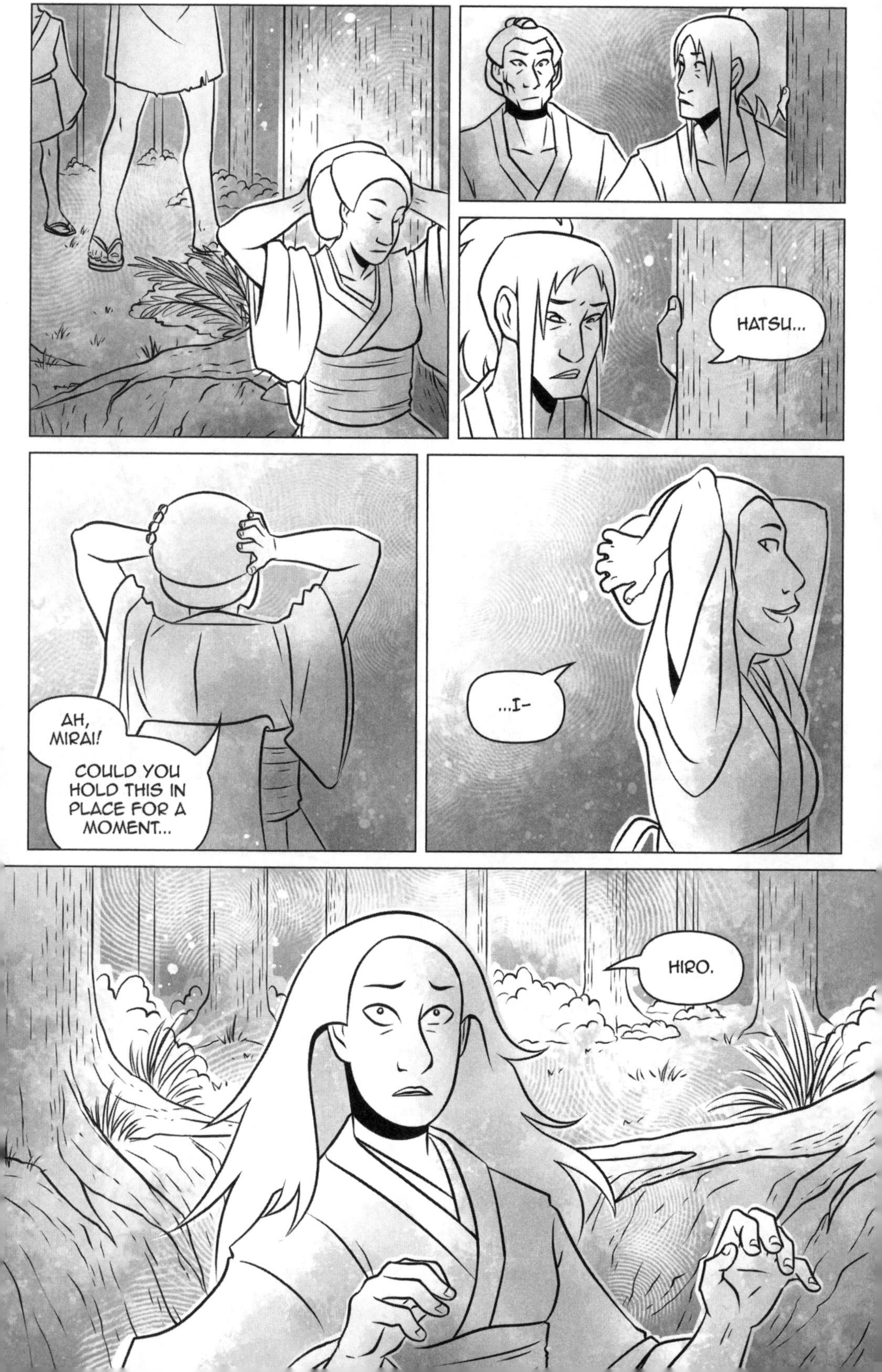
HATSU...
AH, MIRAI!
COULD YOU HOLD THIS IN PLACE FOR A MOMENT...
...I-
HIRO.

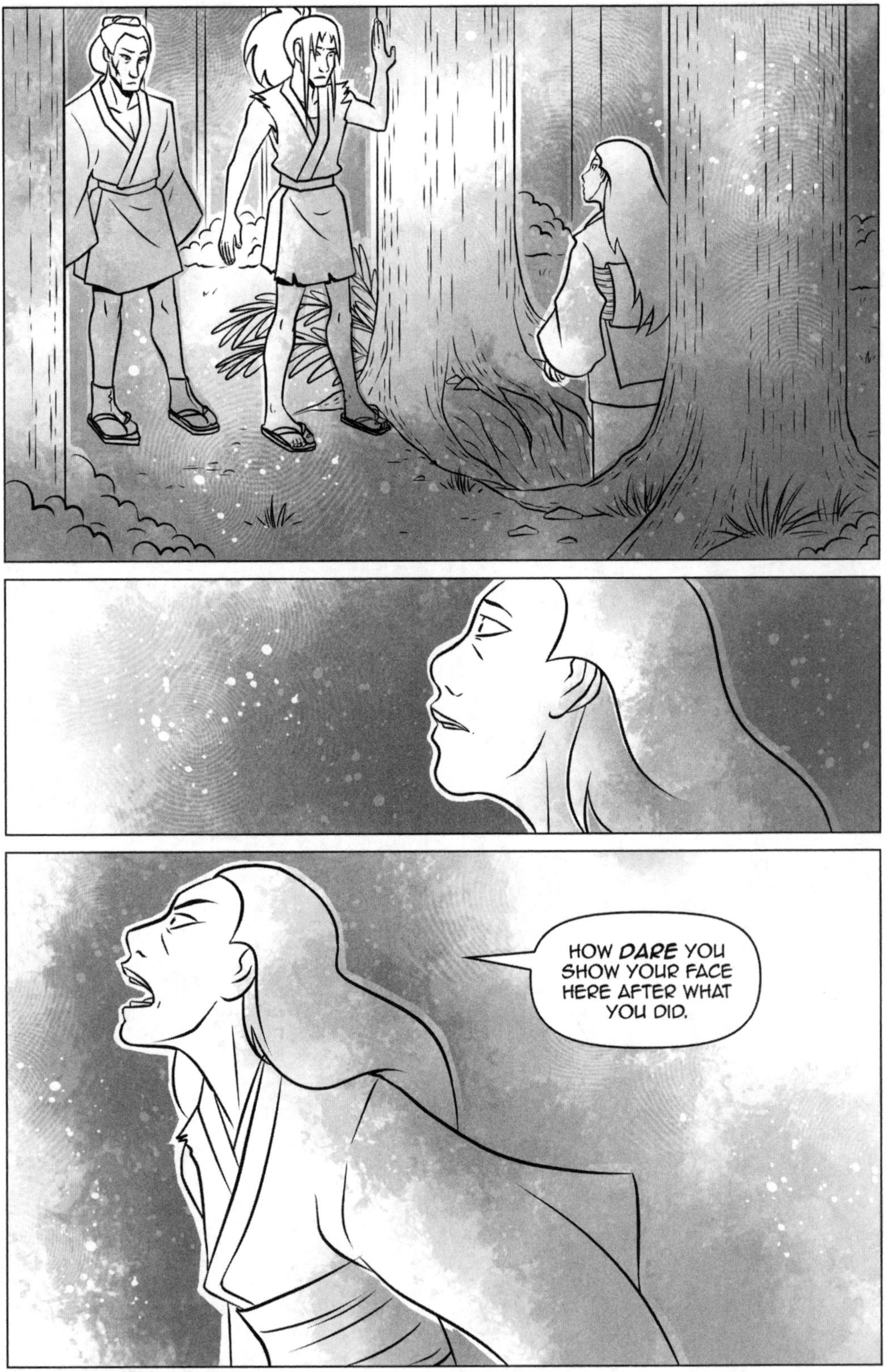
HOW DARE YOU SHOW YOUR FACE HERE AFTER WHAT YOU DID.

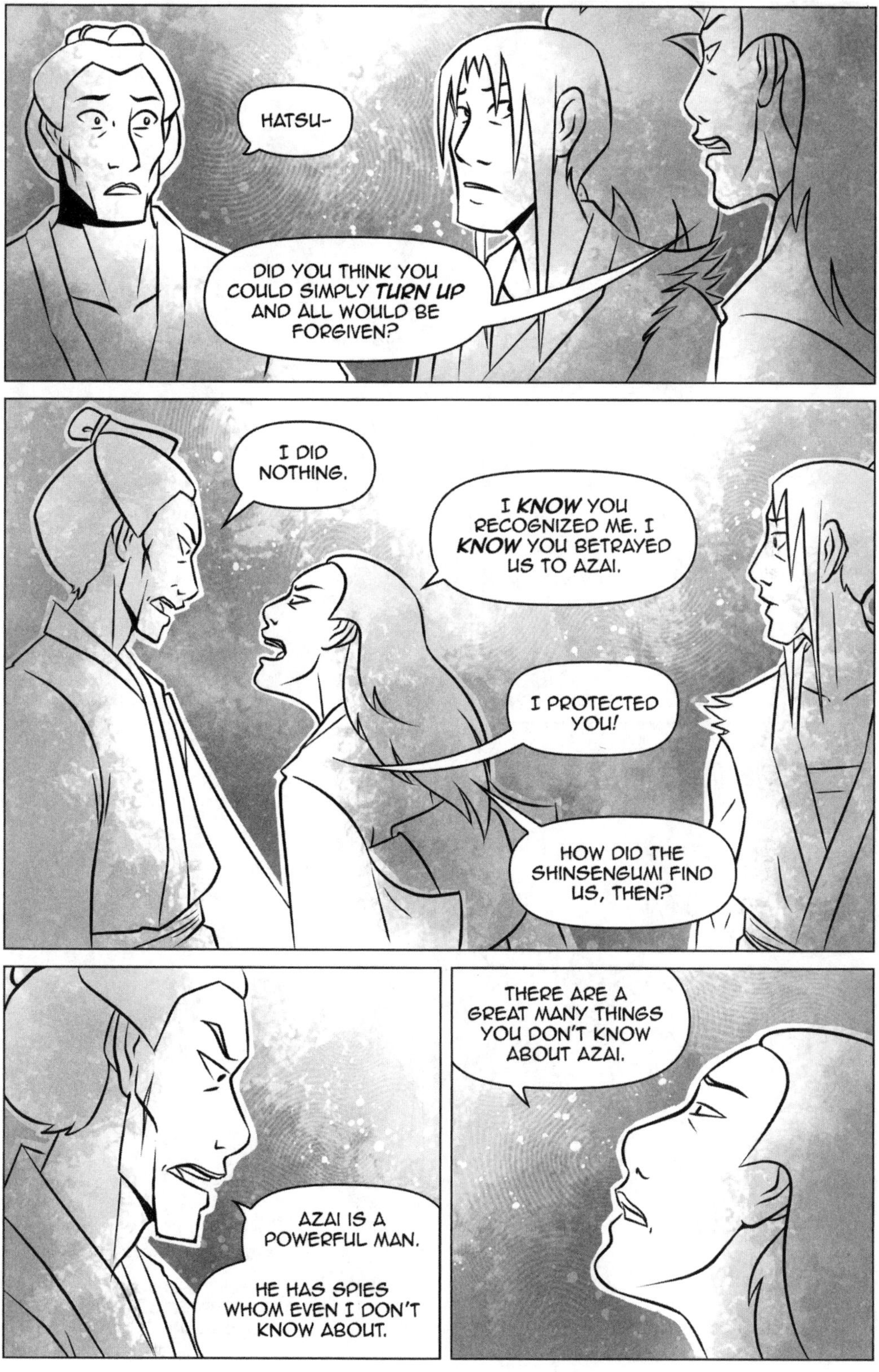
HATSU-
DID YOU THINK YOU COULD SIMPLY *TURN UP* AND ALL WOULD BE FORGIVEN?
I DID NOTHING.
I *KNOW* YOU RECOGNIZED ME. I *KNOW* YOU BETRAYED US TO AZAI.
I PROTECTED YOU!
HOW DID THE SHINSENGUMI FIND US, THEN?
AZAI IS A POWERFUL MAN.
HE HAS SPIES WHOM EVEN I DON'T KNOW ABOUT.
THERE ARE A GREAT MANY THINGS YOU DON'T KNOW ABOUT AZAI.

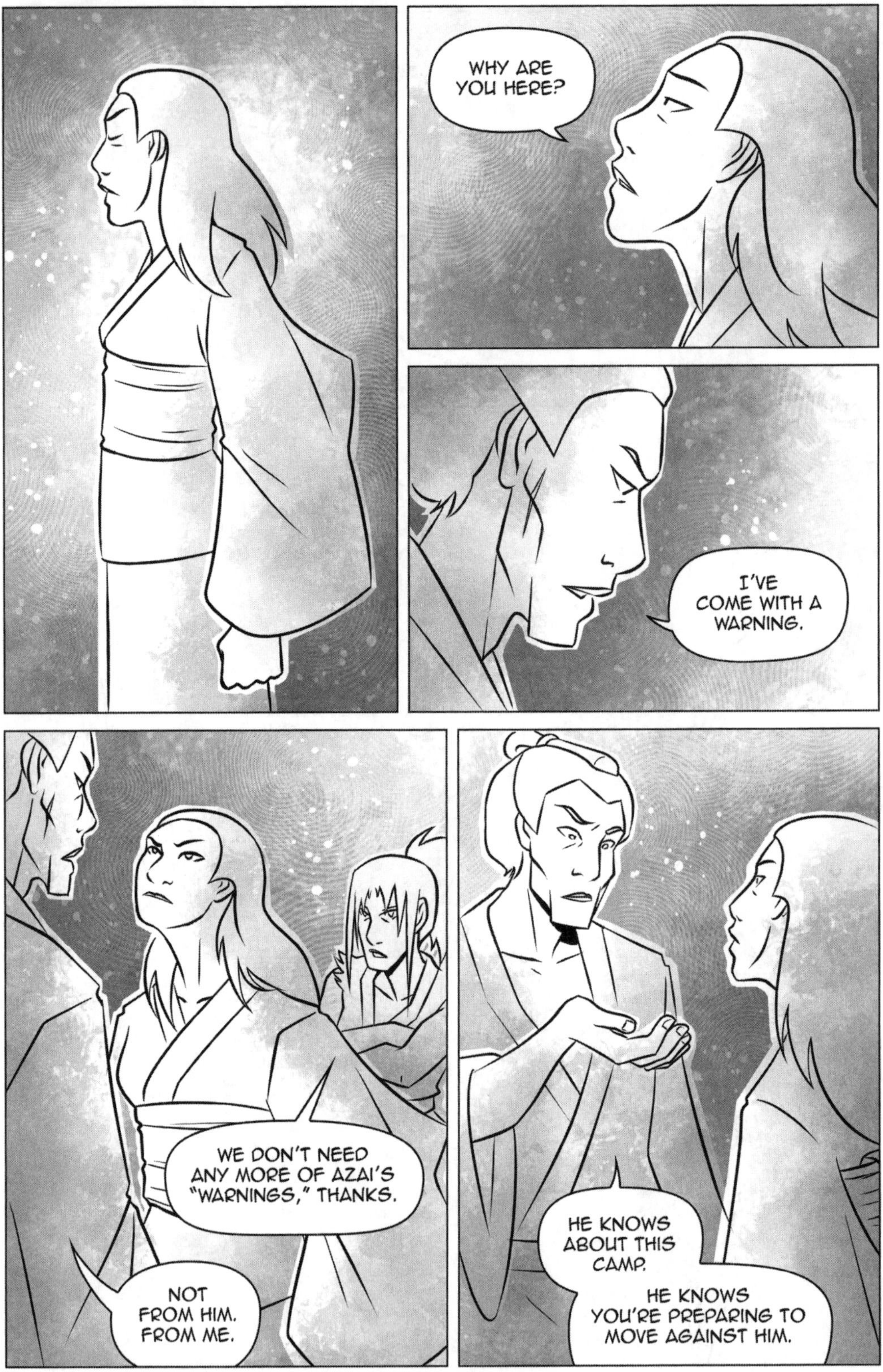
WHY ARE YOU HERE?
I'VE COME WITH A WARNING.
WE DON'T NEED ANY MORE OF AZAI'S "WARNINGS," THANKS.
NOT FROM HIM. FROM ME.
HE KNOWS ABOUT THIS CAMP.
HE KNOWS YOU'RE PREPARING TO MOVE AGAINST HIM.

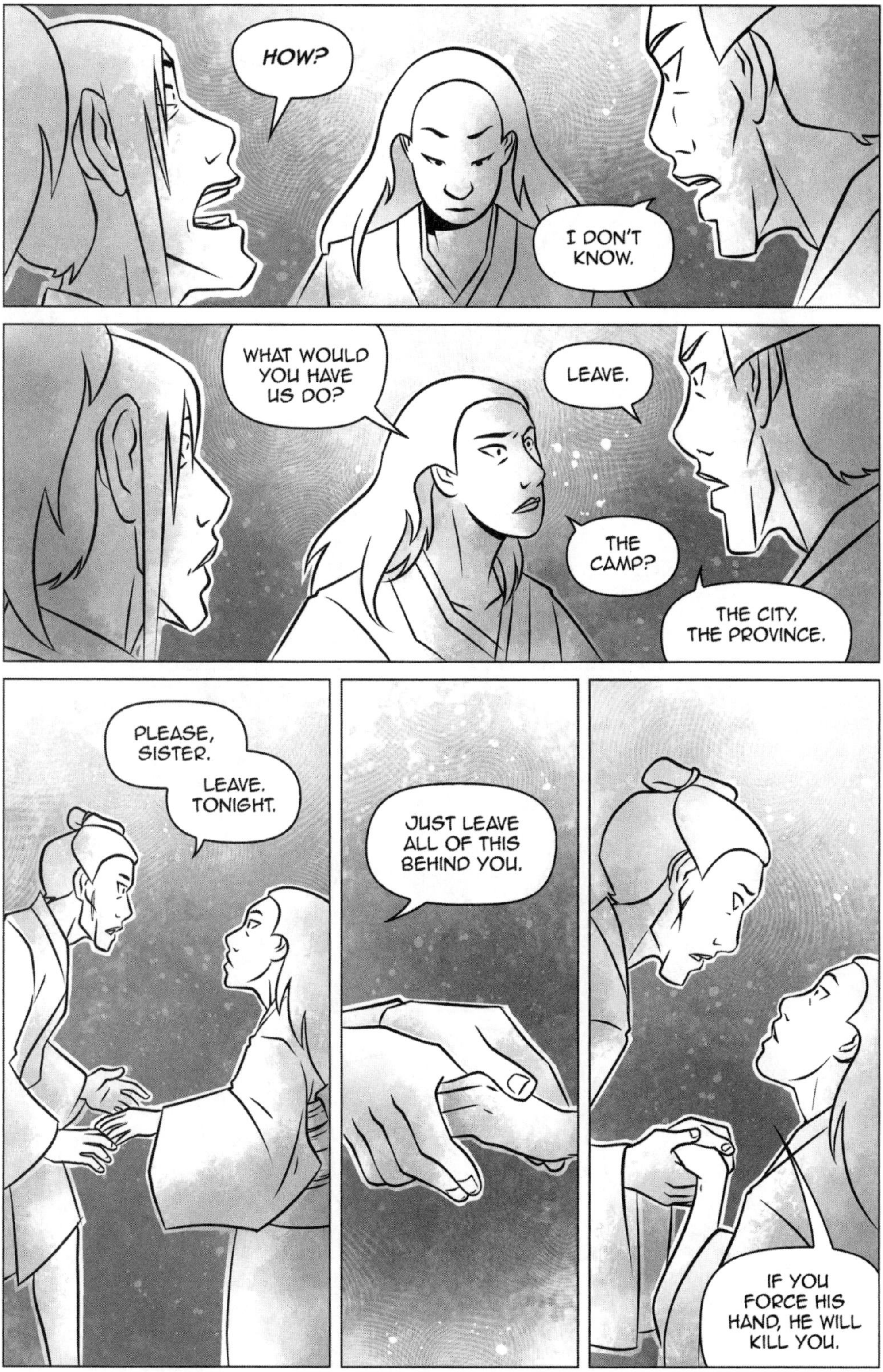
HOW?
I DON'T KNOW.
WHAT WOULD YOU HAVE US DO?
LEAVE.
THE CAMP?
THE CITY. THE PROVINCE.
PLEASE, SISTER.
LEAVE. TONIGHT.
JUST LEAVE ALL OF THIS BEHIND YOU.
IF YOU FORCE HIS HAND, HE WILL KILL YOU.

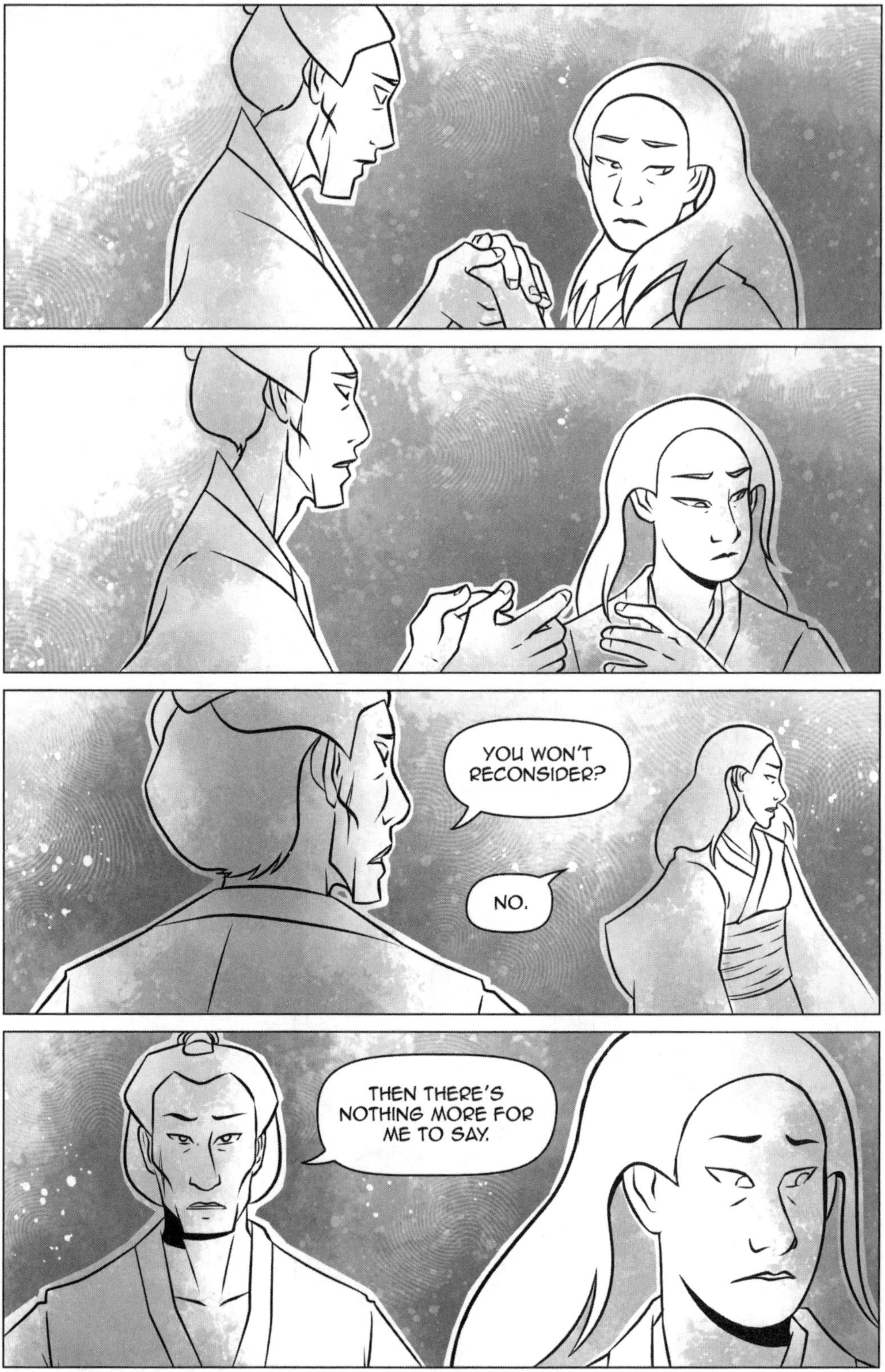
YOU WON'T RECONSIDER?
NO.
THEN THERE'S NOTHING MORE FOR ME TO SAY.

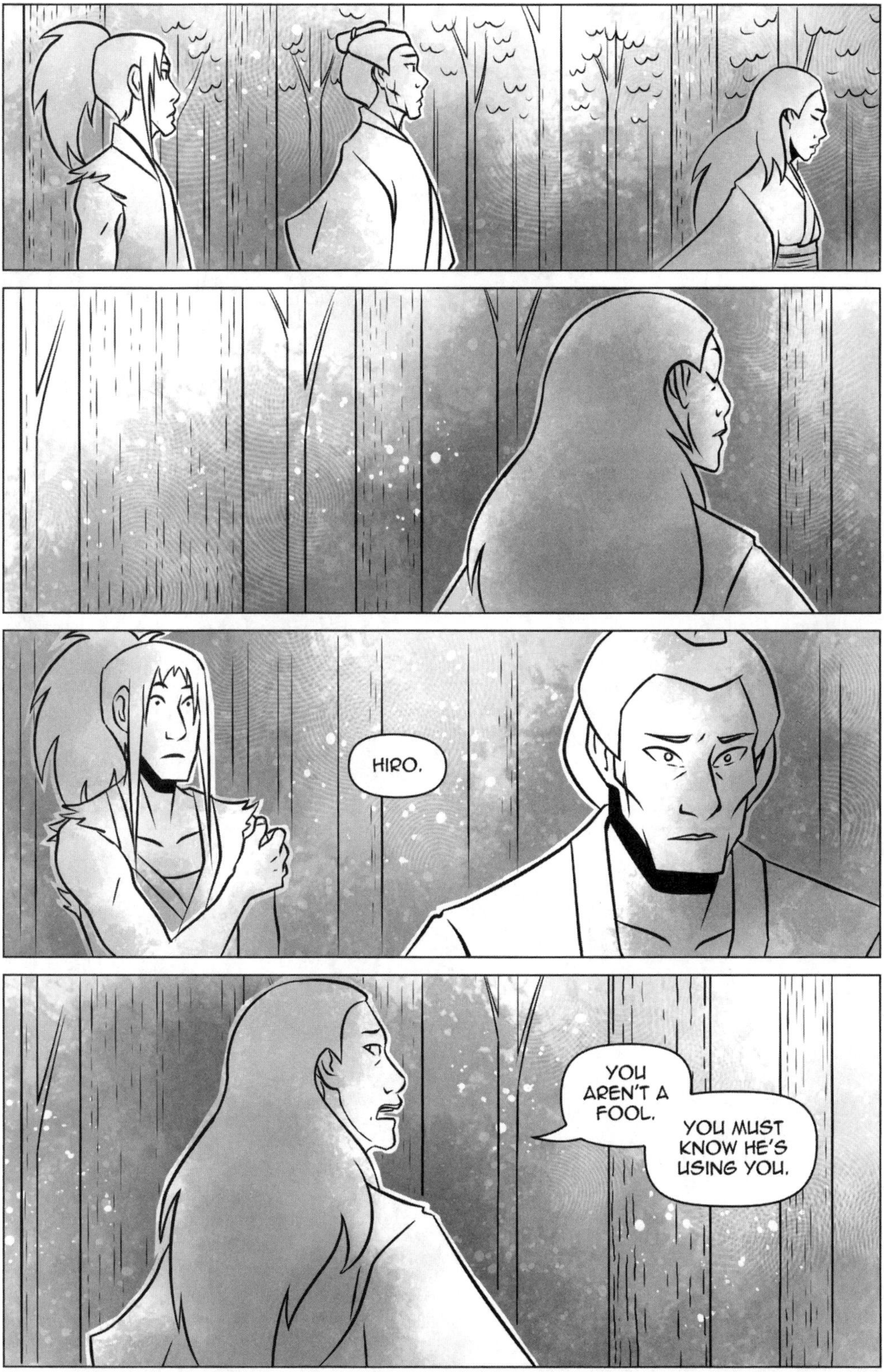
HIRO.
YOU AREN'T A FOOL.
YOU MUST KNOW HE'S USING YOU.

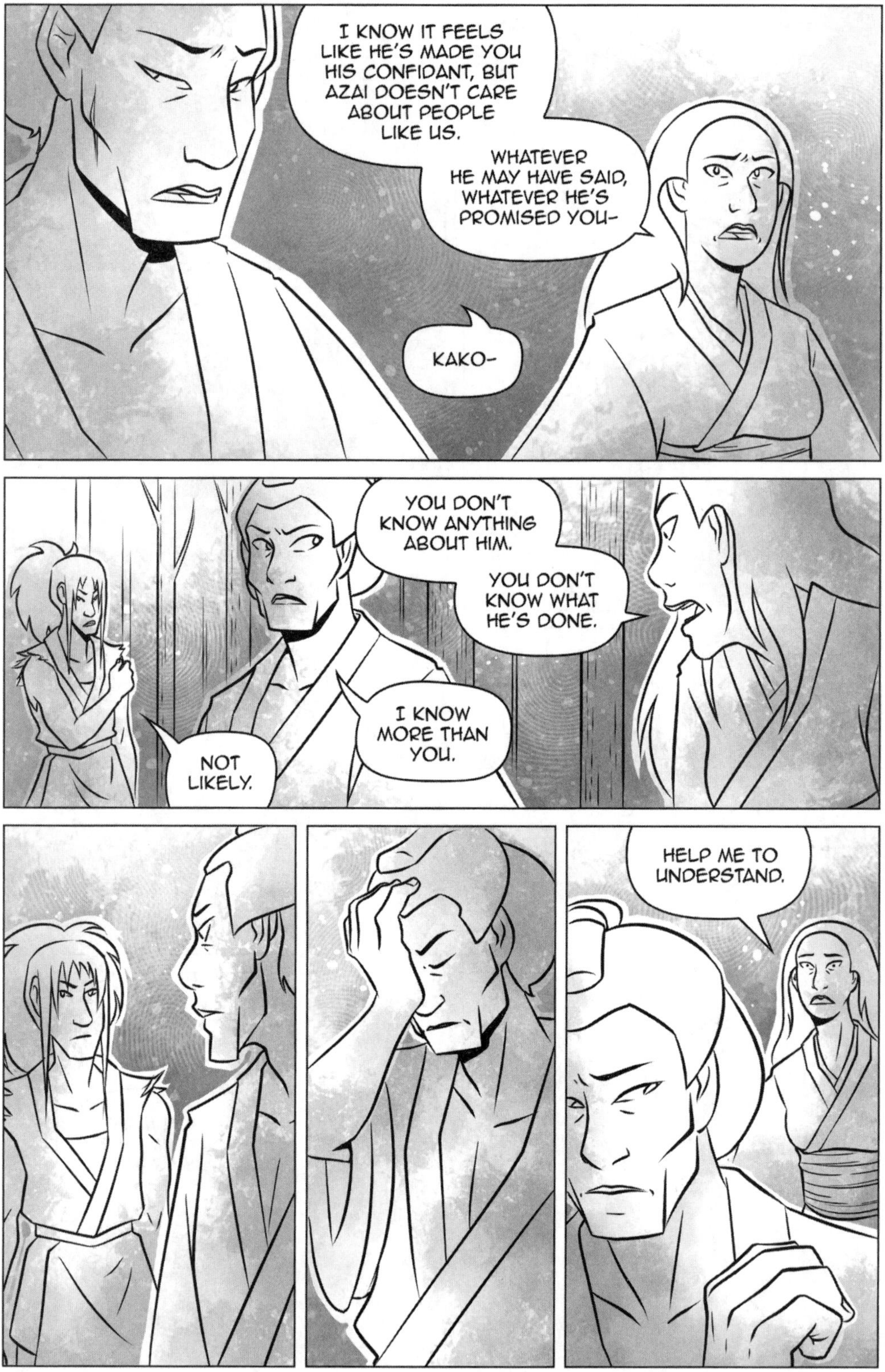
I KNOW IT FEELS LIKE HE'S MADE YOU HIS CONFIDANT, BUT AZAI DOESN'T CARE ABOUT PEOPLE LIKE US.
WHATEVER HE MAY HAVE SAID, WHATEVER HE'S PROMISED YOU-
KAKO-
YOU DON'T KNOW ANYTHING ABOUT HIM.
YOU DON'T KNOW WHAT HE'S DONE.
I KNOW MORE THAN YOU.
NOT LIKELY.
HELP ME TO UNDERSTAND.

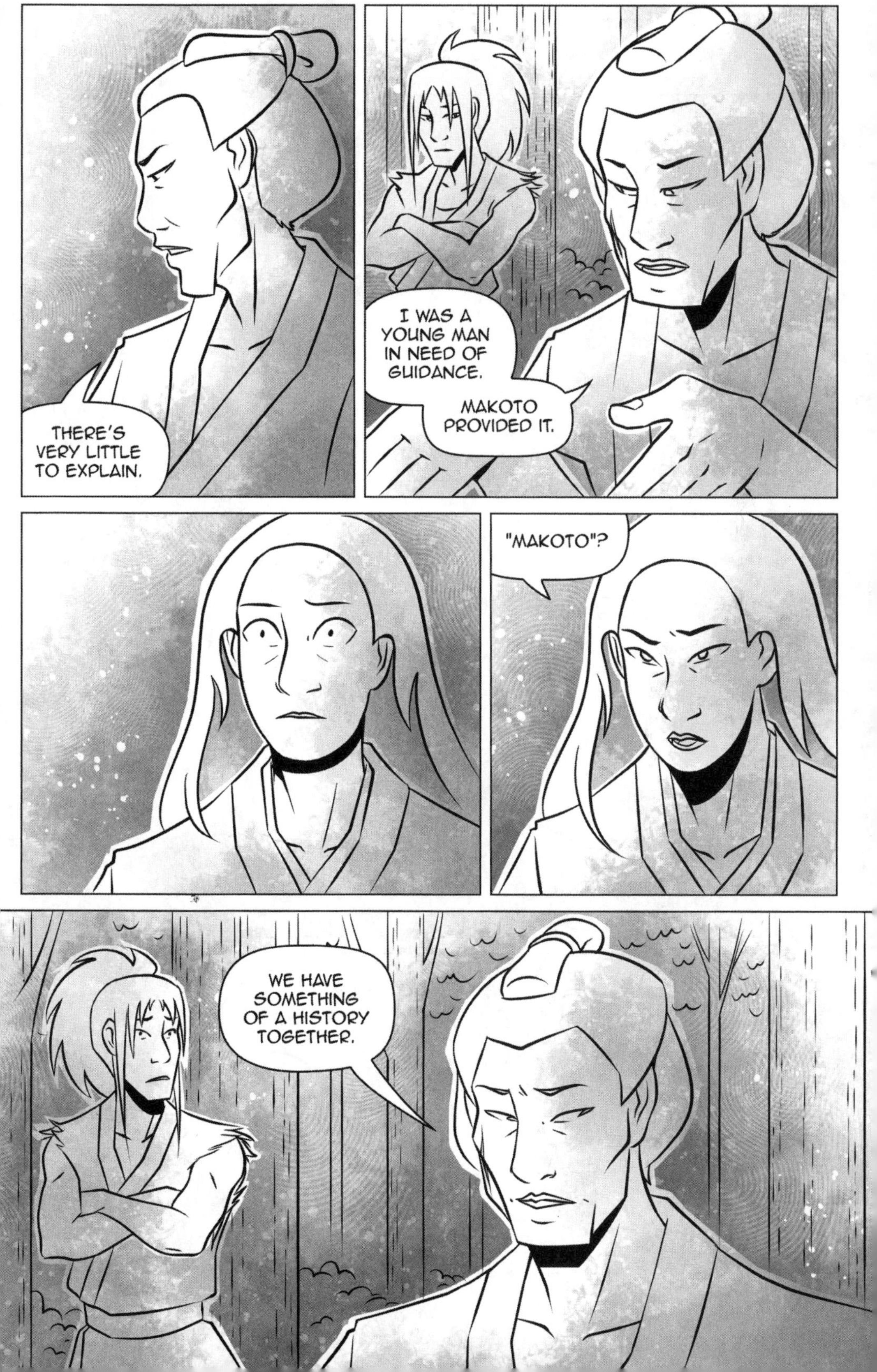
THERE'S VERY LITTLE TO EXPLAIN.
I WAS A YOUNG MAN IN NEED OF GUIDANCE.
MAKOTO PROVIDED IT.
"MAKOTO"?
WE HAVE SOMETHING OF A HISTORY TOGETHER.

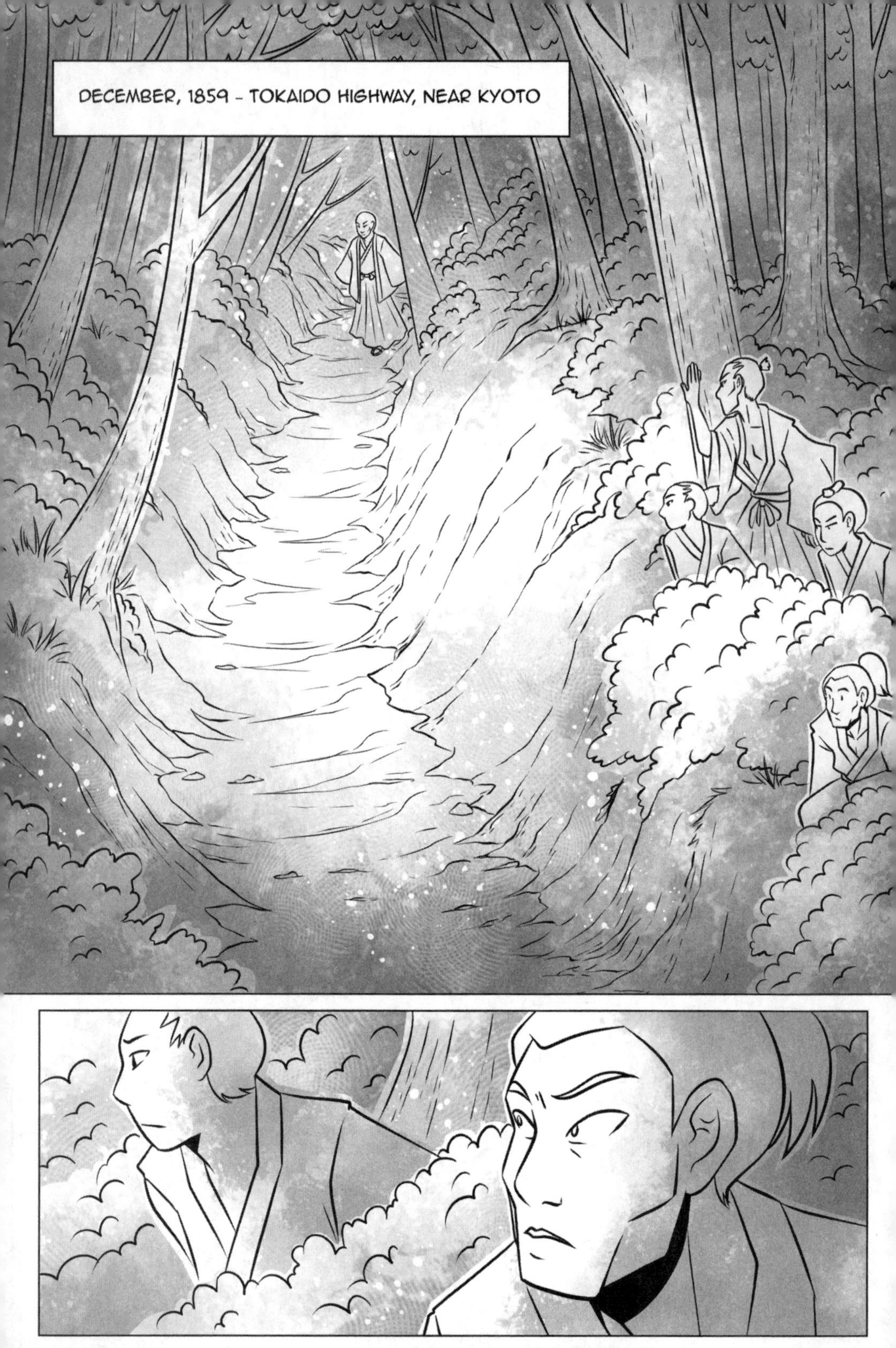
DECEMBER, 1859 - TOKAIDO HIGHWAY, NEAR KYOTO

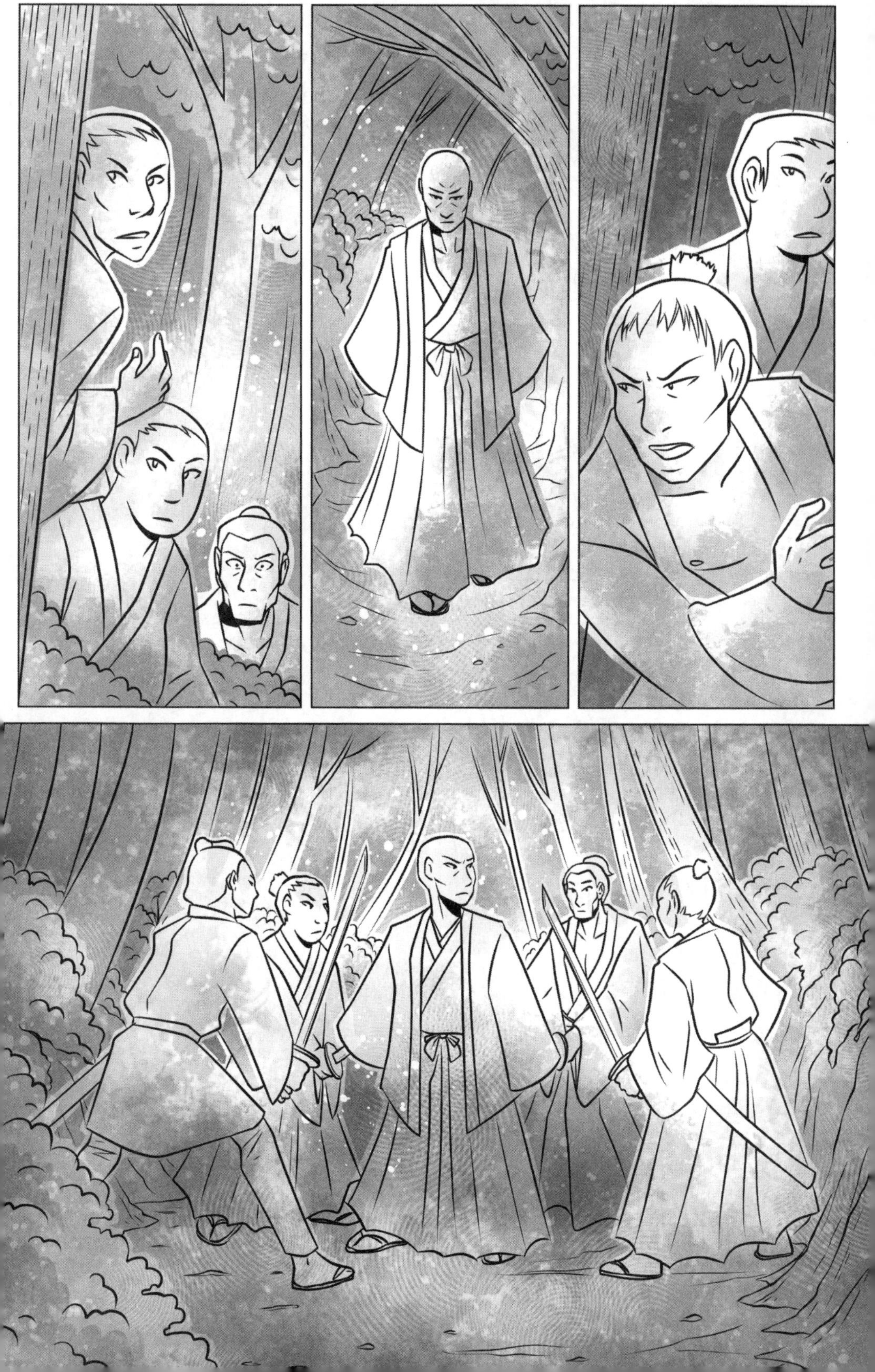

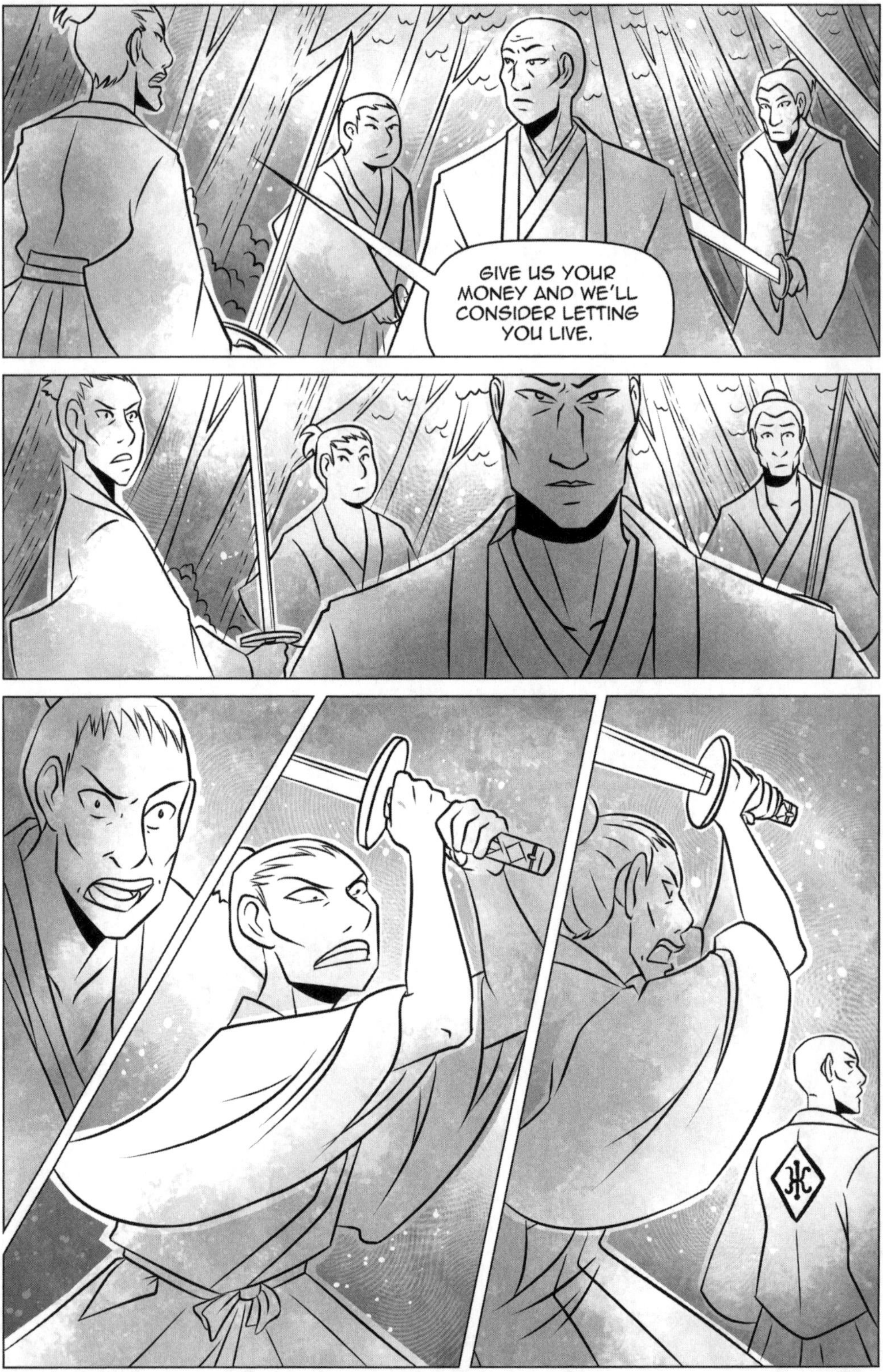
GIVE US YOUR MONEY AND WE'LL CONSIDER LETTING YOU LIVE.

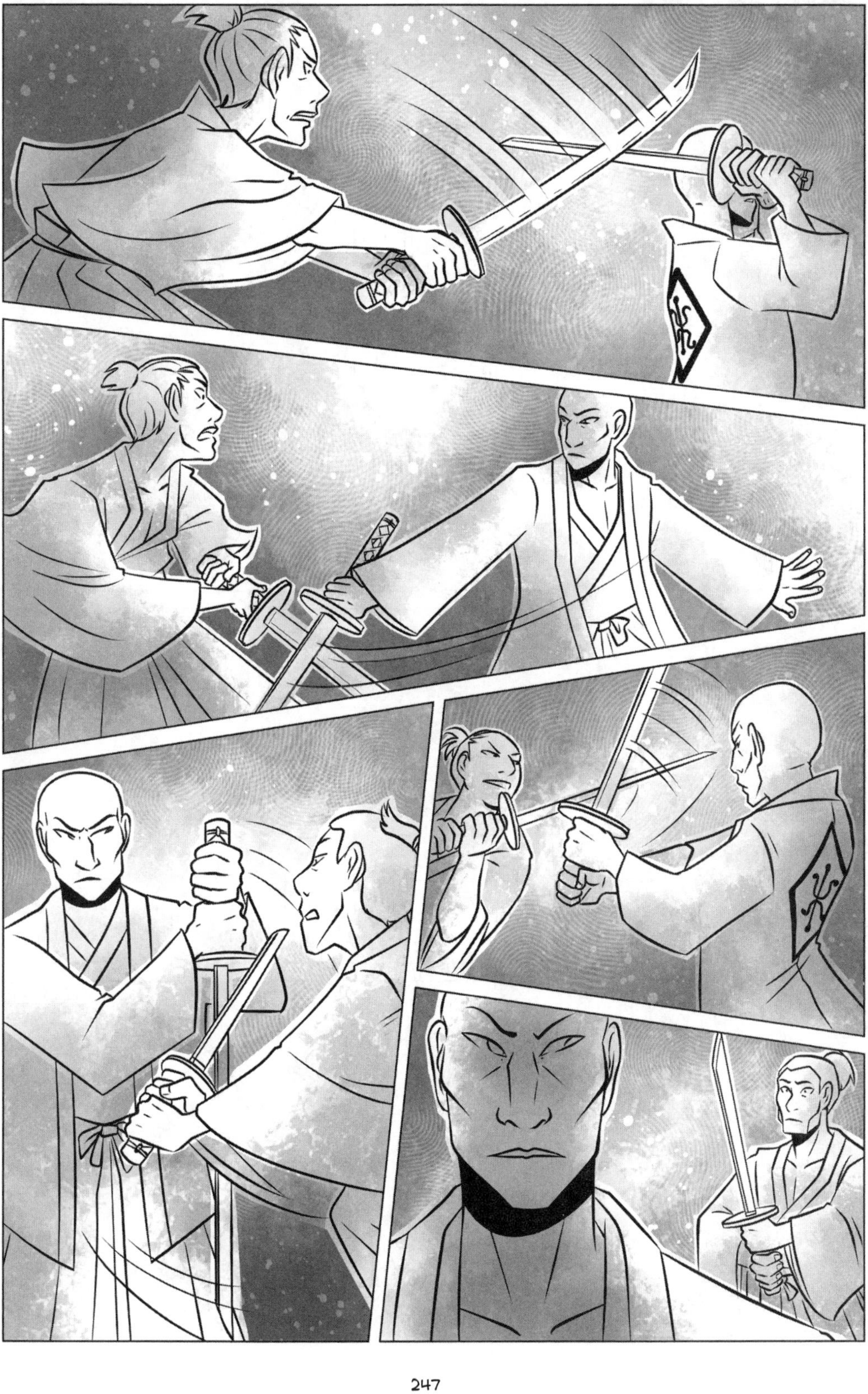

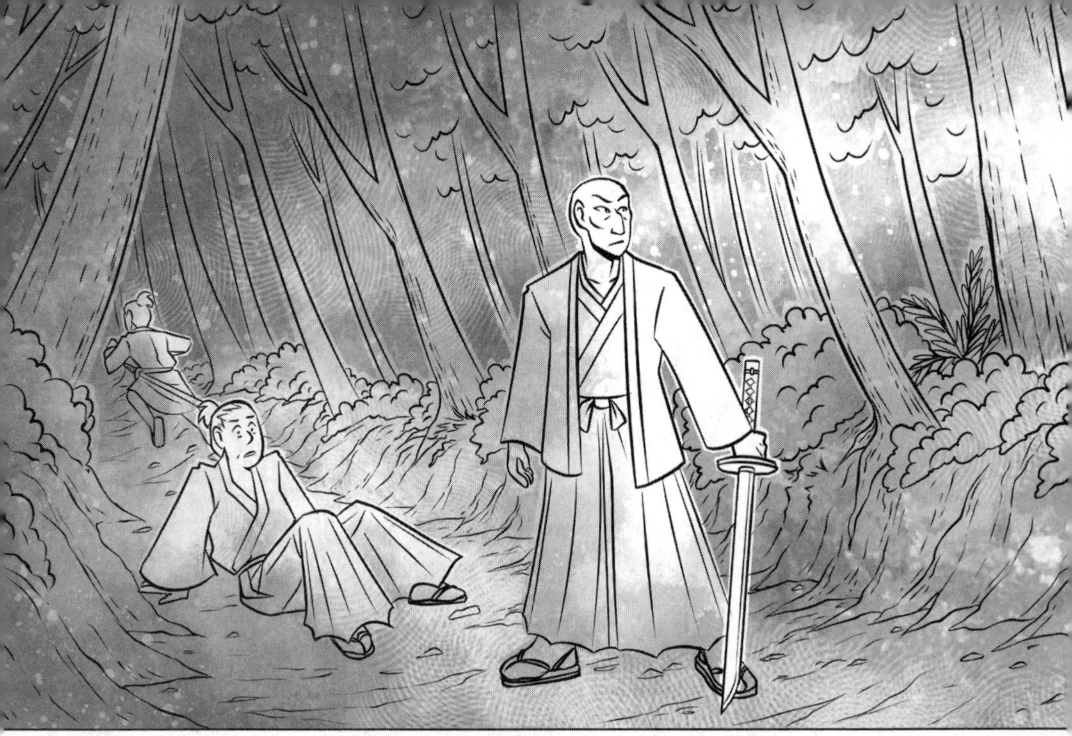

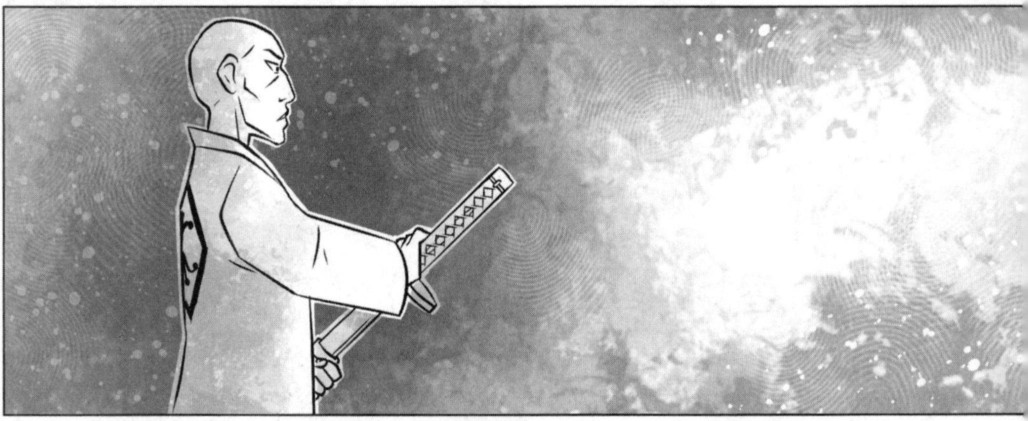

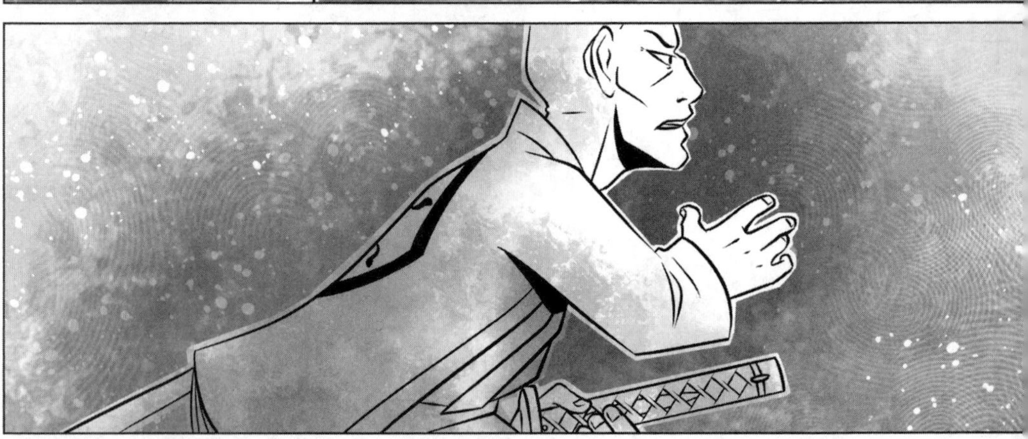

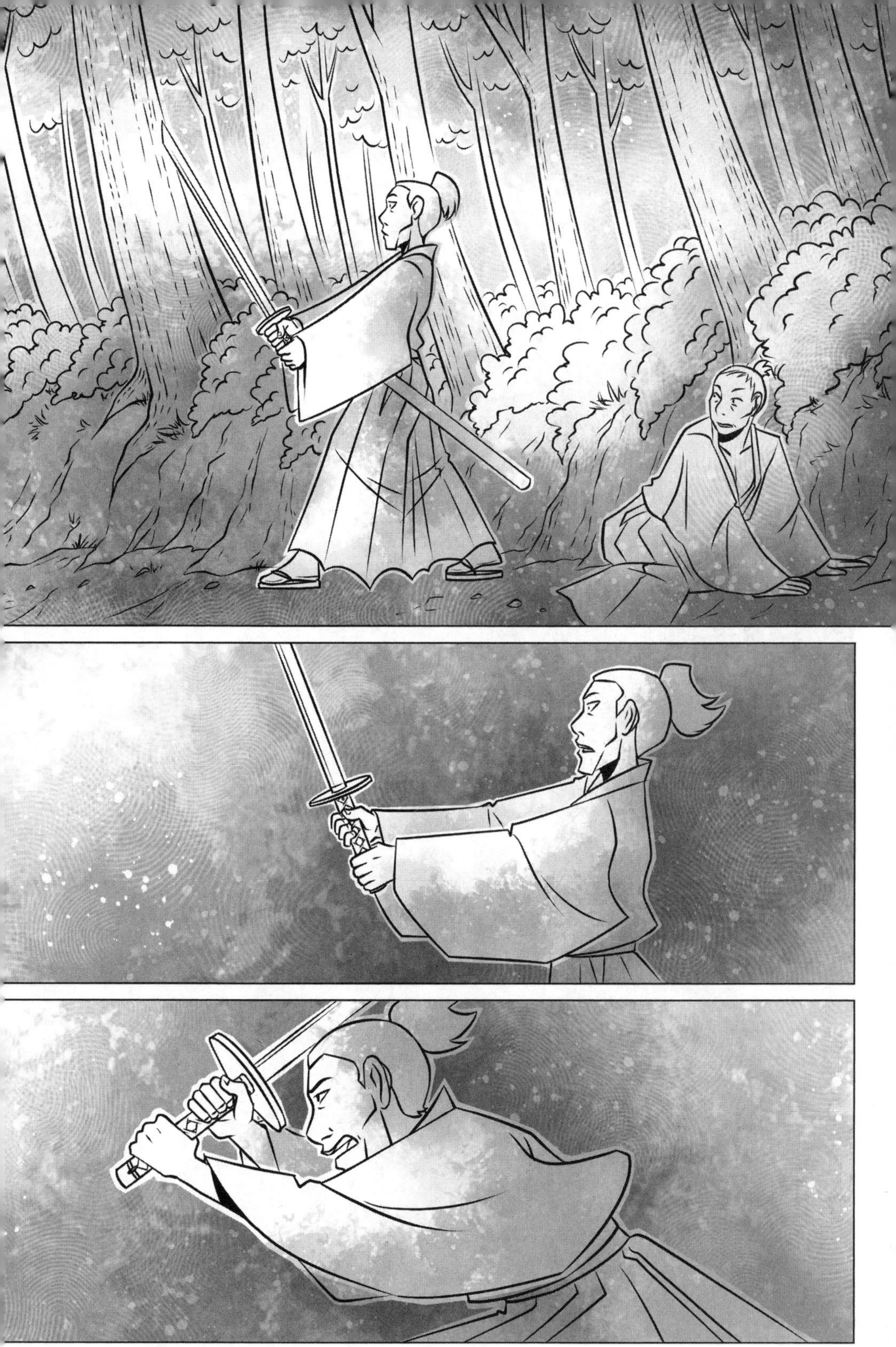

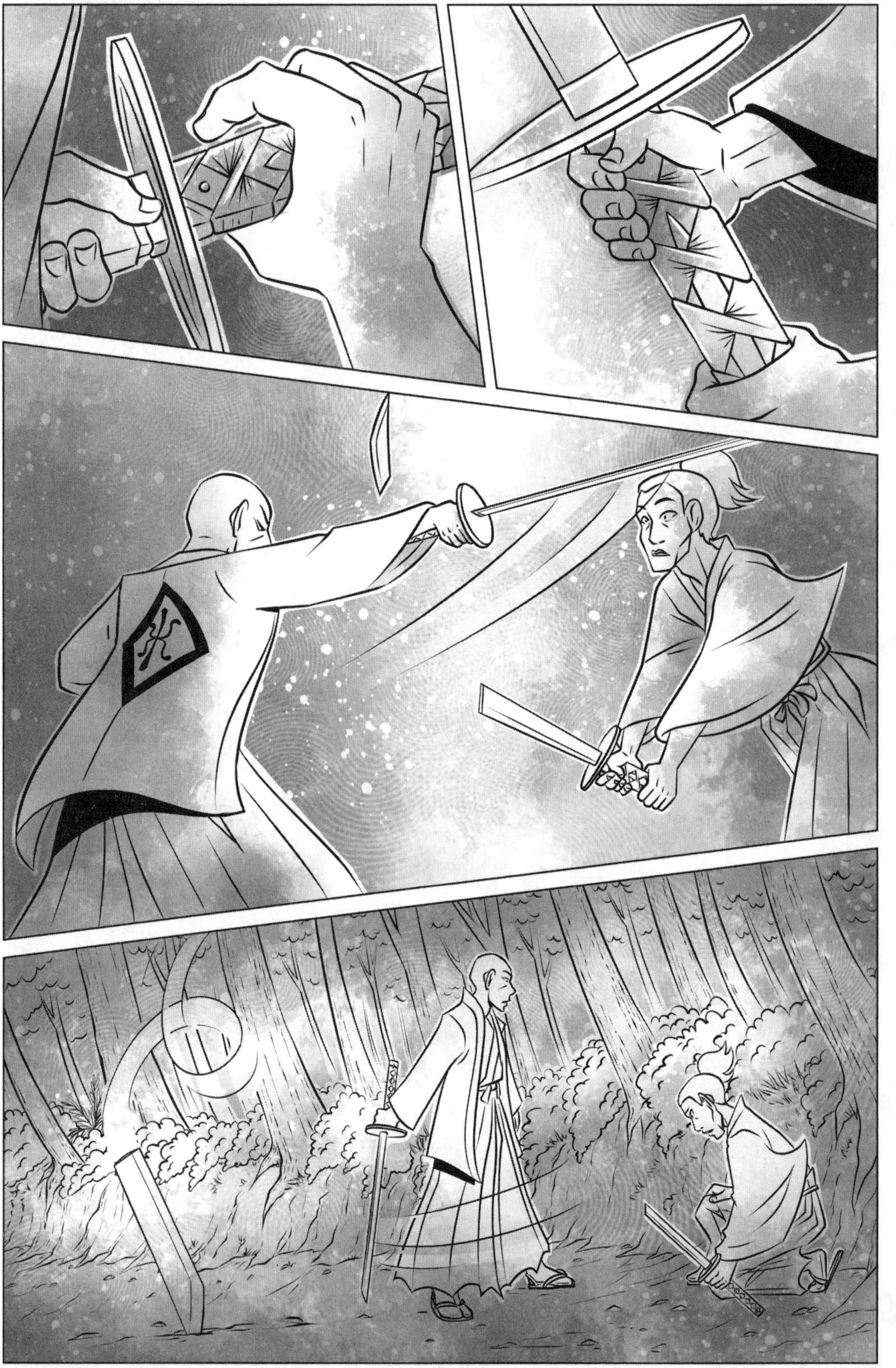

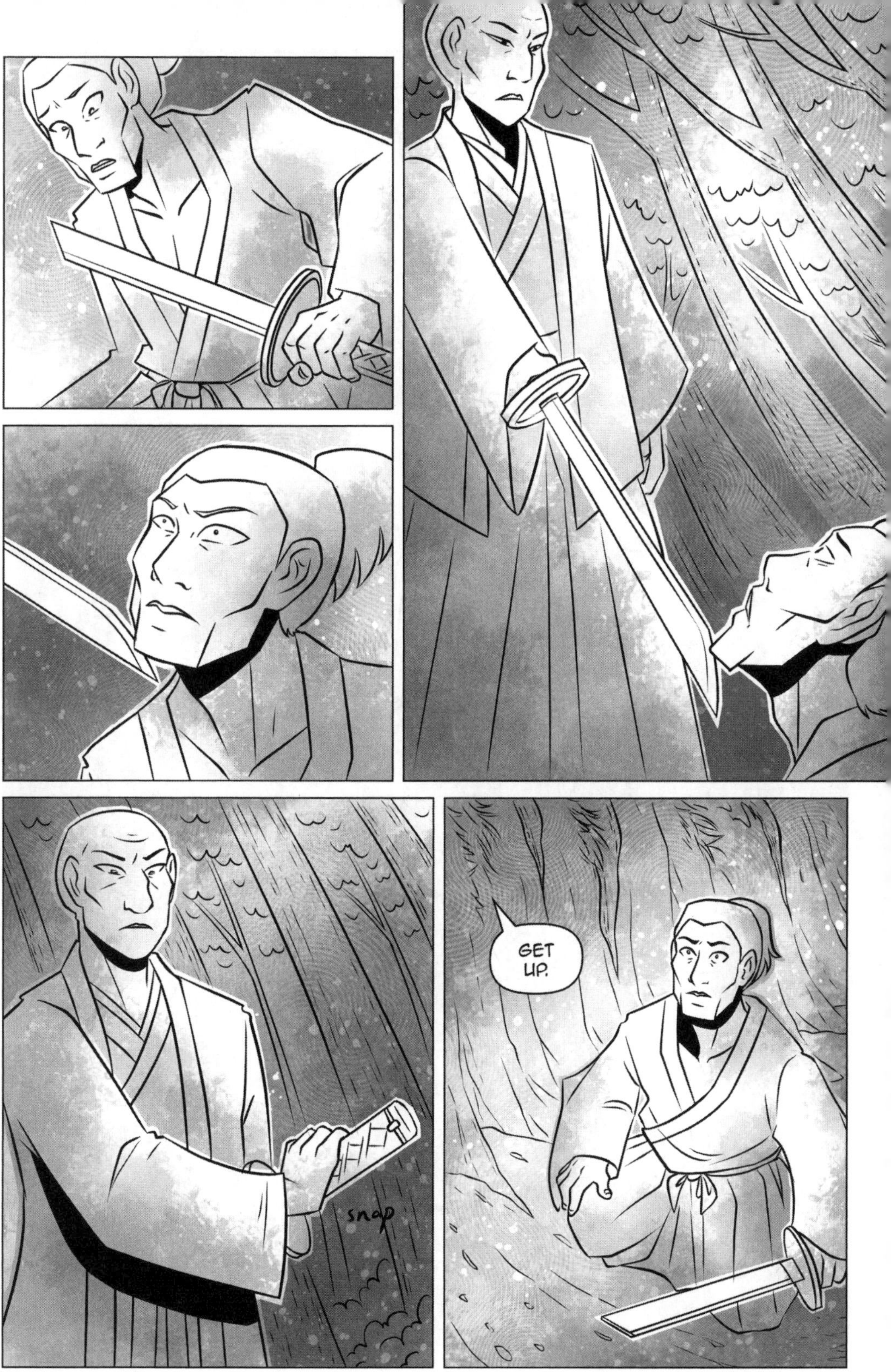
snap
GET UP.

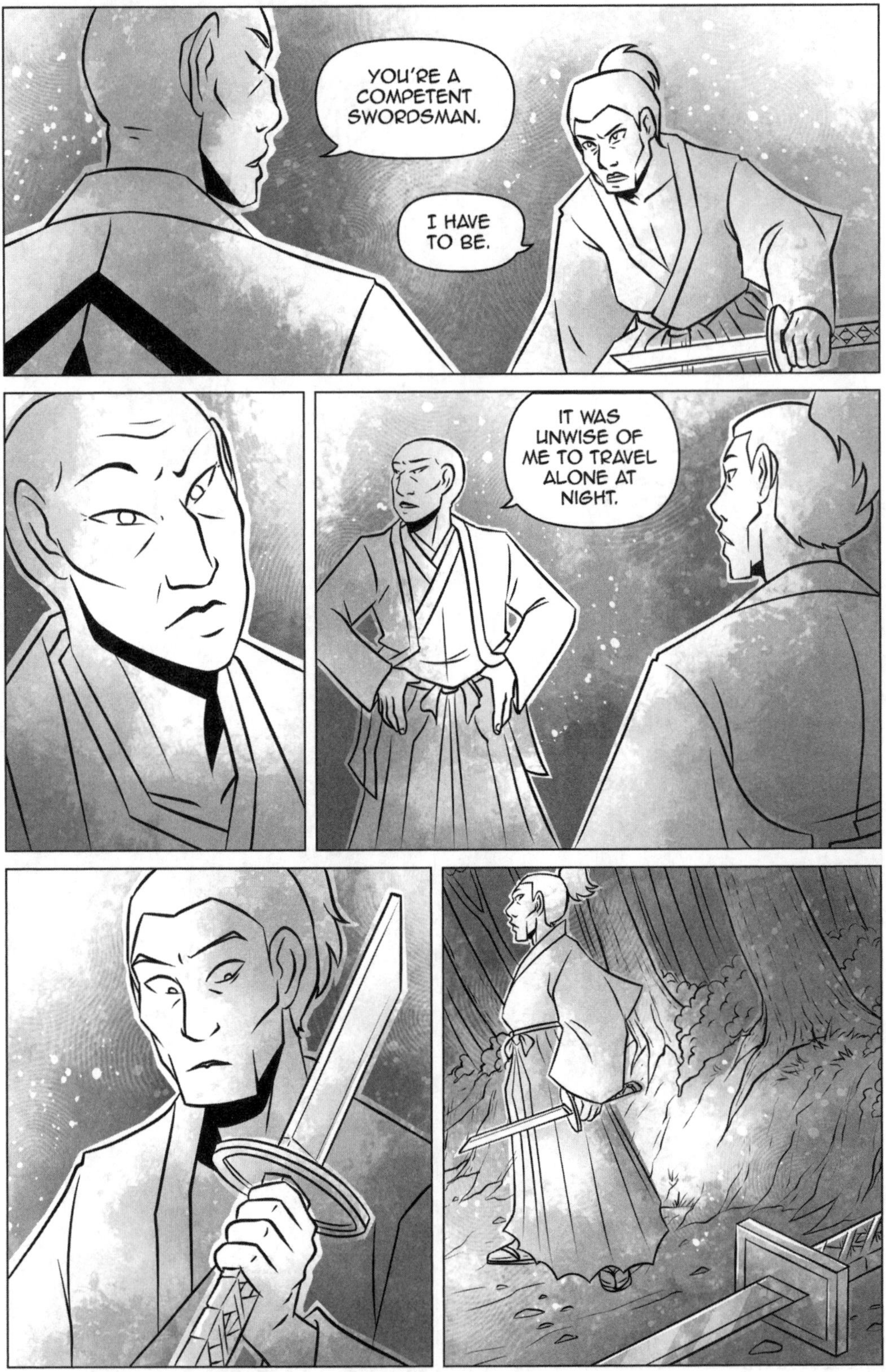
YOU'RE A COMPETENT SWORDSMAN.
I HAVE TO BE.
IT WAS UNWISE OF ME TO TRAVEL ALONE AT NIGHT.

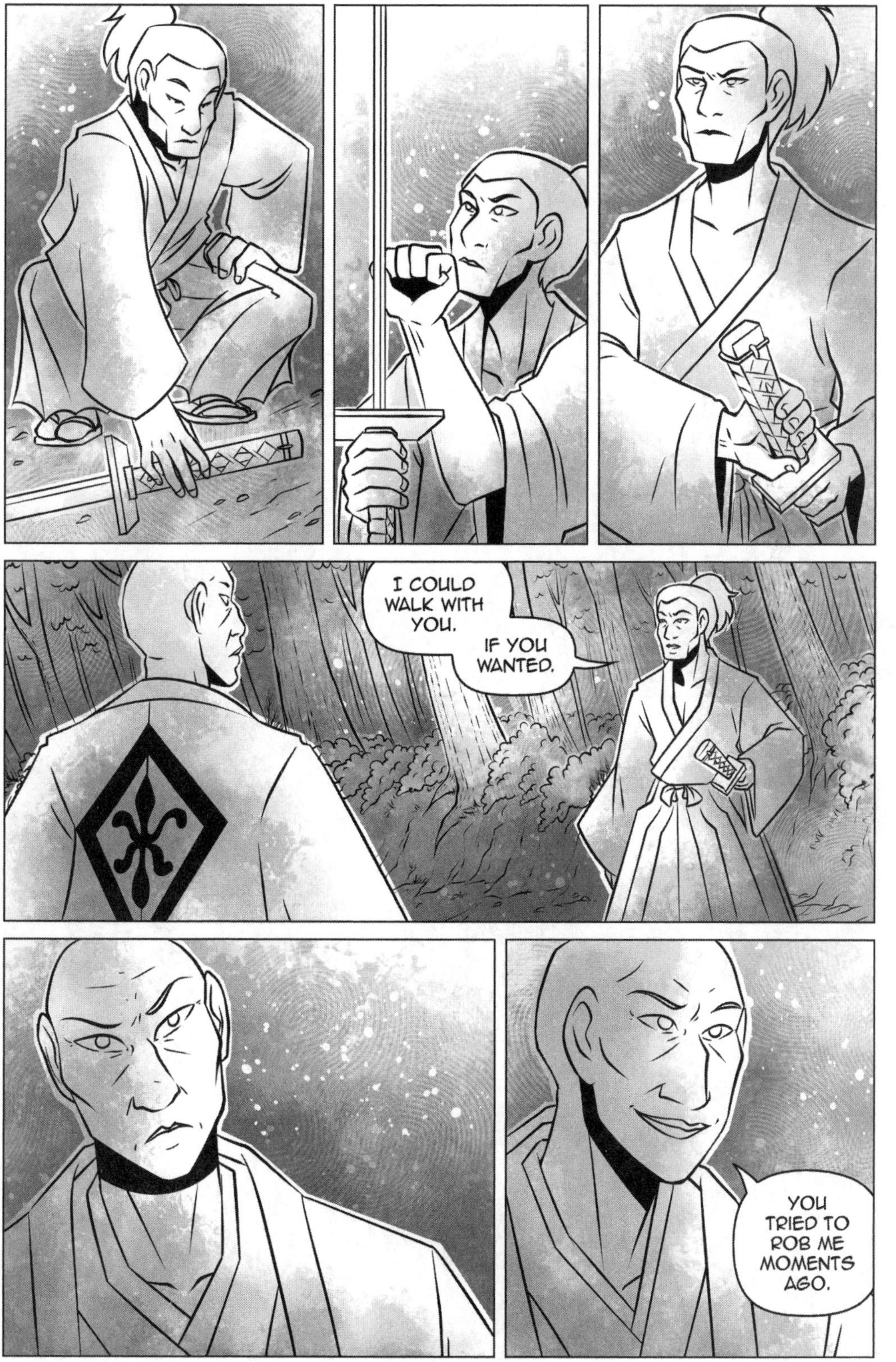
I COULD WALK WITH YOU.
IF YOU WANTED.
YOU TRIED TO ROB ME MOMENTS AGO.

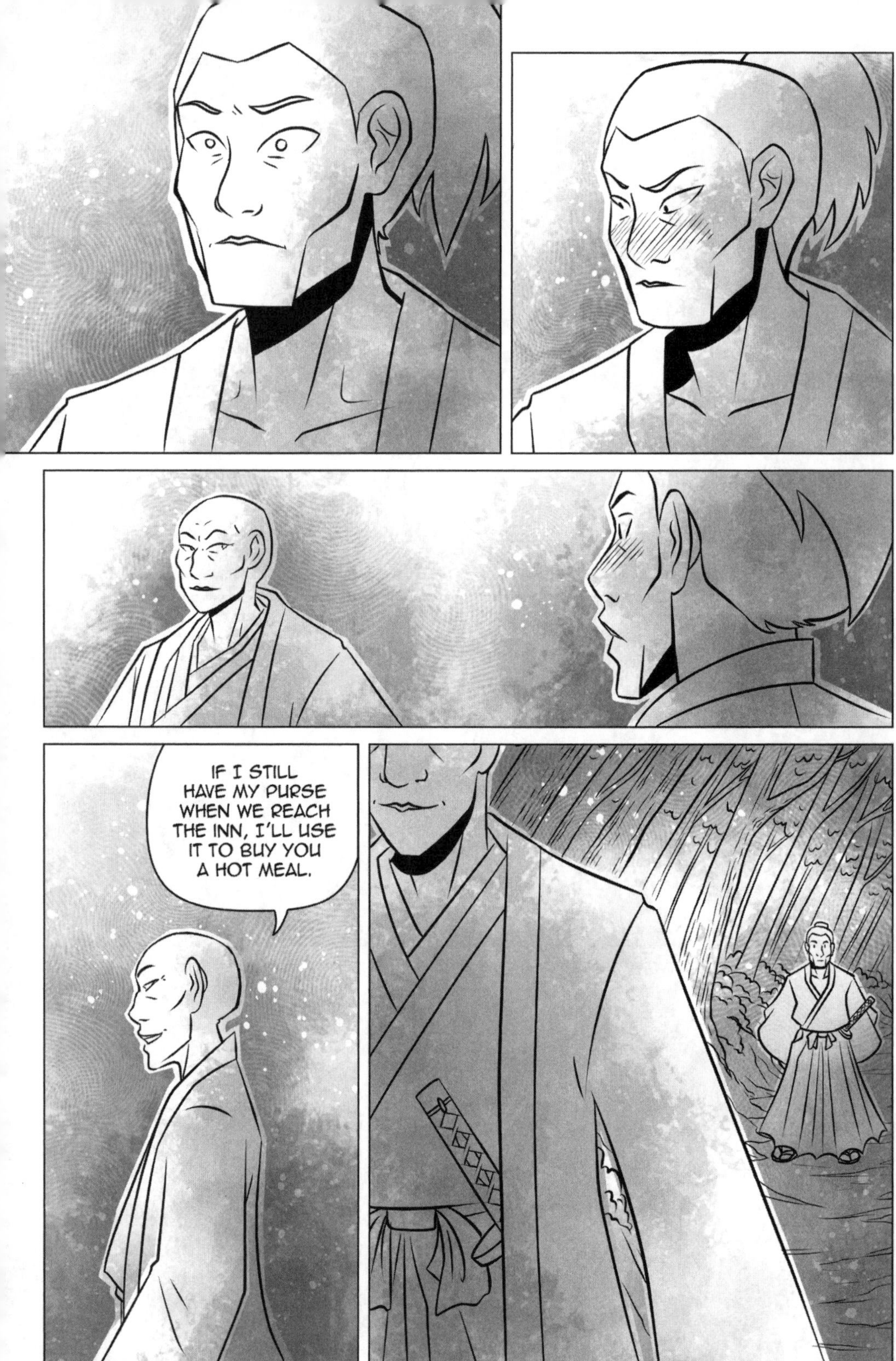
IF I STILL HAVE MY PURSE WHEN WE REACH THE INN, I'LL USE IT TO BUY YOU A HOT MEAL.

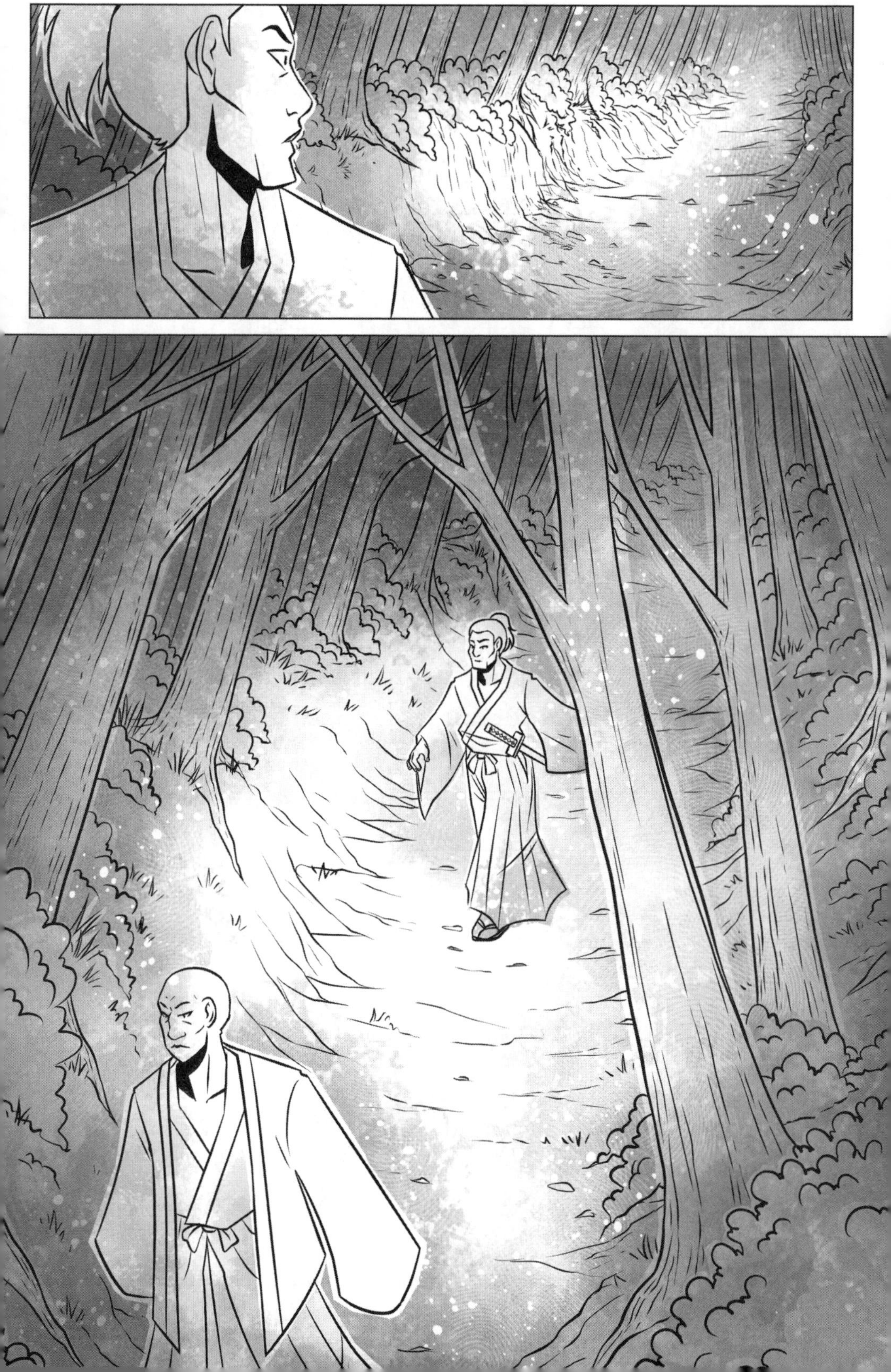

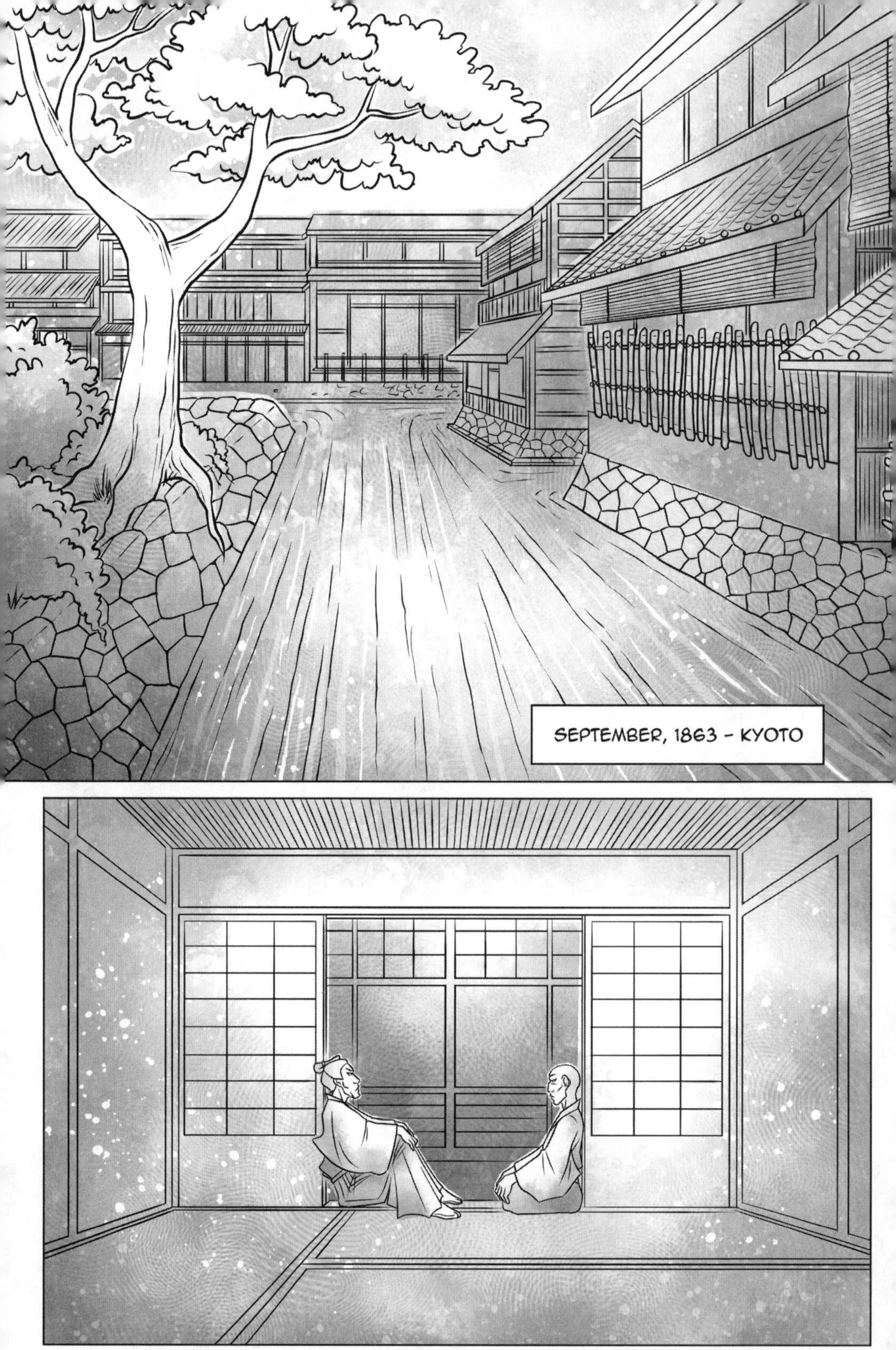
SEPTEMBER, 1863 - KYOTO

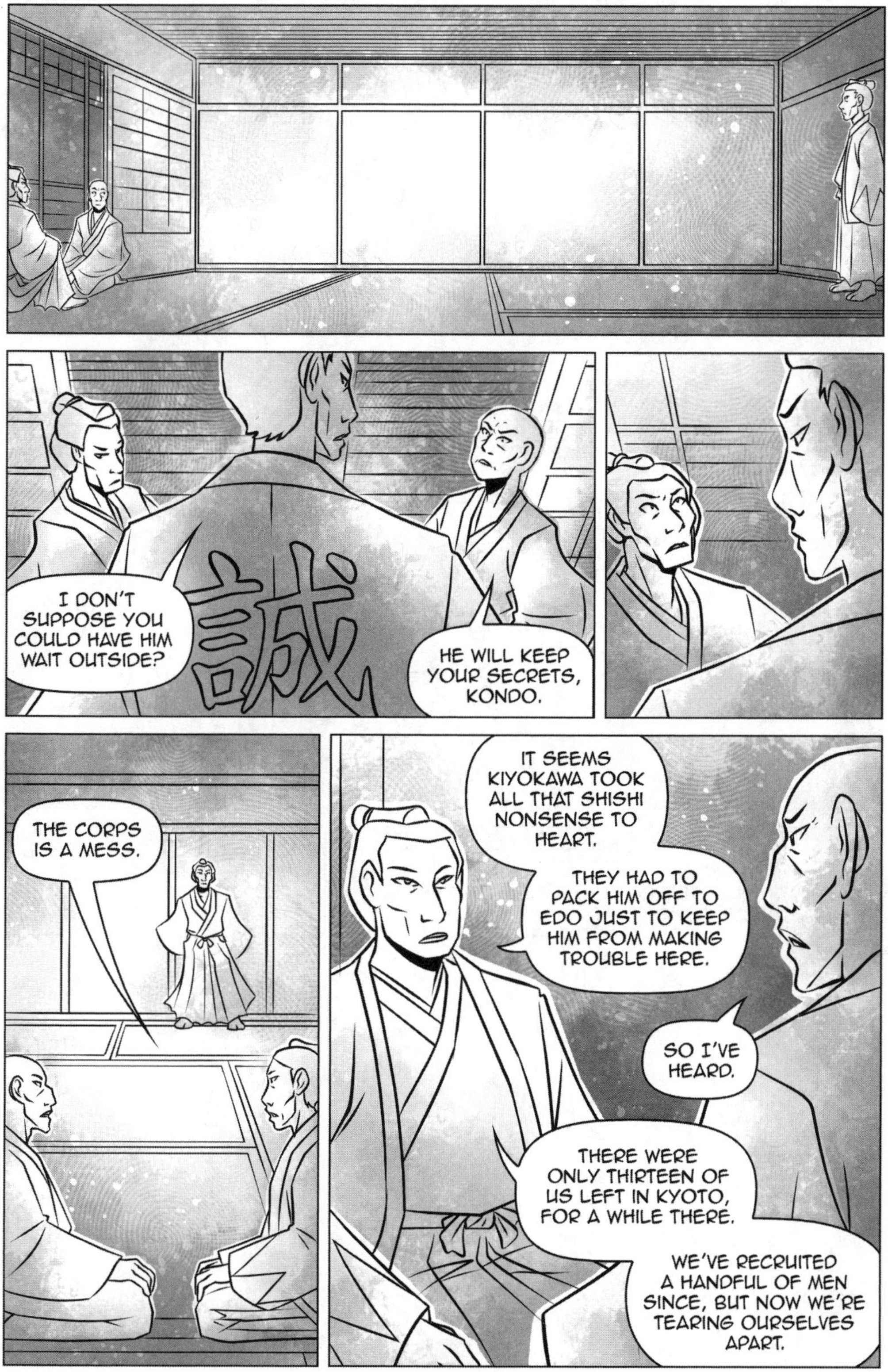
誠
I DON'T SUPPOSE YOU COULD HAVE HIM WAIT OUTSIDE?
HE WILL KEEP YOUR SECRETS, KONDO.
THE CORPS IS A MESS.
IT SEEMS KIYOKAWA TOOK ALL THAT SHISHI NONSENSE TO HEART.
THEY HAD TO PACK HIM OFF TO EDO JUST TO KEEP HIM FROM MAKING TROUBLE HERE.
SO I'VE HEARD.
THERE WERE ONLY THIRTEEN OF US LEFT IN KYOTO, FOR A WHILE THERE.
WE'VE RECRUITED A HANDFUL OF MEN SINCE, BUT NOW WE'RE TEARING OURSELVES APART.

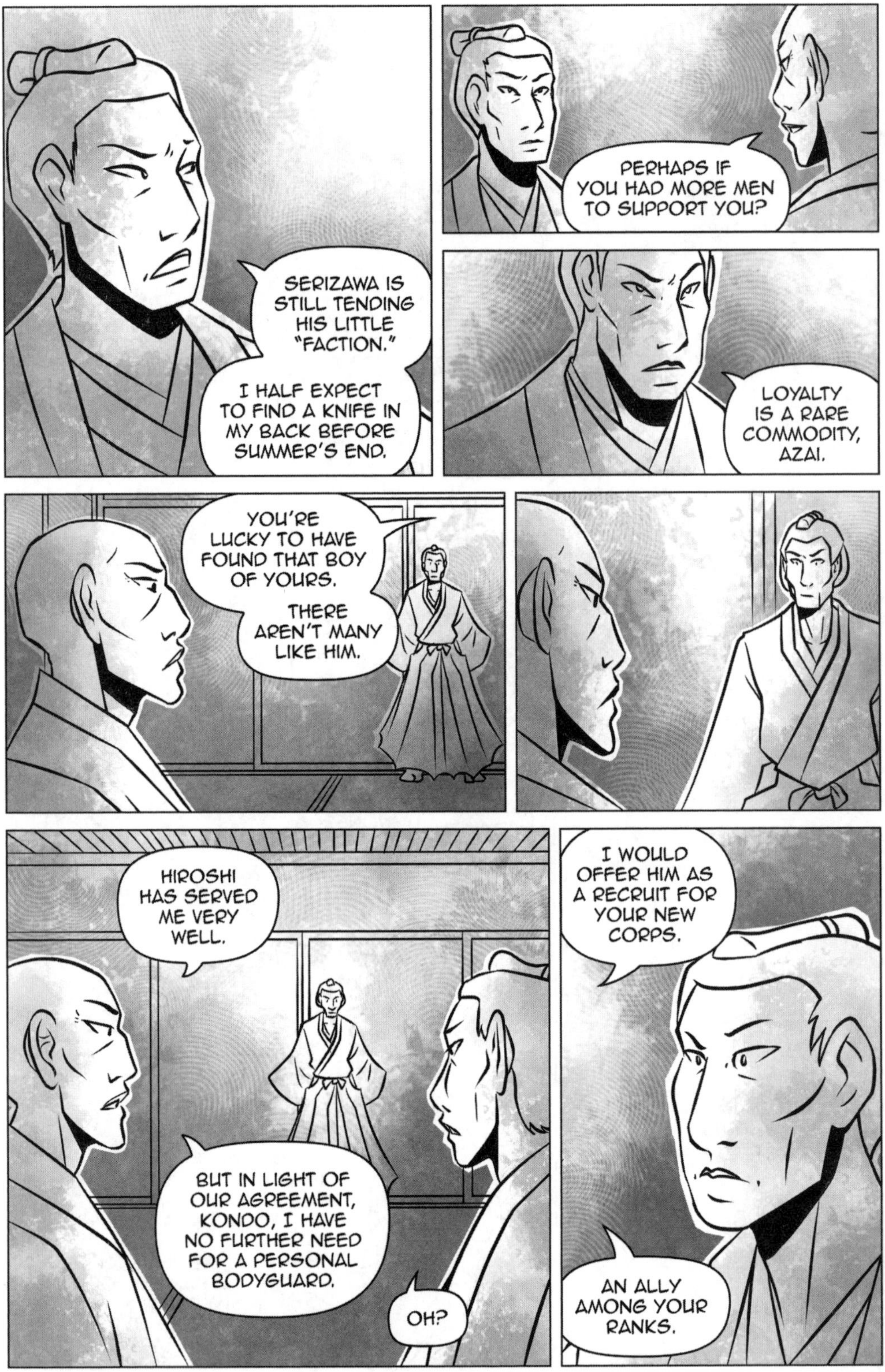
SERIZAWA IS STILL TENDING HIS LITTLE "FACTION."
I HALF EXPECT TO FIND A KNIFE IN MY BACK BEFORE SUMMER'S END.
PERHAPS IF YOU HAD MORE MEN TO SUPPORT YOU?
LOYALTY IS A RARE COMMODITY, AZAI.
YOU'RE LUCKY TO HAVE FOUND THAT BOY OF YOURS.
THERE AREN'T MANY LIKE HIM.
HIROSHI HAS SERVED ME VERY WELL.
BUT IN LIGHT OF OUR AGREEMENT, KONDO, I HAVE NO FURTHER NEED FOR A PERSONAL BODYGUARD.
OH?
I WOULD OFFER HIM AS A RECRUIT FOR YOUR NEW CORPS.
AN ALLY AMONG YOUR RANKS.

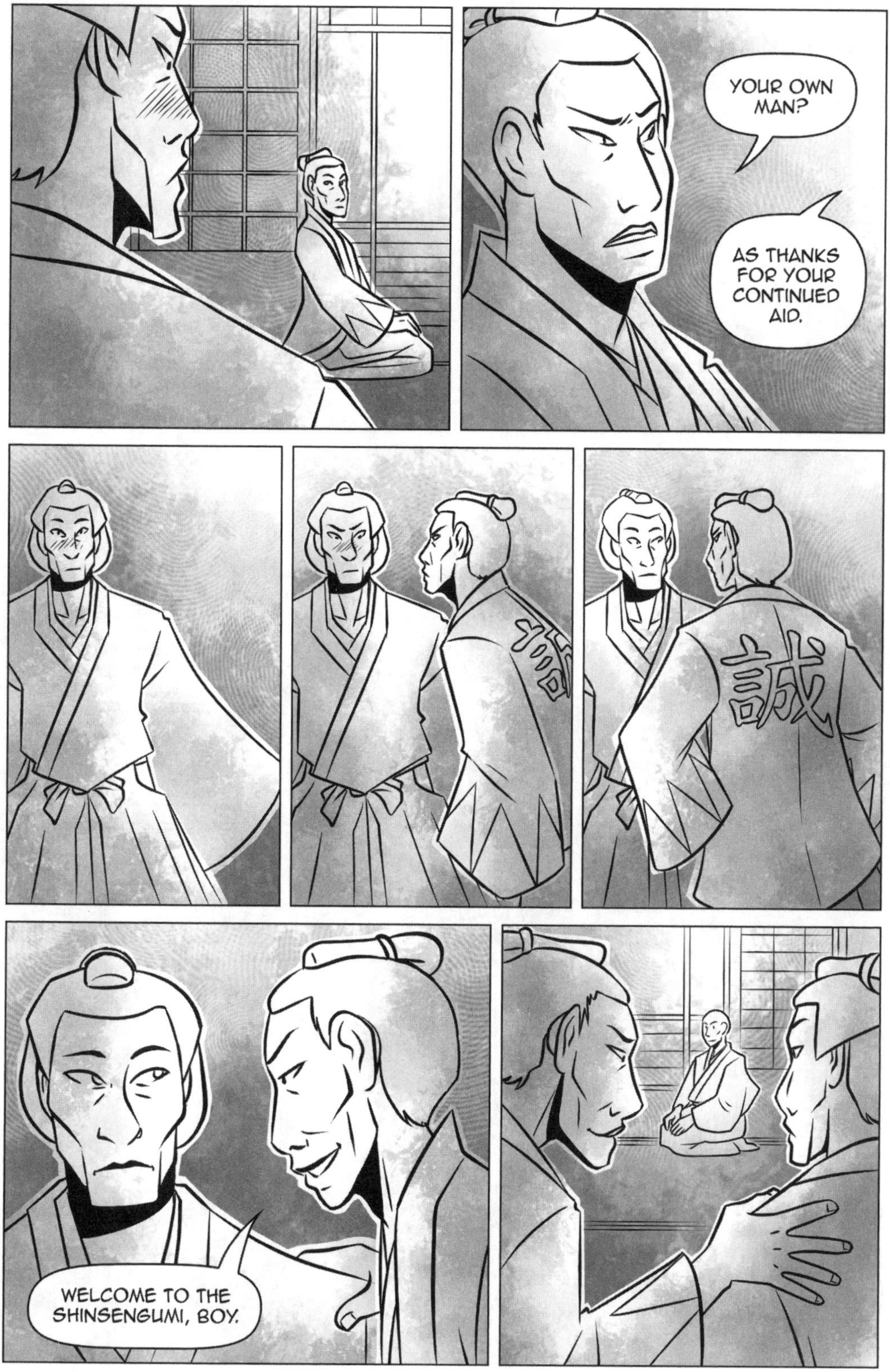
YOUR OWN MAN?
AS THANKS FOR YOUR CONTINUED AID.
誠
誠
WELCOME TO THE SHINSENGUMI, BOY.

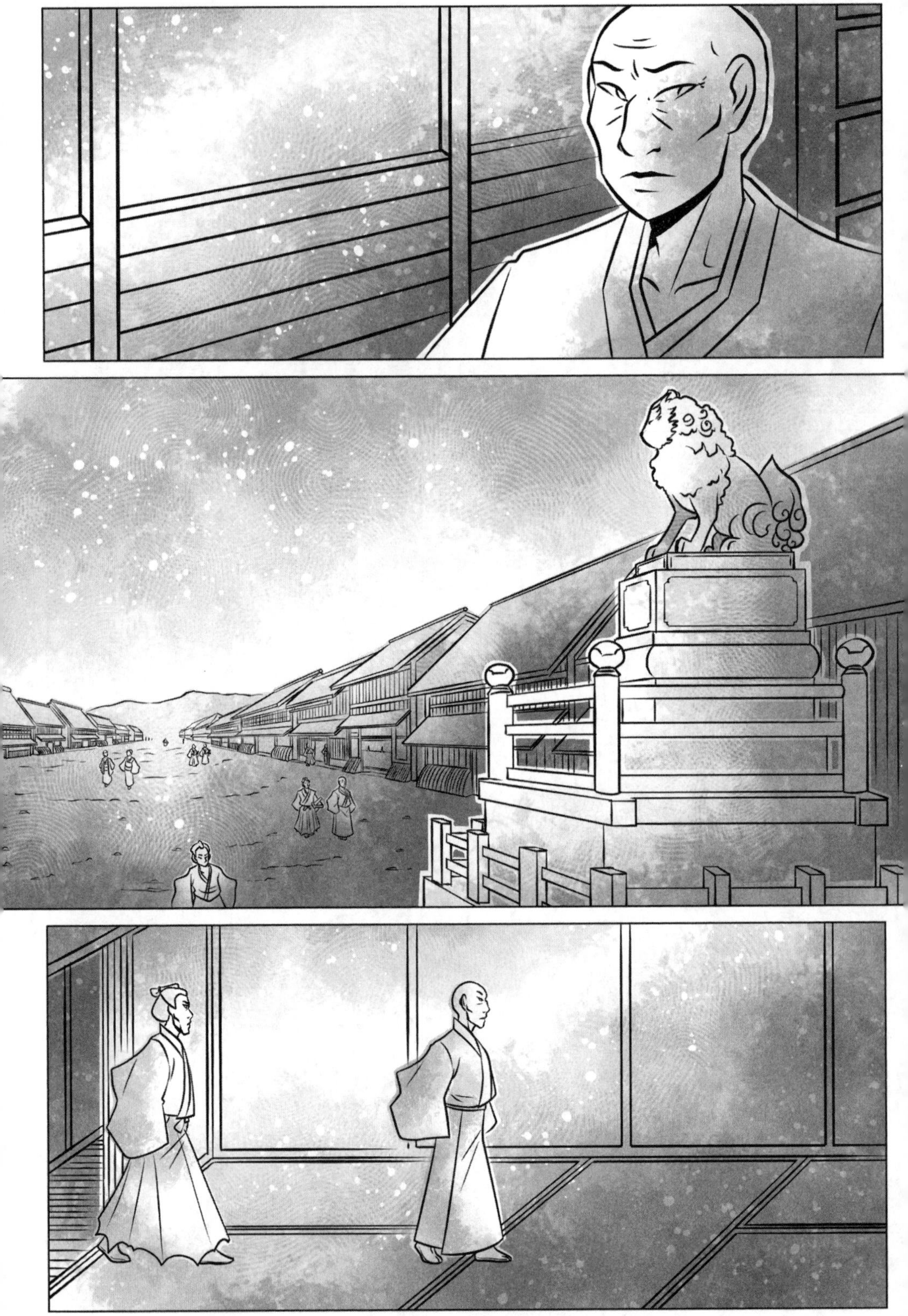

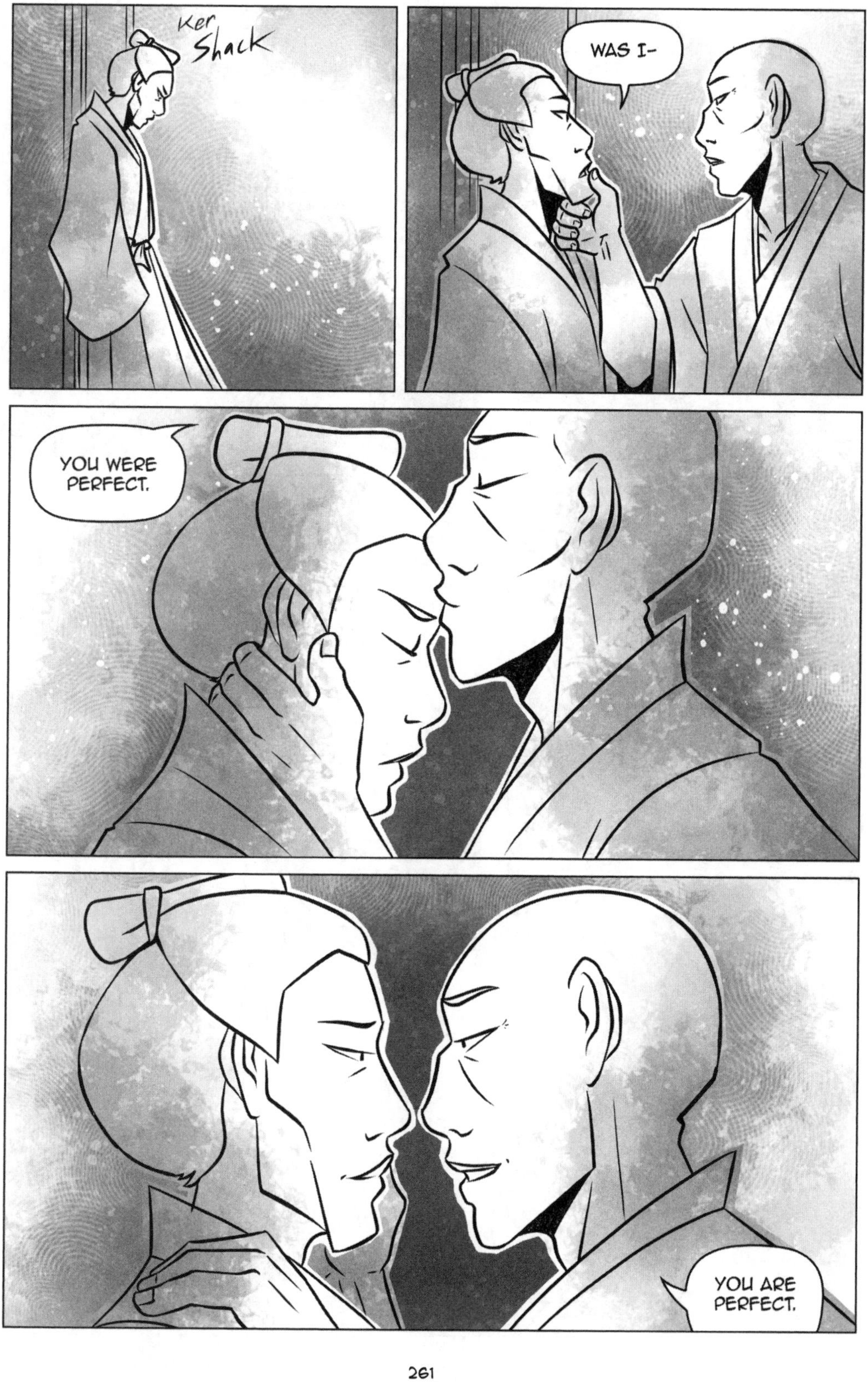
Ker Shack
WAS I-
YOU WERE PERFECT.
YOU ARE PERFECT.

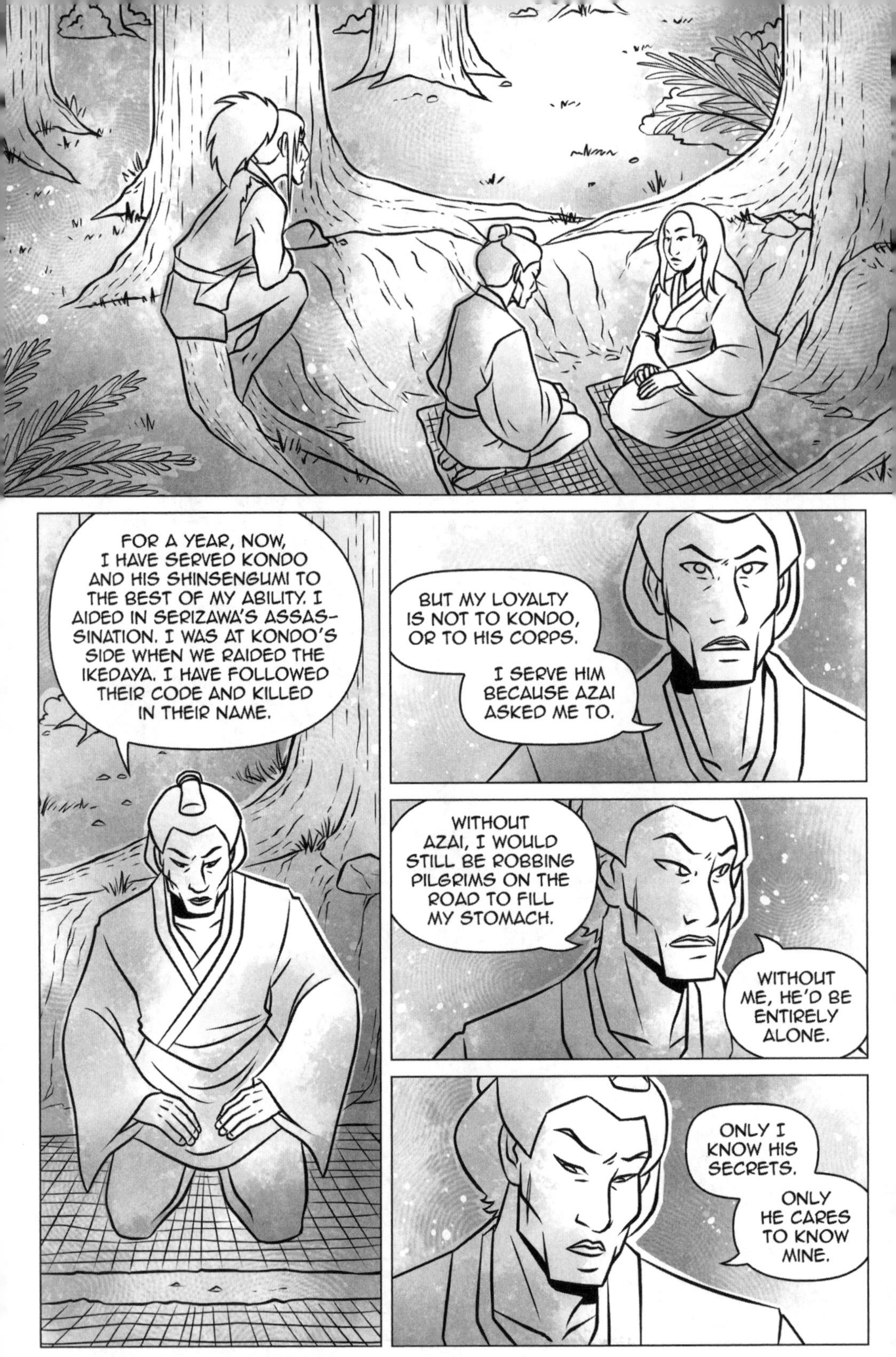

FOR A YEAR, NOW, I HAVE SERVED KONDO AND HIS SHINSENGUMI TO THE BEST OF MY ABILITY. I AIDED IN SERIZAWA'S ASSASSINATION. I WAS AT KONDO'S SIDE WHEN WE RAIDED THE IKEDAYA. I HAVE FOLLOWED THEIR CODE AND KILLED IN THEIR NAME.
BUT MY LOYALTY IS NOT TO KONDO, OR TO HIS CORPS.
I SERVE HIM BECAUSE AZAI ASKED ME TO.
WITHOUT AZAI, I WOULD STILL BE ROBBING PILGRIMS ON THE ROAD TO FILL MY STOMACH.
WITHOUT ME, HE'D BE ENTIRELY ALONE.
ONLY I KNOW HIS SECRETS.
ONLY HE CARES TO KNOW MINE.

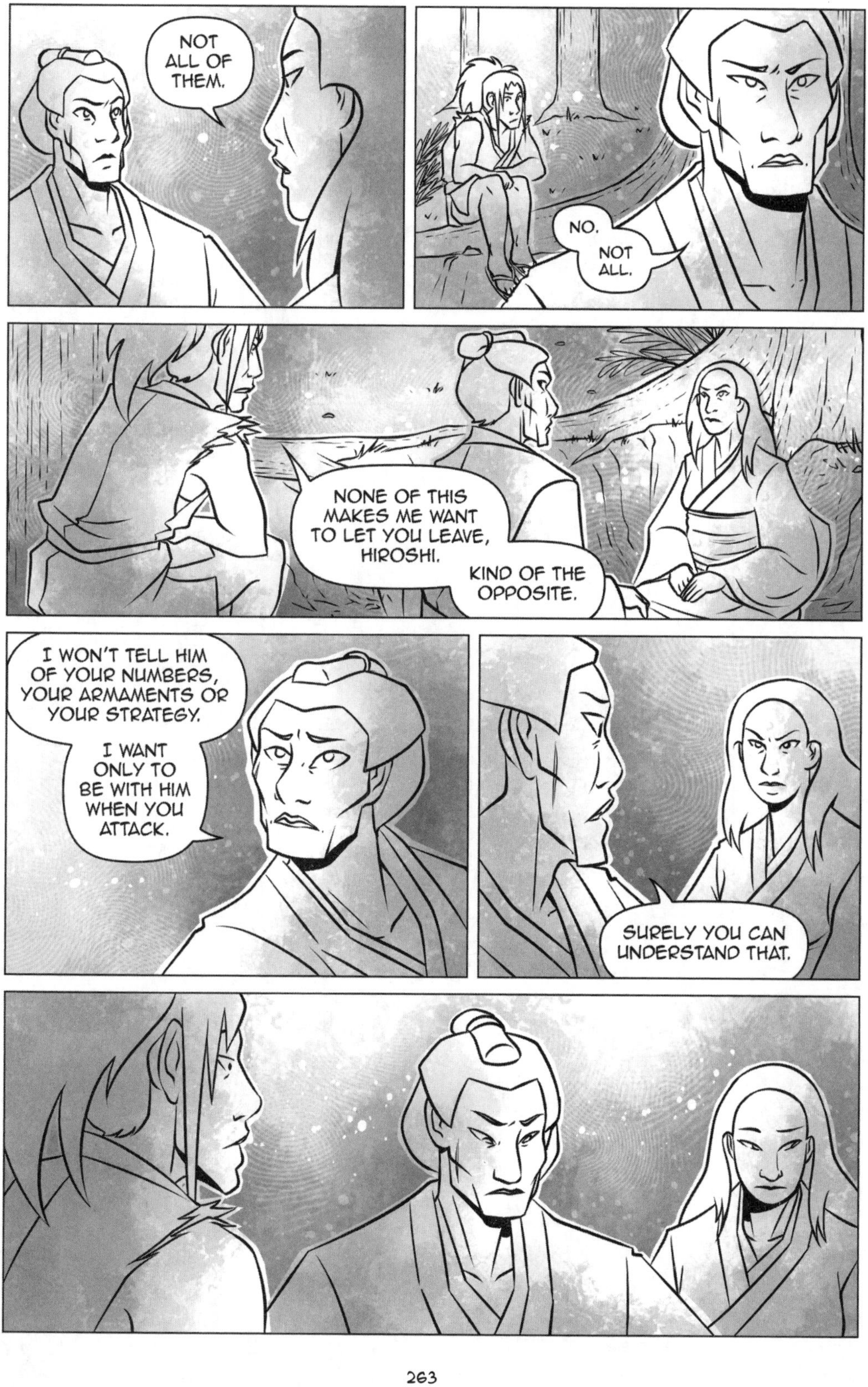
NOT ALL OF THEM.
NO.
NOT ALL.
NONE OF THIS MAKES ME WANT TO LET YOU LEAVE, HIROSHI.
KIND OF THE OPPOSITE.
I WON'T TELL HIM OF YOUR NUMBERS, YOUR ARMAMENTS OR YOUR STRATEGY.
I WANT ONLY TO BE WITH HIM WHEN YOU ATTACK.
SURELY YOU CAN UNDERSTAND THAT.

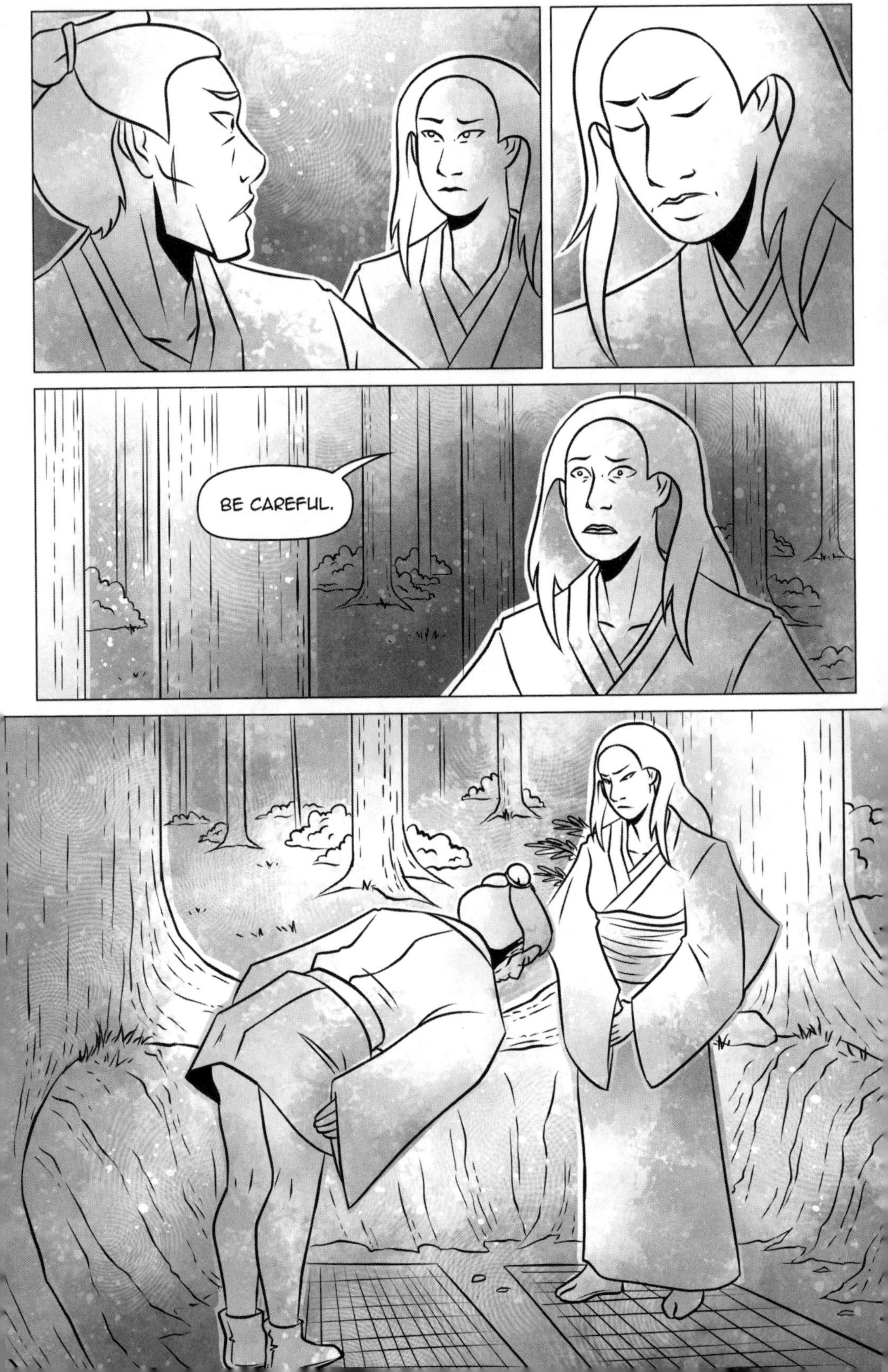
BE CAREFUL.

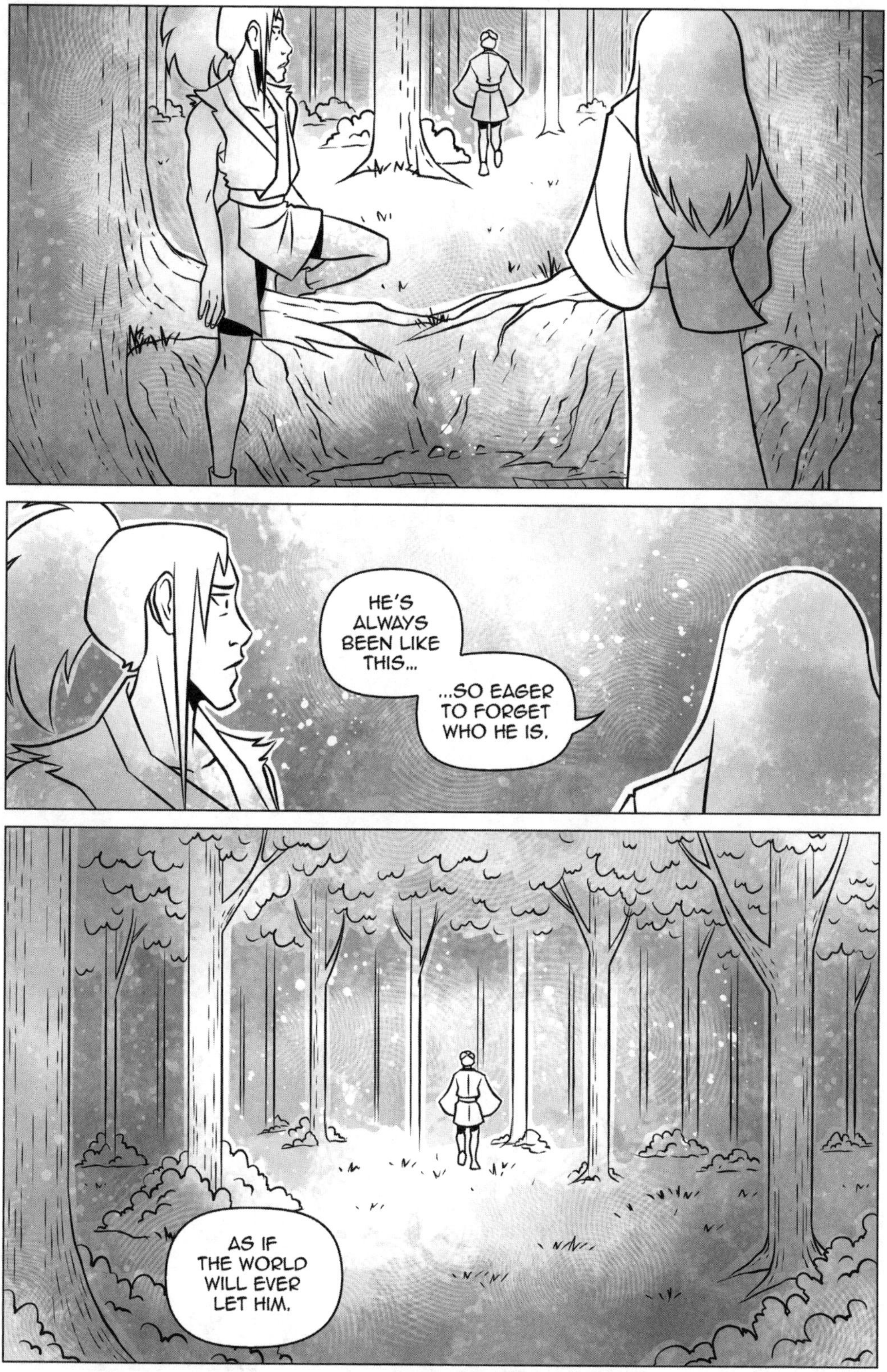
HE'S ALWAYS BEEN LIKE THIS...
...SO EAGER TO FORGET WHO HE IS.
AS IF THE WORLD WILL EVER LET HIM.

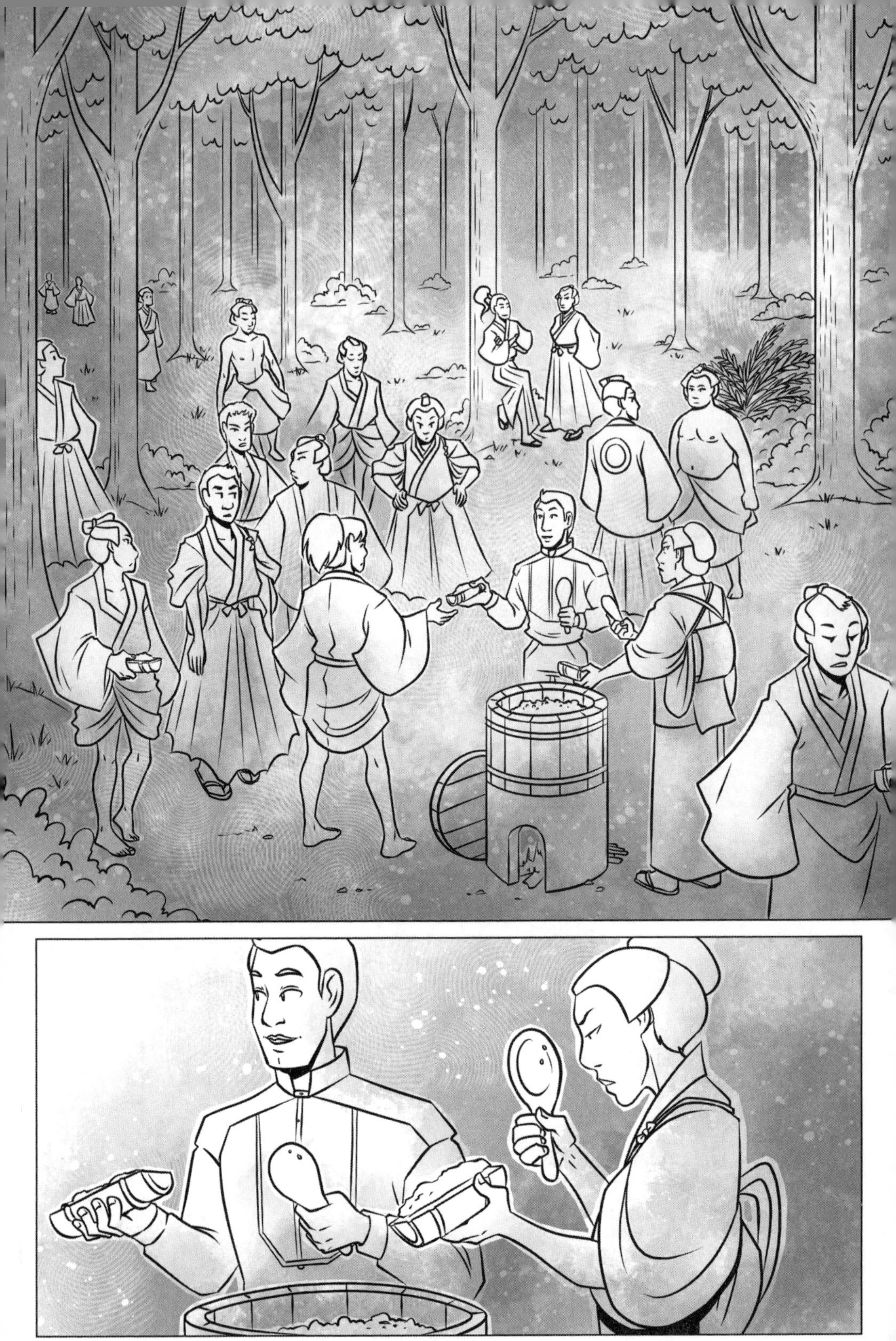

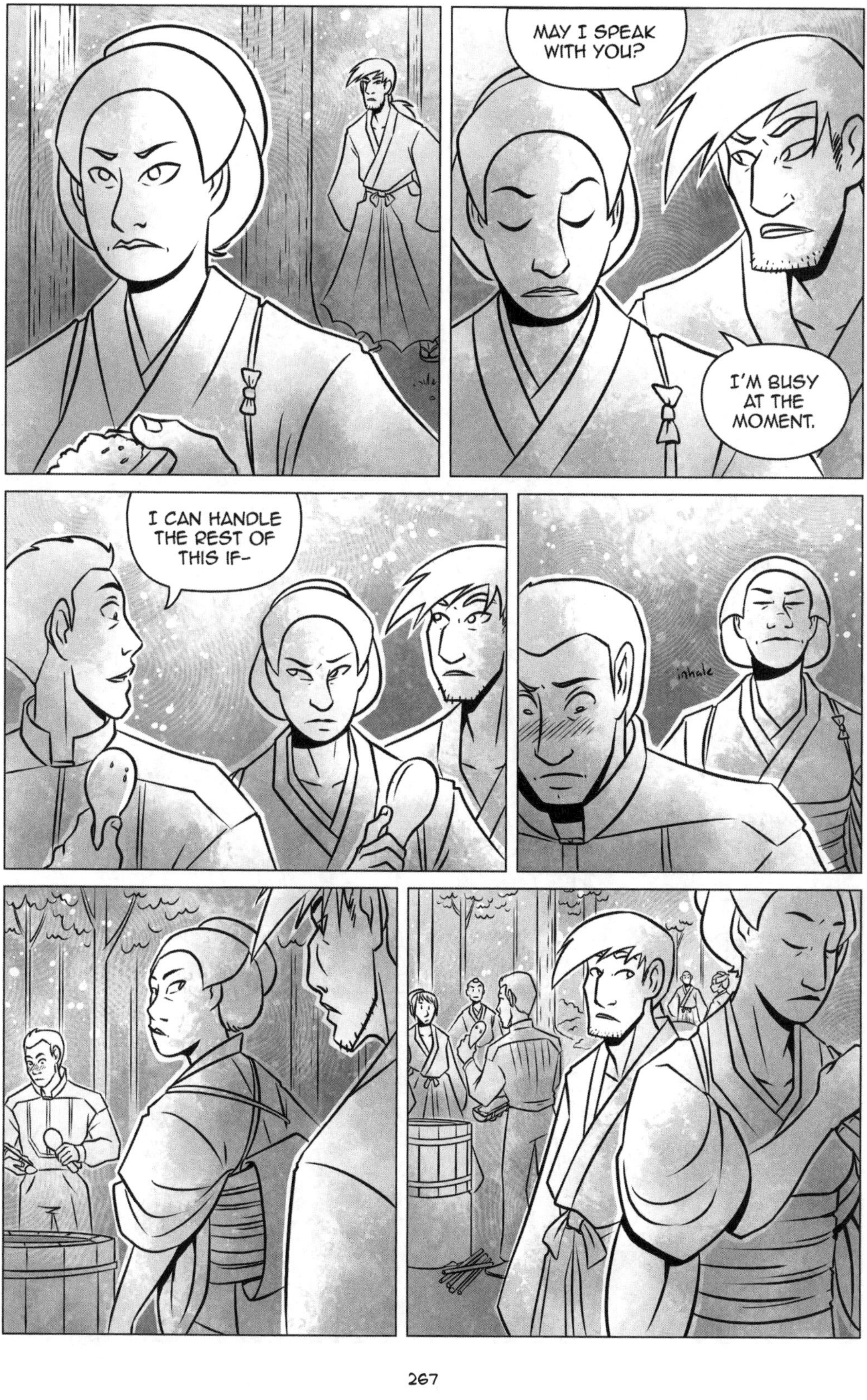
MAY I SPEAK WITH YOU?
I'M BUSY AT THE MOMENT.
I CAN HANDLE THE REST OF THIS IF-
inhale

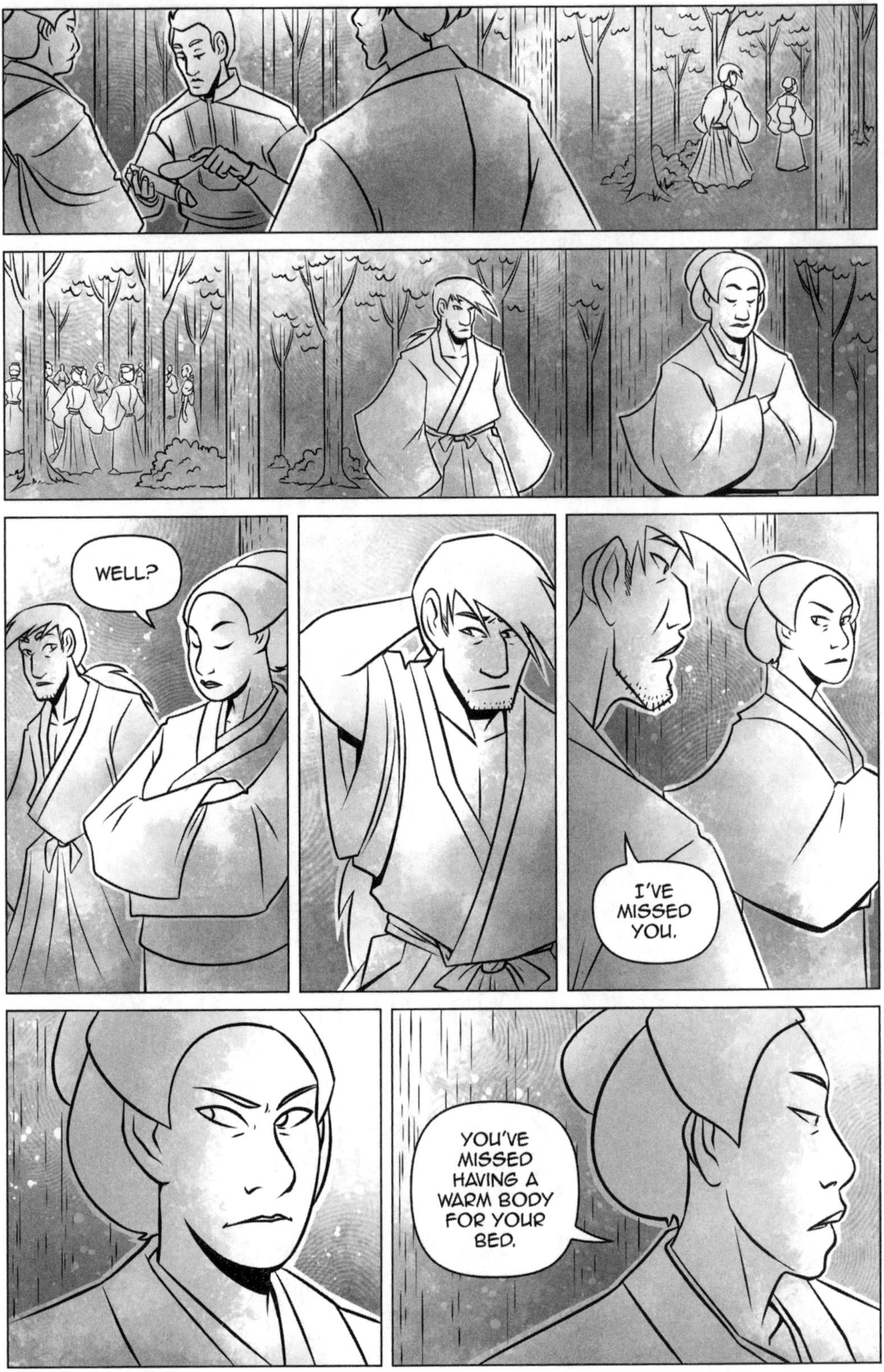

WELL?
I'VE MISSED YOU.
YOU'VE MISSED HAVING A WARM BODY FOR YOUR BED.

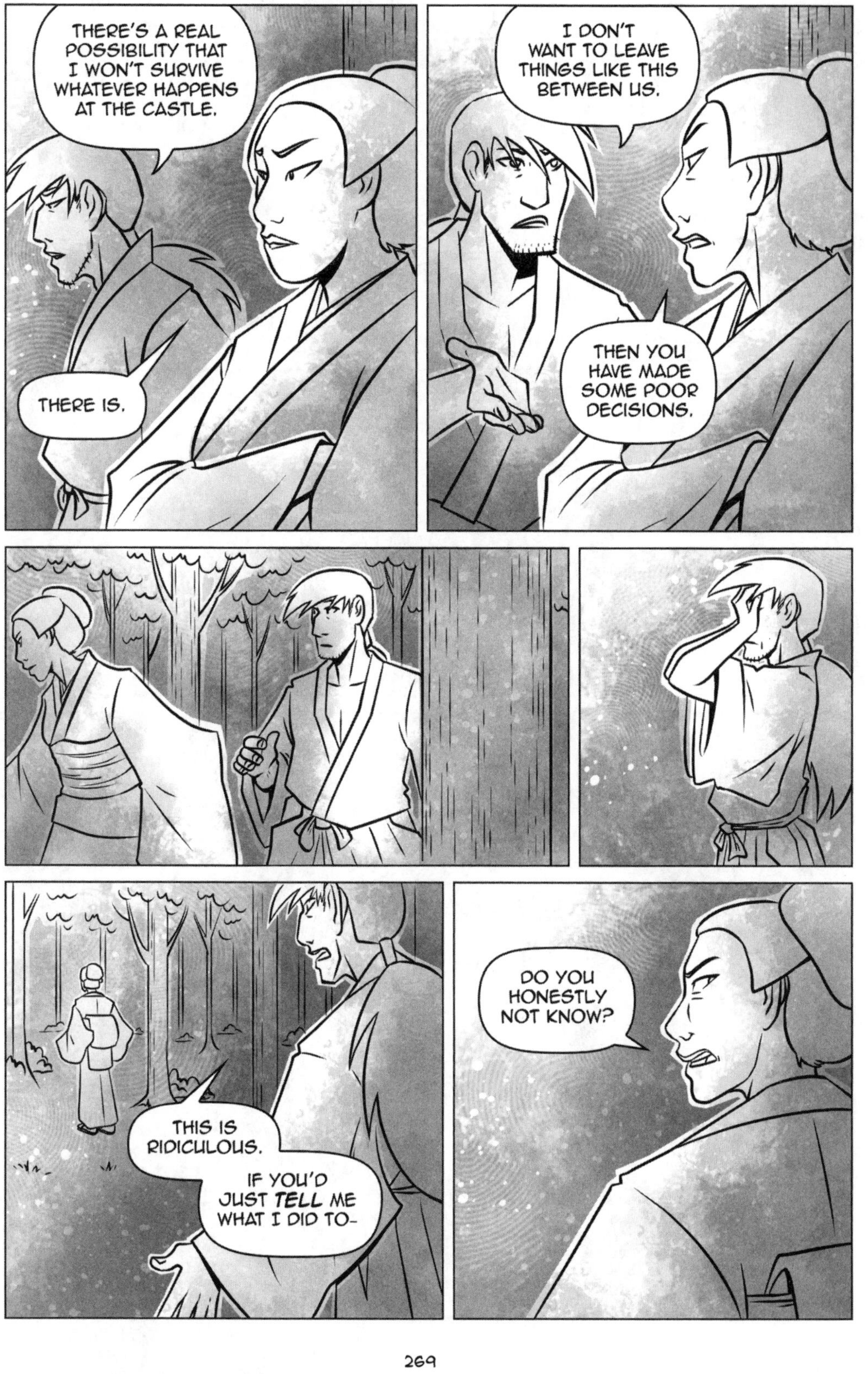
THERE'S A REAL POSSIBILITY THAT I WON'T SURVIVE WHATEVER HAPPENS AT THE CASTLE.
THERE IS.
I DON'T WANT TO LEAVE THINGS LIKE THIS BETWEEN US.
THEN YOU HAVE MADE SOME POOR DECISIONS.
THIS IS RIDICULOUS.
IF YOU'D JUST TELL ME WHAT I DID TO-
DO YOU HONESTLY NOT KNOW?

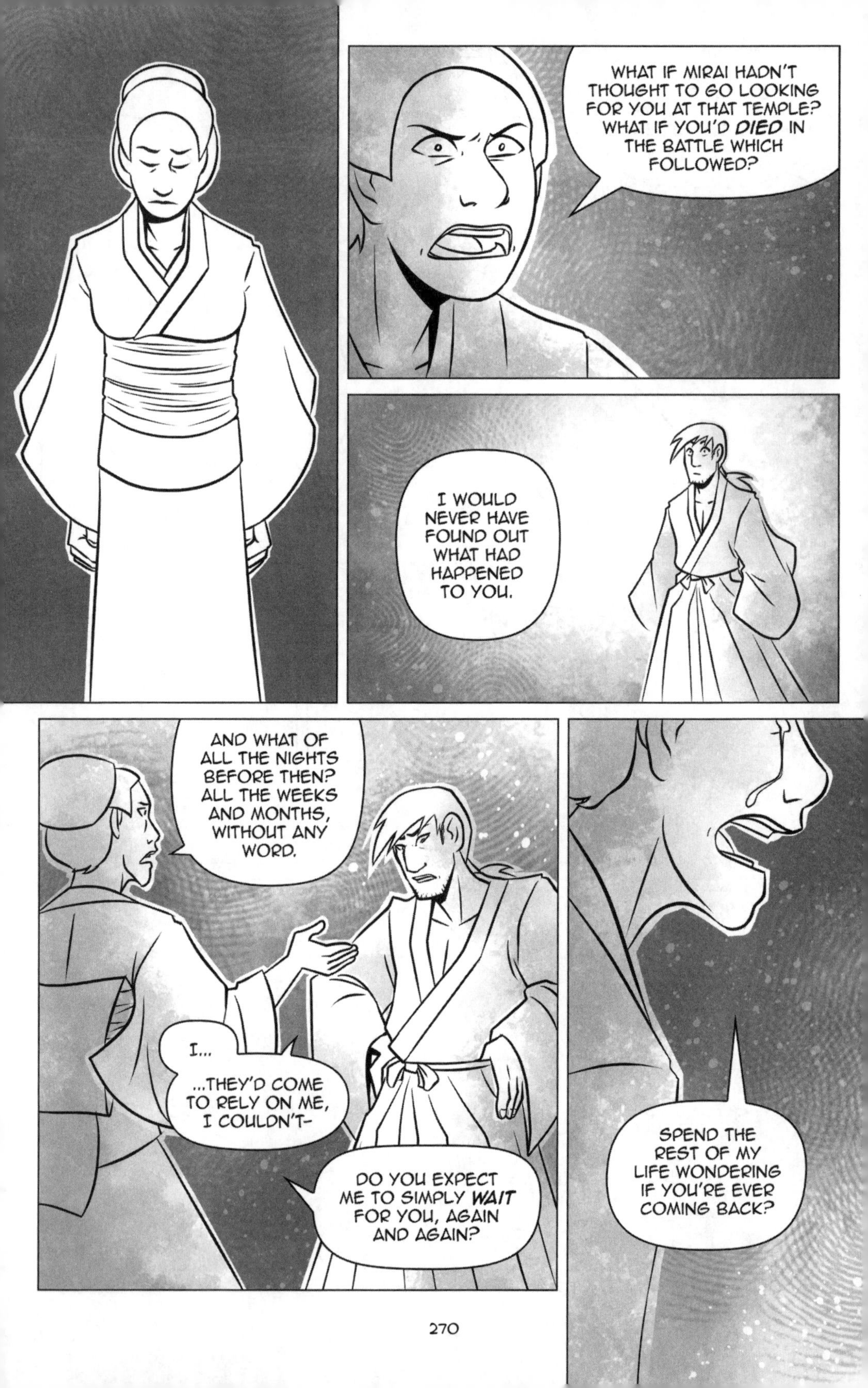
WHAT IF MIRAI HADN'T THOUGHT TO GO LOOKING FOR YOU AT THAT TEMPLE? WHAT IF YOU'D DIED IN THE BATTLE WHICH FOLLOWED?
I WOULD NEVER HAVE FOUND OUT WHAT HAD HAPPENED TO YOU.
AND WHAT OF ALL THE NIGHTS BEFORE THEN? ALL THE WEEKS AND MONTHS, WITHOUT ANY WORD.
I...
...THEY'D COME TO RELY ON ME, I COULDN'T-
DO YOU EXPECT ME TO SIMPLY WAIT FOR YOU, AGAIN AND AGAIN?
SPEND THE REST OF MY LIFE WONDERING IF YOU'RE EVER COMING BACK?

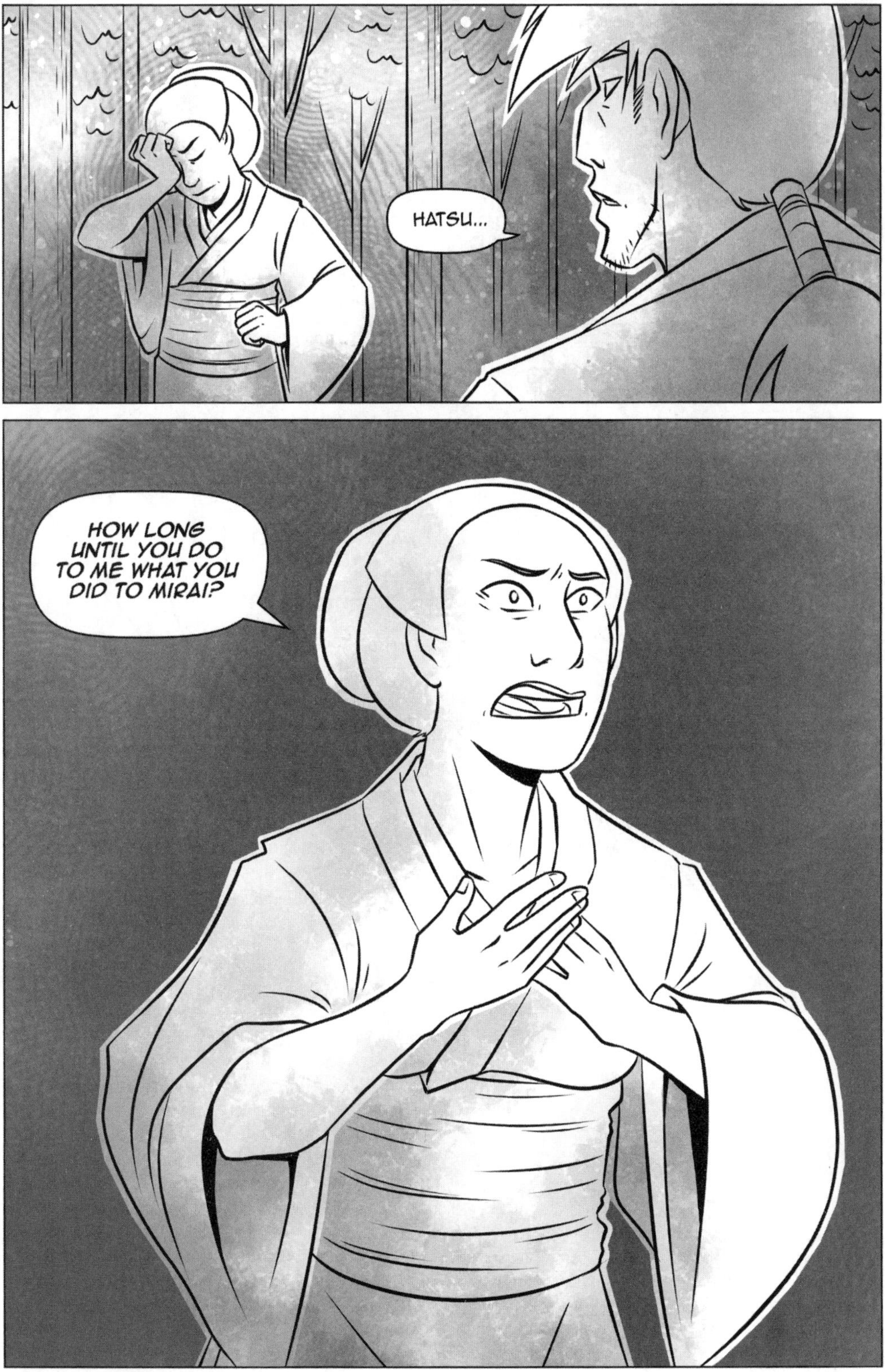
HATSU...
HOW LONG UNTIL YOU DO TO ME WHAT YOU DID TO MIRAI?

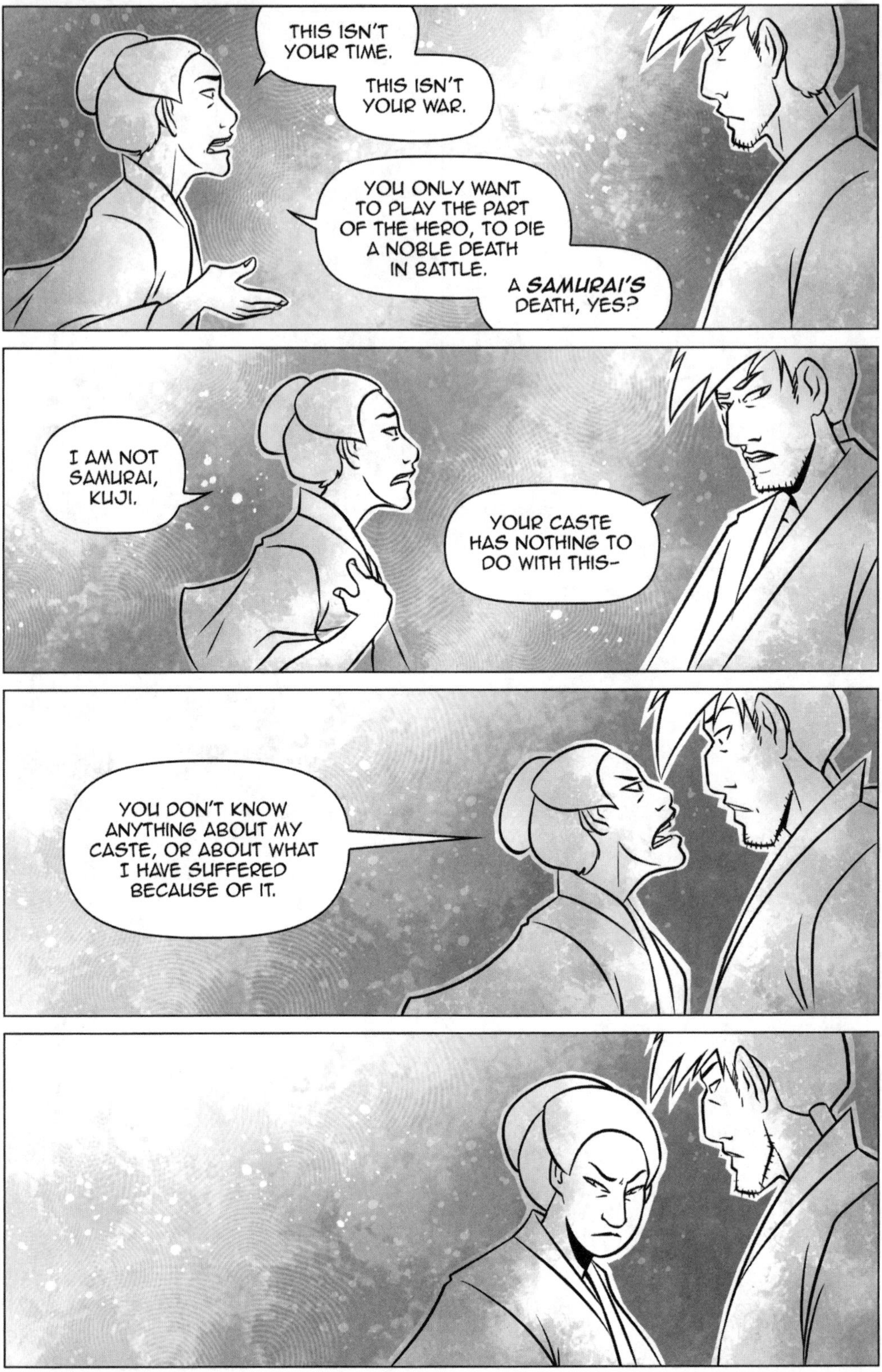
THIS ISN'T YOUR TIME.
THIS ISN'T YOUR WAR.
YOU ONLY WANT TO PLAY THE PART OF THE HERO, TO DIE A NOBLE DEATH IN BATTLE.
A ***SAMURAI'S*** DEATH, YES?
I AM NOT SAMURAI, KUJI.
YOUR CASTE HAS NOTHING TO DO WITH THIS-
YOU DON'T KNOW ANYTHING ABOUT MY CASTE, OR ABOUT WHAT I HAVE SUFFERED BECAUSE OF IT.

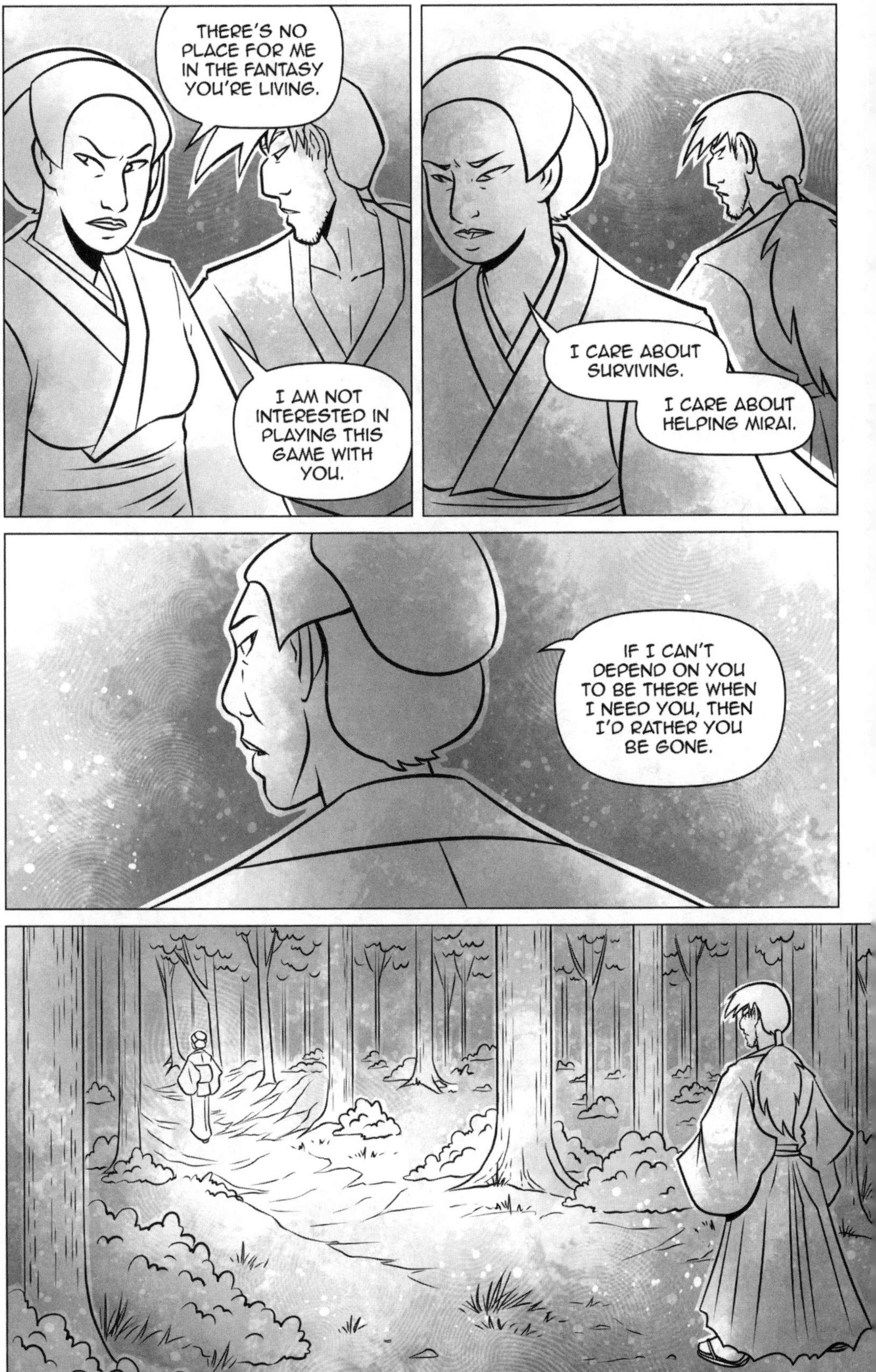
THERE'S NO PLACE FOR ME IN THE FANTASY YOU'RE LIVING.
I AM NOT INTERESTED IN PLAYING THIS GAME WITH YOU.
I CARE ABOUT SURVIVING.
I CARE ABOUT HELPING MIRAI.
IF I CAN'T DEPEND ON YOU TO BE THERE WHEN I NEED YOU, THEN I'D RATHER YOU BE GONE.

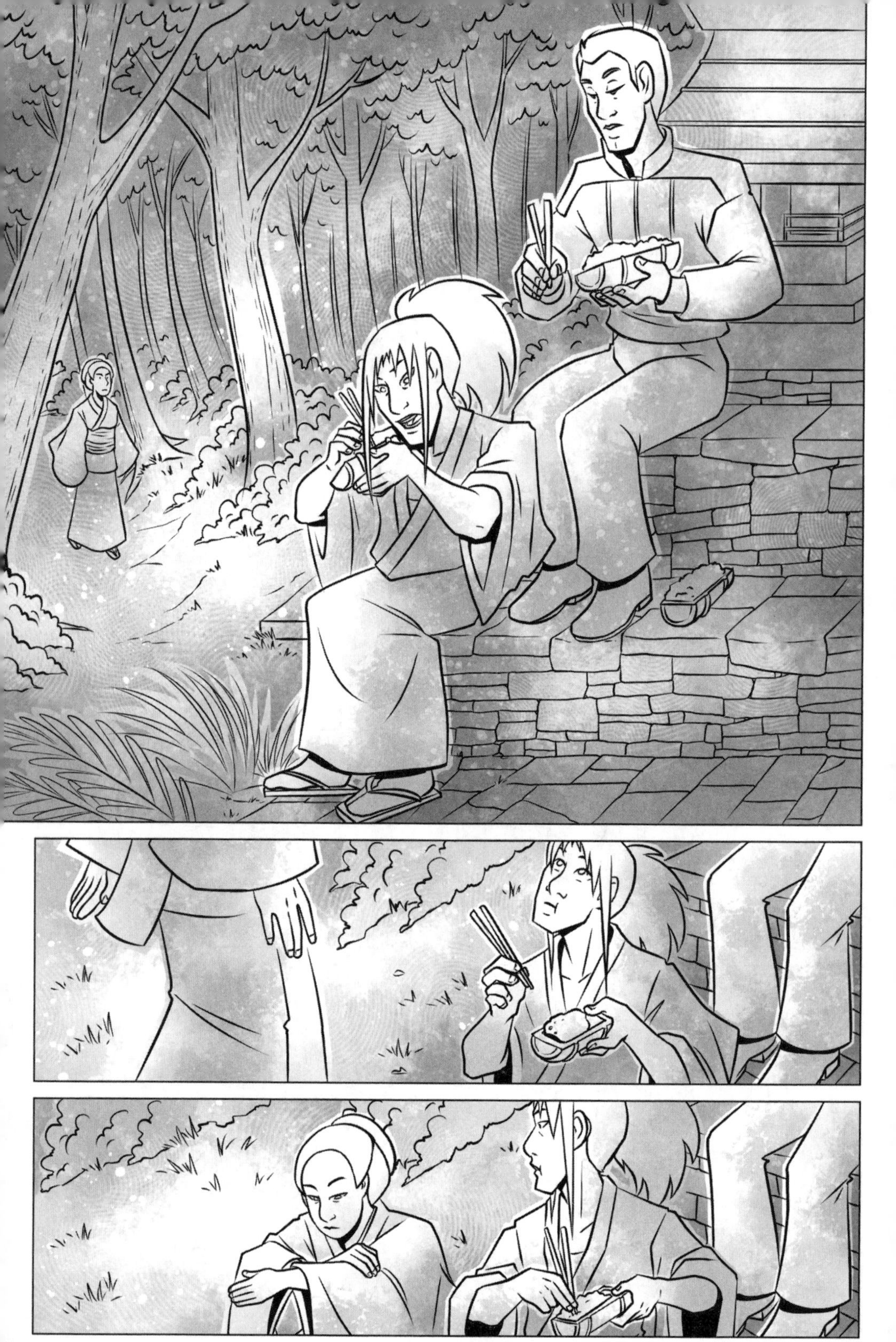

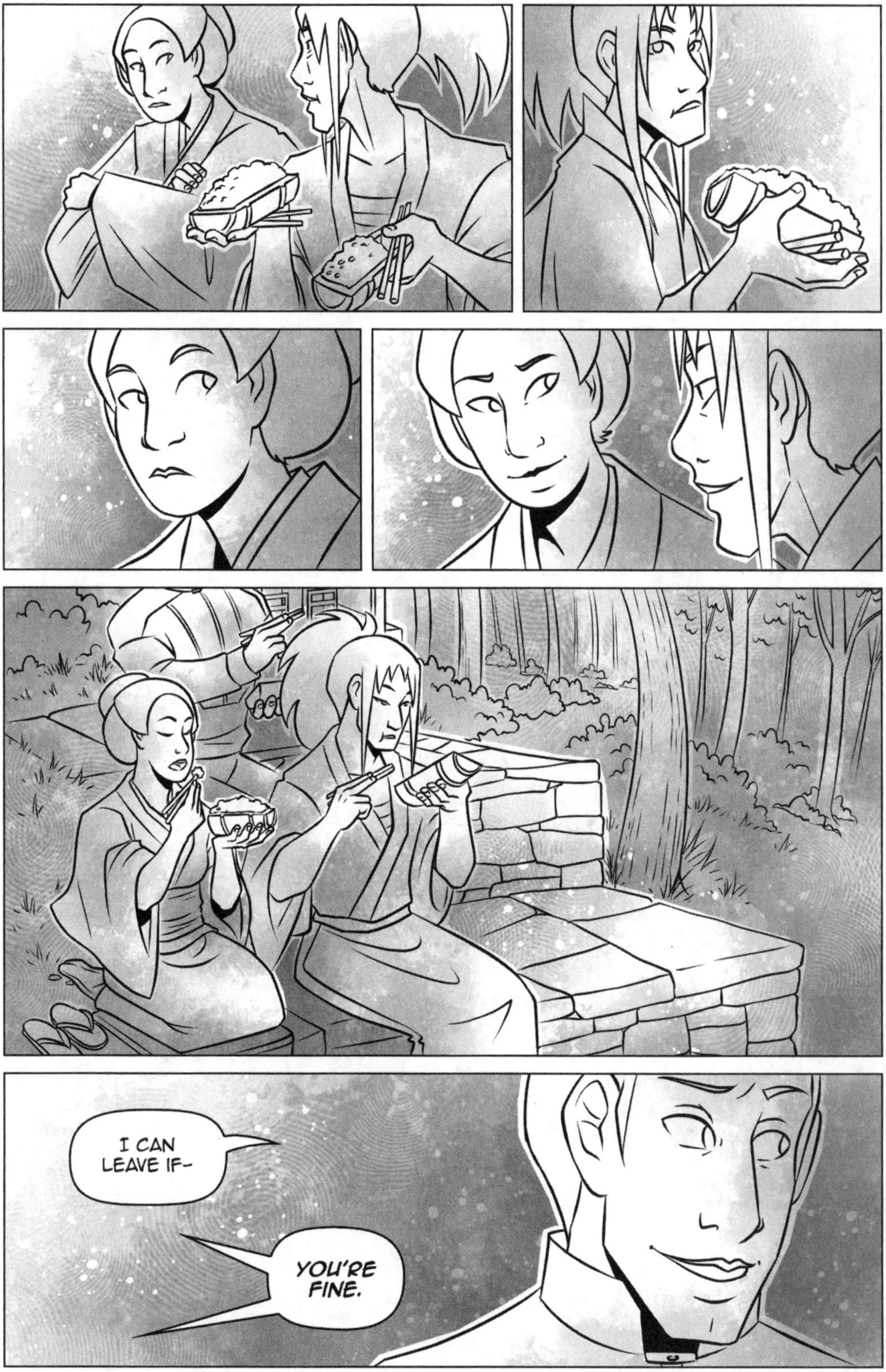
I CAN LEAVE IF-
YOU'RE FINE.

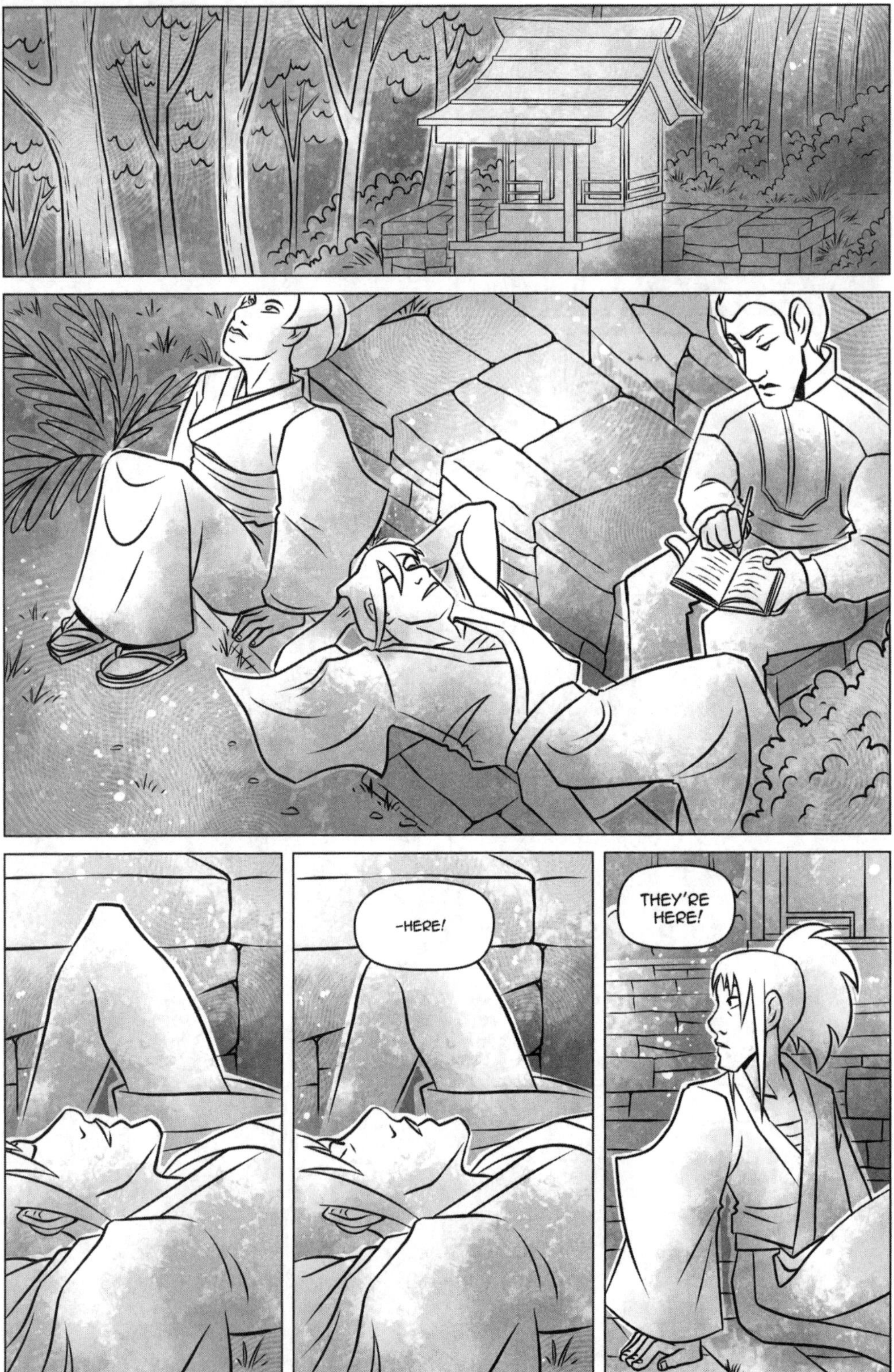
-HERE!
THEY'RE HERE!

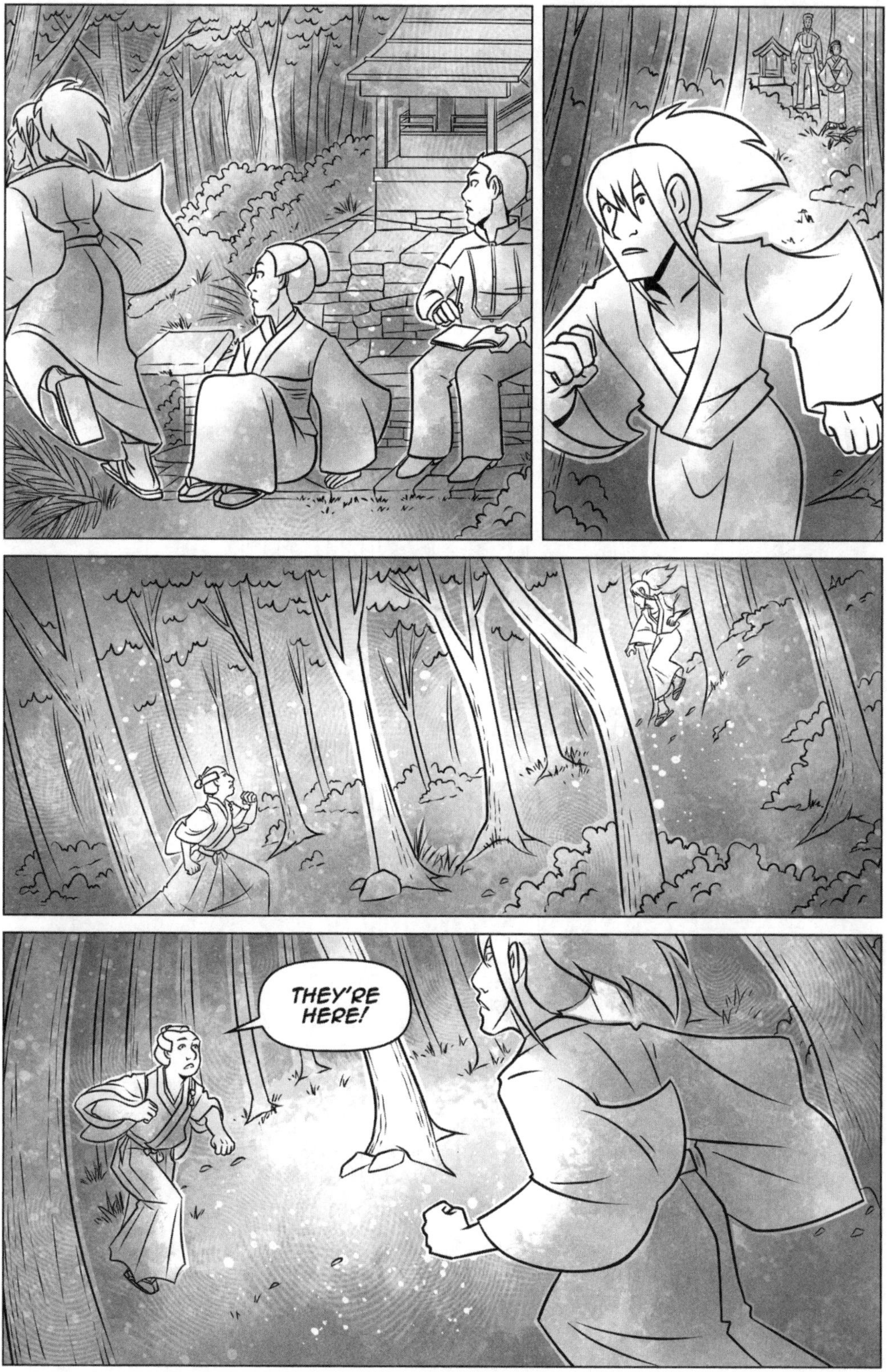
THEY'RE HERE!

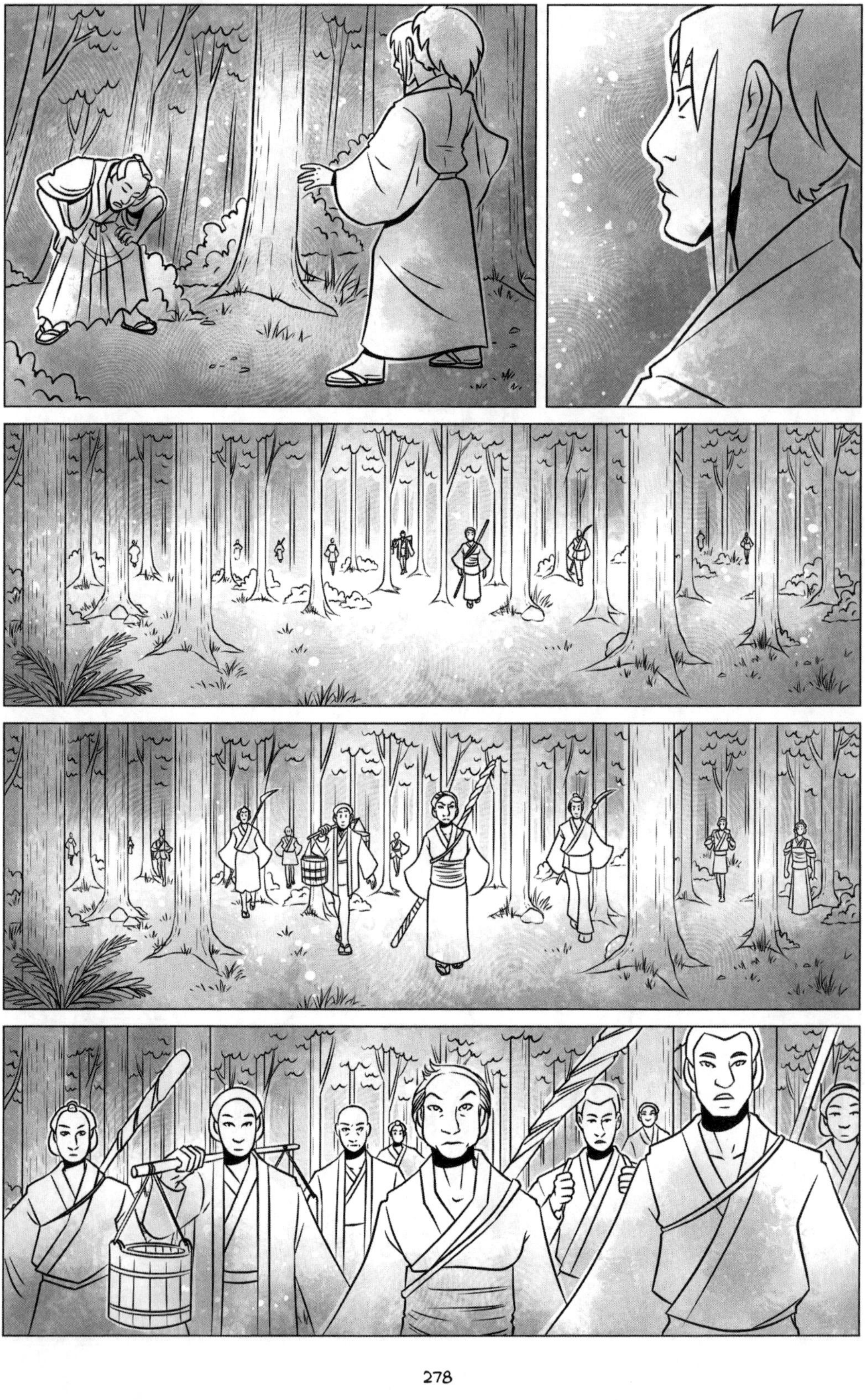

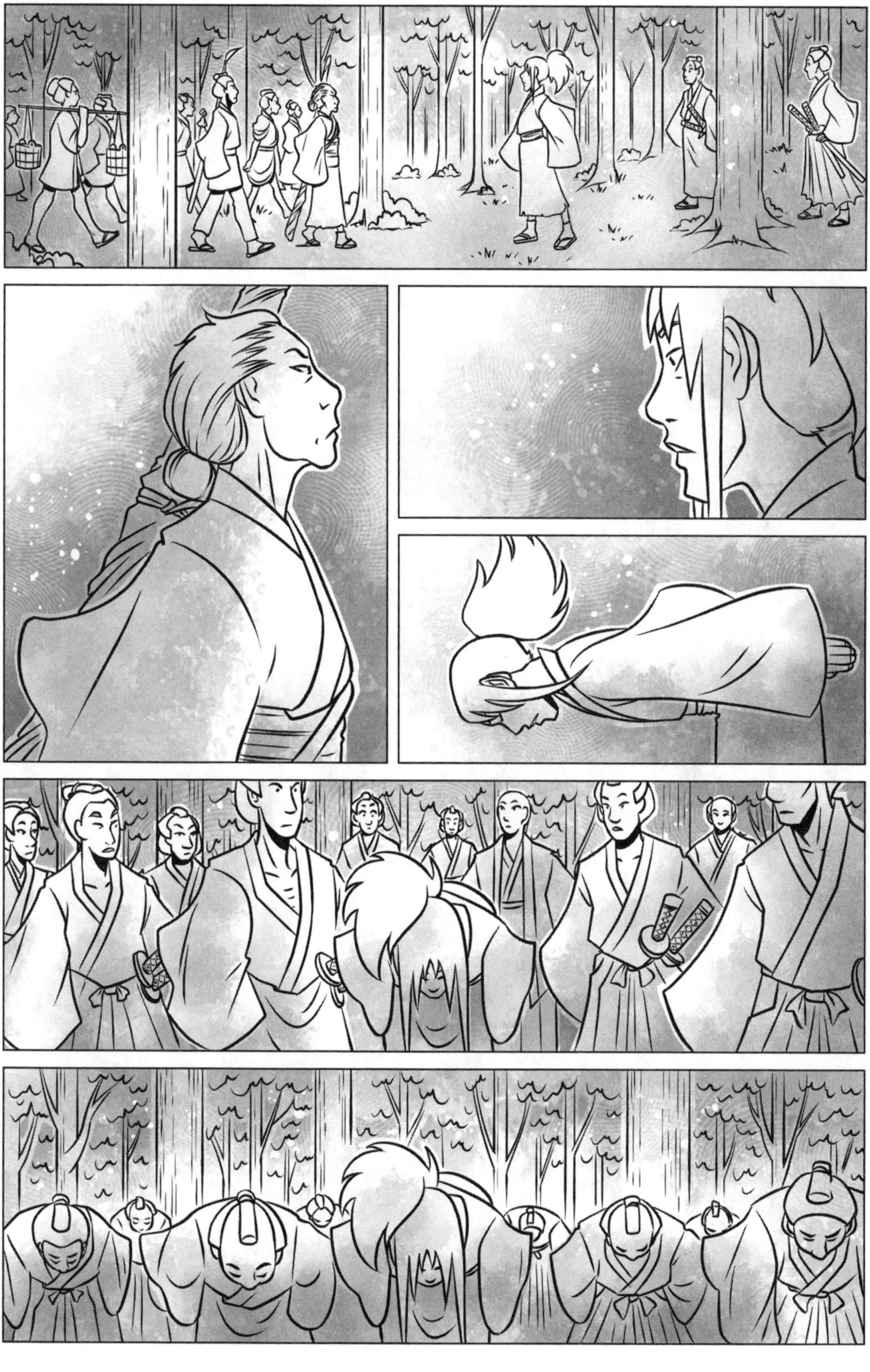

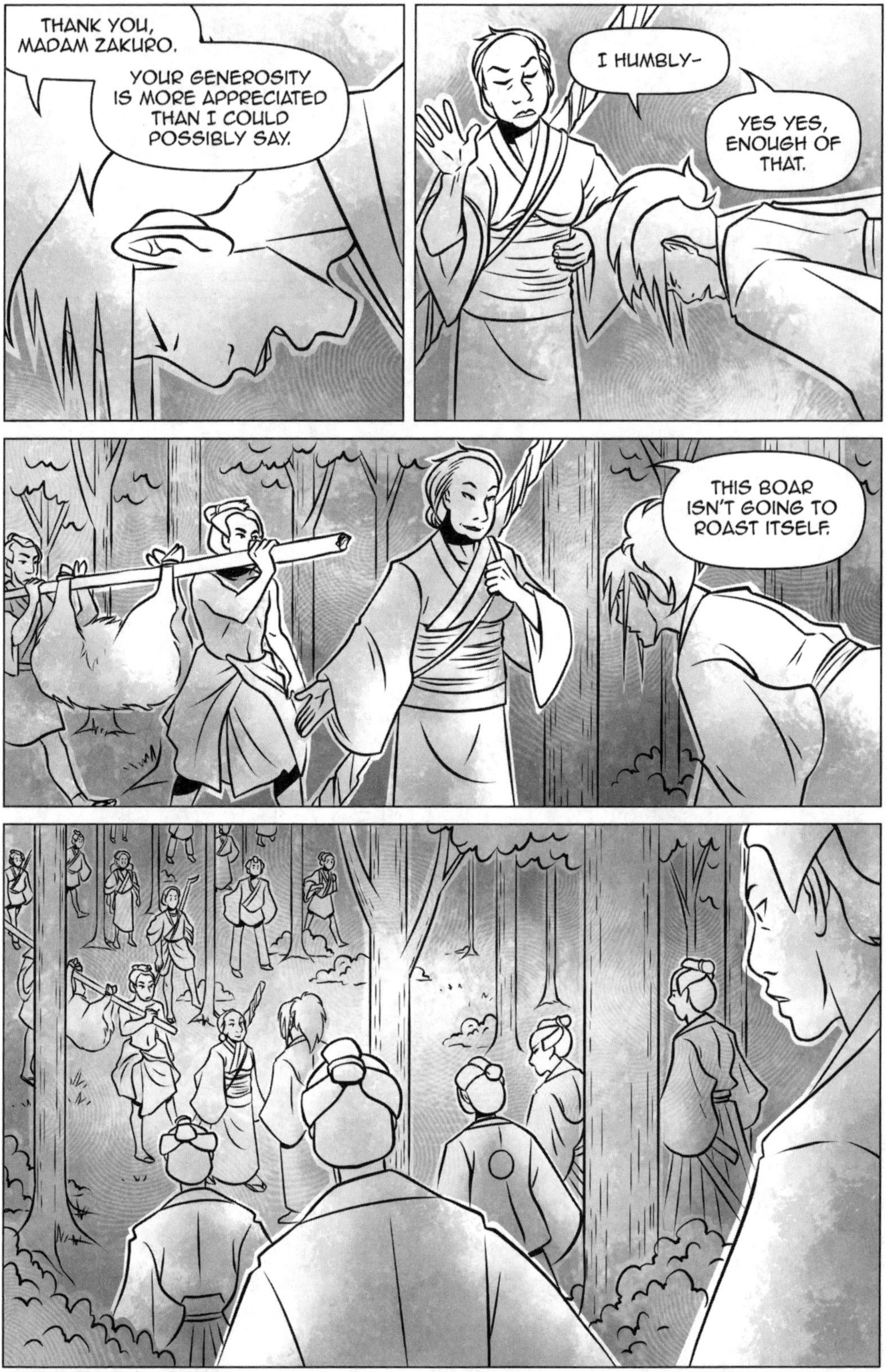
THANK YOU, MADAM ZAKURO.
YOUR GENEROSITY IS MORE APPRECIATED THAN I COULD POSSIBLY SAY.
I HUMBLY-
YES YES, ENOUGH OF THAT.
THIS BOAR ISN'T GOING TO ROAST ITSELF.

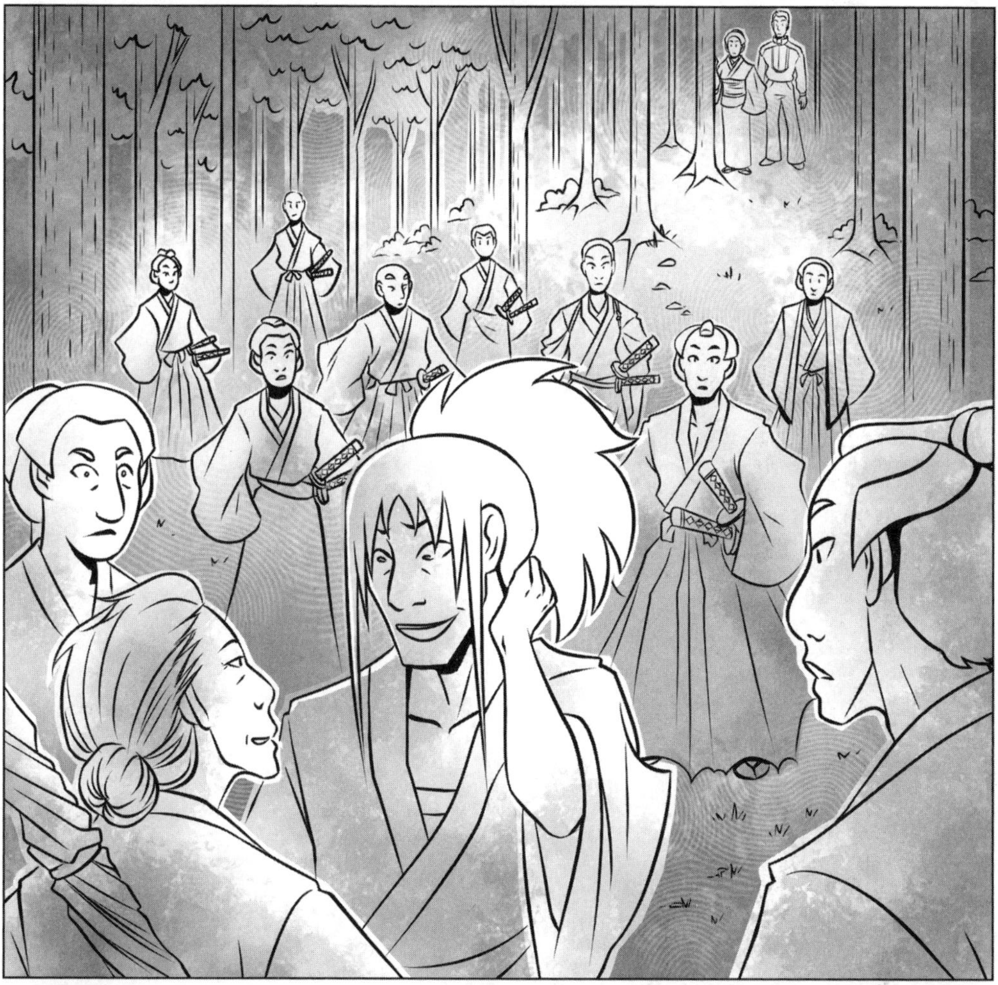

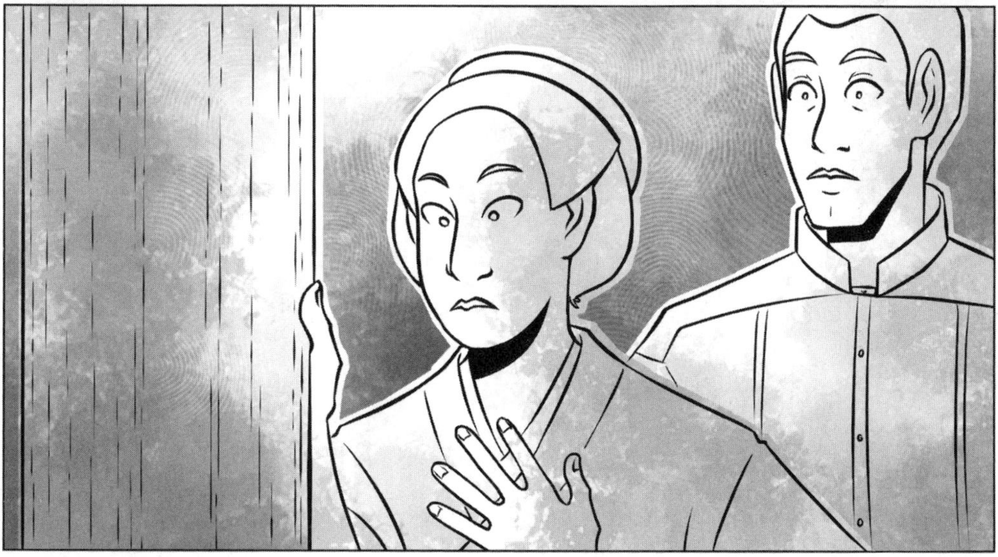

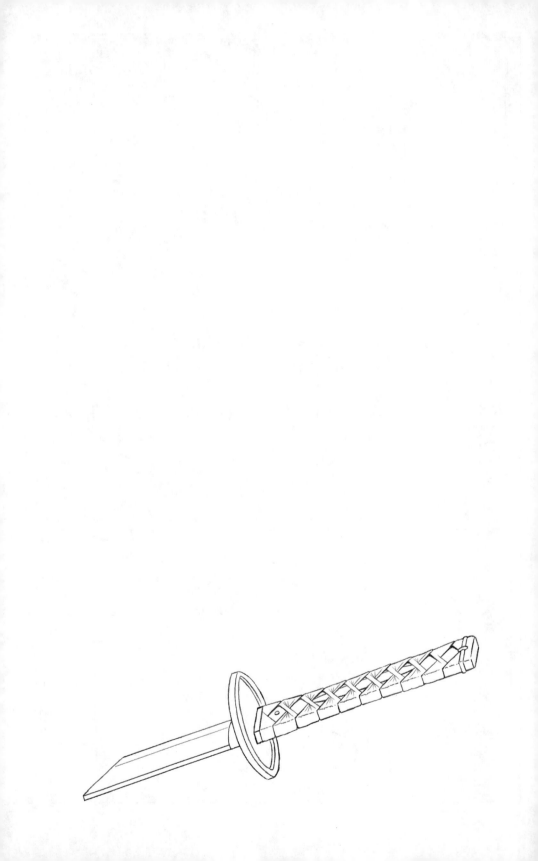

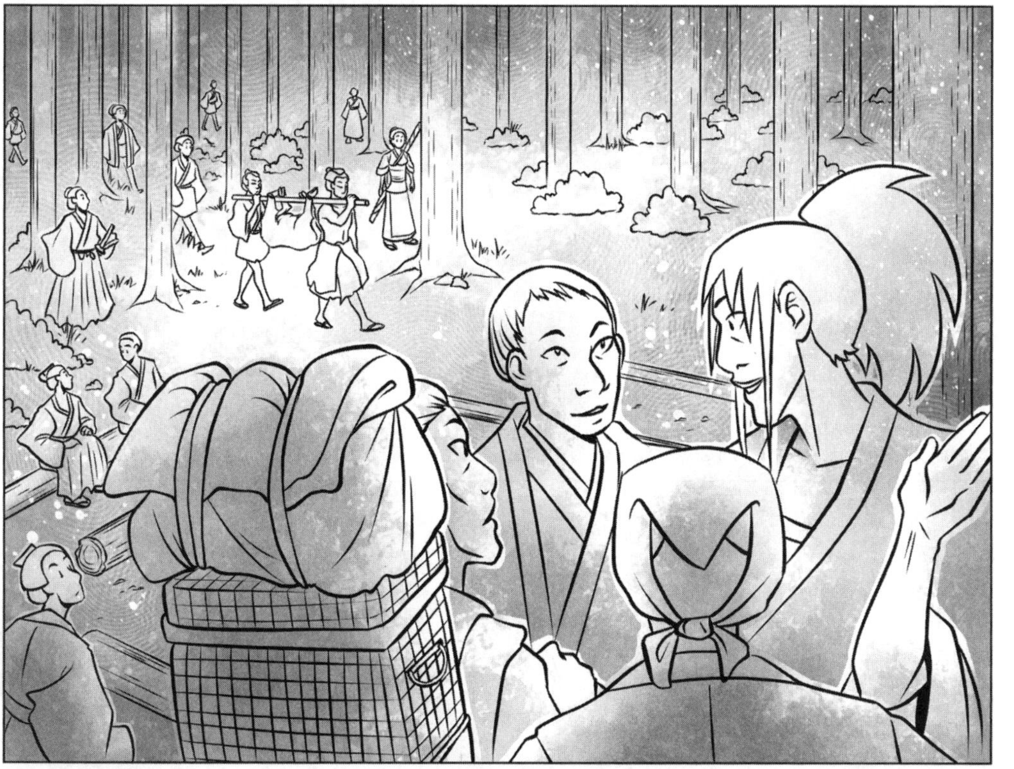

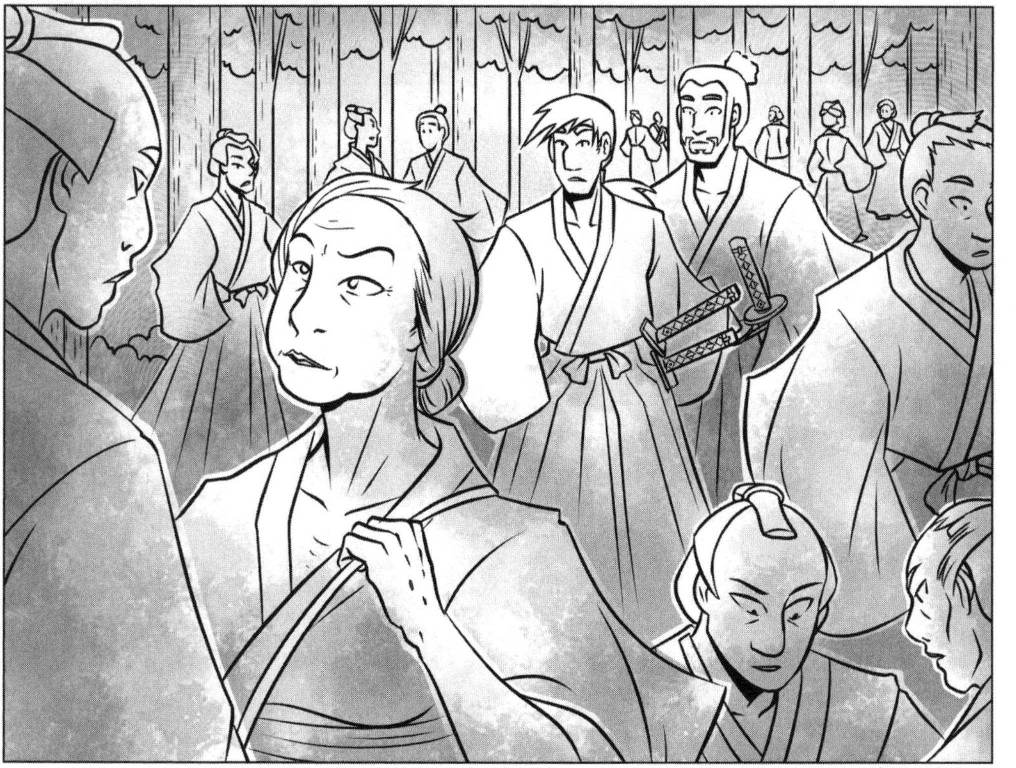

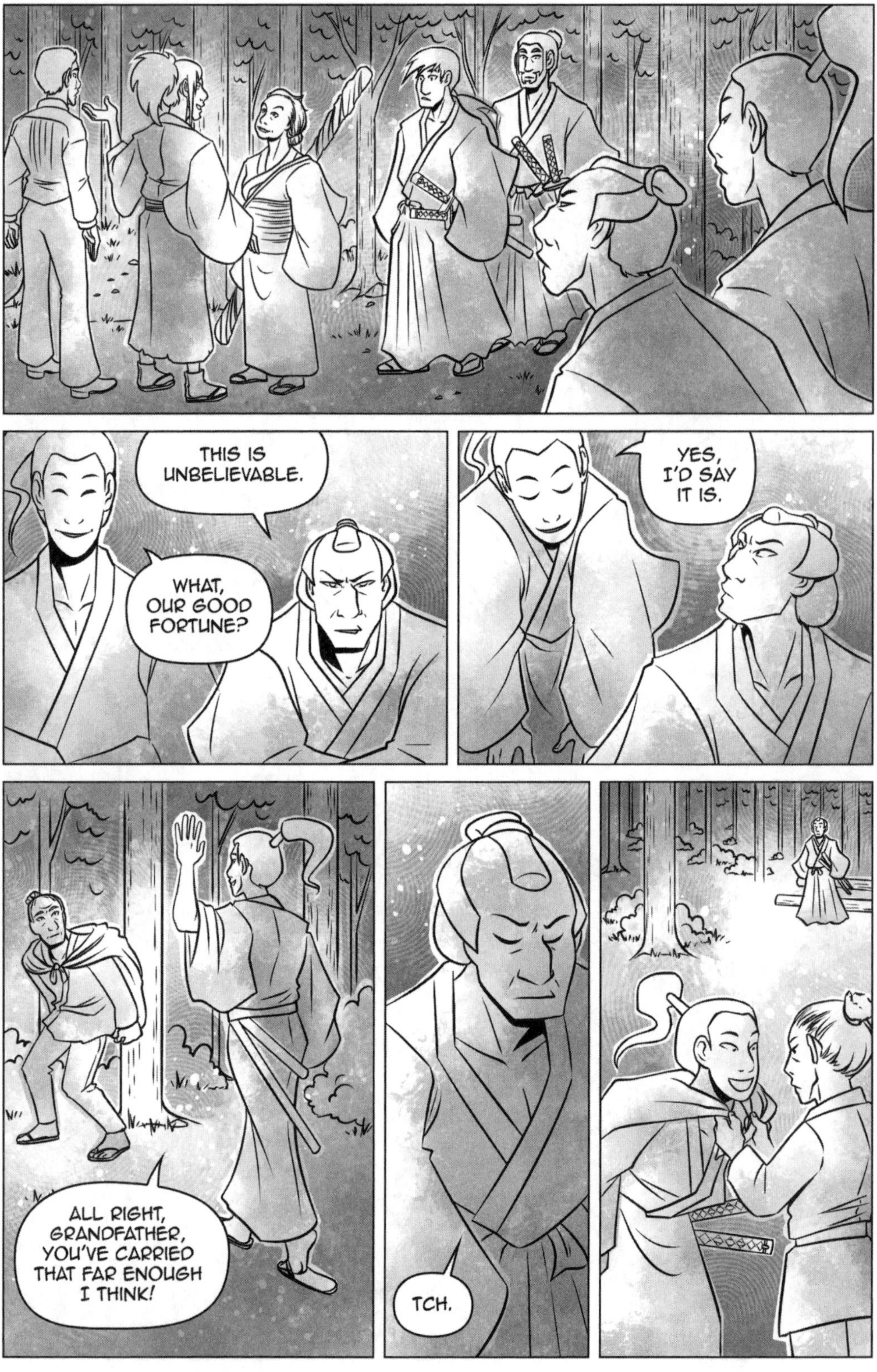
THIS IS UNBELIEVABLE.
WHAT, OUR GOOD FORTUNE?
YES, I'D SAY IT IS.
ALL RIGHT, GRANDFATHER, YOU'VE CARRIED THAT FAR ENOUGH I THINK!
TCH.

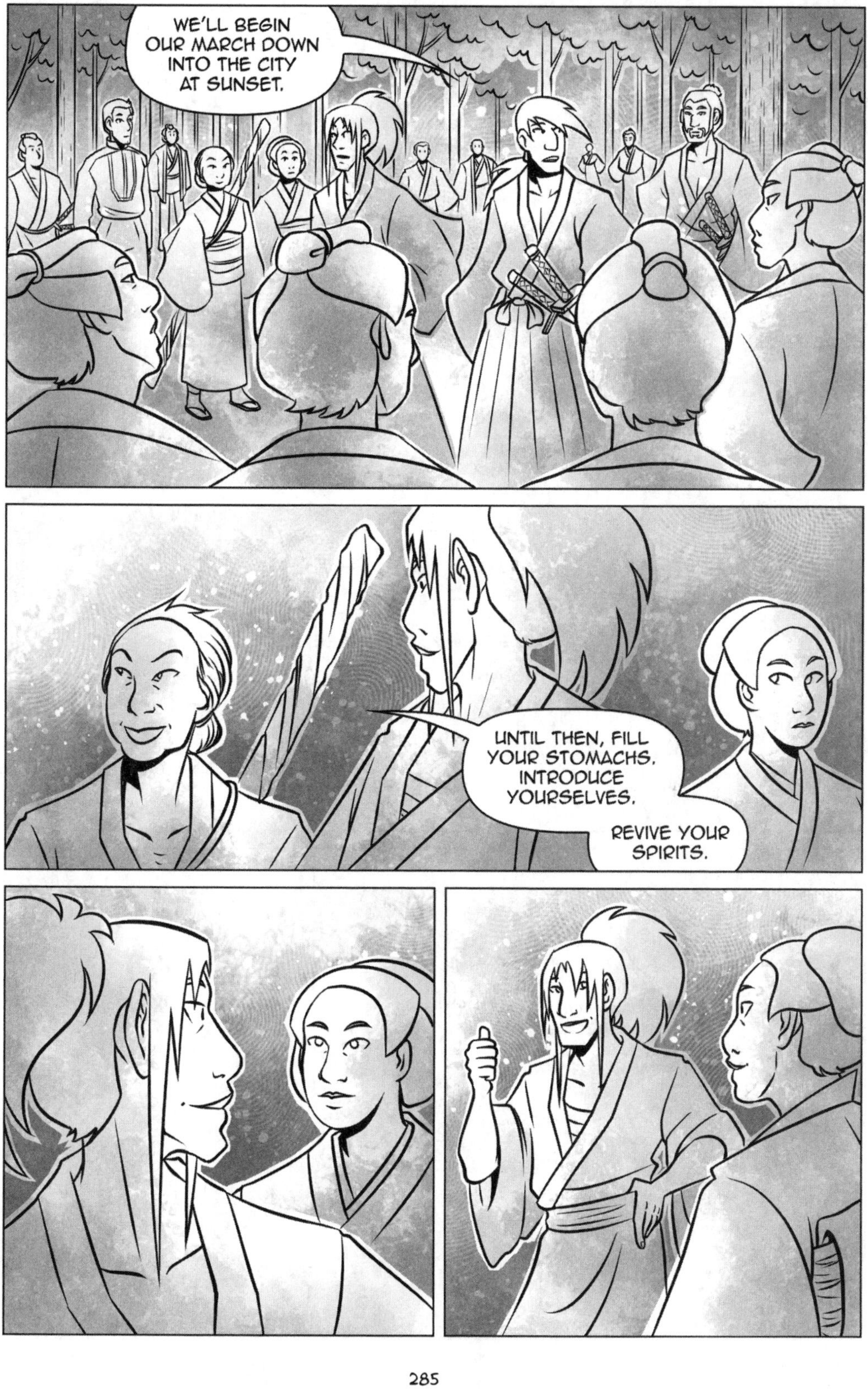
WE'LL BEGIN OUR MARCH DOWN INTO THE CITY AT SUNSET.
UNTIL THEN, FILL YOUR STOMACHS. INTRODUCE YOURSELVES.
REVIVE YOUR SPIRITS.

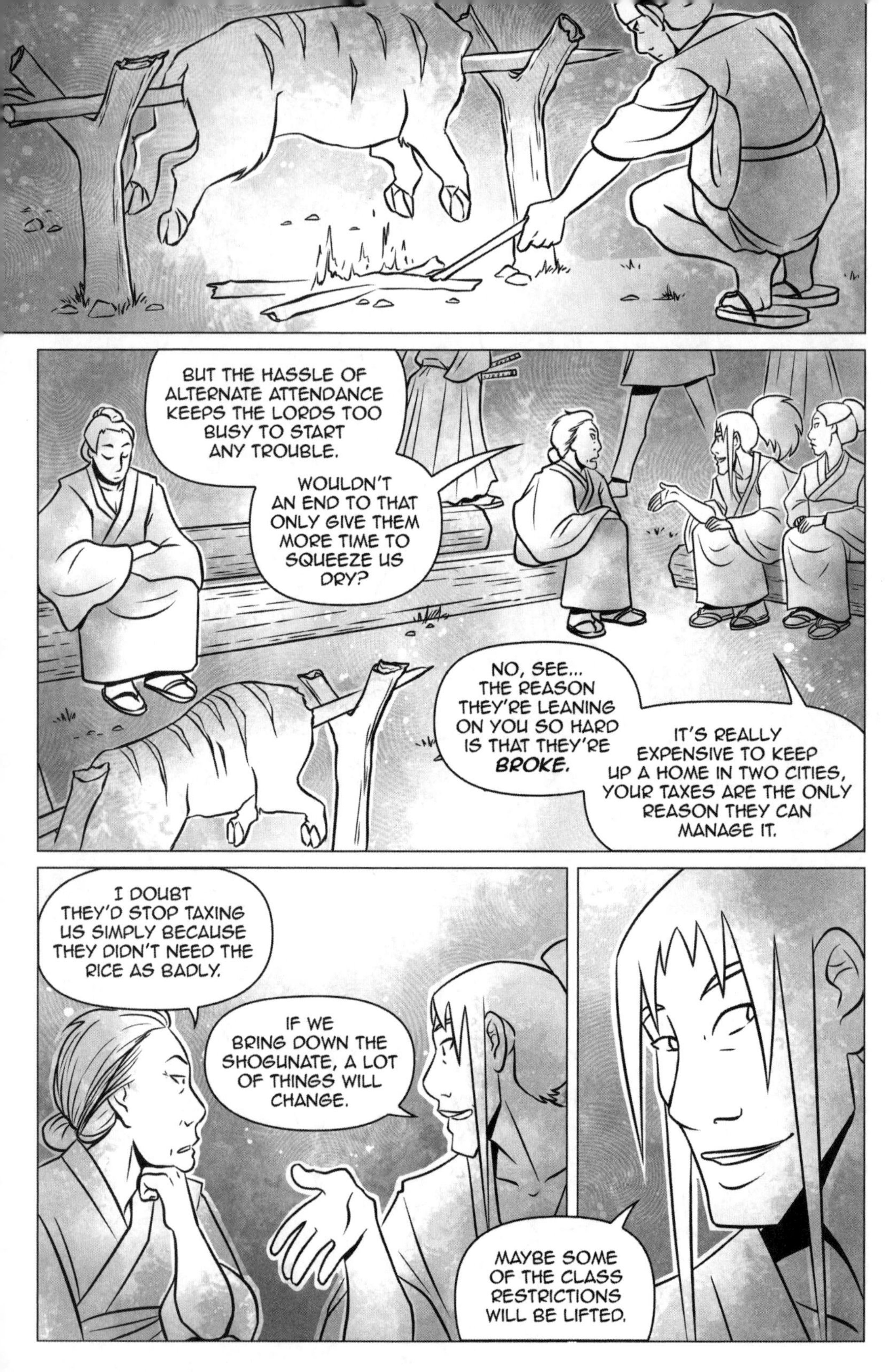
BUT THE HASSLE OF ALTERNATE ATTENDANCE KEEPS THE LORDS TOO BUSY TO START ANY TROUBLE.
WOULDN'T AN END TO THAT ONLY GIVE THEM MORE TIME TO SQUEEZE US DRY?
NO, SEE... THE REASON THEY'RE LEANING ON YOU SO HARD IS THAT THEY'RE BROKE.
IT'S REALLY EXPENSIVE TO KEEP UP A HOME IN TWO CITIES, YOUR TAXES ARE THE ONLY REASON THEY CAN MANAGE IT.
I DOUBT THEY'D STOP TAXING US SIMPLY BECAUSE THEY DIDN'T NEED THE RICE AS BADLY.
IF WE BRING DOWN THE SHOGUNATE, A LOT OF THINGS WILL CHANGE.
MAYBE SOME OF THE CLASS RESTRICTIONS WILL BE LIFTED.

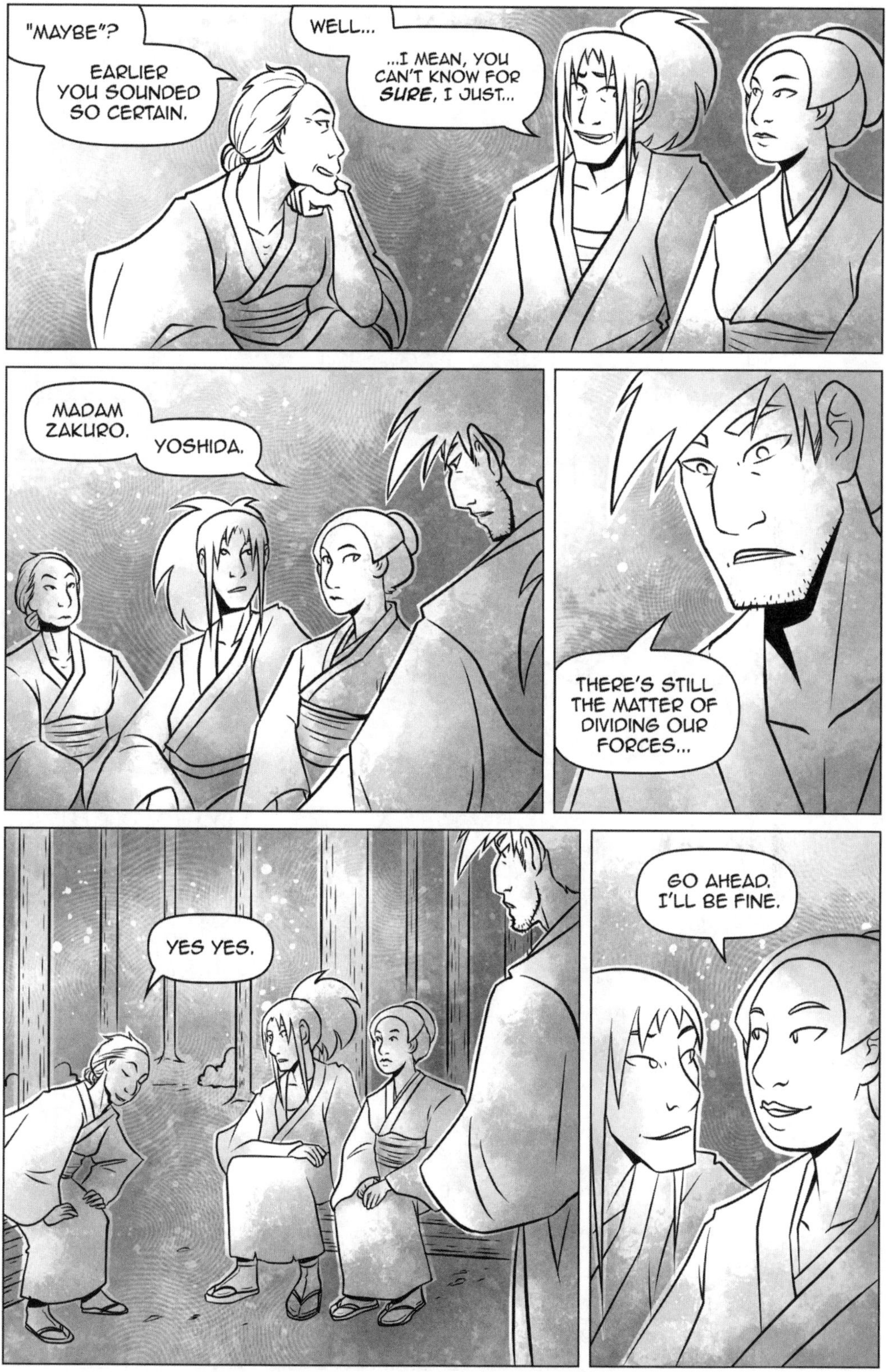
"MAYBE"?
EARLIER YOU SOUNDED SO CERTAIN.
WELL...
...I MEAN, YOU CAN'T KNOW FOR *SURE*, I JUST...
MADAM ZAKURO.
YOSHIDA.
THERE'S STILL THE MATTER OF DIVIDING OUR FORCES...
YES YES.
GO AHEAD. I'LL BE FINE.

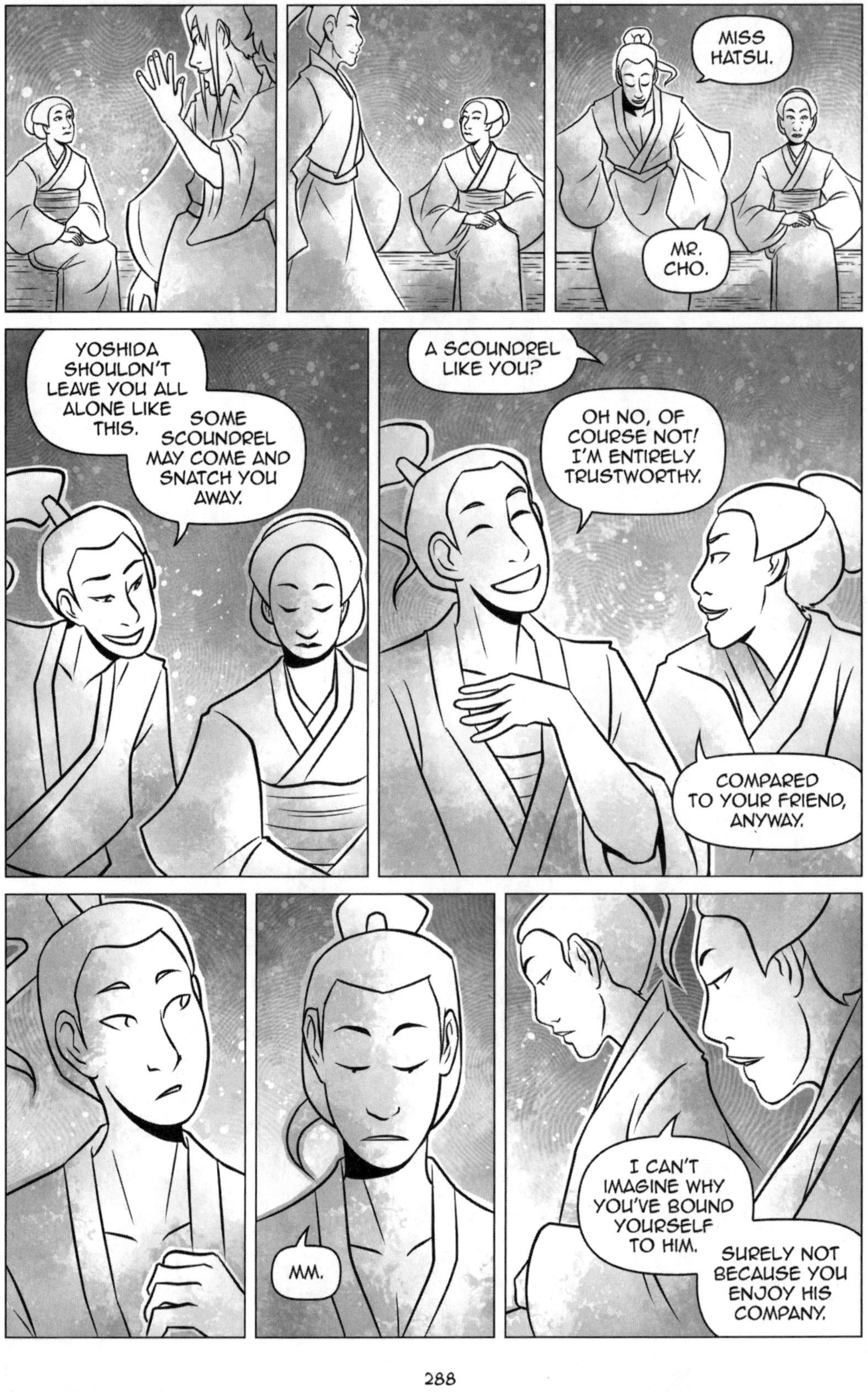
MISS HATSU.
MR. CHO.
YOSHIDA SHOULDN'T LEAVE YOU ALL ALONE LIKE THIS.
SOME SCOUNDREL MAY COME AND SNATCH YOU AWAY.
A SCOUNDREL LIKE YOU?
OH NO, OF COURSE NOT! I'M ENTIRELY TRUSTWORTHY.
COMPARED TO YOUR FRIEND, ANYWAY.
MM.
I CAN'T IMAGINE WHY YOU'VE BOUND YOURSELF TO HIM.
SURELY NOT BECAUSE YOU ENJOY HIS COMPANY.

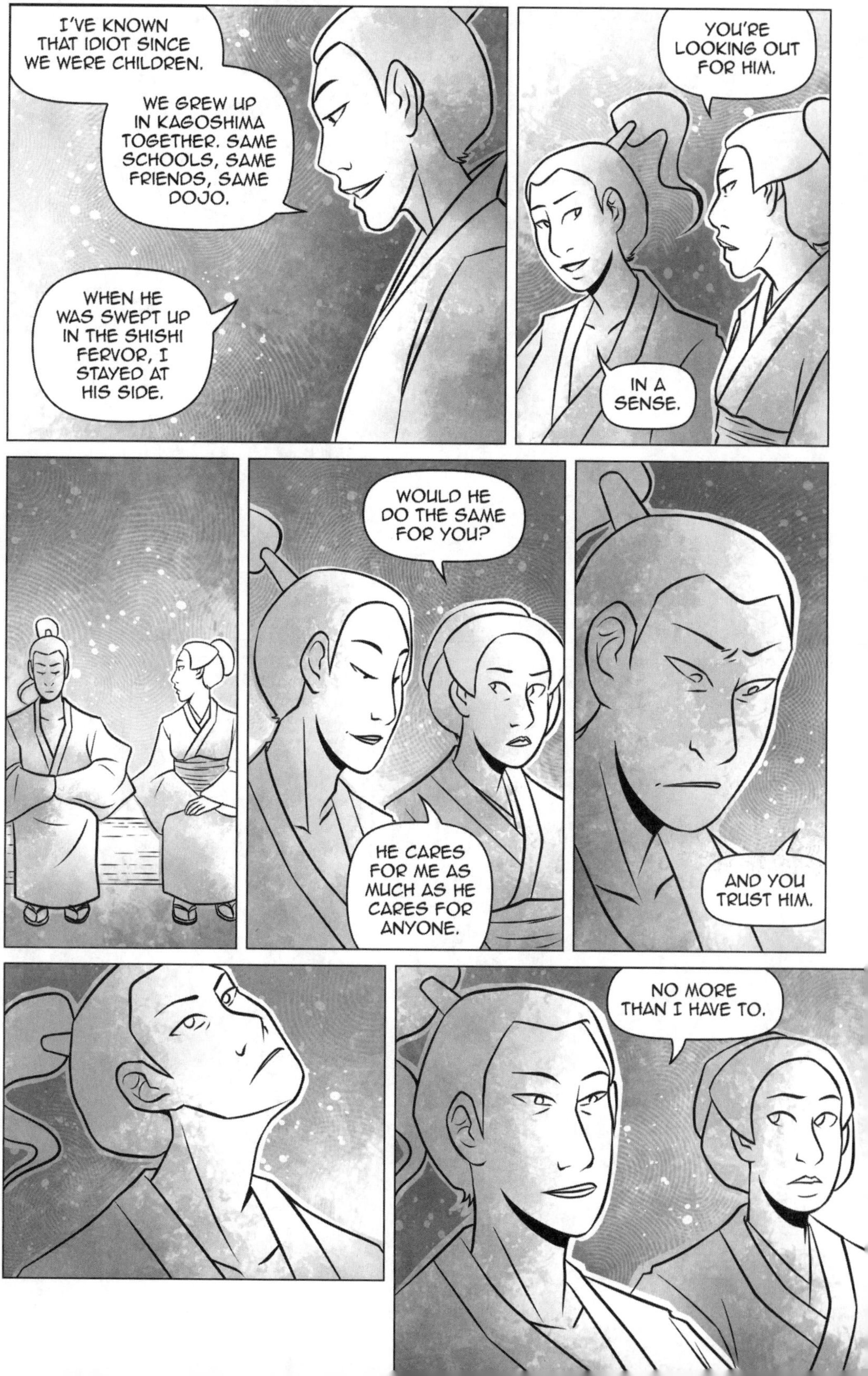
I'VE KNOWN THAT IDIOT SINCE WE WERE CHILDREN.
WE GREW UP IN KAGOSHIMA TOGETHER. SAME SCHOOLS, SAME FRIENDS, SAME DOJO.
WHEN HE WAS SWEPT UP IN THE SHISHI FERVOR, I STAYED AT HIS SIDE.
YOU'RE LOOKING OUT FOR HIM.
IN A SENSE.
WOULD HE DO THE SAME FOR YOU?
HE CARES FOR ME AS MUCH AS HE CARES FOR ANYONE.
AND YOU TRUST HIM.
NO MORE THAN I HAVE TO.

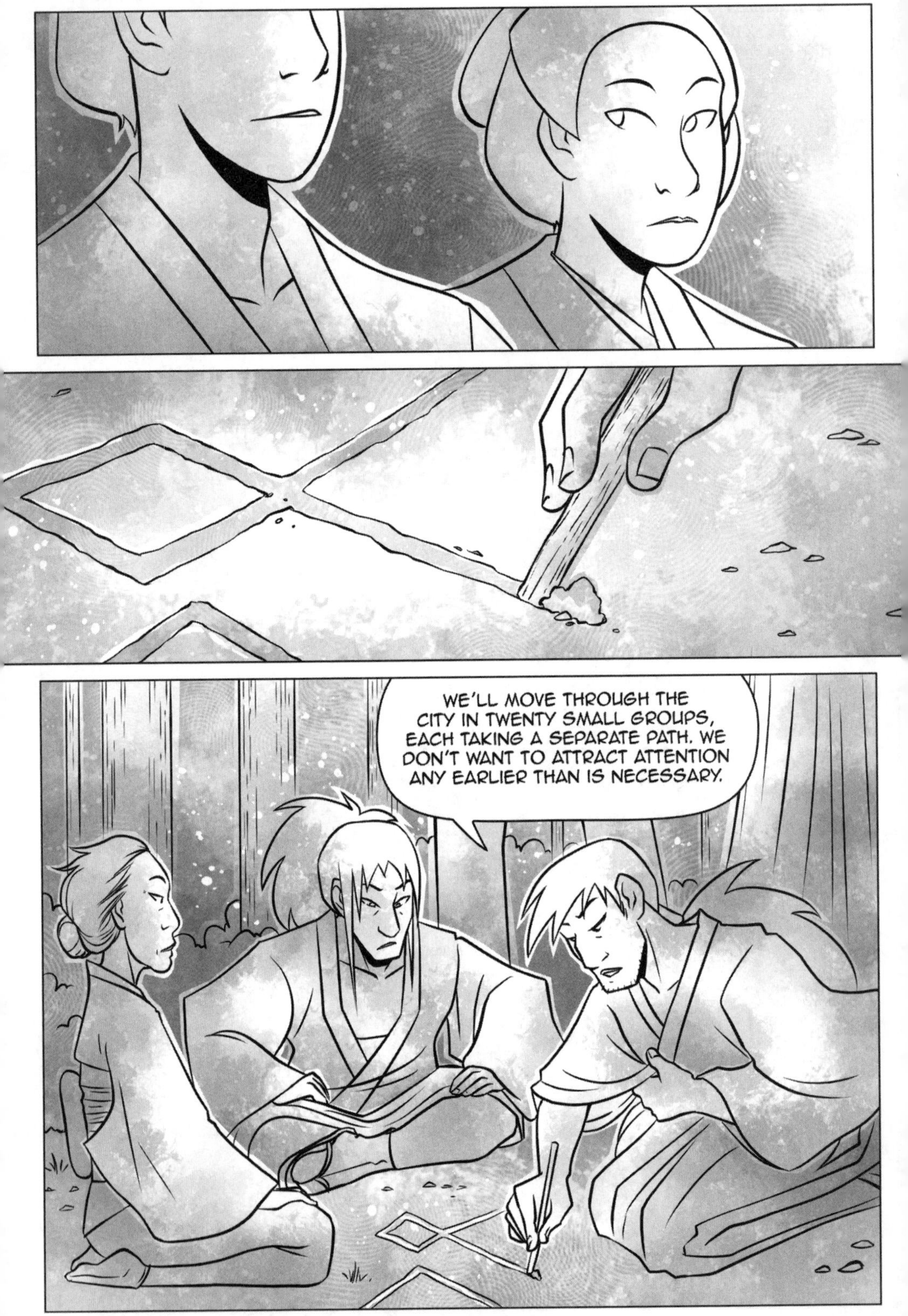
WE'LL MOVE THROUGH THE CITY IN TWENTY SMALL GROUPS, EACH TAKING A SEPARATE PATH. WE DON'T WANT TO ATTRACT ATTENTION ANY EARLIER THAN IS NECESSARY.

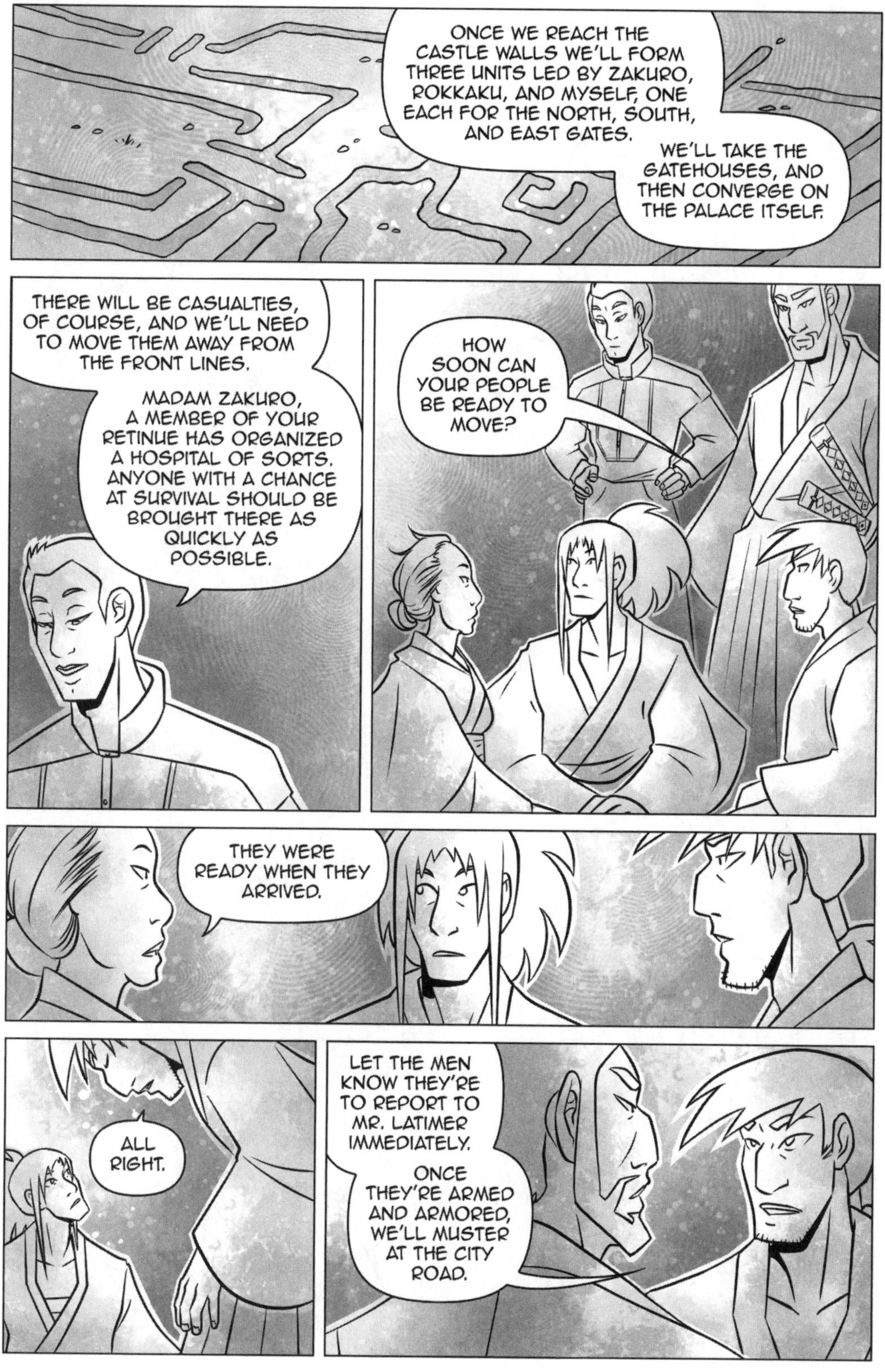
ONCE WE REACH THE CASTLE WALLS WE'LL FORM THREE UNITS LED BY ZAKURO, ROKKAKU, AND MYSELF, ONE EACH FOR THE NORTH, SOUTH, AND EAST GATES.
WE'LL TAKE THE GATEHOUSES, AND THEN CONVERGE ON THE PALACE ITSELF.
THERE WILL BE CASUALTIES, OF COURSE, AND WE'LL NEED TO MOVE THEM AWAY FROM THE FRONT LINES.
MADAM ZAKURO, A MEMBER OF YOUR RETINUE HAS ORGANIZED A HOSPITAL OF SORTS. ANYONE WITH A CHANCE AT SURVIVAL SHOULD BE BROUGHT THERE AS QUICKLY AS POSSIBLE.
HOW SOON CAN YOUR PEOPLE BE READY TO MOVE?
THEY WERE READY WHEN THEY ARRIVED.
ALL RIGHT.
LET THE MEN KNOW THEY'RE TO REPORT TO MR. LATIMER IMMEDIATELY.
ONCE THEY'RE ARMED AND ARMORED, WE'LL MUSTER AT THE CITY ROAD.

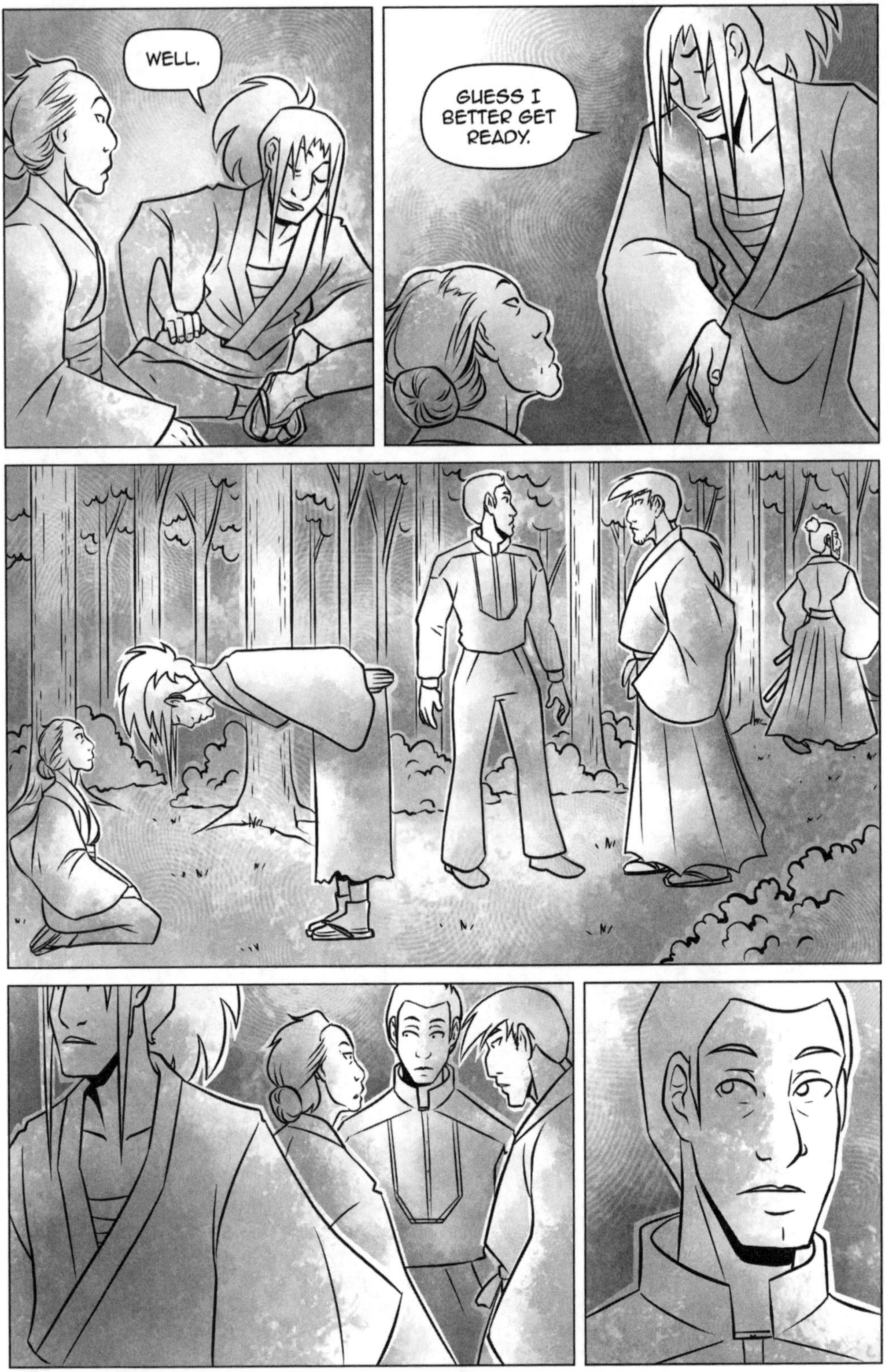
WELL.
GUESS I BETTER GET READY.

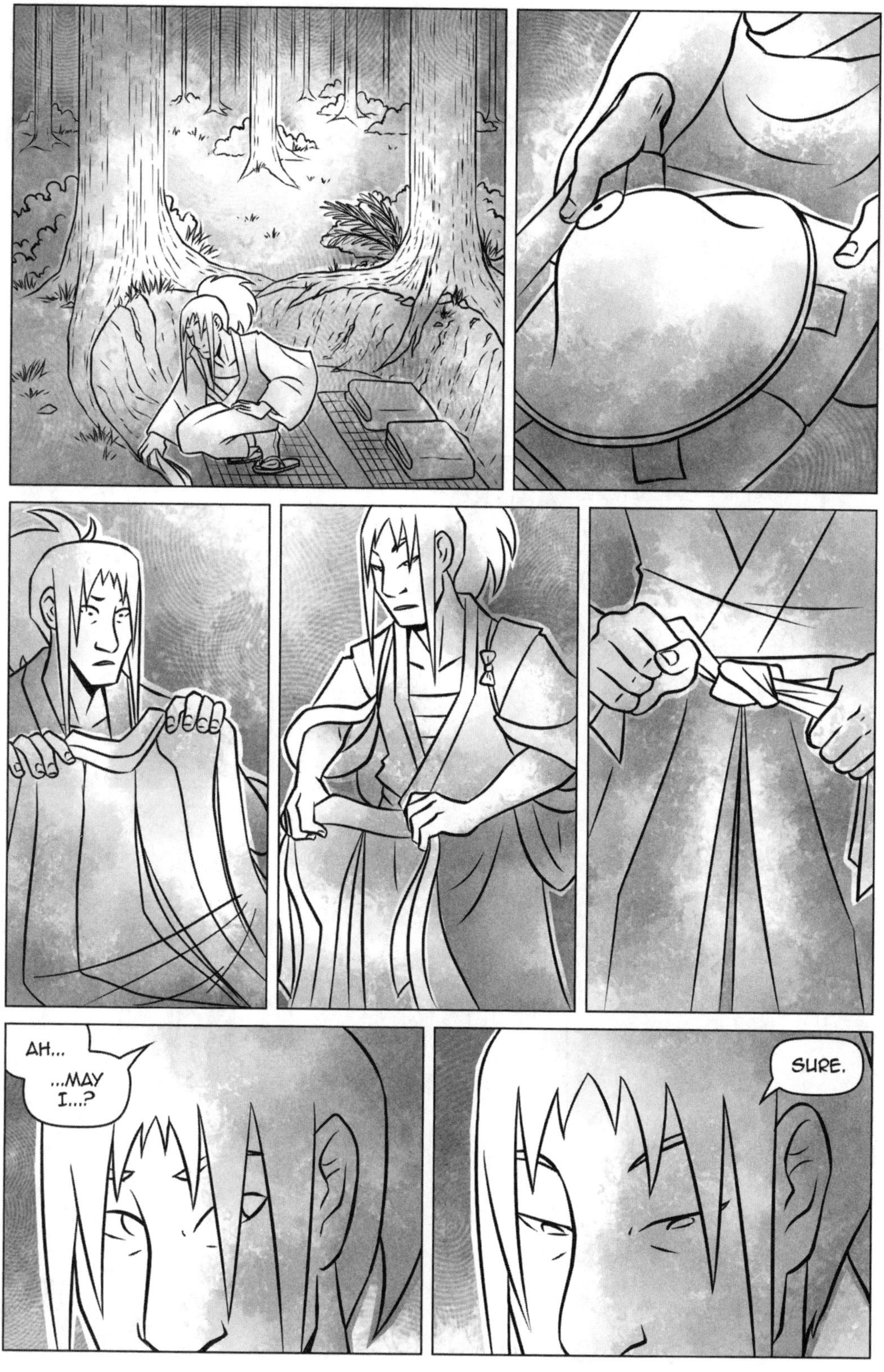
AH...
...MAY I...?
SURE.

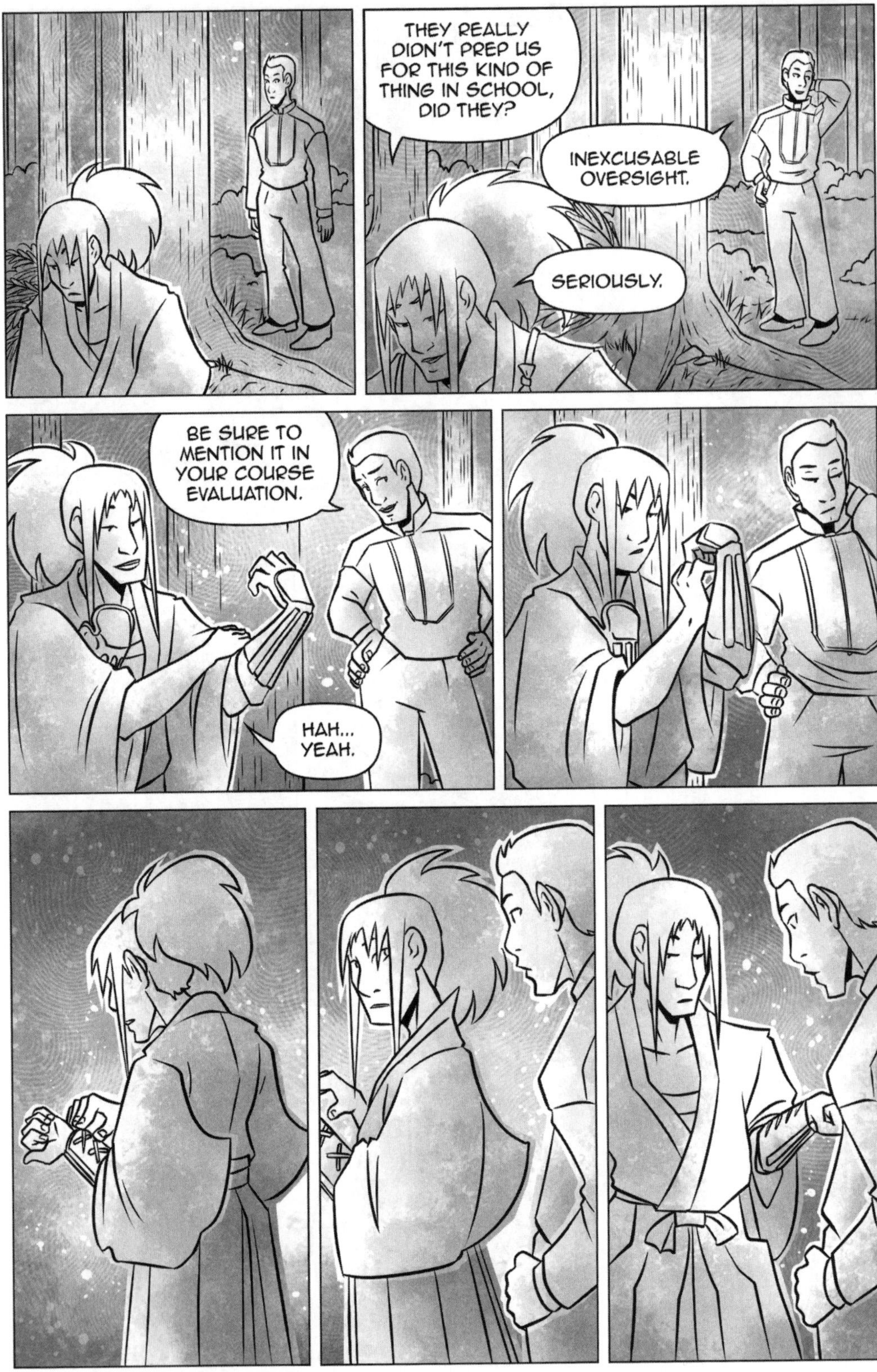
THEY REALLY DIDN'T PREP US FOR THIS KIND OF THING IN SCHOOL, DID THEY?
INEXCUSABLE OVERSIGHT.
SERIOUSLY.
BE SURE TO MENTION IT IN YOUR COURSE EVALUATION.
HAH... YEAH.

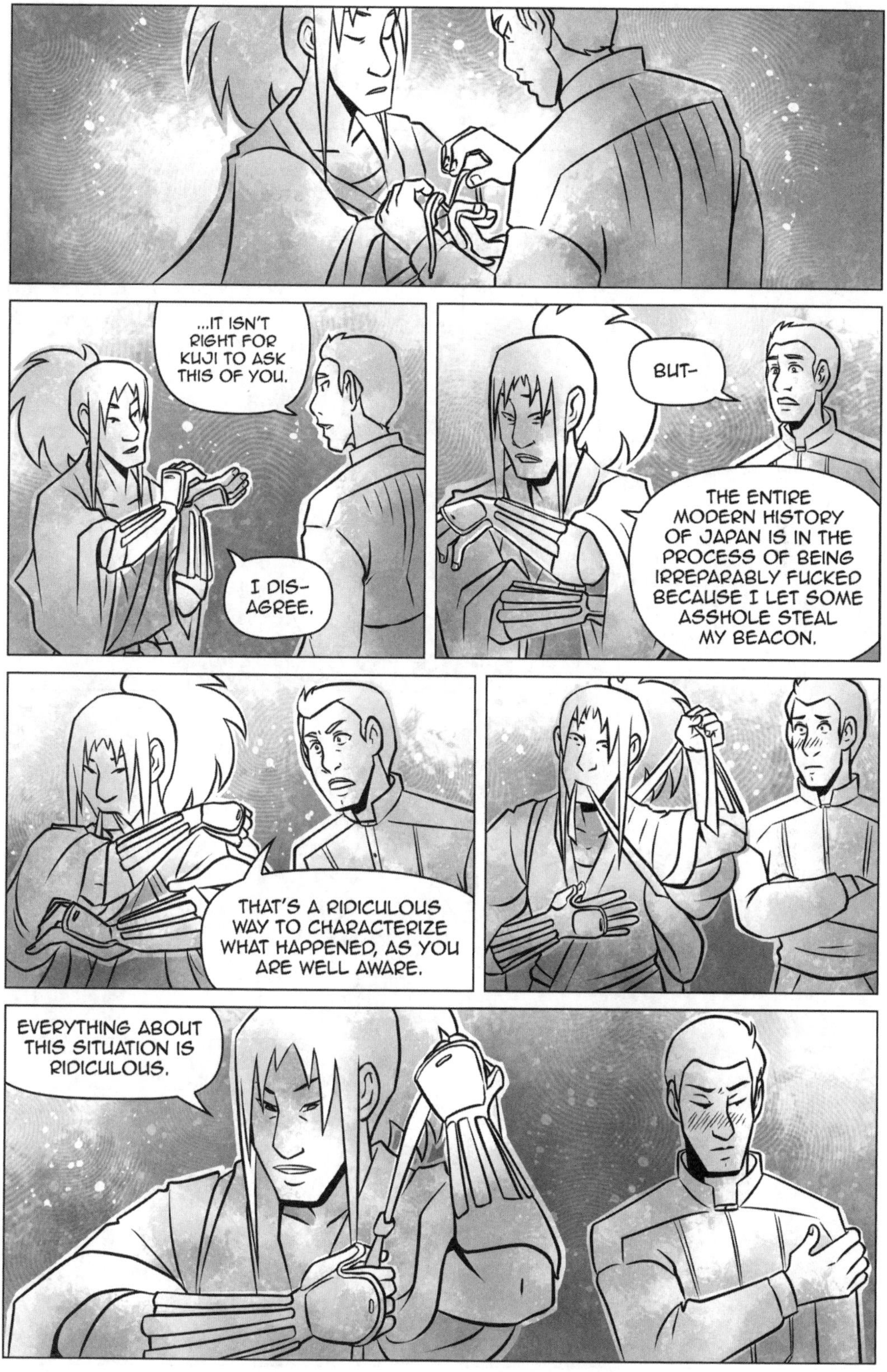
...IT ISN'T RIGHT FOR KUJI TO ASK THIS OF YOU.
I DIS- AGREE.
BUT-
THE ENTIRE MODERN HISTORY OF JAPAN IS IN THE PROCESS OF BEING IRREPARABLY FUCKED BECAUSE I LET SOME ASSHOLE STEAL MY BEACON.
THAT'S A RIDICULOUS WAY TO CHARACTERIZE WHAT HAPPENED, AS YOU ARE WELL AWARE.
EVERYTHING ABOUT THIS SITUATION IS RIDICULOUS.

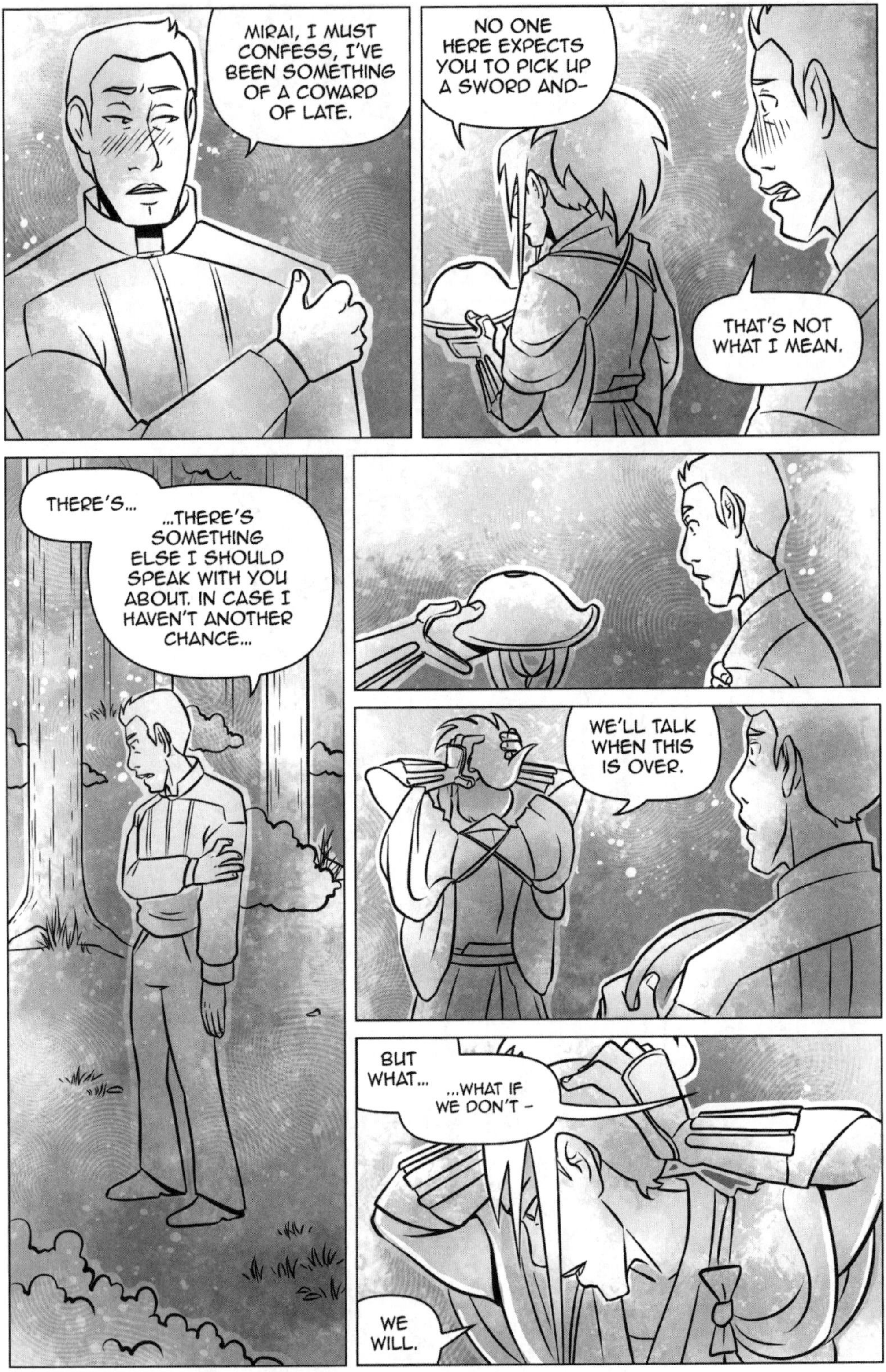
MIRAI, I MUST CONFESS, I'VE BEEN SOMETHING OF A COWARD OF LATE.
NO ONE HERE EXPECTS YOU TO PICK UP A SWORD AND-
THAT'S NOT WHAT I MEAN.
THERE'S...
...THERE'S SOMETHING ELSE I SHOULD SPEAK WITH YOU ABOUT. IN CASE I HAVEN'T ANOTHER CHANCE...
WE'LL TALK WHEN THIS IS OVER.
BUT WHAT...
...WHAT IF WE DON'T -
WE WILL.

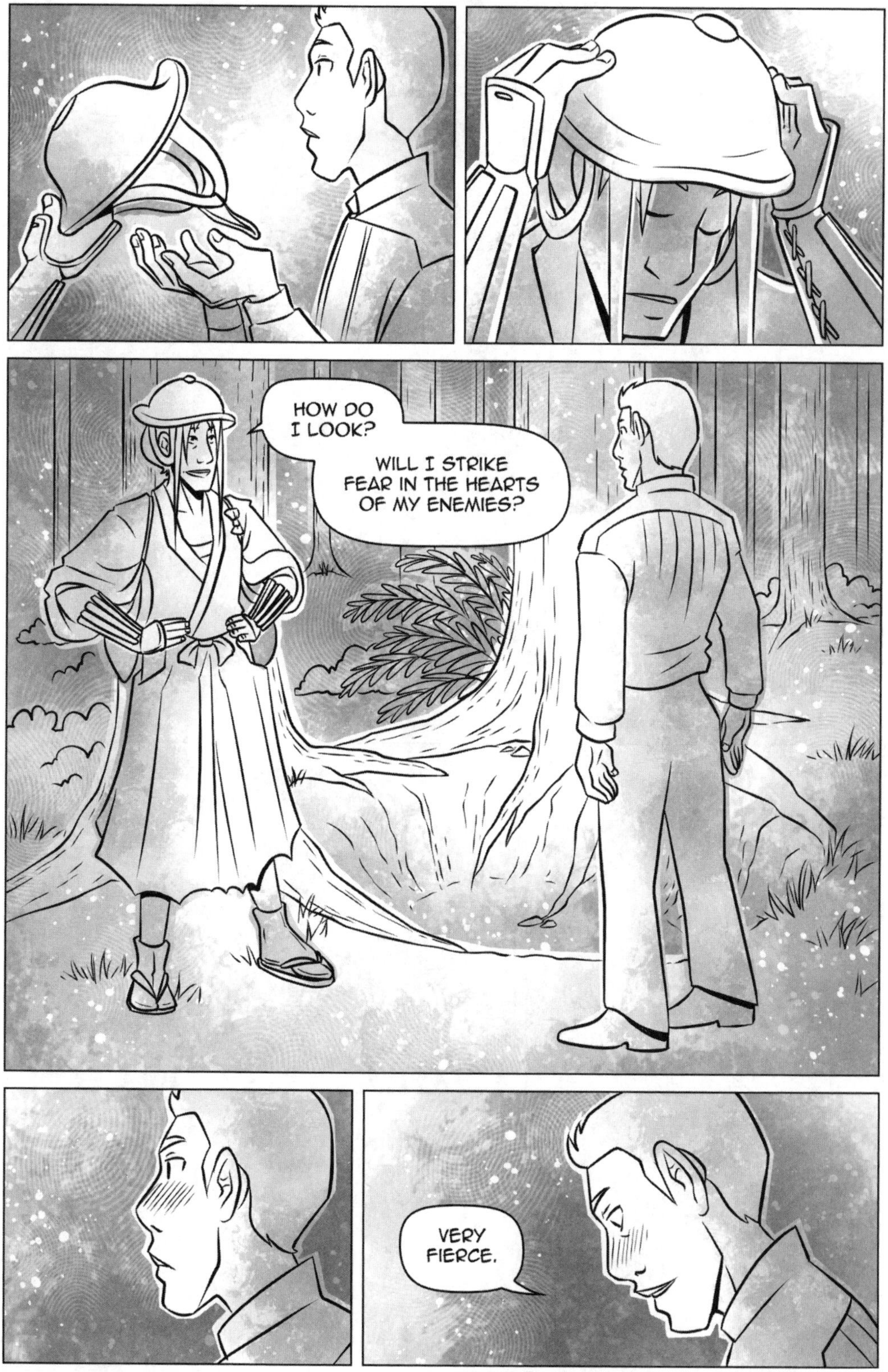
HOW DO I LOOK?
WILL I STRIKE FEAR IN THE HEARTS OF MY ENEMIES?
VERY FIERCE.

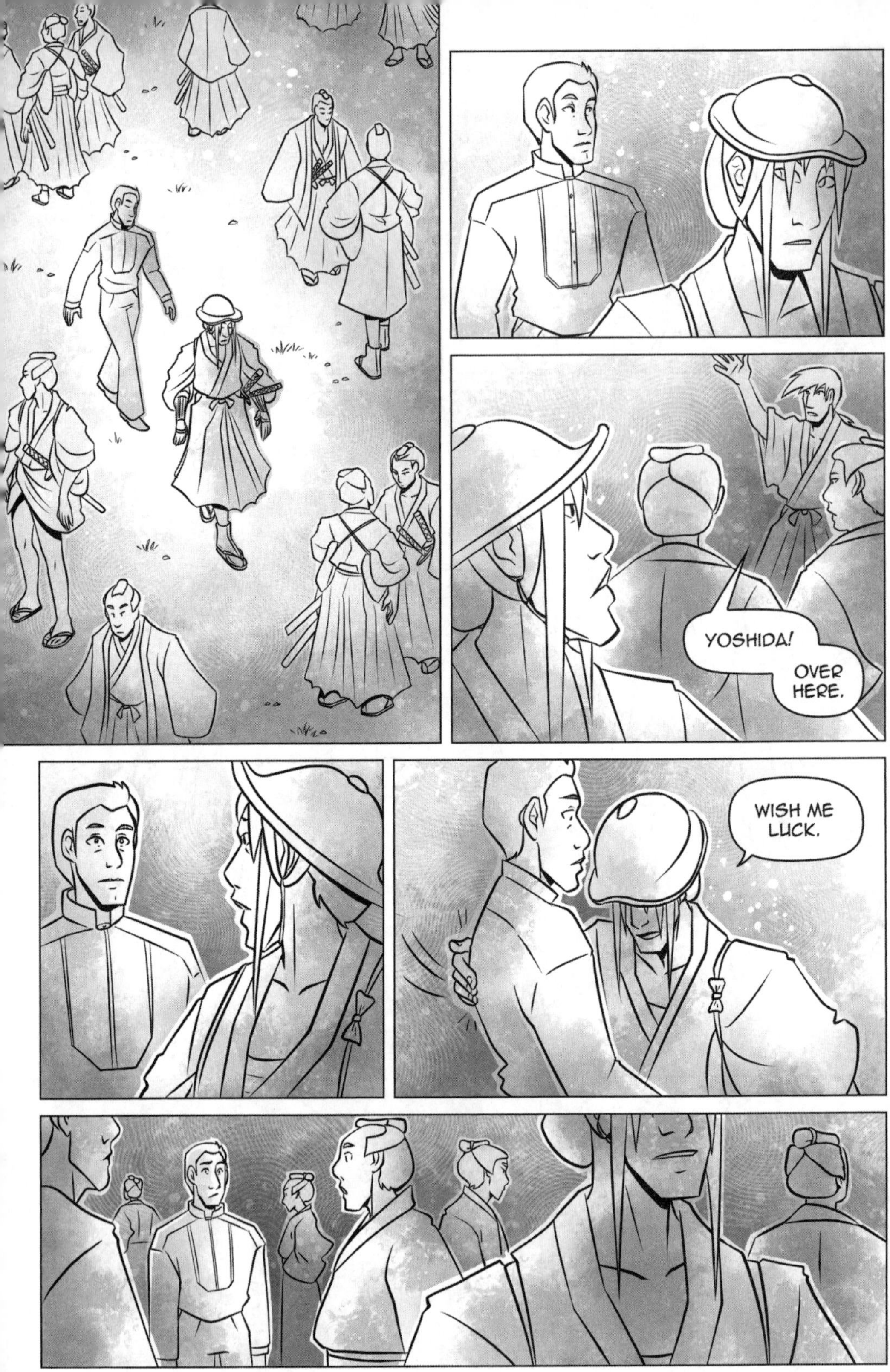
YOSHIDA!
OVER HERE.
WISH ME LUCK.

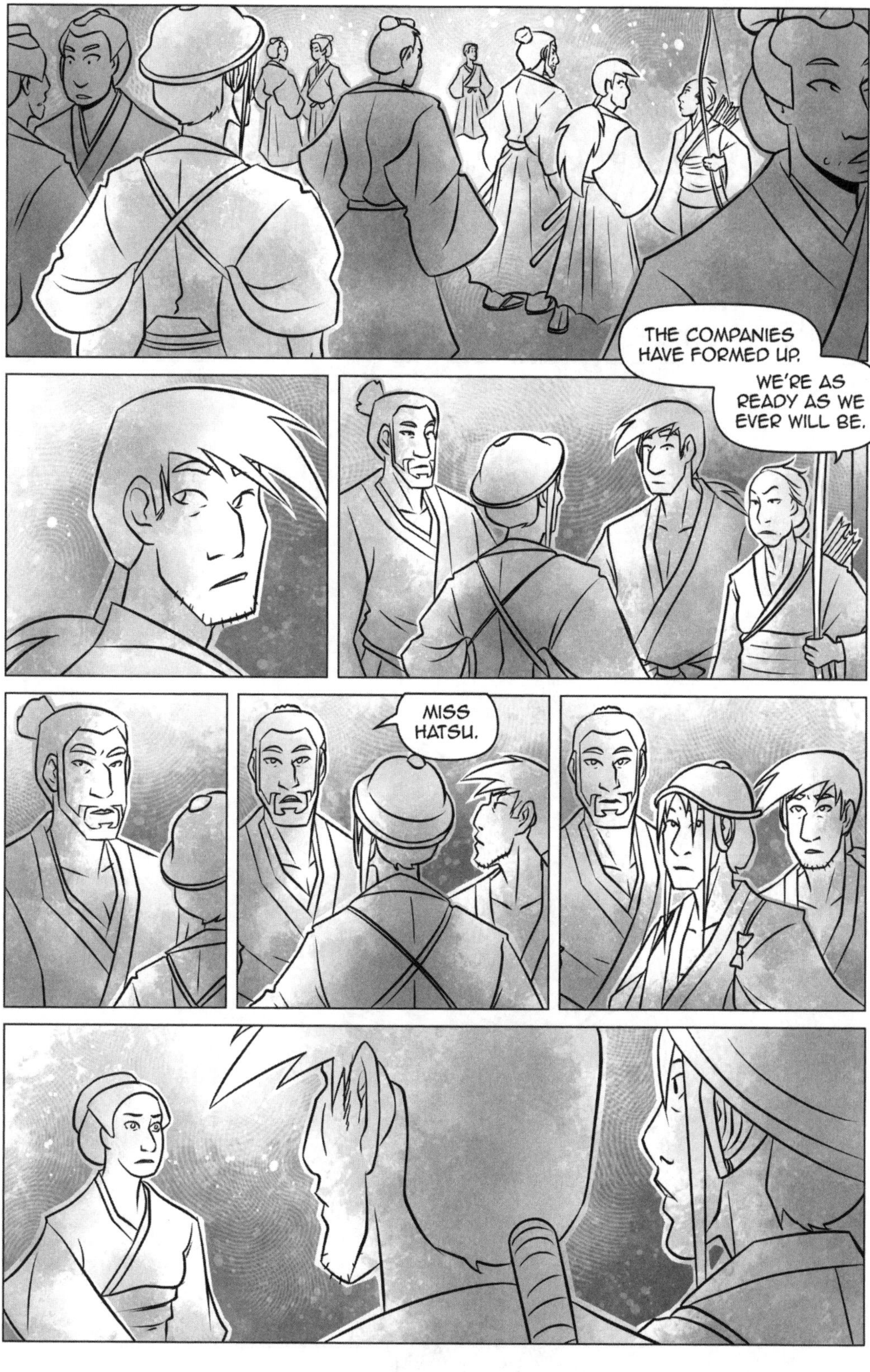
THE COMPANIES HAVE FORMED UP.
WE'RE AS READY AS WE EVER WILL BE.
MISS HATSU.

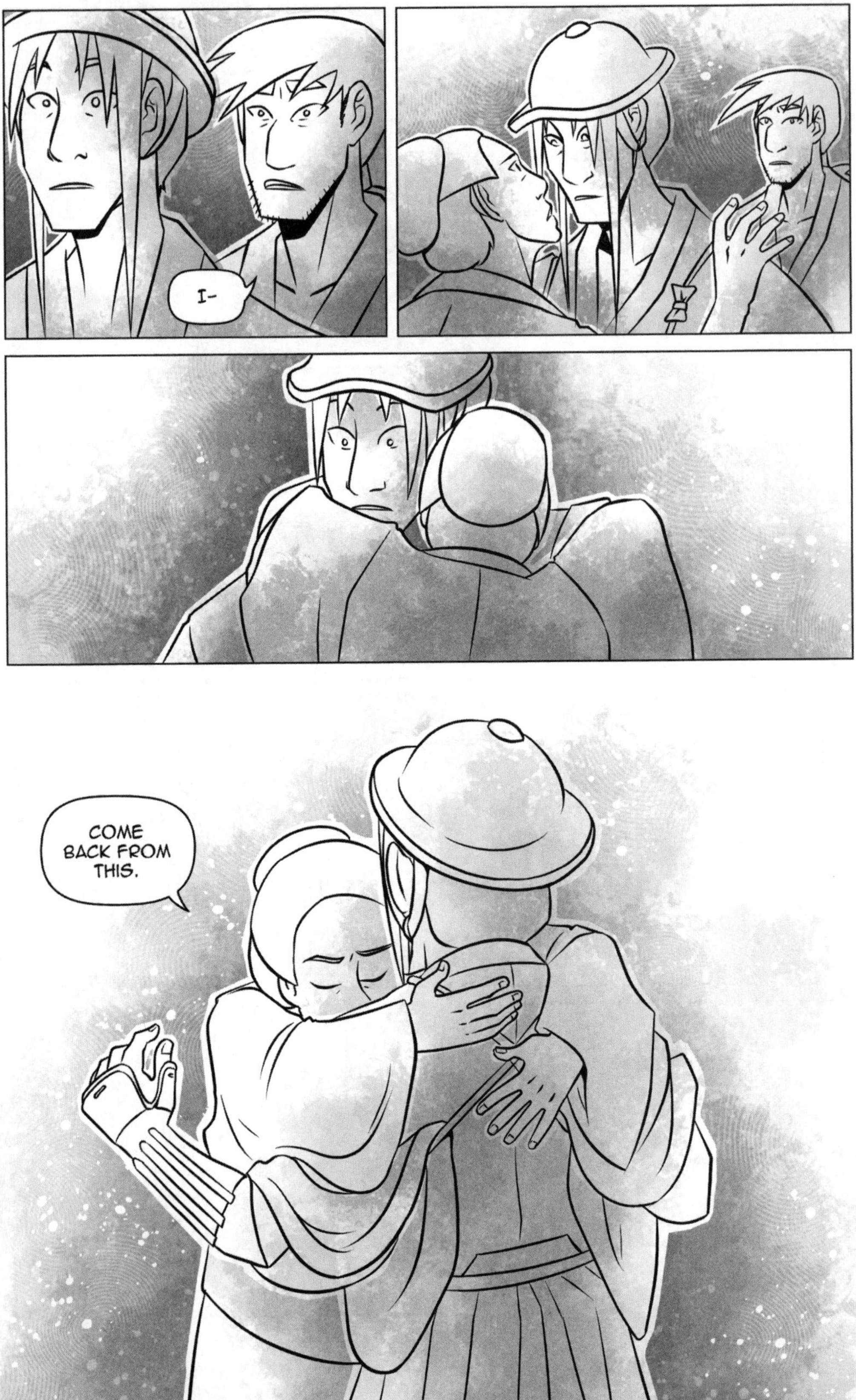
I-
COME BACK FROM THIS.

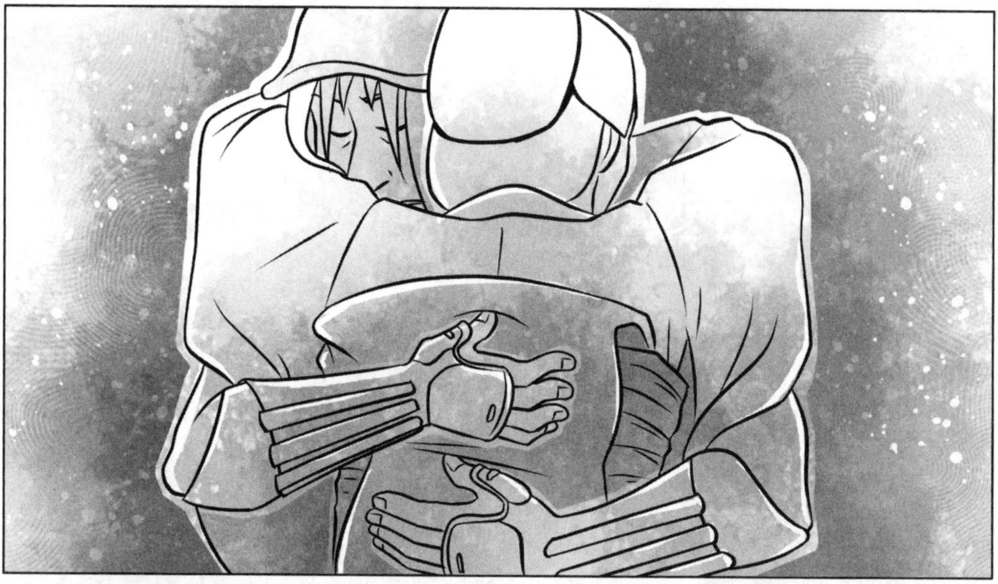

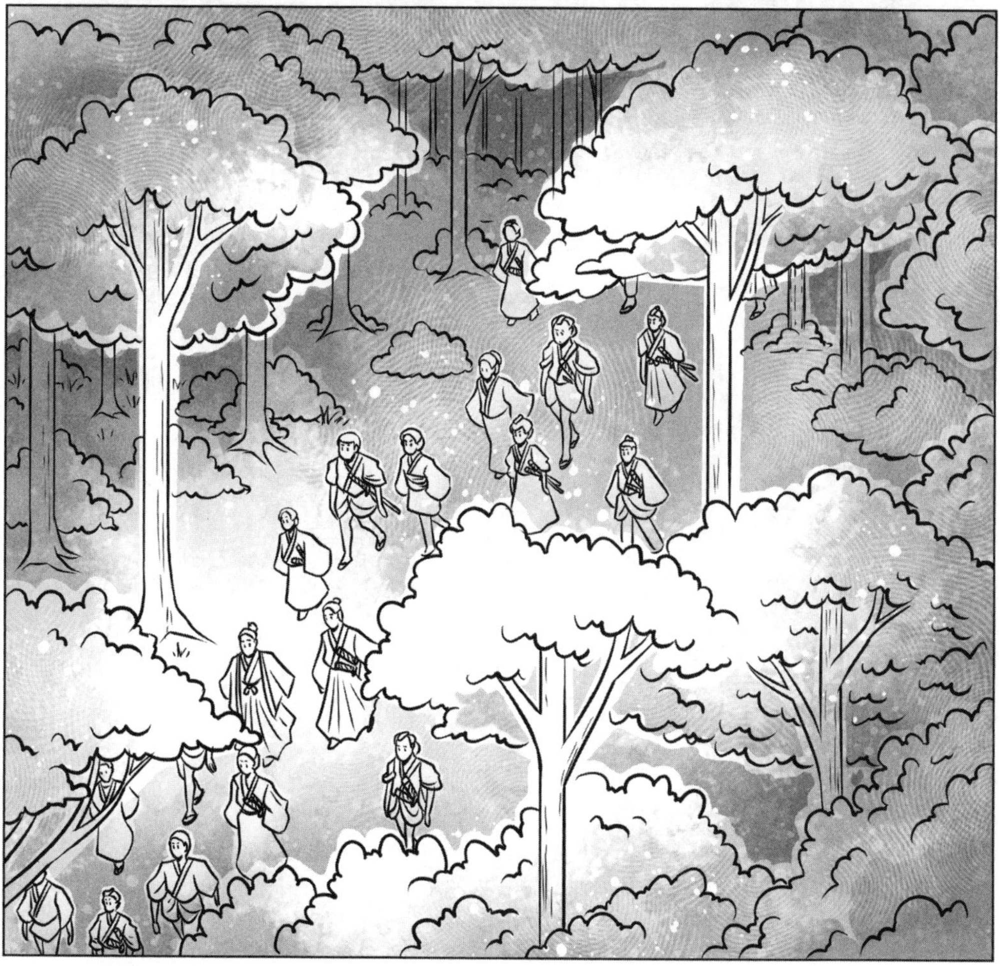

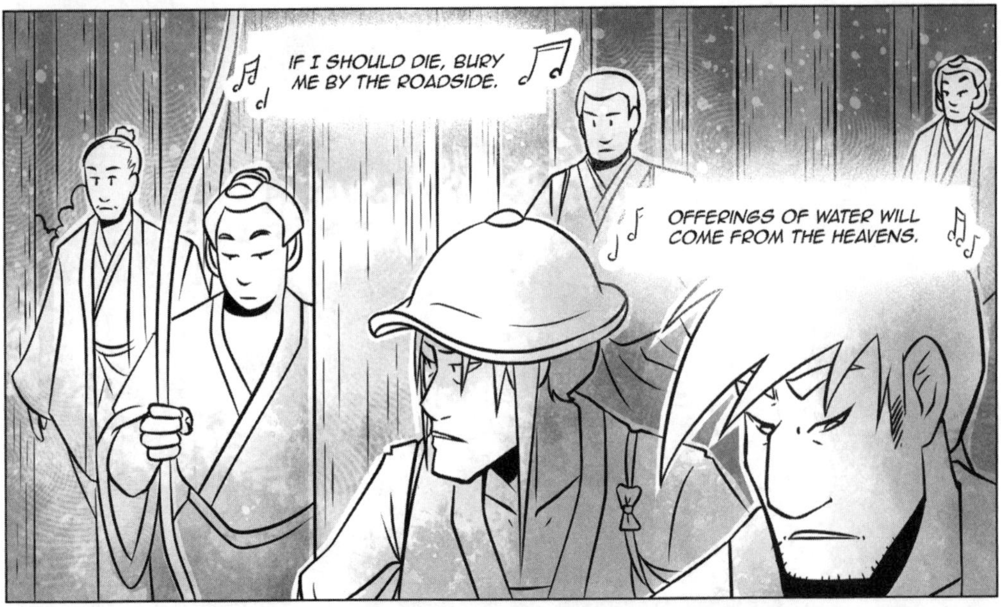
IF I SHOULD DIE, BURY ME BY THE ROADSIDE.
OFFERINGS OF WATER WILL COME FROM THE HEAVENS.

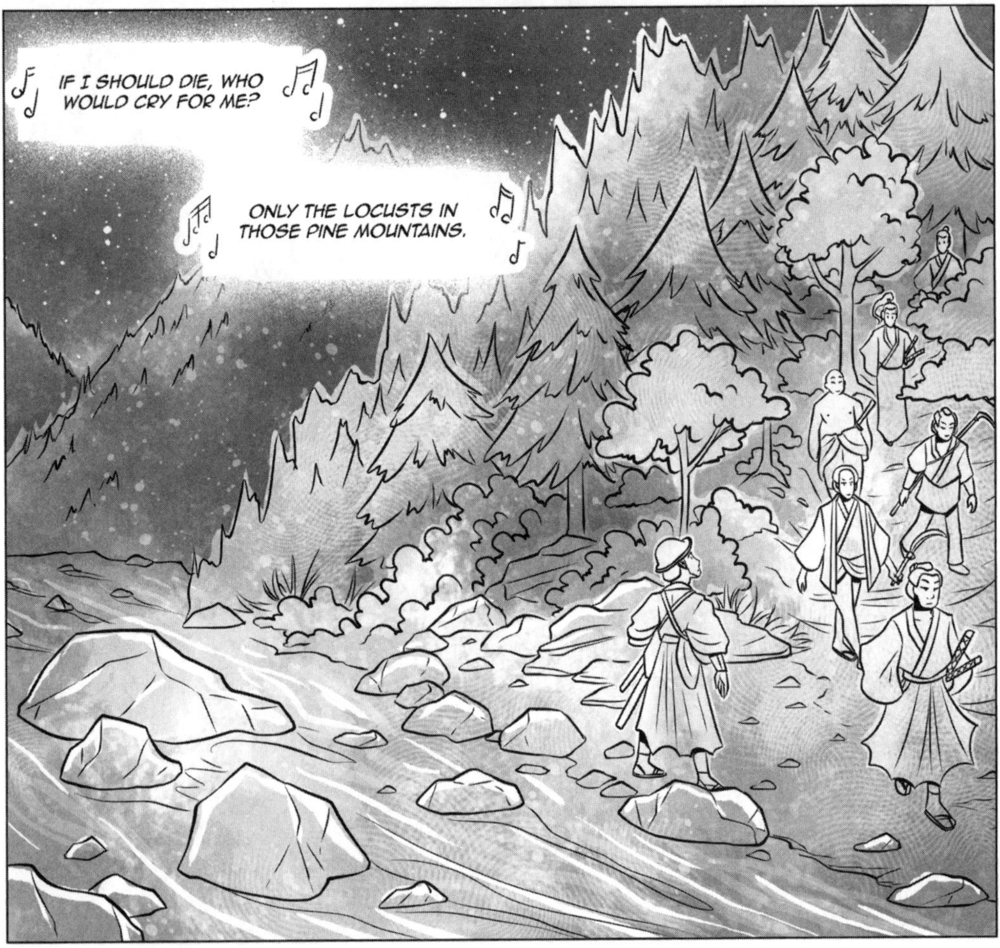
IF I SHOULD DIE, WHO WOULD CRY FOR ME?
ONLY THE LOCUSTS IN THOSE PINE MOUNTAINS.

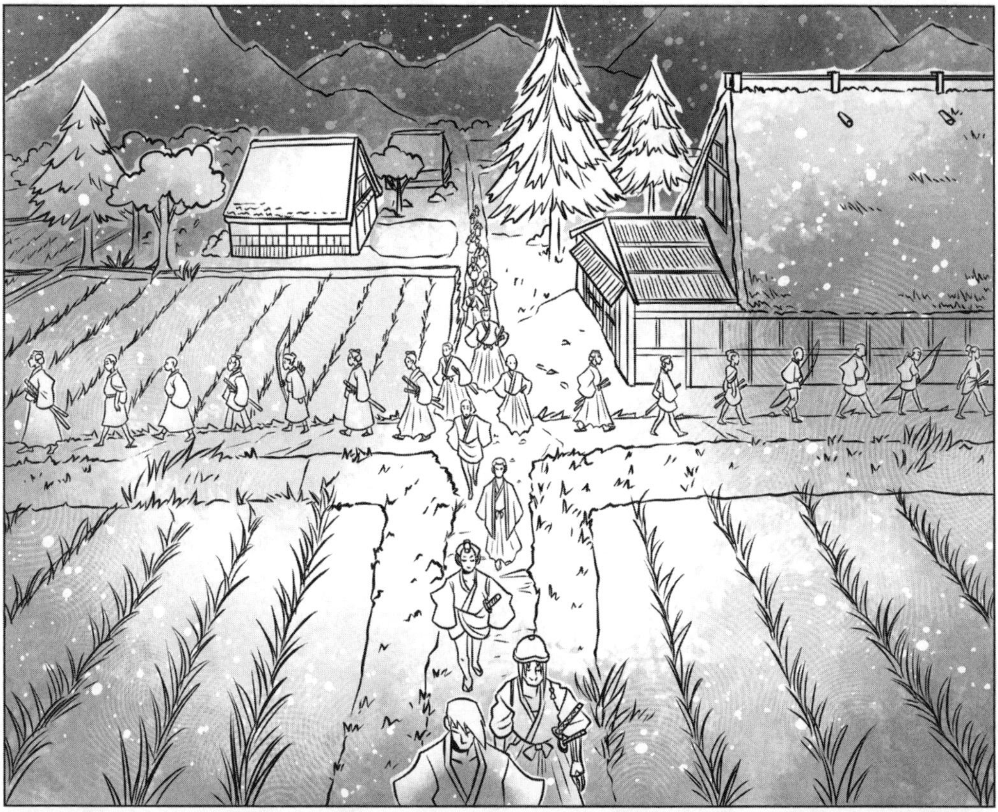

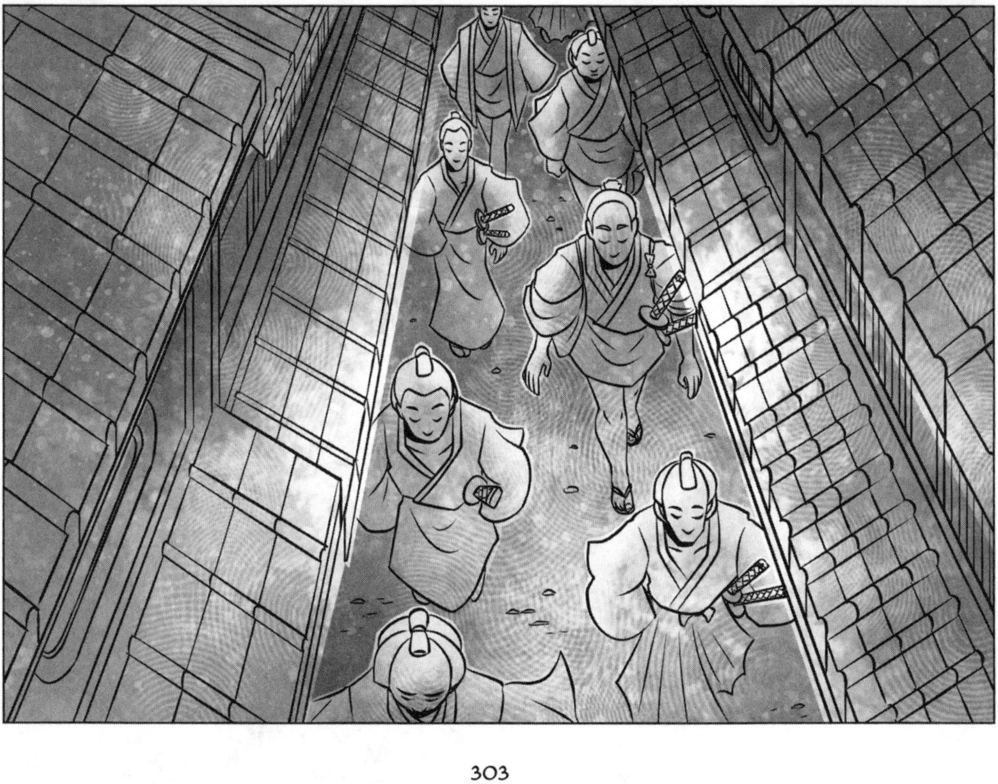

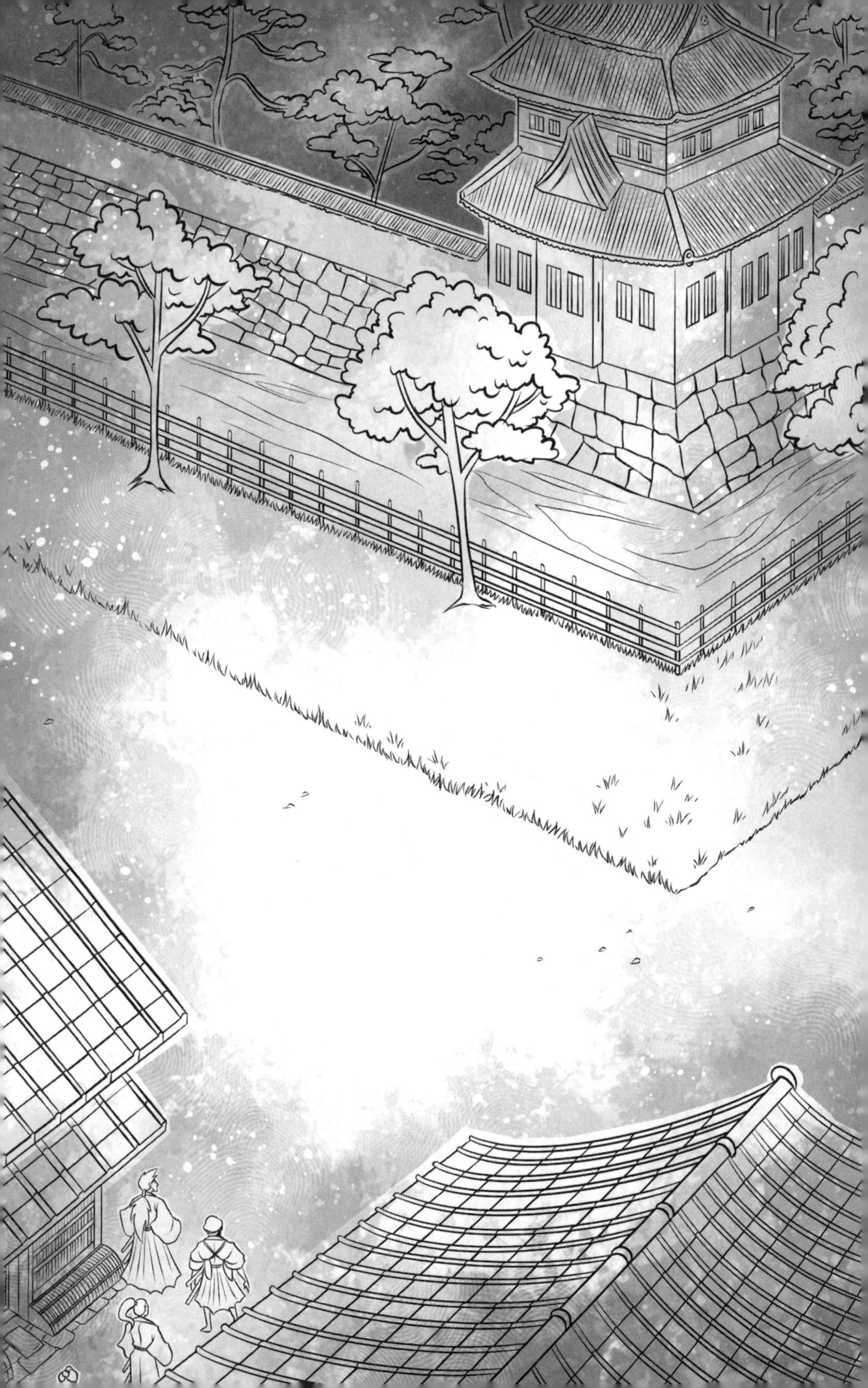

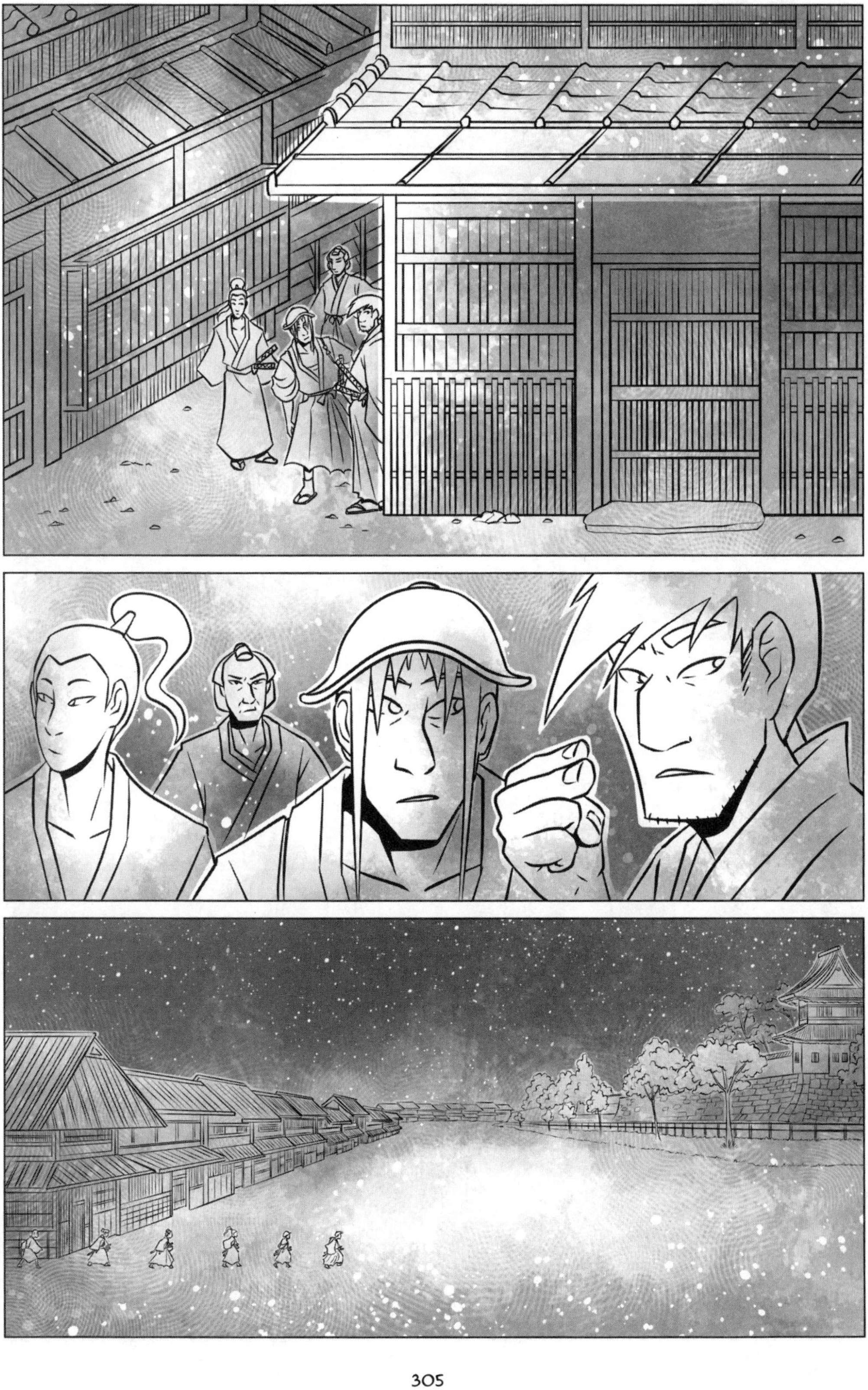

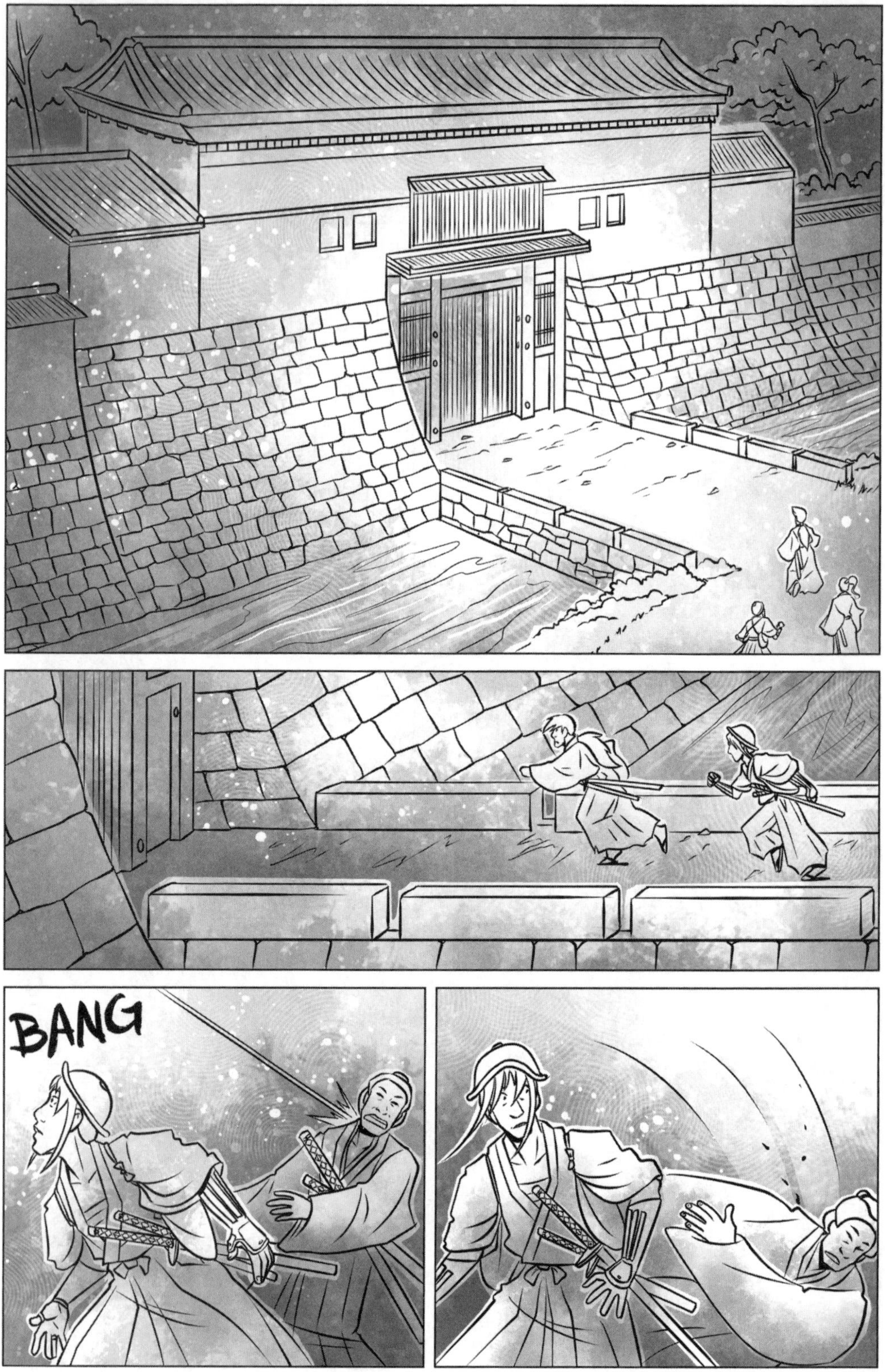
BANG

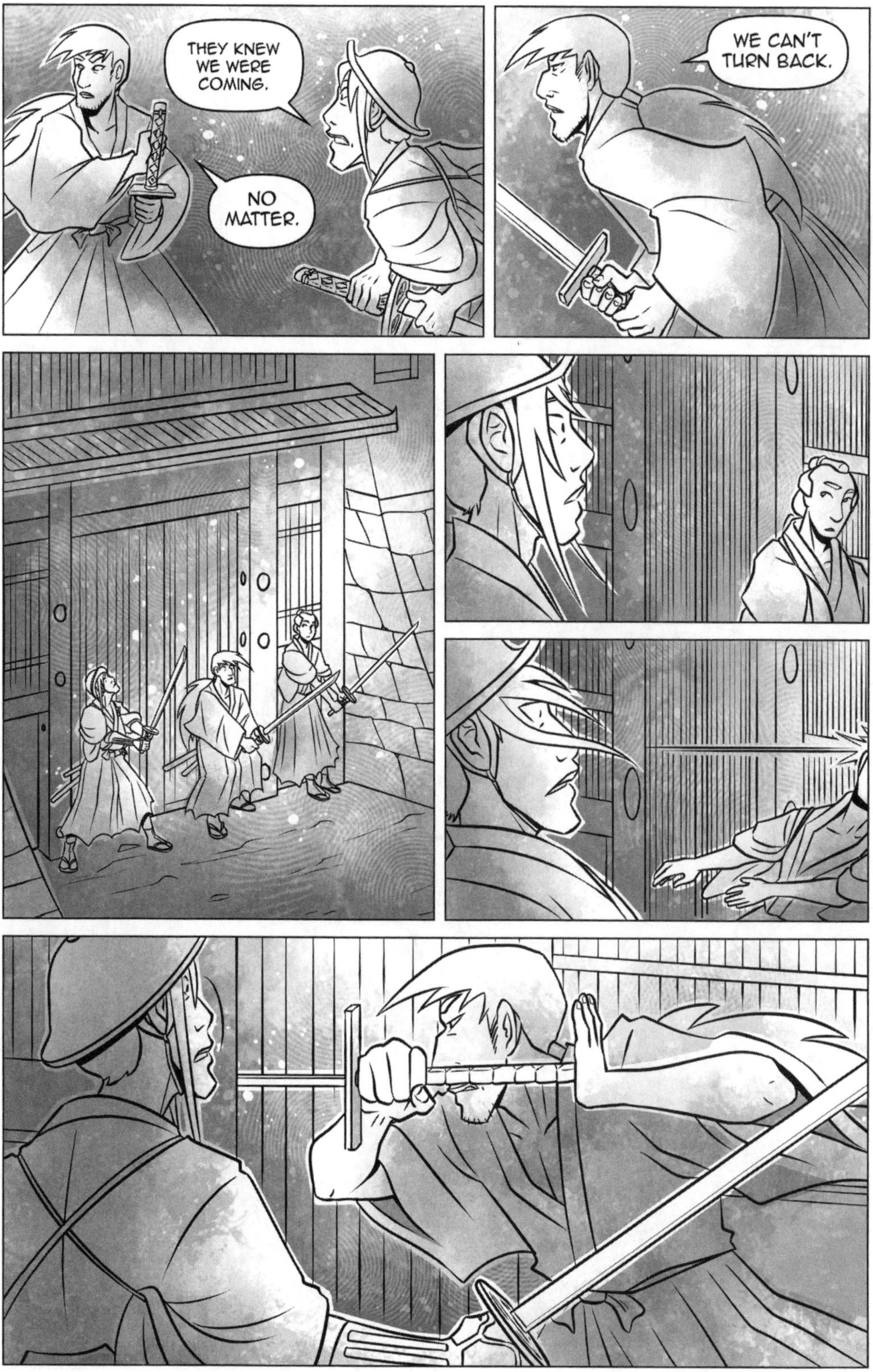
THEY KNEW WE WERE COMING.
NO MATTER.
WE CAN'T TURN BACK.

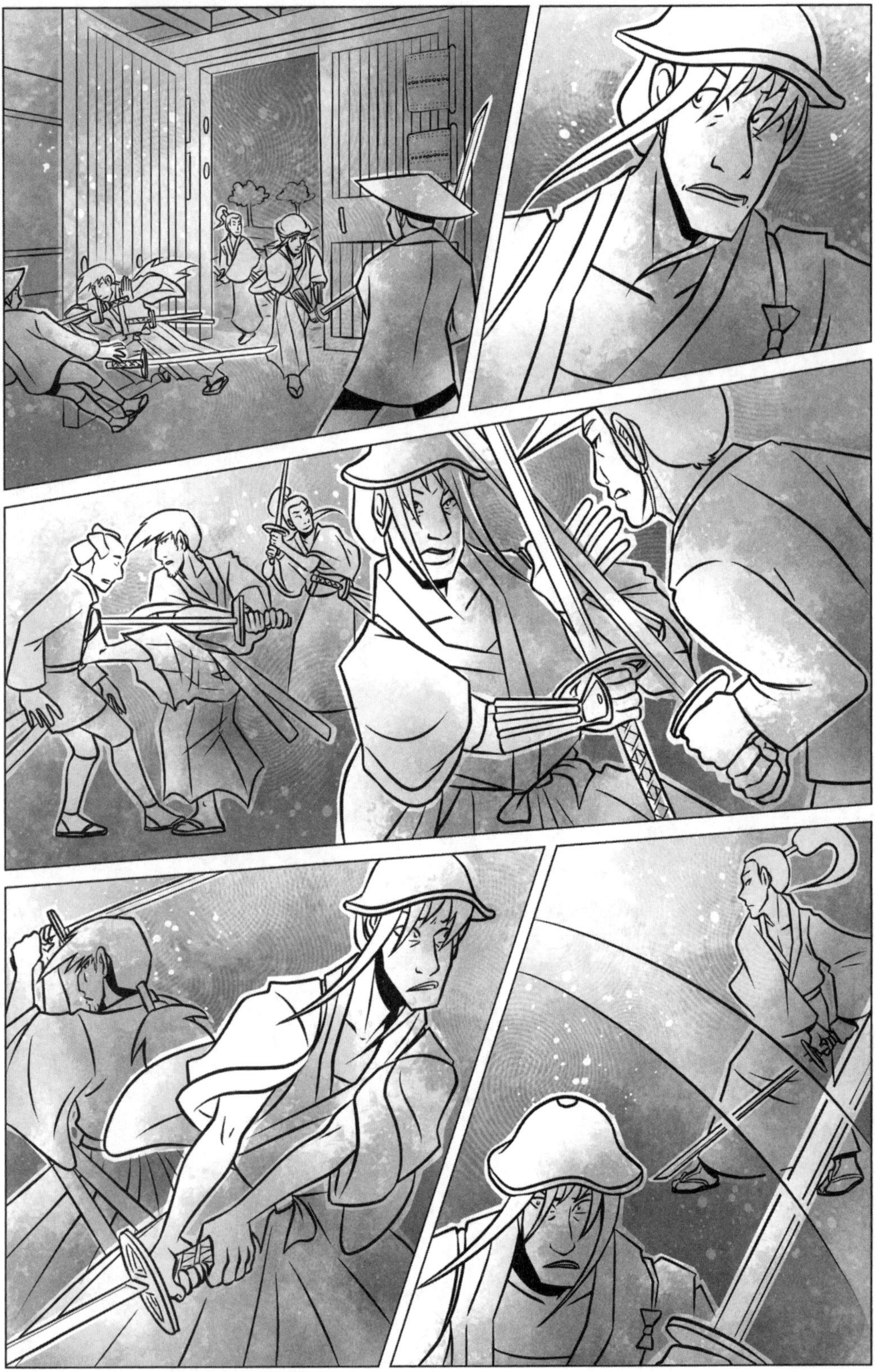

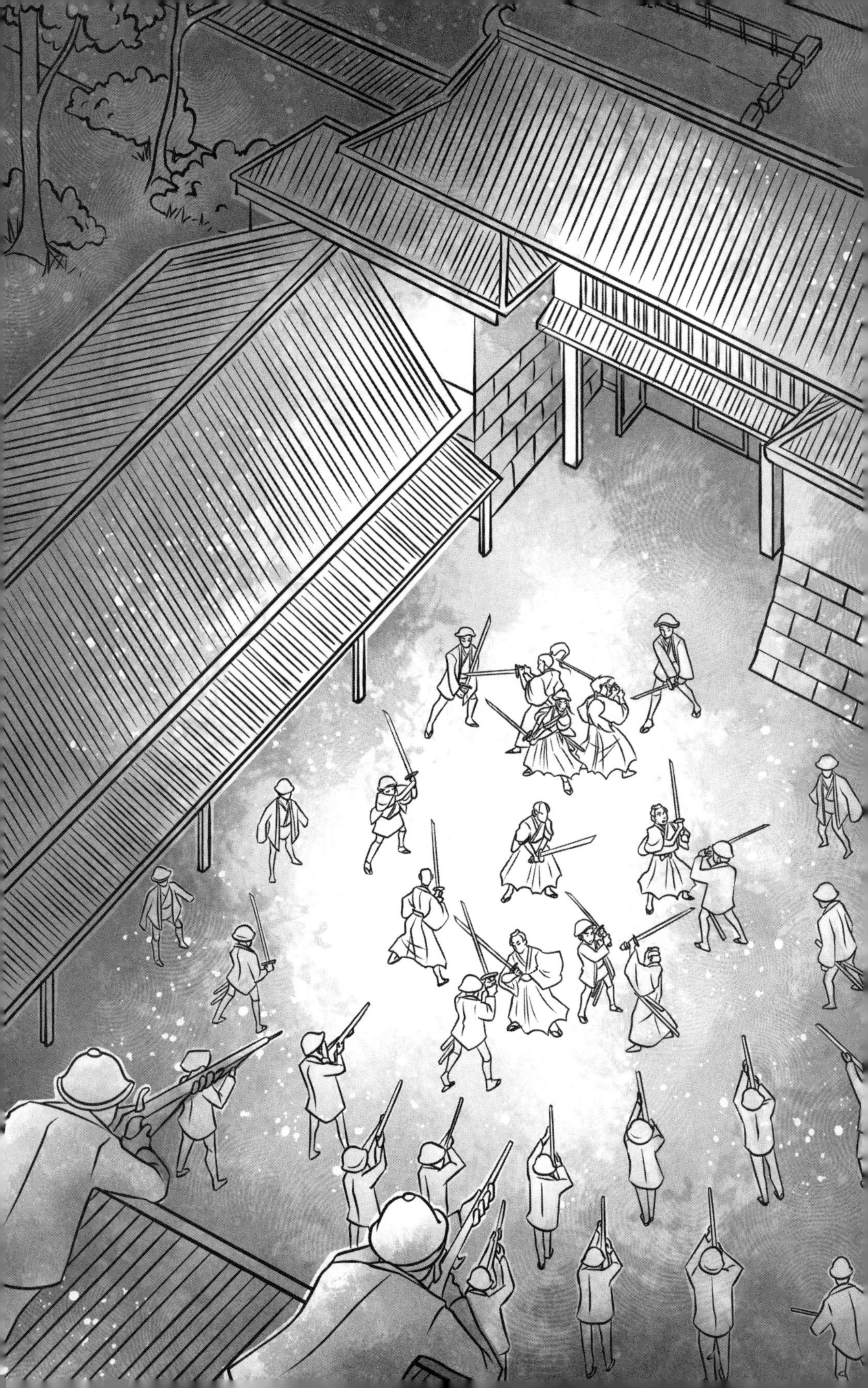

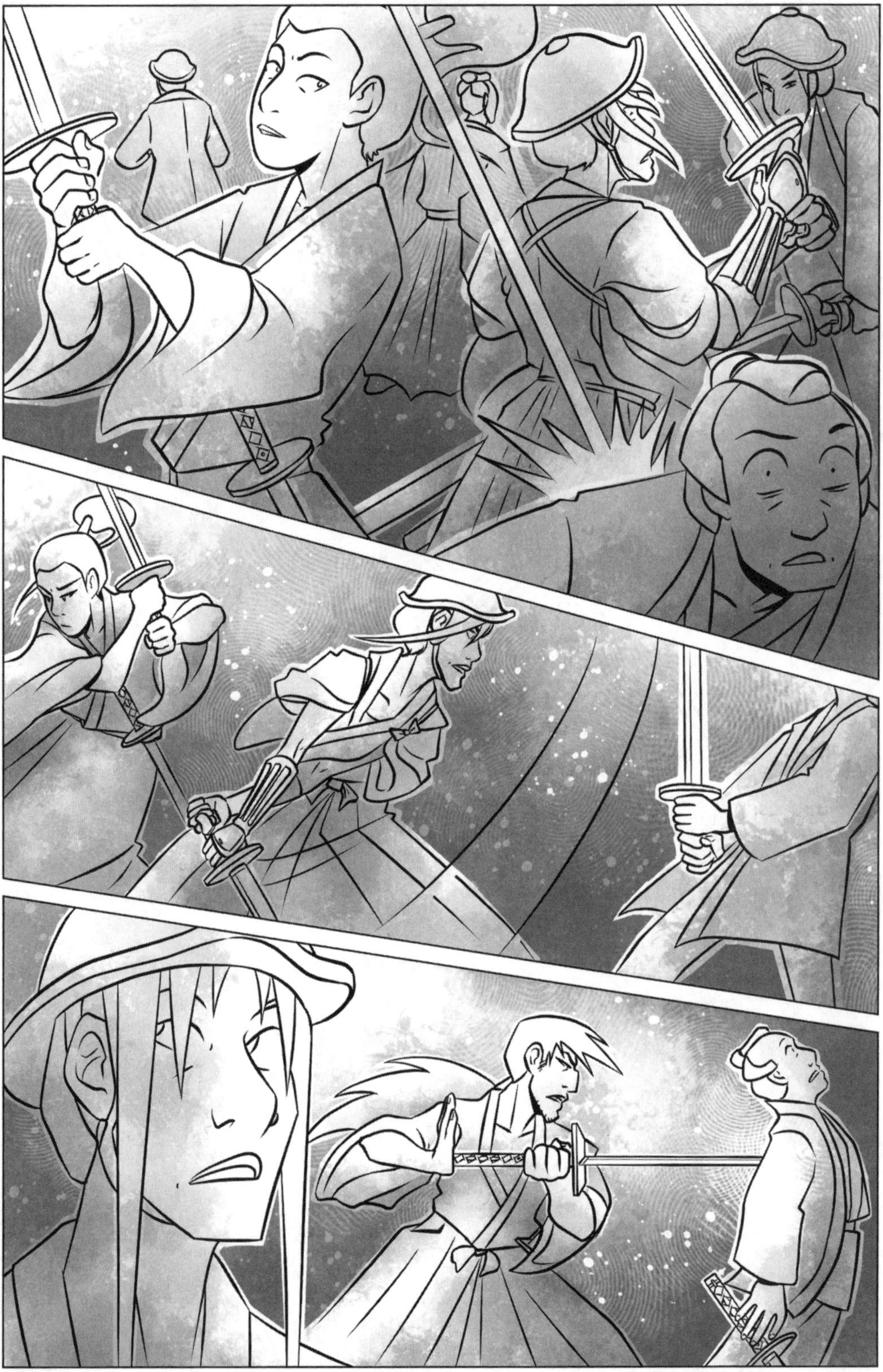

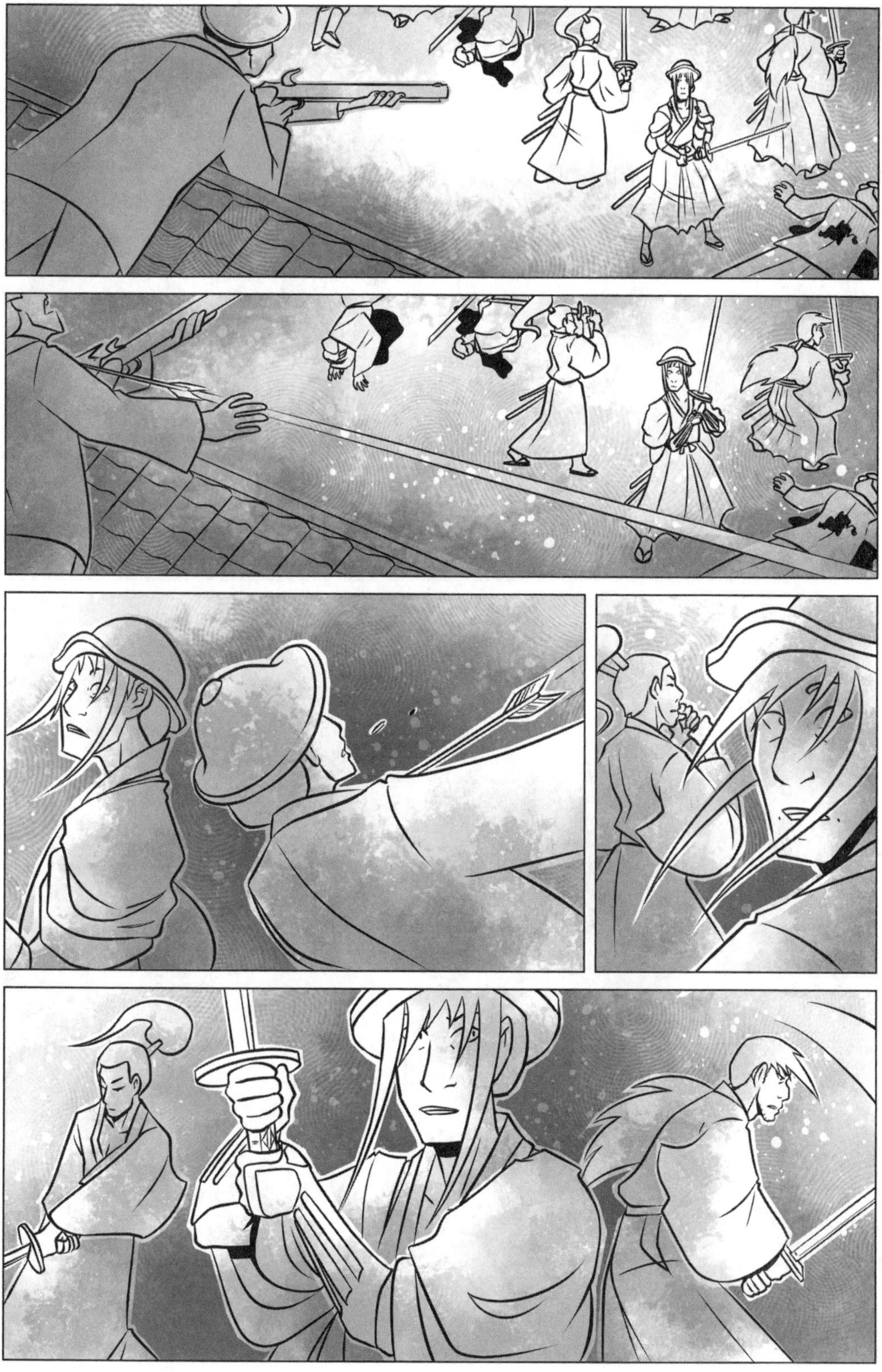

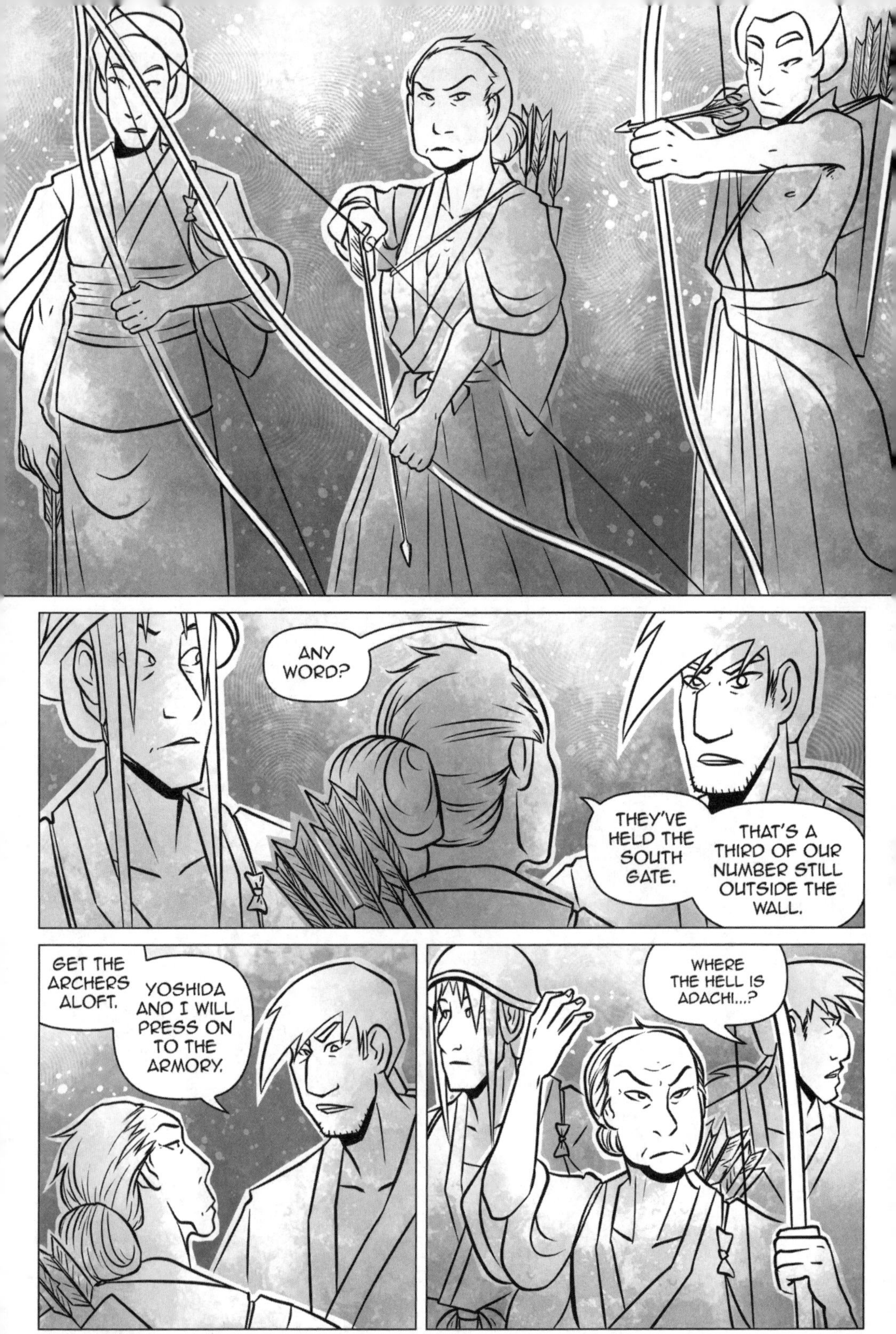
ANY WORD?
THEY'VE HELD THE SOUTH GATE.
THAT'S A THIRD OF OUR NUMBER STILL OUTSIDE THE WALL.
GET THE ARCHERS ALOFT.
YOSHIDA AND I WILL PRESS ON TO THE ARMORY.
WHERE THE HELL IS ADACHI...?

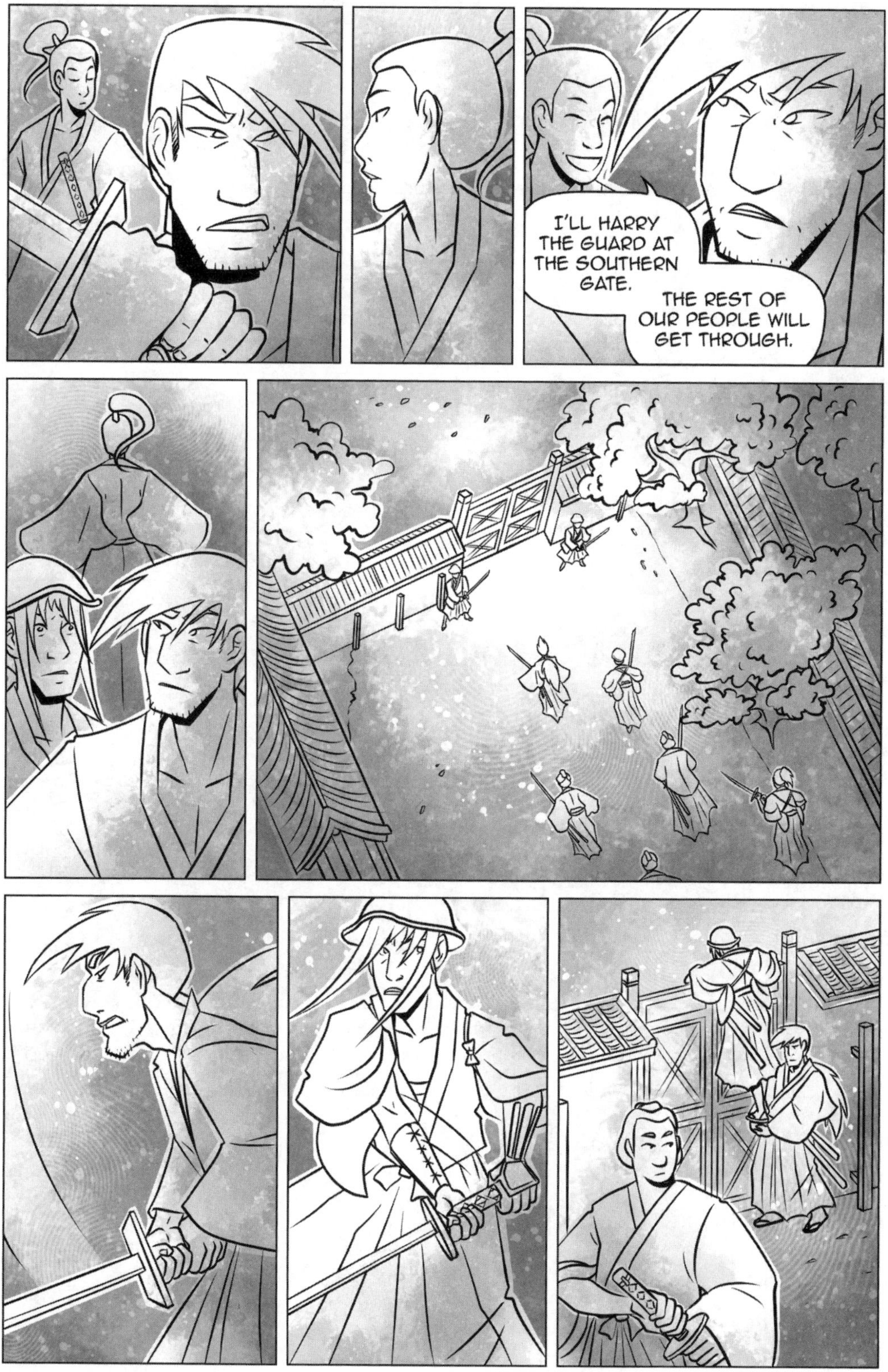
I'LL HARRY THE GUARD AT THE SOUTHERN GATE.
THE REST OF OUR PEOPLE WILL GET THROUGH.

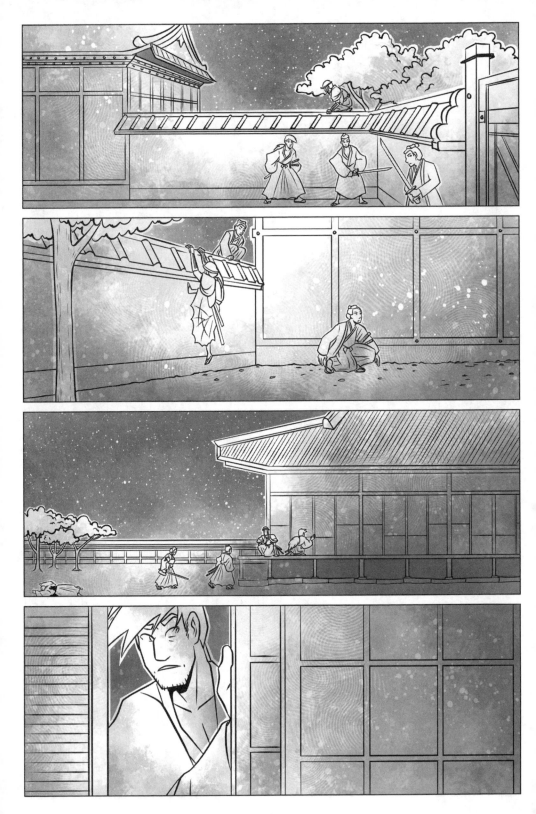

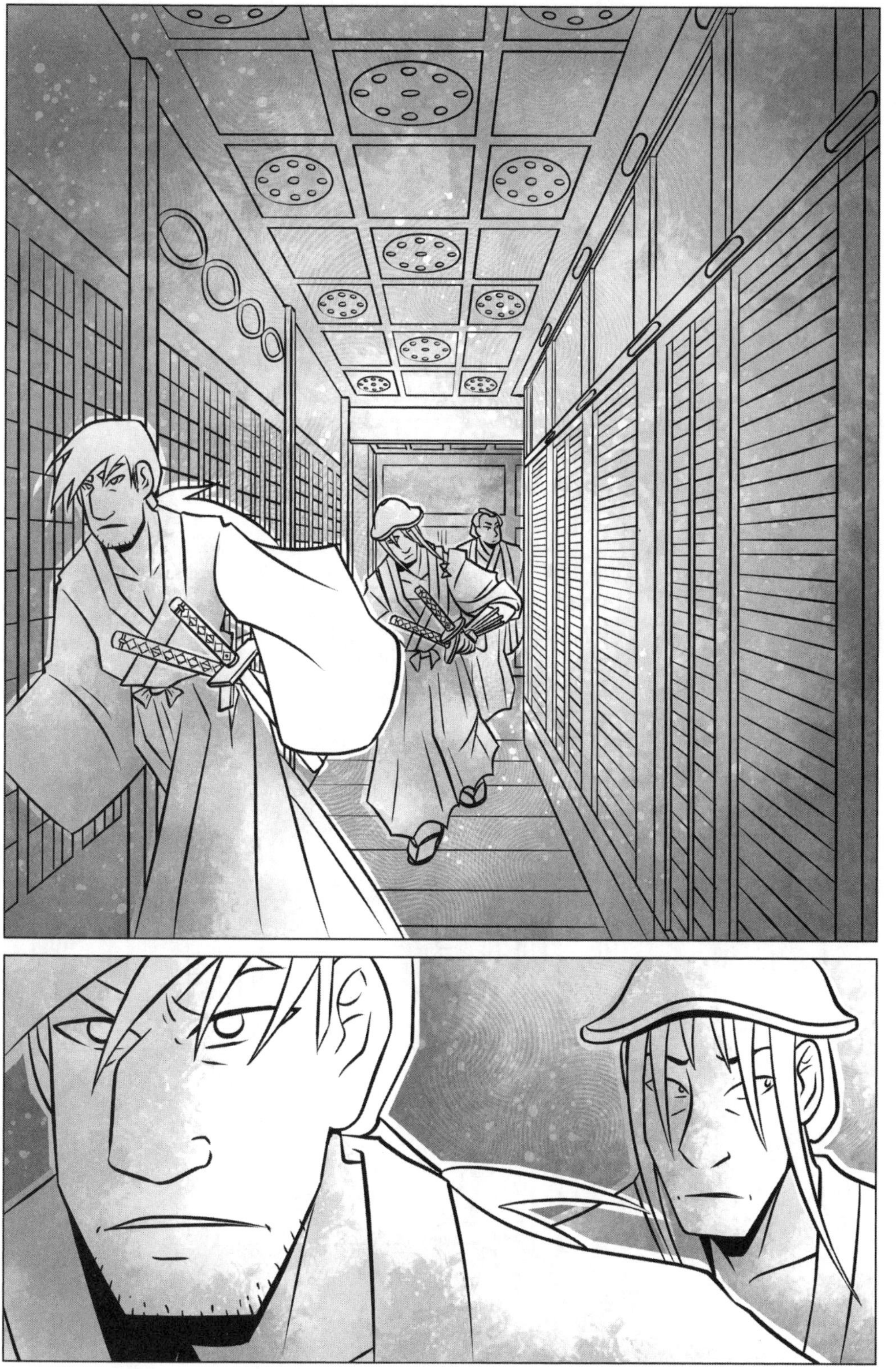

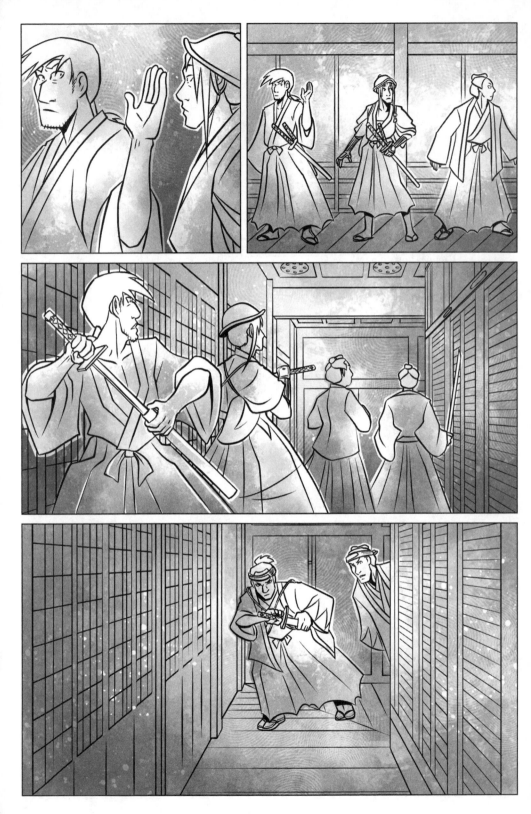

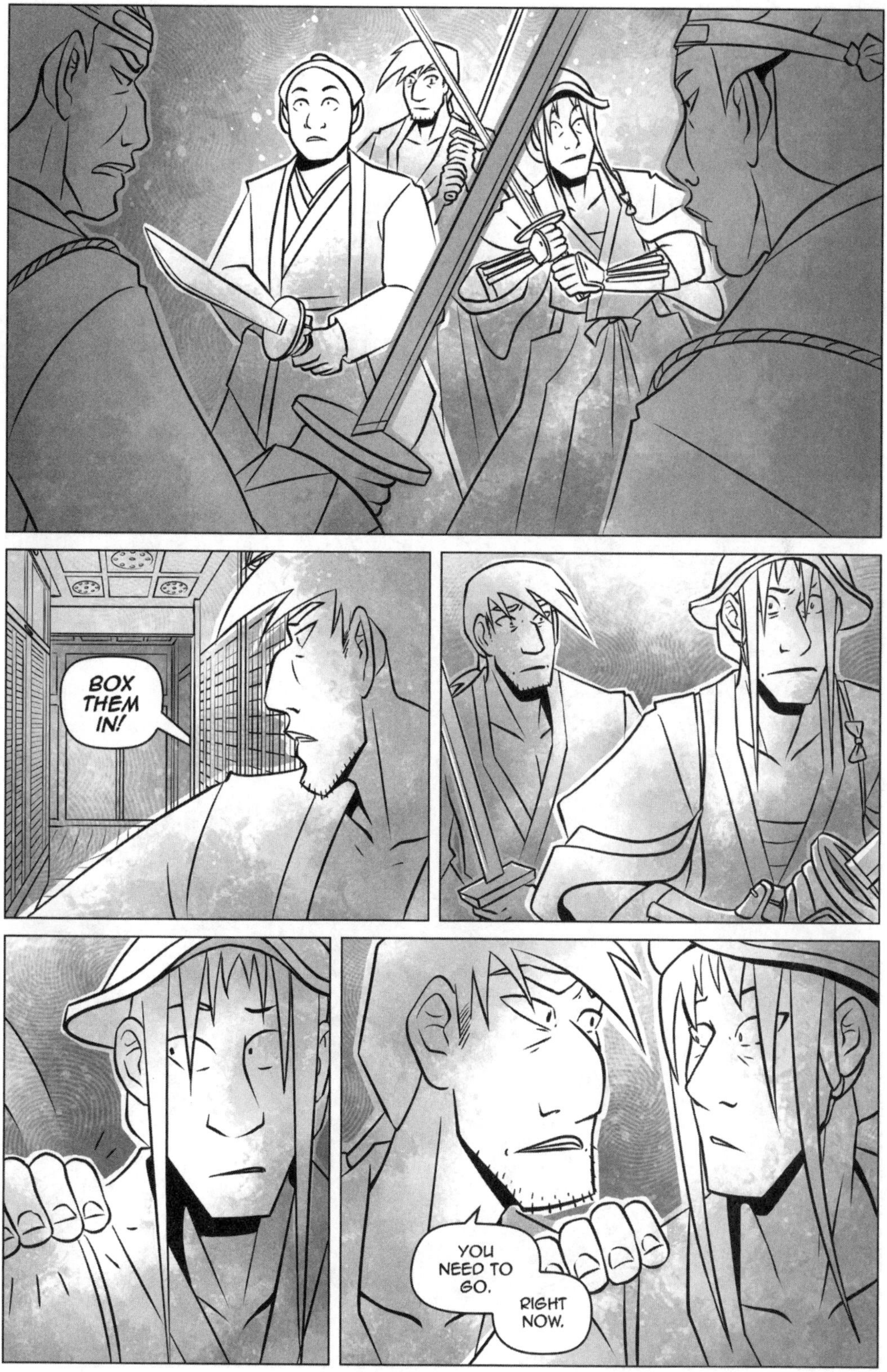
BOX THEM IN!
YOU NEED TO GO.
RIGHT NOW.

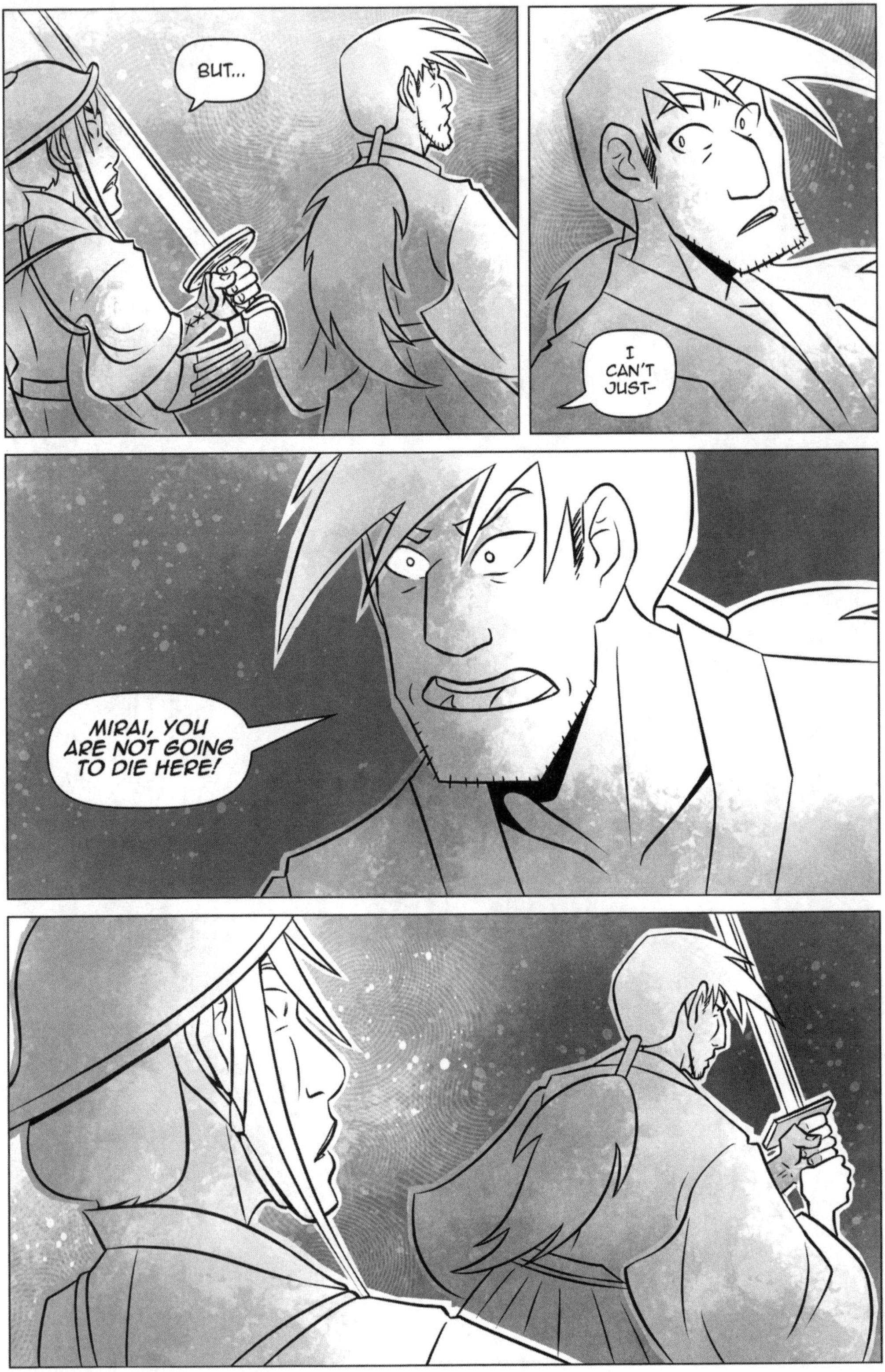
BUT...
I CAN'T JUST-
MIRAI, YOU ARE NOT GOING TO DIE HERE!

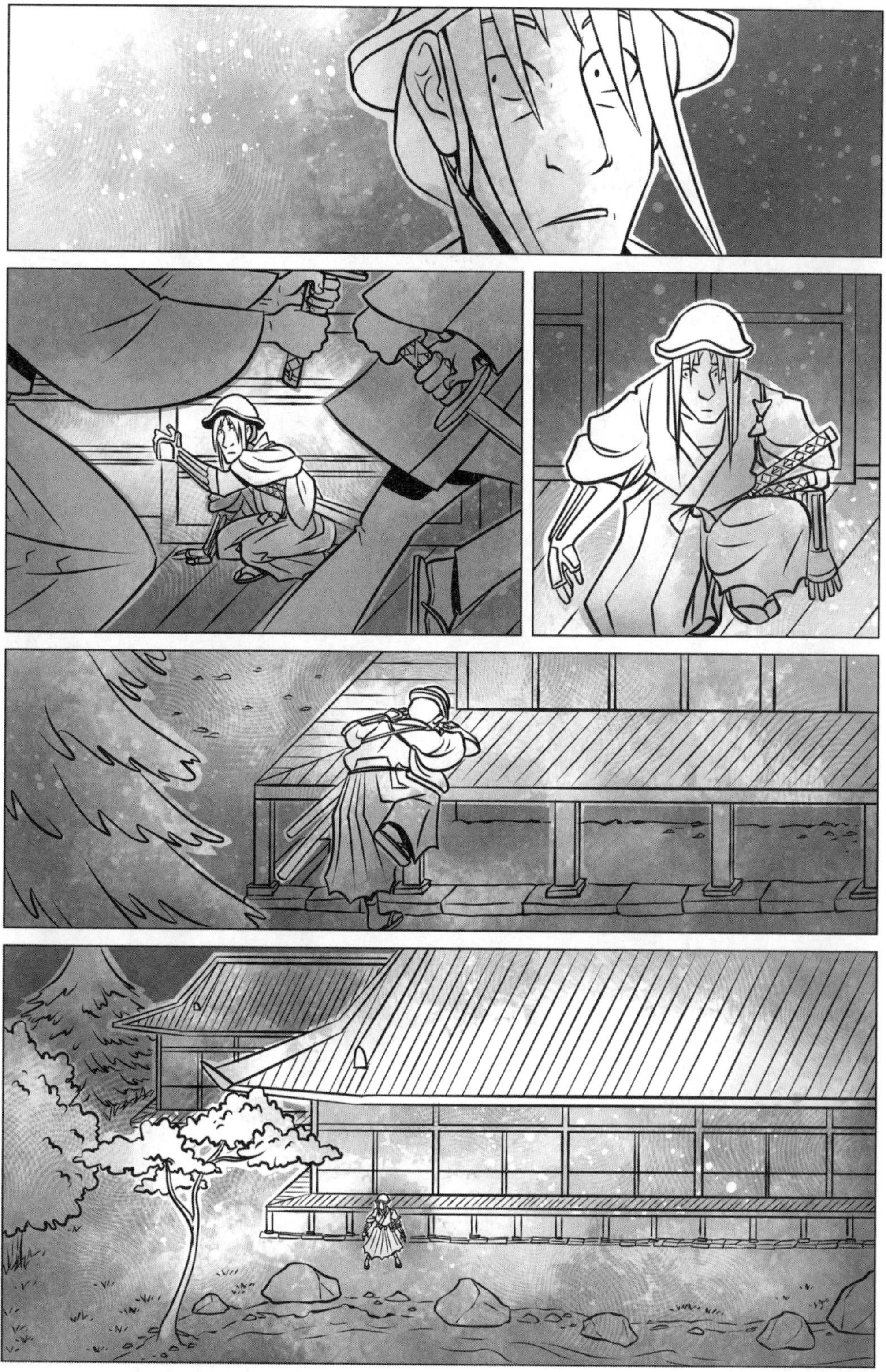

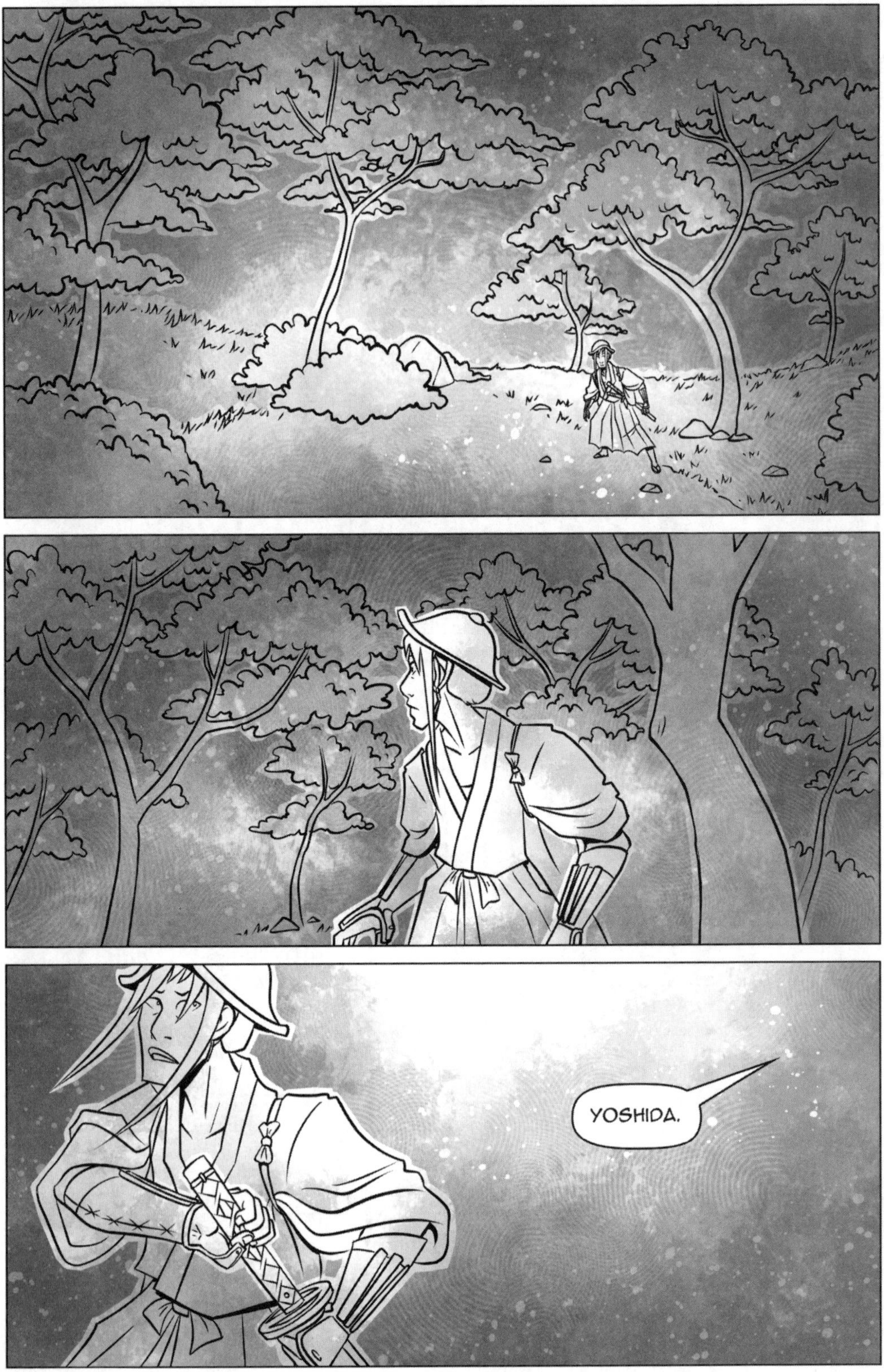
YOSHIDA.

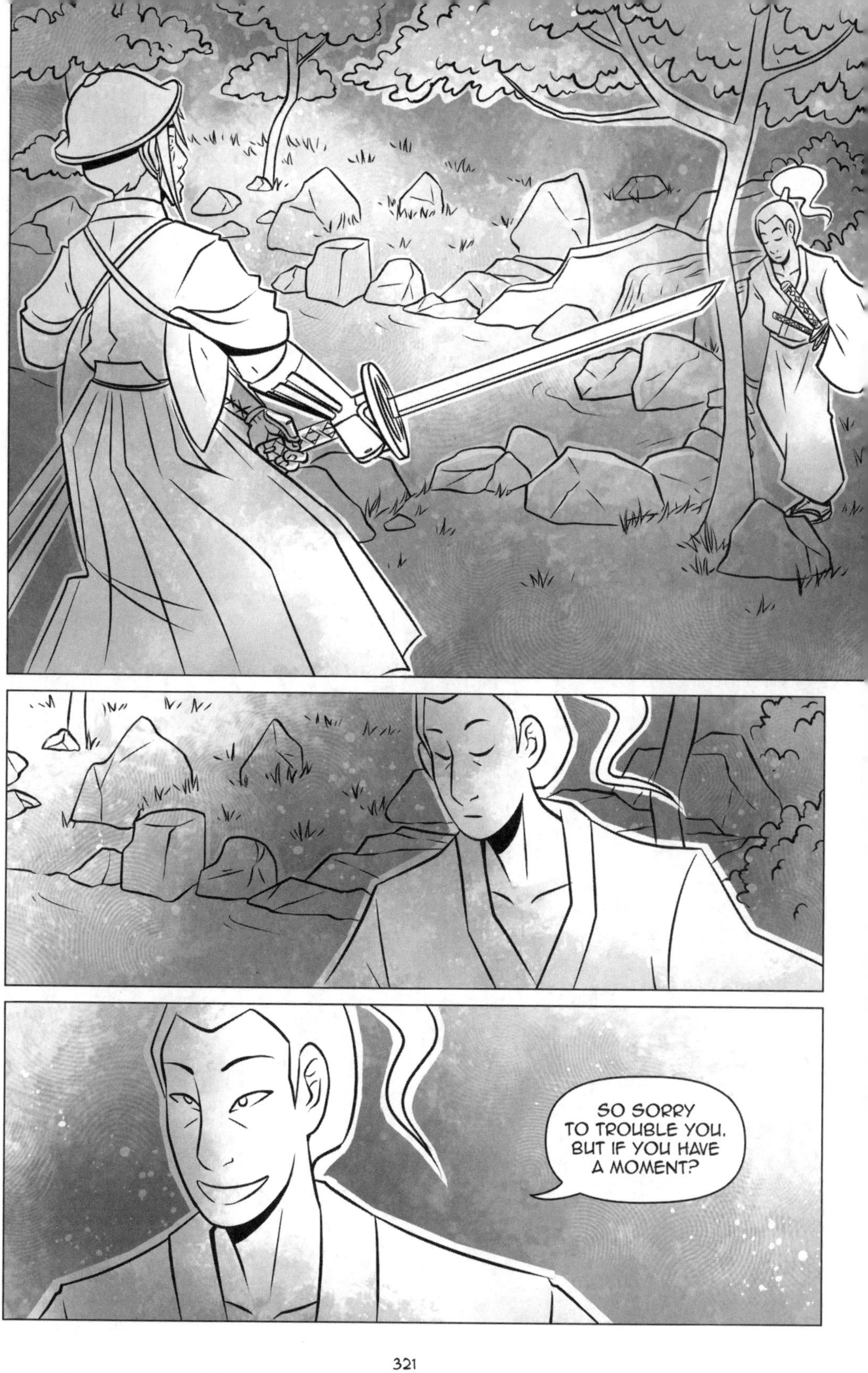
SO SORRY
TO TROUBLE YOU.
BUT IF YOU HAVE
A MOMENT?

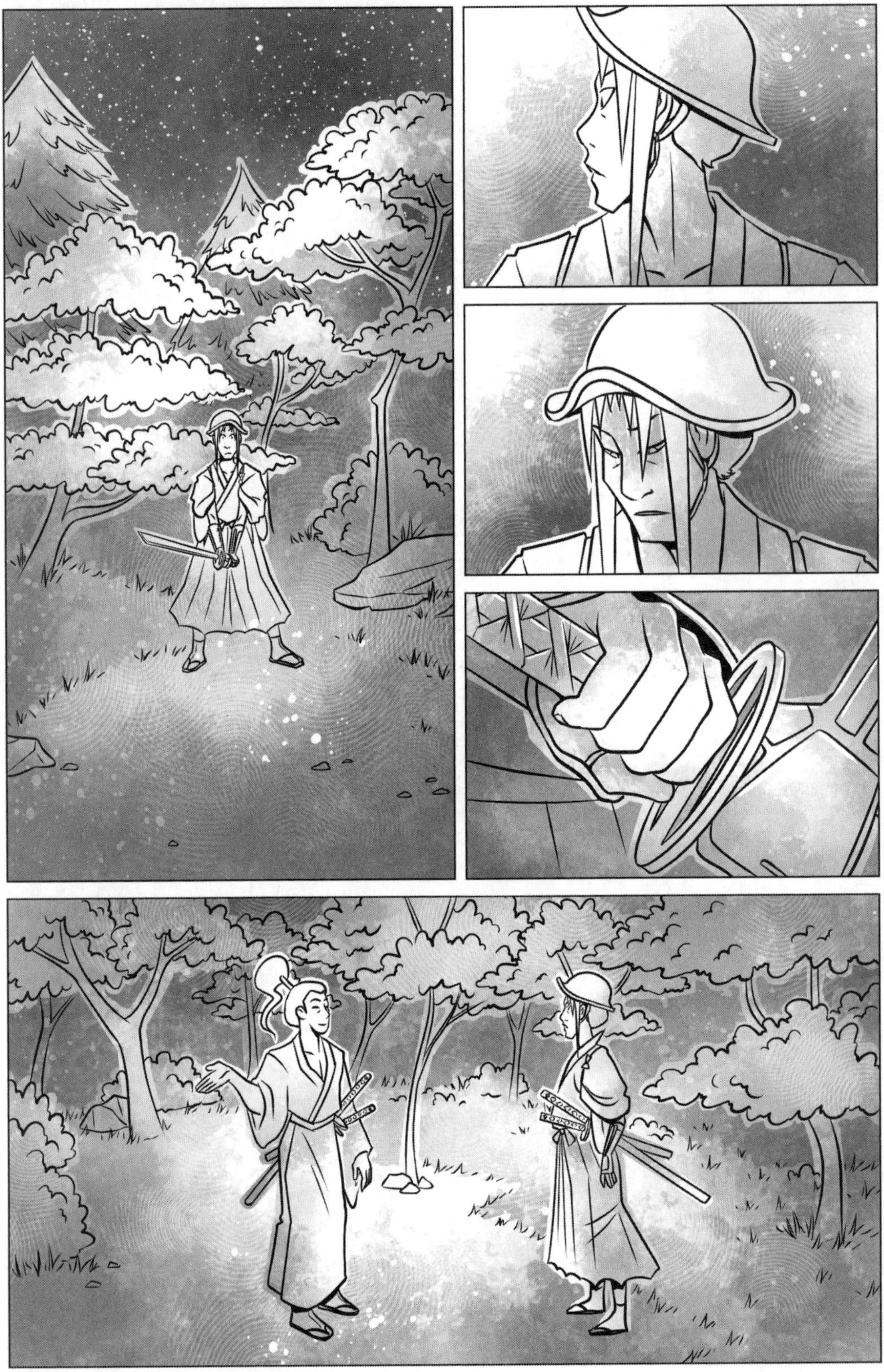

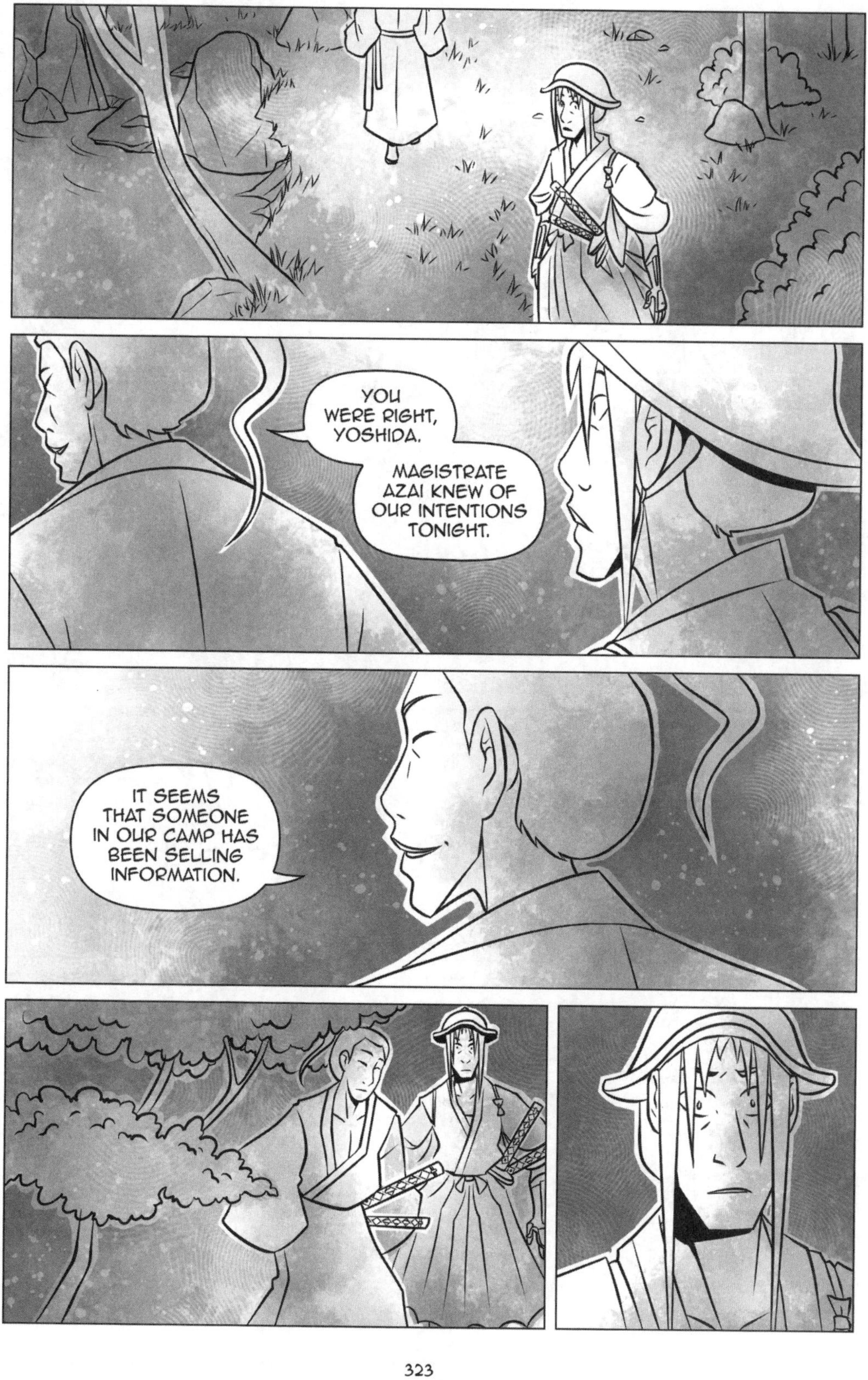
YOU WERE RIGHT, YOSHIDA.
MAGISTRATE AZAI KNEW OF OUR INTENTIONS TONIGHT.
IT SEEMS THAT SOMEONE IN OUR CAMP HAS BEEN SELLING INFORMATION.

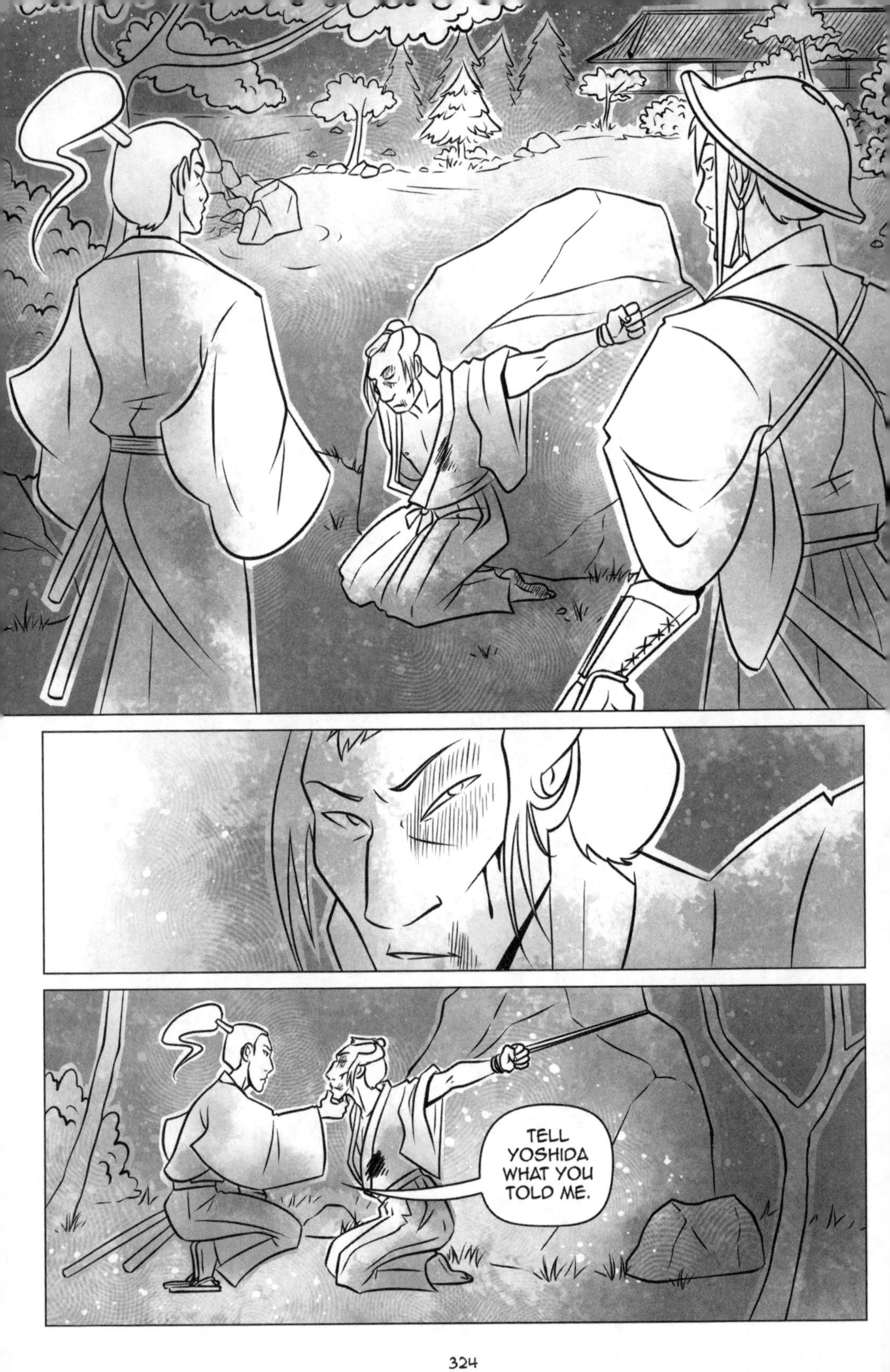
TELL YOSHIDA WHAT YOU TOLD ME.

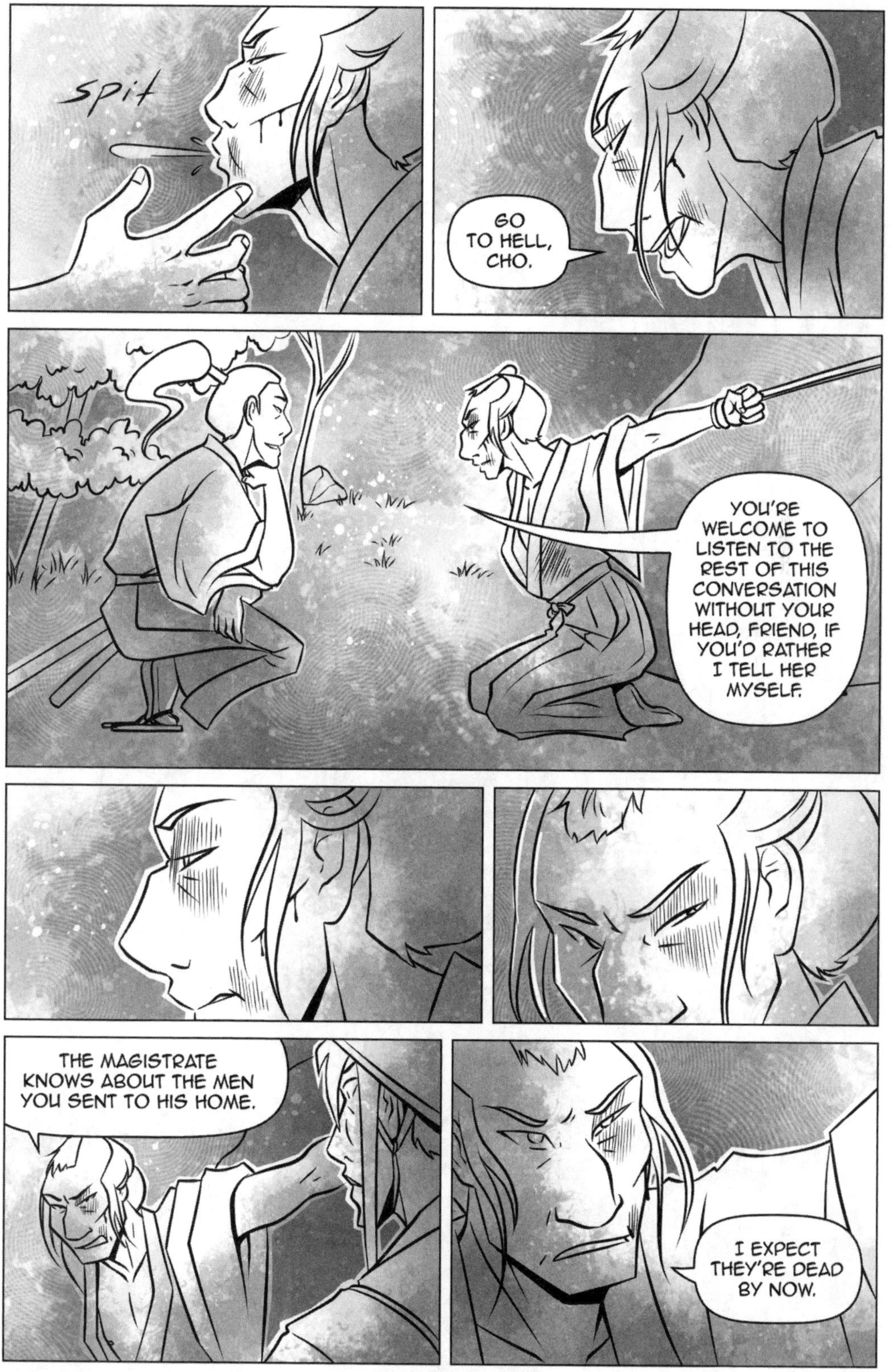
spit
GO TO HELL, CHO.
YOU'RE WELCOME TO LISTEN TO THE REST OF THIS CONVERSATION WITHOUT YOUR HEAD, FRIEND, IF YOU'D RATHER I TELL HER MYSELF.
THE MAGISTRATE KNOWS ABOUT THE MEN YOU SENT TO HIS HOME.
I EXPECT THEY'RE DEAD BY NOW.

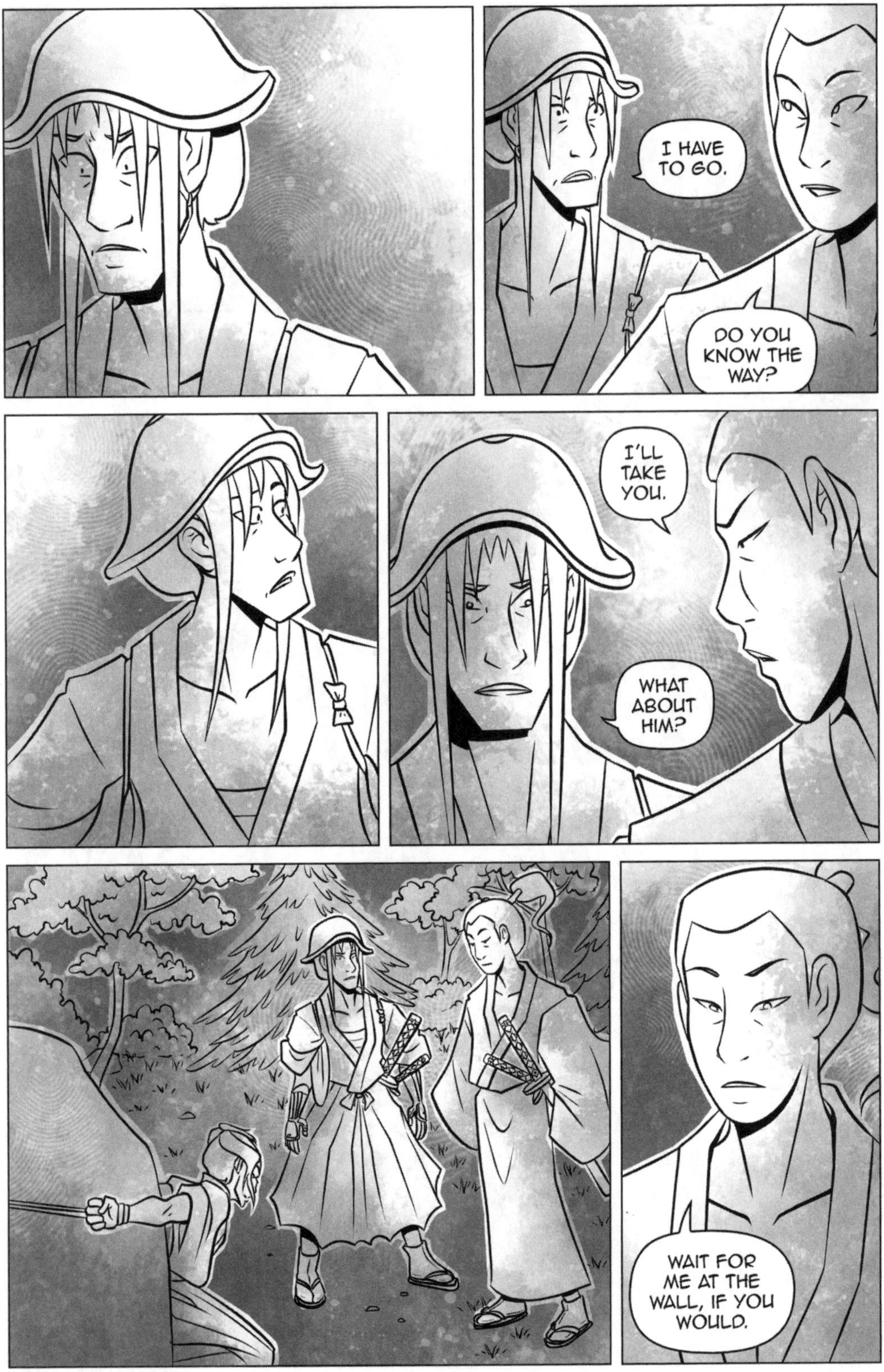
I HAVE TO GO.
DO YOU KNOW THE WAY?
I'LL TAKE YOU.
WHAT ABOUT HIM?
WAIT FOR ME AT THE WALL, IF YOU WOULD.

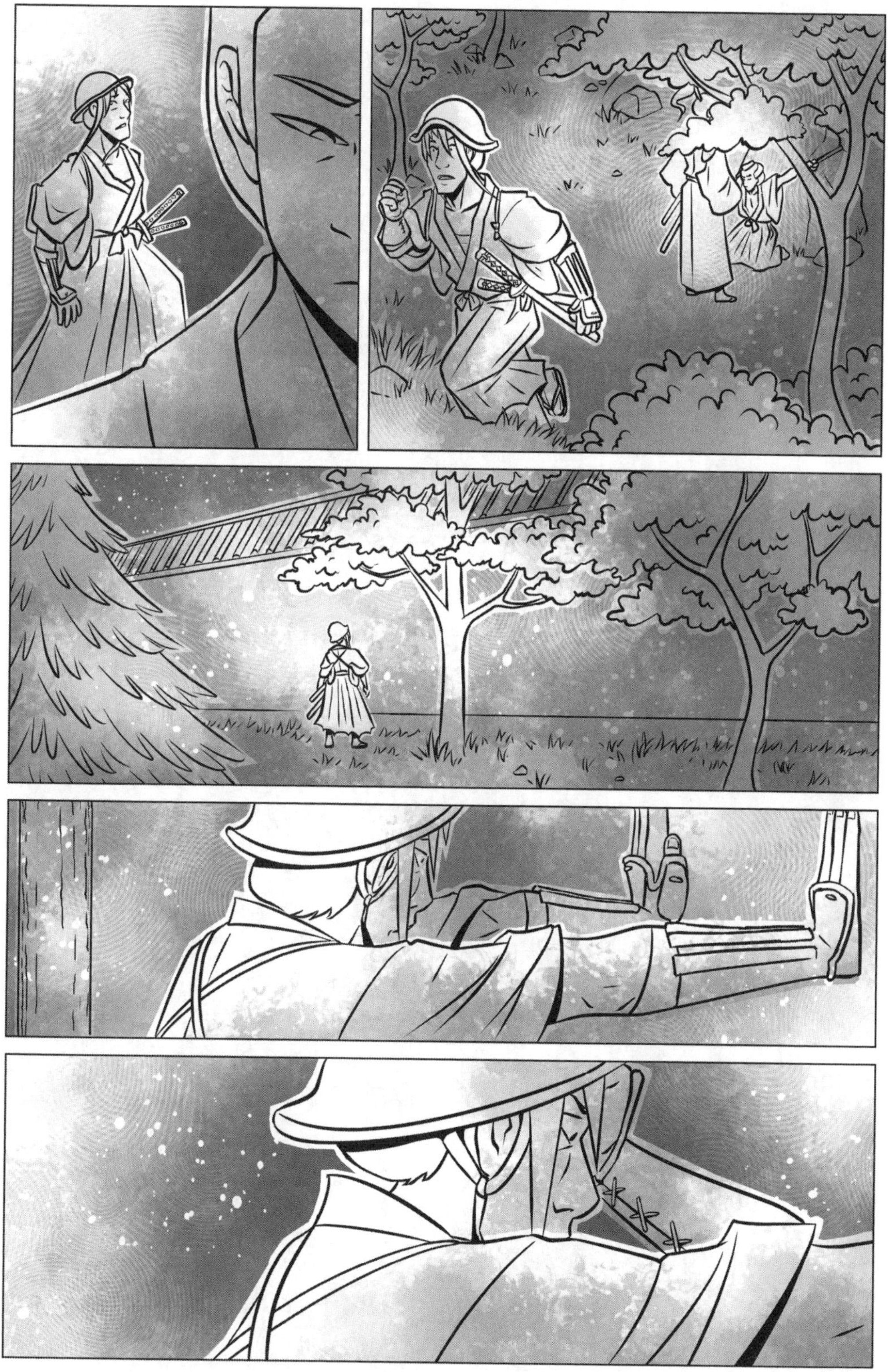

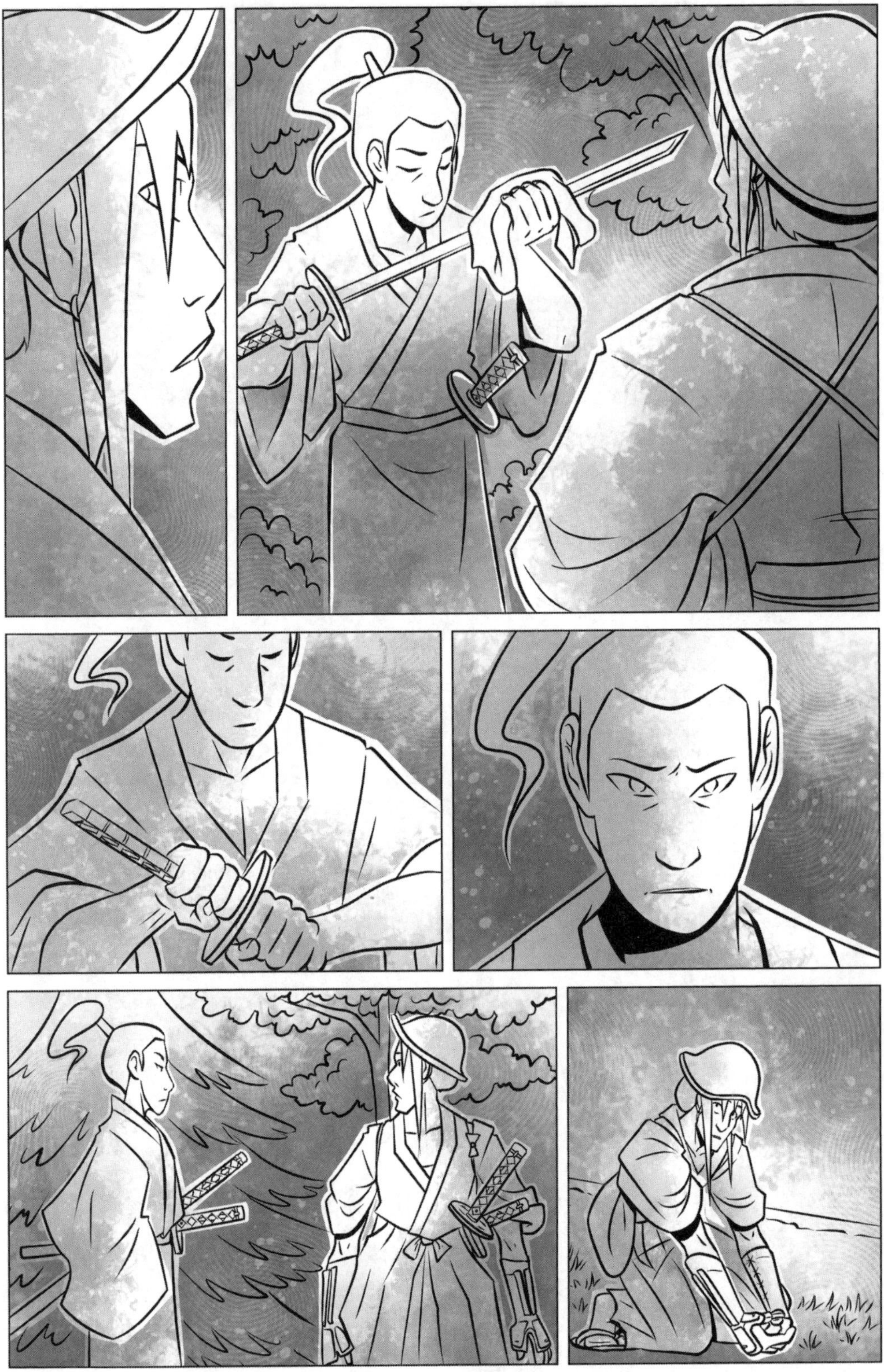

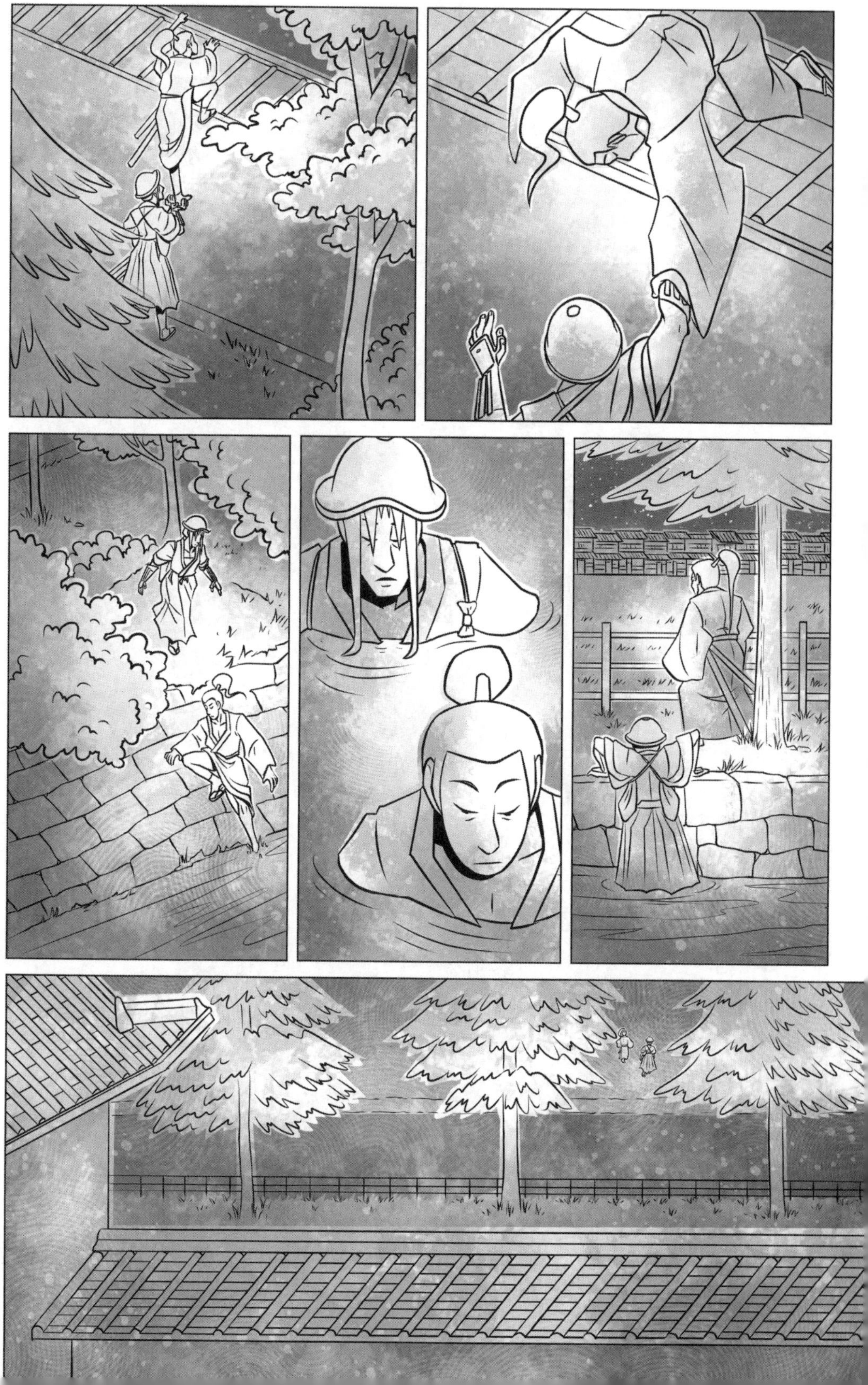

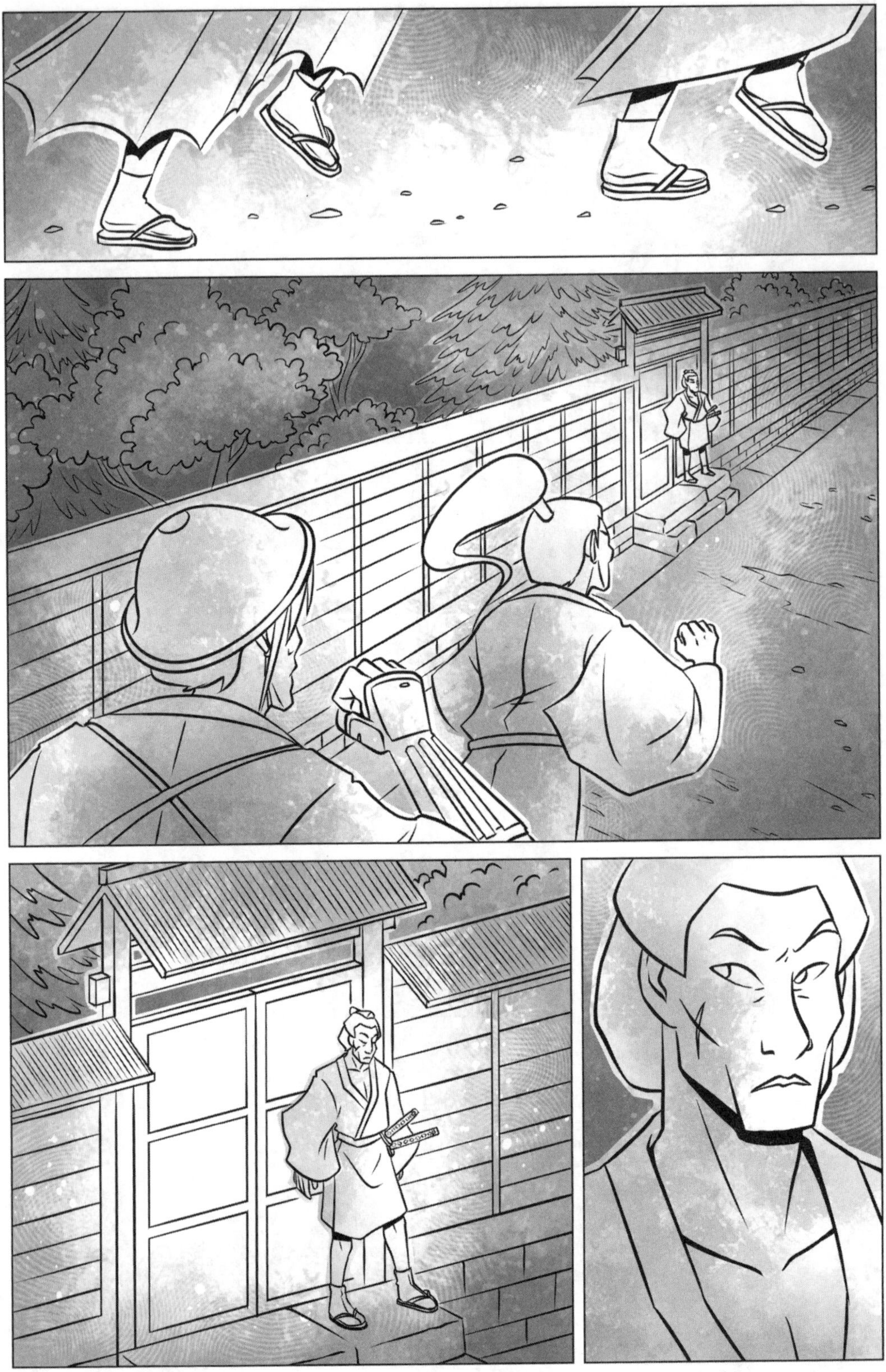

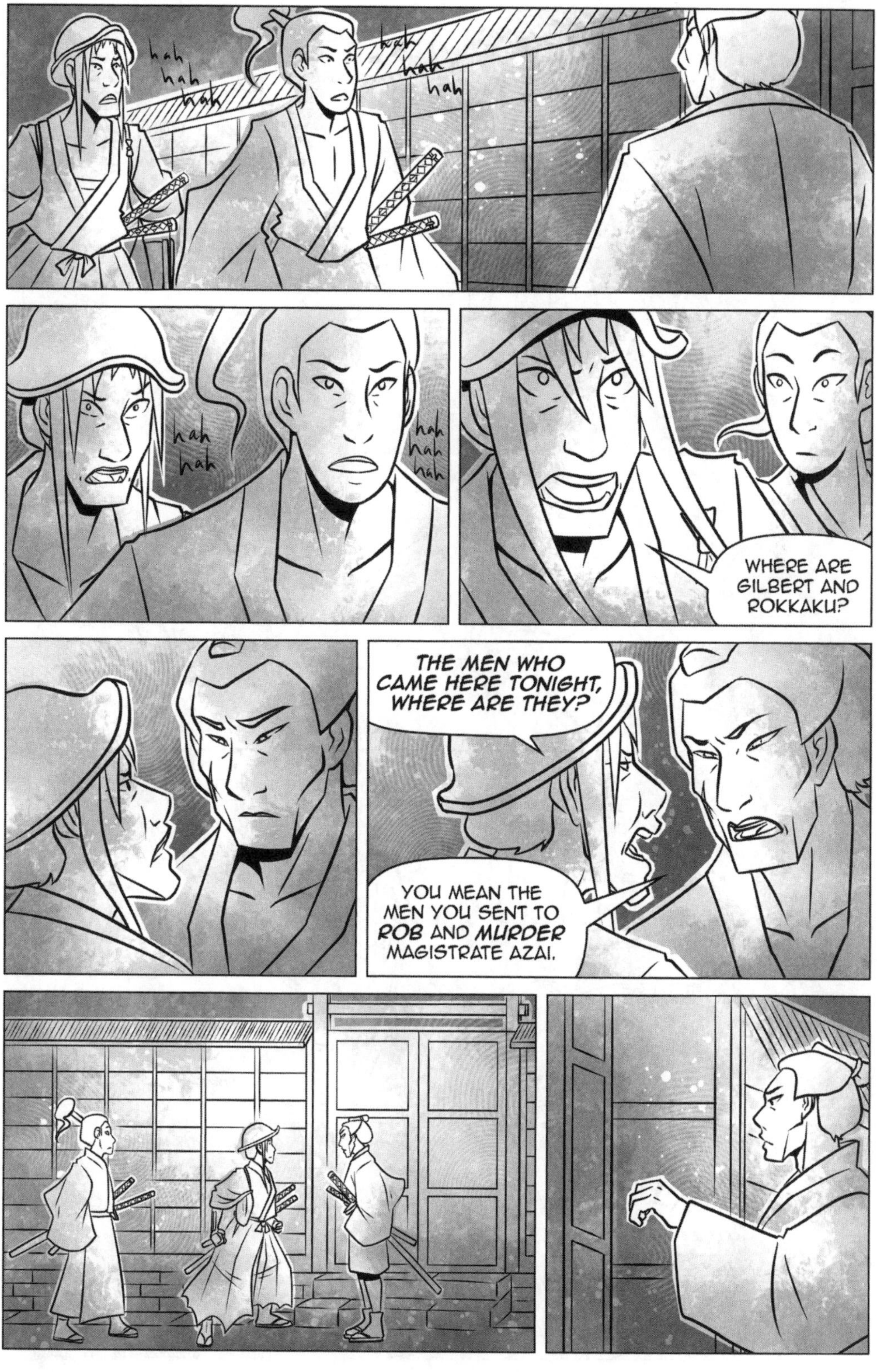
hah hah hah
hah hah hah
hah hah
hah hah hah
WHERE ARE GILBERT AND ROKKAKU?
THE MEN WHO CAME HERE TONIGHT, WHERE ARE THEY?
YOU MEAN THE MEN YOU SENT TO *ROB* AND *MURDER* MAGISTRATE AZAI.

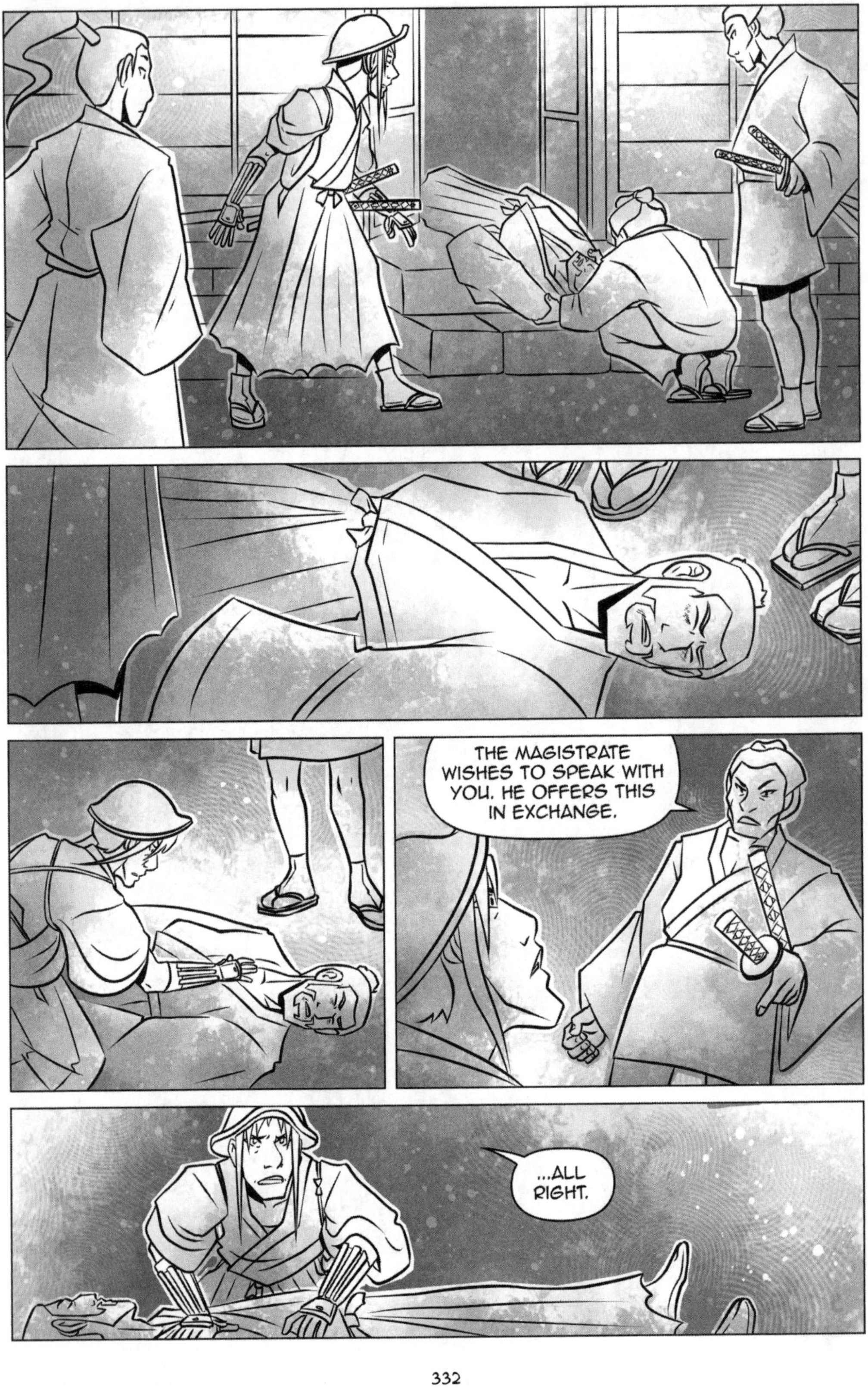
THE MAGISTRATE WISHES TO SPEAK WITH YOU. HE OFFERS THIS IN EXCHANGE.
...ALL RIGHT.

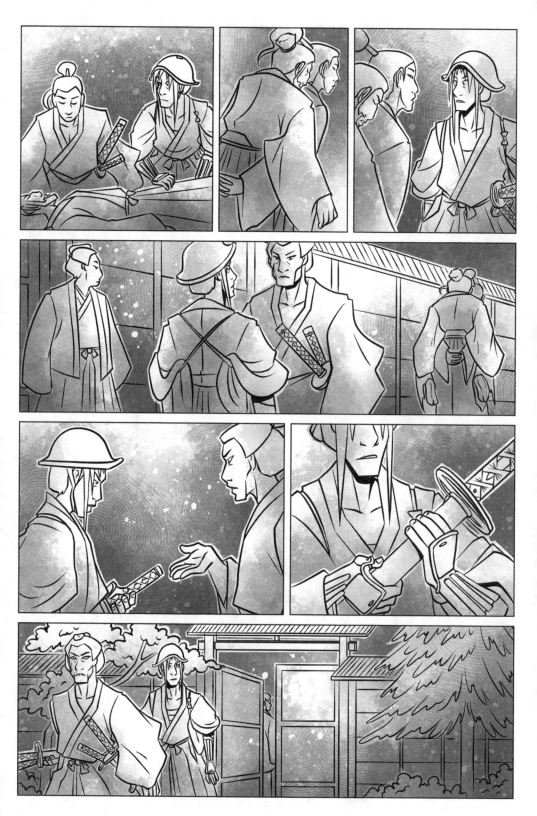

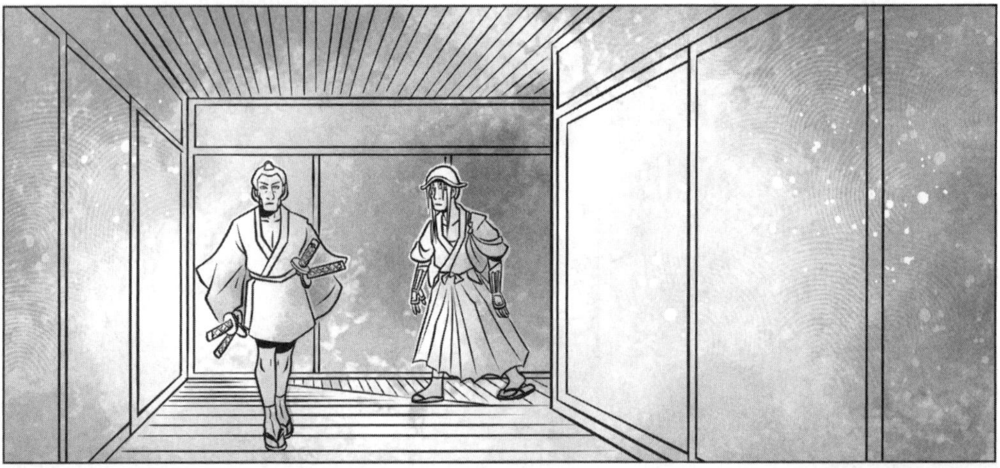
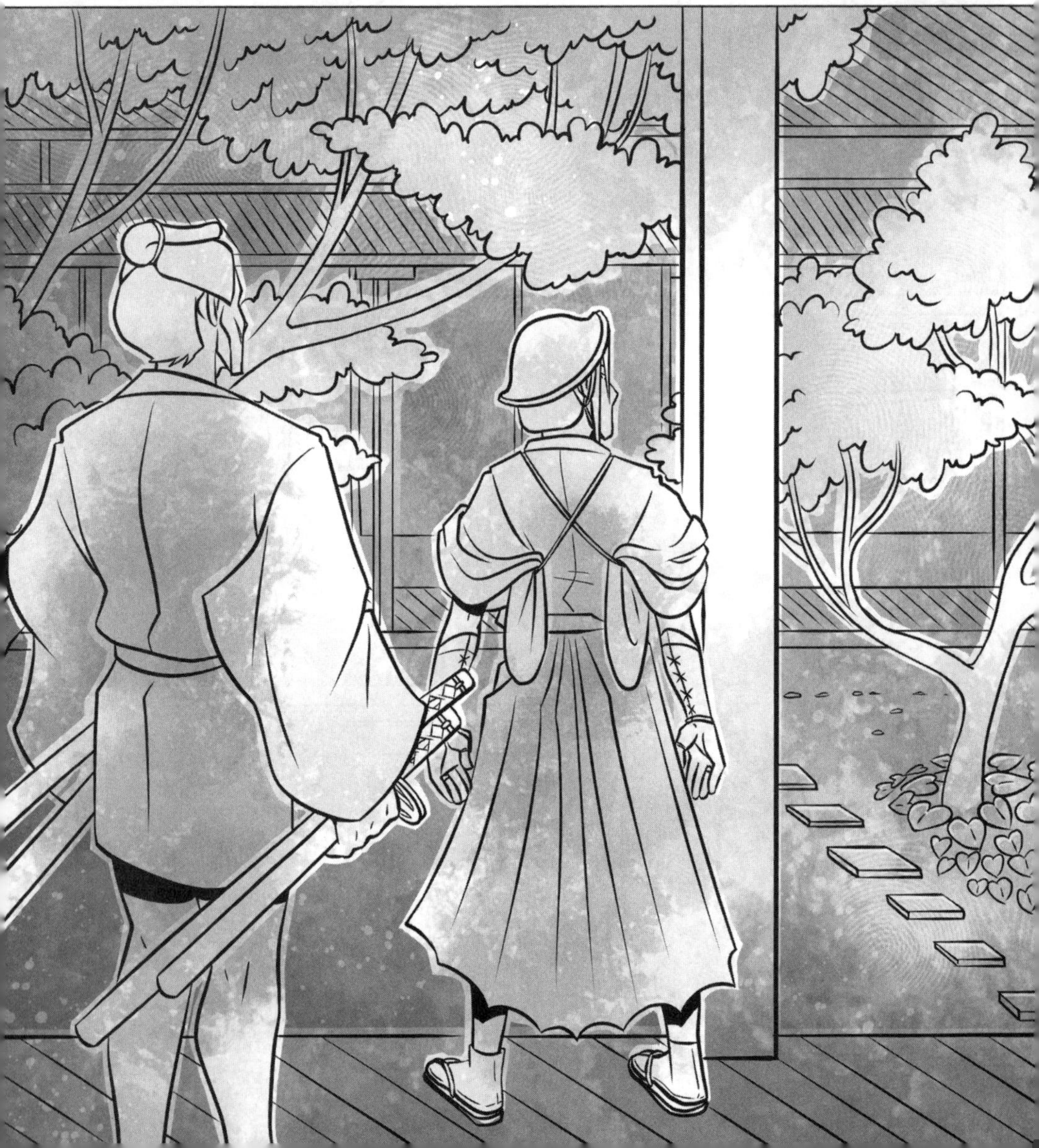

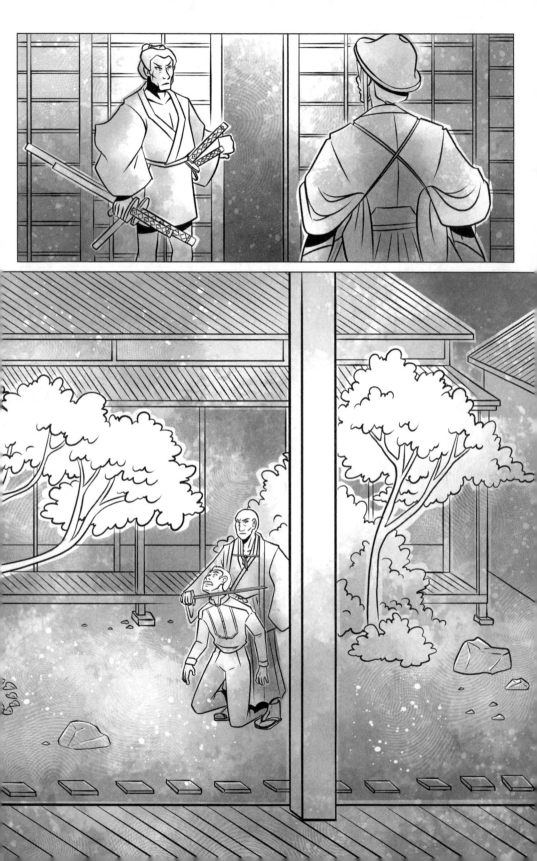

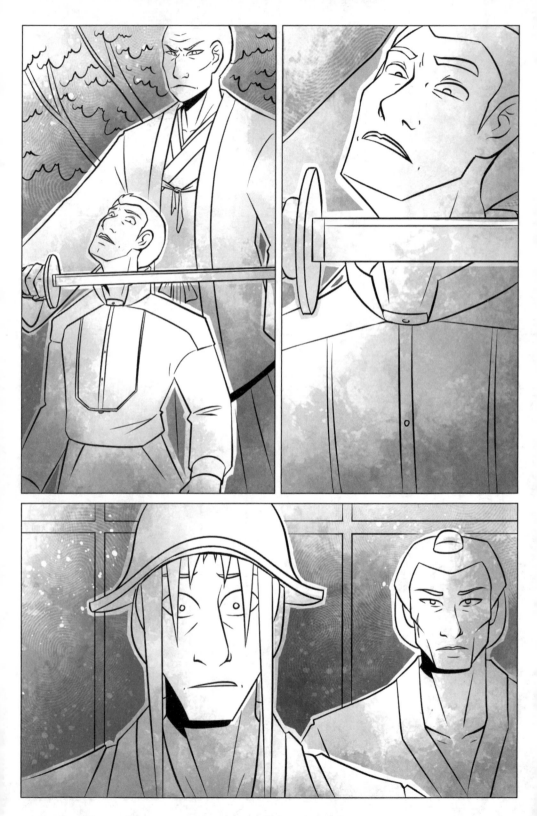

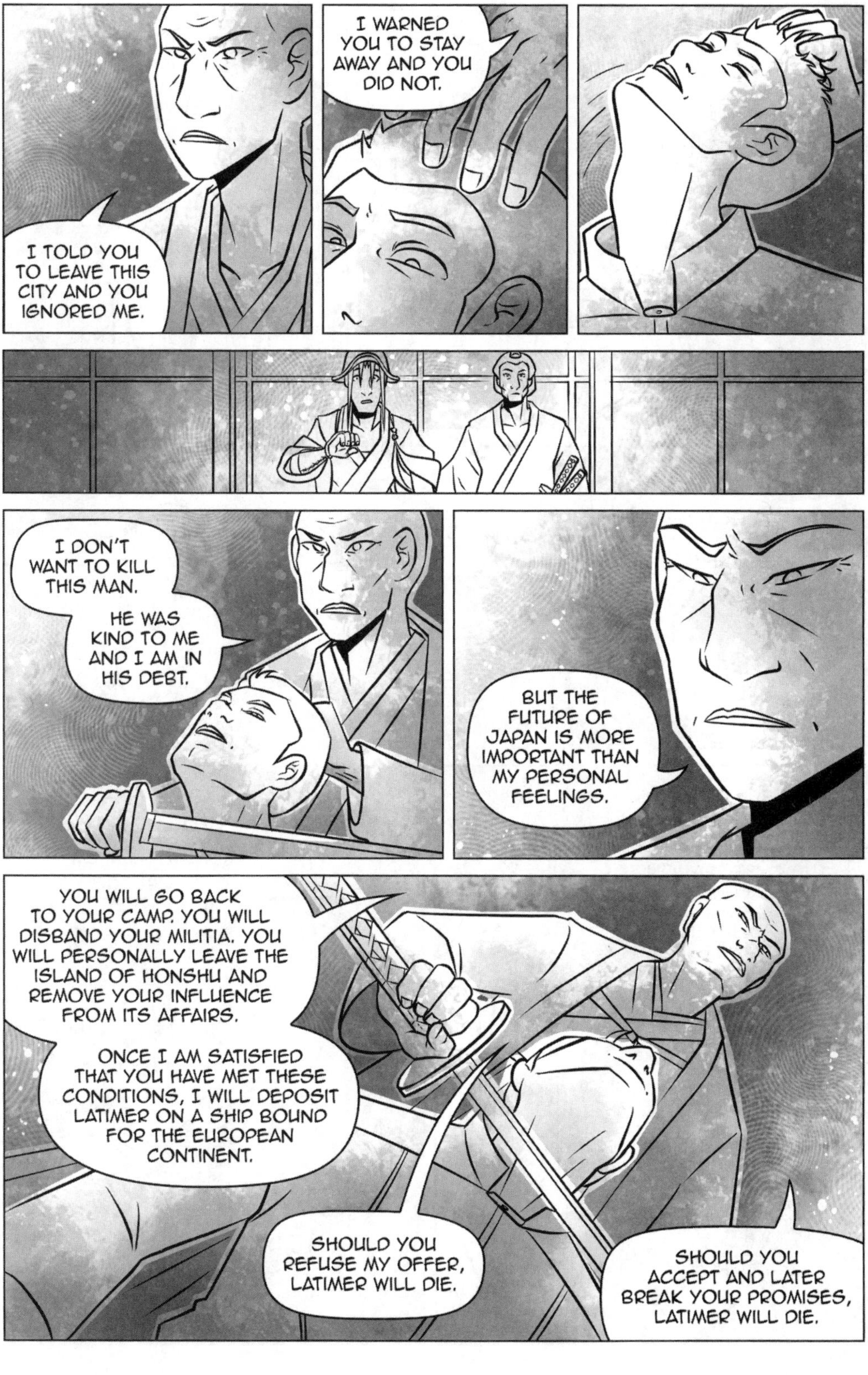
I TOLD YOU TO LEAVE THIS CITY AND YOU IGNORED ME.
I WARNED YOU TO STAY AWAY AND YOU DID NOT.
I DON'T WANT TO KILL THIS MAN.
HE WAS KIND TO ME AND I AM IN HIS DEBT.
BUT THE FUTURE OF JAPAN IS MORE IMPORTANT THAN MY PERSONAL FEELINGS.
YOU WILL GO BACK TO YOUR CAMP. YOU WILL DISBAND YOUR MILITIA. YOU WILL PERSONALLY LEAVE THE ISLAND OF HONSHU AND REMOVE YOUR INFLUENCE FROM ITS AFFAIRS.
ONCE I AM SATISFIED THAT YOU HAVE MET THESE CONDITIONS, I WILL DEPOSIT LATIMER ON A SHIP BOUND FOR THE EUROPEAN CONTINENT.
SHOULD YOU REFUSE MY OFFER, LATIMER WILL DIE.
SHOULD YOU ACCEPT AND LATER BREAK YOUR PROMISES, LATIMER WILL DIE.

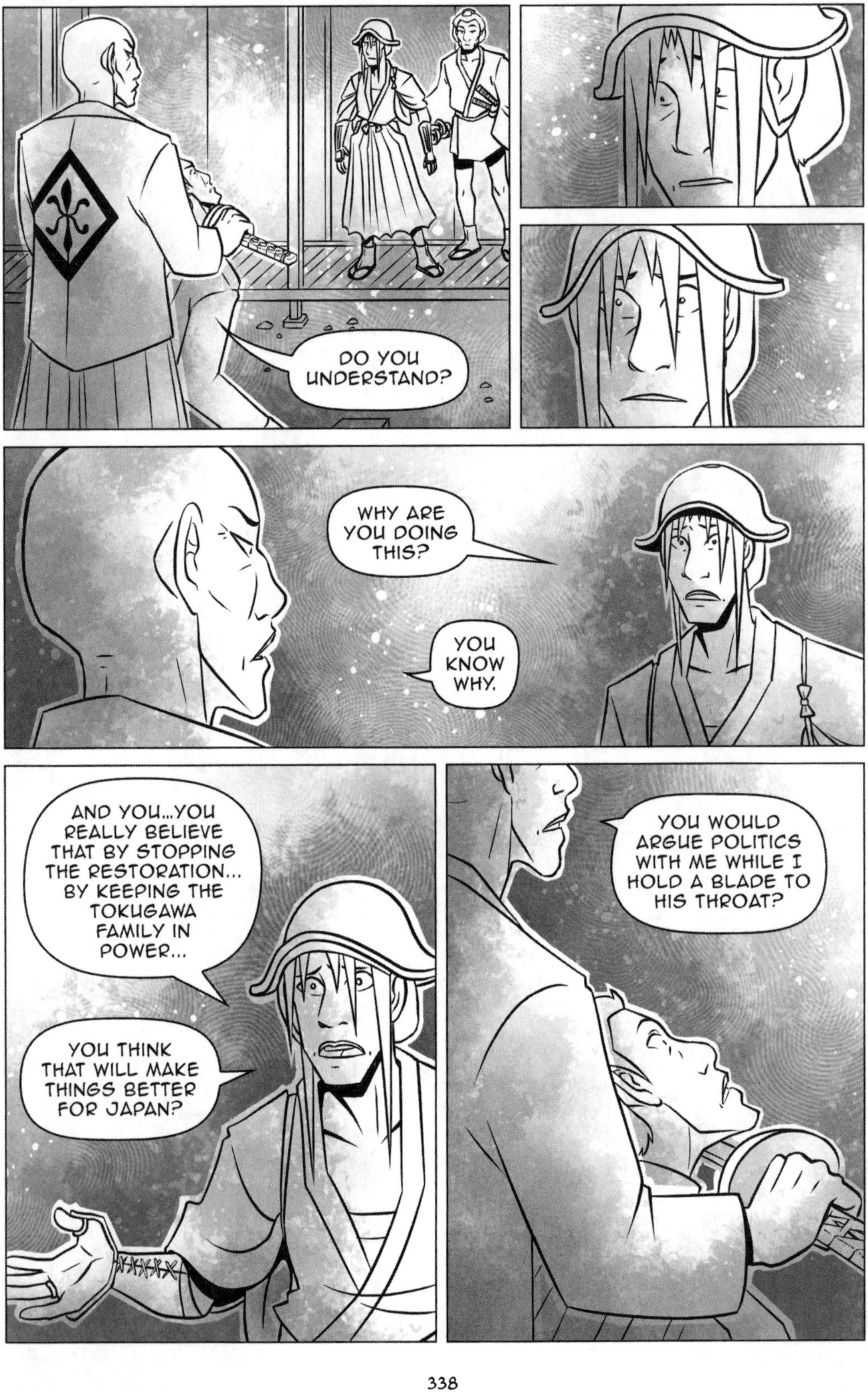
DO YOU UNDERSTAND?
WHY ARE YOU DOING THIS?
YOU KNOW WHY.
AND YOU...YOU REALLY BELIEVE THAT BY STOPPING THE RESTORATION... BY KEEPING THE TOKUGAWA FAMILY IN POWER...
YOU THINK THAT WILL MAKE THINGS BETTER FOR JAPAN?
YOU WOULD ARGUE POLITICS WITH ME WHILE I HOLD A BLADE TO HIS THROAT?

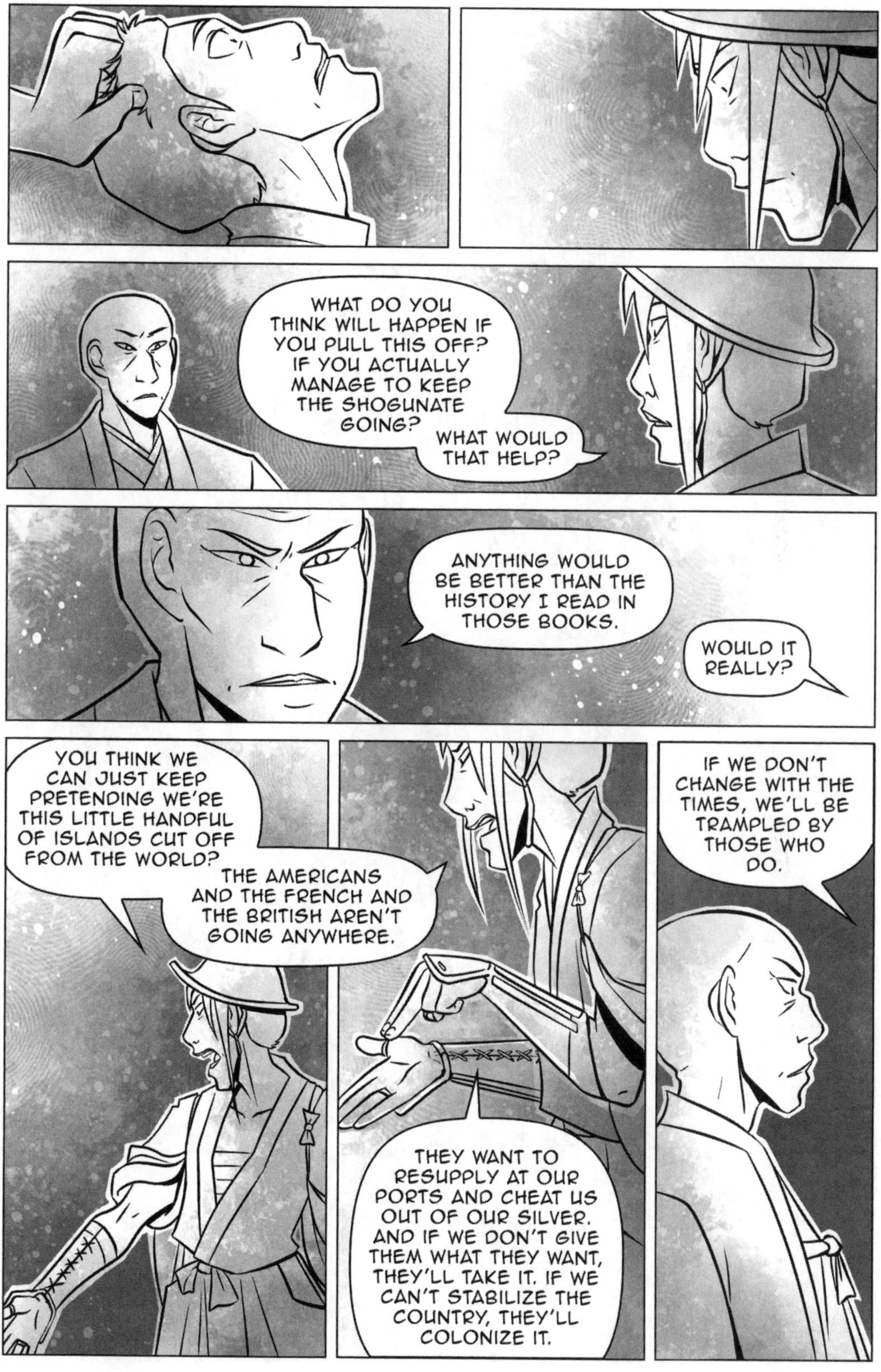

WHAT DO YOU THINK WILL HAPPEN IF YOU PULL THIS OFF? IF YOU ACTUALLY MANAGE TO KEEP THE SHOGUNATE GOING?
WHAT WOULD THAT HELP?
ANYTHING WOULD BE BETTER THAN THE HISTORY I READ IN THOSE BOOKS.
WOULD IT REALLY?
YOU THINK WE CAN JUST KEEP PRETENDING WE'RE THIS LITTLE HANDFUL OF ISLANDS CUT OFF FROM THE WORLD?
THE AMERICANS AND THE FRENCH AND THE BRITISH AREN'T GOING ANYWHERE.
THEY WANT TO RESUPPLY AT OUR PORTS AND CHEAT US OUT OF OUR SILVER. AND IF WE DON'T GIVE THEM WHAT THEY WANT, THEY'LL TAKE IT. IF WE CAN'T STABILIZE THE COUNTRY, THEY'LL COLONIZE IT.
IF WE DON'T CHANGE WITH THE TIMES, WE'LL BE TRAMPLED BY THOSE WHO DO.

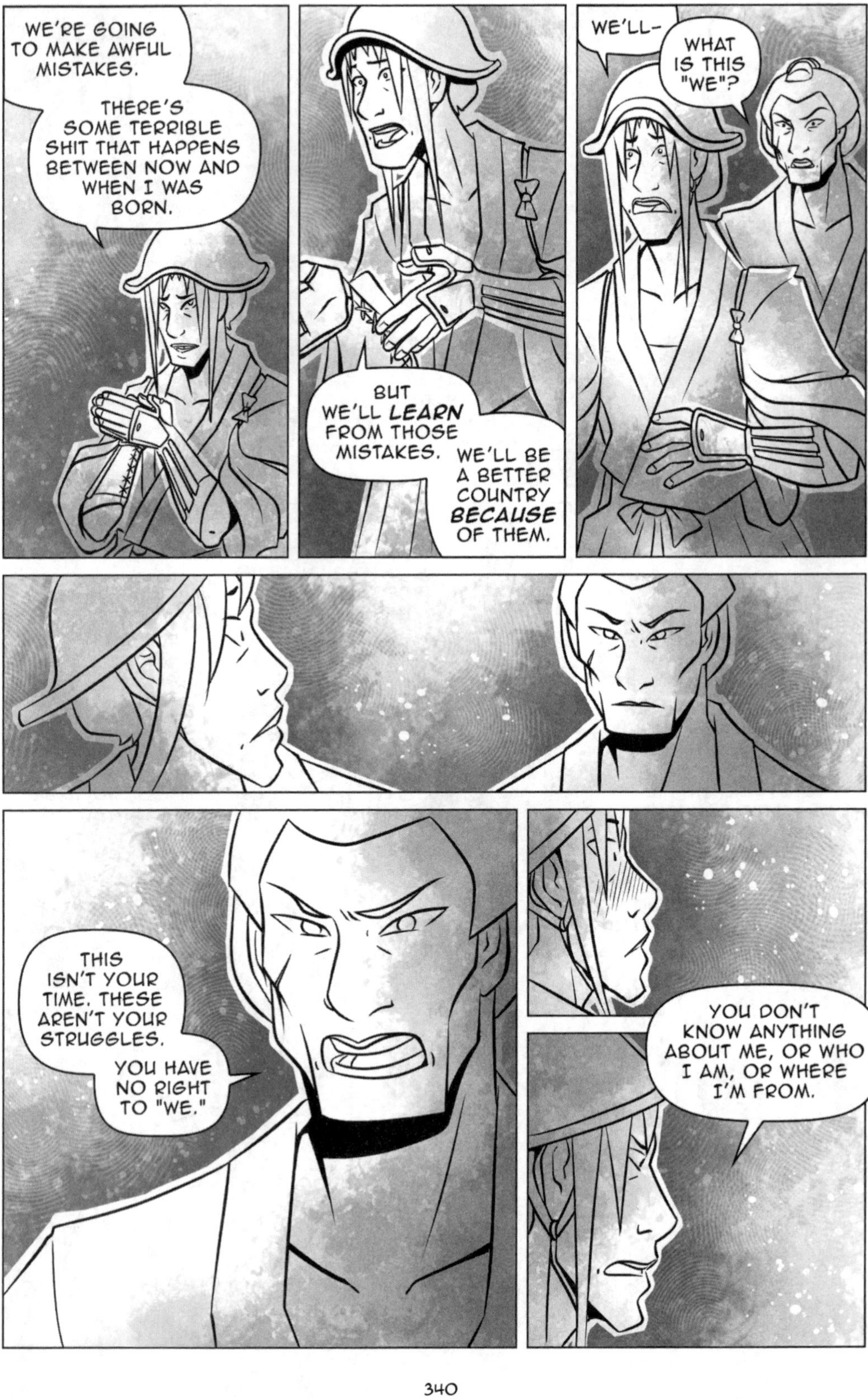
WE'RE GOING TO MAKE AWFUL MISTAKES.
THERE'S SOME TERRIBLE SHIT THAT HAPPENS BETWEEN NOW AND WHEN I WAS BORN.
BUT WE'LL ***LEARN*** FROM THOSE MISTAKES.
WE'LL BE A BETTER COUNTRY ***BECAUSE*** OF THEM.
WE'LL-
WHAT IS THIS "WE"?
THIS ISN'T YOUR TIME. THESE AREN'T YOUR STRUGGLES.
YOU HAVE NO RIGHT TO "WE."
YOU DON'T KNOW ANYTHING ABOUT ME, OR WHO I AM, OR WHERE I'M FROM.

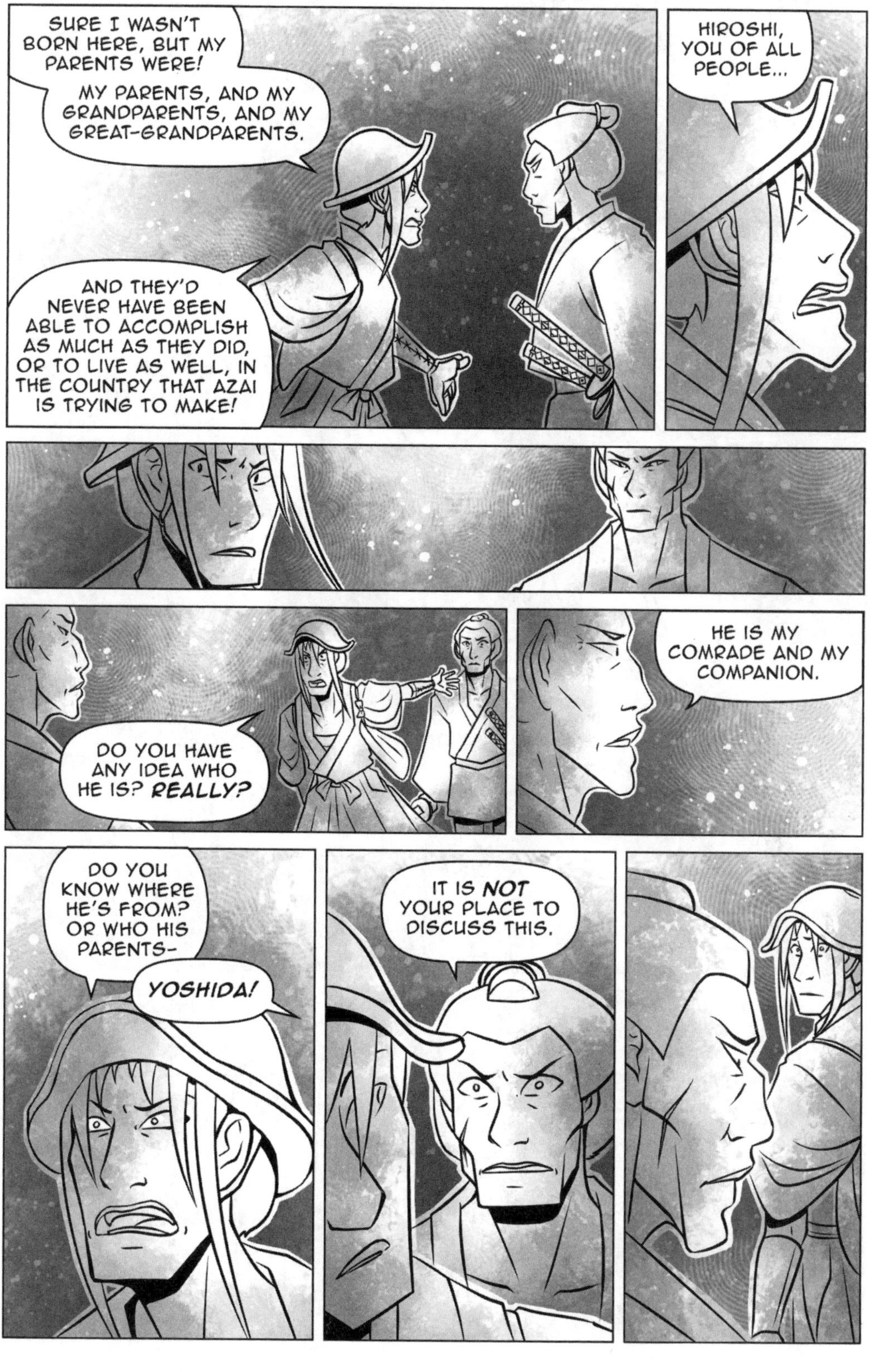
SURE I WASN'T BORN HERE, BUT MY PARENTS WERE!
MY PARENTS, AND MY GRANDPARENTS, AND MY GREAT-GRANDPARENTS.
AND THEY'D NEVER HAVE BEEN ABLE TO ACCOMPLISH AS MUCH AS THEY DID, OR TO LIVE AS WELL, IN THE COUNTRY THAT AZAI IS TRYING TO MAKE!
HIROSHI, YOU OF ALL PEOPLE...
DO YOU HAVE ANY IDEA WHO HE IS? *REALLY?*
HE IS MY COMRADE AND MY COMPANION.
DO YOU KNOW WHERE HE'S FROM? OR WHO HIS PARENTS-
*YOSHIDA!*
IT IS *NOT* YOUR PLACE TO DISCUSS THIS.

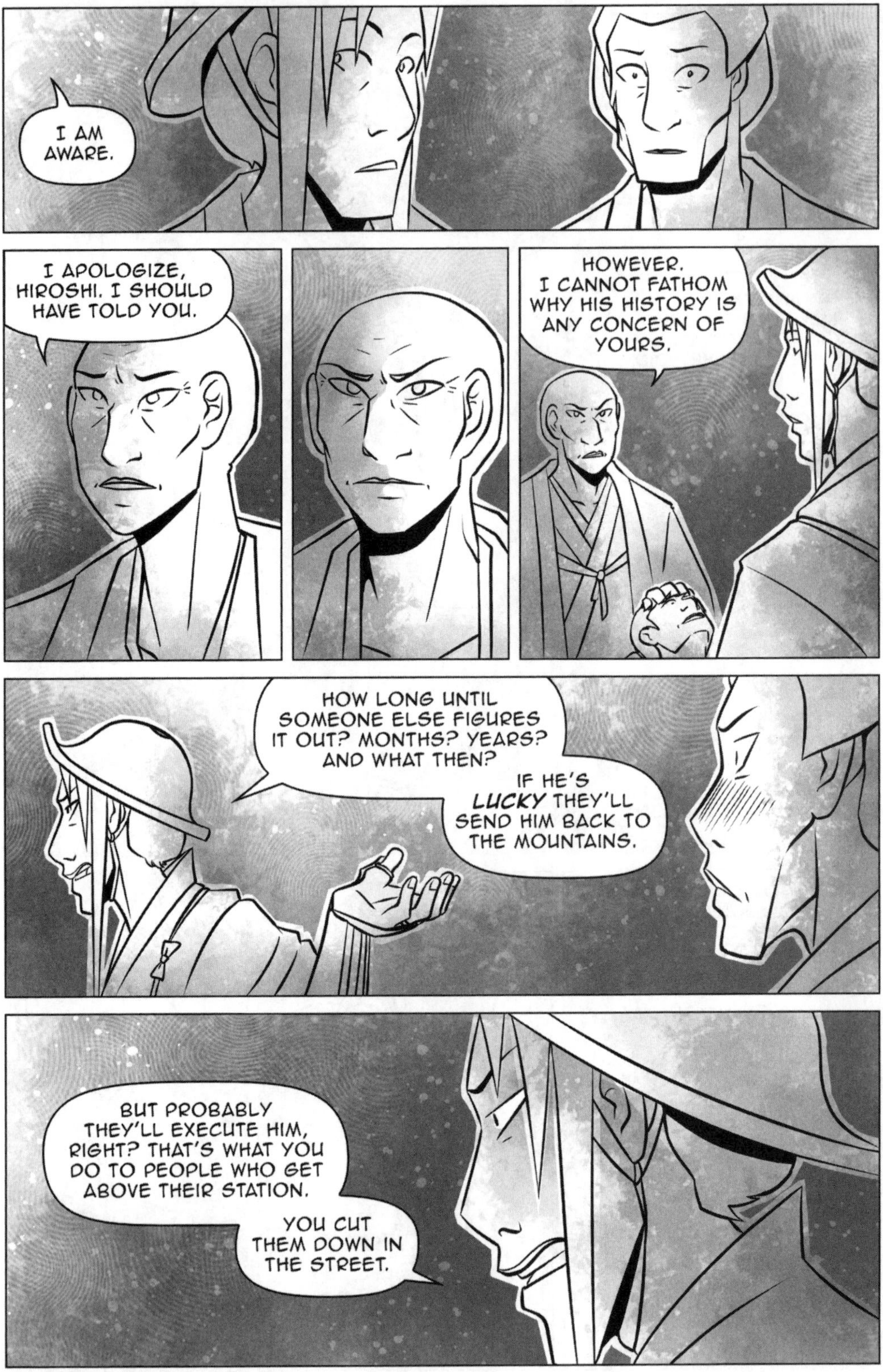
I AM AWARE.
I APOLOGIZE, HIROSHI. I SHOULD HAVE TOLD YOU.
HOWEVER. I CANNOT FATHOM WHY HIS HISTORY IS ANY CONCERN OF YOURS.
HOW LONG UNTIL SOMEONE ELSE FIGURES IT OUT? MONTHS? YEARS? AND WHAT THEN?
IF HE'S *LUCKY* THEY'LL SEND HIM BACK TO THE MOUNTAINS.
BUT PROBABLY THEY'LL EXECUTE HIM, RIGHT? THAT'S WHAT YOU DO TO PEOPLE WHO GET ABOVE THEIR STATION.
YOU CUT THEM DOWN IN THE STREET.

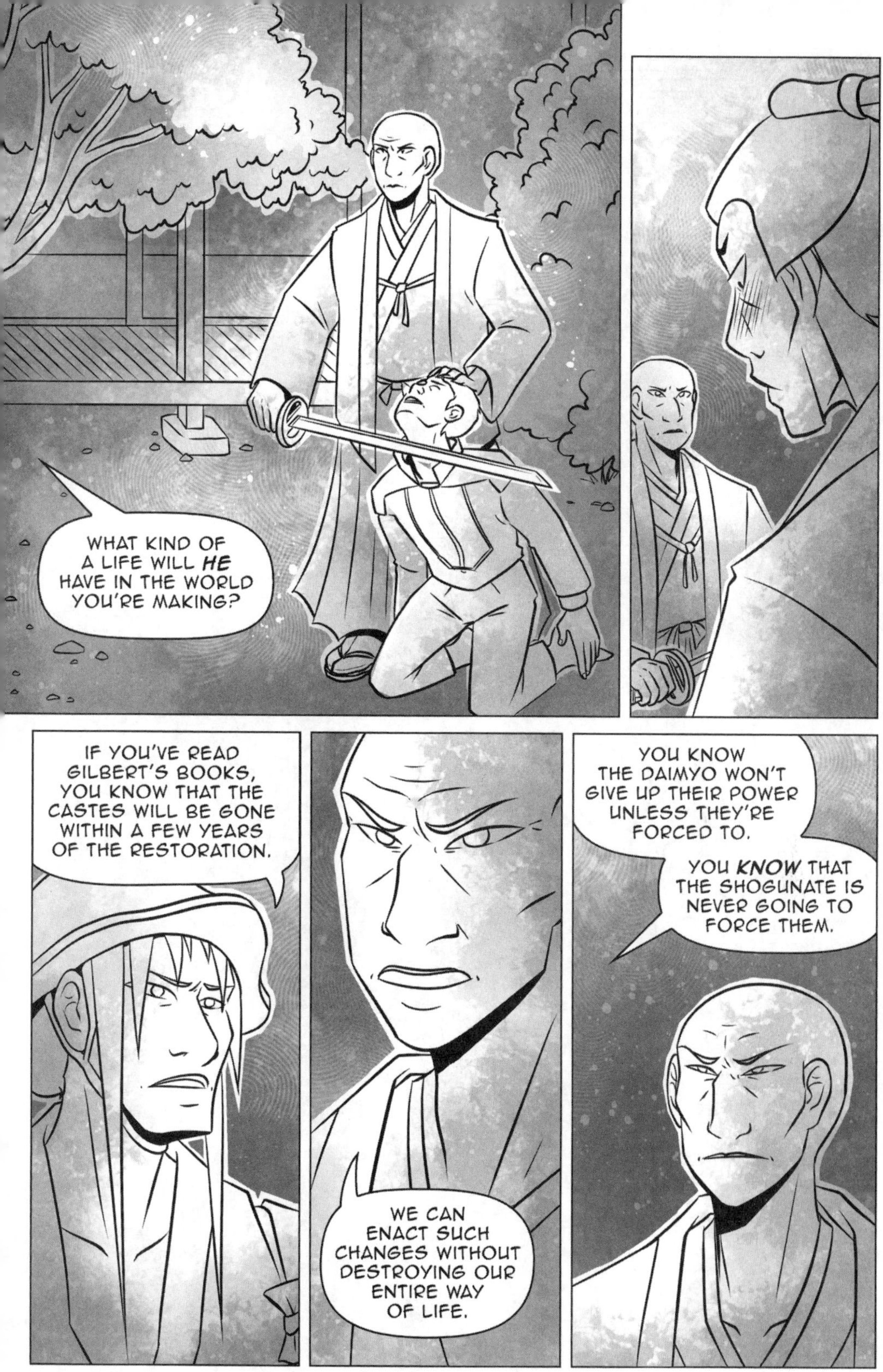
WHAT KIND OF A LIFE WILL **HE** HAVE IN THE WORLD YOU'RE MAKING?
IF YOU'VE READ GILBERT'S BOOKS, YOU KNOW THAT THE CASTES WILL BE GONE WITHIN A FEW YEARS OF THE RESTORATION.
WE CAN ENACT SUCH CHANGES WITHOUT DESTROYING OUR ENTIRE WAY OF LIFE.
YOU KNOW THE DAIMYO WON'T GIVE UP THEIR POWER UNLESS THEY'RE FORCED TO.
YOU **KNOW** THAT THE SHOGUNATE IS NEVER GOING TO FORCE THEM.

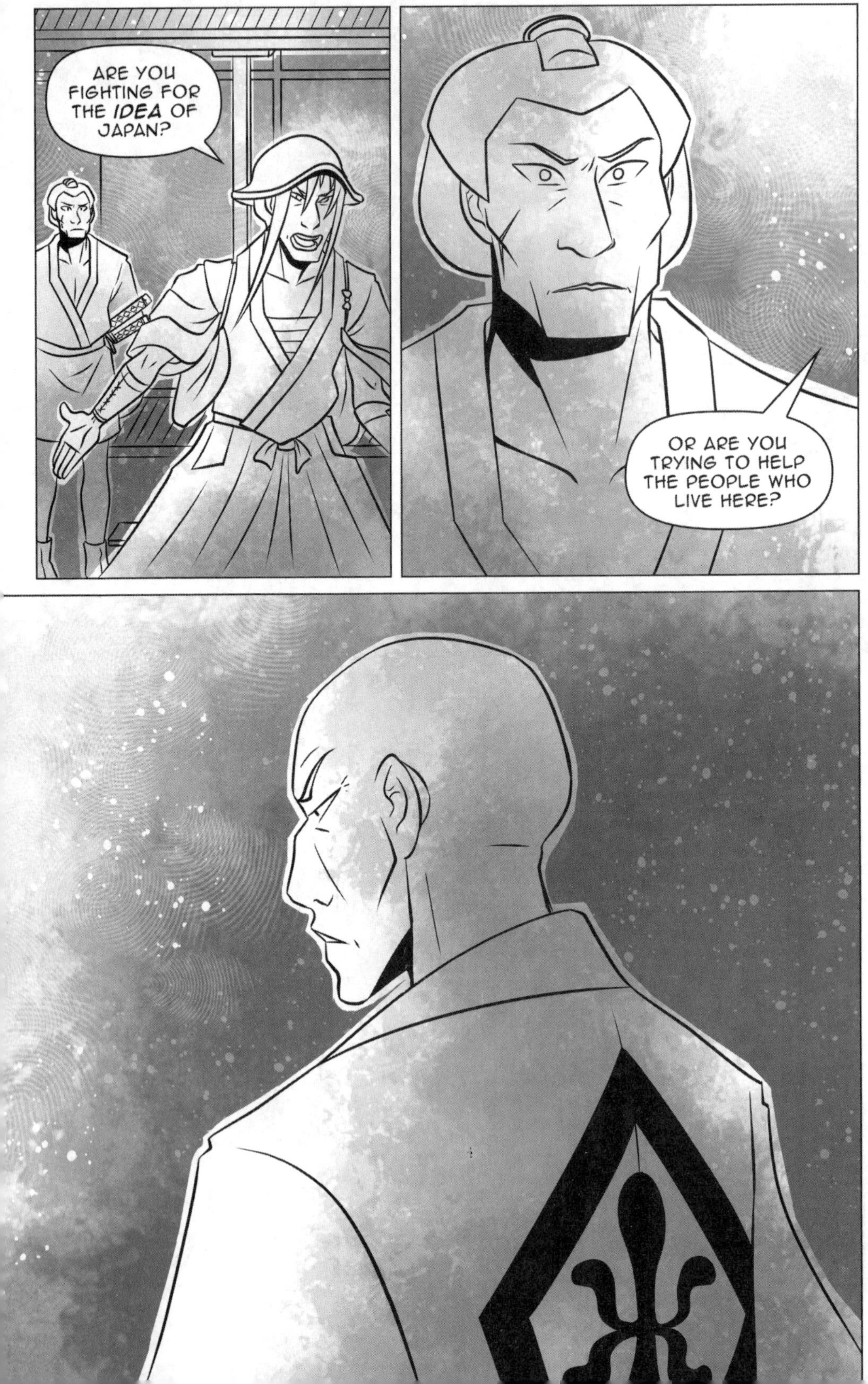
ARE YOU FIGHTING FOR THE *IDEA* OF JAPAN?
OR ARE YOU TRYING TO HELP THE PEOPLE WHO LIVE HERE?

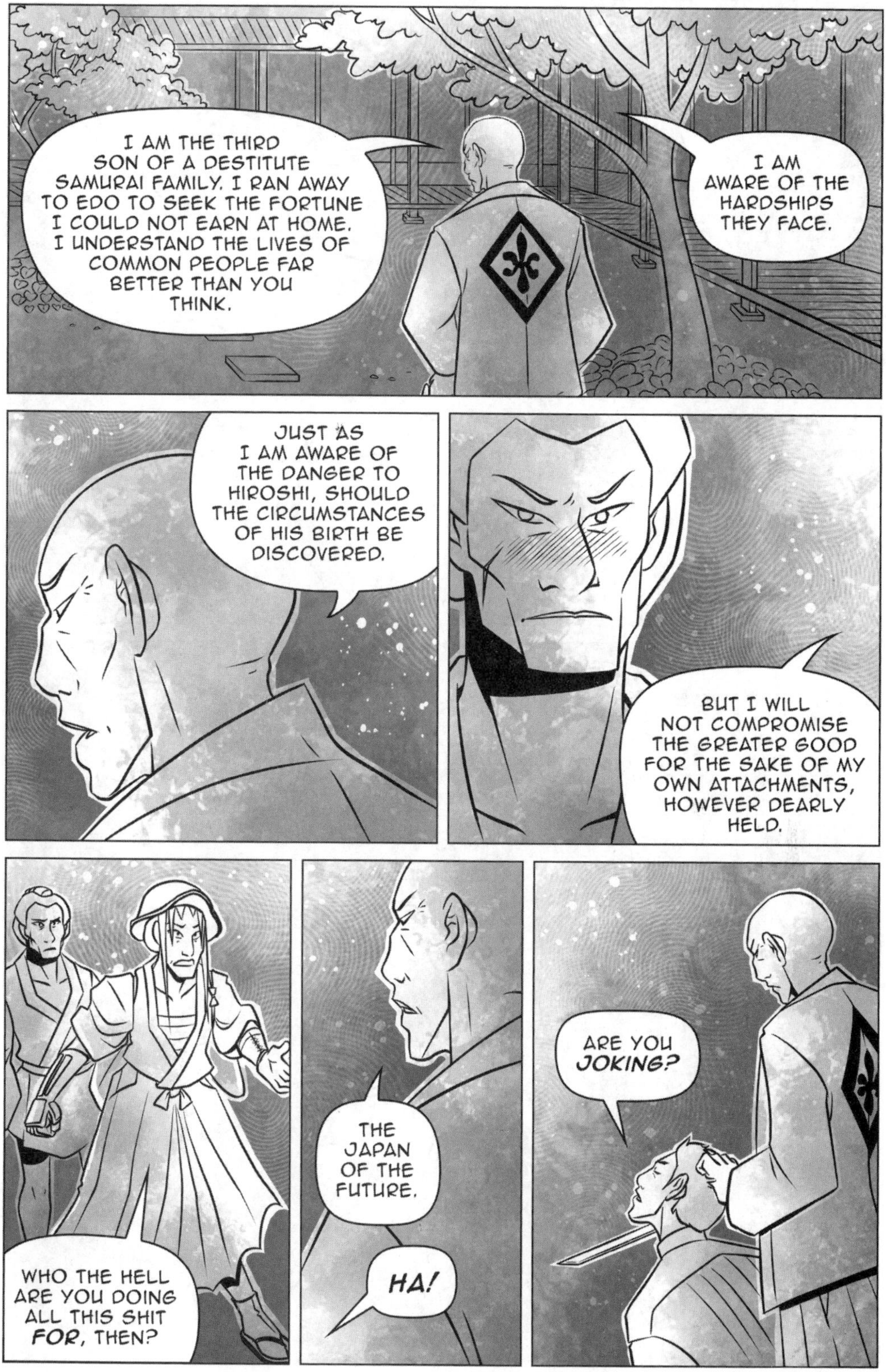
I AM THE THIRD SON OF A DESTITUTE SAMURAI FAMILY. I RAN AWAY TO EDO TO SEEK THE FORTUNE I COULD NOT EARN AT HOME. I UNDERSTAND THE LIVES OF COMMON PEOPLE FAR BETTER THAN YOU THINK.
I AM AWARE OF THE HARDSHIPS THEY FACE.
JUST AS I AM AWARE OF THE DANGER TO HIROSHI, SHOULD THE CIRCUMSTANCES OF HIS BIRTH BE DISCOVERED.
BUT I WILL NOT COMPROMISE THE GREATER GOOD FOR THE SAKE OF MY OWN ATTACHMENTS, HOWEVER DEARLY HELD.
WHO THE HELL ARE YOU DOING ALL THIS SHIT *FOR*, THEN?
THE JAPAN OF THE FUTURE.
*HA!*
ARE YOU *JOKING?*

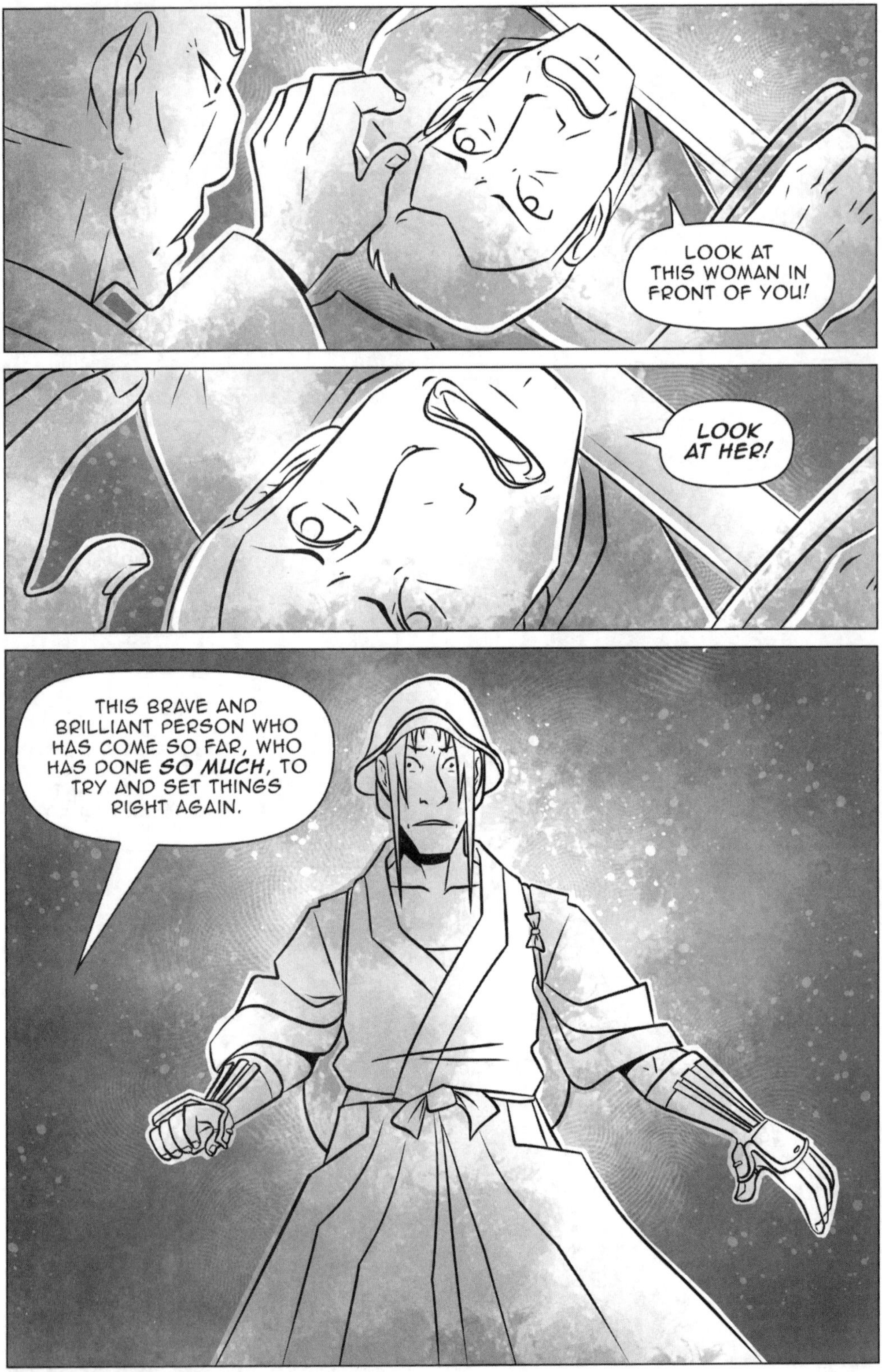
LOOK AT THIS WOMAN IN FRONT OF YOU!
LOOK AT HER!
THIS BRAVE AND BRILLIANT PERSON WHO HAS COME SO FAR, WHO HAS DONE SO MUCH, TO TRY AND SET THINGS RIGHT AGAIN.

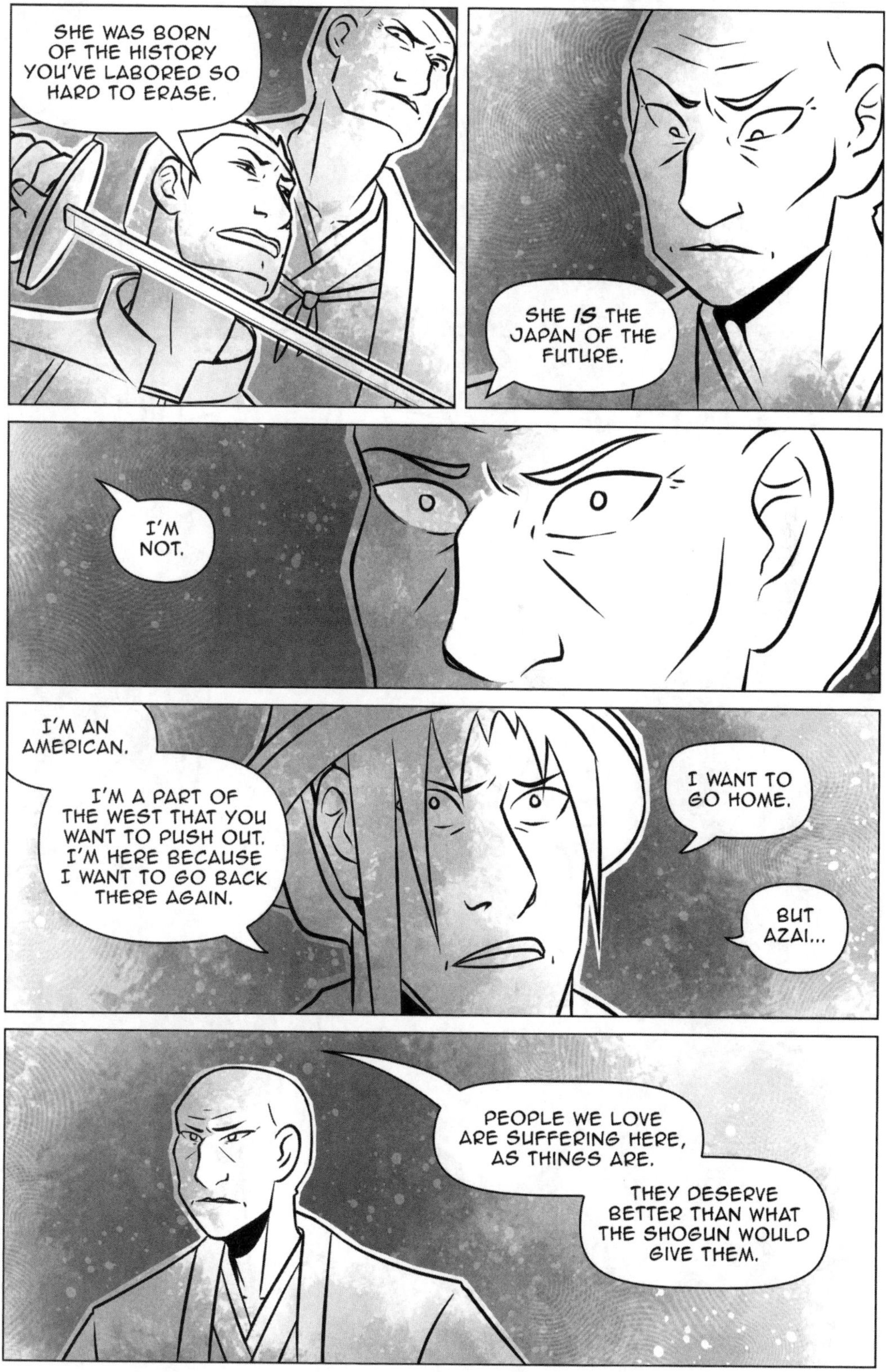
SHE WAS BORN OF THE HISTORY YOU'VE LABORED SO HARD TO ERASE.
SHE *IS* THE JAPAN OF THE FUTURE.
I'M NOT.
I'M AN AMERICAN.
I'M A PART OF THE WEST THAT YOU WANT TO PUSH OUT. I'M HERE BECAUSE I WANT TO GO BACK THERE AGAIN.
I WANT TO GO HOME.
BUT AZAI...
PEOPLE WE LOVE ARE SUFFERING HERE, AS THINGS ARE.
THEY DESERVE BETTER THAN WHAT THE SHOGUN WOULD GIVE THEM.

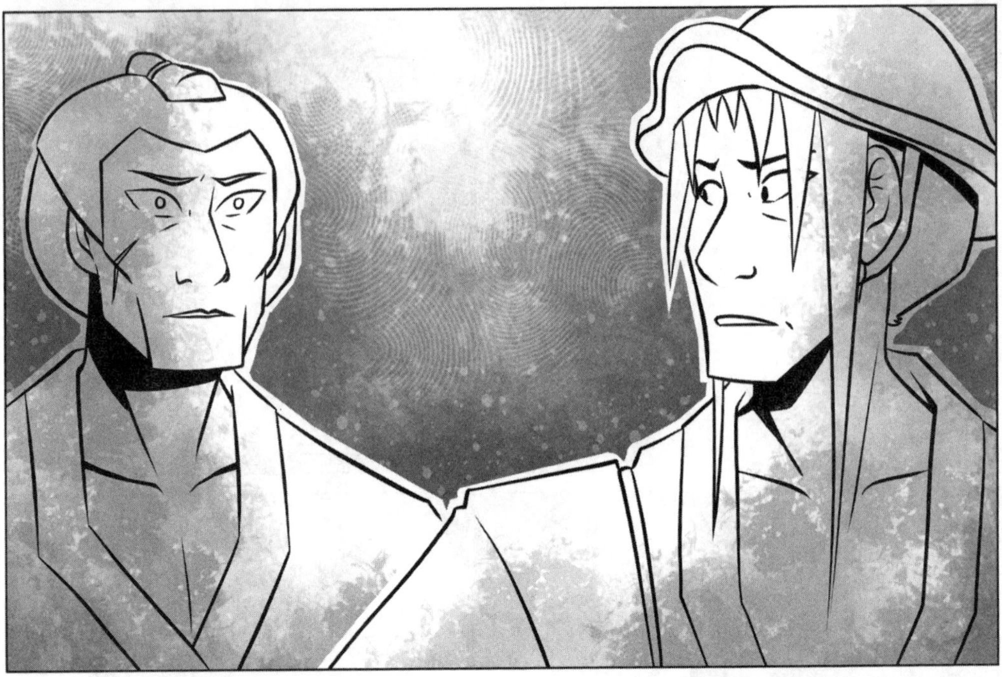

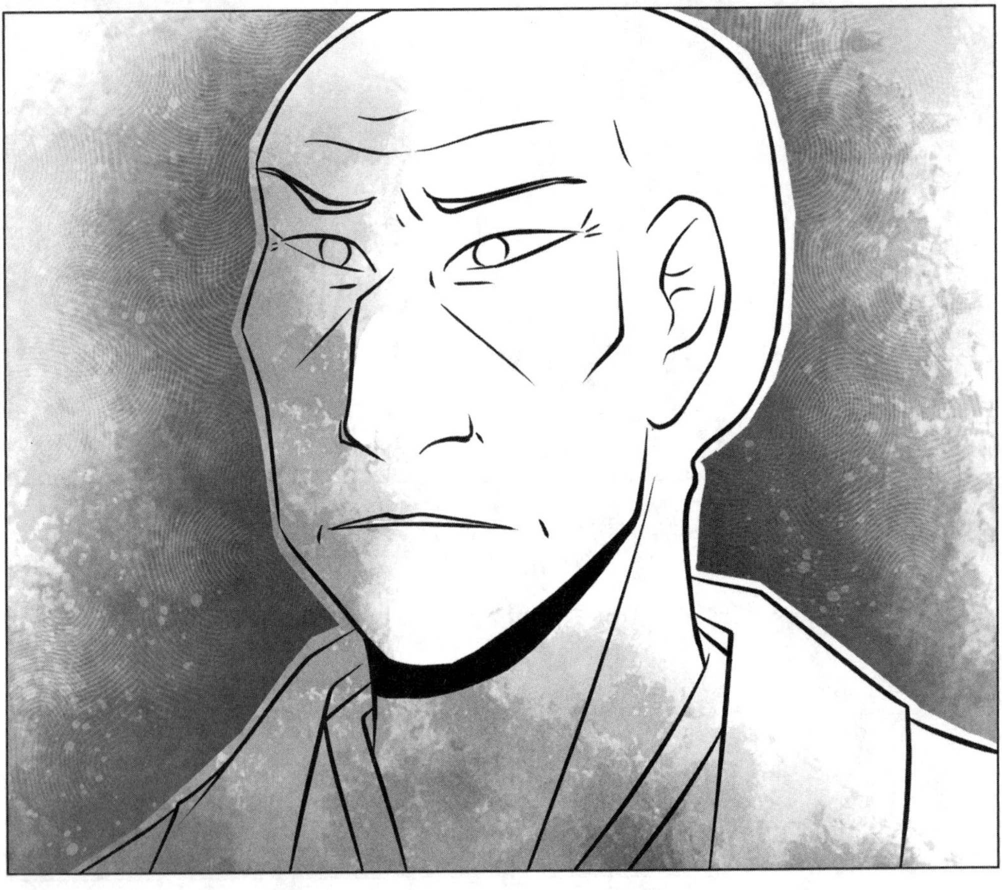

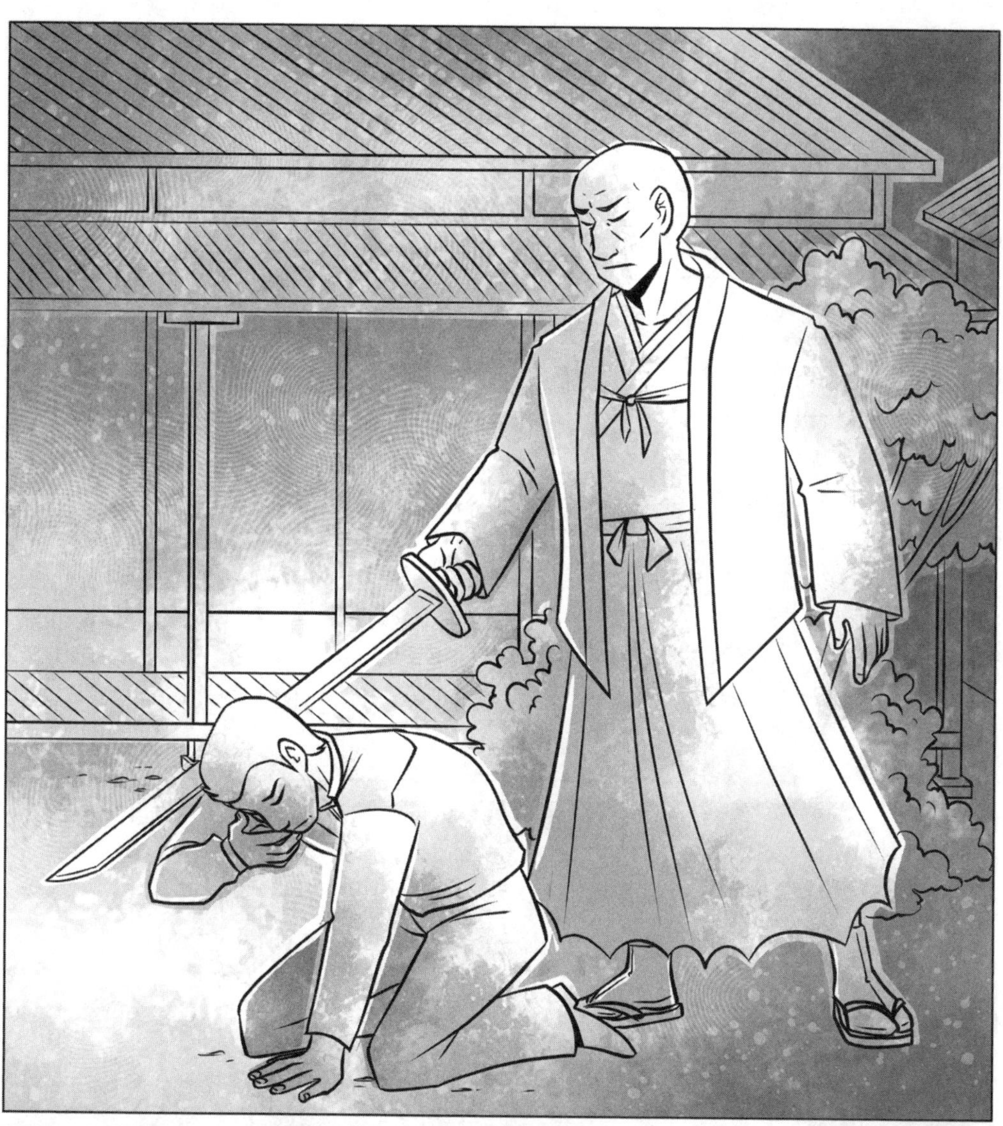

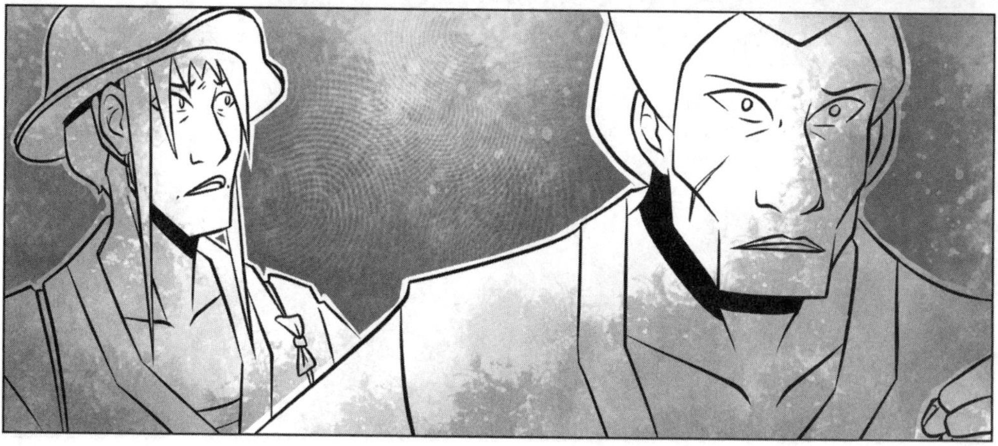

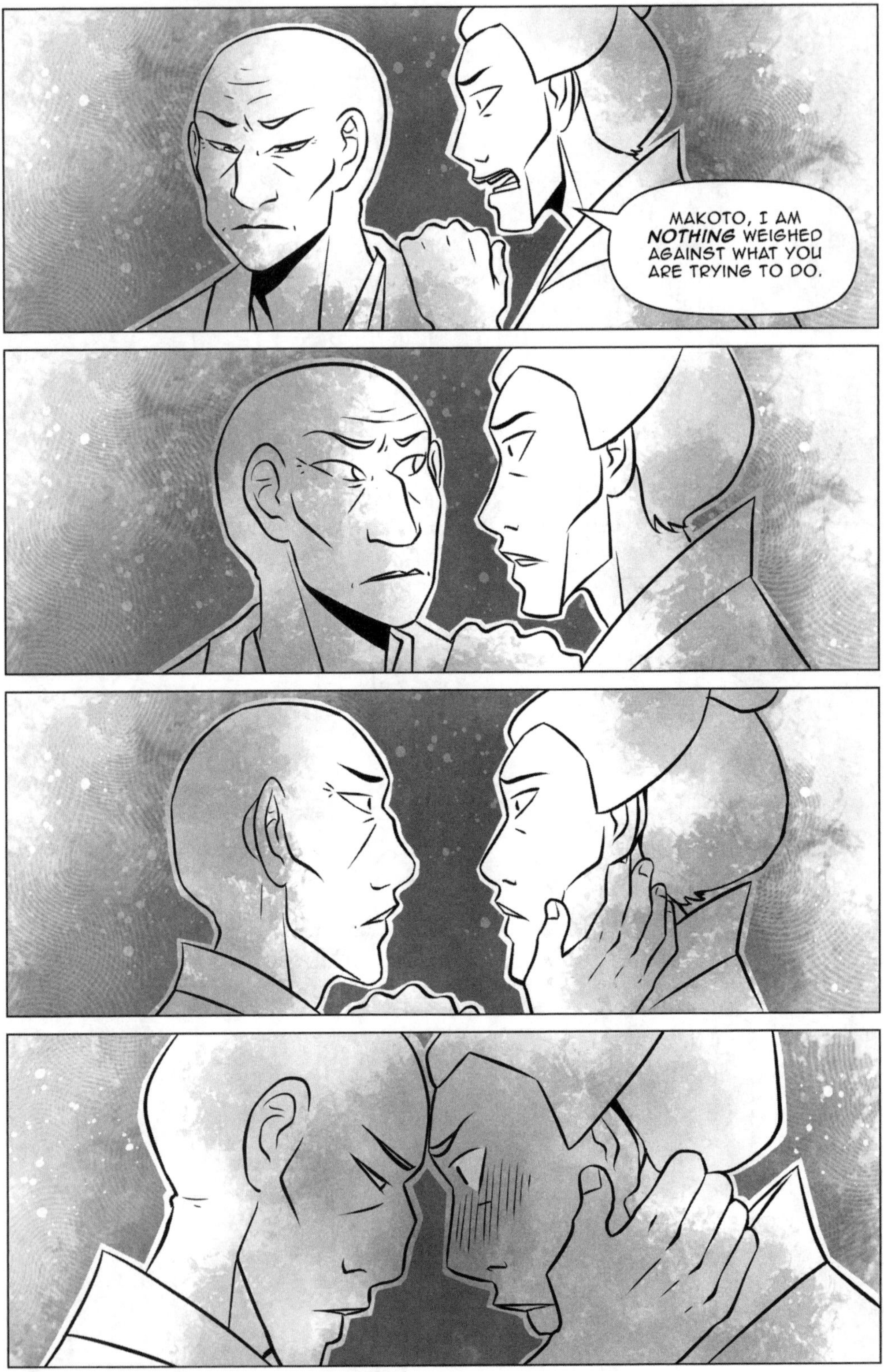
MAKOTO, I AM **NOTHING** WEIGHED AGAINST WHAT YOU ARE TRYING TO DO.

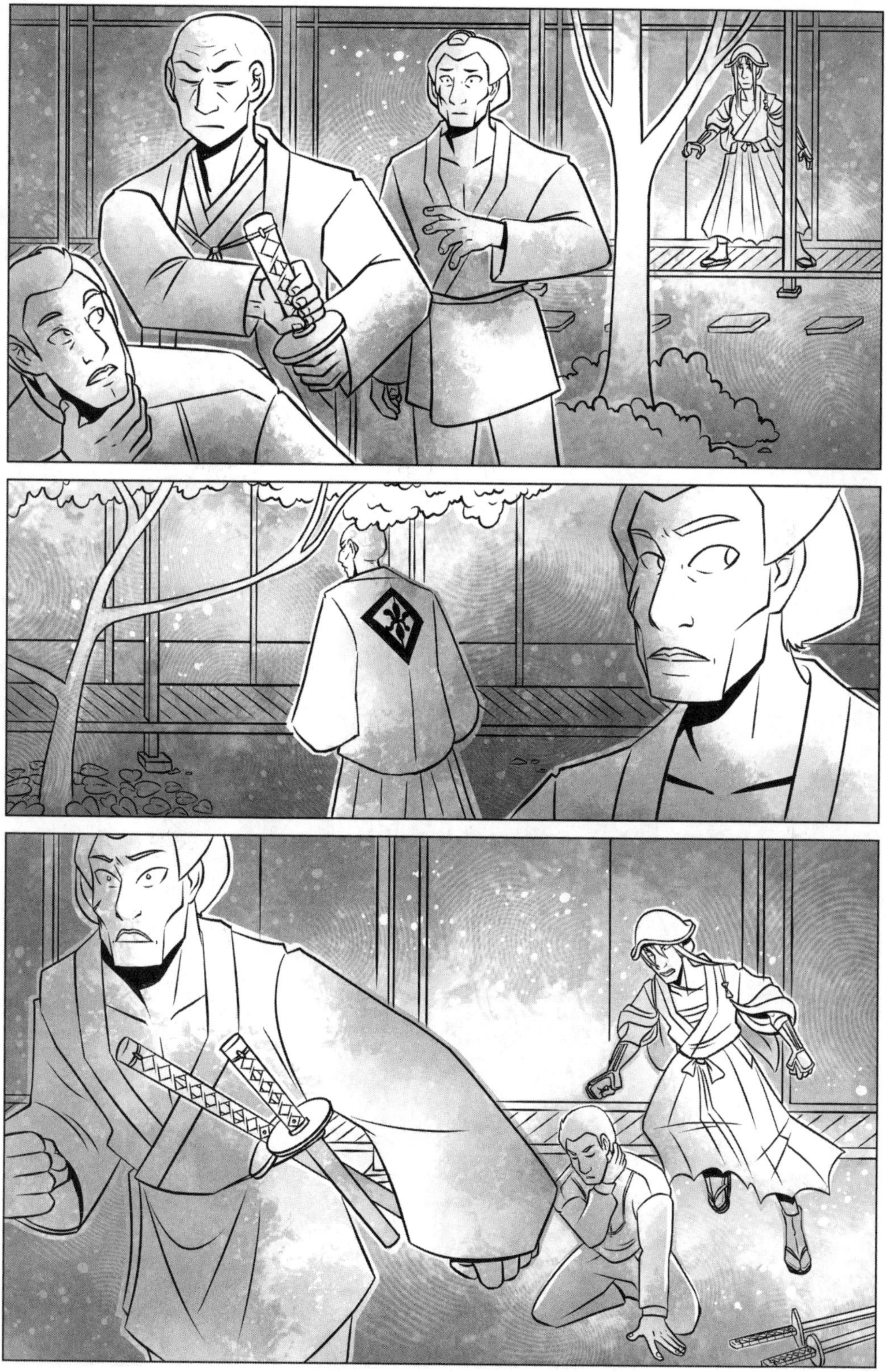

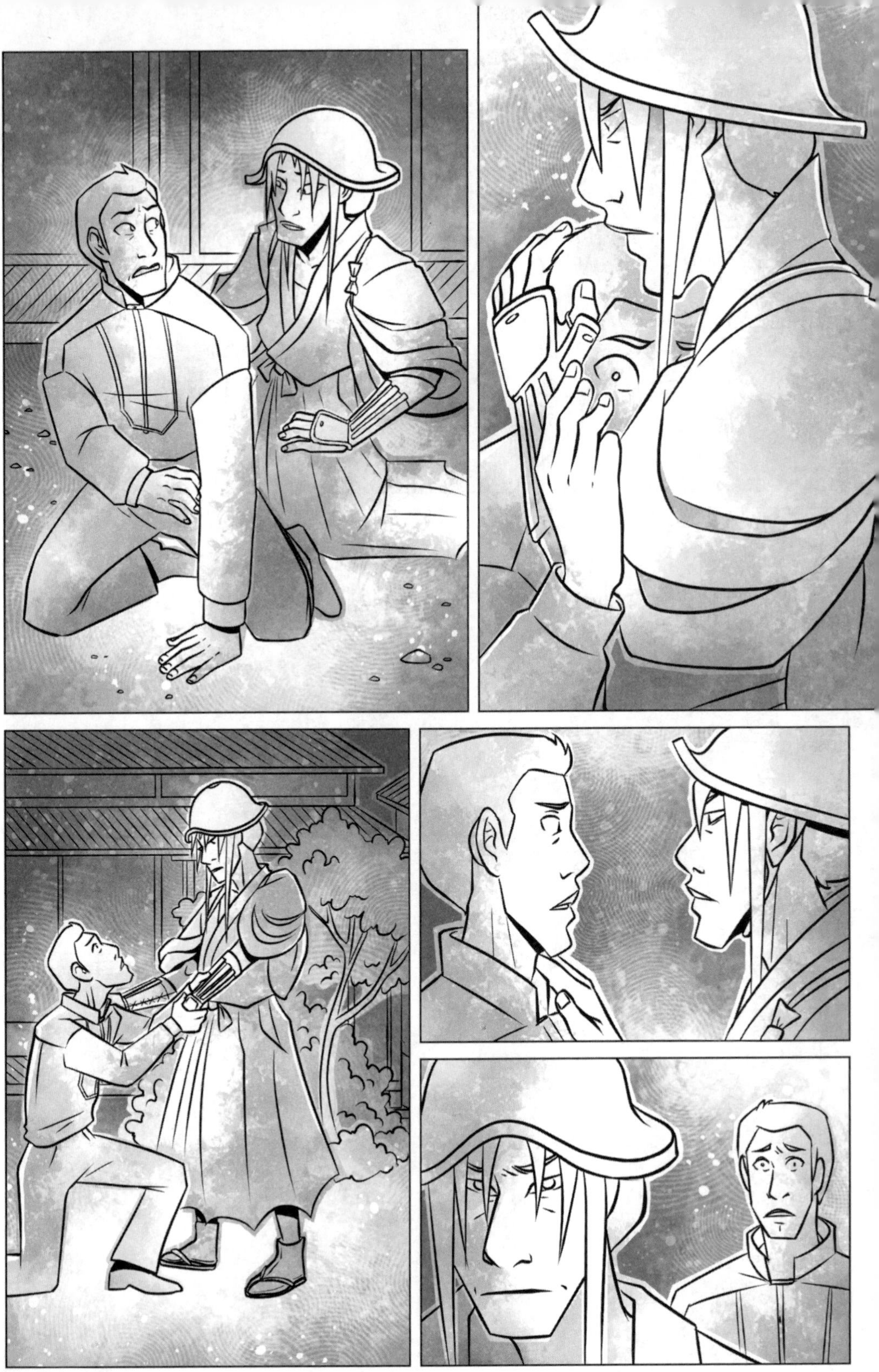

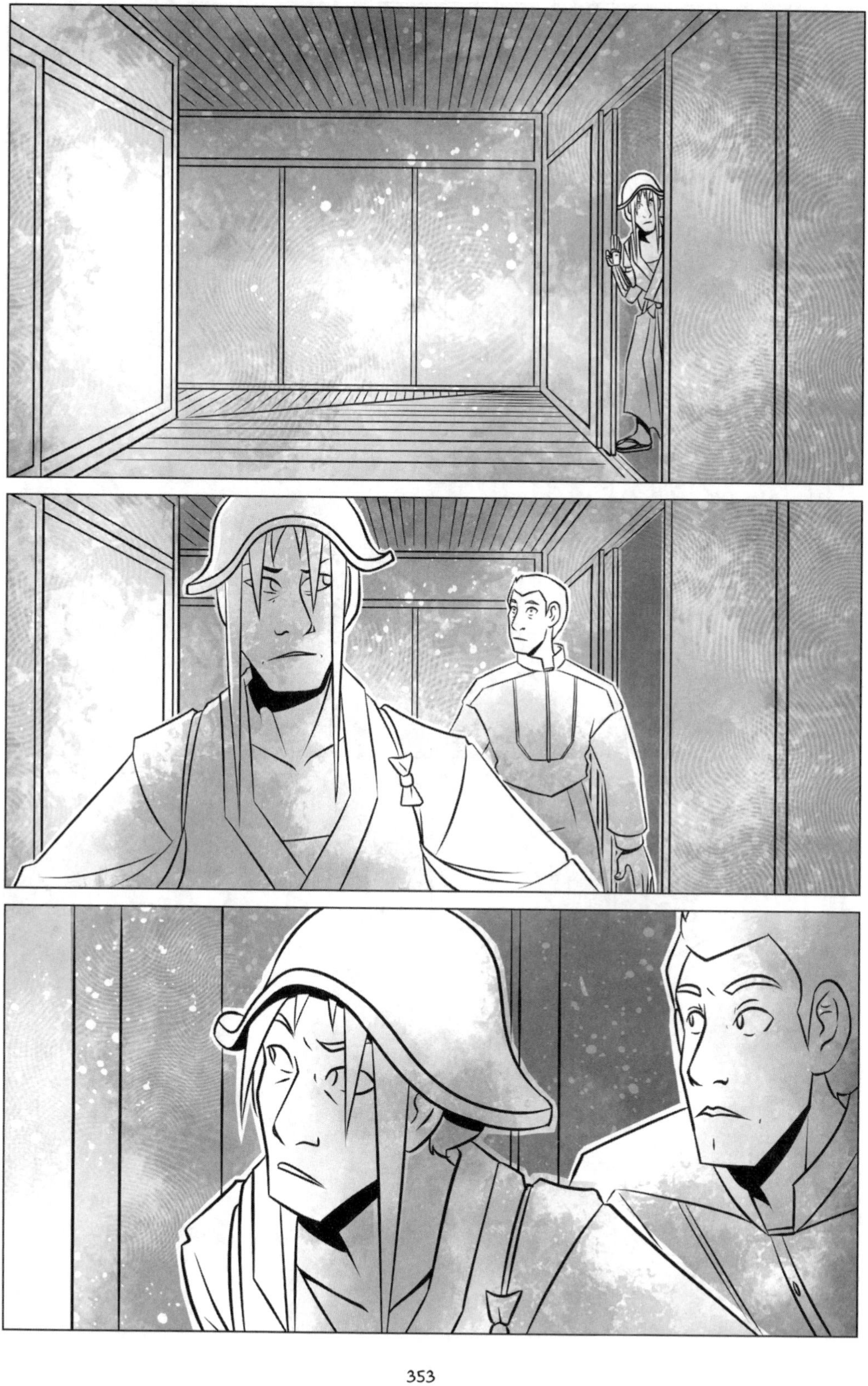

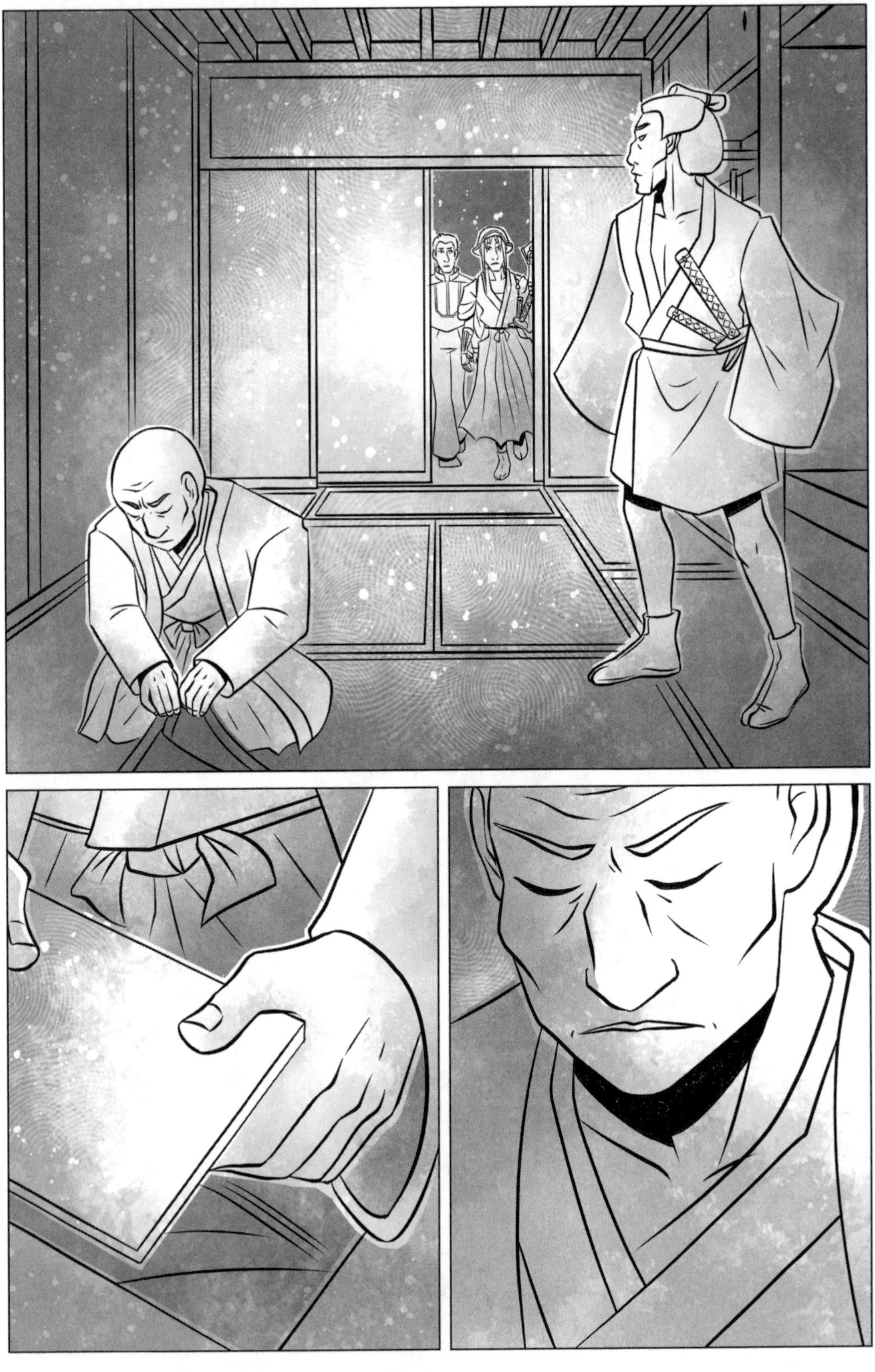

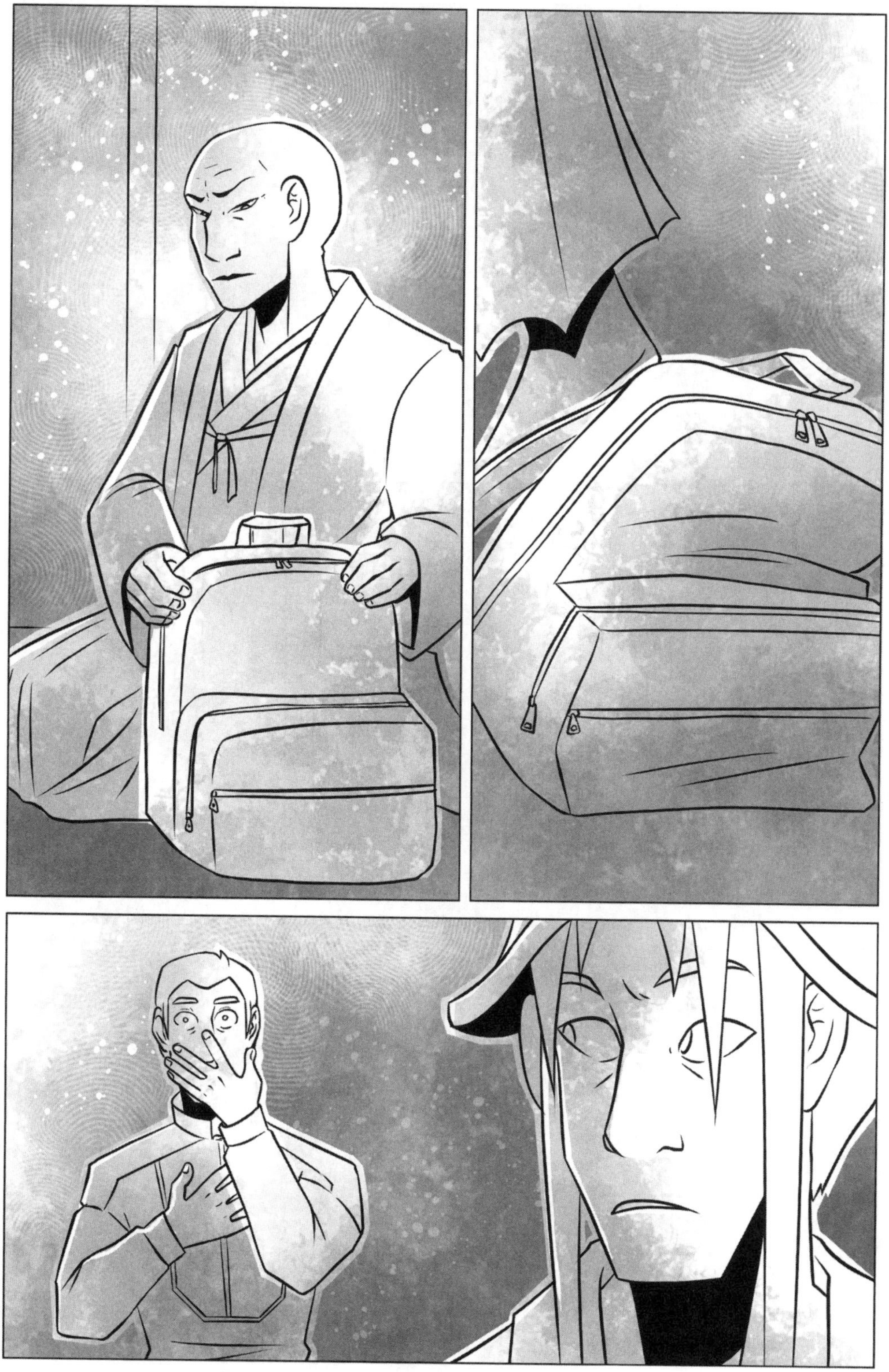

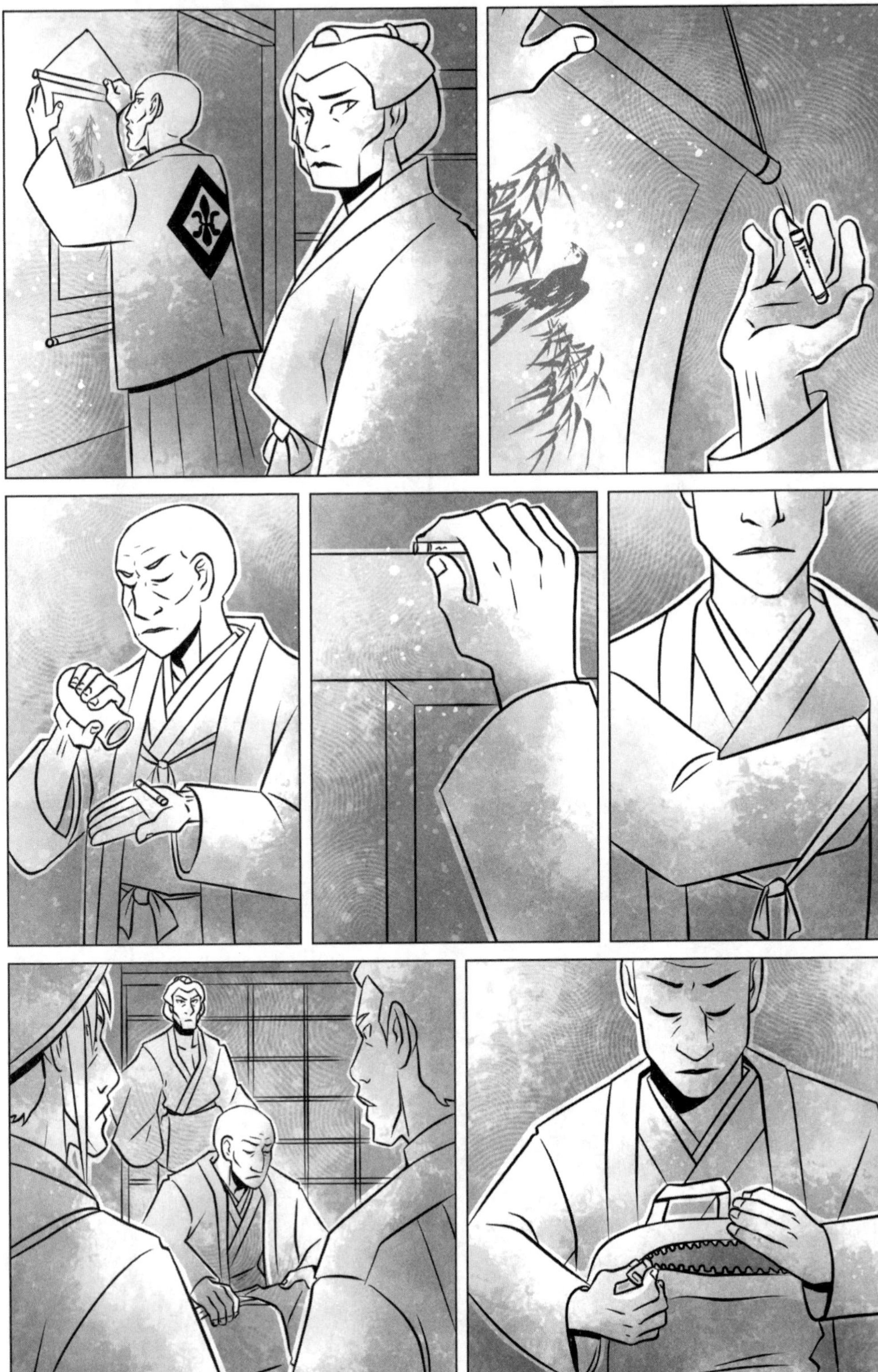

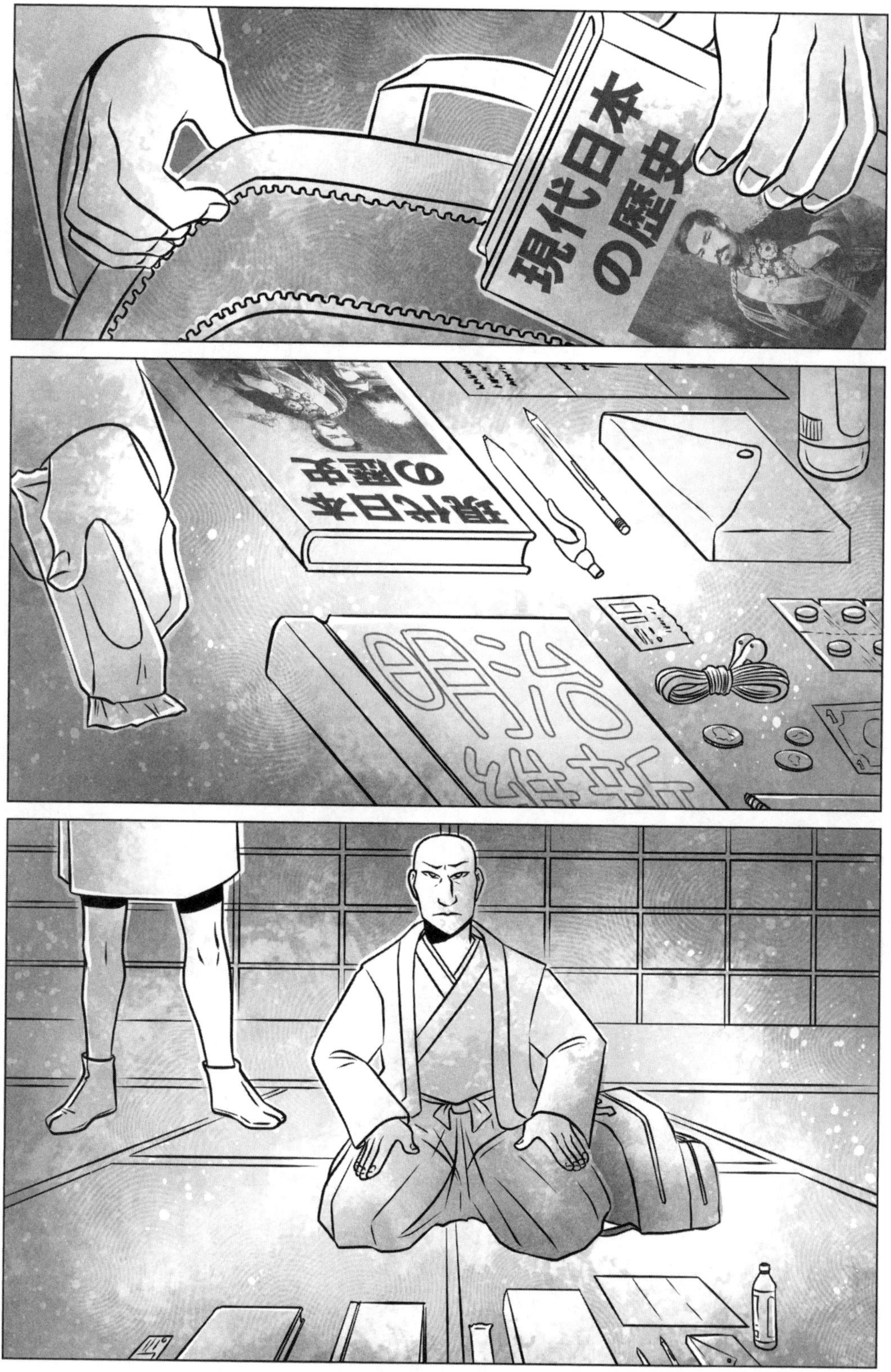
現代日本の歴史
現代日本の歴史

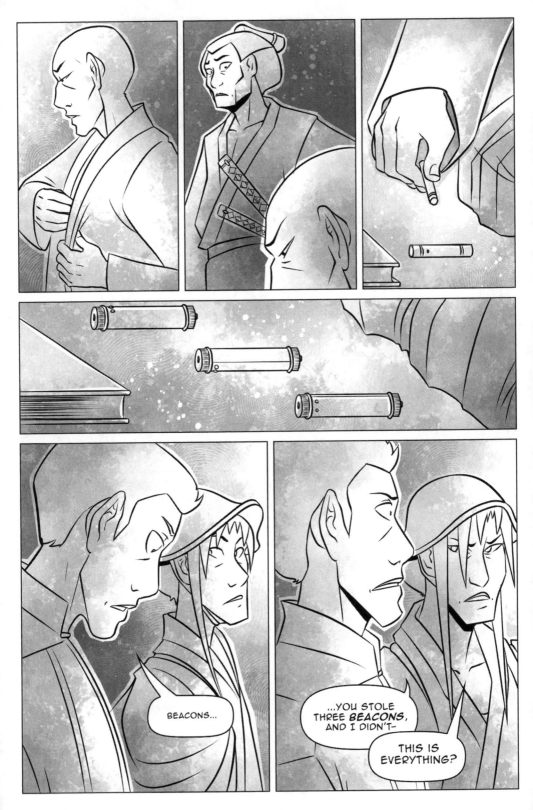

BEACONS...

...YOU STOLE THREE **BEACONS**, AND I DIDN'T—

THIS IS EVERYTHING?

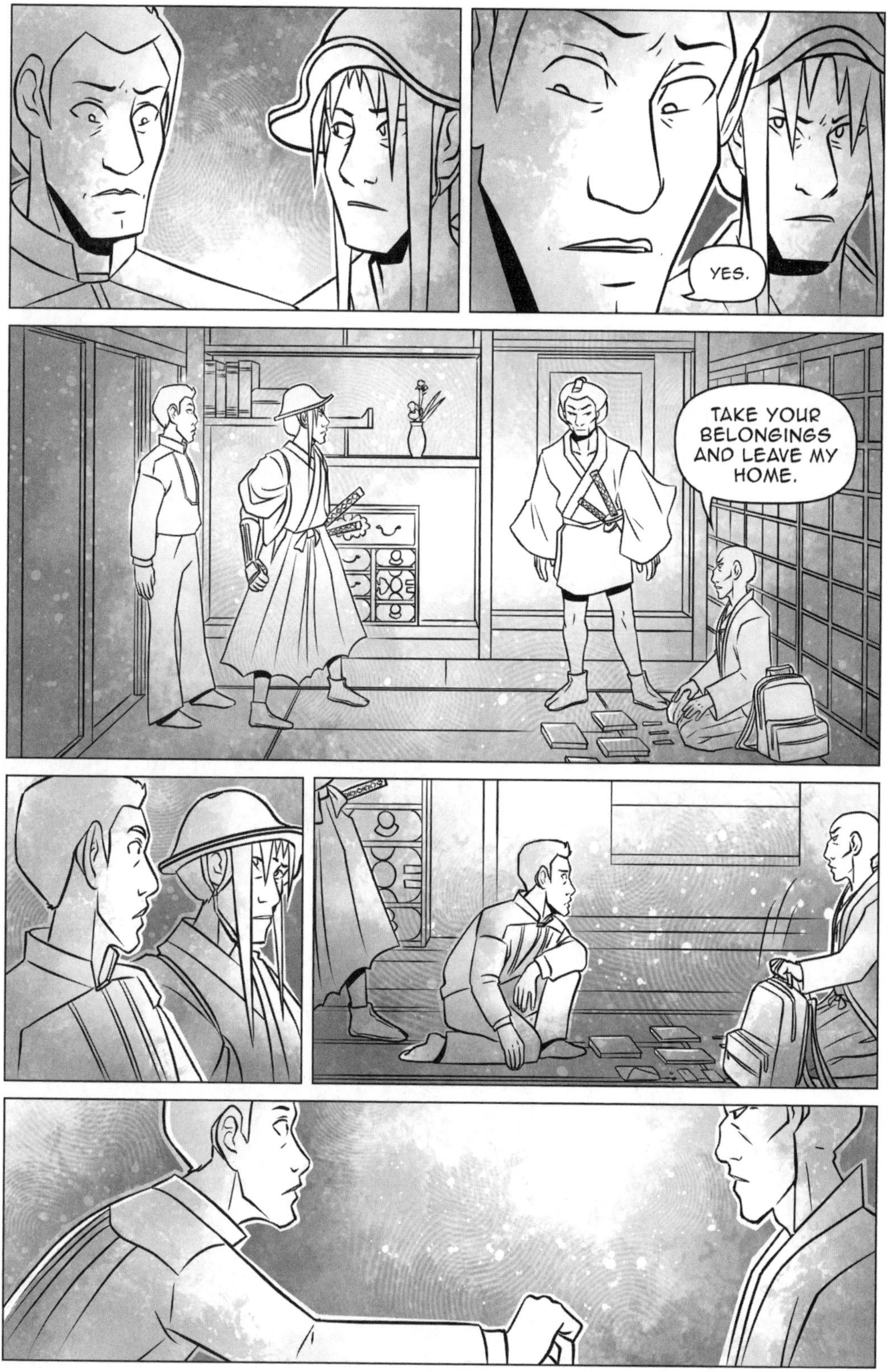
YES.
TAKE YOUR BELONGINGS AND LEAVE MY HOME.

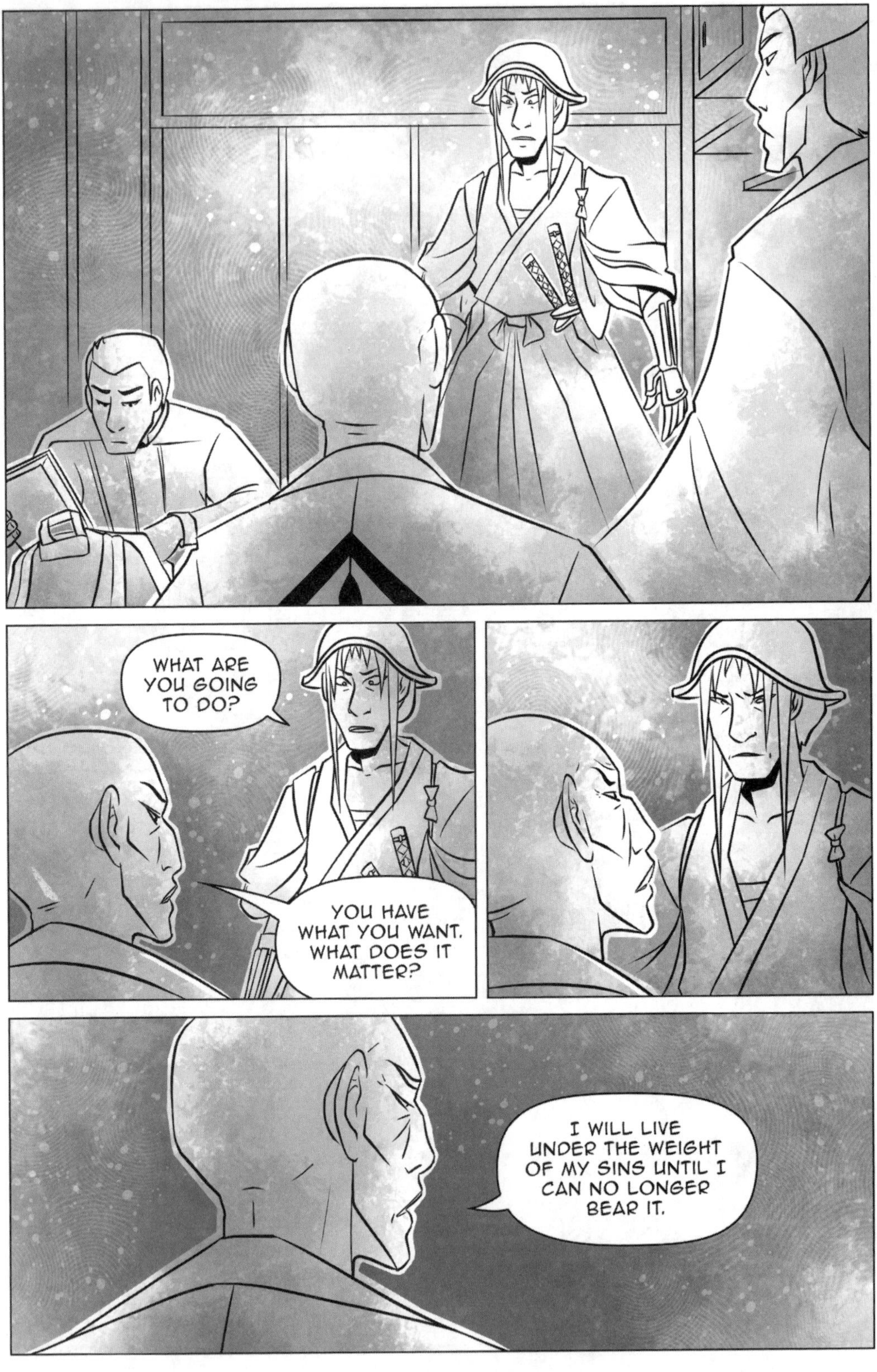
WHAT ARE YOU GOING TO DO?
YOU HAVE WHAT YOU WANT. WHAT DOES IT MATTER?
I WILL LIVE UNDER THE WEIGHT OF MY SINS UNTIL I CAN NO LONGER BEAR IT.

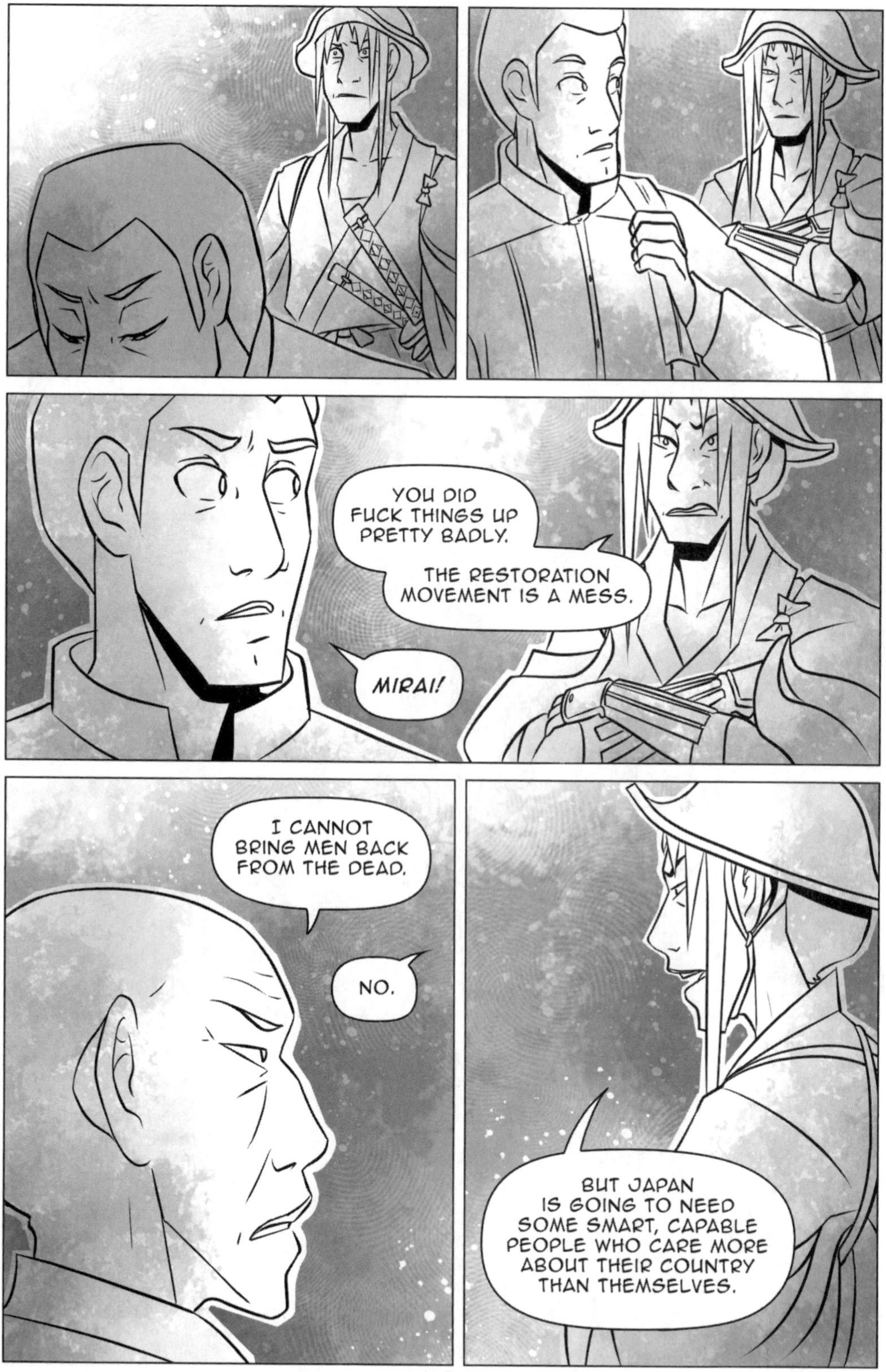
YOU DID FUCK THINGS UP PRETTY BADLY.
THE RESTORATION MOVEMENT IS A MESS.
MIRAI!
I CANNOT BRING MEN BACK FROM THE DEAD.
NO.
BUT JAPAN IS GOING TO NEED SOME SMART, CAPABLE PEOPLE WHO CARE MORE ABOUT THEIR COUNTRY THAN THEMSELVES.

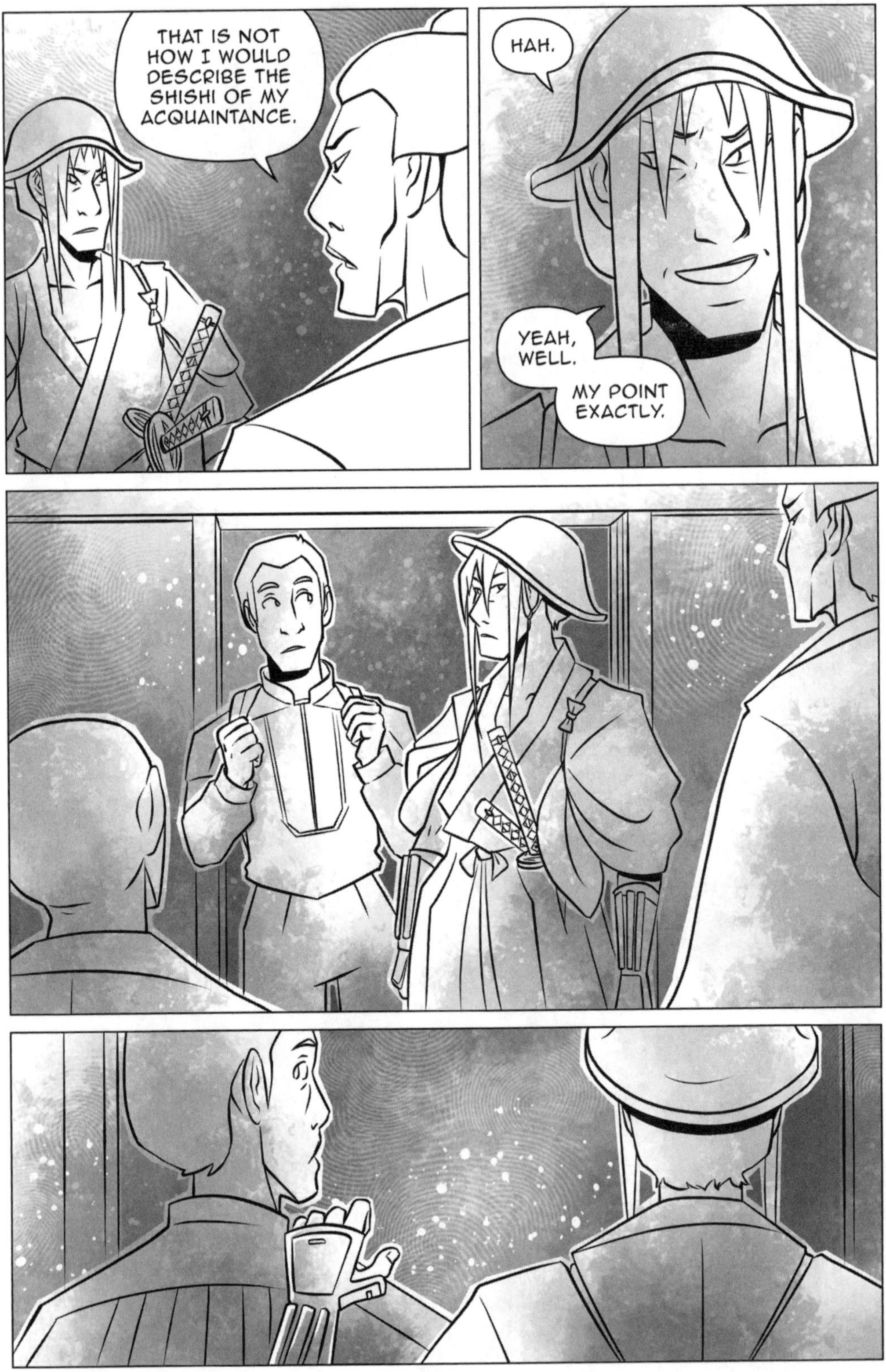
THAT IS NOT HOW I WOULD DESCRIBE THE SHISHI OF MY ACQUAINTANCE.
HAH.
YEAH, WELL.
MY POINT EXACTLY.

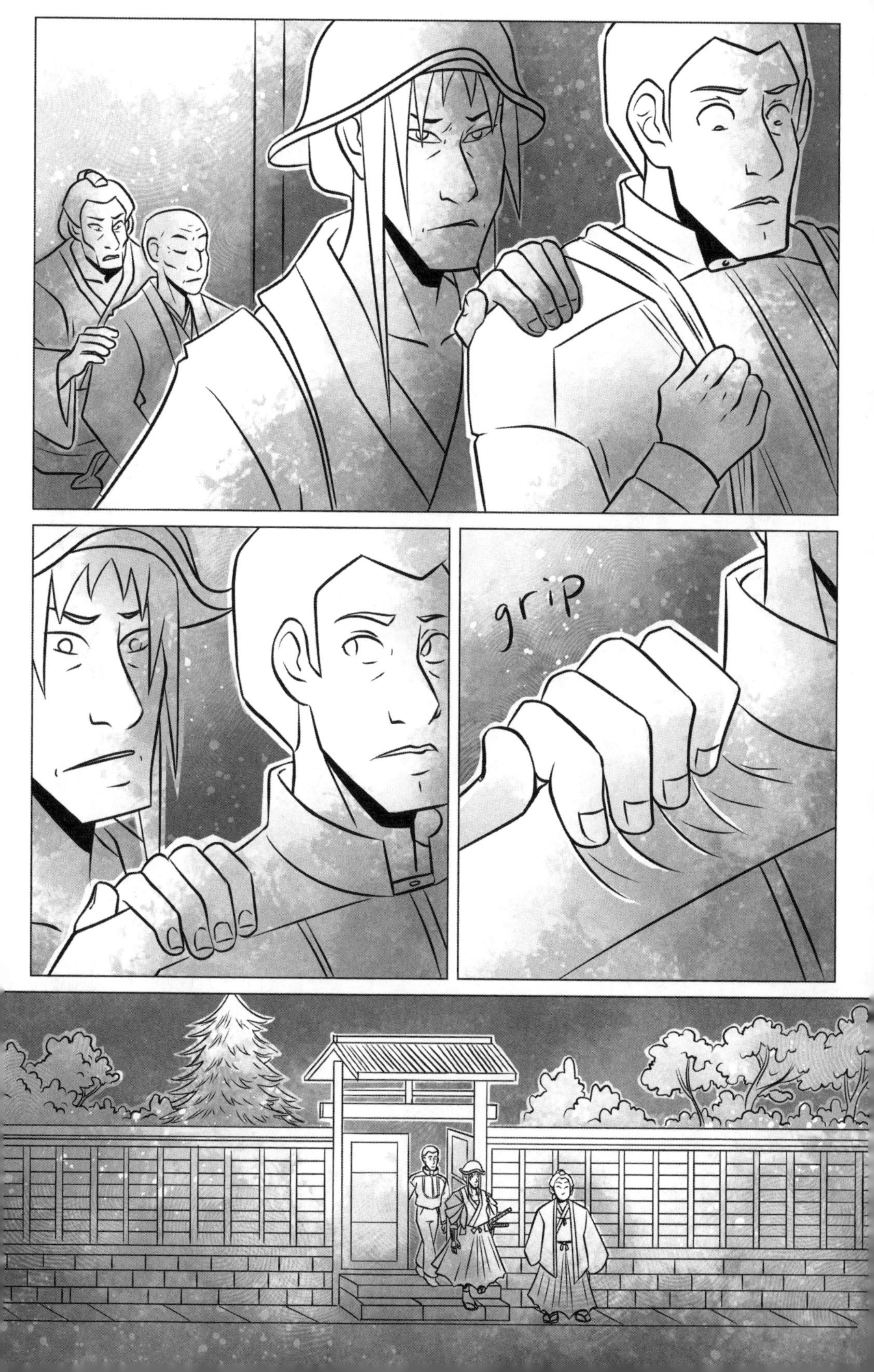
grip

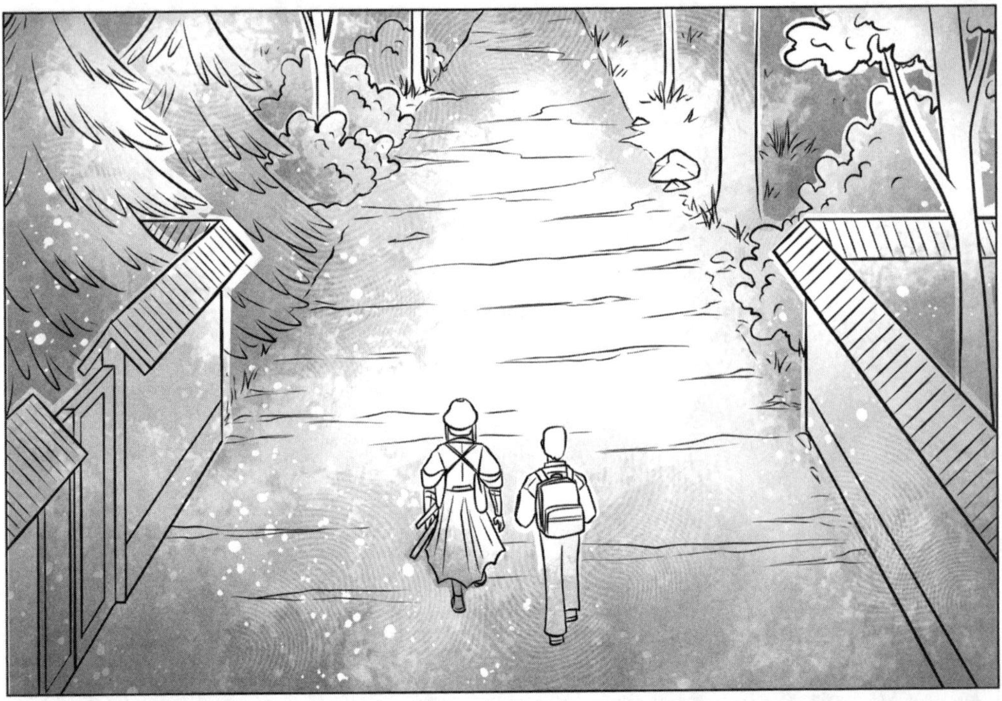

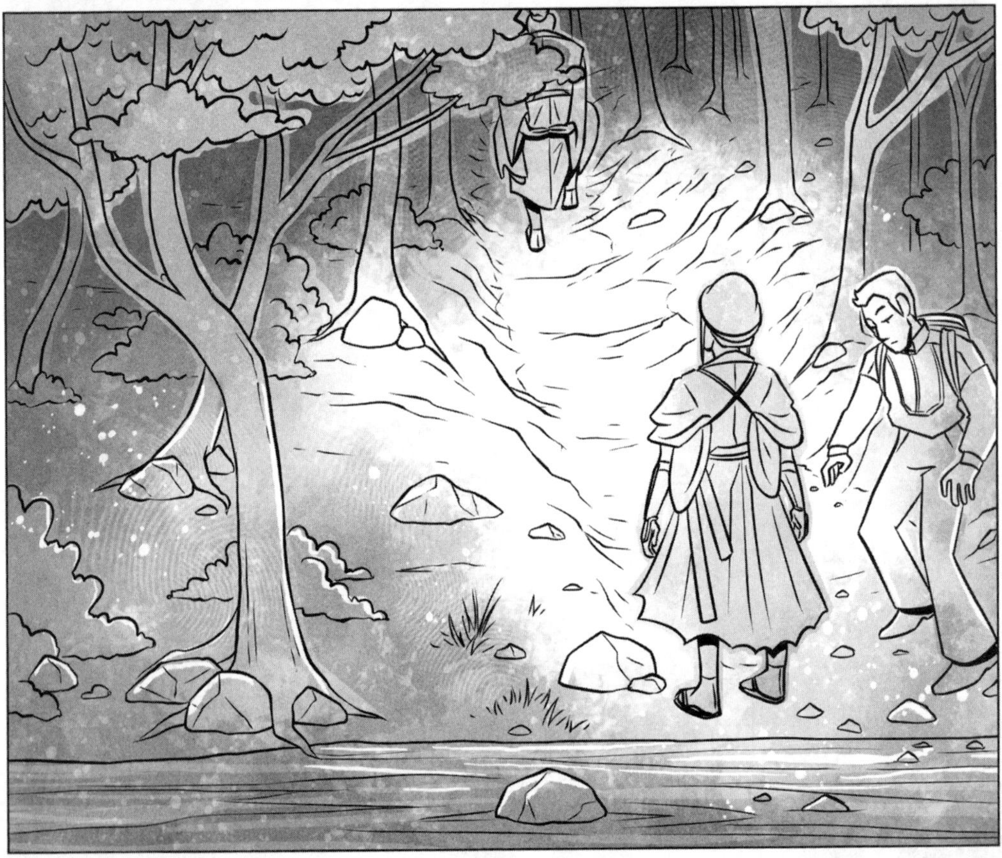

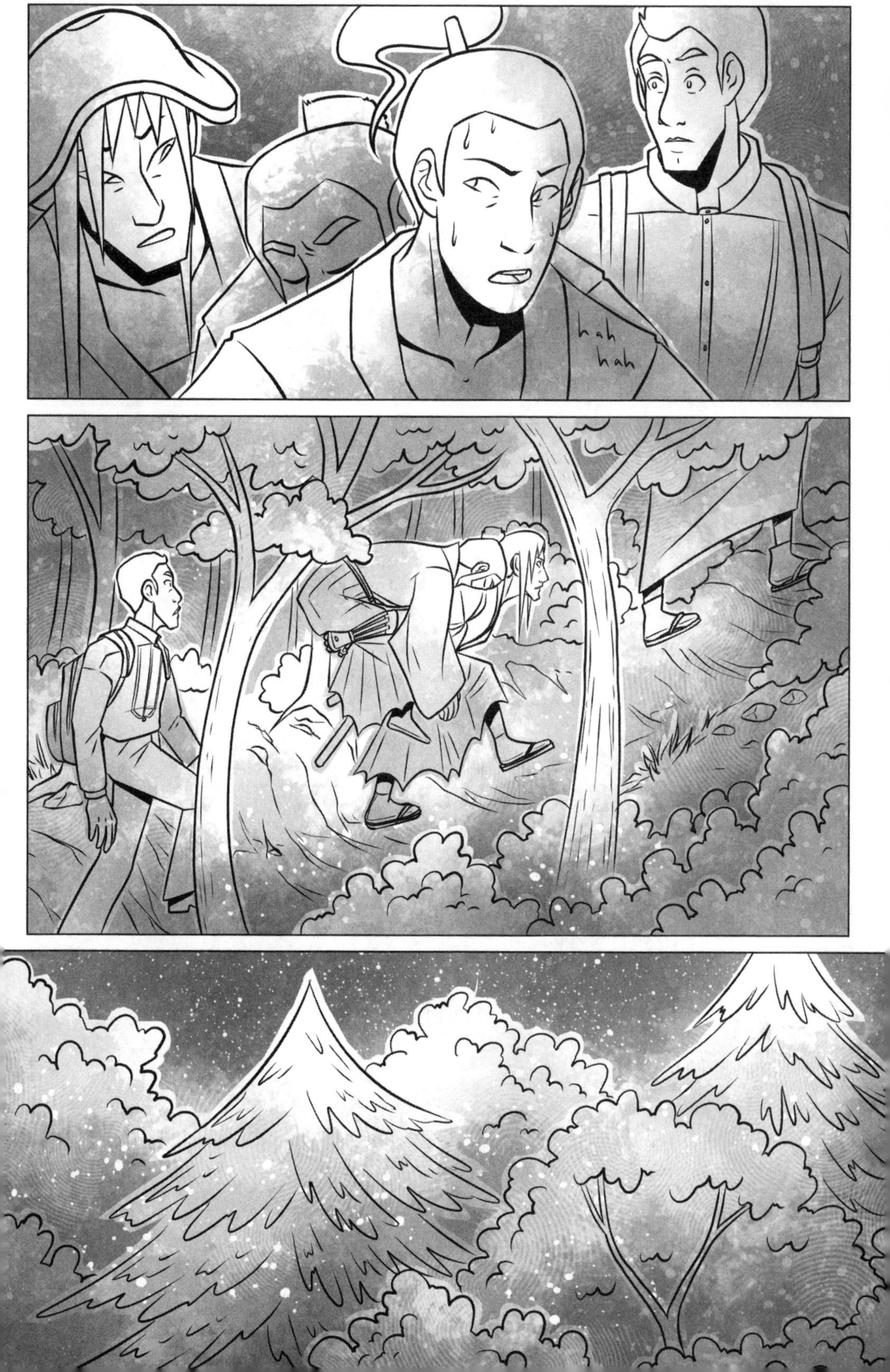
hah
hah

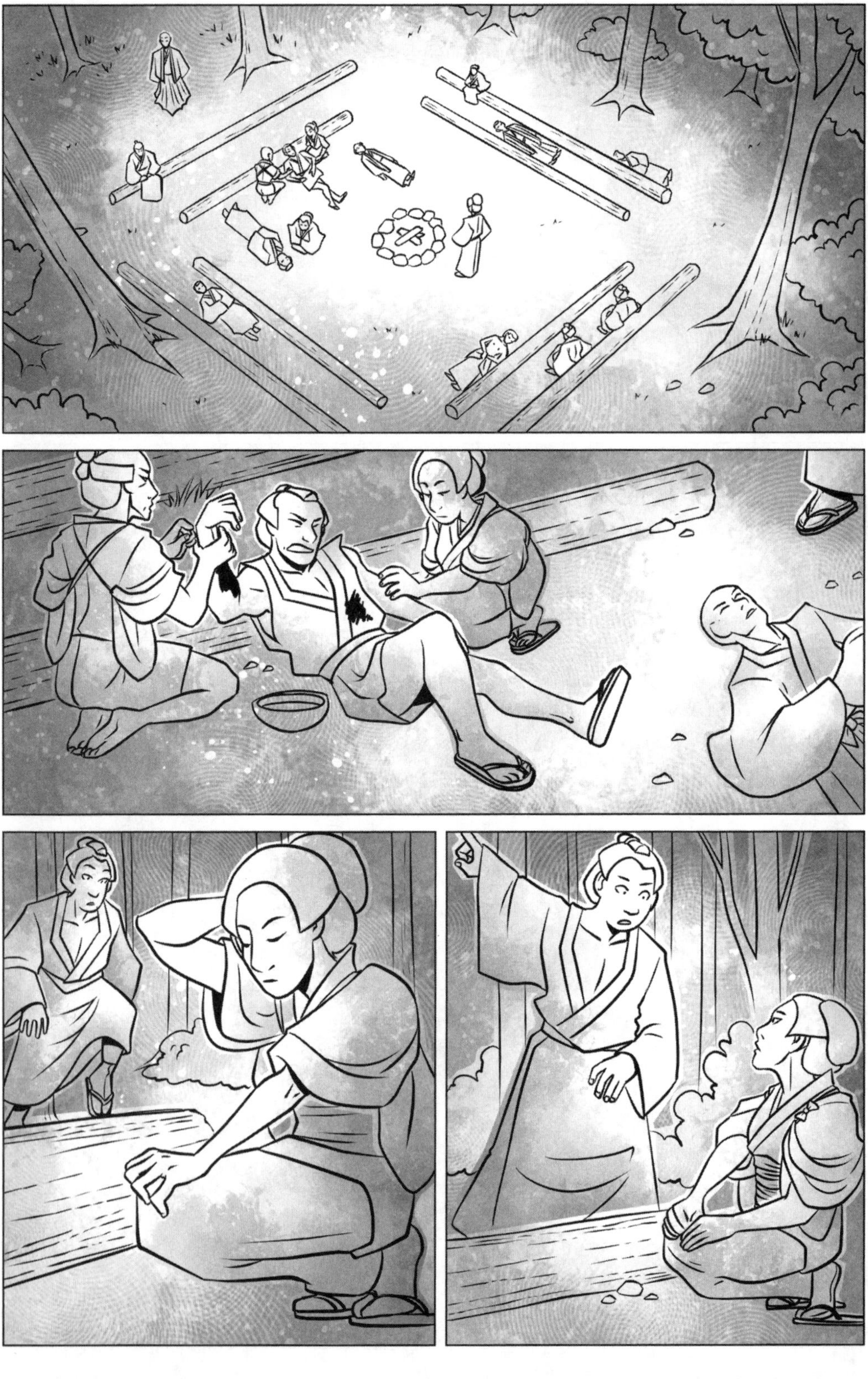

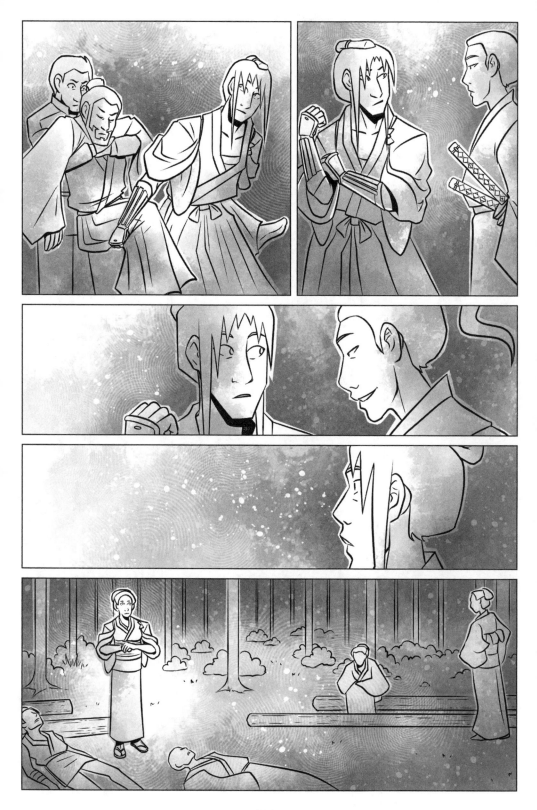

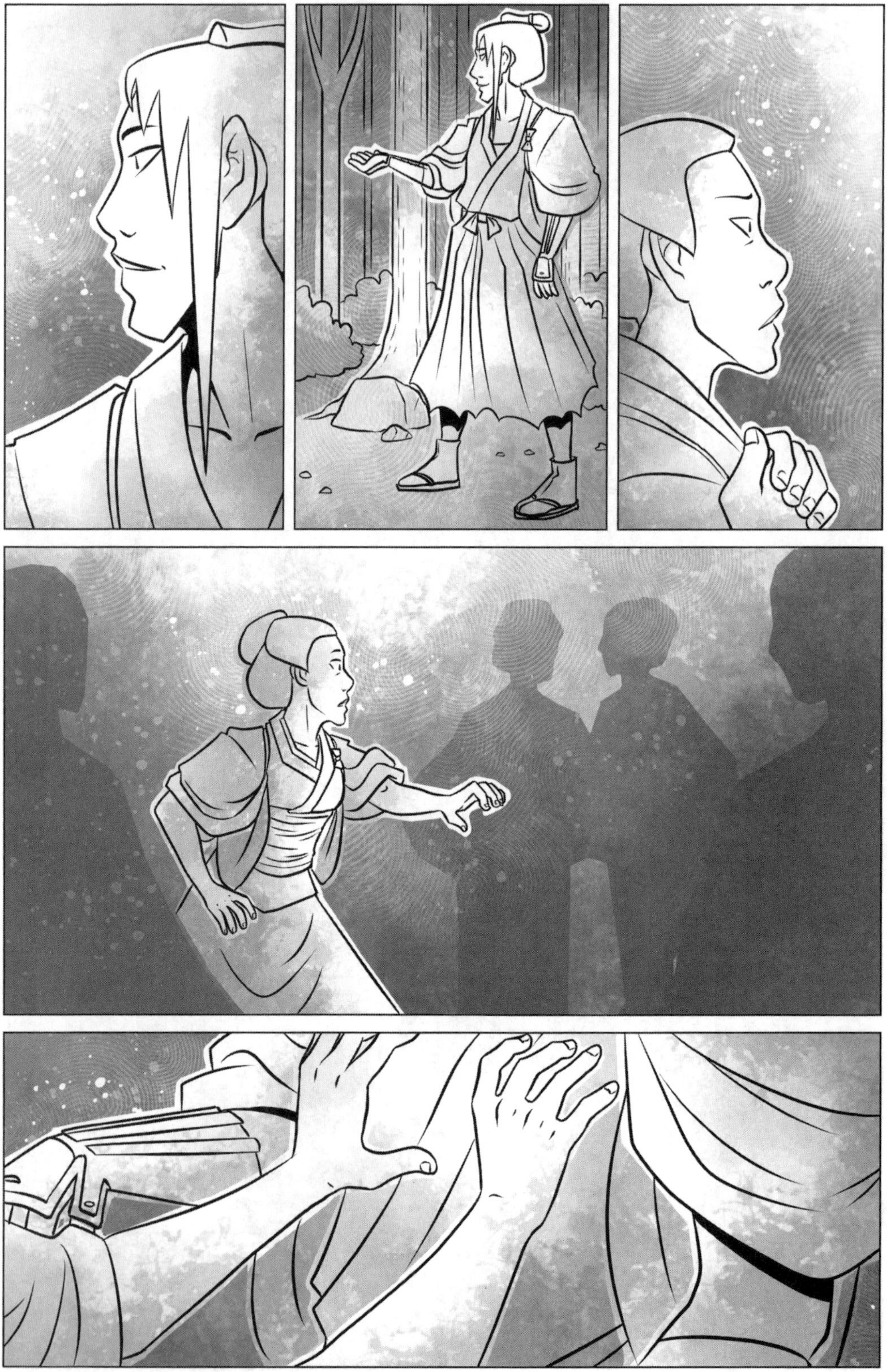

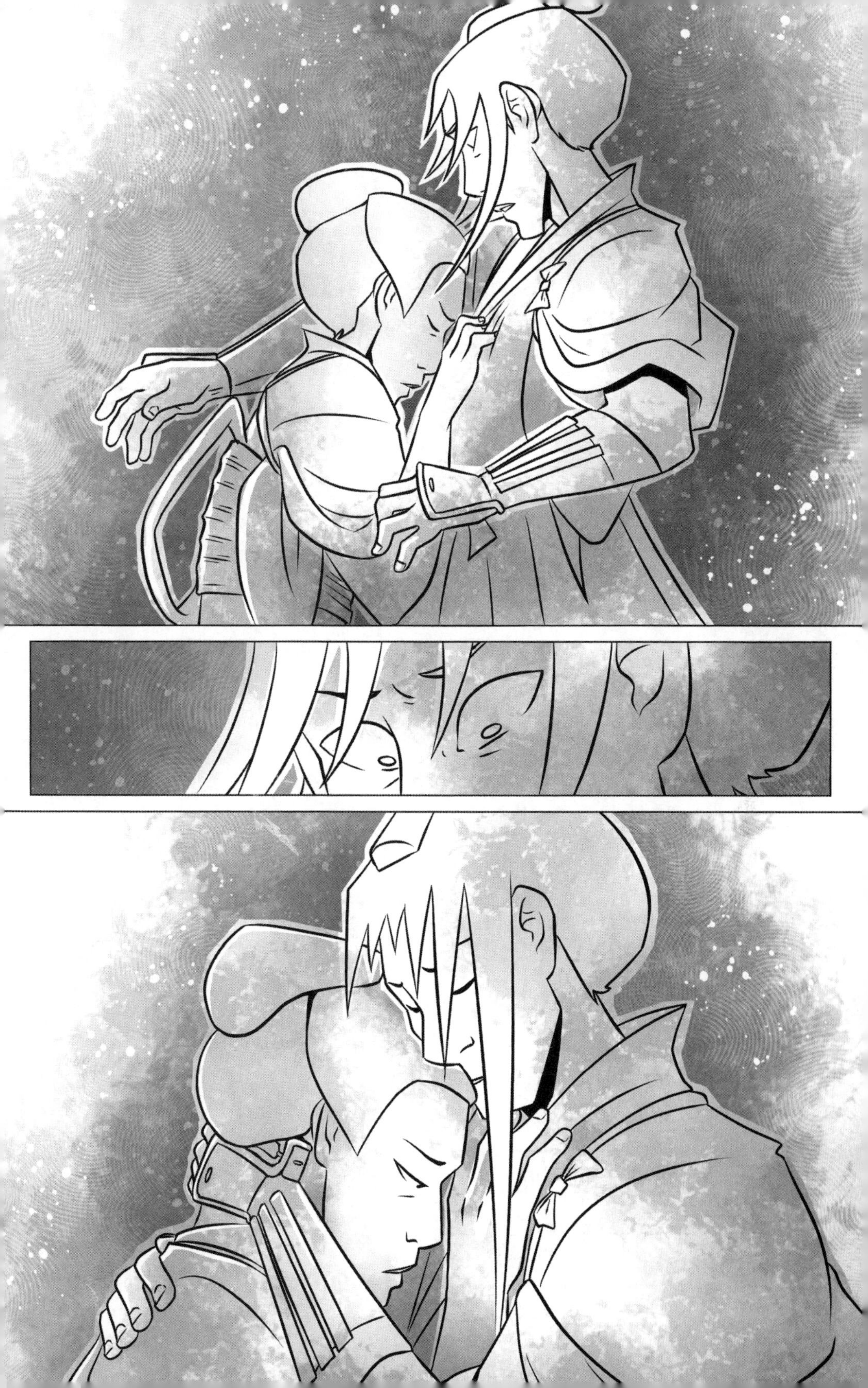

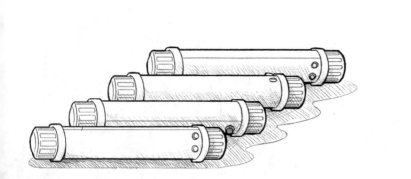

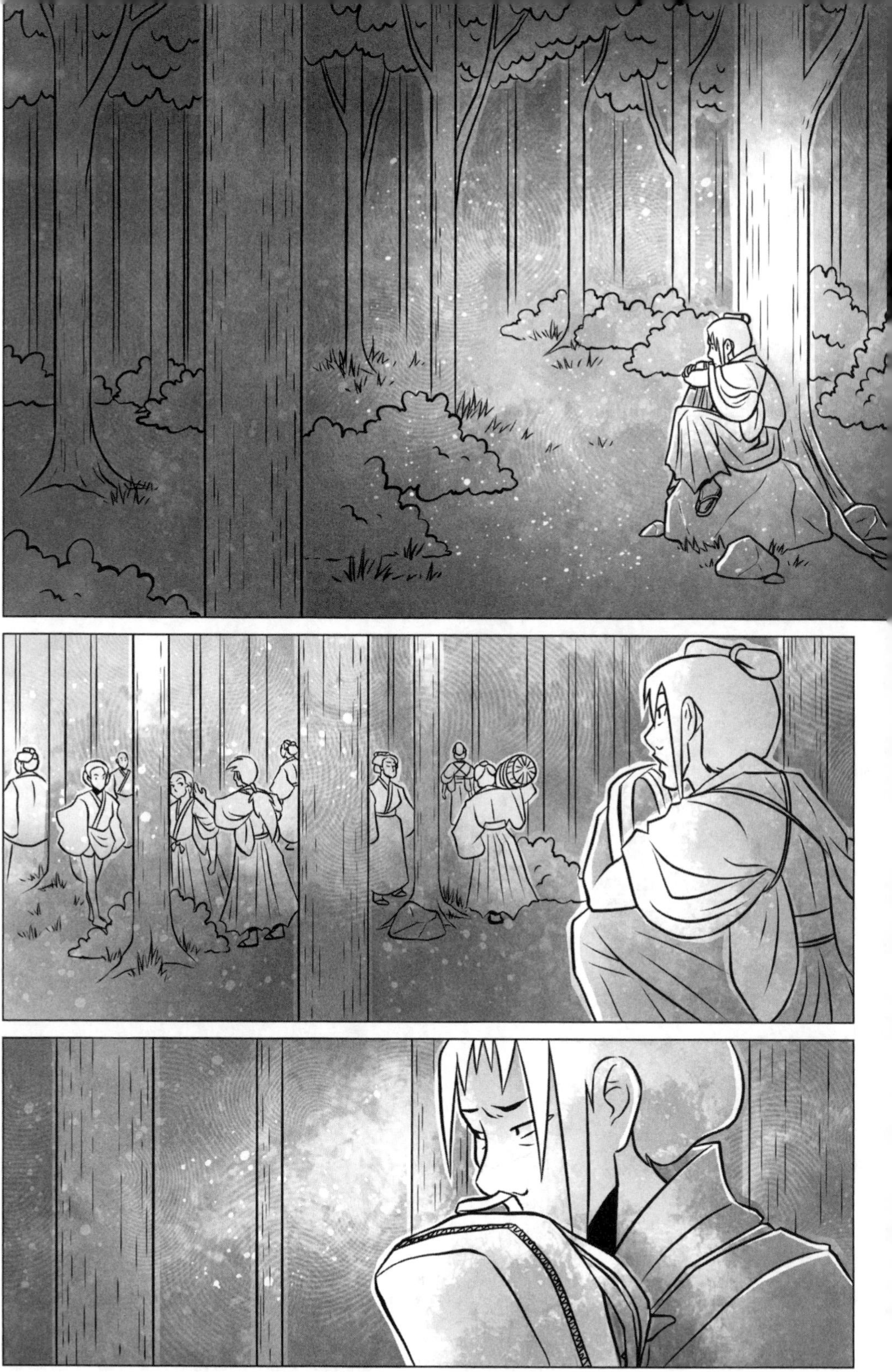

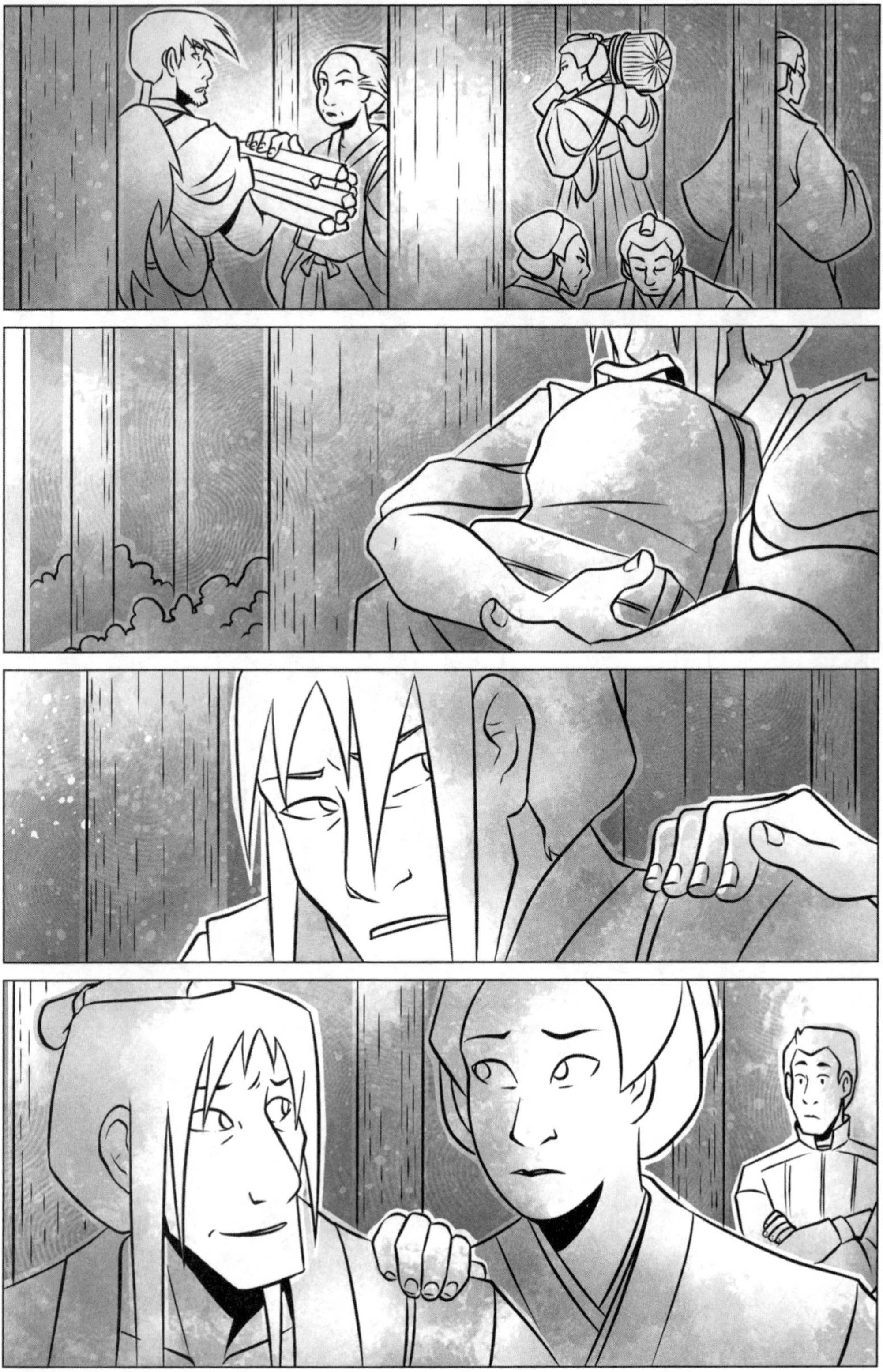

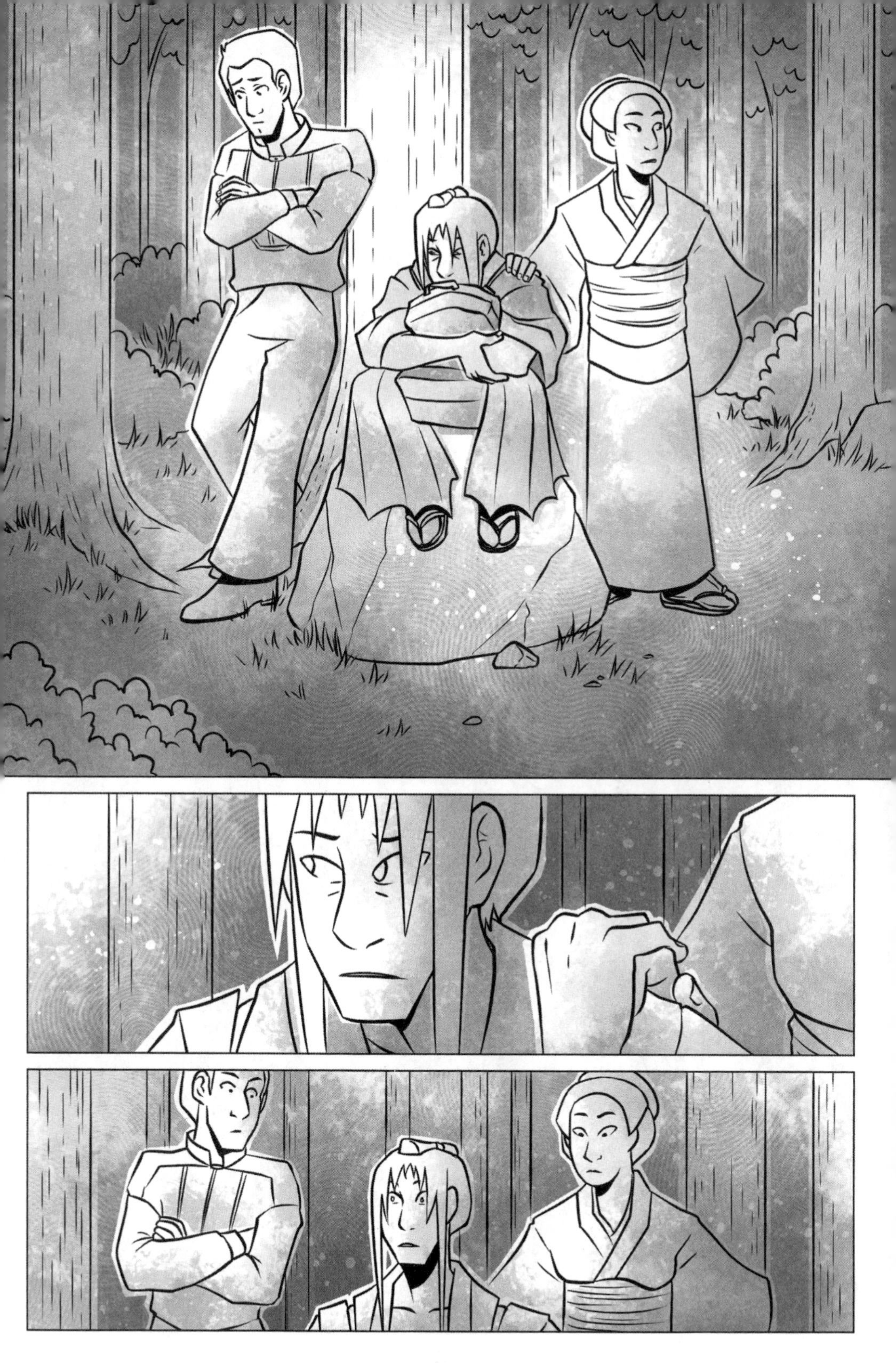

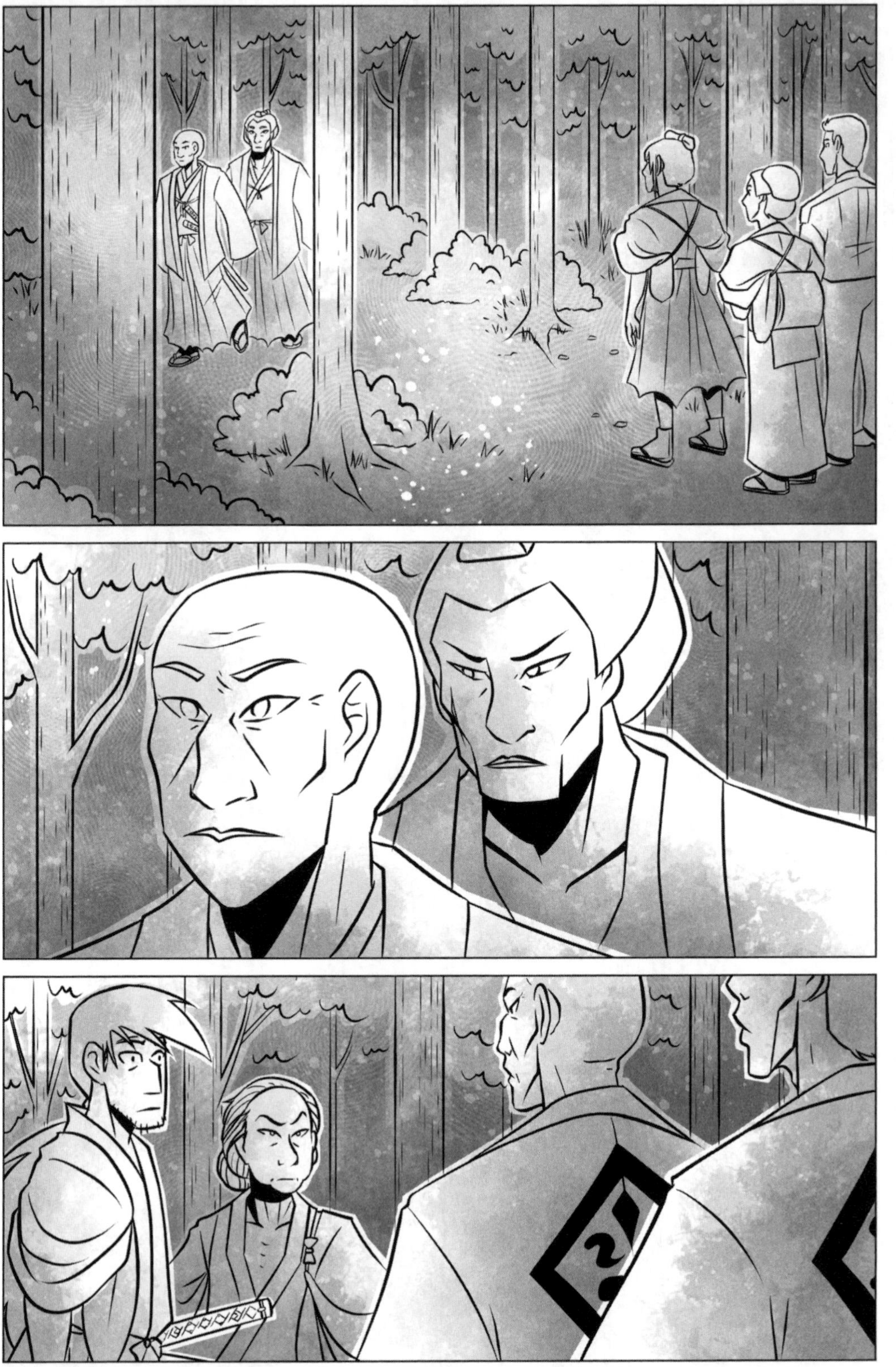

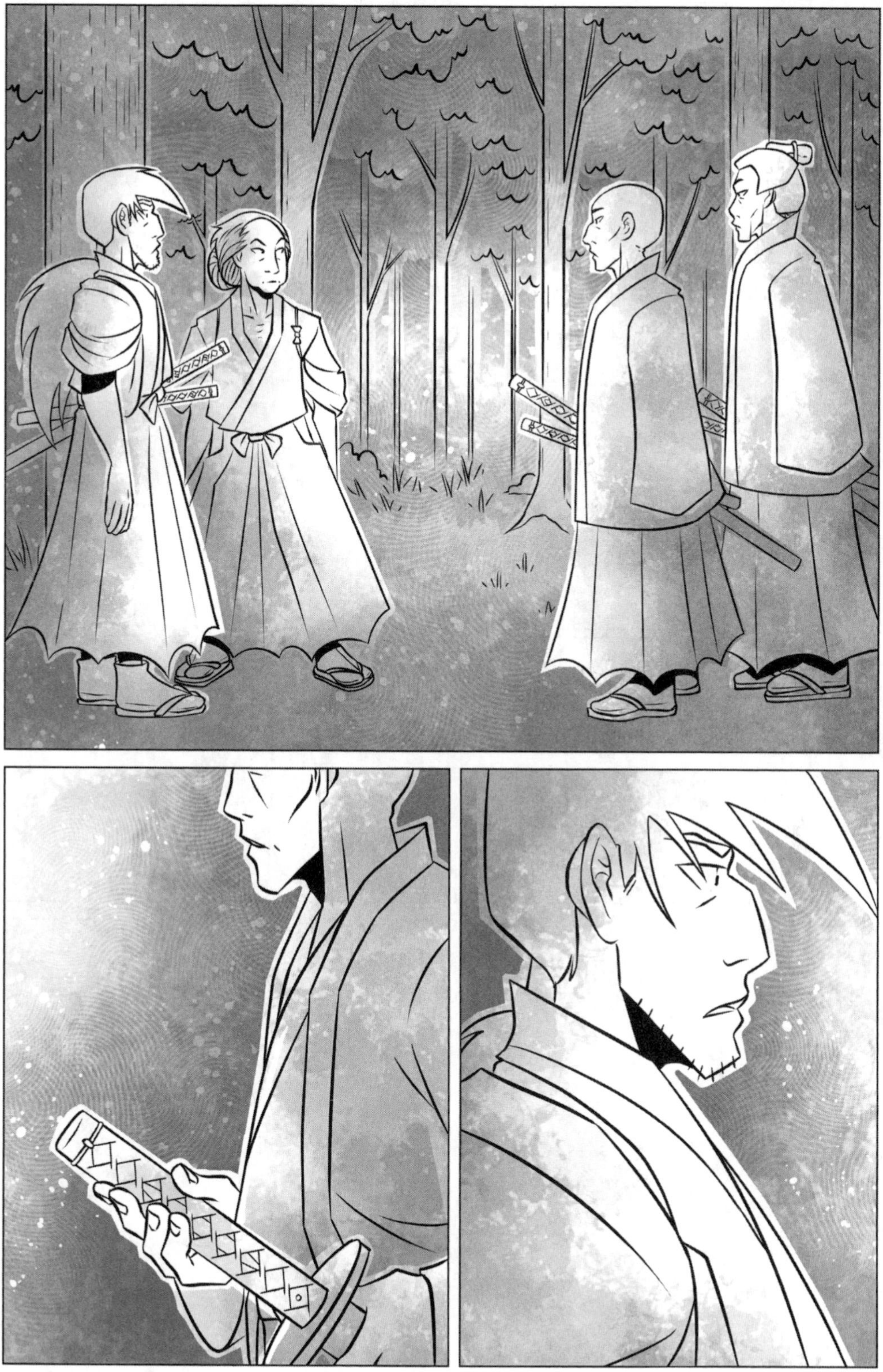

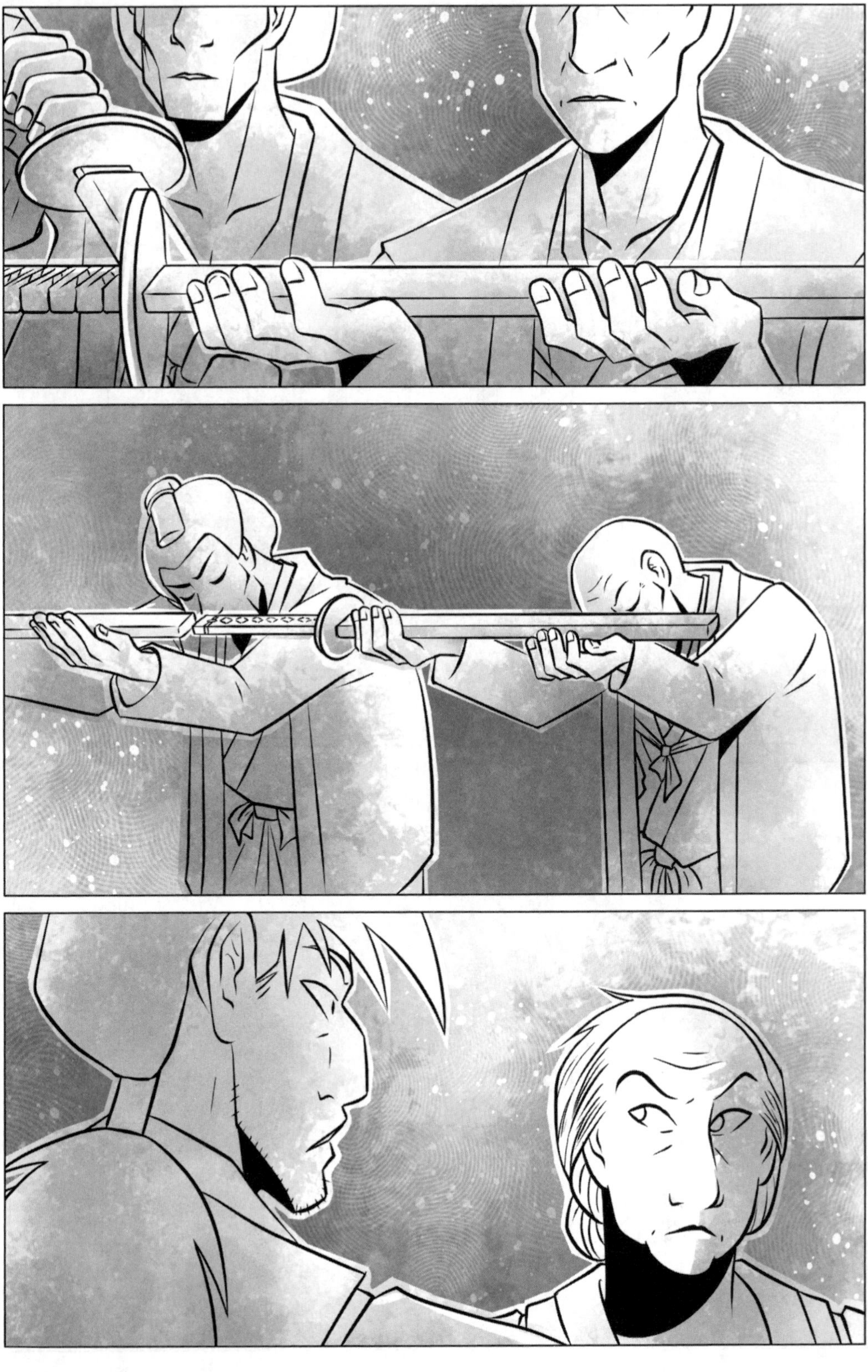

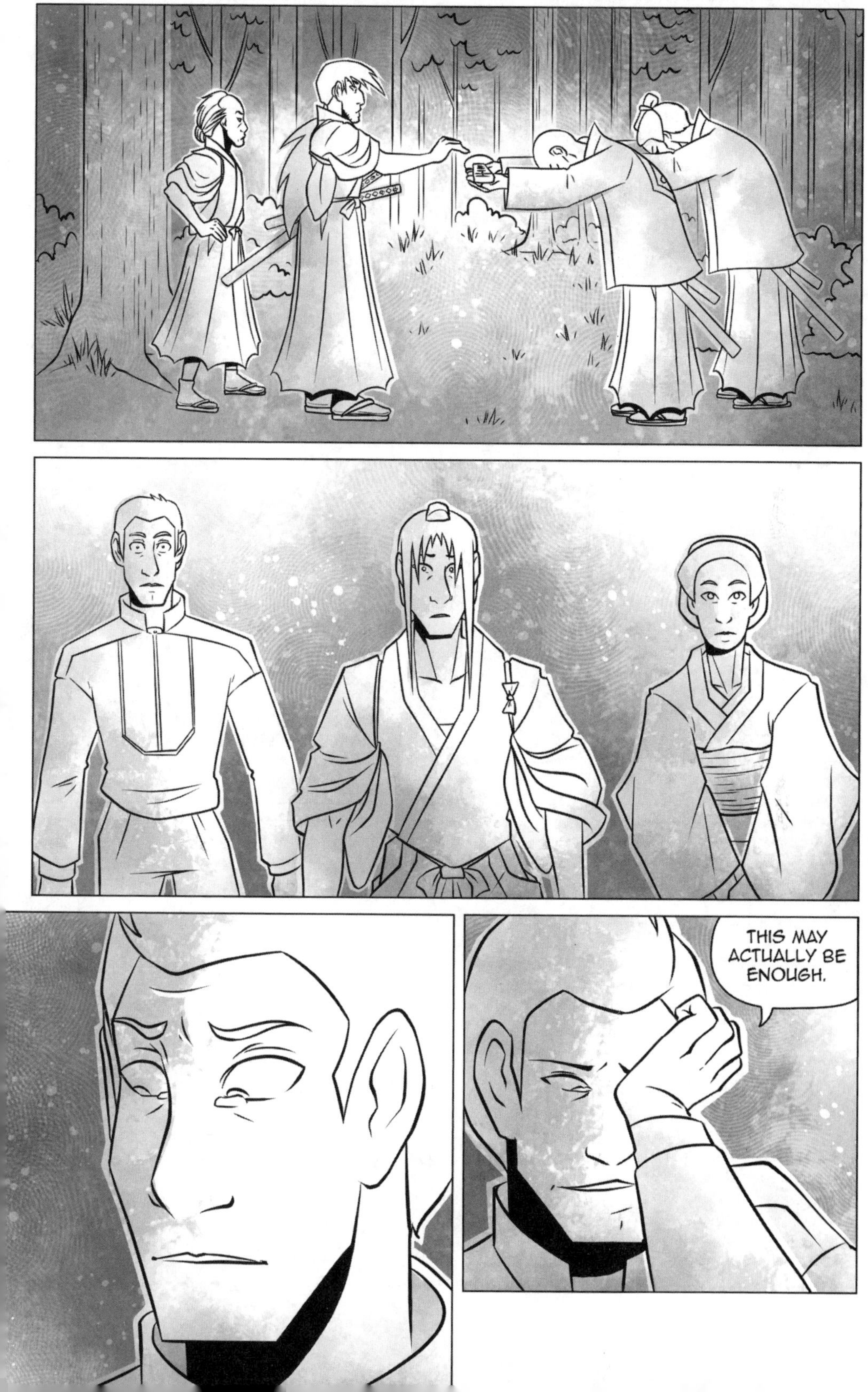
THIS MAY ACTUALLY BE ENOUGH.

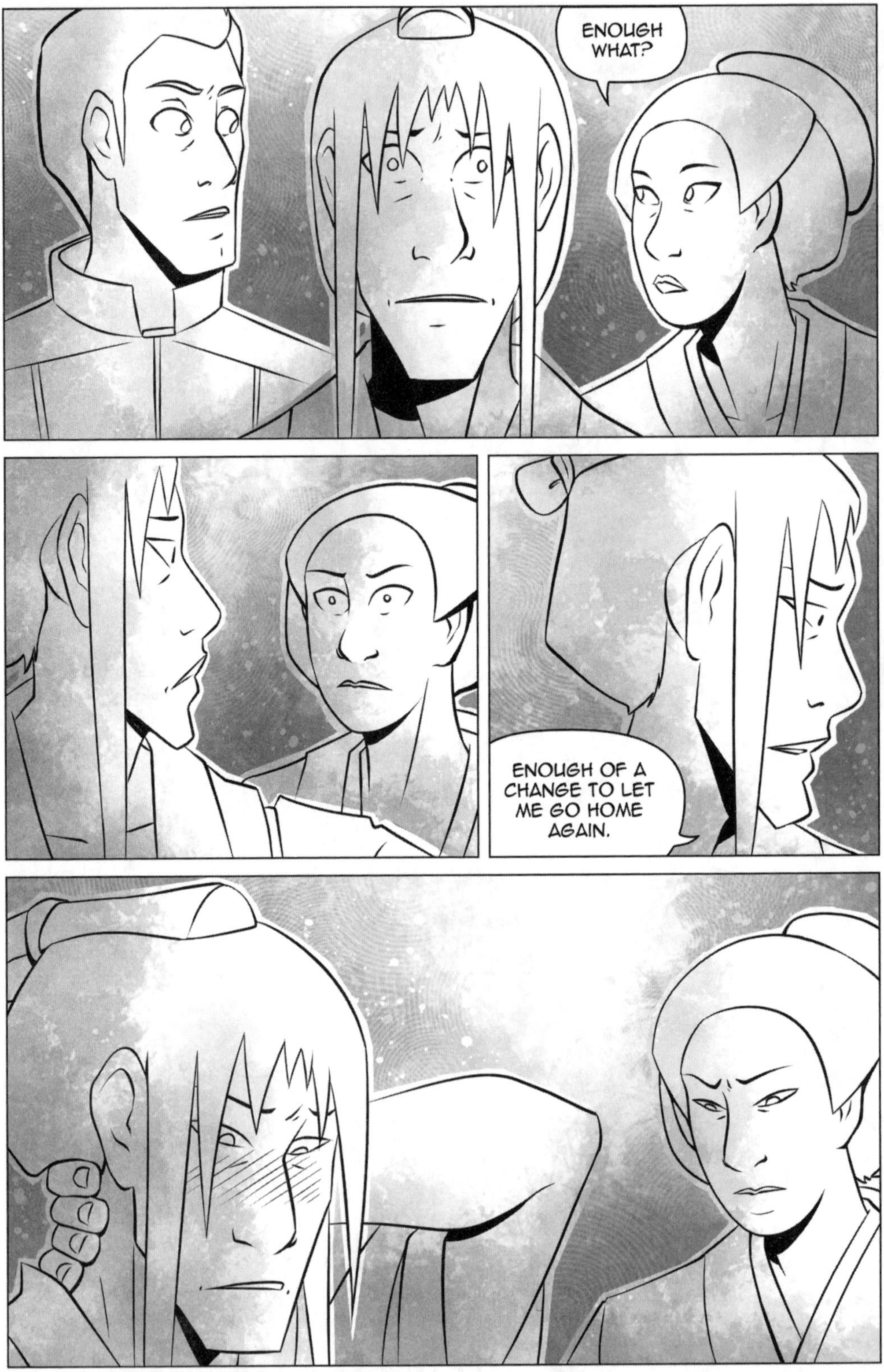
ENOUGH WHAT?
ENOUGH OF A CHANGE TO LET ME GO HOME AGAIN.

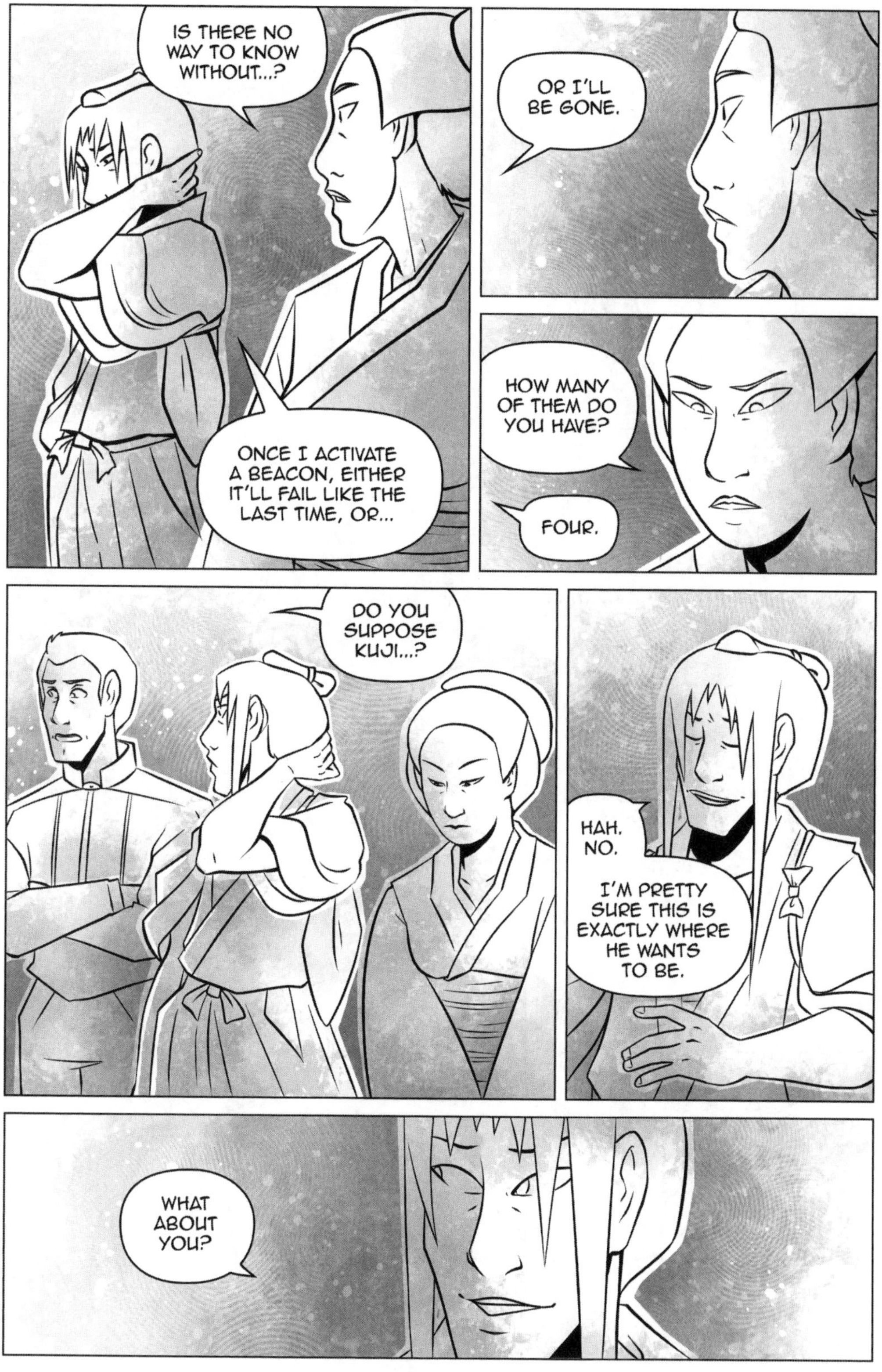
IS THERE NO WAY TO KNOW WITHOUT...?
ONCE I ACTIVATE A BEACON, EITHER IT'LL FAIL LIKE THE LAST TIME, OR...
OR I'LL BE GONE.
HOW MANY OF THEM DO YOU HAVE?
FOUR.
DO YOU SUPPOSE KUJI...?
HAH. NO.
I'M PRETTY SURE THIS IS EXACTLY WHERE HE WANTS TO BE.
WHAT ABOUT YOU?

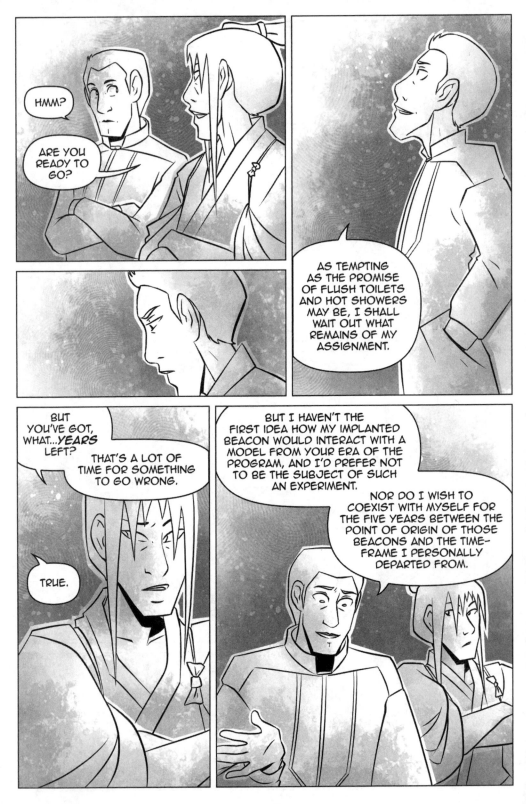

HMM?

ARE YOU READY TO GO?

AS TEMPTING AS THE PROMISE OF FLUSH TOILETS AND HOT SHOWERS MAY BE, I SHALL WAIT OUT WHAT REMAINS OF MY ASSIGNMENT.

BUT YOU'VE GOT, WHAT...*YEARS* LEFT?

THAT'S A LOT OF TIME FOR SOMETHING TO GO WRONG.

TRUE.

BUT I HAVEN'T THE FIRST IDEA HOW MY IMPLANTED BEACON WOULD INTERACT WITH A MODEL FROM YOUR ERA OF THE PROGRAM, AND I'D PREFER NOT TO BE THE SUBJECT OF SUCH AN EXPERIMENT.

NOR DO I WISH TO COEXIST WITH MYSELF FOR THE FIVE YEARS BETWEEN THE POINT OF ORIGIN OF THOSE BEACONS AND THE TIME-FRAME I PERSONALLY DEPARTED FROM.

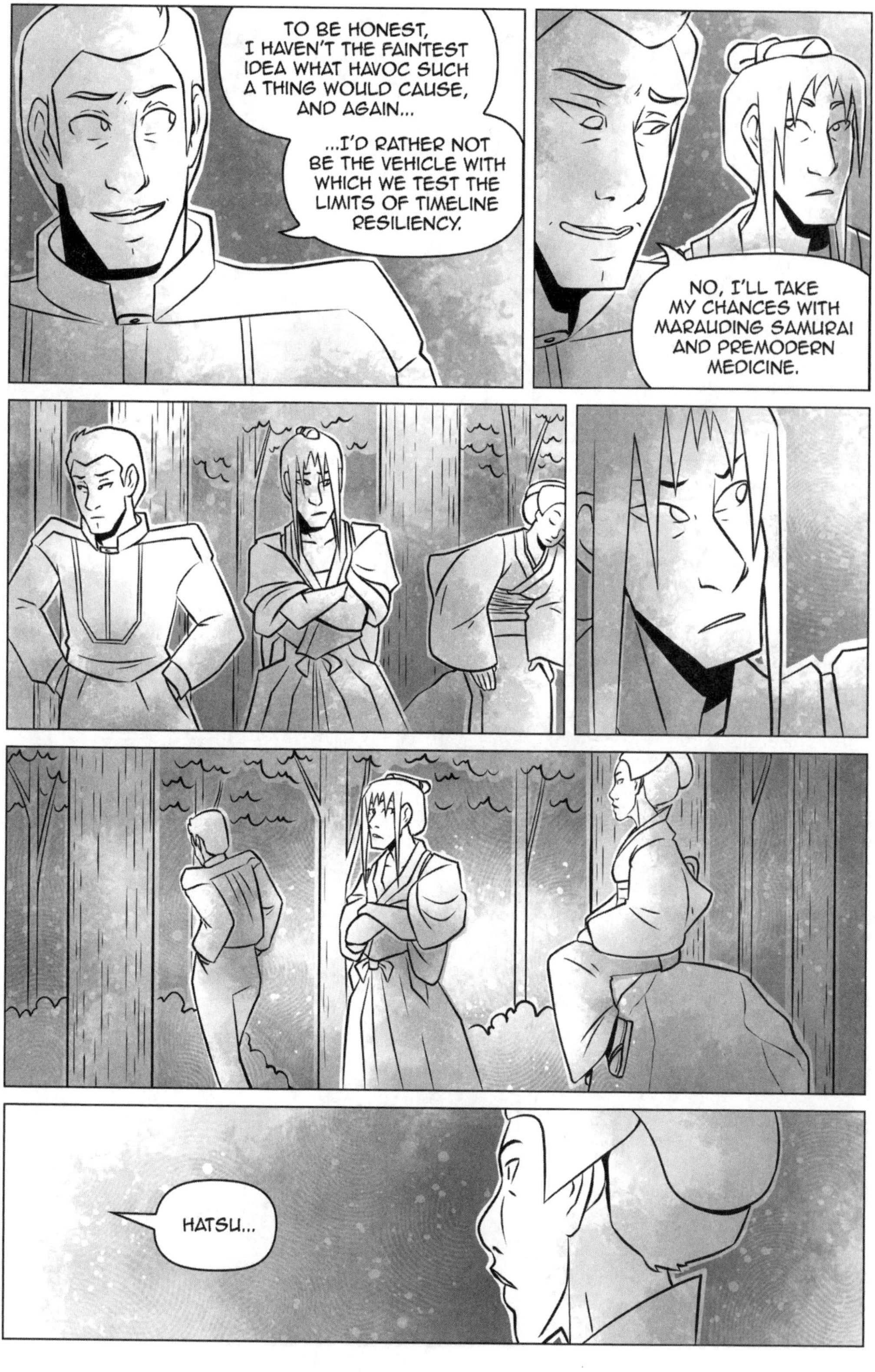
TO BE HONEST, I HAVEN'T THE FAINTEST IDEA WHAT HAVOC SUCH A THING WOULD CAUSE, AND AGAIN...
...I'D RATHER NOT BE THE VEHICLE WITH WHICH WE TEST THE LIMITS OF TIMELINE RESILIENCY.
NO, I'LL TAKE MY CHANCES WITH MARAUDING SAMURAI AND PREMODERN MEDICINE.
HATSU...

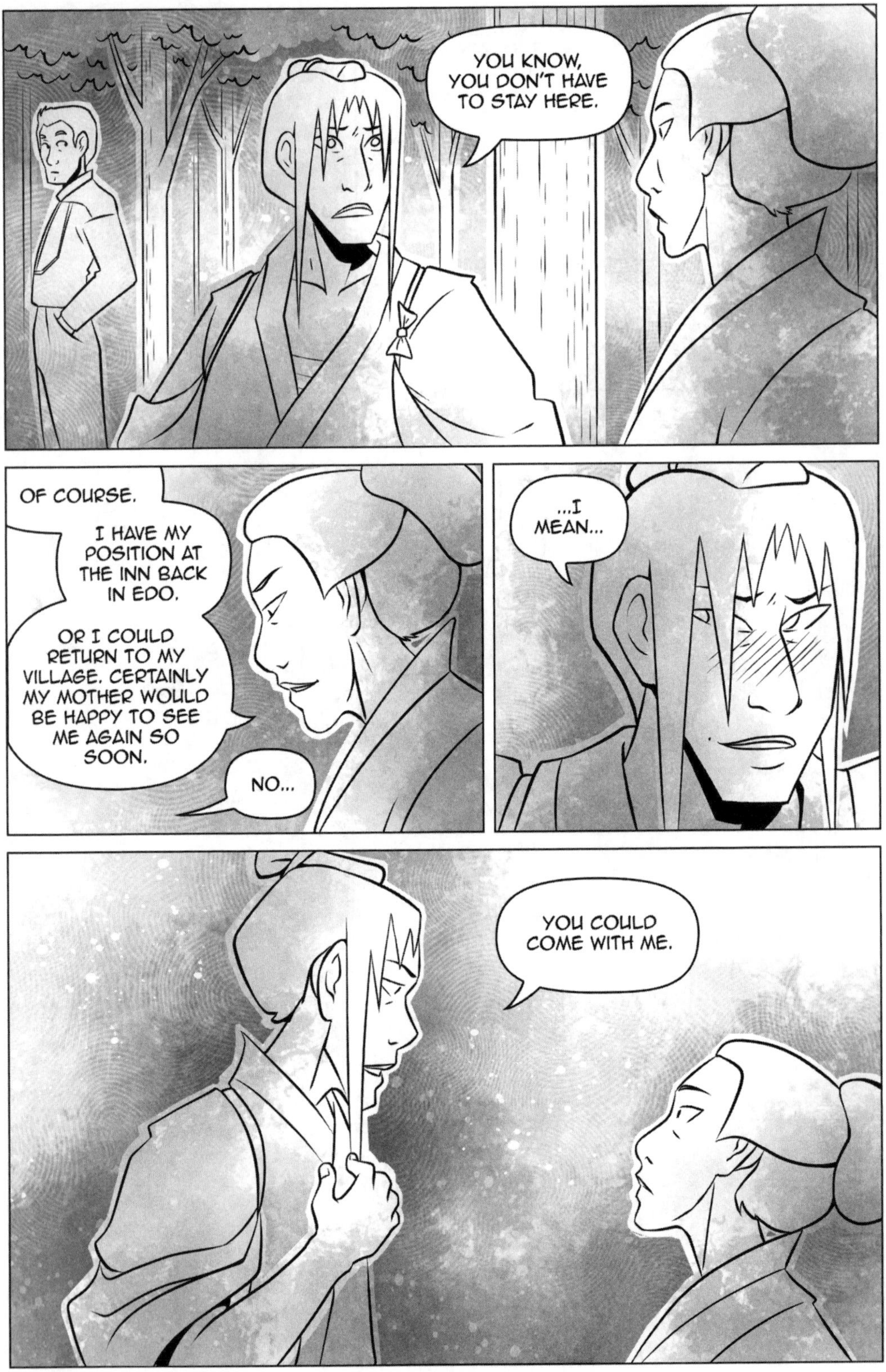
YOU KNOW, YOU DON'T HAVE TO STAY HERE.
OF COURSE.
I HAVE MY POSITION AT THE INN BACK IN EDO.
OR I COULD RETURN TO MY VILLAGE. CERTAINLY MY MOTHER WOULD BE HAPPY TO SEE ME AGAIN SO SOON.
NO...
...I MEAN...
YOU COULD COME WITH ME.

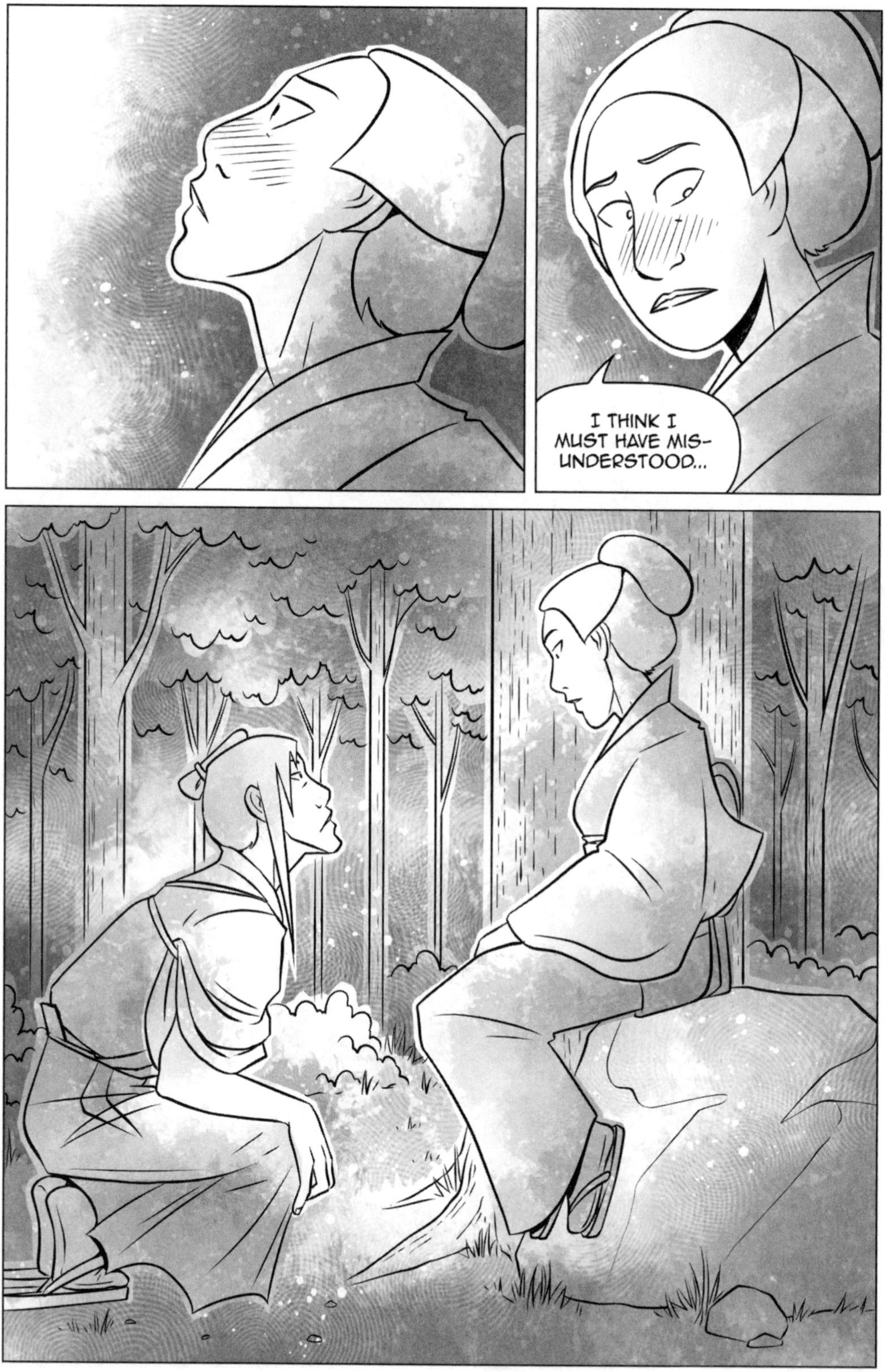
I THINK I MUST HAVE MIS-UNDERSTOOD...

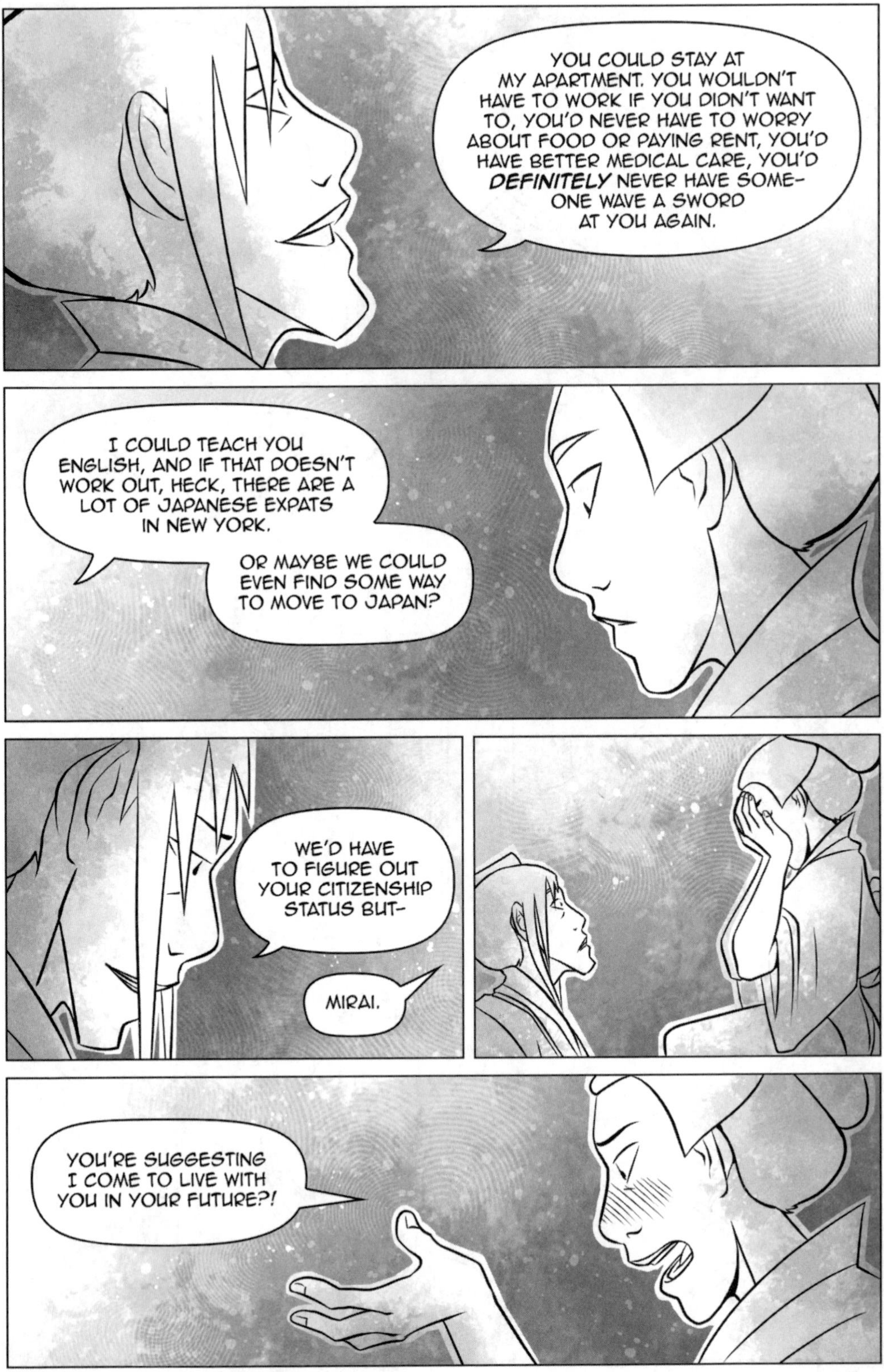
YOU COULD STAY AT MY APARTMENT. YOU WOULDN'T HAVE TO WORK IF YOU DIDN'T WANT TO, YOU'D NEVER HAVE TO WORRY ABOUT FOOD OR PAYING RENT, YOU'D HAVE BETTER MEDICAL CARE, YOU'D ***DEFINITELY*** NEVER HAVE SOME-ONE WAVE A SWORD AT YOU AGAIN.
I COULD TEACH YOU ENGLISH, AND IF THAT DOESN'T WORK OUT, HECK, THERE ARE A LOT OF JAPANESE EXPATS IN NEW YORK.
OR MAYBE WE COULD EVEN FIND SOME WAY TO MOVE TO JAPAN?
WE'D HAVE TO FIGURE OUT YOUR CITIZENSHIP STATUS BUT-
MIRAI.
YOU'RE SUGGESTING I COME TO LIVE WITH YOU IN YOUR FUTURE?!

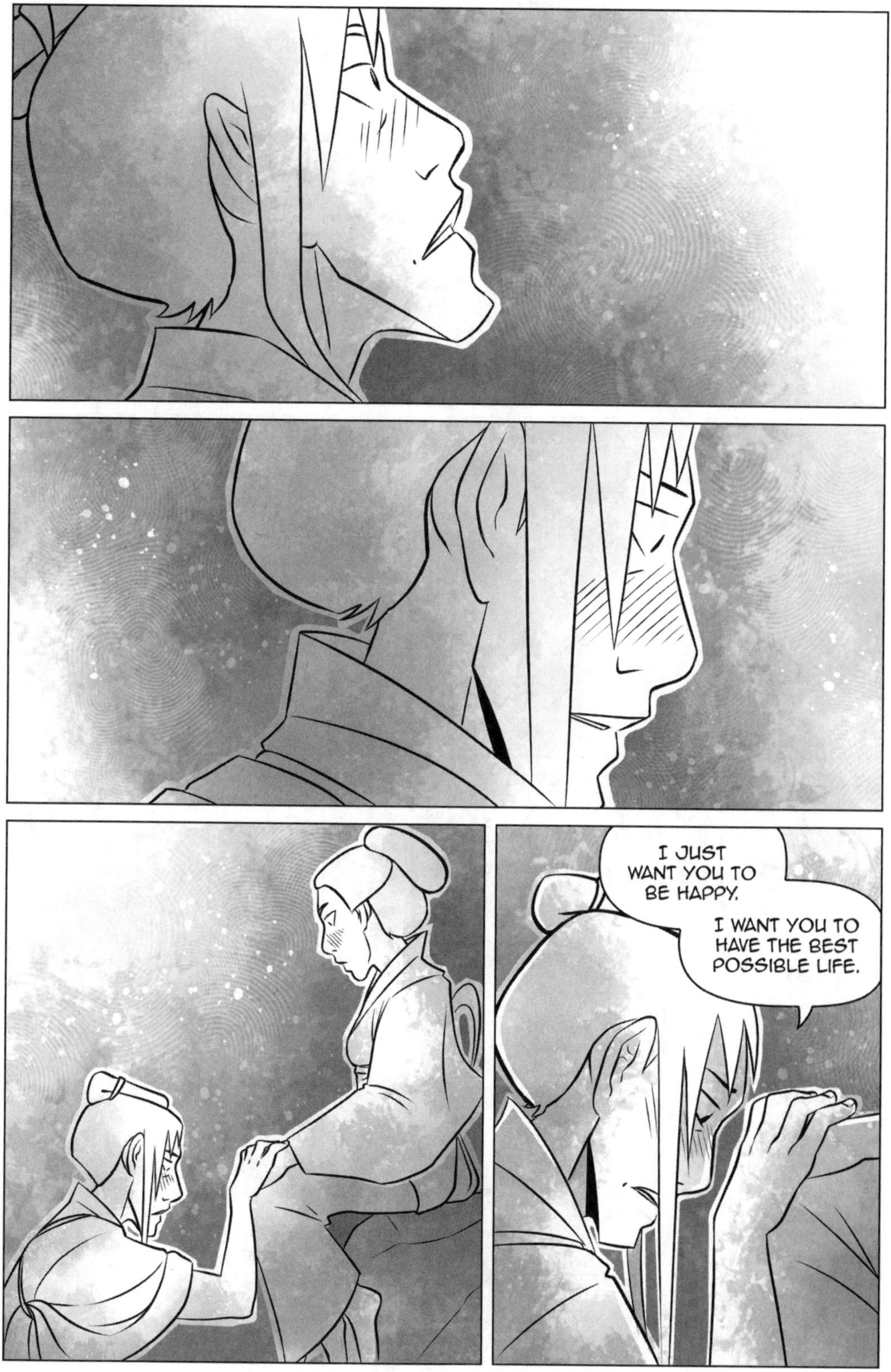
I JUST WANT YOU TO BE HAPPY.
I WANT YOU TO HAVE THE BEST POSSIBLE LIFE.

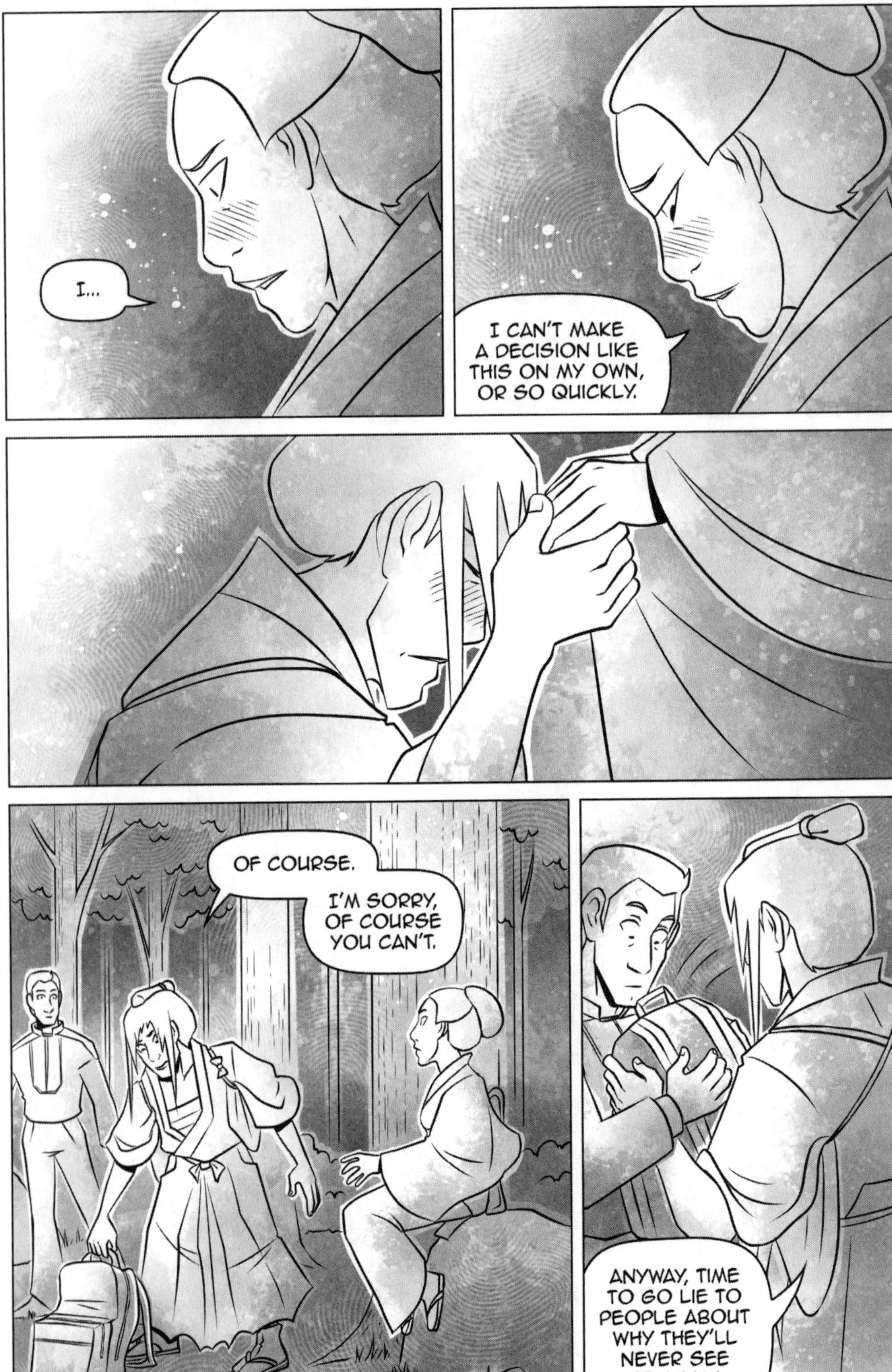
I...
I CAN'T MAKE A DECISION LIKE THIS ON MY OWN, OR SO QUICKLY.
OF COURSE.
I'M SORRY, OF COURSE YOU CAN'T.
ANYWAY, TIME TO GO LIE TO PEOPLE ABOUT WHY THEY'LL NEVER SEE ME AGAIN.

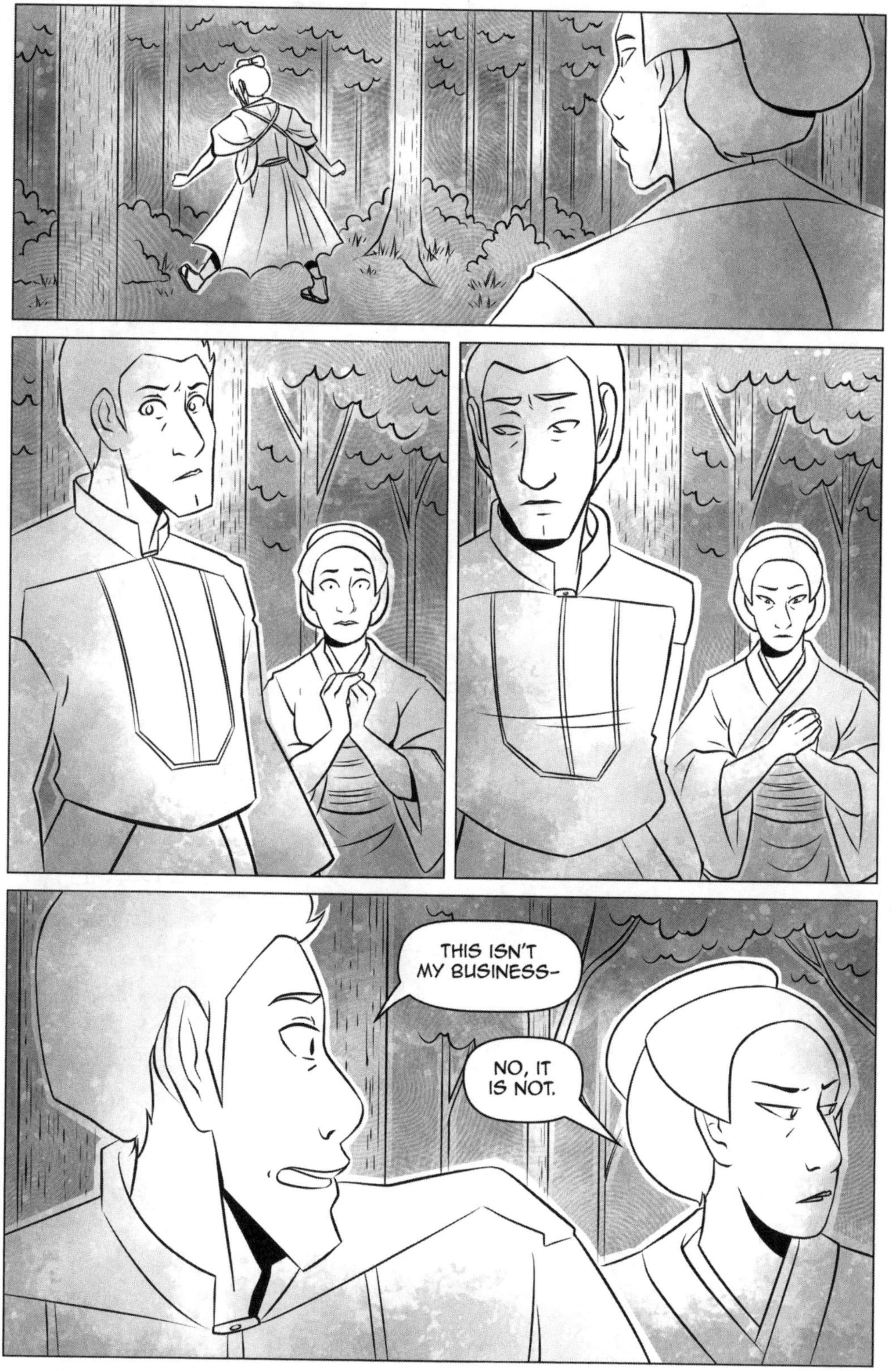
THIS ISN'T MY BUSINESS-
NO, IT IS NOT.

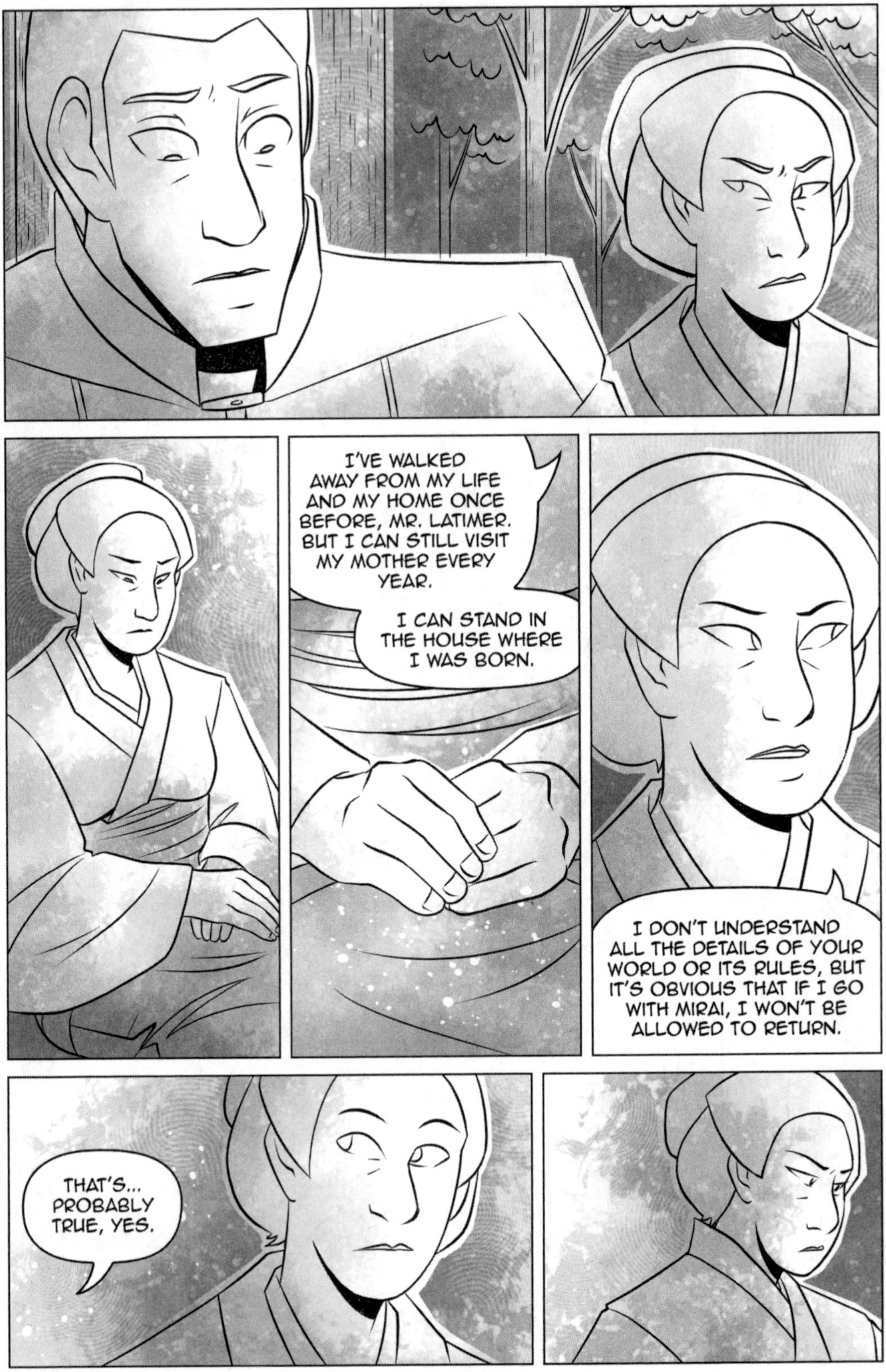
I'VE WALKED AWAY FROM MY LIFE AND MY HOME ONCE BEFORE, MR. LATIMER. BUT I CAN STILL VISIT MY MOTHER EVERY YEAR.
I CAN STAND IN THE HOUSE WHERE I WAS BORN.
I DON'T UNDERSTAND ALL THE DETAILS OF YOUR WORLD OR ITS RULES, BUT IT'S OBVIOUS THAT IF I GO WITH MIRAI, I WON'T BE ALLOWED TO RETURN.
THAT'S... PROBABLY TRUE, YES.

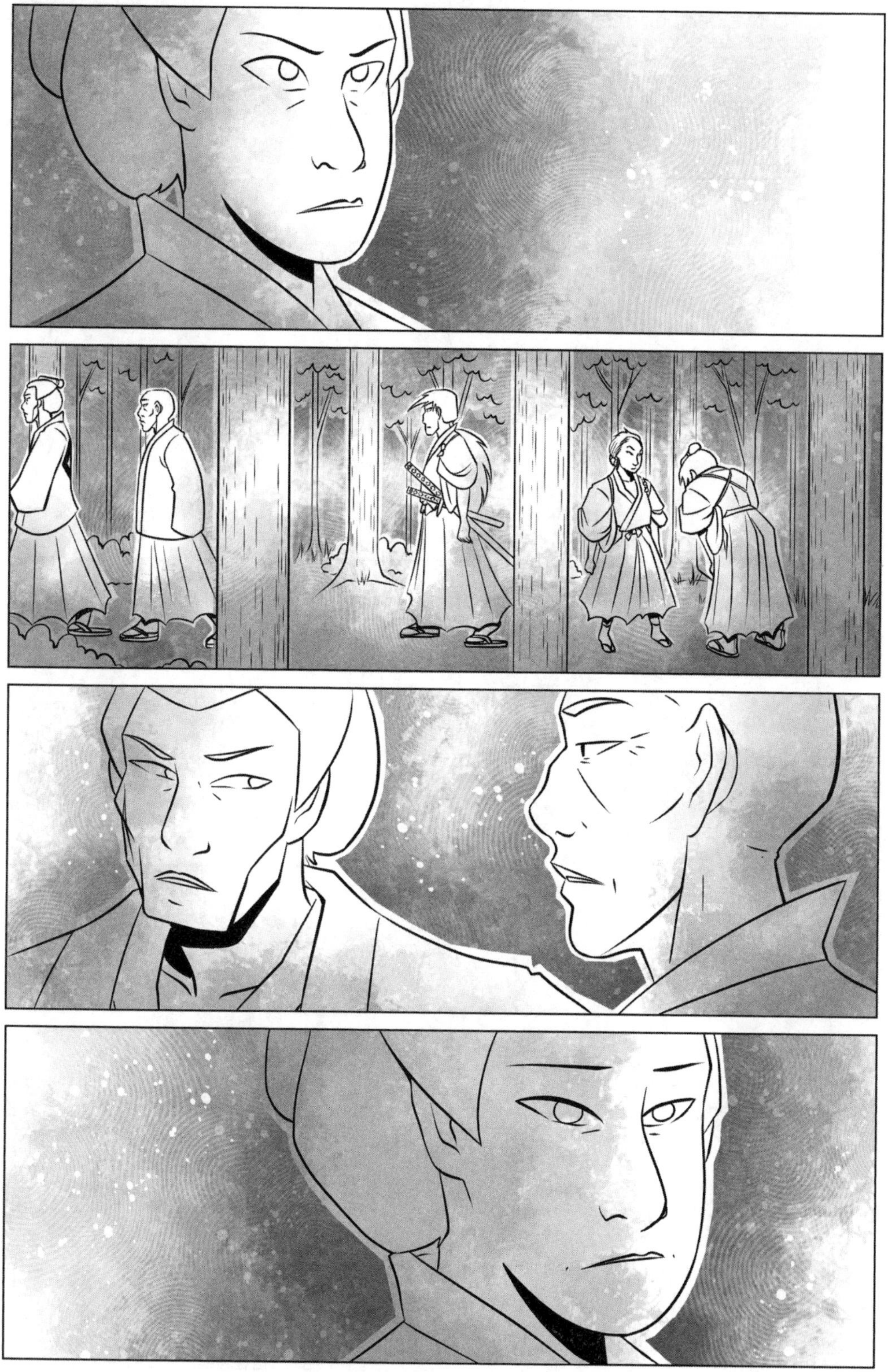

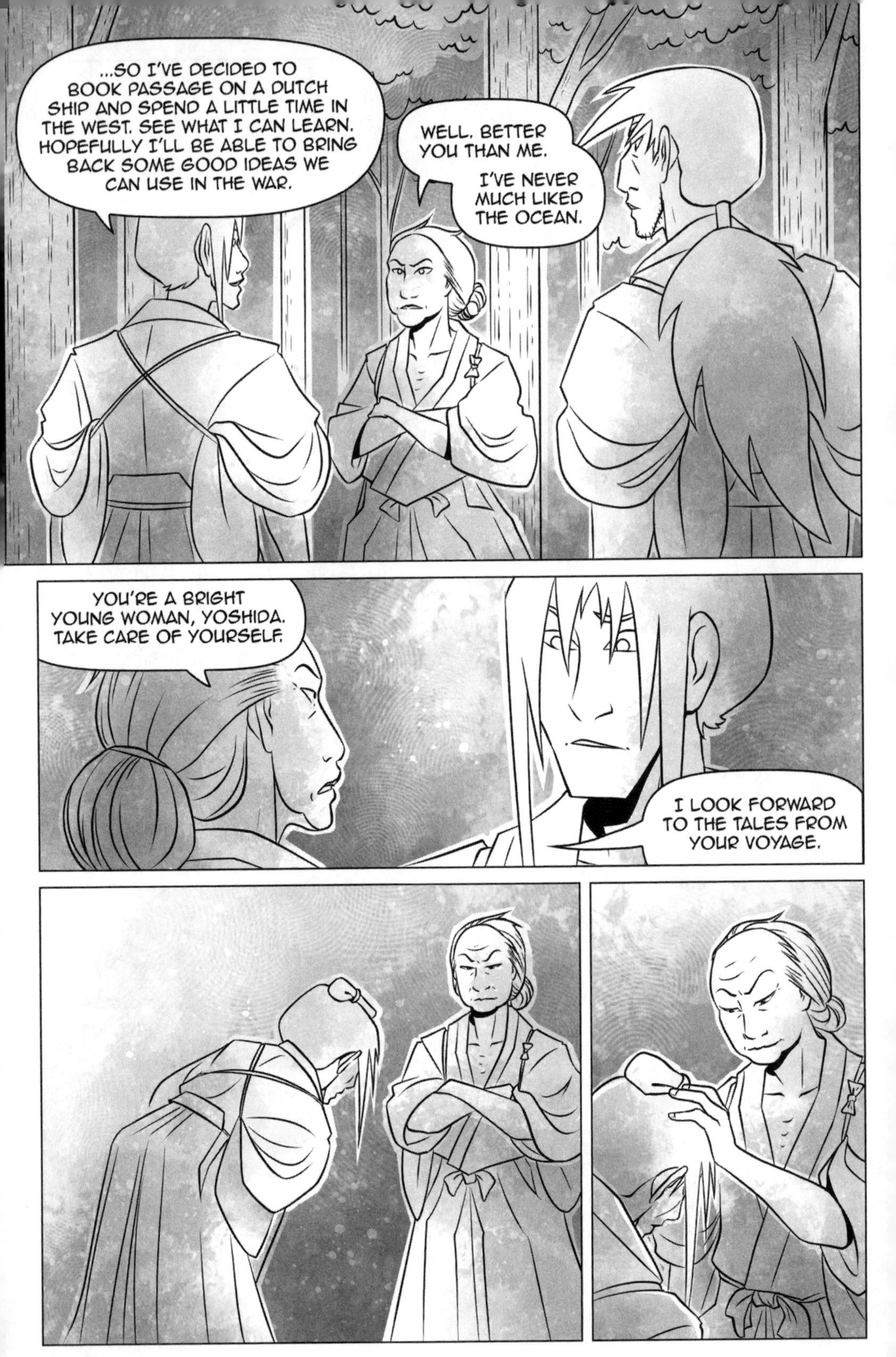
...SO I'VE DECIDED TO BOOK PASSAGE ON A DUTCH SHIP AND SPEND A LITTLE TIME IN THE WEST. SEE WHAT I CAN LEARN. HOPEFULLY I'LL BE ABLE TO BRING BACK SOME GOOD IDEAS WE CAN USE IN THE WAR.
WELL. BETTER YOU THAN ME.
I'VE NEVER MUCH LIKED THE OCEAN.
YOU'RE A BRIGHT YOUNG WOMAN, YOSHIDA. TAKE CARE OF YOURSELF.
I LOOK FORWARD TO THE TALES FROM YOUR VOYAGE.

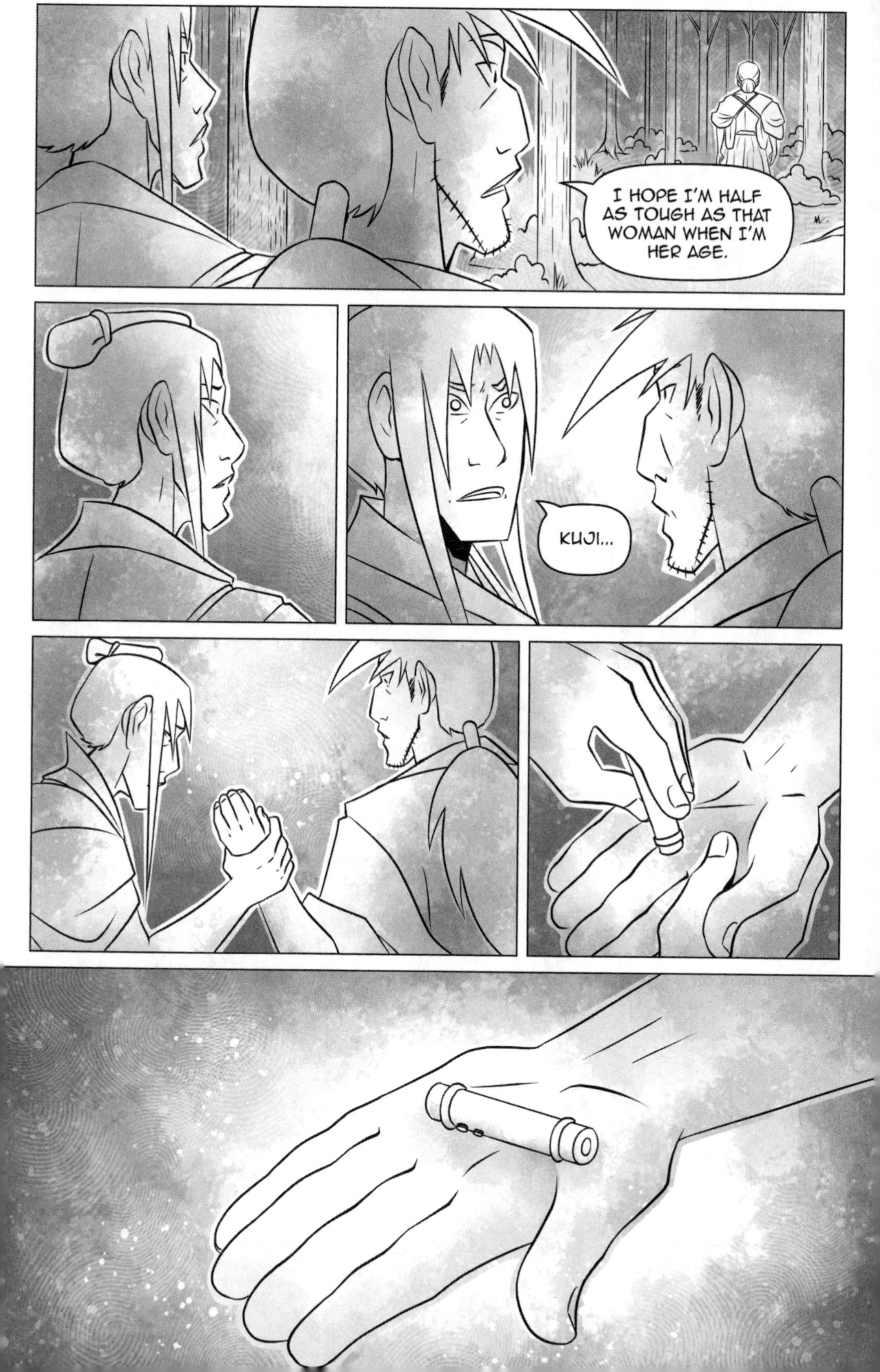
I HOPE I'M HALF AS TOUGH AS THAT WOMAN WHEN I'M HER AGE.
KUJI...

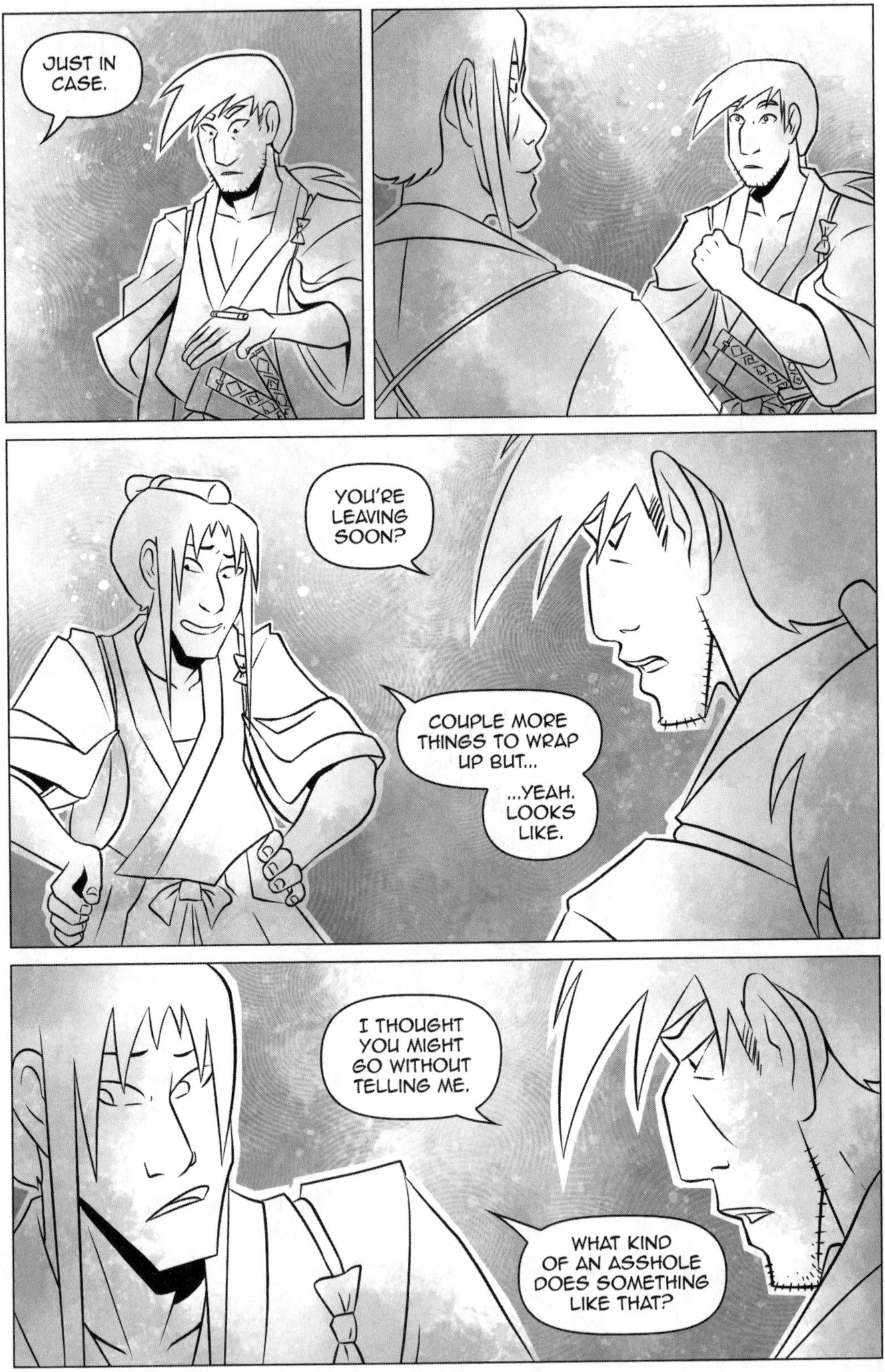
JUST IN CASE.
YOU'RE LEAVING SOON?
COUPLE MORE THINGS TO WRAP UP BUT...
...YEAH. LOOKS LIKE.
I THOUGHT YOU MIGHT GO WITHOUT TELLING ME.
WHAT KIND OF AN ASSHOLE DOES SOMETHING LIKE THAT?

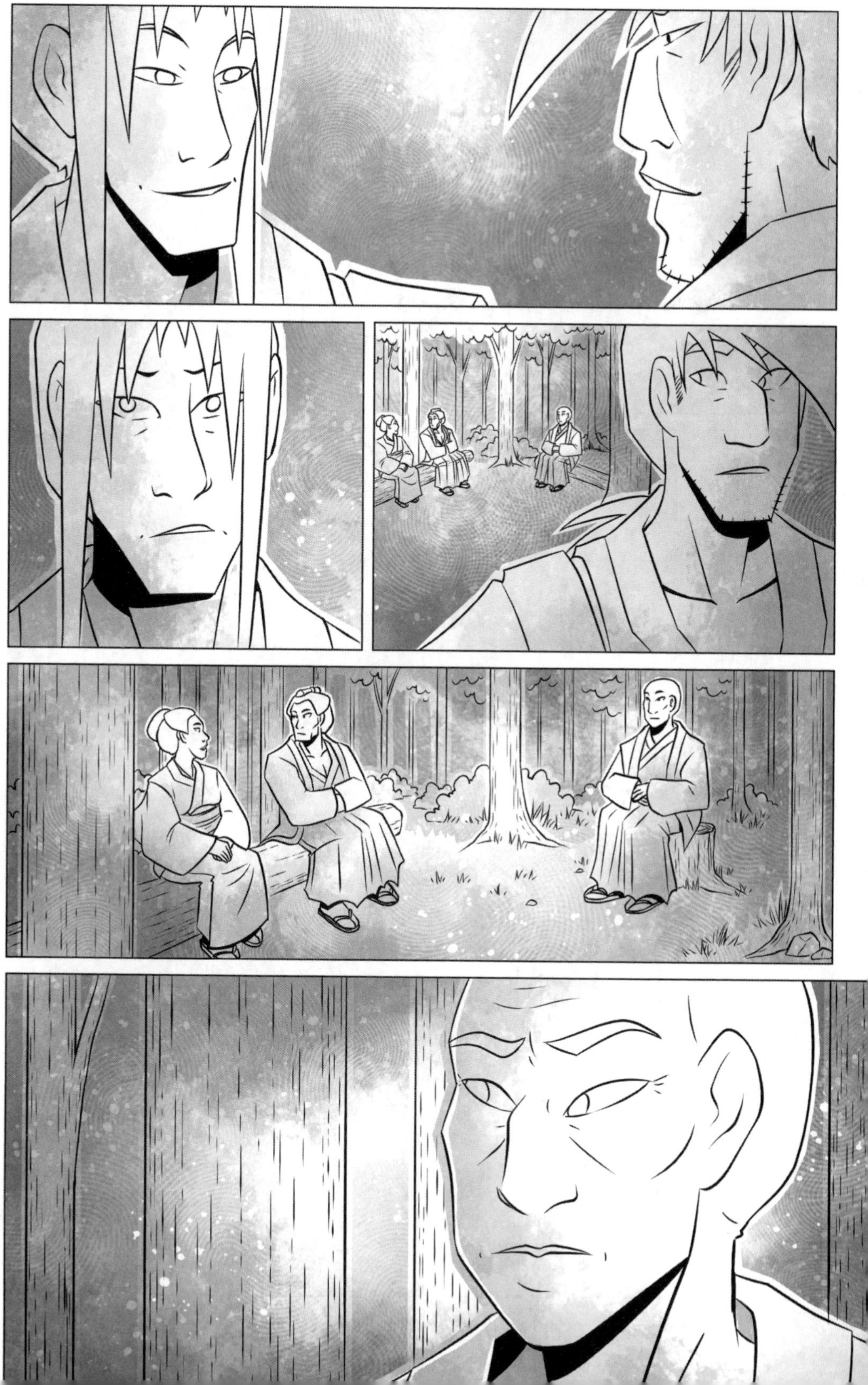

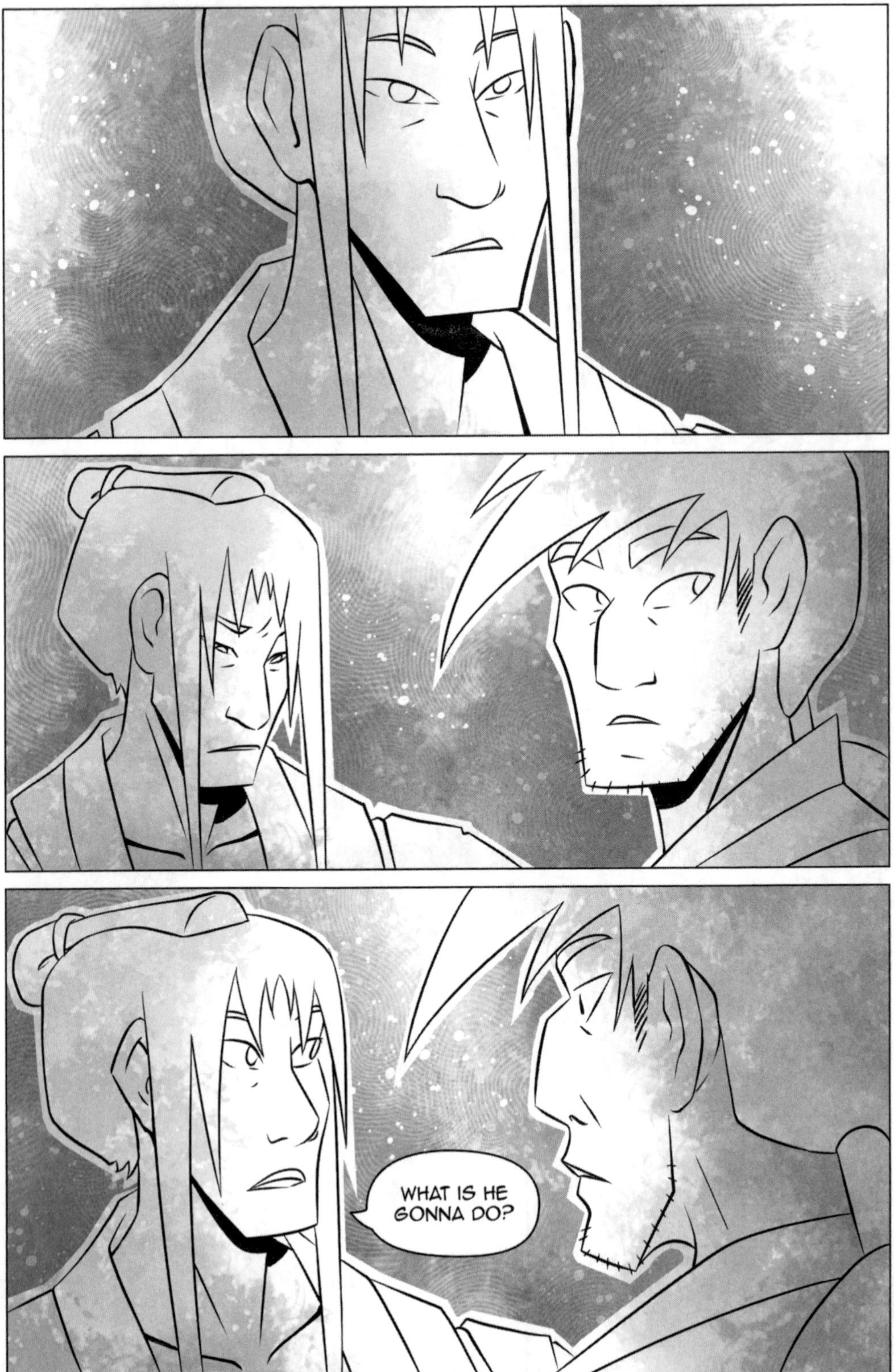
WHAT IS HE GONNA DO?

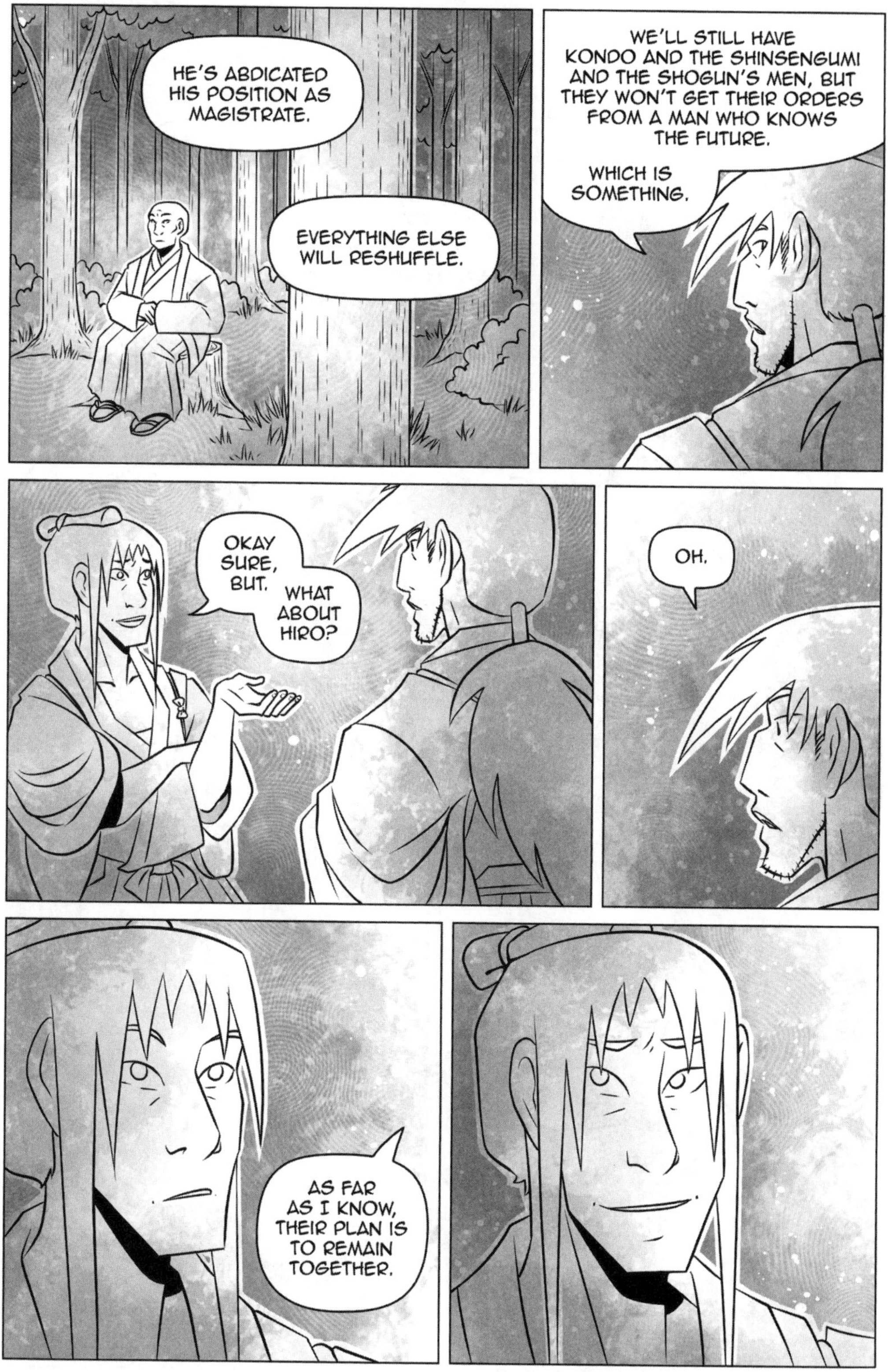
HE'S ABDICATED HIS POSITION AS MAGISTRATE.
EVERYTHING ELSE WILL RESHUFFLE.
WE'LL STILL HAVE KONDO AND THE SHINSENGUMI AND THE SHOGUN'S MEN, BUT THEY WON'T GET THEIR ORDERS FROM A MAN WHO KNOWS THE FUTURE.
WHICH IS SOMETHING.
OKAY SURE, BUT.
WHAT ABOUT HIRO?
OH.
AS FAR AS I KNOW, THEIR PLAN IS TO REMAIN TOGETHER.

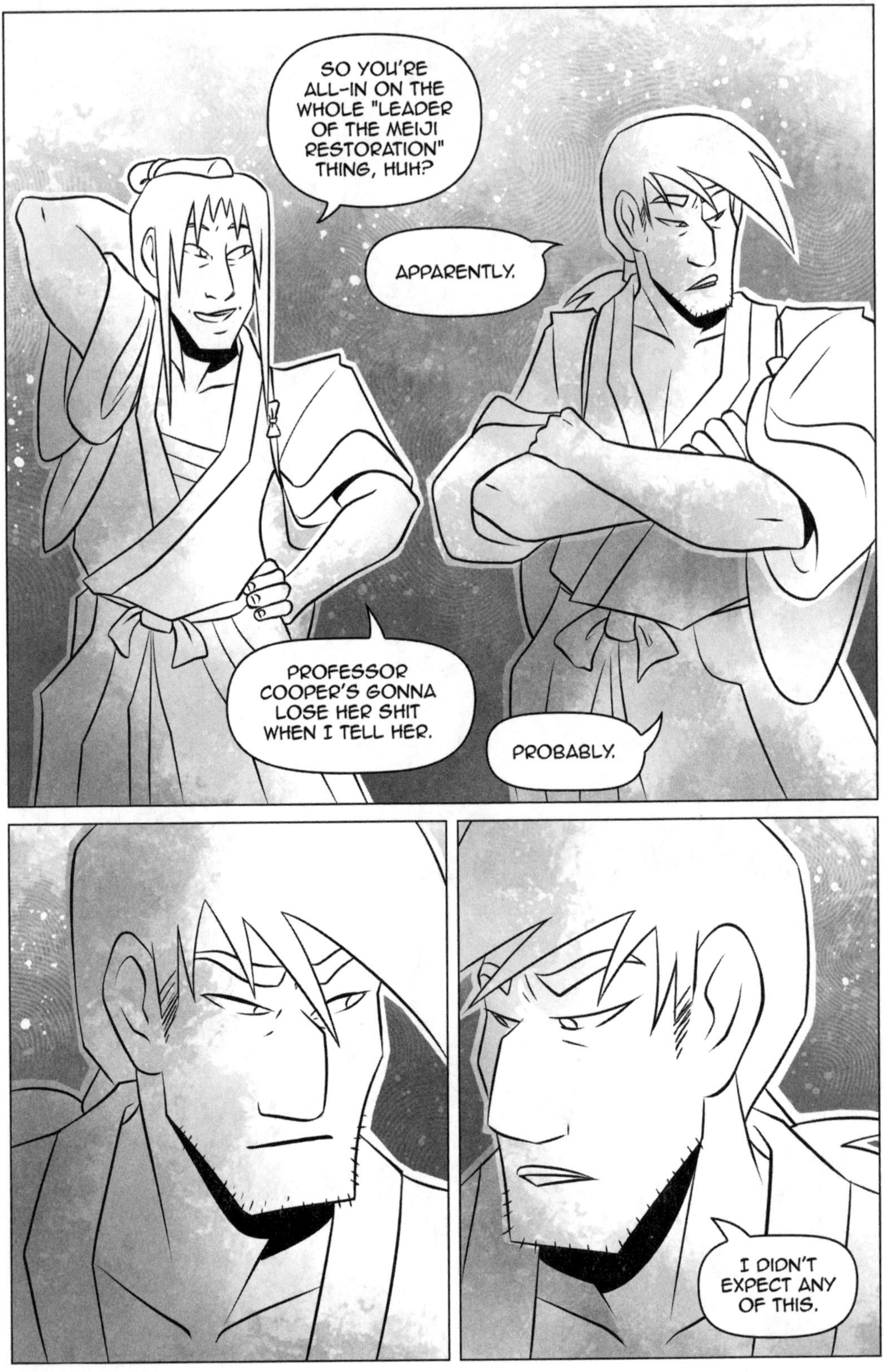
SO YOU'RE ALL-IN ON THE WHOLE "LEADER OF THE MEIJI RESTORATION" THING, HUH?
APPARENTLY.
PROFESSOR COOPER'S GONNA LOSE HER SHIT WHEN I TELL HER.
PROBABLY.
I DIDN'T EXPECT ANY OF THIS.

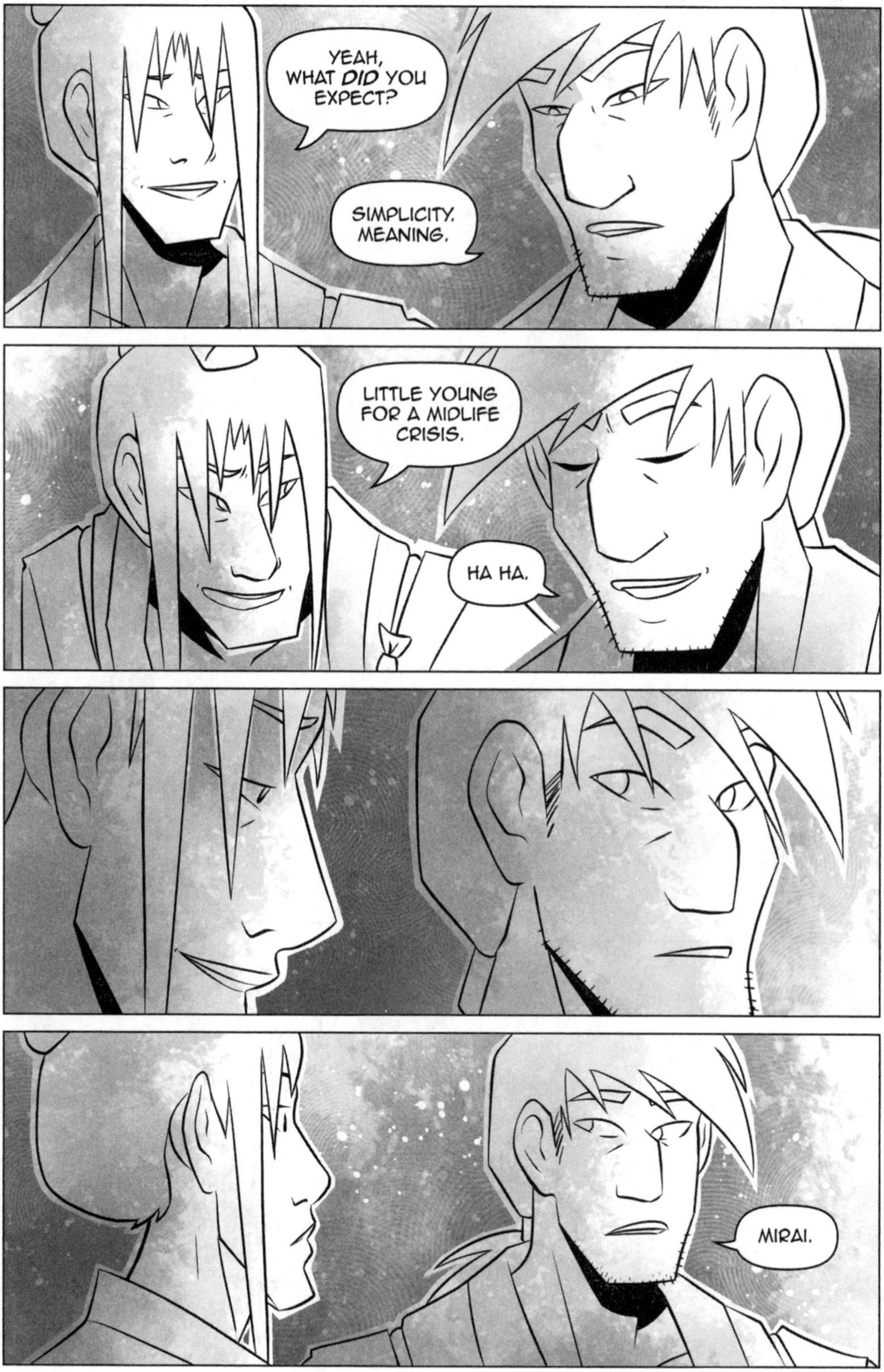
YEAH, WHAT *DID* YOU EXPECT?
SIMPLICITY. MEANING.
LITTLE YOUNG FOR A MIDLIFE CRISIS.
HA HA.
MIRAI.

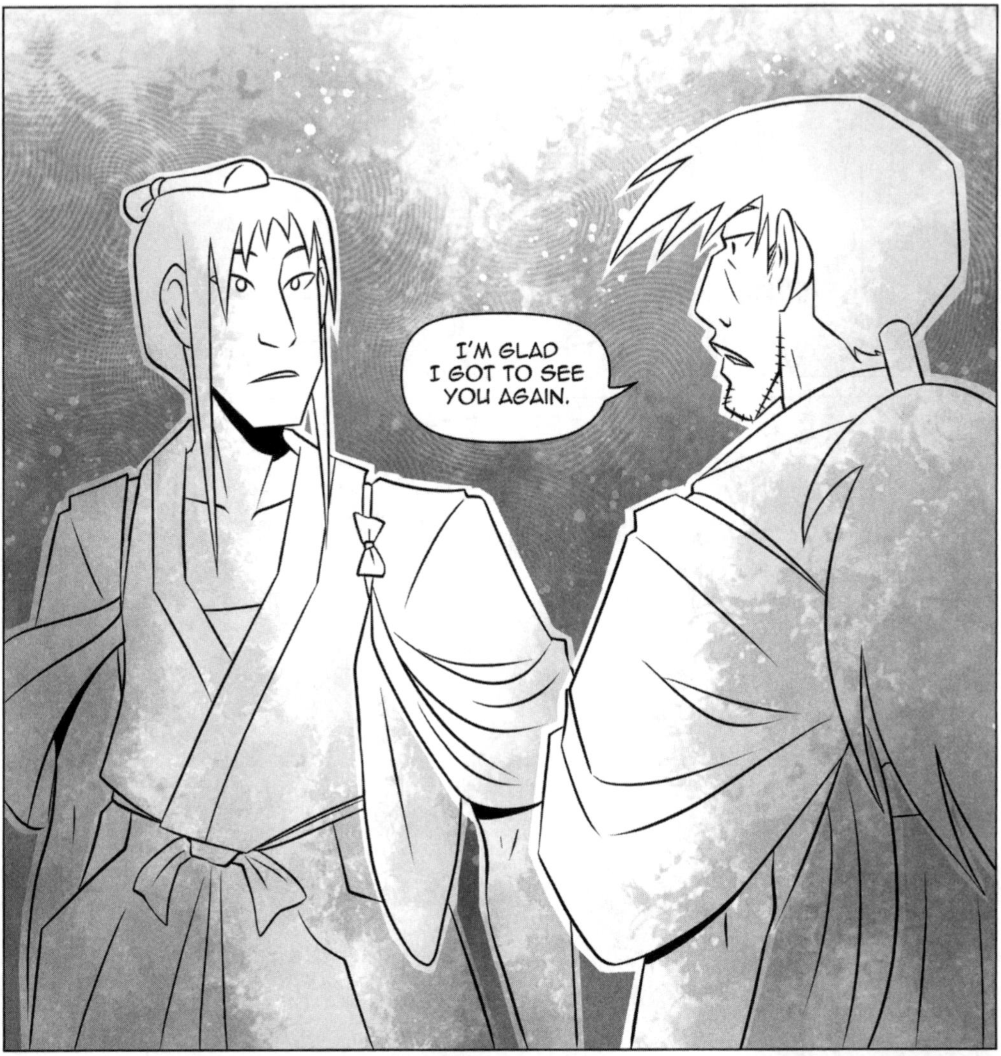
I'M GLAD I GOT TO SEE YOU AGAIN.

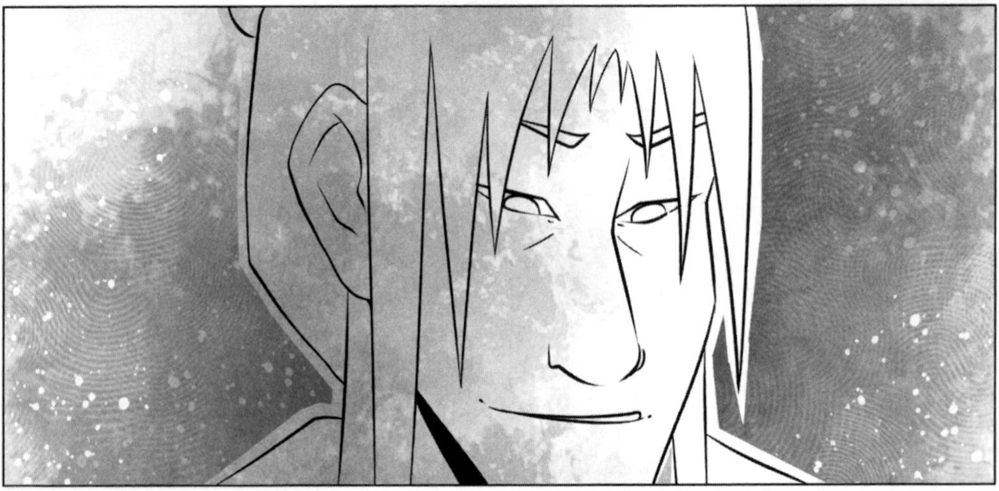

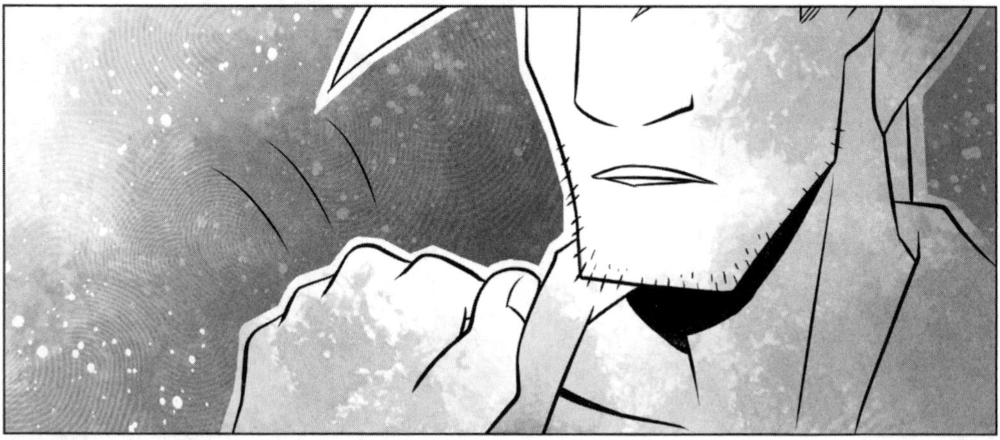

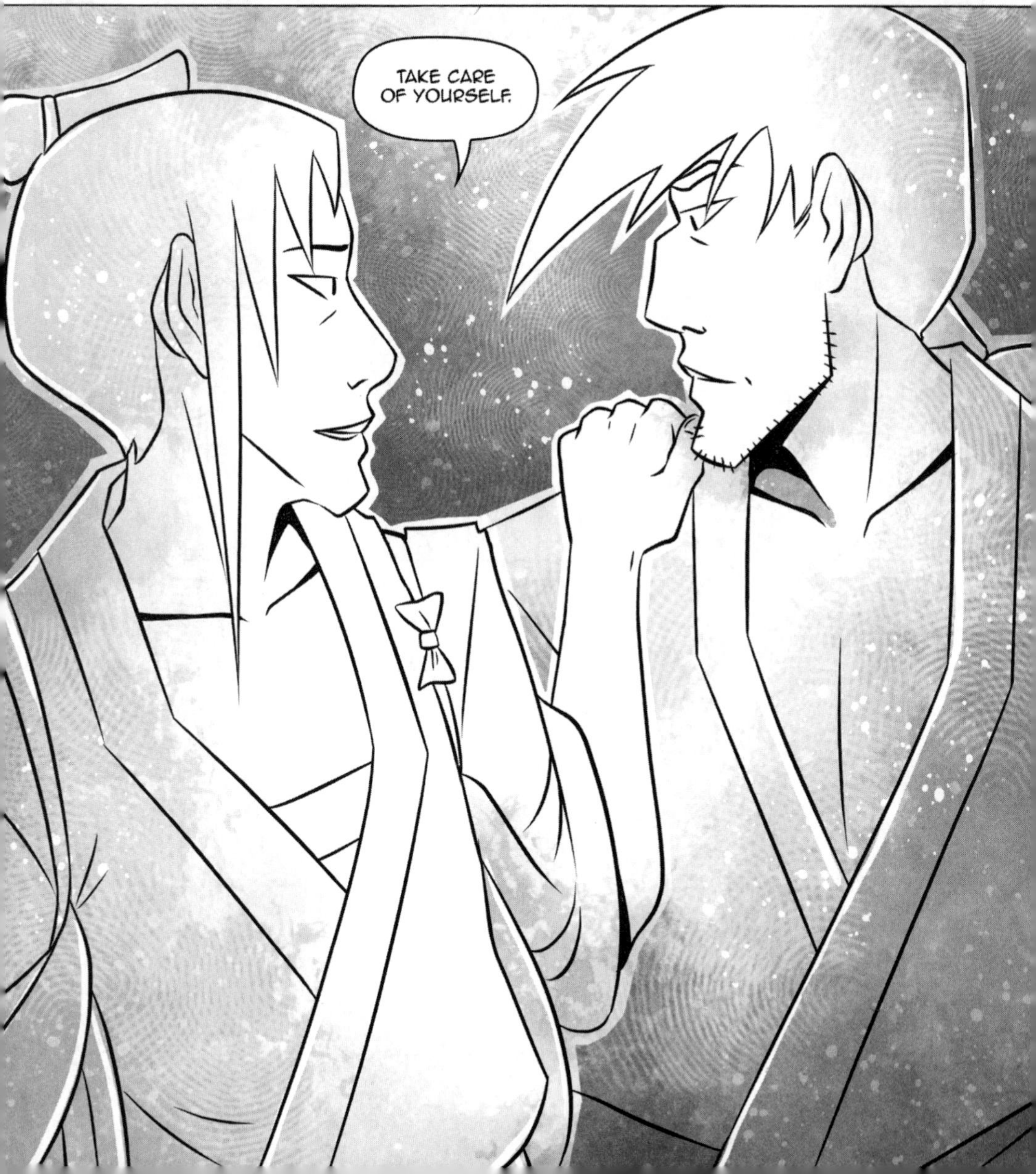
TAKE CARE OF YOURSELF.

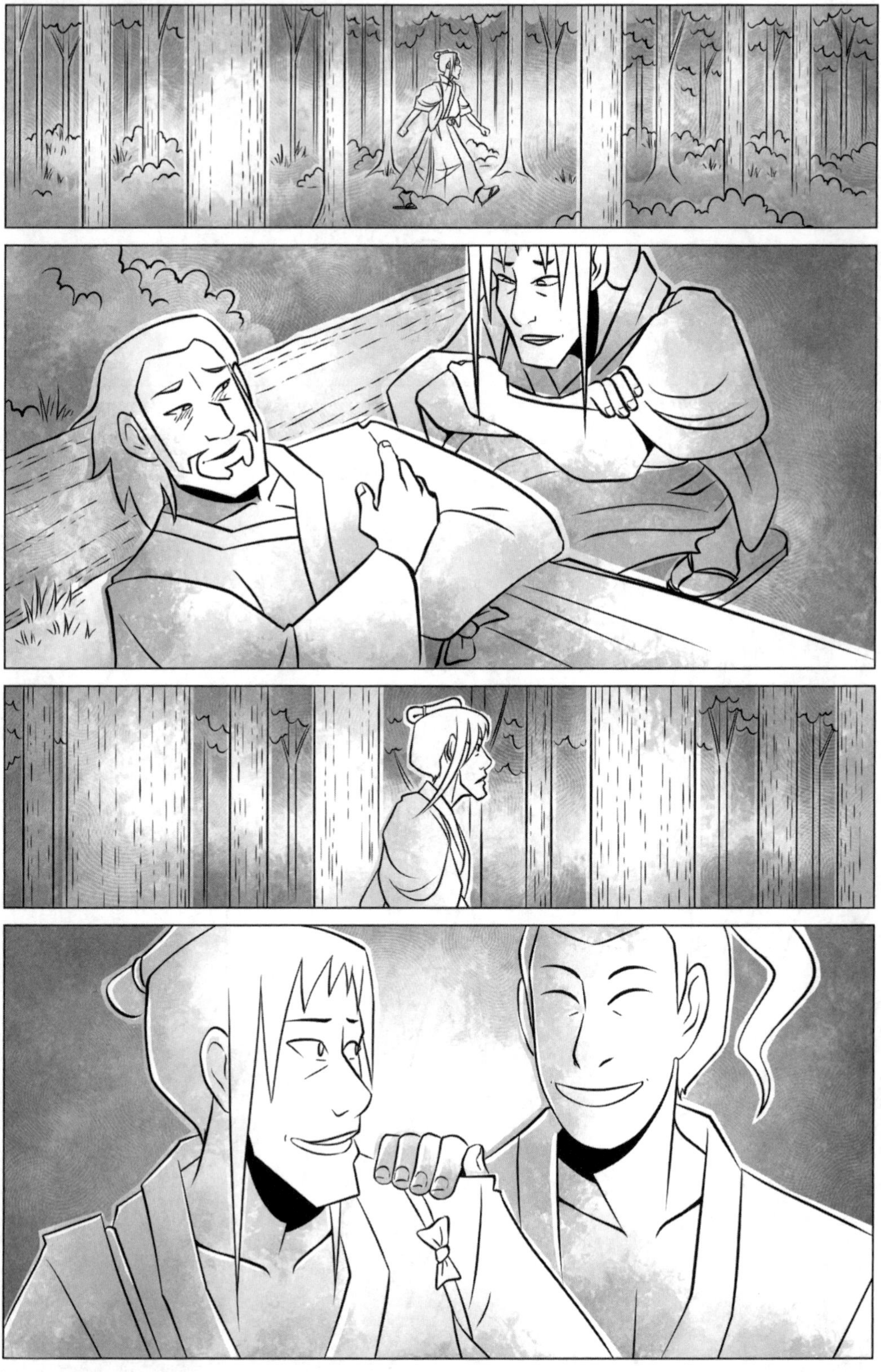

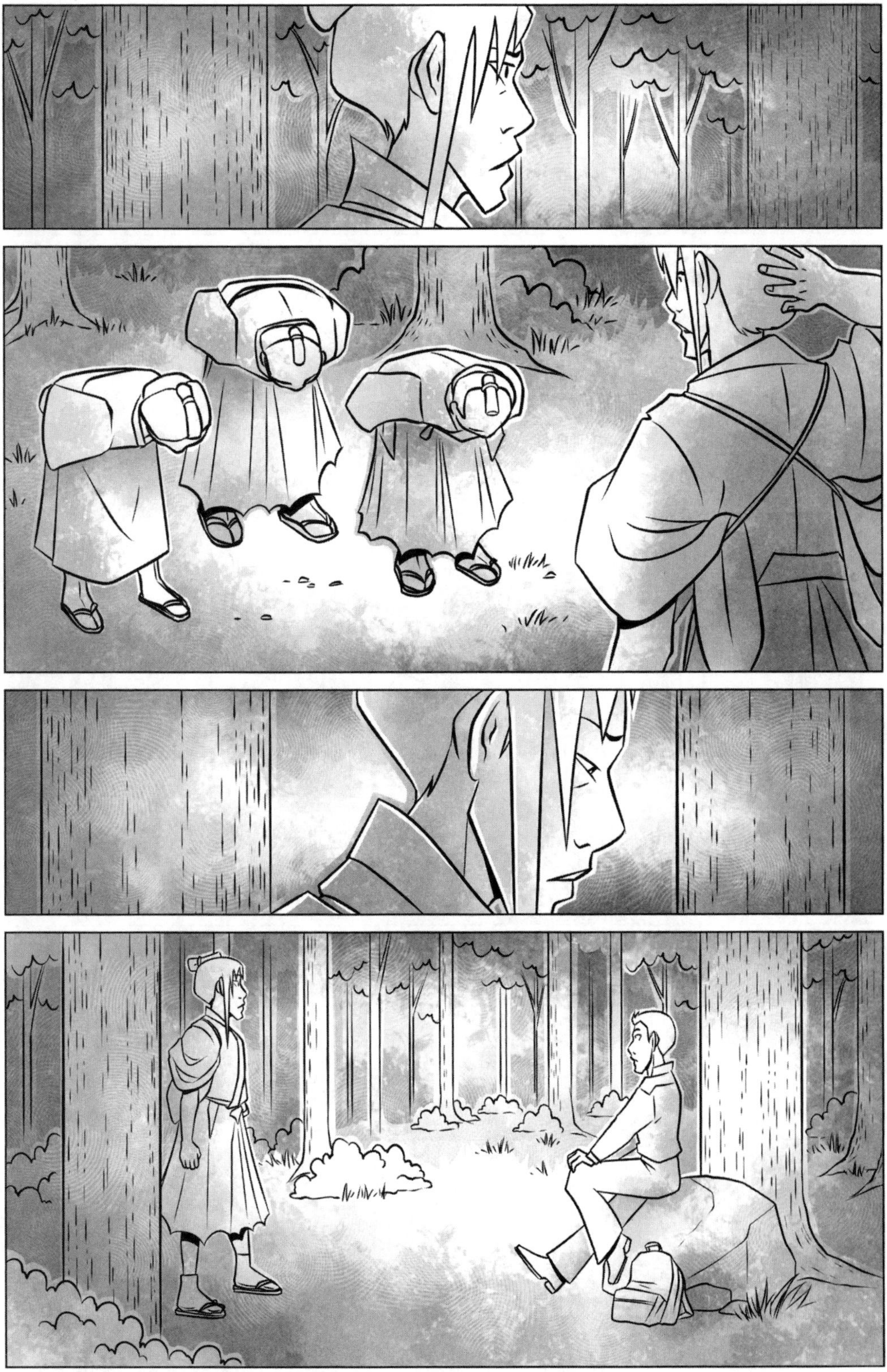

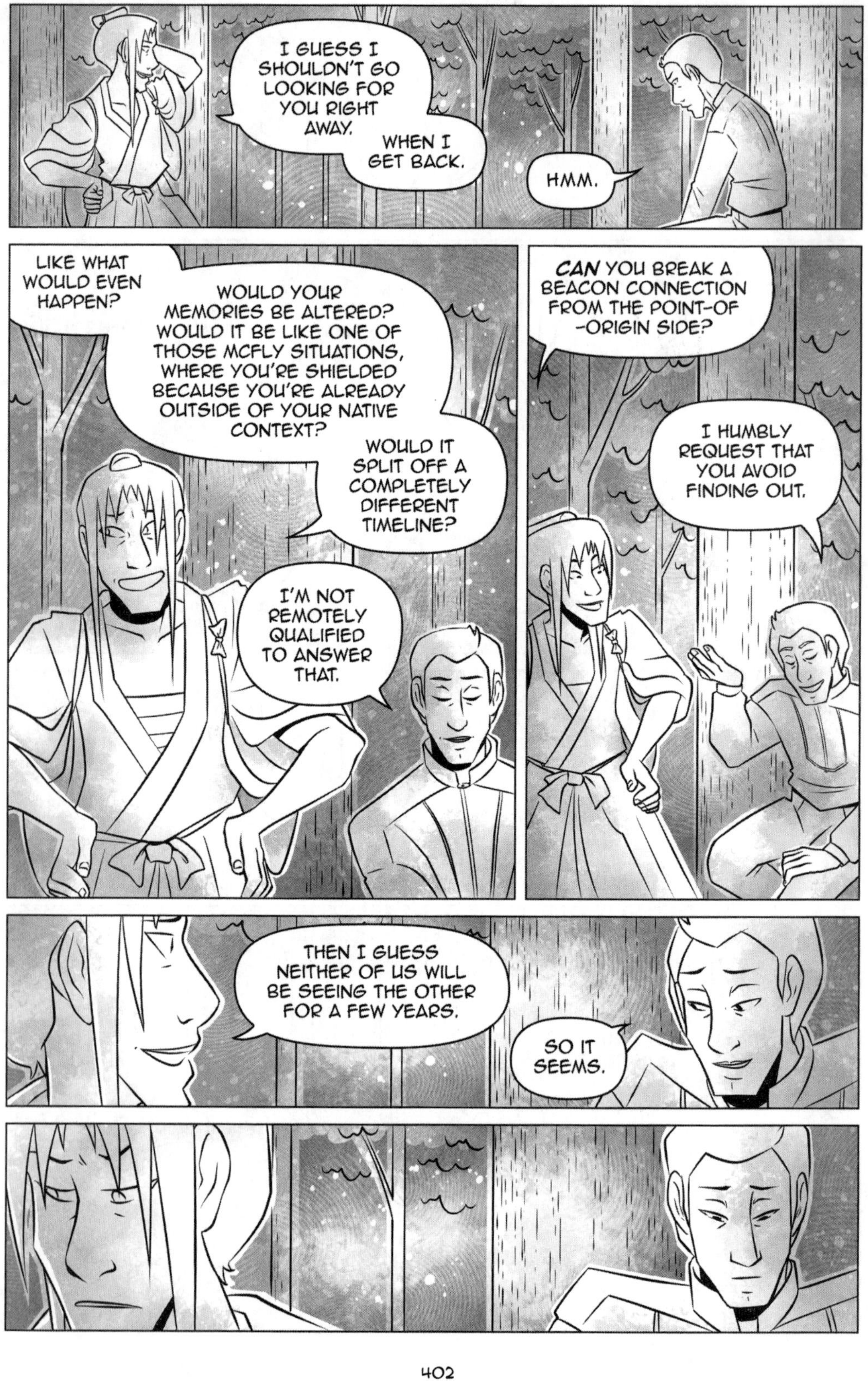
I GUESS I SHOULDN'T GO LOOKING FOR YOU RIGHT AWAY.
WHEN I GET BACK.
HMM.
LIKE WHAT WOULD EVEN HAPPEN?
WOULD YOUR MEMORIES BE ALTERED? WOULD IT BE LIKE ONE OF THOSE MCFLY SITUATIONS, WHERE YOU'RE SHIELDED BECAUSE YOU'RE ALREADY OUTSIDE OF YOUR NATIVE CONTEXT?
WOULD IT SPLIT OFF A COMPLETELY DIFFERENT TIMELINE?
I'M NOT REMOTELY QUALIFIED TO ANSWER THAT.
*CAN* YOU BREAK A BEACON CONNECTION FROM THE POINT-OF-ORIGIN SIDE?
I HUMBLY REQUEST THAT YOU AVOID FINDING OUT.
THEN I GUESS NEITHER OF US WILL BE SEEING THE OTHER FOR A FEW YEARS.
SO IT SEEMS.

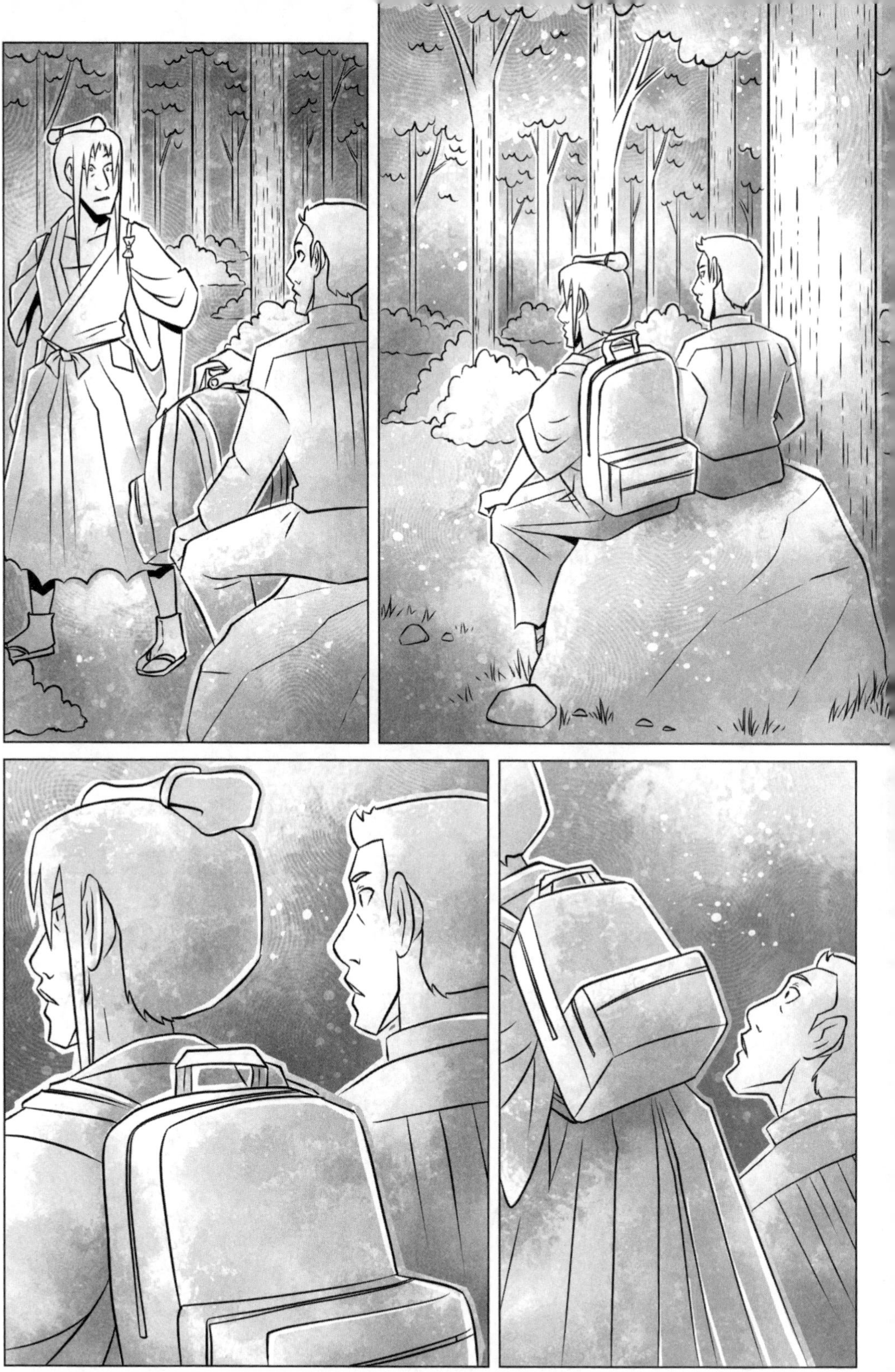

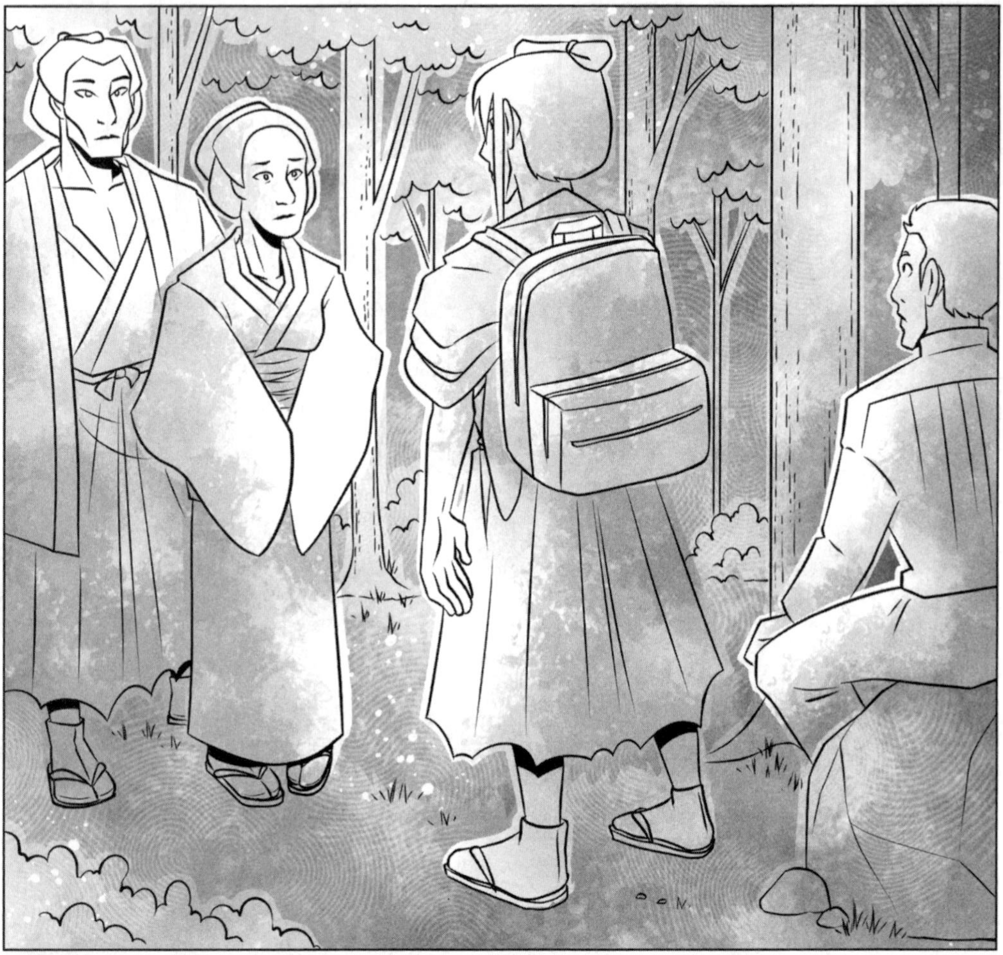

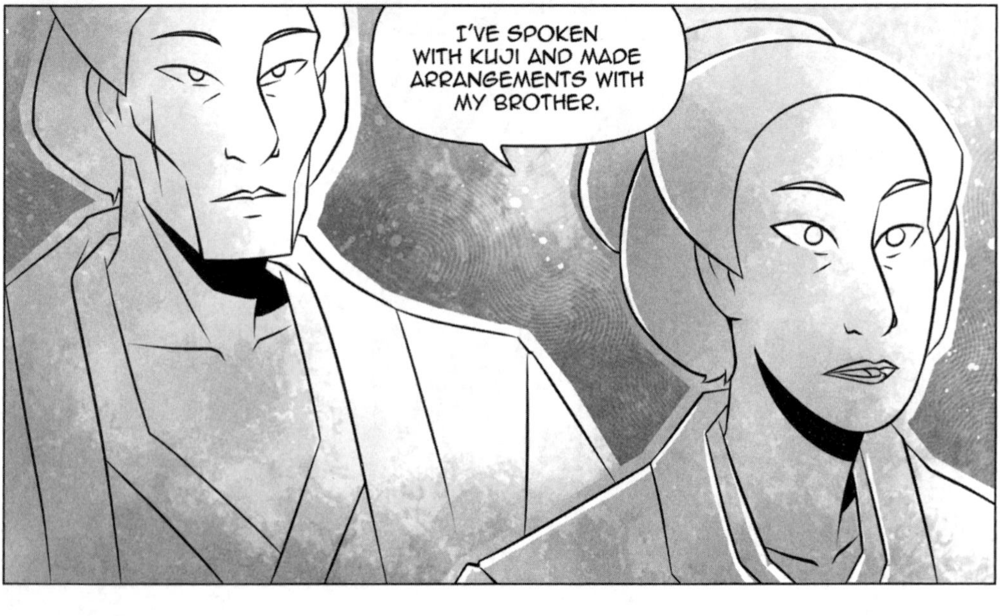
I'VE SPOKEN WITH KUJI AND MADE ARRANGEMENTS WITH MY BROTHER.

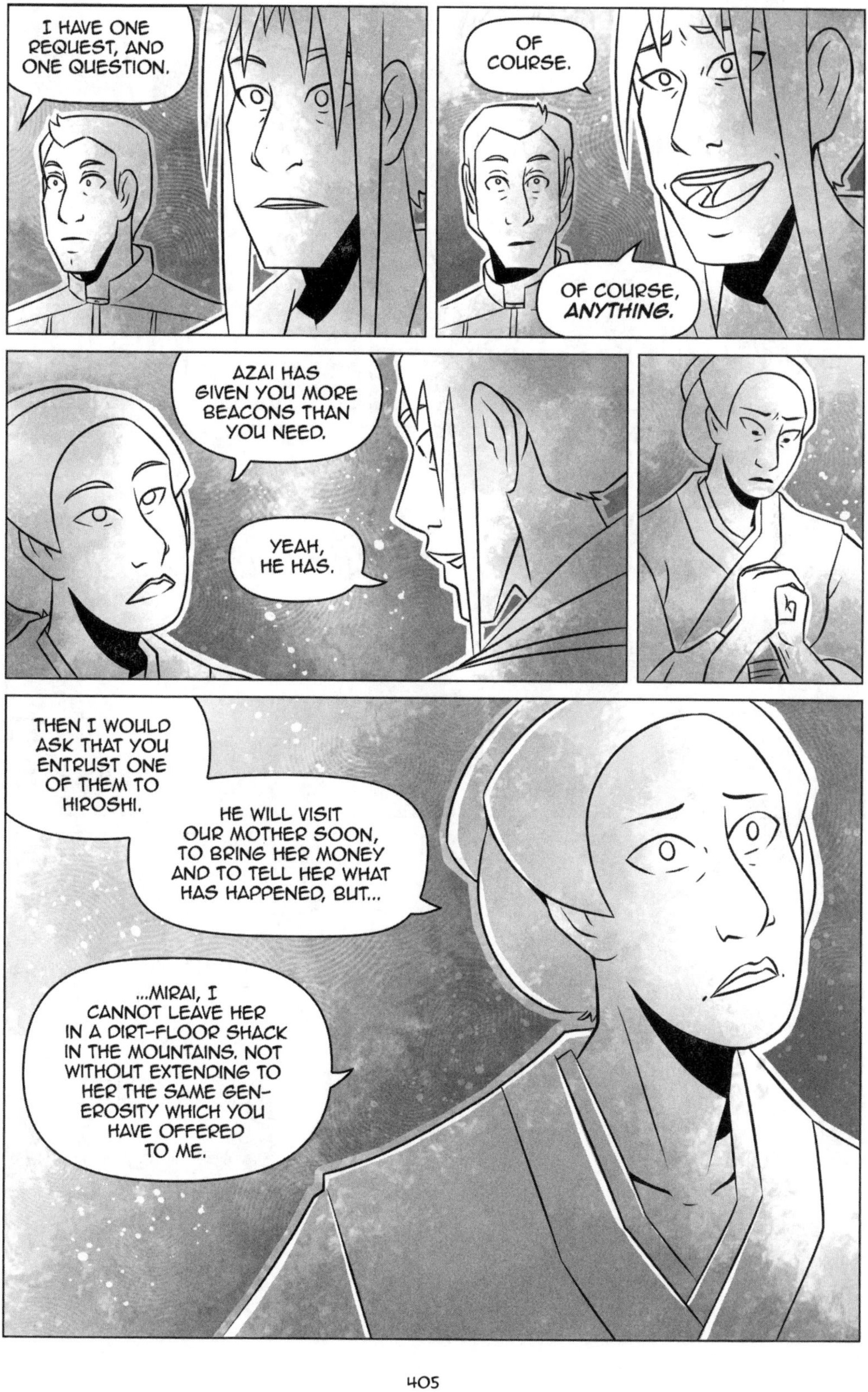
I HAVE ONE REQUEST, AND ONE QUESTION.
OF COURSE.
OF COURSE, ANYTHING.
AZAI HAS GIVEN YOU MORE BEACONS THAN YOU NEED.
YEAH, HE HAS.
THEN I WOULD ASK THAT YOU ENTRUST ONE OF THEM TO HIROSHI.
HE WILL VISIT OUR MOTHER SOON, TO BRING HER MONEY AND TO TELL HER WHAT HAS HAPPENED, BUT...
...MIRAI, I CANNOT LEAVE HER IN A DIRT-FLOOR SHACK IN THE MOUNTAINS. NOT WITHOUT EXTENDING TO HER THE SAME GEN-EROSITY WHICH YOU HAVE OFFERED TO ME.

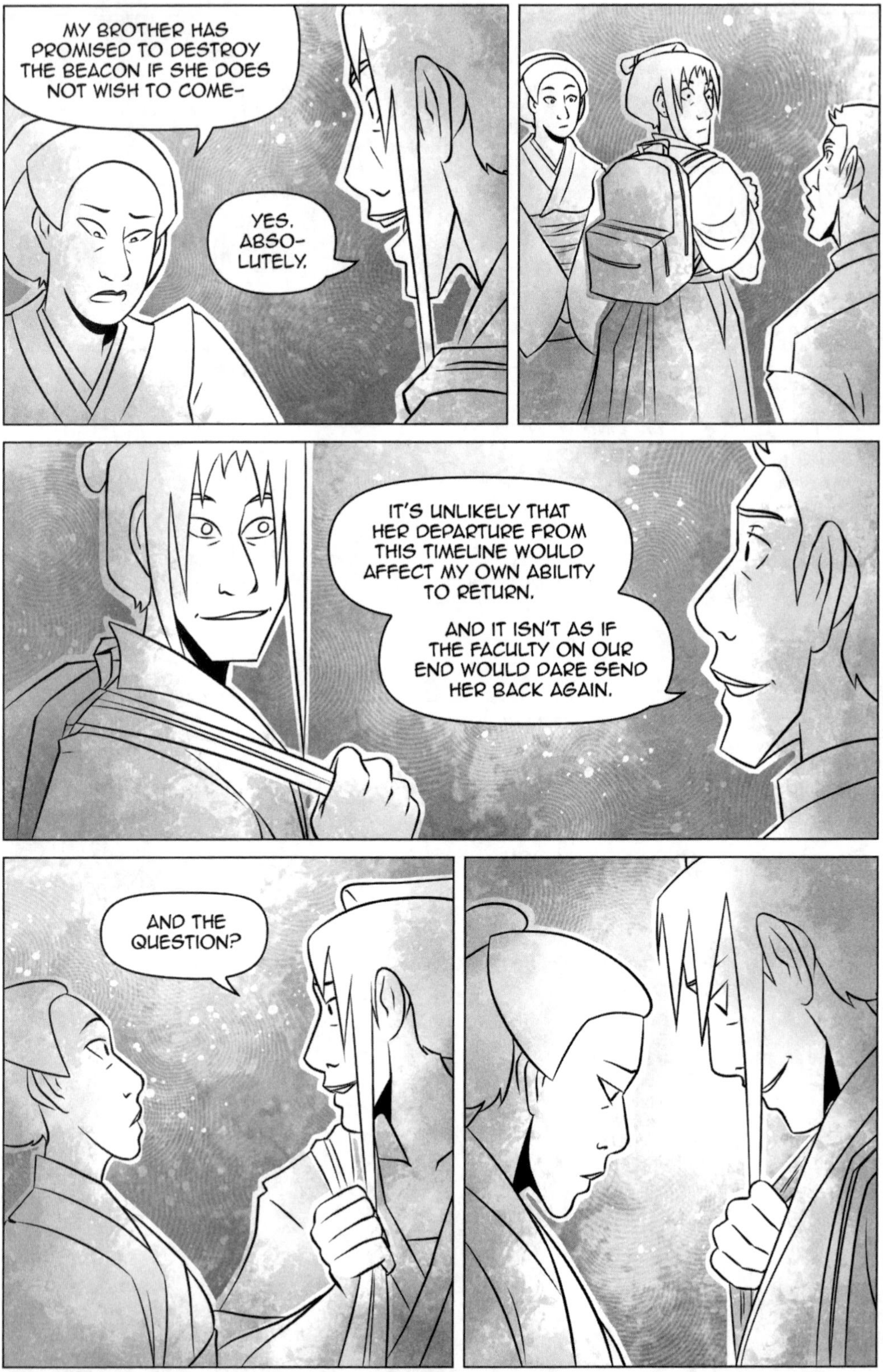
MY BROTHER HAS PROMISED TO DESTROY THE BEACON IF SHE DOES NOT WISH TO COME-
YES. ABSO-LUTELY.
IT'S UNLIKELY THAT HER DEPARTURE FROM THIS TIMELINE WOULD AFFECT MY OWN ABILITY TO RETURN.
AND IT ISN'T AS IF THE FACULTY ON OUR END WOULD DARE SEND HER BACK AGAIN.
AND THE QUESTION?

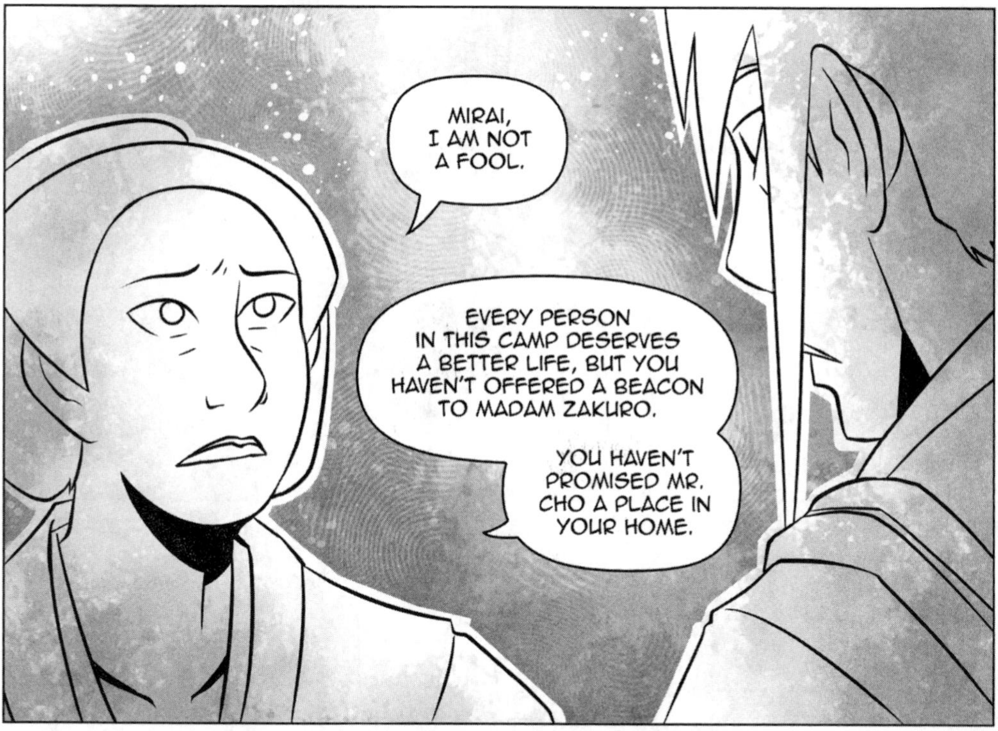
MIRAI, I AM NOT A FOOL.
EVERY PERSON IN THIS CAMP DESERVES A BETTER LIFE, BUT YOU HAVEN'T OFFERED A BEACON TO MADAM ZAKURO.
YOU HAVEN'T PROMISED MR. CHO A PLACE IN YOUR HOME.

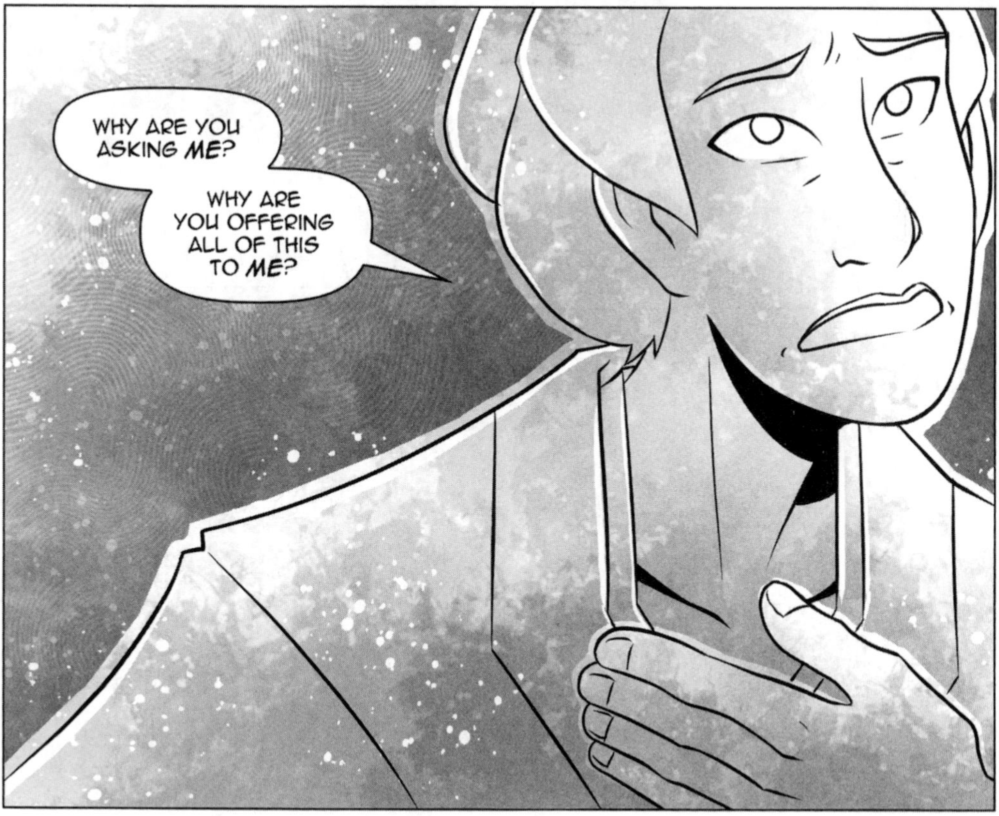
WHY ARE YOU ASKING *ME*?
WHY ARE YOU OFFERING ALL OF THIS TO *ME*?

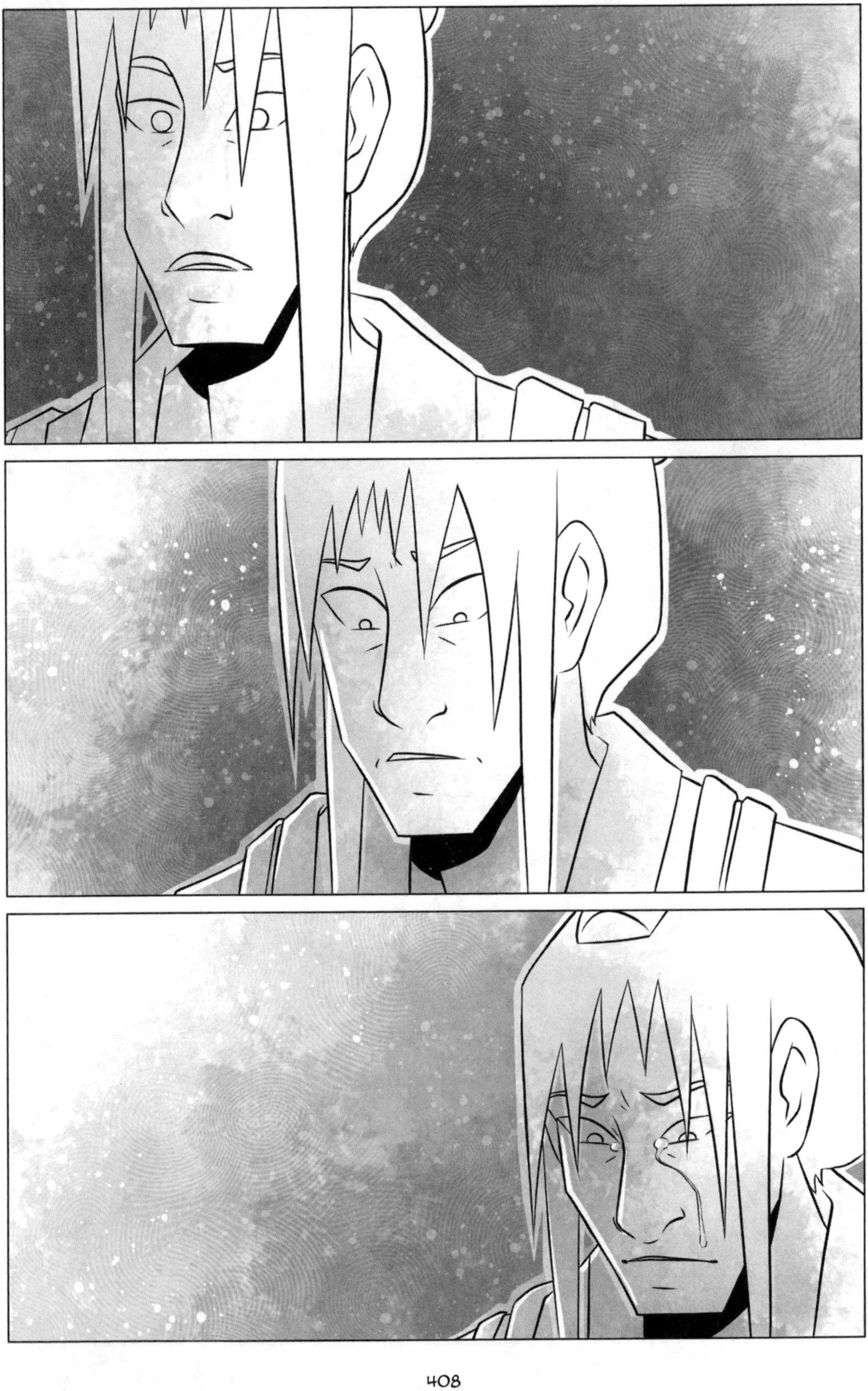

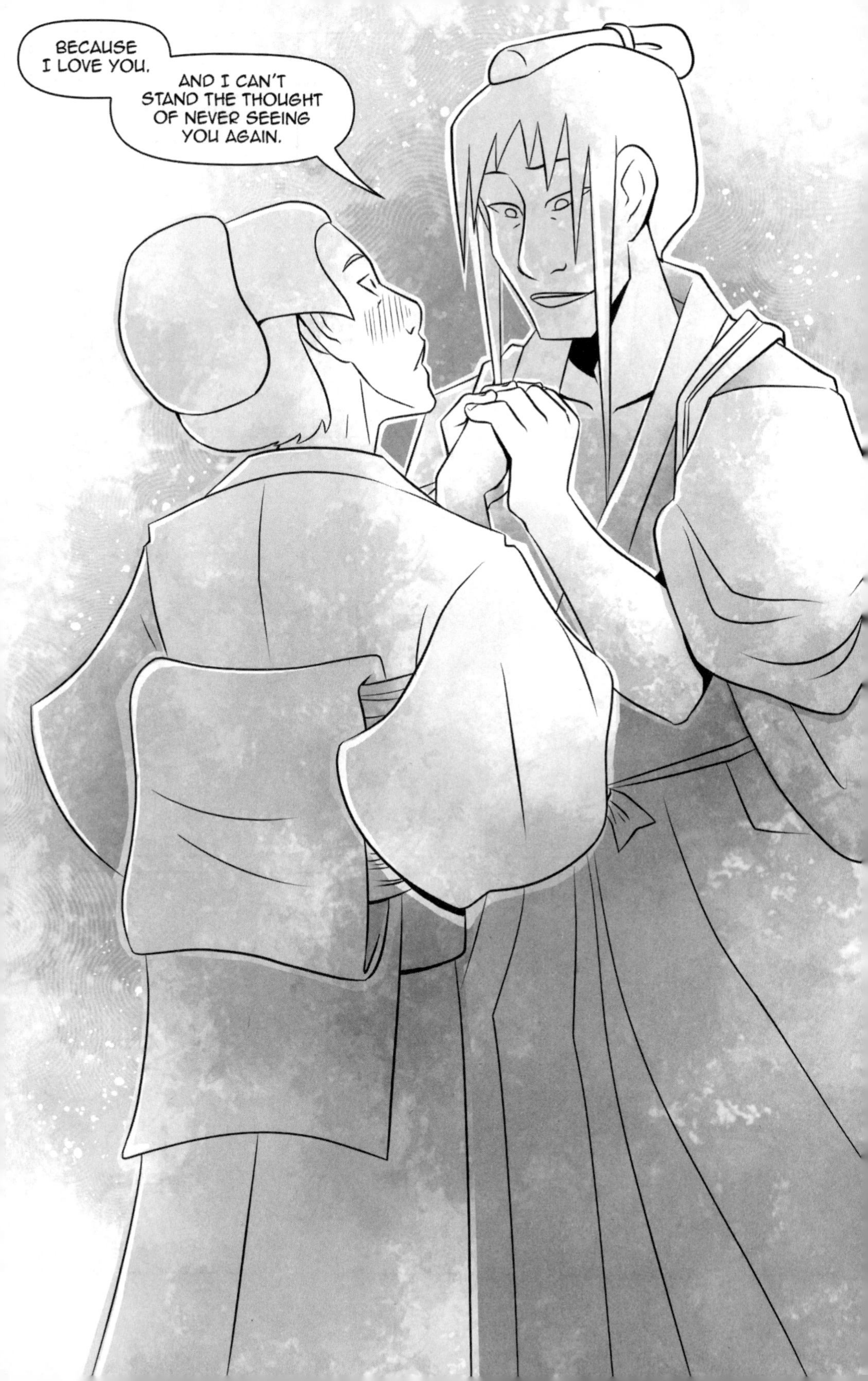
BECAUSE I LOVE YOU.
AND I CAN'T STAND THE THOUGHT OF NEVER SEEING YOU AGAIN.

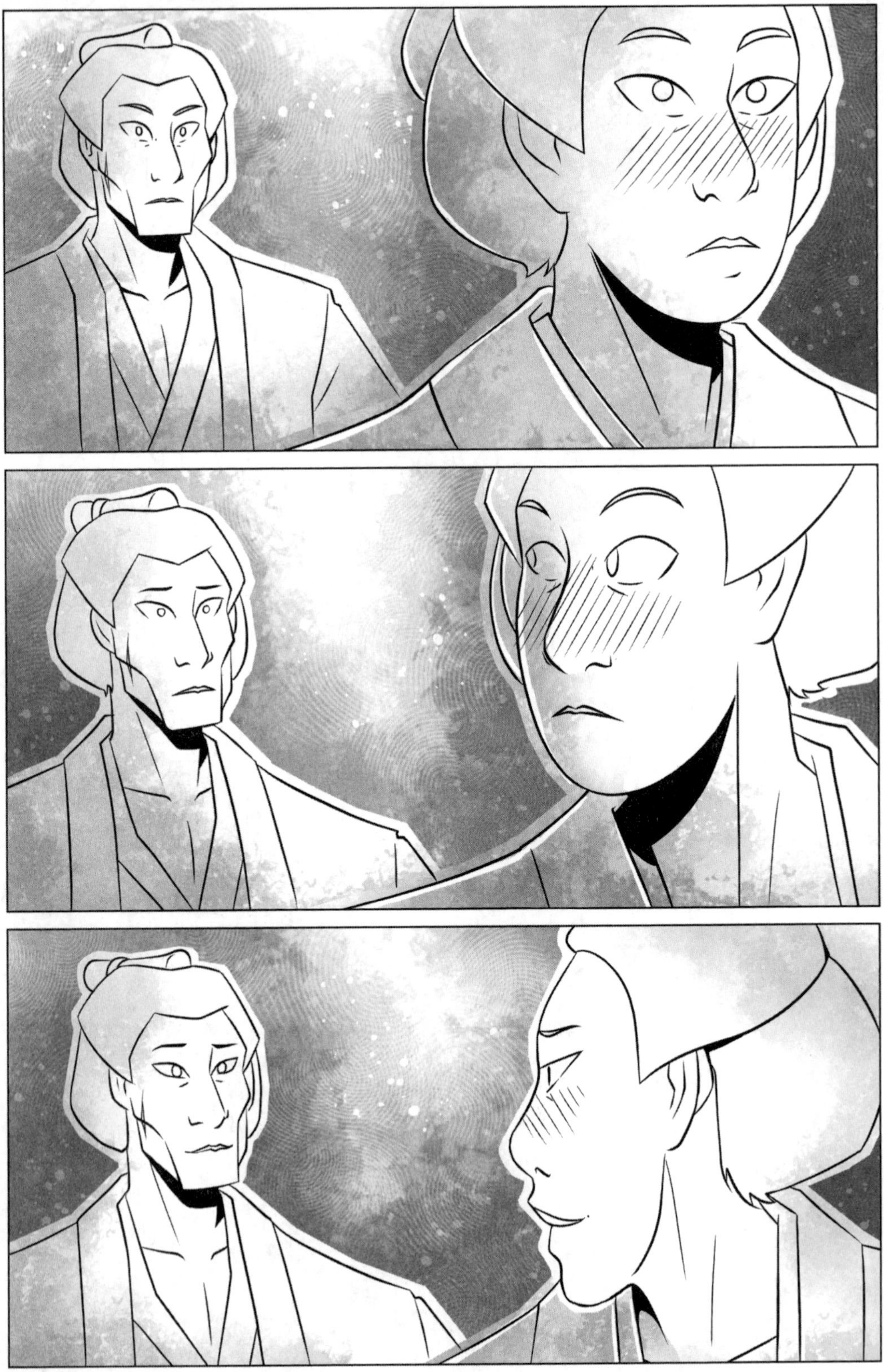

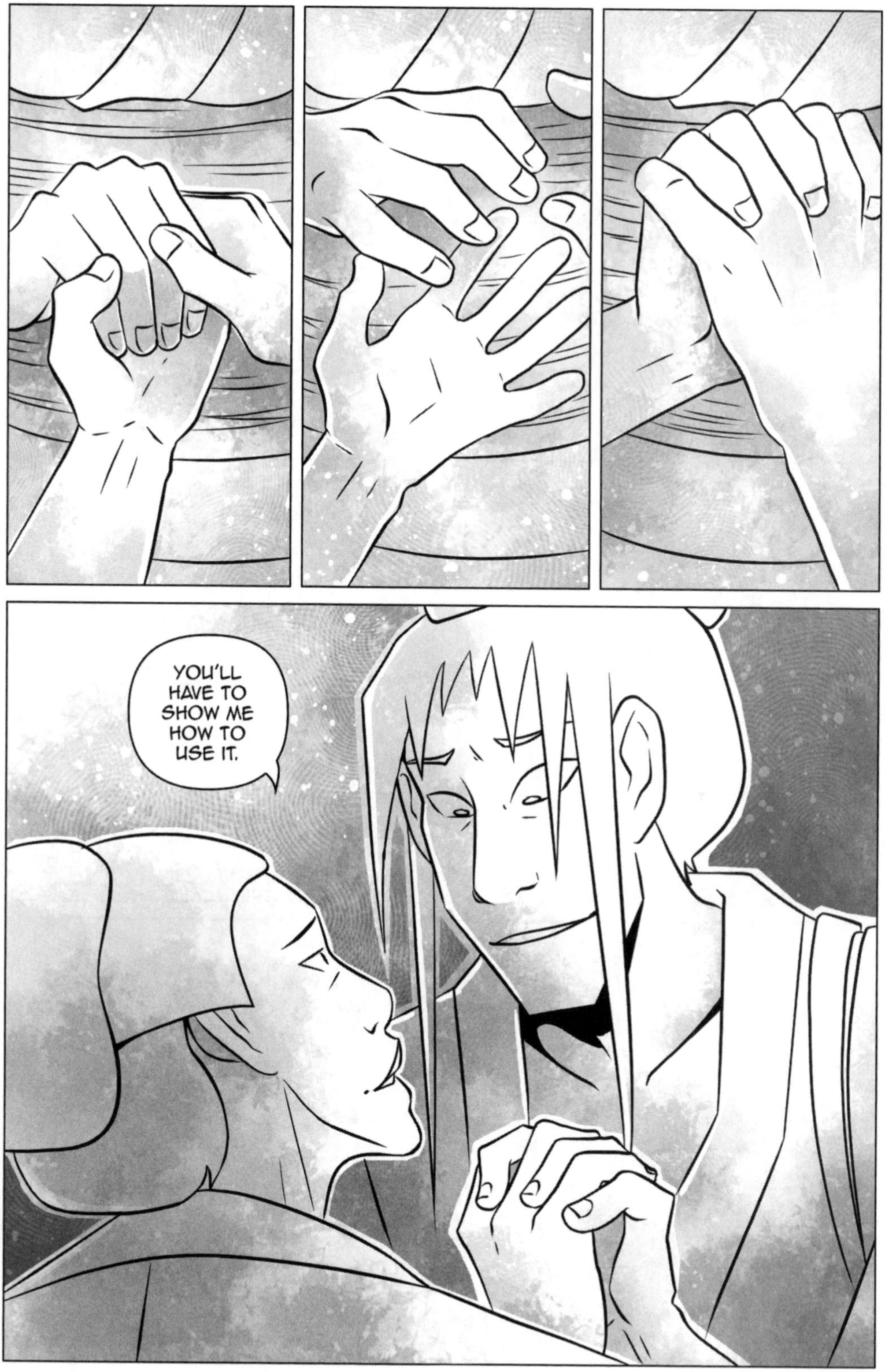
YOU'LL HAVE TO SHOW ME HOW TO USE IT.

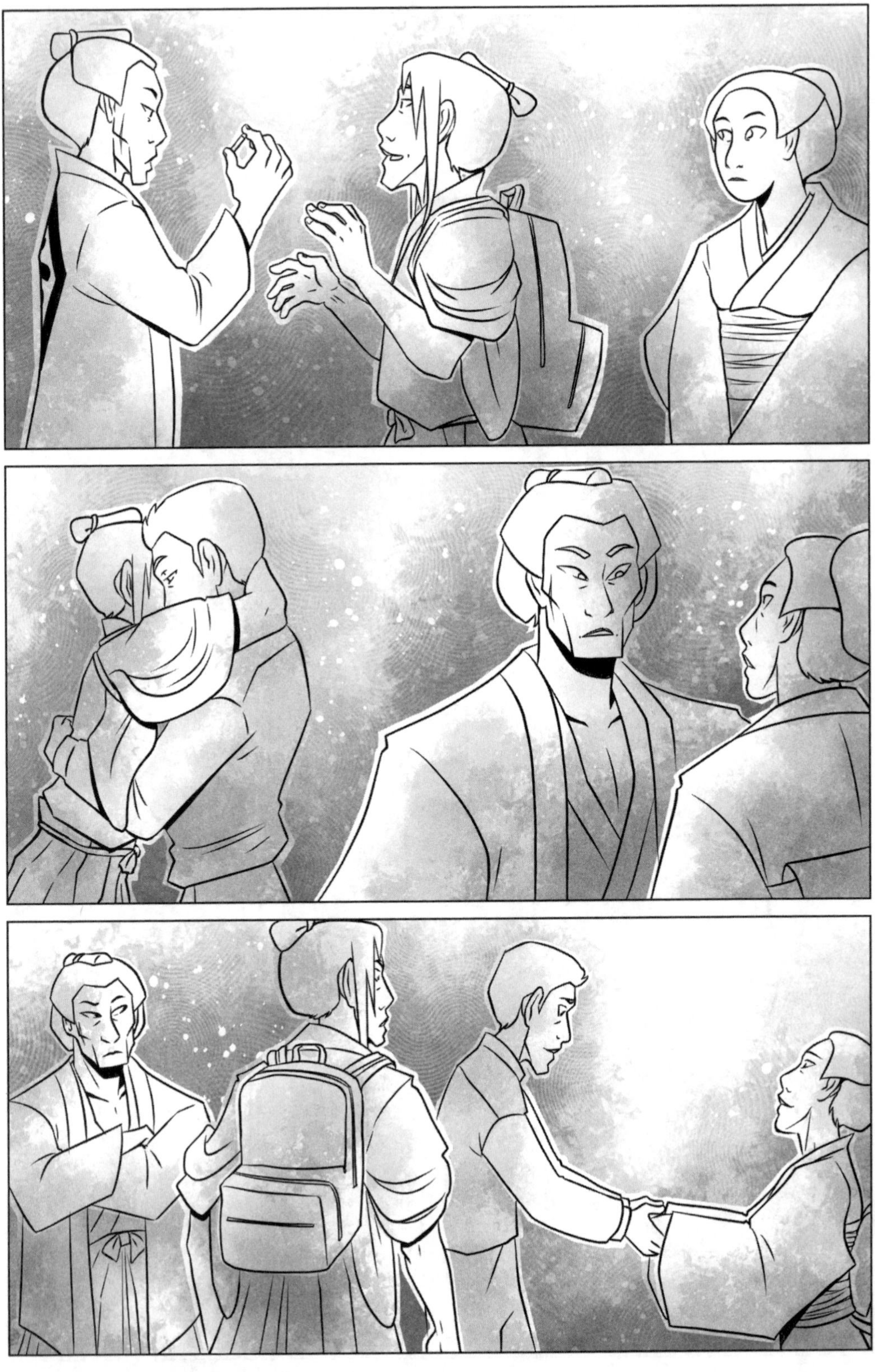

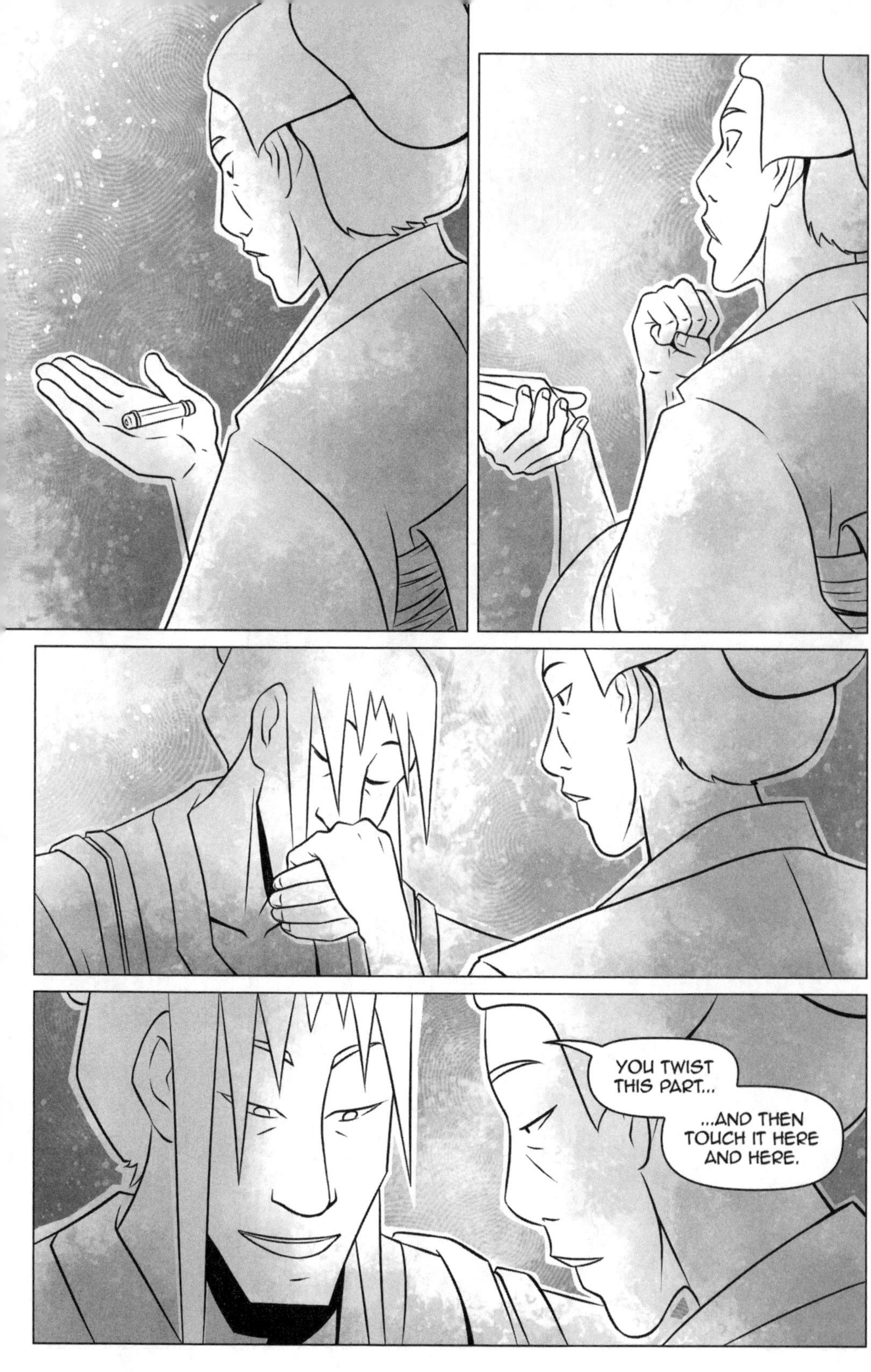
YOU TWIST THIS PART...
...AND THEN TOUCH IT HERE AND HERE.

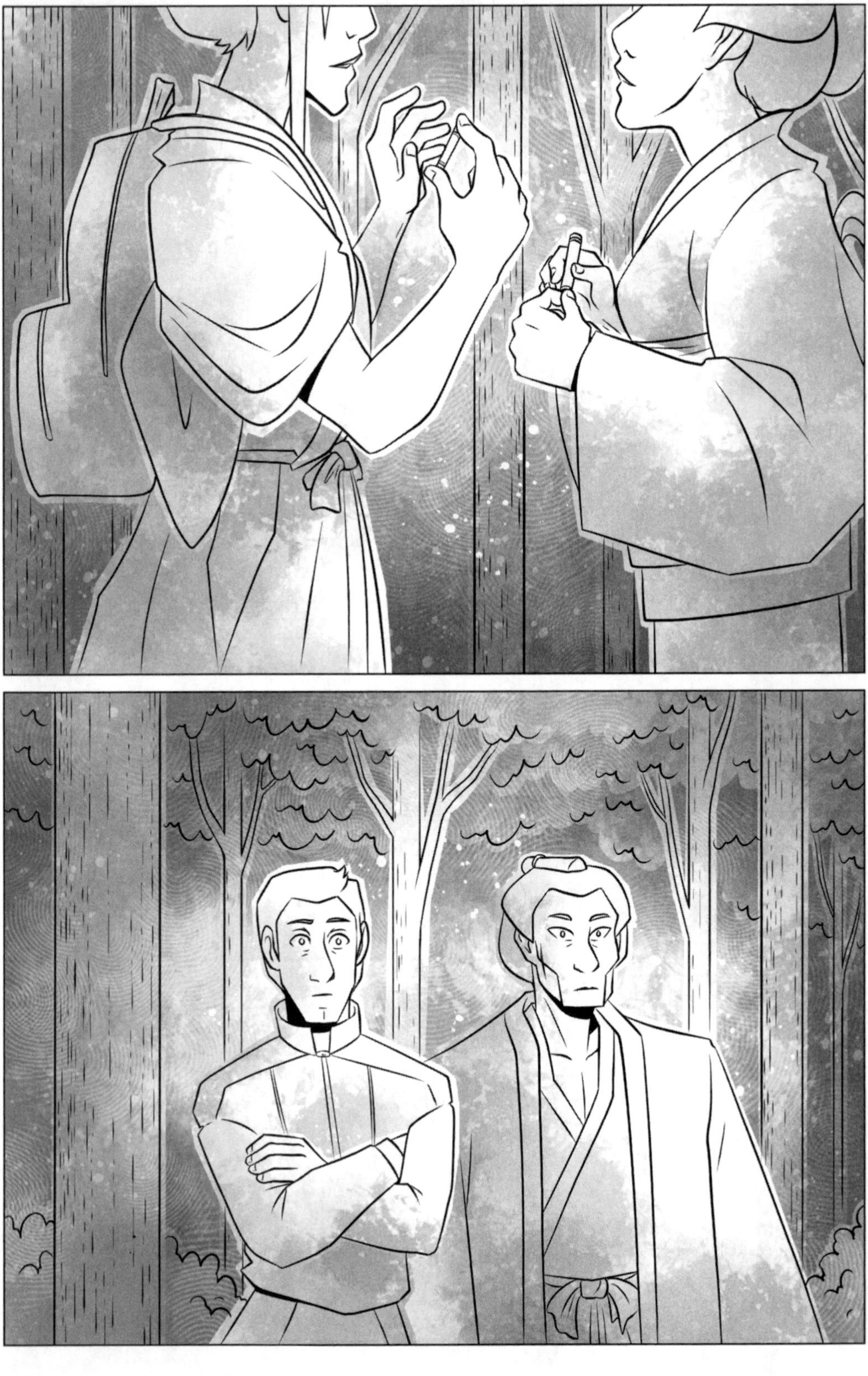

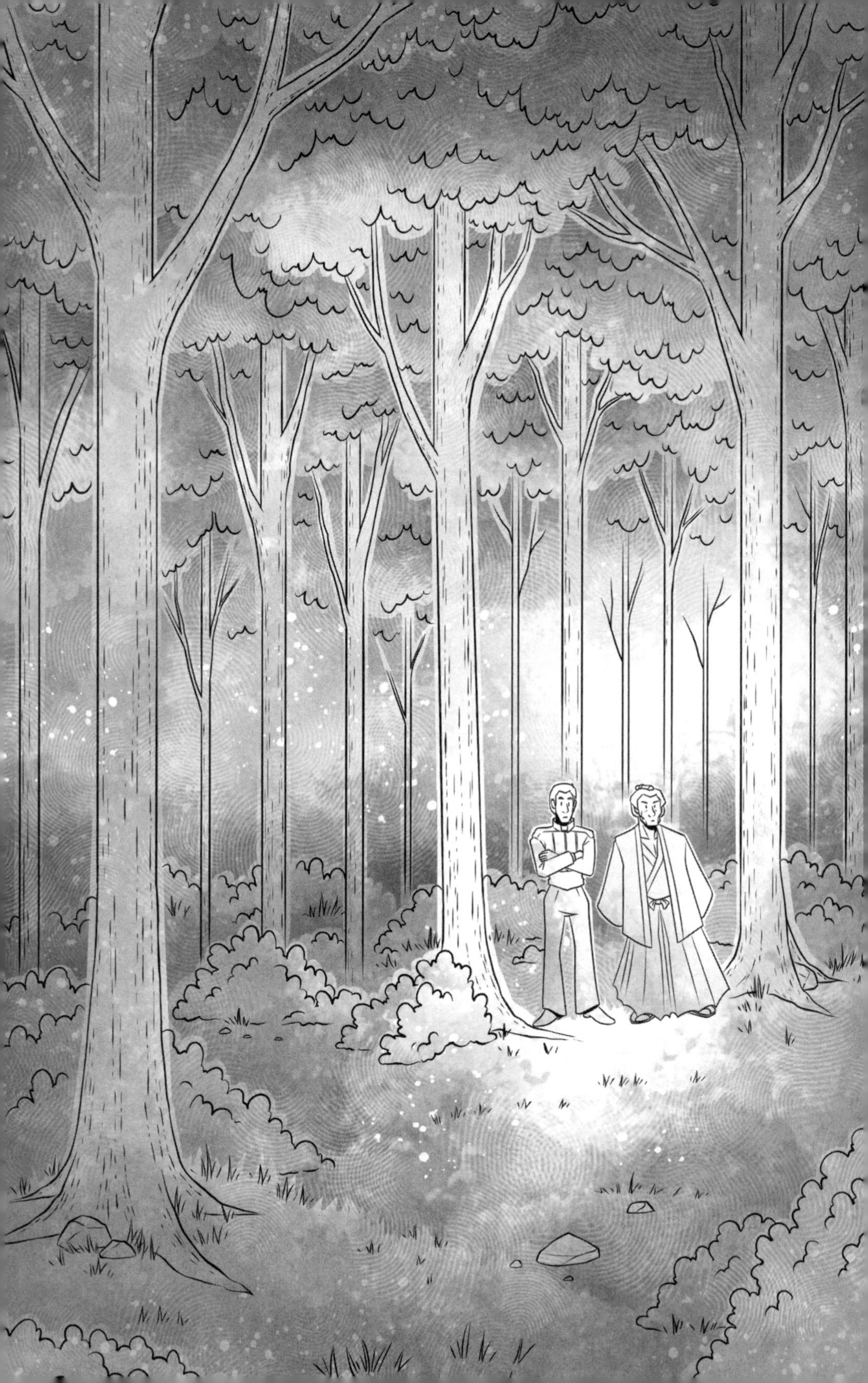

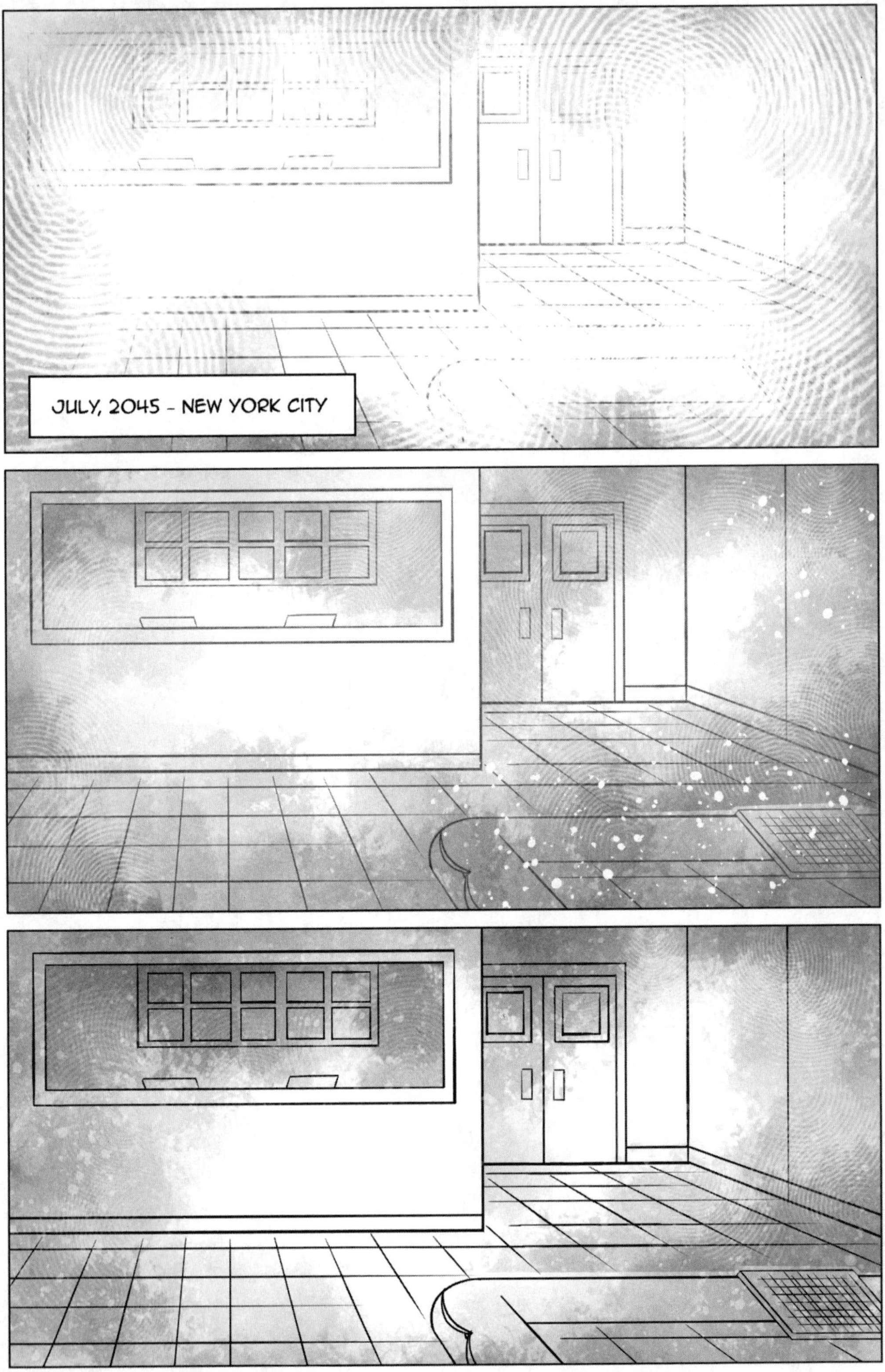
JULY, 2045 - NEW YORK CITY

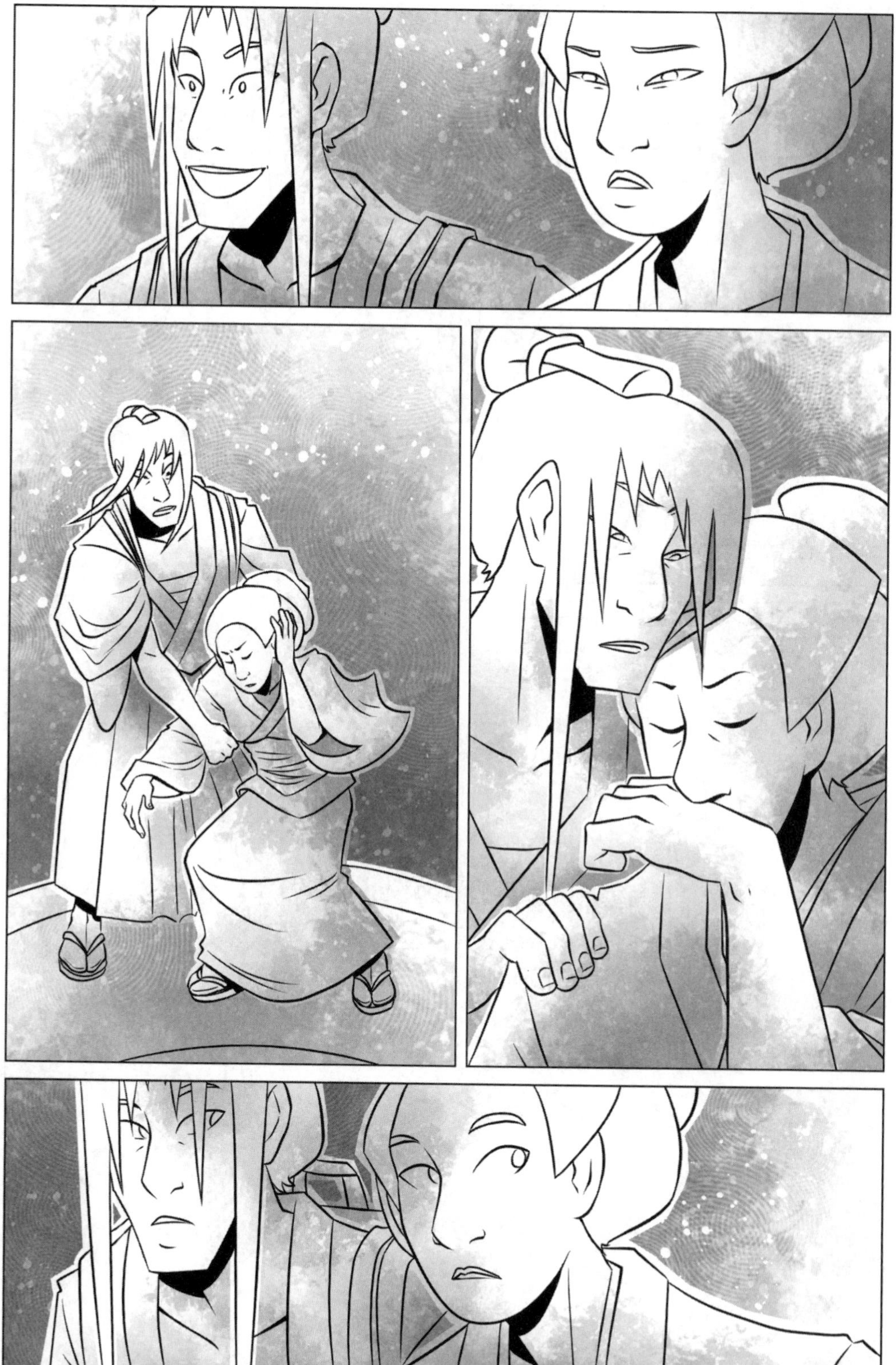

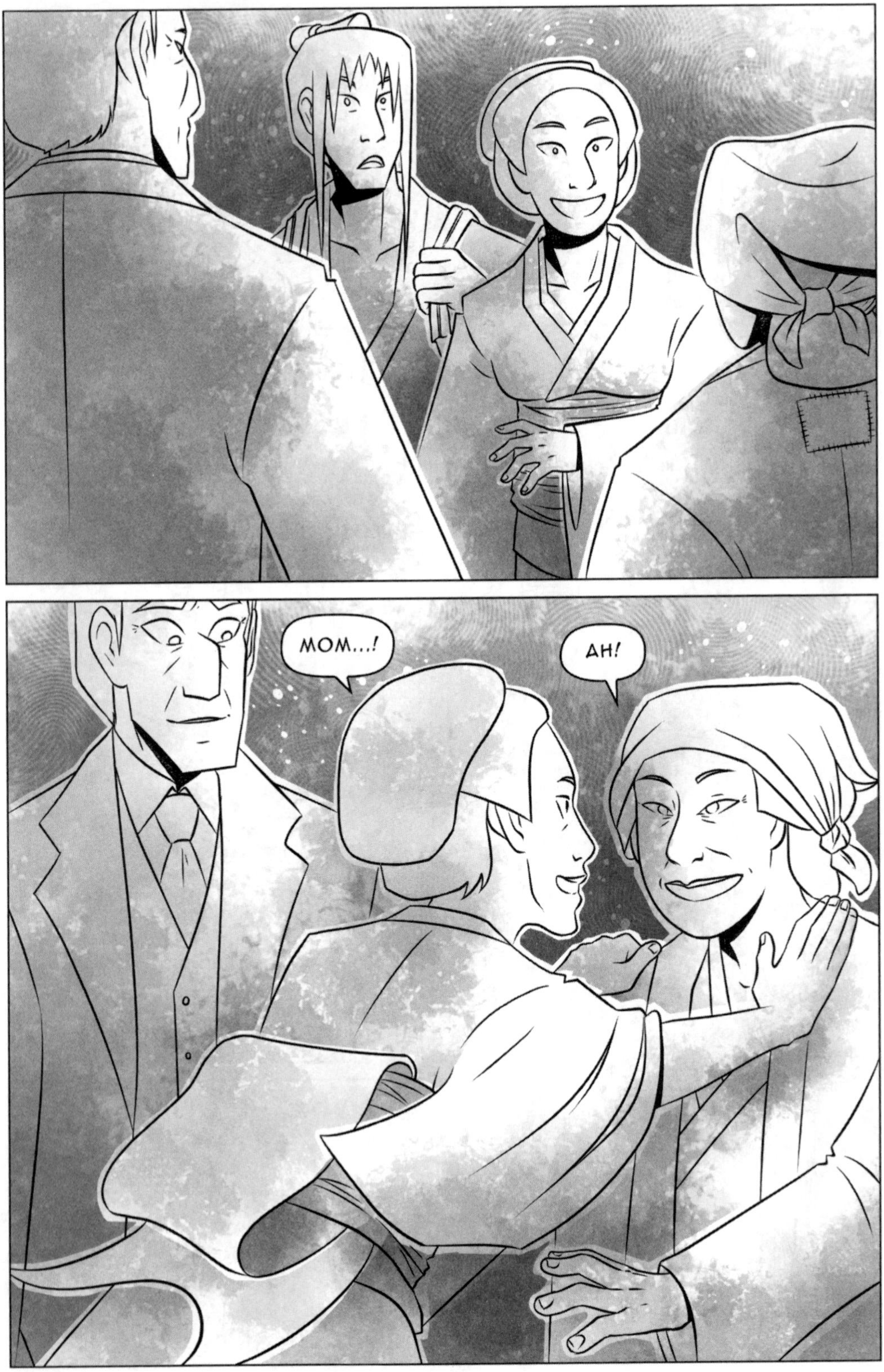
MOM...!
AH!

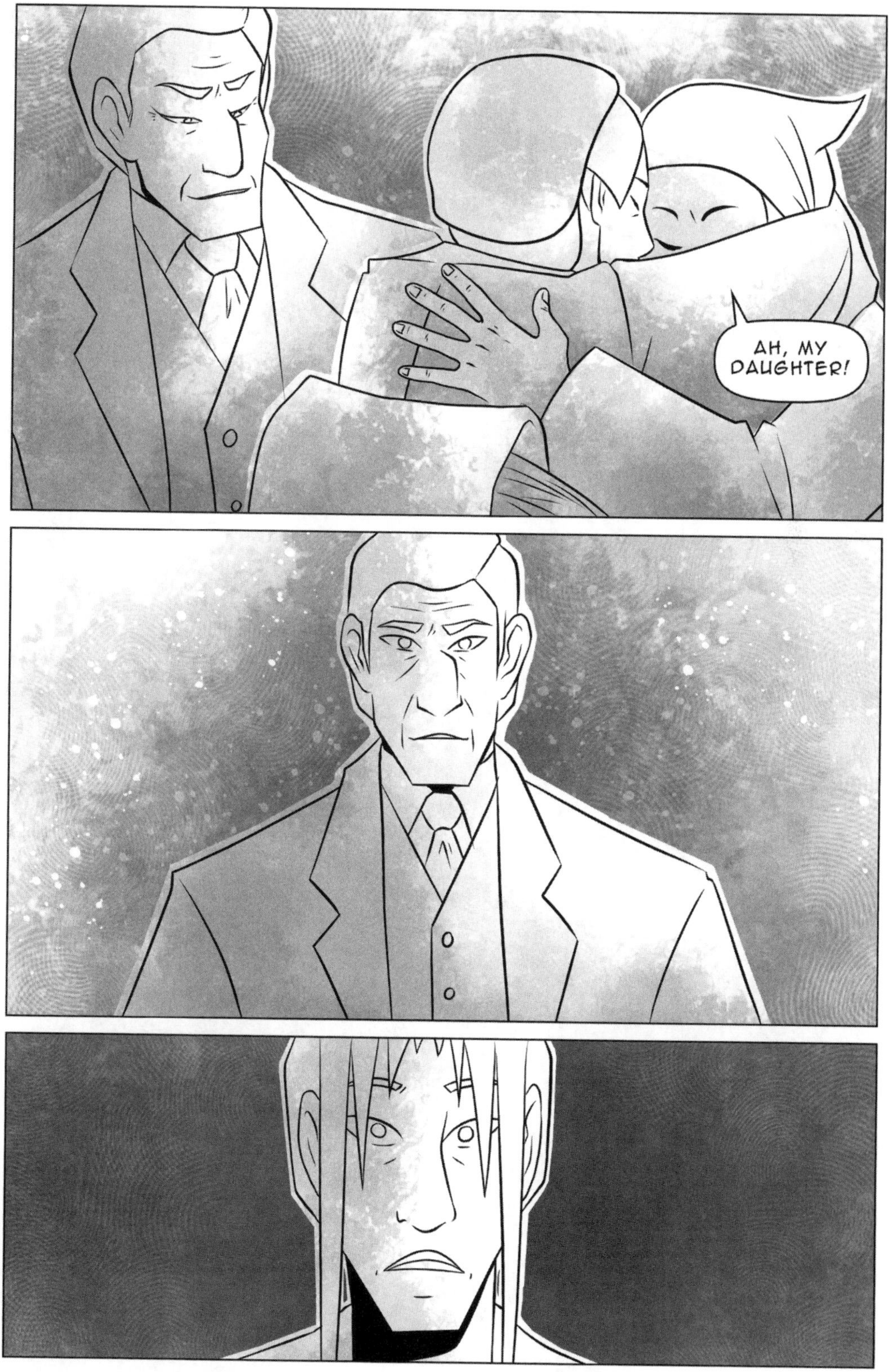
AH, MY DAUGHTER!

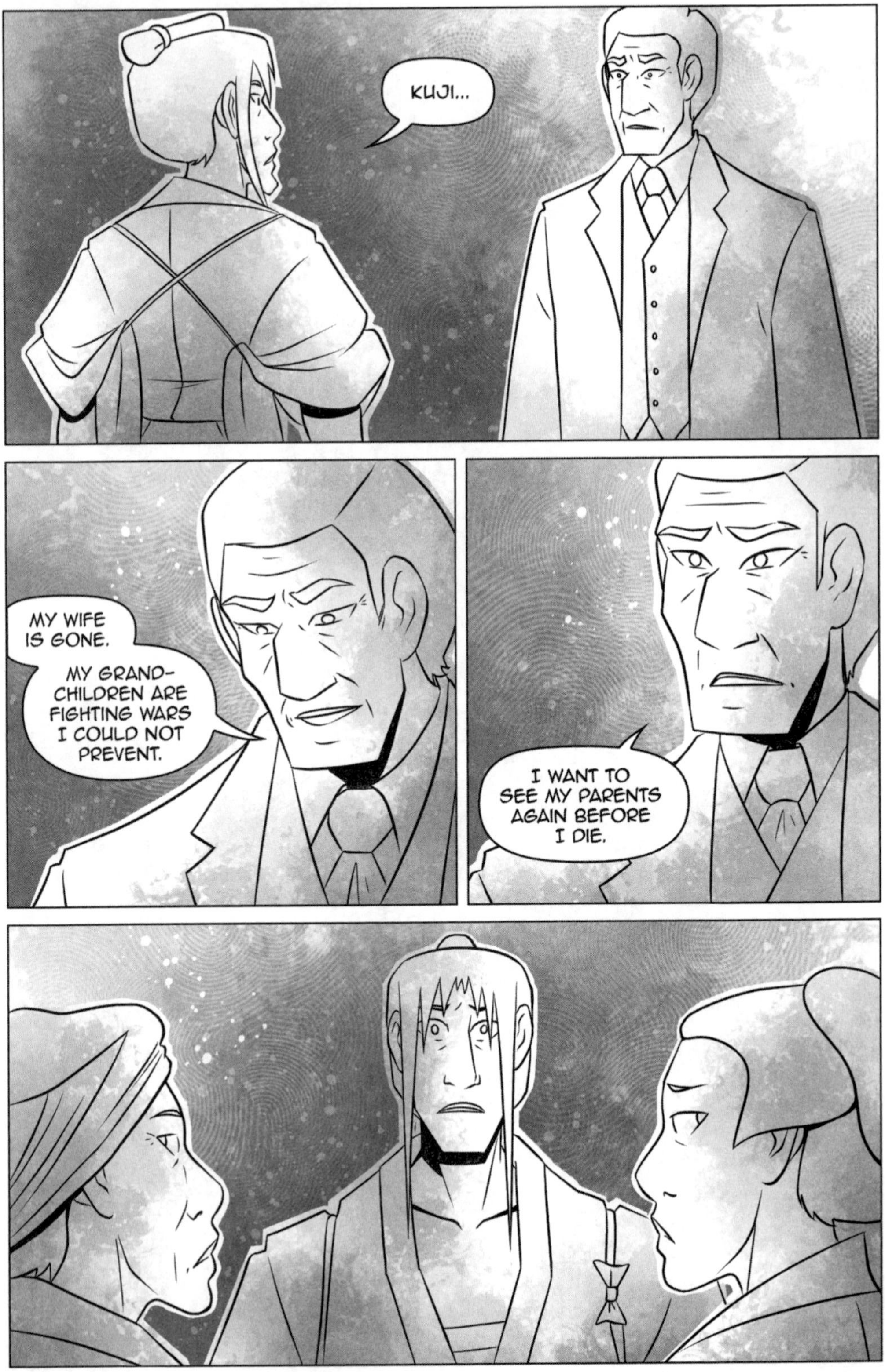
KUJI...
MY WIFE IS GONE.
MY GRAND-CHILDREN ARE FIGHTING WARS I COULD NOT PREVENT.
I WANT TO SEE MY PARENTS AGAIN BEFORE I DIE.

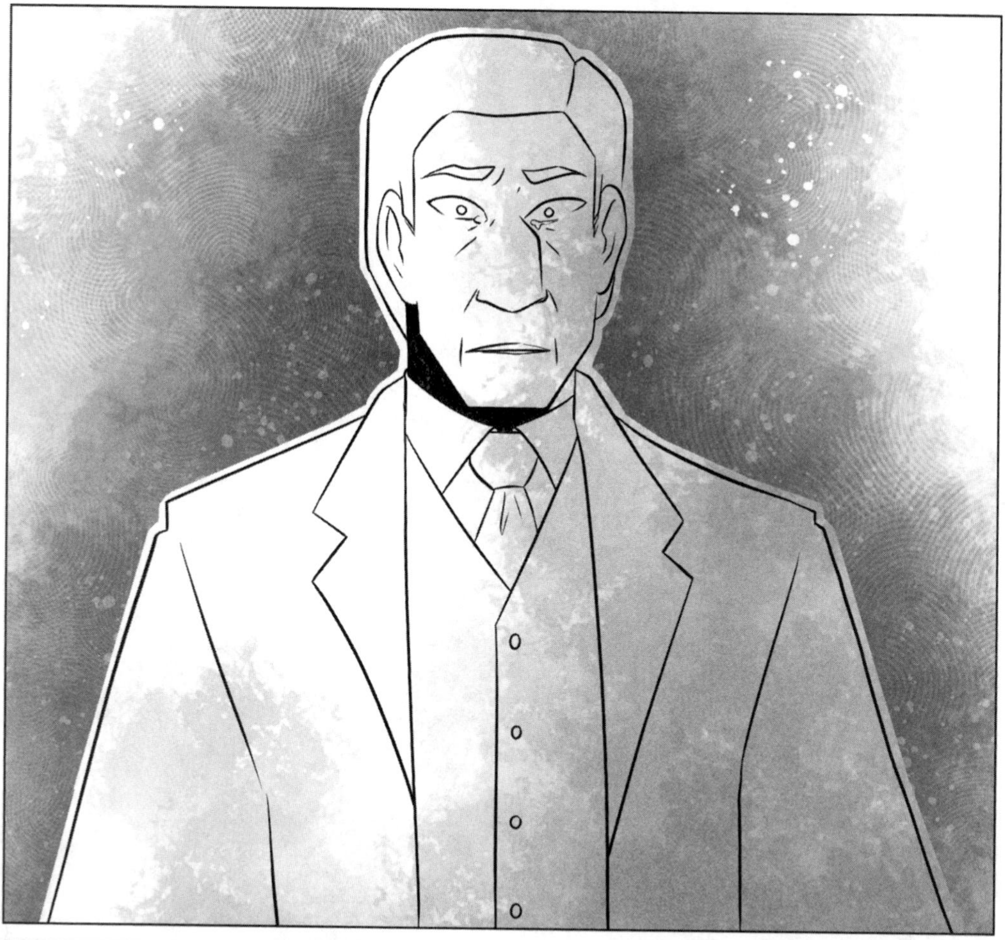

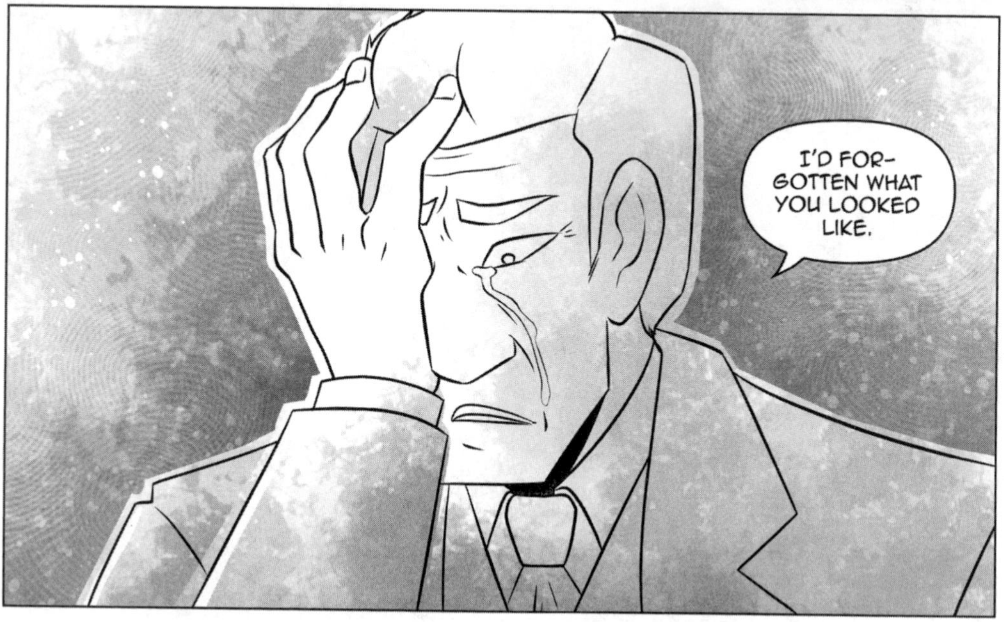
I'D FOR-GOTTEN WHAT YOU LOOKED LIKE.

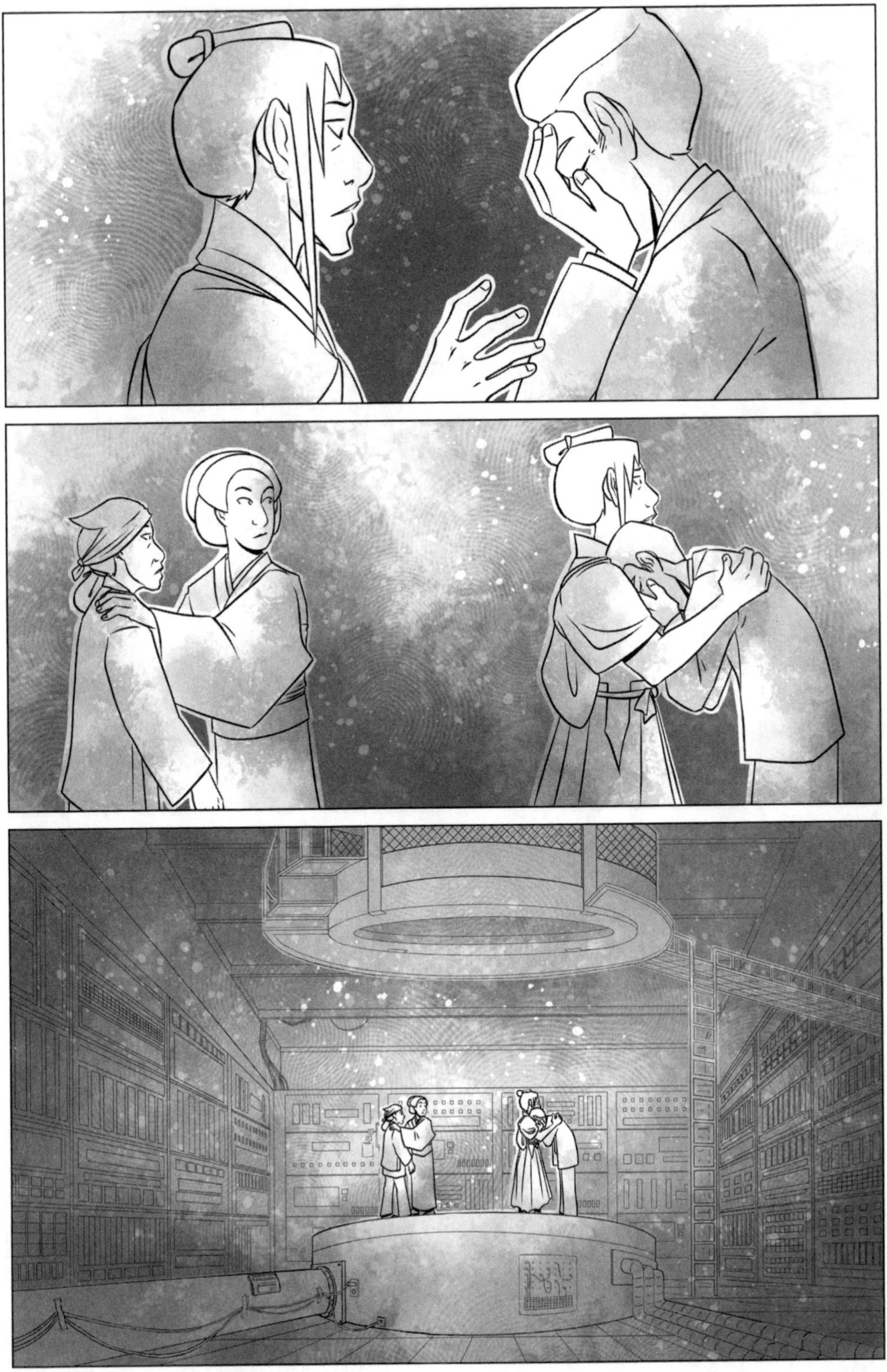

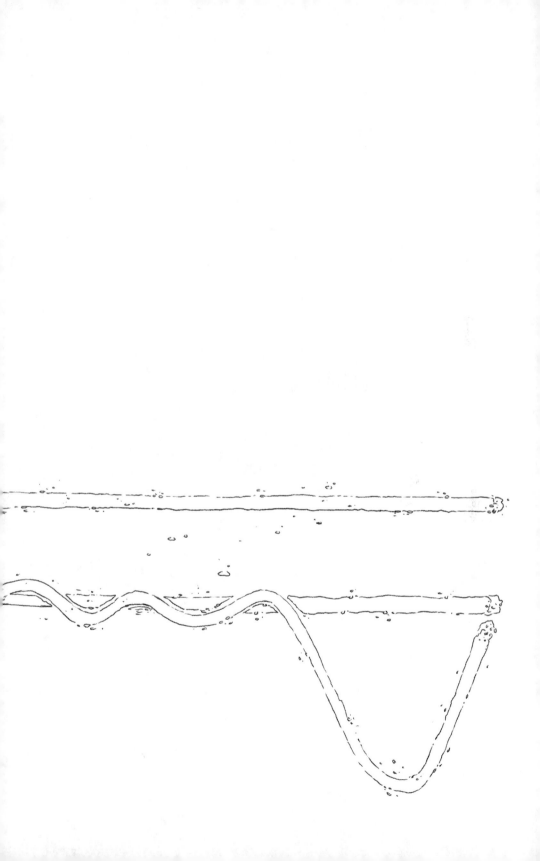

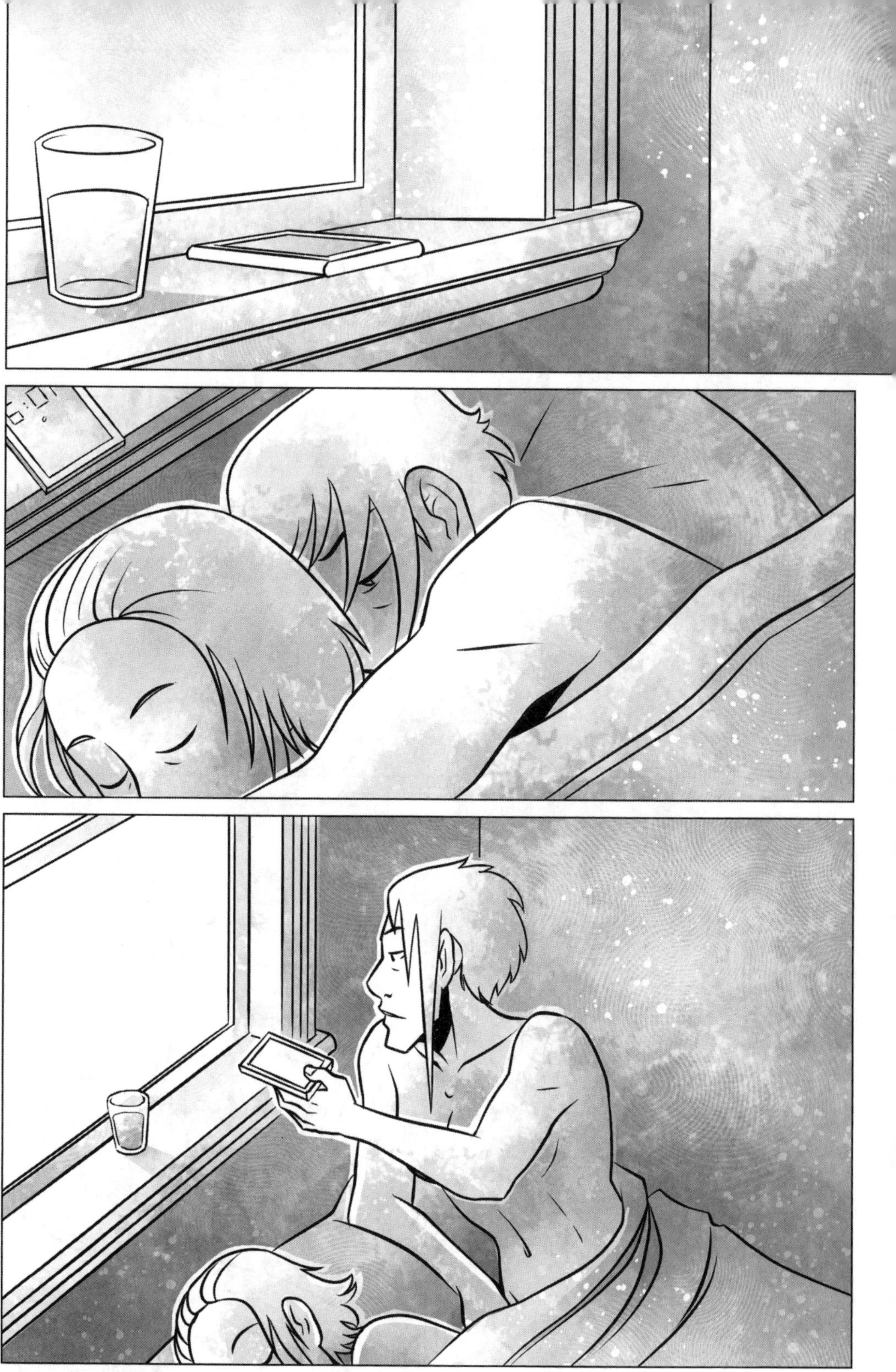

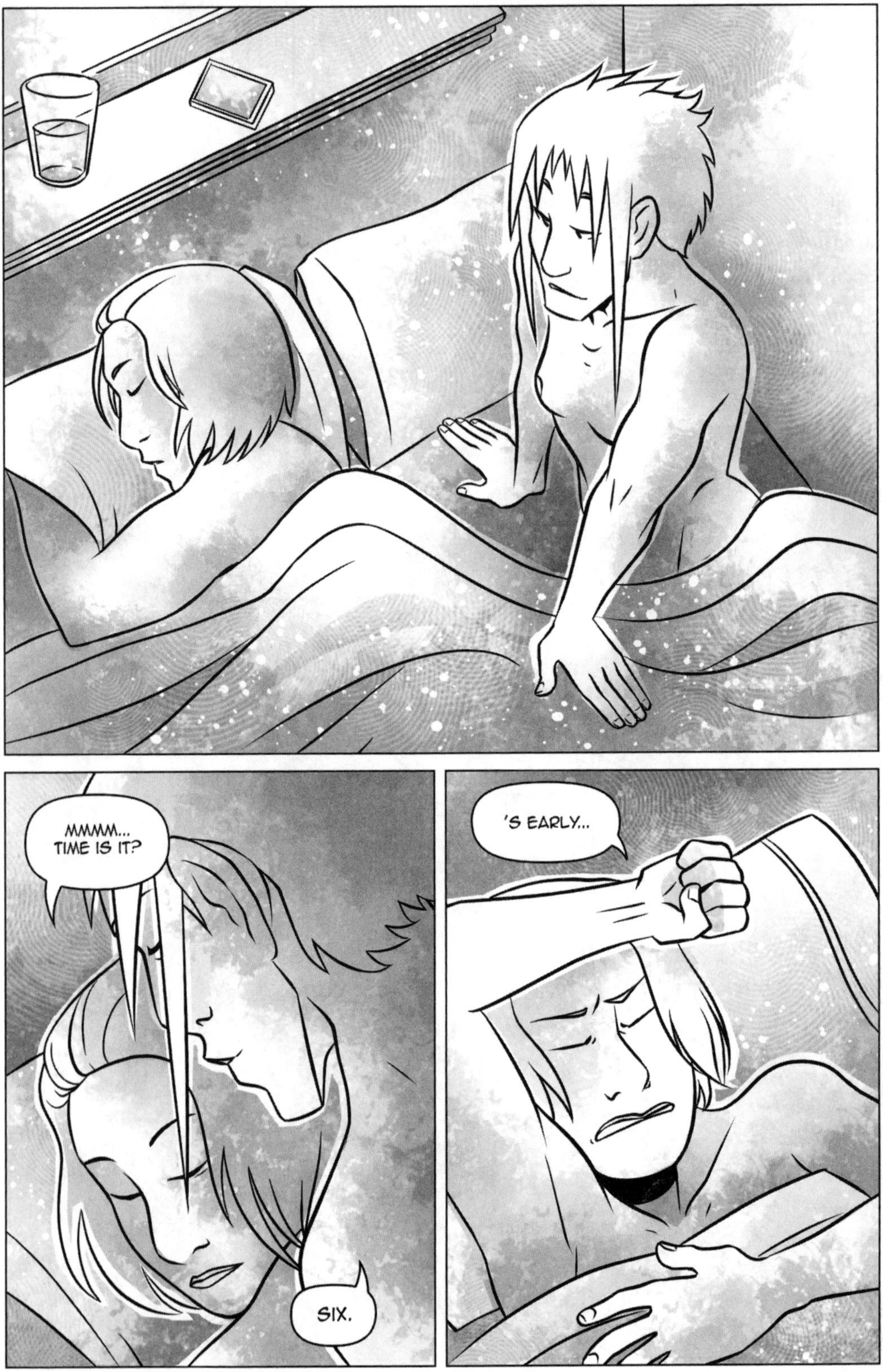
MMMM...
TIME IS IT?
SIX.
'S EARLY...

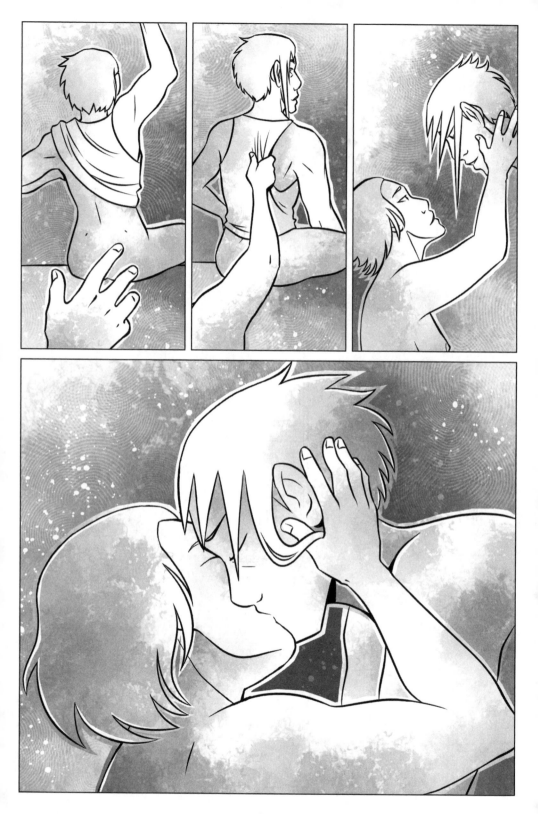

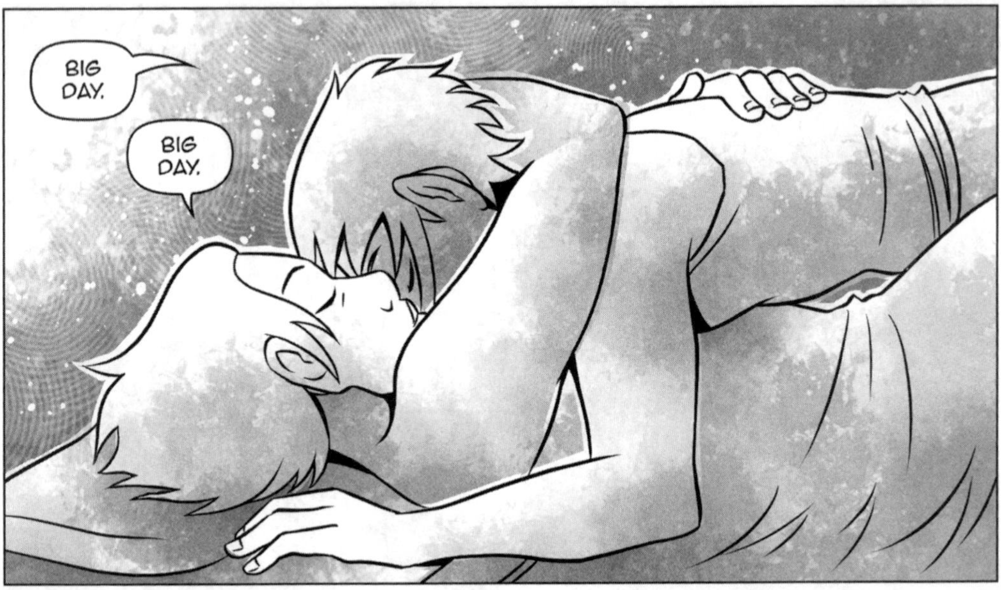
BIG DAY.
BIG DAY.
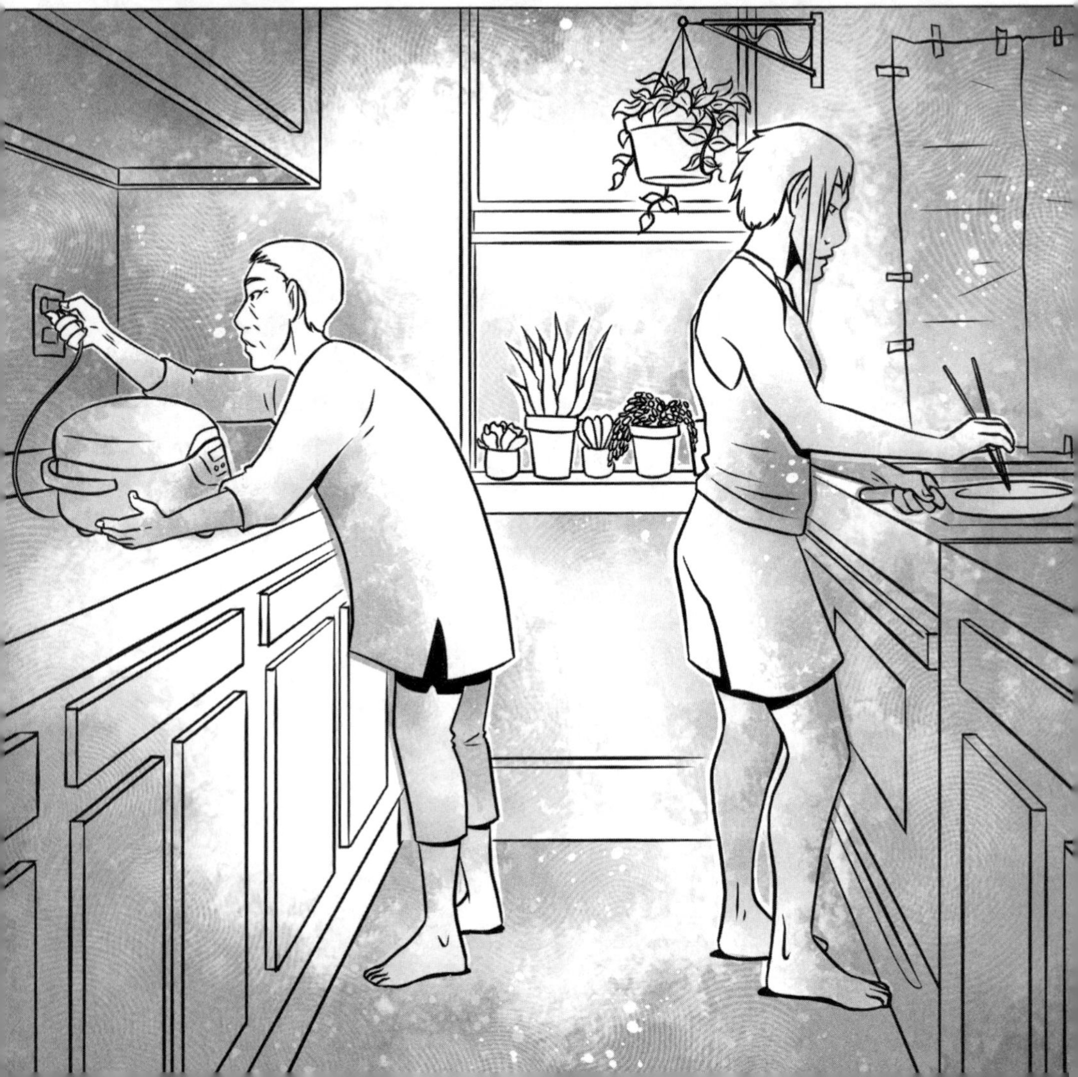

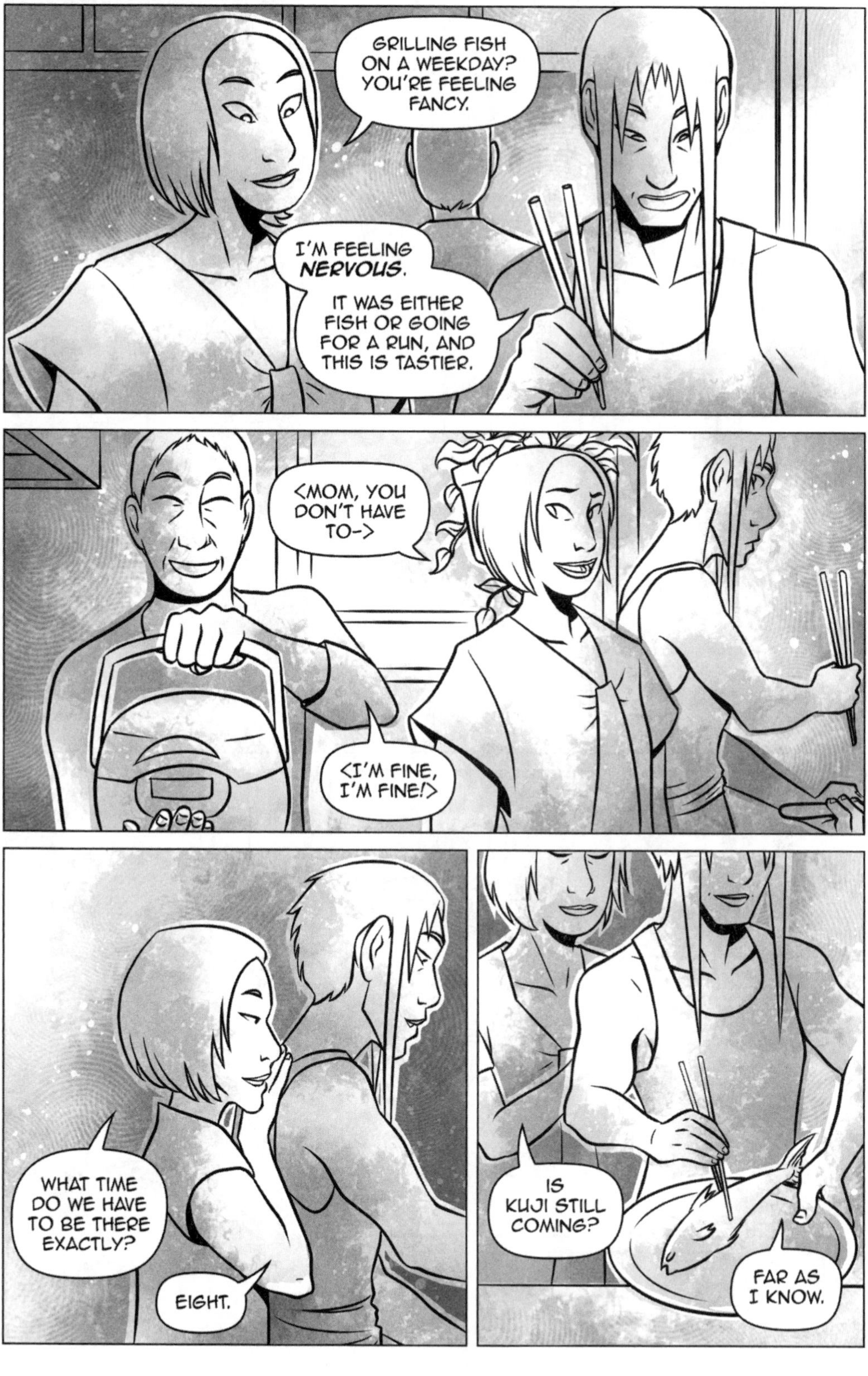
GRILLING FISH ON A WEEKDAY? YOU'RE FEELING FANCY.
I'M FEELING **NERVOUS**.
IT WAS EITHER FISH OR GOING FOR A RUN, AND THIS IS TASTIER.
<MOM, YOU DON'T HAVE TO->
<I'M FINE, I'M FINE!>
WHAT TIME DO WE HAVE TO BE THERE EXACTLY?
EIGHT.
IS KUJI STILL COMING?
FAR AS I KNOW.

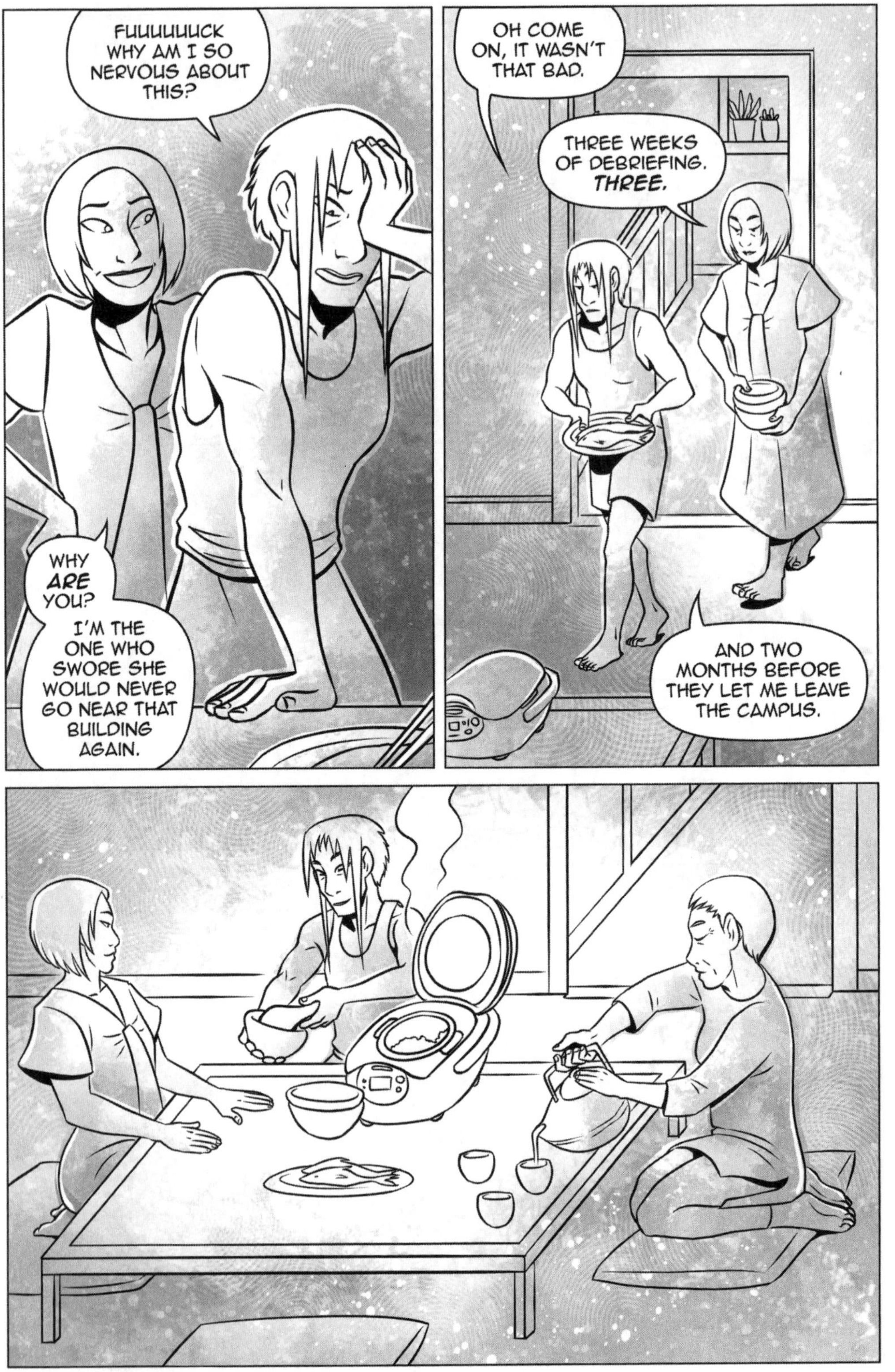
FUUUUUUCK WHY AM I SO NERVOUS ABOUT THIS?
WHY **ARE** YOU?
I'M THE ONE WHO SWORE SHE WOULD NEVER GO NEAR THAT BUILDING AGAIN.
OH COME ON, IT WASN'T THAT BAD.
THREE WEEKS OF DEBRIEFING. ***THREE.***
AND TWO MONTHS BEFORE THEY LET ME LEAVE THE CAMPUS.

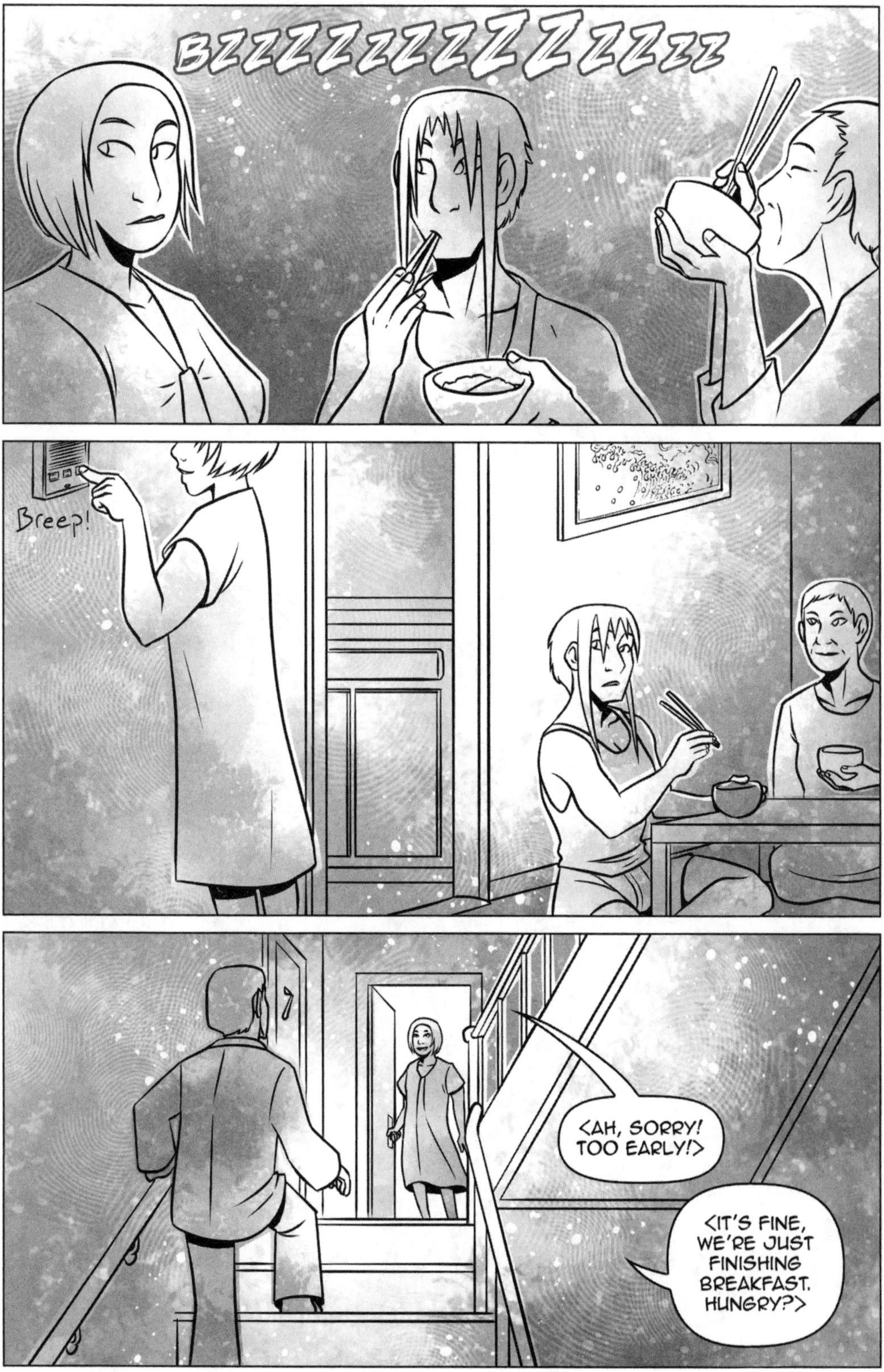
BZZZZZZZZZZZZZZ
Breep!
<AH, SORRY! TOO EARLY!>
<IT'S FINE, WE'RE JUST FINISHING BREAKFAST. HUNGRY?>

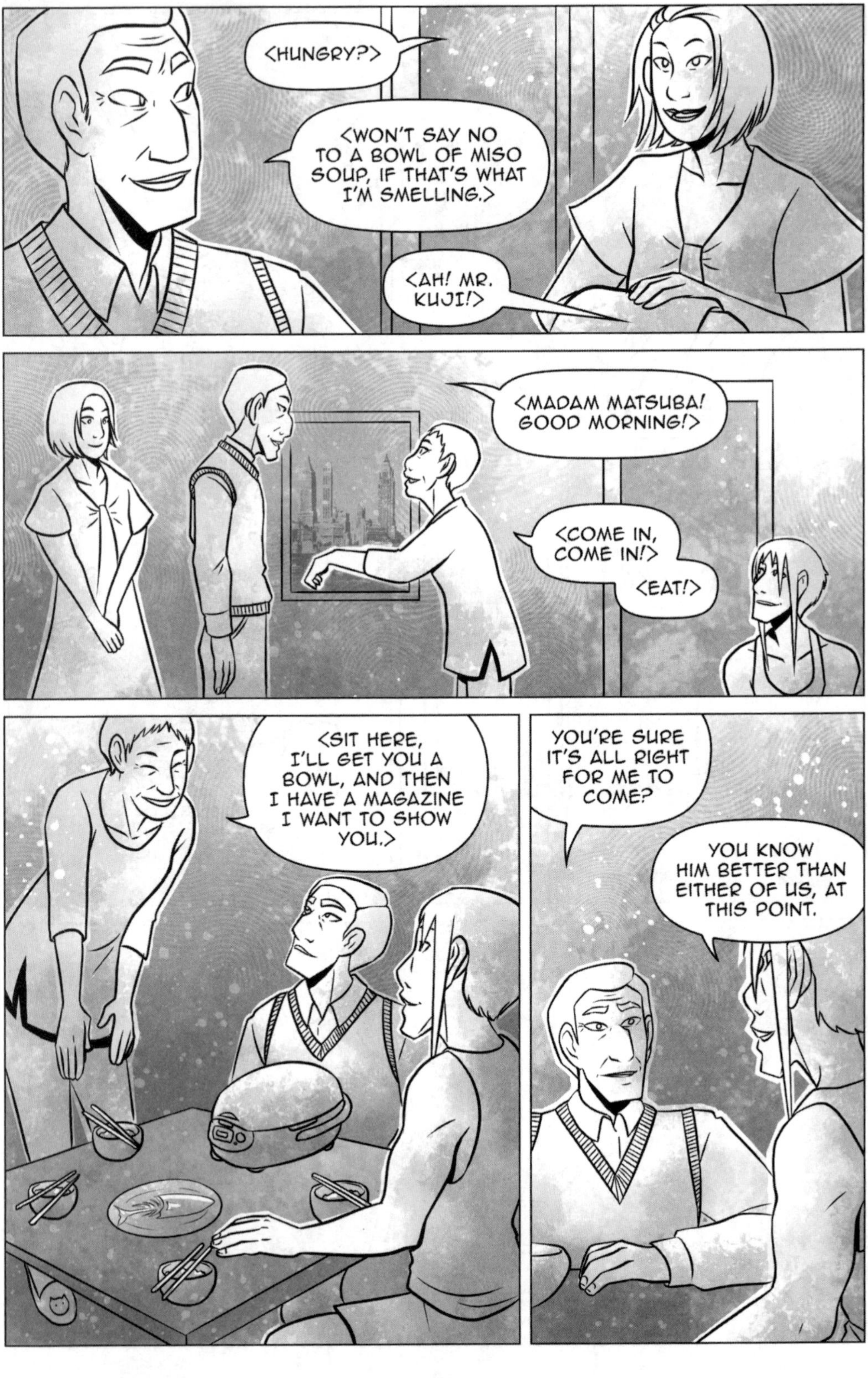
<HUNGRY?>
<WON'T SAY NO TO A BOWL OF MISO SOUP, IF THAT'S WHAT I'M SMELLING.>
<AH! MR. KUJI!>
<MADAM MATSUBA! GOOD MORNING!>
<COME IN, COME IN!>
<EAT!>
<SIT HERE, I'LL GET YOU A BOWL, AND THEN I HAVE A MAGAZINE I WANT TO SHOW YOU.>
YOU'RE SURE IT'S ALL RIGHT FOR ME TO COME?
YOU KNOW HIM BETTER THAN EITHER OF US, AT THIS POINT.

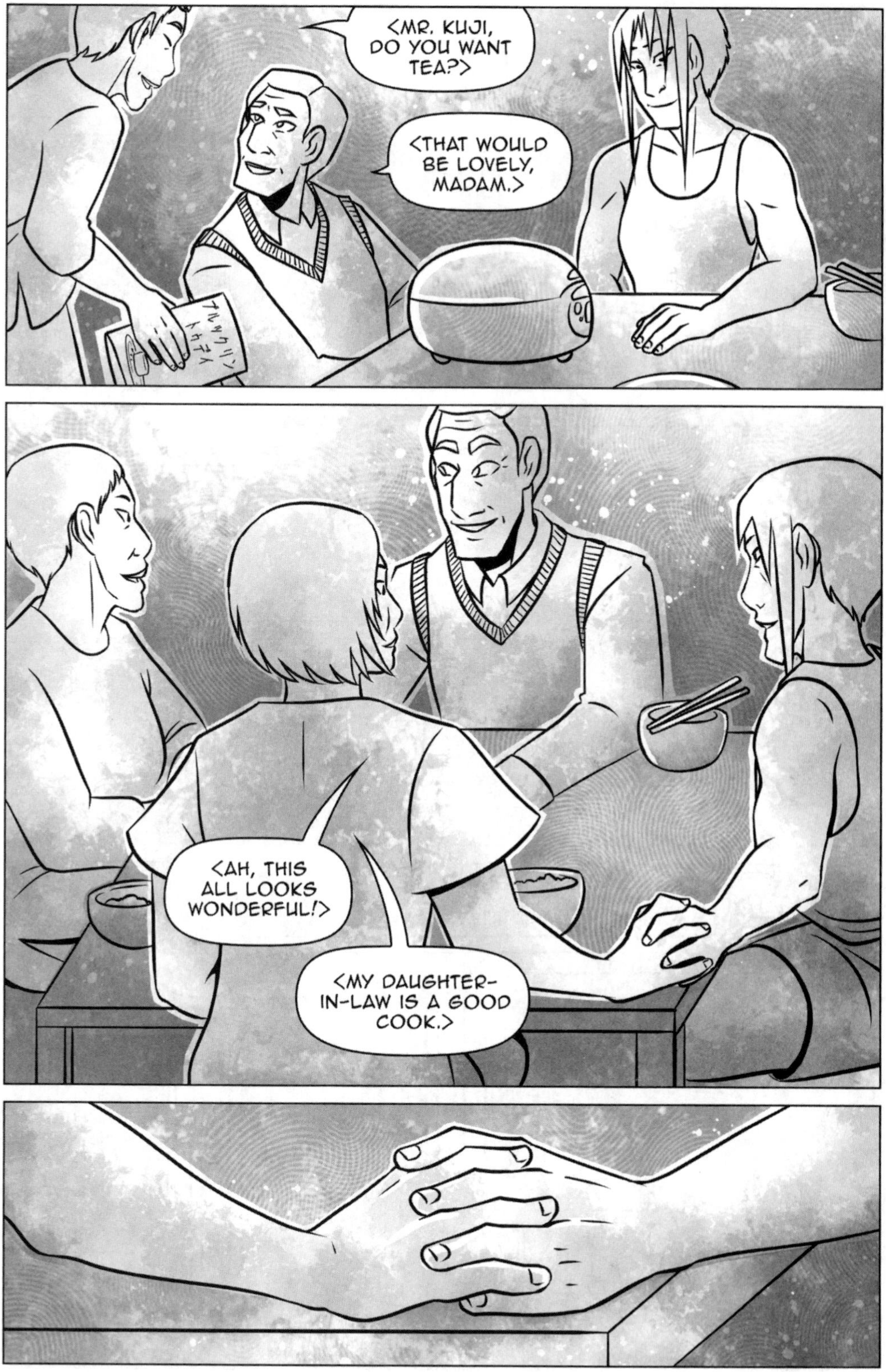
<MR. KUJI, DO YOU WANT TEA?>
<THAT WOULD BE LOVELY, MADAM.>
<AH, THIS ALL LOOKS WONDERFUL!>
<MY DAUGHTER-IN-LAW IS A GOOD COOK.>

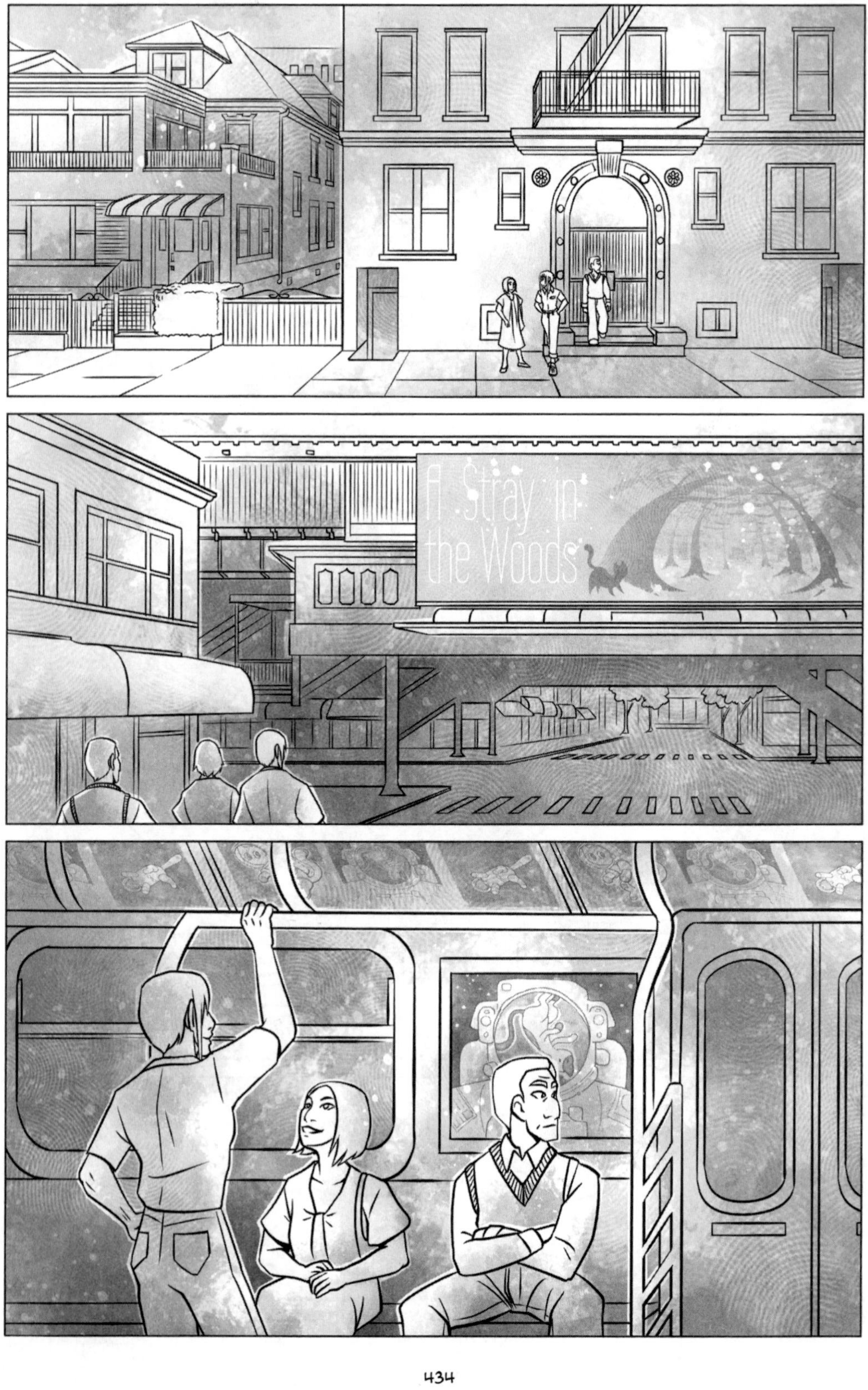
A Stray in the Woods

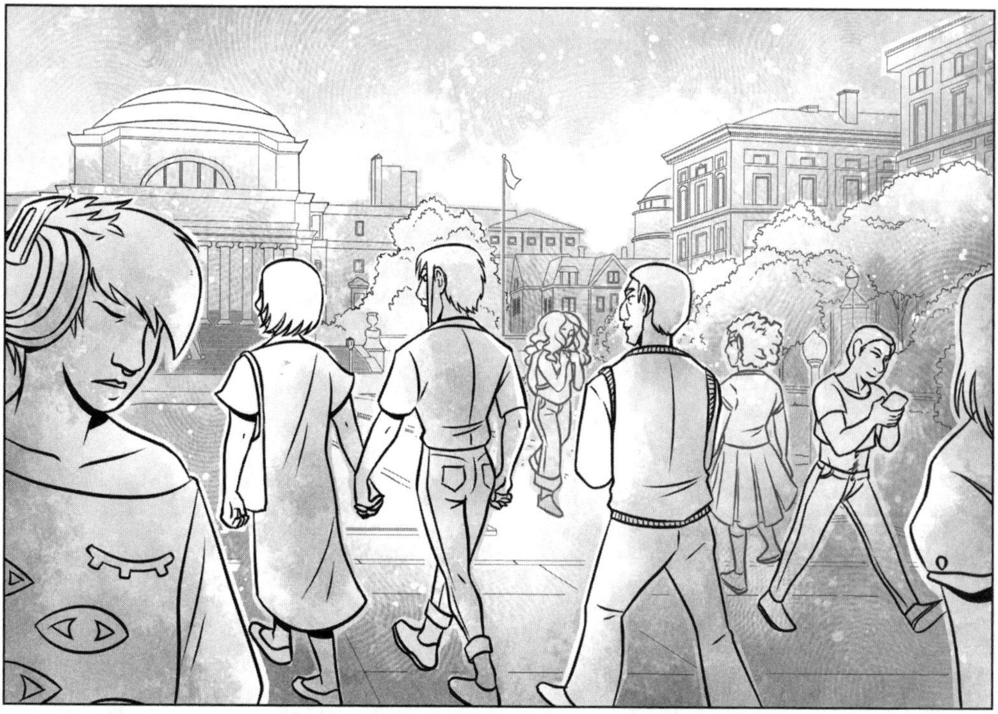

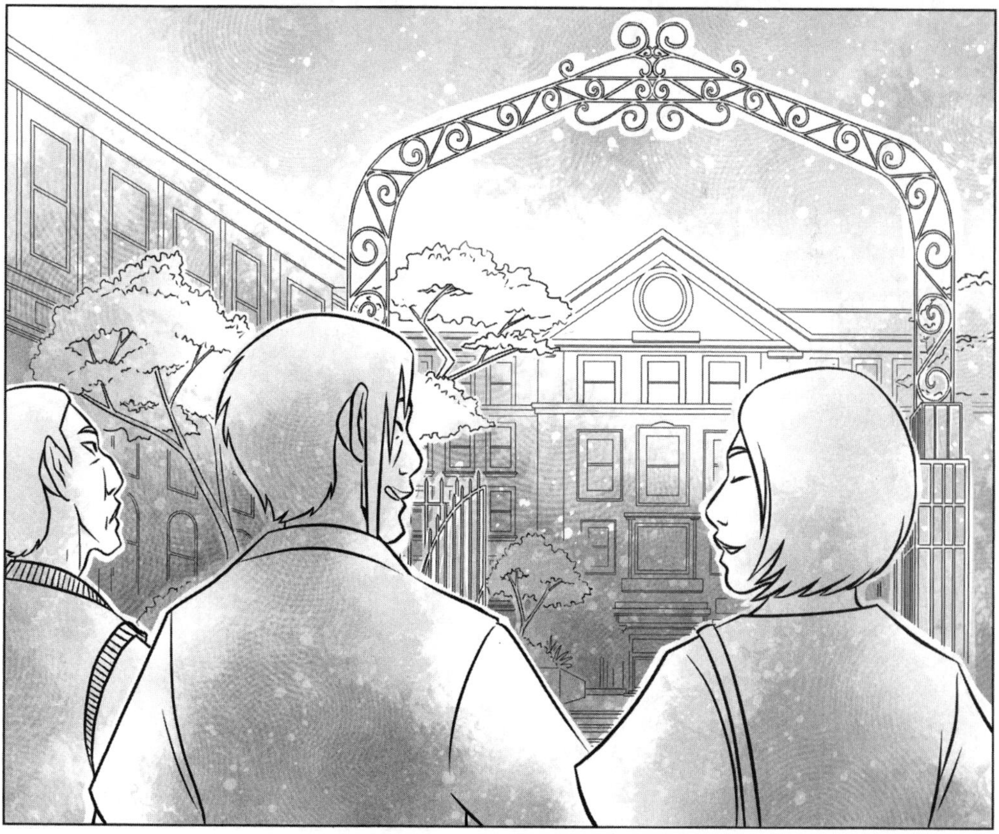

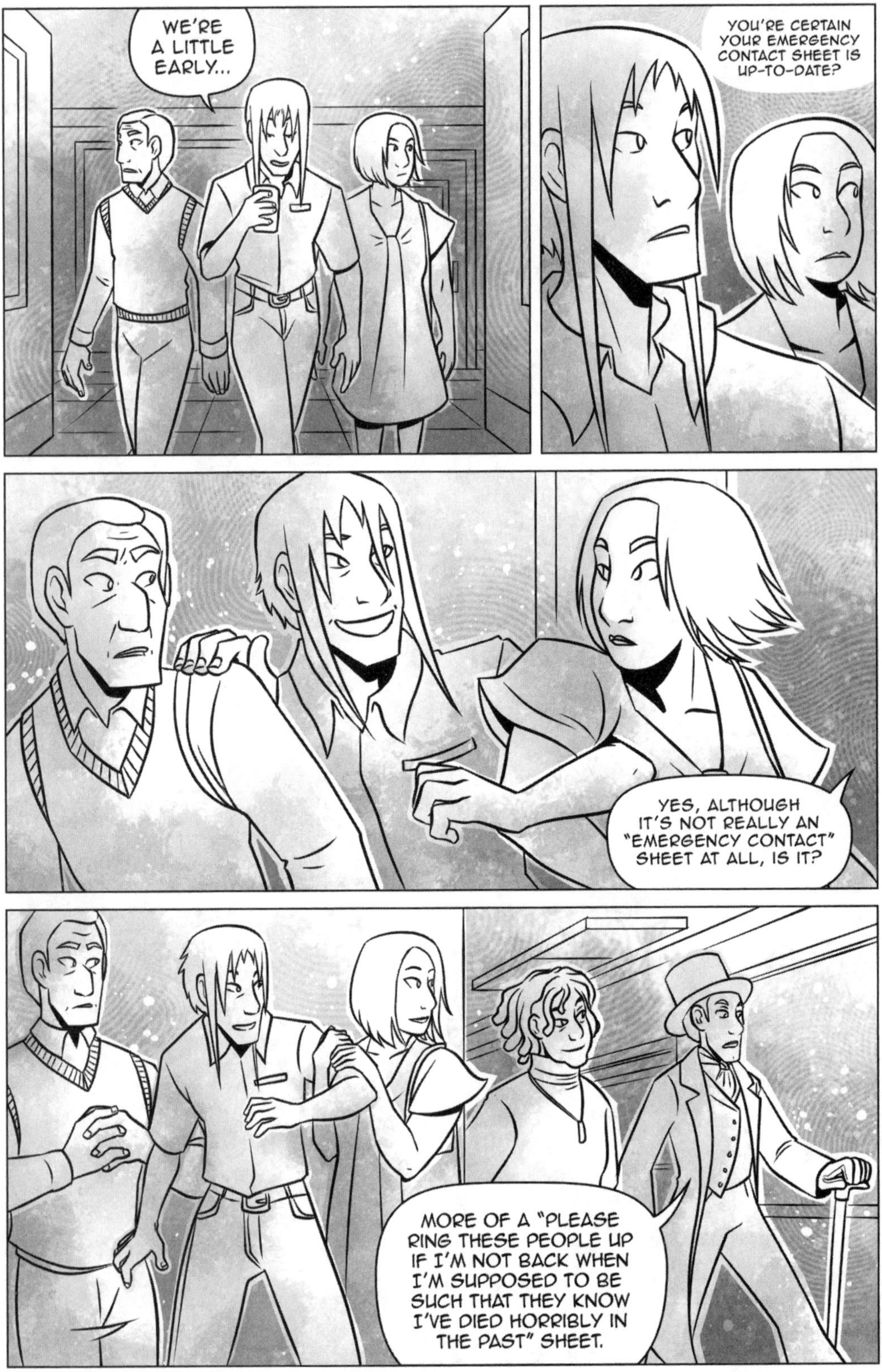
WE'RE A LITTLE EARLY...
YOU'RE CERTAIN YOUR EMERGENCY CONTACT SHEET IS UP-TO-DATE?
YES, ALTHOUGH IT'S NOT REALLY AN "EMERGENCY CONTACT" SHEET AT ALL, IS IT?
MORE OF A "PLEASE RING THESE PEOPLE UP IF I'M NOT BACK WHEN I'M SUPPOSED TO BE SUCH THAT THEY KNOW I'VE DIED HORRIBLY IN THE PAST" SHEET.

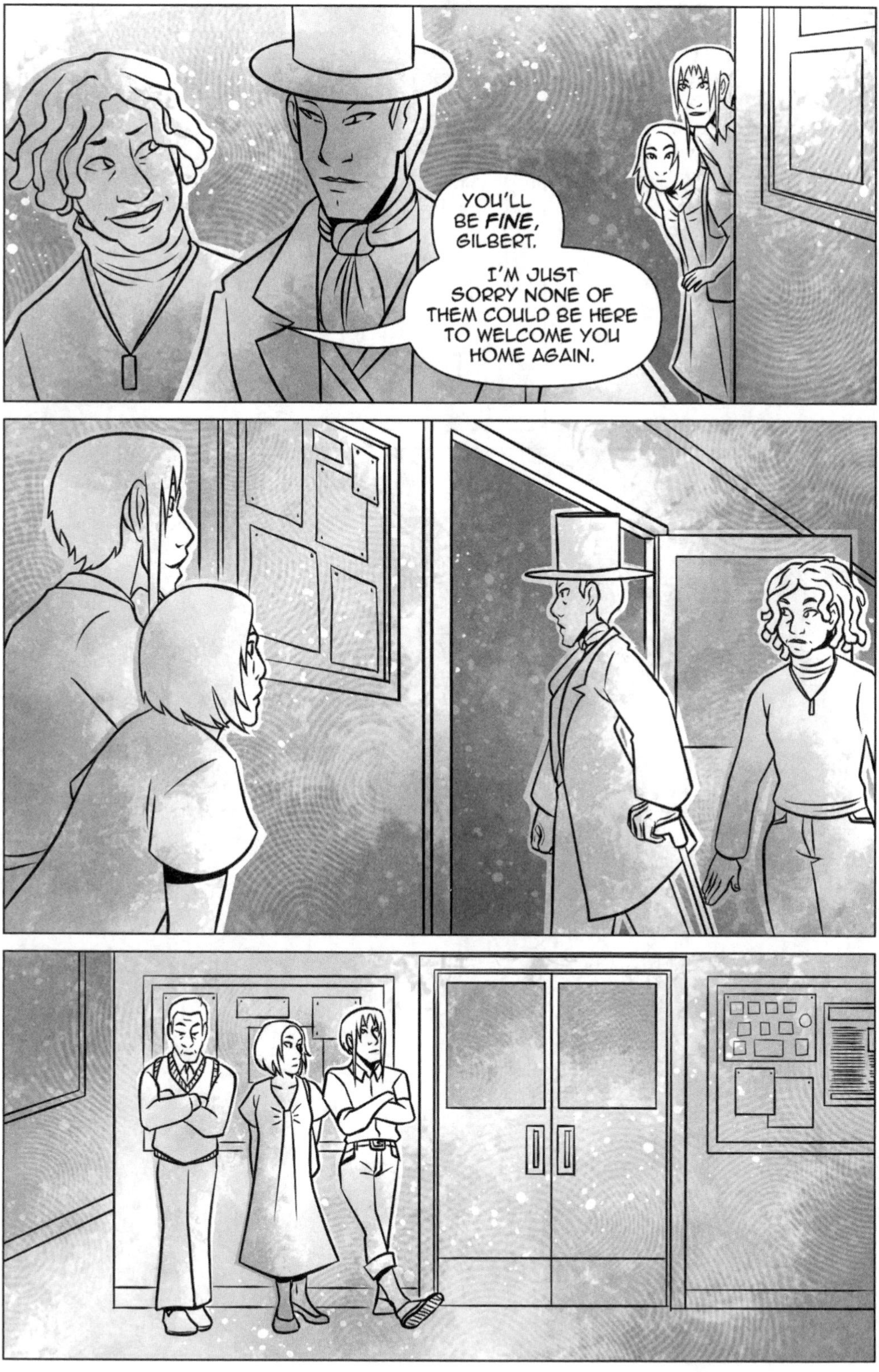
YOU'LL BE FINE, GILBERT.
I'M JUST SORRY NONE OF THEM COULD BE HERE TO WELCOME YOU HOME AGAIN.

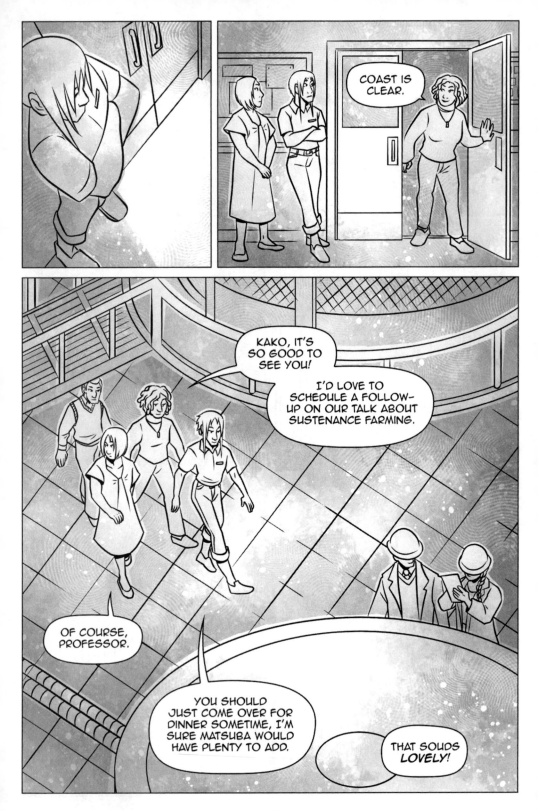

COAST IS CLEAR.

KAKO, IT'S SO GOOD TO SEE YOU!

I'D LOVE TO SCHEDULE A FOLLOW-UP ON OUR TALK ABOUT SUSTENANCE FARMING.

OF COURSE, PROFESSOR.

YOU SHOULD JUST COME OVER FOR DINNER SOMETIME, I'M SURE MATSUBA WOULD HAVE PLENTY TO ADD.

THAT SOUDS *LOVELY!*

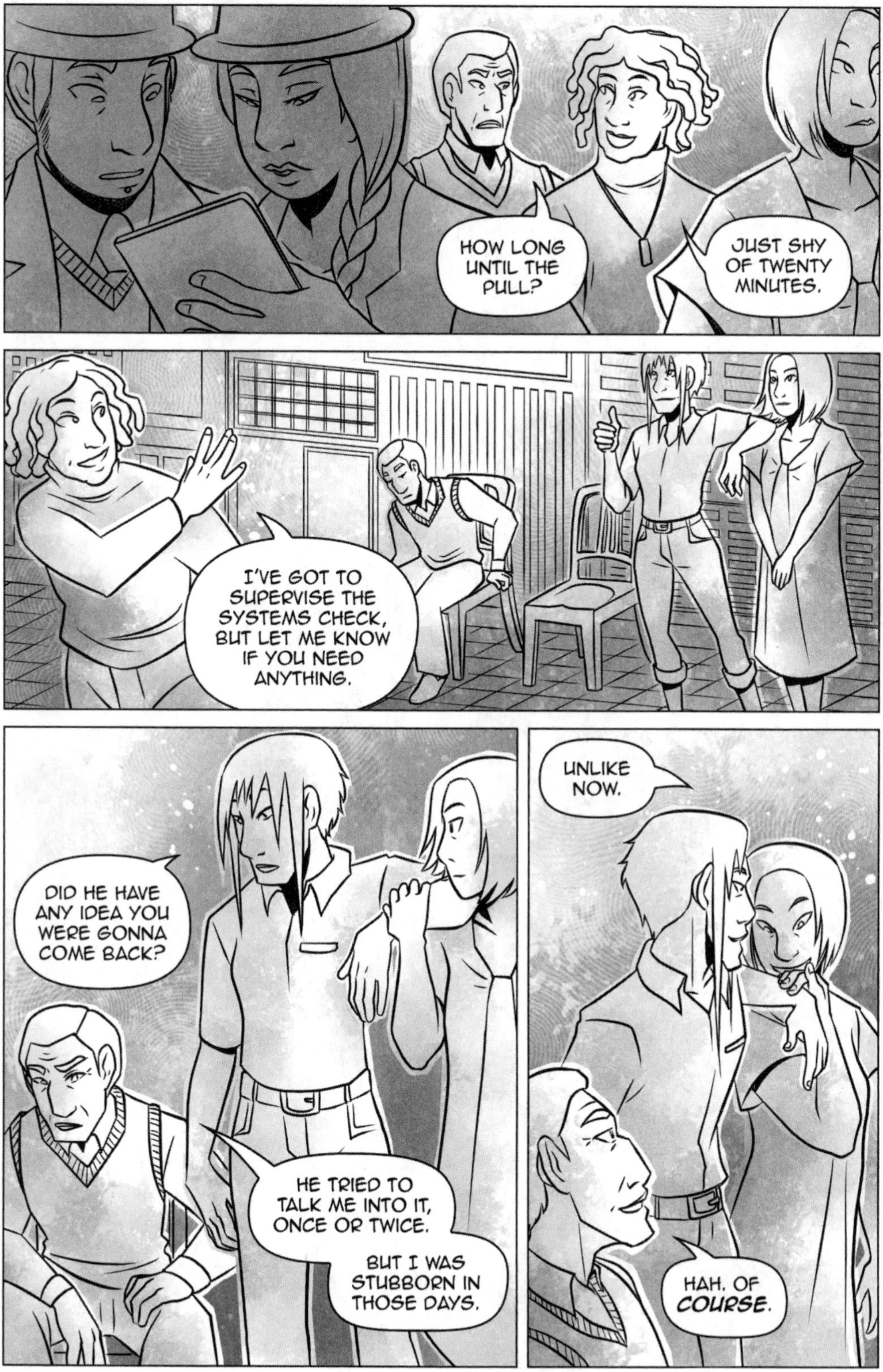
HOW LONG UNTIL THE PULL?
JUST SHY OF TWENTY MINUTES.
I'VE GOT TO SUPERVISE THE SYSTEMS CHECK, BUT LET ME KNOW IF YOU NEED ANYTHING.
DID HE HAVE ANY IDEA YOU WERE GONNA COME BACK?
HE TRIED TO TALK ME INTO IT, ONCE OR TWICE.
BUT I WAS STUBBORN IN THOSE DAYS.
UNLIKE NOW.
HAH. OF *COURSE*.

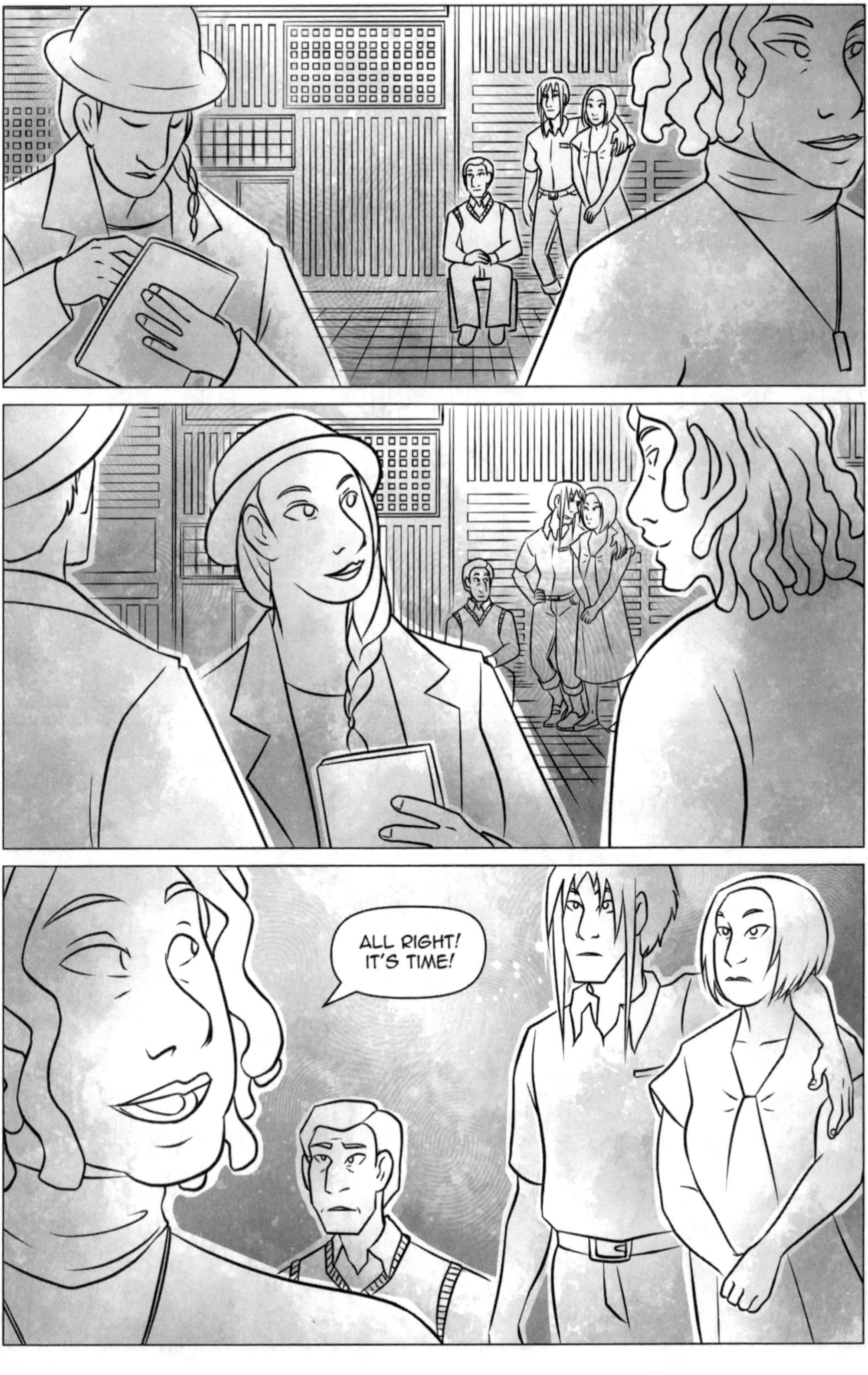
ALL RIGHT! IT'S TIME!

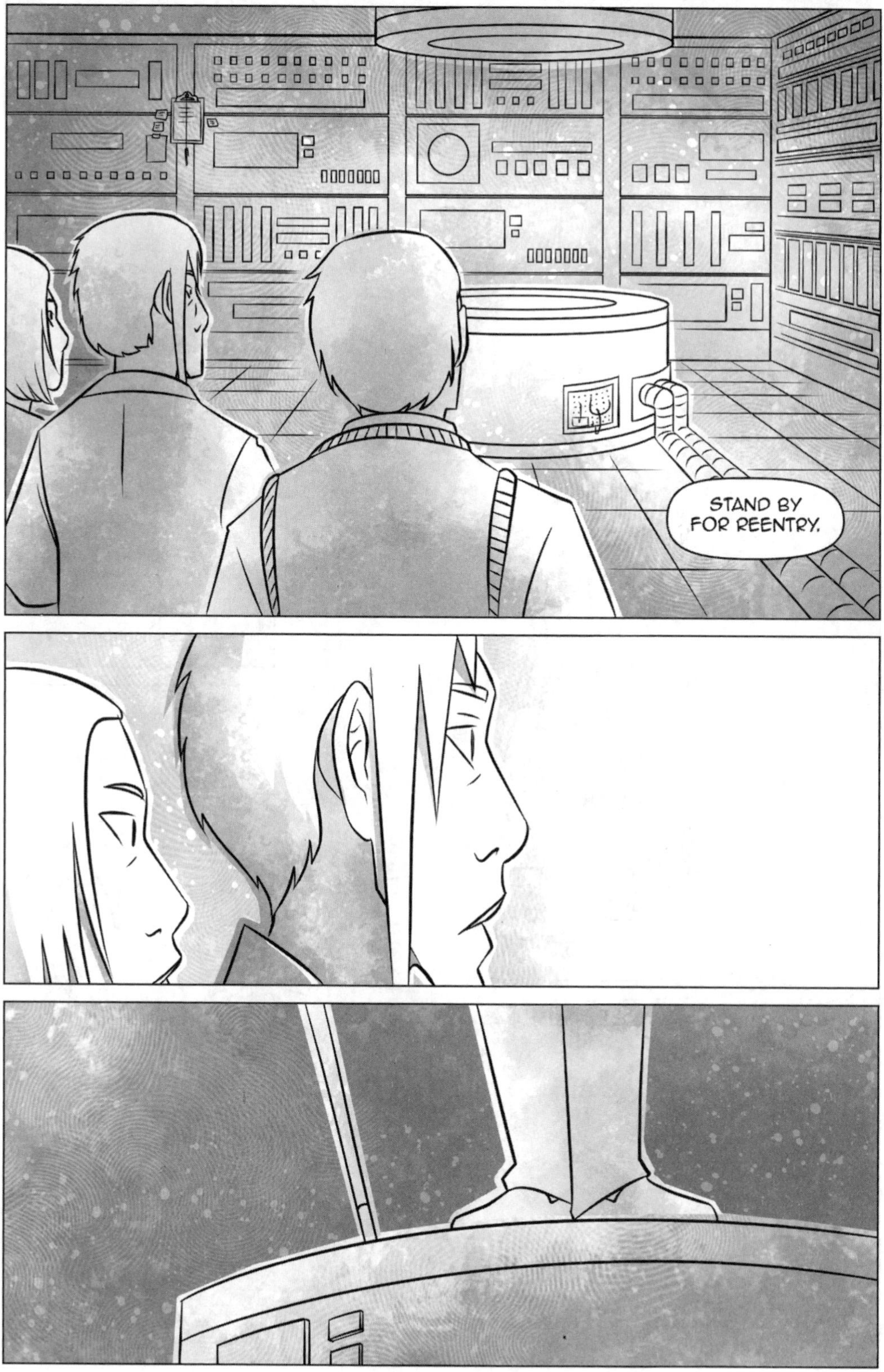
STAND BY
FOR REENTRY.

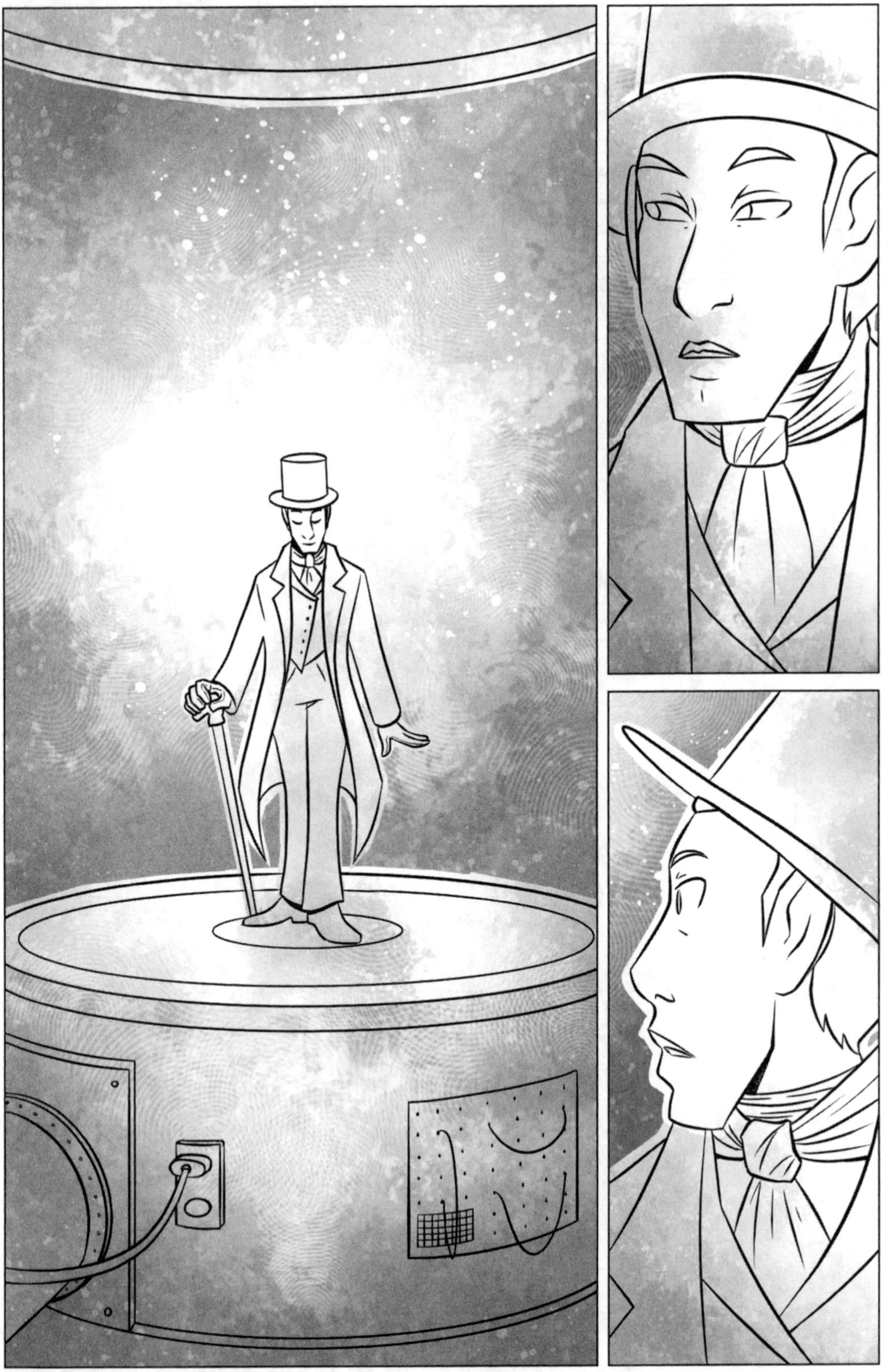

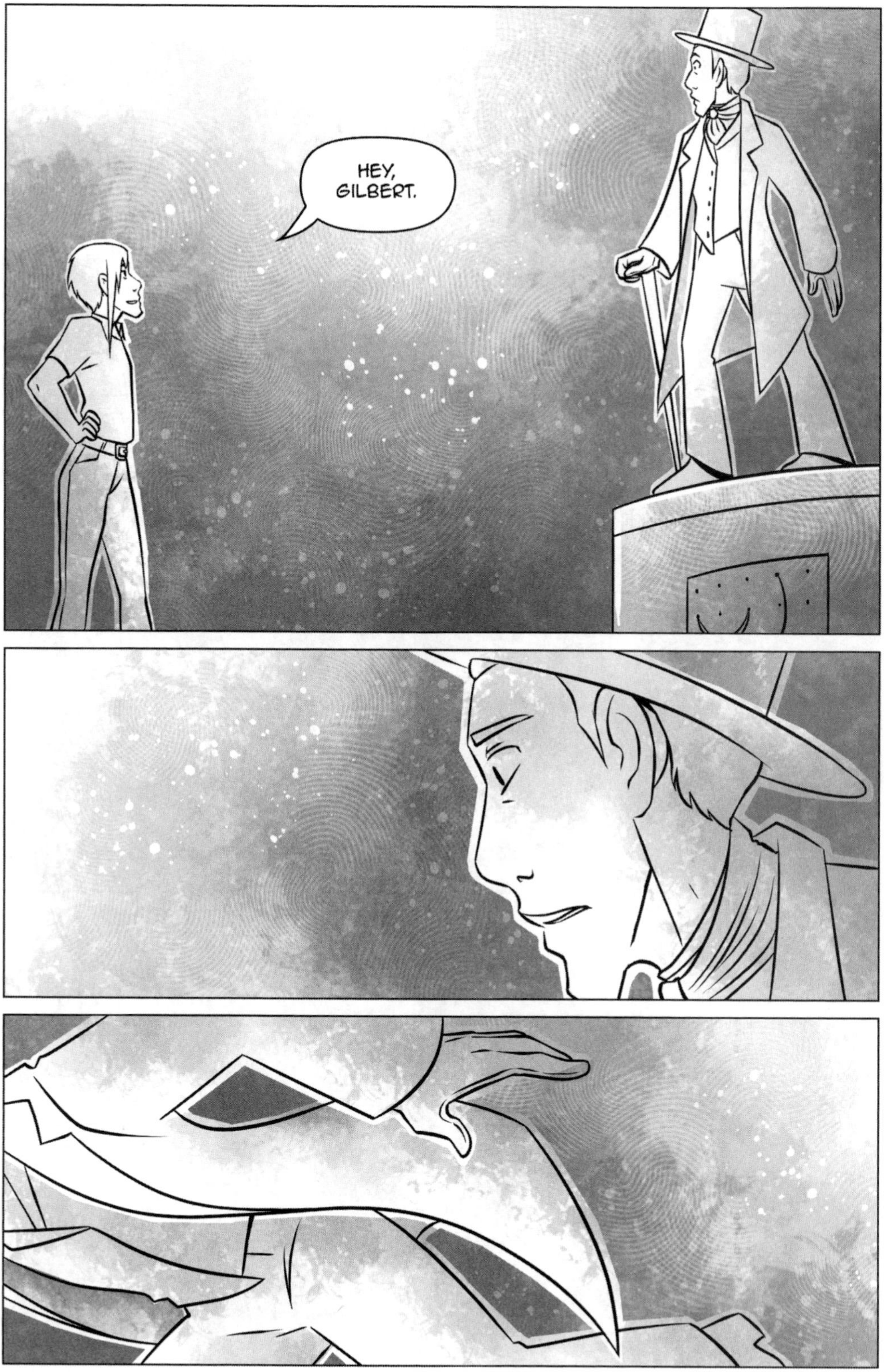
HEY, GILBERT.

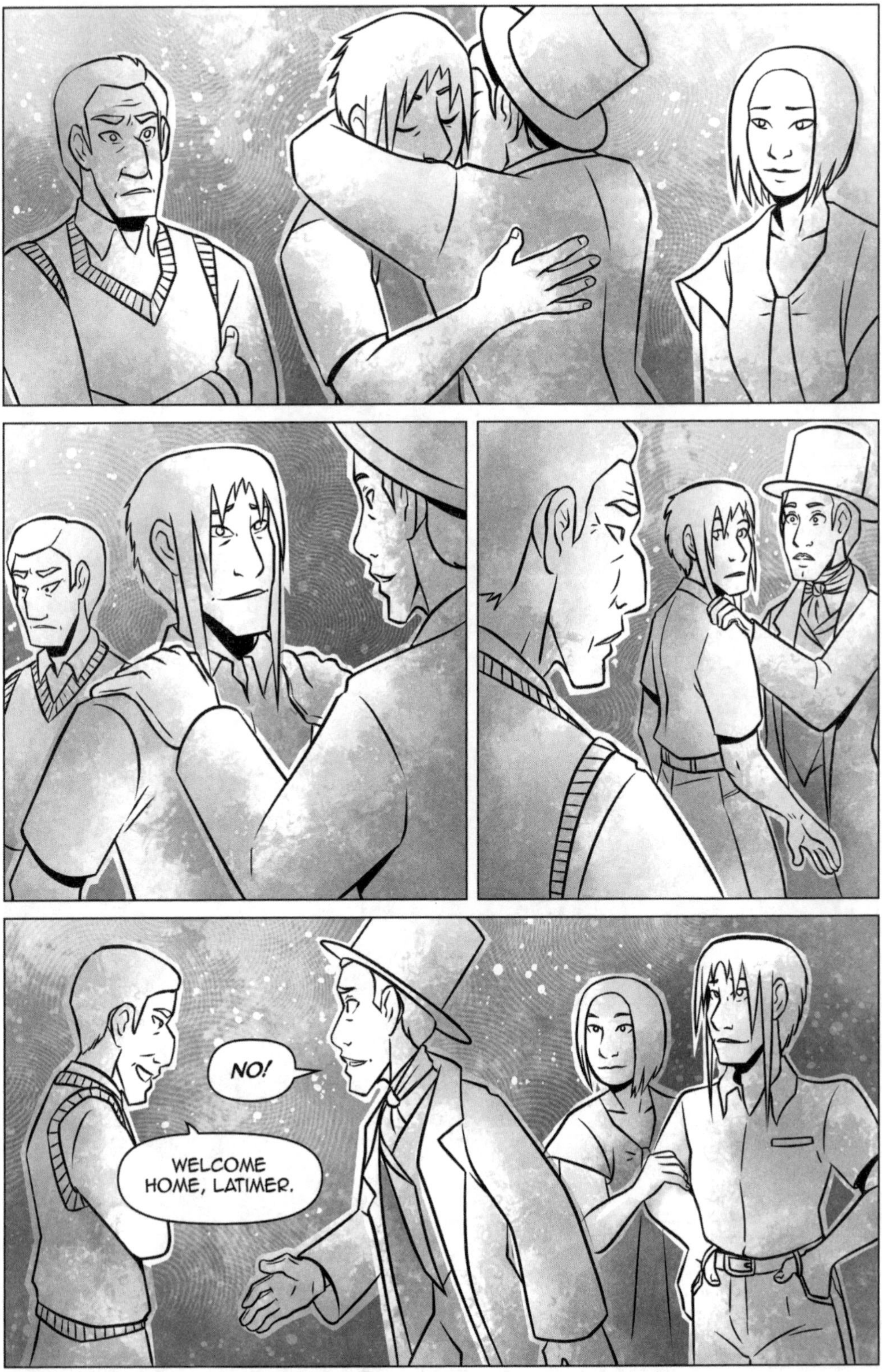
NO!
WELCOME HOME, LATIMER.

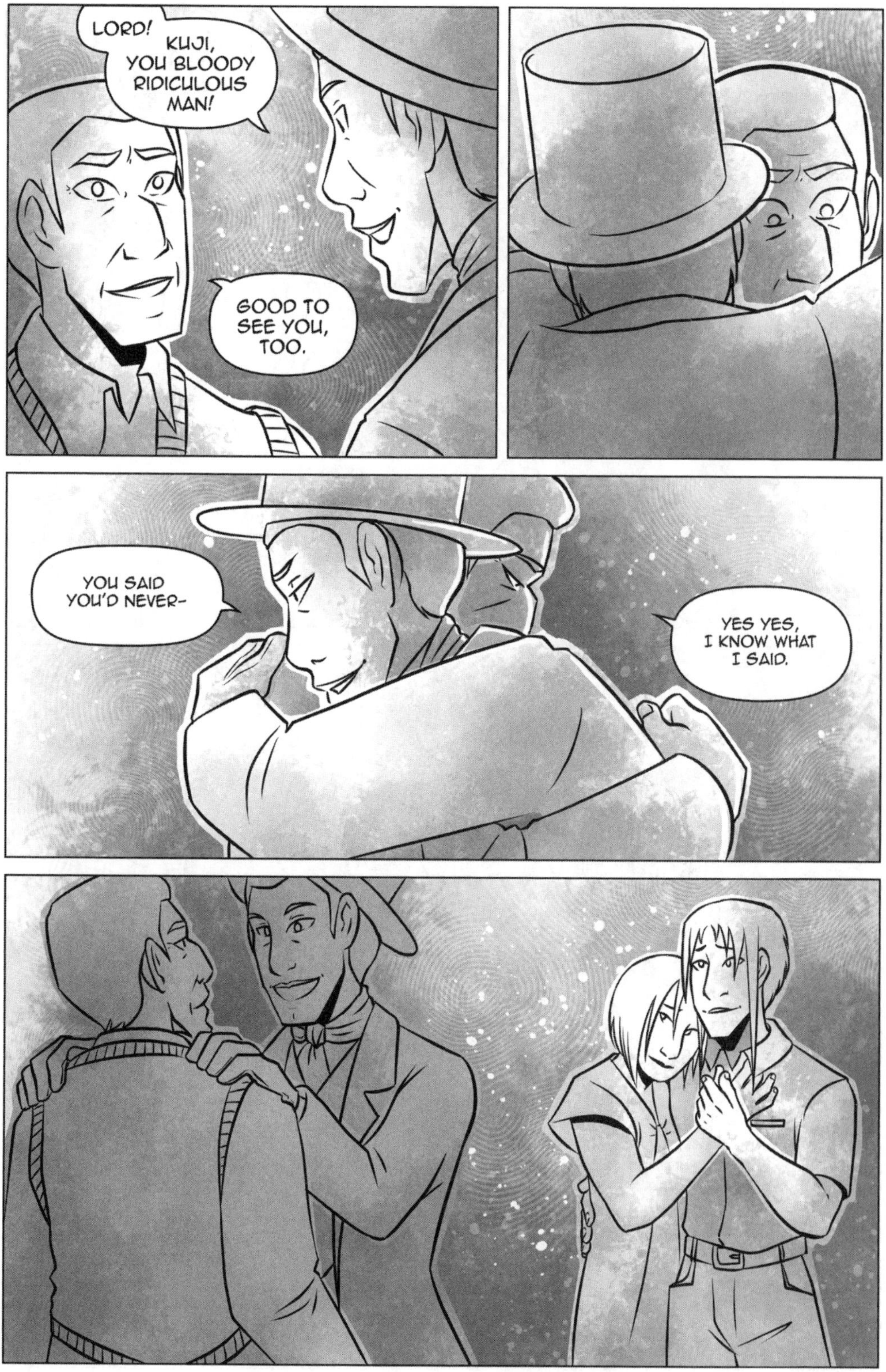
LORD!
KUJI, YOU BLOODY RIDICULOUS MAN!
GOOD TO SEE YOU, TOO.
YOU SAID YOU'D NEVER-
YES YES, I KNOW WHAT I SAID.

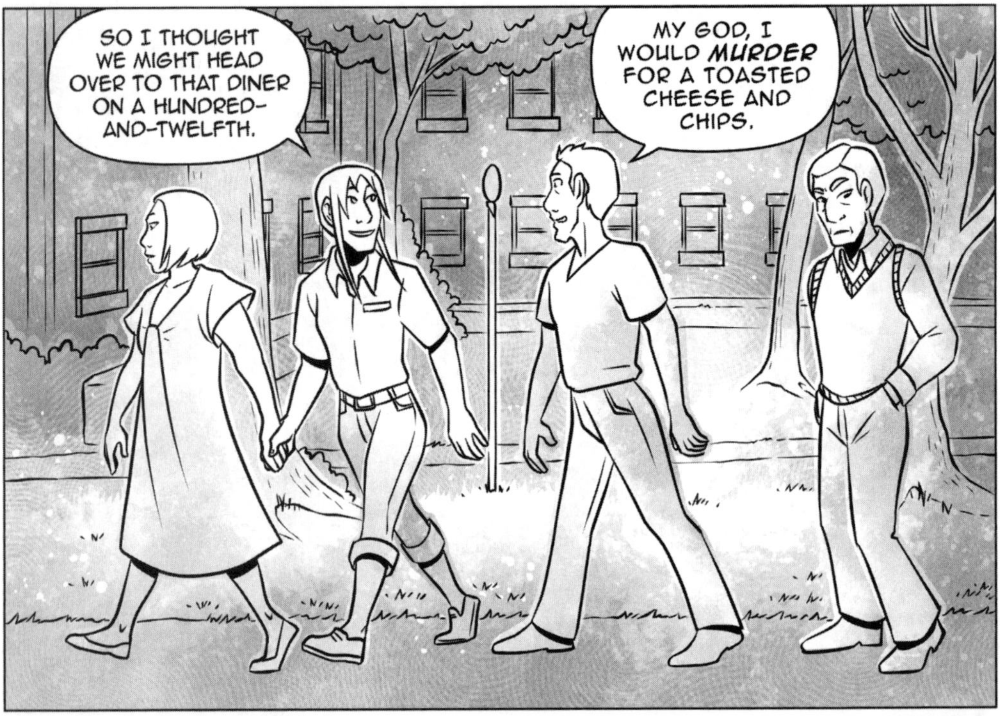
SO I THOUGHT WE MIGHT HEAD OVER TO THAT DINER ON A HUNDRED-AND-TWELFTH.
MY GOD, I WOULD *MURDER* FOR A TOASTED CHEESE AND CHIPS.

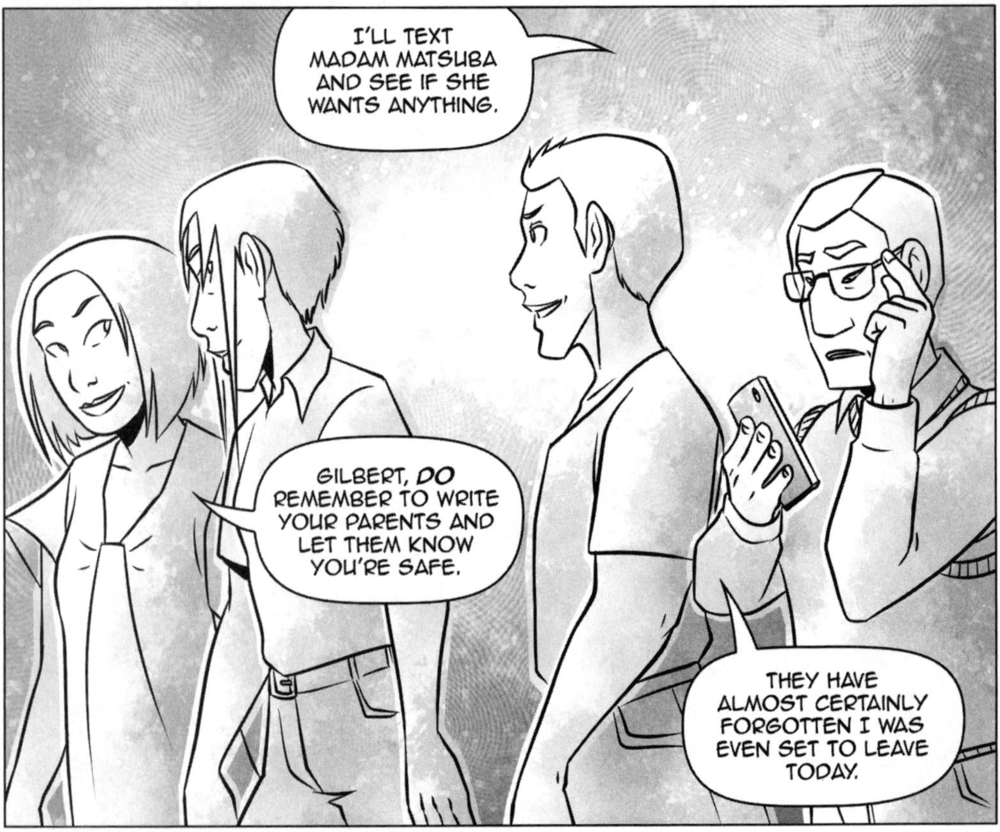
I'LL TEXT MADAM MATSUBA AND SEE IF SHE WANTS ANYTHING.
GILBERT, *DO* REMEMBER TO WRITE YOUR PARENTS AND LET THEM KNOW YOU'RE SAFE.
THEY HAVE ALMOST CERTAINLY FORGOTTEN I WAS EVEN SET TO LEAVE TODAY.

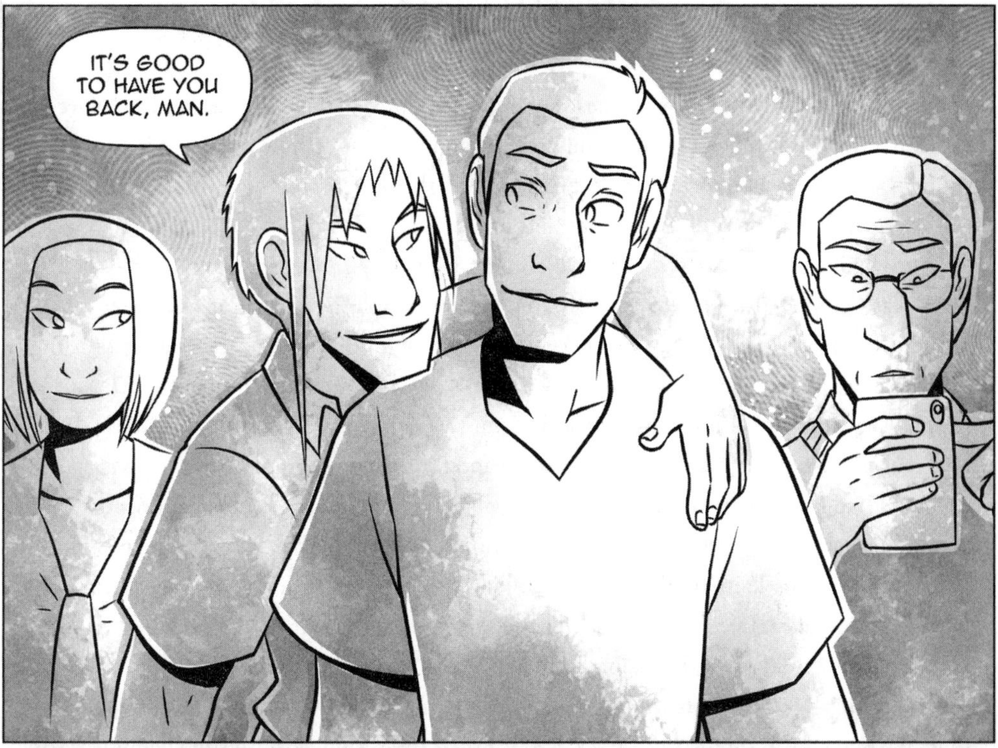
IT'S GOOD TO HAVE YOU BACK, MAN.

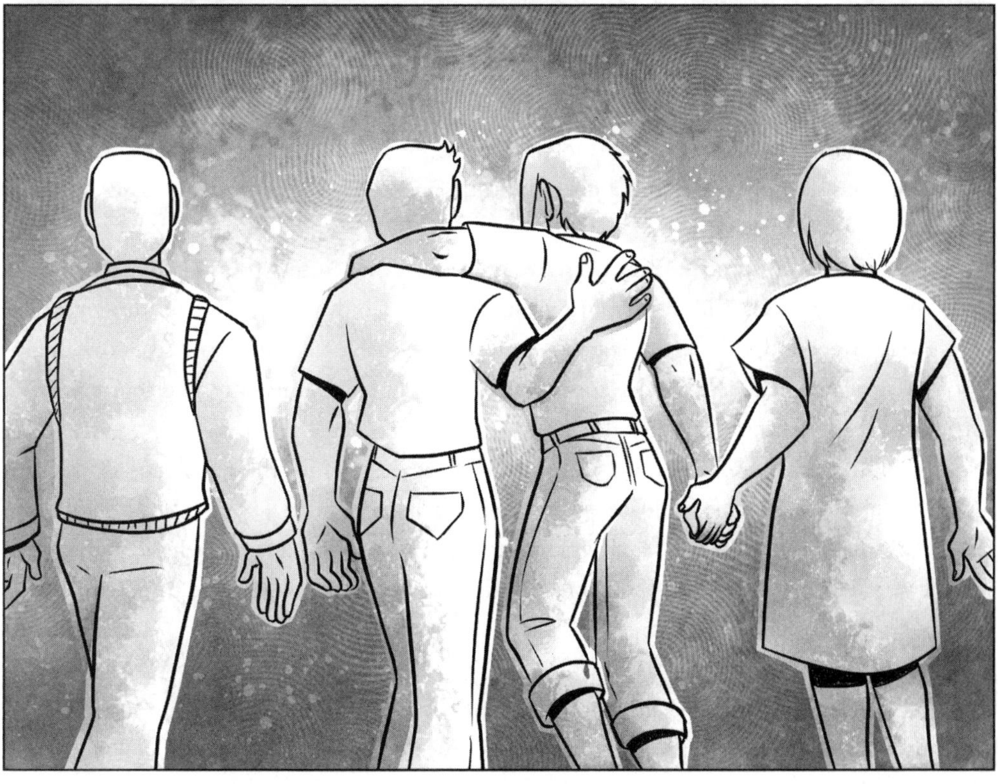

# ACKNOWLEDGMENTS

I started to work on this story in earnest sometime in 2007. I'm typing these words in November of 2018, hours after finishing the manuscript. I cannot overstate how strange it is to be done.

*Chronin* is a graphic novel in two parts, and the acknowledgments below are also a sort of "Volume 2," continuing from where I left off.

Unlike the previous volume, which I chipped away at over the course of a decade, this book was completed in just over two years. That turnaround would not have been possible without the help of my fantastic inker, Niki Smith, who did an amazing job astonishingly quickly. She's also a talented and prolific cartoonist, and I highly recommend purchasing and reading every one of her books as soon as you put this one down. Thank you, Niki, for your lines and your professionalism and your friendship, and for saving me from myself.

Thank you to everyone whose loving yells gave me the strength to drag my poor carcass across the finish line, particularly Aatmaja, Aimee, Arthur, Barbara, Carey, Chris, Clio, EK, Elissa, Emily, Eric, Faith, Gale, GG, Gina, Jay, Jaye, Jesse, John, JoXn, Kari, Kel, Kori, Kory, Kou, Kristin, Laura, Lee, Lisa, Meg, Melanie, Miranda, MK, Mo, Molly B, Molly O, Momo, Natalie, Niki, Paul, Phil, Pola, Raina, Rebecca, Sarah, Scott, Sfé, Shelli, Shing, Smo, and Tim. Thanks especially to Carey, Kori, and Paul for soldiering through thumbnails and rough pencils to let me know I was on the right track, and for their reassuring enthusiasm when it was sorely needed.

Thank you to Robyn and Wyeth for being patient with me when my labors on this book interfered with our journey to Mars.

Thank you to Paul and Scott for convincing me to buy an iPad Pro, which allowed me to pencil the second half of this book without being stuck at home at my desk and thus dissolving into madness.

Thank you to my editor, Diana Pho, for believing in me; to my publicist, Desirae Friesen, for her tireless aid in promoting this series; to Cindy De la Cruz, for designing my gorgeous covers; and to the entire team at Tor for taking such excellent care of my books. Thank you to my agent, Eddie Schneider, for his aid and advice and enthusiasm, and to everyone at JABberwocky for having my back.

Thank you to Indiana Scarlet Brown and Iori Kusano for their generous, exhaustive, thoughtful, and invaluable feedback—*Chronin* is much better for it.

Thank you to Carey, Clio, Elissa, Gina, Kari, Kori, and Laura for helping me weather some very dark days. Thank you to Mom and Kim for being themselves, and being in my life.

Thank you to Scott for his kindness and patience through late nights, missed vacations, and a general vibe of "Sorry, I gotta work."

Thank you to the queer comics community, who have been nothing but supportive of this poor idiot who took thirty-something years to see the truth of herself.

Thank *you*, reader, for picking up this book. I hope it took good care of you.

*—Alison*